Digital Image Analysis

Springer Science+Business Media, LLC

Walter G. Kropatsch   Horst Bischof
Editors

Digital Image Analysis

Selected Techniques
and Applications

With 150 Illustrations

 Springer

Walter G. Kropatsch
Pattern Recognition and
    Image Processing Group
Institute of Computer Aided
    Automation
Vienna University of Technology
Favoritenstrasse 9/183/2
Vienna A-1040
Austria
krw@prip.tuwien.ac.at

Horst Bischof
Pattern Recognition and
    Image Processing Group
Institute of Computer Aided
    Automation
Vienna University of Technology
Favoritenstrasse 9/183/2
Vienna A-1040
Austria
bis@prip.tuwien.ac.at

Additional material to this book can be downloaded from http://extras.springer.com.

ISBN 978-1-4757-7517-4   ISBN 978-0-387-21643-0 (eBook)
DOI 10.1007/978-0-387-21643-0

Library of Congress Cataloging-in-Publication Data
    Digital image analysis: selected techniques and applications/editors, Walter G.
Kropatsch, Horst Bischof.
        p. cm.
    Includes bibliographical references and index.

    1. Image processing—Digital techniques. 2. Image analysis. I. Kropatsch, W. (Walter).
II. Bischof, Horst.
  TA1637.D517 2001
  621.36'7—dc21   00-052278

Printed on acid-free paper.

Production managed by Frank McGuckin; manufacturing supervised by Jeffrey Taub.
Camera-ready copy prepared from the authors' LaTeX2e files using Springer's svsing2e.sty macro.

9 8 7 6 5 4 3 2 1

SPIN 10770712

Preface

The human visual system as a functional unit including the eyes, the nervous system, and the corresponding parts of the brain certainly ranks among the most important means of human information processing. The efficiency of the biological systems is beyond the capabilities of today's technical systems, even with the fastest available computer systems.

However, there are areas of application where digital image analysis systems produce acceptable results. Systems in these areas solve very specialized tasks, they operate in a limited environment, and high speed is often not necessary. Several factors determine the economical application of technical vision systems: cost, speed, flexibility, robustness, functionality, and integration with other system components. Many of the recent developments in digital image processing and pattern recognition show some of the required achievements. Computer vision enhances the capabilities of computer systems

- in autonomously collecting large amounts of data,

- in extracting relevant information,

- in perceiving its environment, and

- in automatic or semiautomatic operation in this environment.

The development of computer systems in general shows a steadily increasing need in computational power, which comes with decreasing hardware costs.

About This Book

This book is the result of the Austrian Joint Research Program (JRP) 1994–1999 on "Theory and Applications of Digital Image Processing and Pattern Recognition". This program was initiated by the Austrian Science Foundation (FWF) and funded research in 11 labs all over Austria for more than 5 years. Because the program has produced many scientific results in many different areas and communities, we collected the most important results in one volume. The development of practical solutions involving digital images requires the **cooperation** of specialists from many different scientific fields. The wide range of fields covered by the participating institutions fulfills this important requirement. Furthermore, the often very specialized vocabulary in the different disciplines makes it necessary to have experts in the different areas, which are in close contact and often exchange ideas. For this reason, active cooperation among the different groups has been declared an important goal of the research program. It has stimulated the research activities for each of the participating groups (and beyond) in a way that has a positive long-term effect for activities in this field in Austria. More details about the joint research program and the participating labs can be found on the CD included in this book.

This book is not a collection of research papers; it brings together the research results of the joint research program in a uniform manner, thereby making the contents of the more than 300 scientific papers accessible to the nonspecialist. The main motivation for writing this book was to bridge the gap between the basic knowledge available in standard textbooks and the newest research results published in scientific papers.

In particular the book was written with the following goals in mind:

- presentation of the research results of the joint research program in a unified manner;

- together with the accompanying CD, the book provides a quick overview of the research in digital image processing and pattern recognition in Austria from 1994–1999;

- parts of this book can serve as advanced courses in selected chapters in pattern recognition and image processing.

The book is organized in five parts, each dealing with a special topic. The parts are written in an independent manner and can be read in any order. Each part consists of several chapters and has its own bibliography. Each part focuses on a specific topic in image processing and describes new methods developed within the research program, but it also demonstrates selected applications showing the benefits of the methods. Parts I, III, and IV are more focused on methodological developments, and Parts II and V are more application oriented. New mathematical methods centered around the topic of image transformations is the main subject of Part I. Part II is mainly devoted to the computer science aspect of image processing, in particular how to handle this huge amount of information in a reasonable time. Parts III and IV are centered around algorithmic issues in image processing. Part III deals with graph-based and robust methods, whereas Part IV is focused on information fusion. 3D information is the main topic of Part V. Table 1 gives a concise overview of the parts and presents the main methods and selected applications for each part.

The Compact Disc

The CD included with this book presents the research program from a multimedia perspective. The CD contains a collection of html-files, which can be viewed by common Web-browsers. The CD has following features:

- the structure of the research program;

- the main topics of research;

- a collection of scientific papers produced during the research program;

- WWW-links to demo pages, which are maintained by the different labs;

- information about the participating labs; and

- the people working on the various projects.

The WWW-links to the demos on the CD should add to the "static" content of the book access to the latest developments of active research done in the labs. Although we are aware of the difficulties of maintaining Internet links over long periods, we have decided for this dynamic solution in order to communicate up-to-date results in such rapidly evolving technology as digital image processing.

Acknowledgments

This work was supported by the Austrian Science Foundation under grant S-70 and the Austrian national bank. We are indebted to Dr. Niel from FWF for continuing support. We would like to thank all our colleagues who have worked under the Joint Research Program S-70 for more than 5 years and who have produced the results in this book and on the CD. Special thanks go to Karin Hraby at the Pattern Recognition and Image Processing Lab who has supported the research program from the administrative side; without her invaluable help we would have spent much more time on administration than on research. For the production of the CD we would like to thank the Hagenberg team at the Fachhochschule Multimedia Design, especially Wilhelm Burger for producing the CD with his students. Special thanks to Tatjana Elssenwenger, Daniela Kreiss, and Manuela Mittermayr for their excellent work in preparing the CD and for their patience for working with us. Finally we would like to express our sincere thanks to all contributors to this book for their professional work and timely delivery of the chapters.

Vienna, Austria   *Walter G. Kropatsch*
January 2001   *Horst Bischof*

TABLE 1. Overview of the Book Parts

Methods	Selected Applications
I Mathematical Methods for Image Analysis	
Time-frequency methods	Echocardiography
Signal approximation	Geophysics
Gabor analysis	Image reconstruction
Wavelet analysis	Shape classification
Stochastic shape theory	Image compression
Non-linear optimizations	Image encryption
Multilevel interpolation	Watermarking
Chaotic Kolmogorov flows	
II Data Handling	
Parallelization	Remote sensing
Distributed processing	Radar data
Data management	Art history
Image databases	
III Robust and Adaptive Image Understanding	
Graphs	Technical drawings
Image pyramids	Line images
Irregular pyramids	Range images
Robust methods	
Minimum Description Length	
Object recognition	
Structural features	
Grouping and Indexing	
Machine learning	
IV Information Fusion and Radiometric Models for Image Understanding	
Active fusion	Remote sensing
Active recognition	Car recognition
Reinforcement learning	View planning
Generic object recognition	Land cover classification
Radiometric models	
Sub-pixel analysis	
V 3D Reconstruction	
Image matching	Remote sensing
Object reconstruction	Target localization
Topographic mapping	Building extraction
Vision-based navigation	Space exploration
Rotating CCD cameras	Digital elevation models
	Surveying

Contributors

Andreu, Jean-Philippe
Joanneum Research
The Institute of Digital Image Processing (DIB)
Wastiangasse 6
A-8010 Graz, Austria
jean-philippe.andreu@joanneum.ac.at

Bachmann, Dieter
Graz University of Technology
Computer Graphics and Vision
Inffeldgasse 16
A-8010 Graz, Austria
bachmann@icg.tu-graz.ac.at

Bartl, Renate
University of Agricultural Sciences
Institute of Surveying, Remote Sensing and Land Information
Peter-Jordan-Str. 82
A-1190 Vienna, Austria
renate.bartl@debis.at

Bischof, Horst
Vienna University of Technology
Institute of Computer Aided Automation
Favoritenstr. 9/1832
A-1040 Vienna, Austria
bis@prip.tuwien.ac.at

Blurock, Edward
Johannes Kepler University
Research Institute for Symbolic Computation
Altenbergerstrasse 69
A-4040 Linz, Austria
blurock@risc.uni-linz.ac.at

Borotschnig, Hermann
European Patent Office
D-80298 Munich, Germany
hborotschnig@epo.org

Burge, Mark
Armstrong Atlantic University
Department of Computer Science
11935 Abercorn Street
Savannah, Georgia 31419-1997, USA
mburge@acm.org

Burger, Wilhelm
FH-Studiengang Medientechnik und -design
Hauptstrasse 117
A-4232 Hagenberg, Austria
wilbur@ieee.org

Cenker, Christian
University of Vienna
Department of Statistics and Decision Support Systems
Universitätsstr. 5
A-1010 Vienna, Austria
christian.cenker@univie.ac.at

Englert, Roman
DeTeMobil–Deutsche Telekom MobilNet GmbH
Landgrabenweg 151
D-53227 Bonn, Germany
Roman.Englert@t-mobil.de

Feichtinger, Hans G.
University of Vienna
Department of Mathematics
Strudlhofg. 4
A-1090 Vienna, Austria
hans.georg.feichtinger@univie.ac.at

Ganster, Harald
Graz University of Technology
Electrical Measurement and Measurement Signal Processing
Schiesstattg. 14b
A-8010 Graz, Austria
ganster@emt.tu-graz.ac.at

Glantz, Roland
Vienna University of Technology
Institute of Computer Aided Automation
Favoritenstr. 9/1832
A-1040 Vienna, Austria
glz@prip.tuwien.ac.at

Glendinning, Ian
European Centre for Parallel Computing at Vienna (VCPC)
Liechtensteinstr. 22
A-1090 Vienna, Austria
ian@vpc.univie.ac.at

Goller, Alois
Department of Electrical and Computer Engineering
Chalmers Lindholmen University College
P.O. Box 8873
SE-402 72 Goeteborg, Sweden
algo@chl.chalmers.se

Kahmen, Heribert
Vienna University of Technology
Department of Applied and Engineering Geodesy
Gusshausstr. 27-29/128/3
A-1040 Vienna, Austria
Heribert.Kahmen@tuwien.ac.at

Kalliany, Rainer
Graz University of Technology
Computer Graphics and Vision
Inffeldgasse 16
A-8010 Graz, Austria
kalliany@icg.tu-graz.ac.at

Kropatsch, Walter G.
Vienna University of Technology
Institute of Computer Aided Automation
Favoritenstr. 9/1832
A-1040 Vienna, Austria
krw@prip.tuwien.ac.at

Leonardis, Aleš
University of Ljubljana
Faculty of CIS
Trzaska 25
SI-1001 Ljubljana, Slovenia
Ales.Leonardis@fri.uni-lj.si

Mayer Manfred
University of Vienna
Department of Statistics and Decision Support Systems
Universitätsstr. 5
A-1010 Vienna, Austria
m3mayer@ibm.net

Niederl Franz
akaryon Niederl & Bußwald OEG
Grazer Straße 77
A-8665 Langenwang, Austria
niederl@akaryon.com

Niessner, Anton
Vienna University of Technology
Department of Applied and Engineering Geodesy
Gusshausstr. 27-29/128/3
A-1040 Vienna, Austria
aniessne@pop.tuwien.ac.at

Paar, Gerhard
Joanneum Research
The Institute of Digital Image Processing (DIB)
Wastiangasse 6
A-8010 Graz, Austria
gerhard.paar@joanneum.ac.at

Paletta, Lucas
Joanneum Research
The Institute of Digital Image Processing (DIB)
Wastiangasse 6
A-8010 Graz, Austria
lucas.paletta@joanneum.ac.at

Pflug, Georg
University of Vienna
Department of Statistics and Decision Support Systems
Universitätsstr. 5
A-1010 Vienna, Austria
georg.pflug@univie.ac.at

Pinz, Axel
Graz University of Technology
Electrical Measurement and Measurement Signal Processing
Schiesstattg. 14b
A-8010 Graz, Austria
pinz@emt.tu-graz.ac.at

Pölzleitner, Wolfgang
Sensotech Forschungs- und Entwicklungs GesmbH
Scheigergasse 74
A-8010 Graz, Austria
wp@sensotech.at

Prantl, Manfred
Alicona GdbR
Koch-Sternfeldstr. 5
D-83471 Berchtesgaden, Germany
prantl@alicona.com

Rottensteiner, Franz
Vienna University of Technology
Institute of Photogrammetry and Remote Sensing
Gusshausstr. 27-29
A-1040 Vienna, Austria
fr@ipf.tuwien.ac.at

Saraceno, Caterina
Starlab NV
Boulevard St.-Michel 47
B-1040 Brussels, Belgium
saraceno@starlab.net

Scharinger, Josef
Johannes Kepler University
Institute of Systems Science, Systems Theory and Information Technology
Altenbergerstrasse 69
A-4040 Linz, Austria
js@cast.uni-linz.ac.at

Schneider, Werner
University of Agricultural Sciences
Institute of Surveying, Remote Sensing and Land Information
Peter-Jordan-Str. 82
A-1190 Vienna, Austria
werner.schneider@boku.ac.at

Steinwendner, Joachim
University of Agricultural Sciences
Institute of Surveying, Remote Sensing and Land Information
Peter-Jordan-Str. 82
A-1190 Vienna, Austria
Steinwendner@boku.ac.at

Seixas, Andrea de
Vienna University of Technology
Department of Applied and Engineering Geodesy
Gusshausstr. 27-29/128/3
A-1040 Vienna, Austria
aseixas@pop.tuwien.ac.at

Strohmer, Thomas
University of California, Davis
Department of Mathematics
1 Shield Avenue
Davis California 95616-8633, USA
strohmer@math.ucdavis.edu

Contents

9   Structural Object Recognition   237
M. Burge and W. Burger

10 Machine Learning   251
E. Blurock

References   265

V   3D Reconstruction   367

List of Figures

List of Tables

Part I

Mathematical Methods
for
Image Analysis

Introduction to Part I

Signal and image analysis deals with the description of one- or multidimensional signals, e.g., speech, music, images and image sequences, and multimedia data. On the one hand, some features of the analyzed signals are often known, e.g., smoothness, frequency band, and number of colors; on the other hand, general tools for the description of families of signals by features have to be developed. Fourier and spline techniques are often used to describe (approximate) a signal or to extract special properties from a signal. Drawbacks of these techniques are bad time-frequency concentration, in the case of Fourier methods, and the piecewise and polygonal character of splines.

All these approximation techniques represent the signal with the help of basis functions, which can easily be generated. In addition to the approximation properties, the computational performance of the algorithms are of essential interest.

Furthermore, not only the extraction of important information from a signal or signal "encoding" is of interest, but also fast, reliable, and secure transmission of the signal and information itself, as the amount of data transmitted and the size of the signals increase. Thus, signal compression and encoding are also of major interest.

In this part of the book we concentrate on new time-frequency techniques that circumvent some of the drawbacks of classical time-frequency-analysis, and we develop new algorithms for signal approximation and description, feature extraction, and signal compression and image coding.

Standard mathematical methods used for signal approximation in pattern recognition often use only orthonormal bases for series expansions as they produce an exact and unique representation of the analyzed signal. We develop algorithms for more general classes of bases, so-called *frames*. Strictly speaking, frames provide families of functions (atoms) that deal as building blocks of signals and images. These families can be, but do not have to be, Riesz bases, bases, or even orthonormal bases. The choice of an overcomplete family of atoms implies a redundancy which is often preferred to an orthonormal basis, as perturbations of the signal do not have too much influence on the analysis of the signal.

Special instances of frames are Gabor frames and wavelets. They come from different techniques of generating the entire set of functions from just one basis function (atom). Gabor frames use time and frequency shifts of one function (on a not necessarily regular grid), i.e., shift and modulation operators; wavelets use time shifts and dilations. From an algebraic point of view, both Gabor frames and wavelets are generated by elements of a subset of a group acting on one basis function. The Weyl-Heisenberg group of (time) shift and modulation operators represents Gabor frames; the affine group of shift and dilation operators represents wavelets.

Due to the different generation methods, given an atom the (essential) supports of the basis functions in the time-frequency plane look different with wavelets and Gabor frames, covering all of the time-frequency plane (cf. Figure 2). For an introduction and overview of recent work on Gabor frames, see [FS98a], a fine tutorial of the theory and applications of wavelets is [Chu92c].

In Chapter 1 we concentrate on Gabor analysis and synthesis of signals. We present

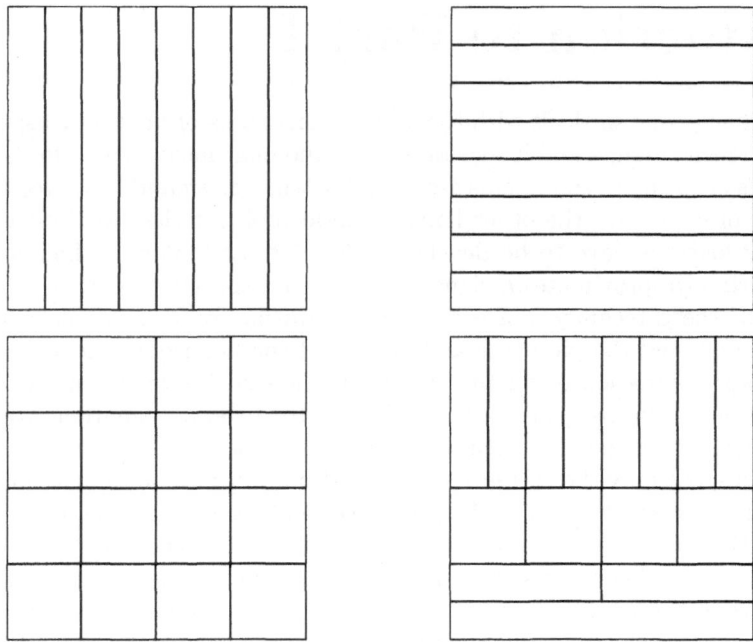

FIGURE 1. Time-frequency grids (horizontal time axes, and vertical frequency axes). The cells are the supports of the basis functions. From left to right and top to bottom: Shannon grid, Fourier grid, Gabor grid, Wavelet grid.

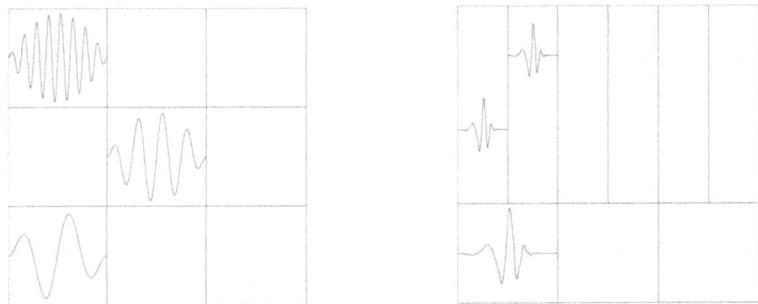

FIGURE 2. Gabor and Wavelet grids and basis functions.

the development of Gabor frames, starting with the Fourier transform and complete with a theoretical section on Gabor frames on groups, and the development of algorithms for image analysis. Numerical Gabor methods are developed and applied to recover and reconstruct images or parts of images.

In Chapter 2 we deal with the shape of objects, presenting the stochastic "deformable templates" model. Furthermore, wavelet analysis is used to extract features from shapes, modeling standard statistic pattern recognition methods in the "wavelet packet domain". The notation of wavelets, wavelet packets, and their connection to frames are introduced. A section on stochastic global optimization is added, which presents a method for *template matching* , that has to be used with the methods presented earlier in this chapter.

Finally, in Chapter 3 methods for image compression, (lossy and nonlossy) and for data encryption are presented, developed, and compared. We only refer to the JPEG 2000 standard, which connects this chapter with the two previous ones, i.e., with frames and wavelets.

1

Numerical Harmonic Analysis and Image Processing

Hans G. Feichtinger
Thomas Strohmer

Signal processing has become an essential part of contemporary scientific and technological activity and even of everyday life. It is used in telecommunications, medical imaging, geophysics, and the transmission and analysis of satellite images. The objectives of signal processing are analysis and diagnostics, coding and compression, and transmission and reconstruction.

Common to all these objectives is the extraction of information of a signal, which is present but hidden in its complex representation. Thus, a major issue is to represent the given data as well as possible. Clearly, the optimal representation of a signal has to be tied to an objective goal. A signal representation that is optimal for compression can be disastrous for analysis. A transform that is optimal for one class of signals can yield modest results for a different class of signals.

In the last decade a number of new tools have been developed to analyze, compress, transmit, and reconstruct digital signals. In this chapter we present an overview of methods from numerical harmonic analysis that have proven to be useful in digital image processing.

In the first part of this chapter we discuss numerical methods designed for the restoration of missing data in digital images and the reconstruction of an image from scattered data. We describe efficient and robust numerical algorithms for the reconstruction of multidimensional (essentially) band-limited signals. We demonstrate the performance of the proposed methods by applying them to reconstruction problems in areas as diverse as medical imaging, exploration geophysics, and digital image restoration.

In the second part we focus on image analysis and optimal image representation. Time-frequency methods, such as wavelets and Gabor expansions, have been recognized as powerful tools for various tasks in image processing. We give an overview of recent developments in Gabor theory.

1.1 Gabor Analysis and Digital Signal Processing

In order to analyze and describe complicated phenomena, mathematicians, engineers and physicists like to represent these as superpositions of simple, well-understood objects. A significant part of research has gone into the development of methods to find such representations. These methods have become important in many areas of scientific

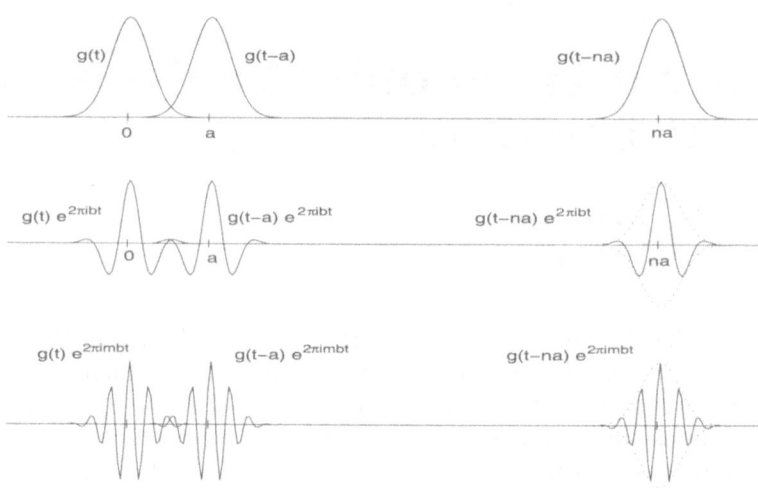

FIGURE 1.1. Gabor's elementary functions $g_{m,n}(t) = e^{2\pi imbt} g(t - na)$ are shifted and modulated copies of a single building block g (a and b denoting the time-shift and frequency-shift parameter, respectively). Each $g_{m,n}$ has the same envelope (up to translation); its shape is given by g. In this figure only the real part of the functions $g_{m,n}$ is shown in order to make the plot more readable.

and technological activity. They are used, for example, in telecommunications, medical imaging, geophysics, and engineering. An important aspect of many of these representations is the chance to extract relevant information from a signal or the underlying process, which is present but hidden in its complex representation. For example, we apply linear transformations with the aim that the information can be read off more easily from the new representation of the signal. Such transformations are used for many different tasks, such as analysis and diagnostics, compression and coding, and transmission and reconstruction.

For many years Fourier transform was the main tool in applied mathematics and signal processing for these purposes. But due to the large diversity of problems with which science is confronted on a regular basis, it is clear that there is not a single universal method that is well adapted to all those problems. Now there are many efficient analysis tools at our disposal. In this chapter we concentrate on methods that can be summarized under the name *Gabor analysis*, an area of research that is both theoretically appealing and successfully used in applications.

1.1.1   From Fourier to Gabor Expansions

Motivated by the study of heat diffusion, Fourier asserted that an arbitrary function f in $[0, 1)$ identified with its periodic extension to the full real line can be represented by a trigonometric series

$$f(t) = \sum_{n \in \mathbb{Z}} \hat{f}(n) e^{2\pi i n t} \tag{1.1}$$

with

$$\hat{f}(n) = \int_0^1 f(t) e^{-2\pi i n t} dt. \tag{1.2}$$

Much mathematical analysis developed since then was devoted to the attempt to make Fourier's statement precise. Despite the delicate problems of convergence, Fourier series are a powerful and widely used tool in mathematics, engineering, physics, and other areas. The existence of the fast Fourier transform has extended the practical usefulness of Fourier theory enormously in the past thirty years, with a wide range of areas where it has become important. Fourier expansions are not only useful to study single functions or to characterize the smoothness of elements of various function spaces in terms of the decay of their Fourier transform, but they are also important to study operators between function spaces. It is a well-known fact that the trigonometric basis $\{e^{2\pi i n t}, n \in \mathbb{Z}\}$ diagonalizes translation-invariant operators on the interval $[0, 1)$, identified with the torus. However, the Fourier system is not adapted to represent local information in time of a function or operator, because the representation functions themselves are not localized in time; we have $|e^{2\pi i n t}| = 1$ for all n and t. A small and very local perturbation of $f(t)$ may result in a perturbation of all expansion coefficients $\hat{f}(\omega)$. Roughly speaking, the same remarks apply to the Fourier transform. Indeed, if some noise concentrated on a finite interval is added the change on the Fourier transform will be in the form of the addition of an analytic function, and therefore no single interval of positive length can stay unaffected by such a modification.

Although the Fourier transform is a suitable tool for studying stationary signals or stationary processes (of which the properties are statistically invariant over time), we have to admit that many physical processes and signals are nonstationary; they evolve with time. Think of a speech signal or a musical melody, which can be seen as prototypical signals with well-defined local frequency content, that changes over time.

Let us take a short part of Mozart's Magic Flute, say thirty seconds, and the corresponding number of samples, as they are stored on a CD. If we represent this piece of music as a function of time, we may be able to perceive the transition from one note to the next, but we get little insight about which notes are played. On the other hand, the Fourier representation may give us a clear indication about the prevailing notes in terms of the corresponding frequencies, but information about the moment of emission and duration of the notes is masked in the phases. Both representations are mathematically correct, but we do not have to be members of the Vienna Philharmonic Orchestra to find neither of them satisfying. According to our hearing sensations we would intuitively prefer a representation that is local, in both time and frequency, like a musical score, which tells the musician which note to play at a given time. Additionally, such a local time-frequency representation should be discrete, so that it is better adapted to applications.

Dennis Gabor had similar considerations in mind when he introduced a method to represent a one-dimensional signal in two dimensions, with time and frequency as coordinates, in his "Theory of Communication" in 1946 [Gab46]. Gabor's research in communication theory was driven by the question of how to represent a time signal by a finite number of suitably chosen coefficients in the best possible way, despite the fact that, mathematically speaking, every interval requires uncountably many real numbers $f(t)$ to describe the signal f perfectly on that interval. He was strongly influenced by developments in quantum mechanics, in particular by Heisenberg's *uncertainty principle* and the fundamental results of Nyquist [Nyq24] and Hartley [Har28] on the limits for the transmission of information over a channel.

Gabor proposed expanding a function f into a series of elementary functions constructed from a single building block by translation and modulation (i.e., translation in the frequency domain). More precisely, he suggested representing f by the series

$$f(t) = \sum_{n,m \in \mathbb{Z}} c_{m,n}\, g_{m,n}(t) \tag{1.3}$$

in which the elementary functions $g_{m,n}$ are given by

$$g_{m,n}(t) = e^{2\pi imbt} g(t - na), \quad m, n \in \mathbb{Z} \tag{1.4}$$

for a fixed function g and *time-frequency shift parameters* $a, b > 0$. Although Gabor suggested the use of a Gauss function many other choices of g are now considered reasonable and possible, and any g chosen in this context is called a *Gabor atom*. A typical set of Gabor elementary functions is illustrated in Figure 1.1.

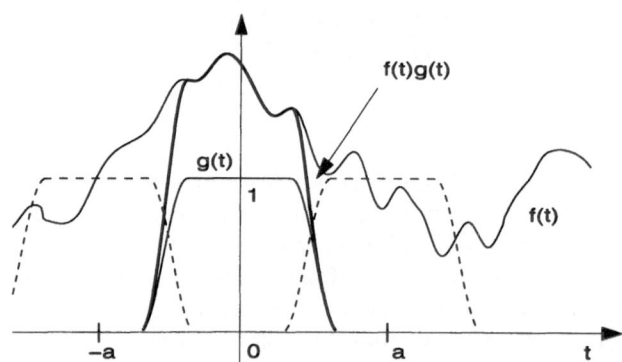

FIGURE 1.2. For fixed t_0 the short-time Fourier transform of a function $f(t)$ describes the local spectral content of $f(t)$ near t_0, as a function of ω. It is defined as the Fourier transform of $f(t)g(t - t_0)$, $g(t)$ is a (often compactly supported) window function, localized around the origin. Moving the center of the window g along the real line allows us to obtain "snapshots" of the time-frequency behavior of f. We depict a collection of such shifted windows, with $t_0 = -a, 0, a$.

In other words the $g_{m,n}$ in (1.4) are obtained by shifting g along a *lattice* $\Lambda = a\mathbb{Z} \times b\mathbb{Z}$ in the *time-frequency plane* (TF plane, for short). If g and its Fourier transform $\hat{g}$ are essentially localized at the origin, then $g_{m,n}$ is essentially localized at (na, mb) in the time-frequency plane, in the sense that $g_{m,n}$ is mostly concentrated near na whereas its Fourier transform $\widehat{g_{m,n}}$ is concentrated around mb. Using the concept of a Short-Time Fourier transform (STFT, see (1.7)) with respect to any other "window" having essentially the same properties, we see that the STFT of $g_{m,n}$ is essentially supported by a region around the point (na, mb) in the TF plane.

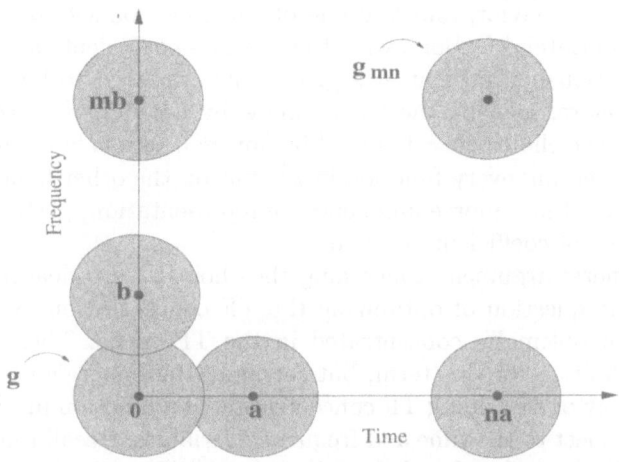

FIGURE 1.3. If g is localized at the origin in the time-frequency plane, then $g_{m,n}$ is localized at the point (na, mb). For appropriate lattice constants a, b the $g_{m,n}$ cover the time-frequency plane.

According to Gabor's interpretation of the situation each elementary function $g_{m,n}$ essentially occupies a certain area ("logon") in the time-frequency plane. Each of the expansion coefficients $c_{m,n}$, associated with the corresponding area of the time-frequency plane via $g_{m,n}$, represents one *quantum of information*. It is not hard to understand (at least qualitatively) that it will not be possible to cover the full time-frequency plane if the lattice constants chosen are too large, and correspondingly certain signals having most of their energy concentrated in the points far away from their centers (in the sense of the TF plane) will have no representation. However, for properly chosen shift parameters a, b the $g_{m,n}$ will cover the time-frequency plane in the appropriate sense. Figure 1.3 visualizes this general idea, although we have to admit that this argument is only heuristic and is not used in any formal mathematical proofs which actually confirm Gabor's intuition to some extent (but not fully).

Indeed, Gabor proposed using the Gauss function and its translations and modulations with shift parameters $ab = 1$ as elementary signals, because they "assure the best utilization of the information area in the sense that they possess the smallest product of effective duration by effective width" [Gab46]. First he argued that the family $\{g_{m,n}\}$ would be too sparse for the case $ab > 1$; certain elements would not be representable. This turned out to be valid in the following slightly stronger sense: Whatever g is chosen, for any pair of lattice constants (a, b) with $ab > 1$ there will always be some L^2-functions f that cannot even be approximated by finite linear combinations from such a Gabor family (in the sense of L^2-norm). On the other hand, he indicated that the choice of $ab < 1$ (at least for the case of the Gauss function) would result in ambiguities of the representation; in other words, for such dense lattices we can — to give a typical example — skip any one of the involved elements and replace it by a suitable (infinite, but fast converging) sum of the remaining elements. Consequently every function f has an many different series expansions of the form (1.3), showing completely different behavior, and any one of them can be set to zero if the other's are adjusted appropriately! Gabor's wish to use those coefficients as indications about the "amount" of frequency present at a given time appeared to be strongly hindered in this case. Therefore, he took the (as we know by now, cf. [GP92]) overoptimistic point of view that the choice $ab = 1$ should be optimal, seriously hoping to achieve the possibility of representing every function in L^2, but on the other hand (working at the border line of lattices that enforce uniqueness of representation) getting into a situation in which uniqueness of coefficients is valid.

Besides this general argument concerning the choice of an ideal lattice Gabor was concerned with the question of optimizing the TF concentration by using a building block that is itself optimally concentrated in the TF plane. There is no unique or logical evident definition for this term, but certainly Heisenberg's uncertainty relation is a very natural way of describing TF concentration of a function in L^2 in a way that is symmetric with respect to the time and frequency variables. Recall that the *uncertainty inequality* [Ben94] states that for all functions $f \in L^2(\mathbb{R})$ and all points (t_0, ω_0) in the time-frequency plane

$$\|f\|_2^2 \le 4\pi \|(t - t_0)f(t)\|_2 \, \|(\omega - \omega_0)\hat{f}(\omega)\|_2 \qquad (1.5)$$

in which equality is achieved only by functions of the form

$$g(t) = Ce^{2\pi it\omega_0}e^{-s(t-t_0)^2}, \quad C \in \mathbb{C}, \, s > 0, \qquad (1.6)$$

i.e., by translated and modulated Gaussians. The Fourier transform of the Gauss function is of the same analytic form, hence its sharpness is reciprocal.

It is obvious that time series and Fourier series are limiting cases of Gabor's series expansion. The first may be obtained by letting $s \to 0$ in (1.6), in which case the $g_{m,n}$ approximate the delta distribution δ; in the second case, the $g_{m,n}$ become ordinary sine and cosine waves for $s \to \infty$.

The idea of representing a function f in terms of the time-frequency shifts of a single atom g did not originate in communication theory; about 15 years earlier it was considered in quantum mechanics. In an attempt to expand general functions (quantum mechanical states) with respect to states with minimal uncertainty, in 1932 John von Neumann [vN55] introduced a set of *coherent states* on a lattice, with lattice constants $ab = \hbar$, in the *phase space* with position and momentum as coordinates ($\hbar$ is *Planck's constant*). Consequently, this lattice is known as the von Neumann lattice; a cell of the lattice is called a *Gibbs cell*. Observing that different units are used in that context it turns out that this corresponds exactly to Gabor's "critical" case $ab = 1$, which can be intrinsically characterized by the fact that the involved time respectively frequency-shift operators commute.

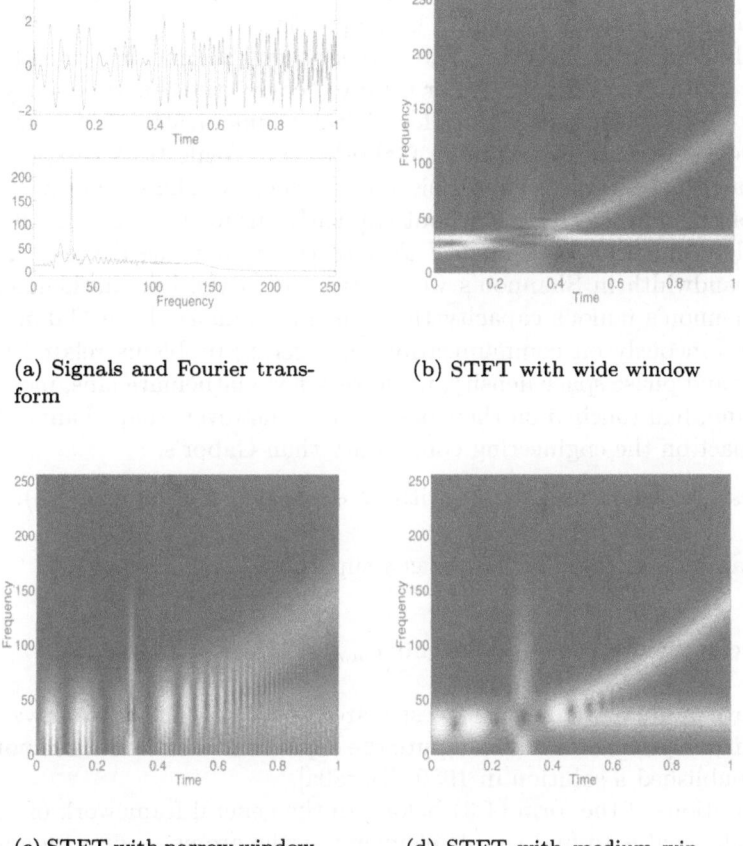

(a) Signals and Fourier transform

(b) STFT with wide window

(c) STFT with narrow window

(d) STFT with medium window

FIGURE 1.4. A signal, its Fourier transform, and short-time Fourier transform with windows of different duration: (a) The signal itself consists of a constant sine wave (with 35 Hz), a quadratic chirp (starting at time 0 with 25 Hz and ending after one second at 140 Hz), and a short pulse (appearing after 0.3 sec). (b) Using a wide window for the STFT leads to good frequency resolution. The constant frequency term can be clearly seen, as can the quadratic chirp. However, the short pulse is hardly visible. (c) Using a narrow window gives good time resolution, clearly localizing the short pulse at 0.3 sec, but the information about the constant harmonic gets very unsharp. (d) In this situation a medium-width window yields a satisfactory resolution in both time and frequency.

These states, associated with the *Weyl-Heisenberg group*, are in principle the same as these used by Gabor. Therefore, the system $\{g_{m,n}\}$ is also called a *Weyl-Heisenberg system*. We recommend the book by Klauder and Skagerstam for an excellent review on coherent states [KS85].

Only two years after Gabor's paper, Shannon published "A Mathematical Theory of Communication" [Sha48]. It should be emphasized that the temporal coincidence is not the only connection between Gabor theory and Shannon's principles of information theory. Both Shannon and Gabor tried to "cover" the time-frequency plane with a set of functions: transmission signals for digital communication in Shannon's case, and building blocks for natural signals in Gabor's case. While Gabor explicitly suggested the Gaussian function and a Weyl-Heisenberg structure, Shannon only emphasized the relevance of orthonormal bases without explicitly suggesting a signal set design. However, the determination of a *critical density* (referred to as degrees of freedom per time and bandwidth in Shannon's work) was one of the key mathematical prerequisites for Shannon's famous capacity theorem. In summary, both Gabor and Shannon workedsimultaneously on communication engineering problems related to Heisenberg uncertainty and phase space density, while very few mathematicians, most prominently von Neumann, had touched on their basics. Note, however, that Shannon's work had a greater impact on the engineering community than Gabor's.

Two questions arise immediately with an expansion of the form (1.3):

- Can any $f \in L^2(\mathbb{R})$ be written as a superposition of such $g_{m,n}$s?

- How can the expansion coefficients $c_{m,n}$ of (1.3) be computed?

Gabor gave an iterative method to estimate the $c_{m,n}$, which was analyzed in [GP92]. However, an analytic method to compute the expansion coefficients was not known until Bastiaans published a solution in 1980 [Bas80a].

Representations of the form (1.3) belong to the general framework of *atomic decompositions*. The goal is to find simple elements — the atoms — of a function space and the "assembly rule" which allows reconstruction of all the elements of the function space using these atoms. Thus, in our context the building block g is also called a *Gabor atom*. See [CR80] for atomic decompositions in function spaces of entire functions and [FG89a, FG89b, FG92b] for atomic decompositions in connection with Gabor analysis.

While Gabor was awarded the Nobel Prize in Physics in 1971 for the conception of holography, his paper on "Theory of Communication" went almost unnoticed until the early 1980s, when the work of Bastiaans and Janssen refreshed the interest of mathematicians and engineers in Gabor analysis. The connection to wavelet theory — in wavelet literature the functions $g_{m,n}$ are often referred to as *Gabor wavelets* — and the increasing interest of scientists in signal analysis and frame theory was then very much influenced by the work of Ingrid Daubechies [DGM86, Dau90, Dau92c]. But before we proceed to the 1980s let us go back to the 1930s and 1940s and follow the development of Gabor theory from the signal analytical point of view.

1.1.2   Local Time-Frequency Analysis and Short-Time Fourier Transform

Time-frequency analysis plays a central role in signal analysis. Long ago it was recognized that a global Fourier transform of a long time signal is of little practical value to analyze the frequency spectrum of a signal. High frequency bursts, for example, cannot be read off easily from $\hat{f}$. Transient signals, which are evolving in time in an unpredictable way (like a speech signal or an EEG signal), necessitate the notion of frequency analysis that is local in time.

In 1932, Wigner derived a distribution over the phase space in quantum mechanics [Wig32].

It is a well-known fact that the *Wigner distribution* of an L^2-function f is the *Weyl symbol* of the orthogonal projection operator onto f [Fol89]. Some 15 years later, Ville, searching for an "instantaneous spectrum" — influenced by the work of Gabor — introduced the same transform in signal analysis [Vil48]. Unfortunately, the nonlinearity of the Wigner distribution causes many interference phenomena, which makes it less attractive for many purposes [Coh95].

A different approach to obtain a local time-frequency analysis (suggested by various scientists, including Ville), is to first cut the signal into slices and then do a Fourier analysis on these slices. But the functions obtained by this crude segmentation are not periodic, which will be reflected in large Fourier coefficients at high frequencies, because the Fourier transform will interpret this jump at the boundaries as a discontinuity or an abrupt variation of the signal. To avoid these artifacts, the concept of windowing has been introduced. Instead of localizing f by means of a rectangle function, one uses a smooth window function for the segmentation, which is close to 1 near the center and decays toward zero at the edges. Popular windows that have been proposed for this purpose are associated with the names Hamming, Hanning, Bartlett, and Kaiser. If the window is in C^∞ (i.e., infinitely differentiable), one finds that for any C^∞-function f the localized Fourier coefficients show at least polynomial decay in the frequency direction.

The resulting local time-frequency analysis procedure is referred to as (continuous) *short-time Fourier transform* or *windowed Fourier transform* [AR77]. It is schematically represented in Figure 1.2. In mathematical notation, the short-time Fourier transform (STFT) of an arbitrary function $f \in L^2(\mathbb{R})$ with respect to a given window g is defined as

$$\mathcal{V}_g f(t,\omega) = \int_{\mathbb{R}} f(s)\overline{g(s-t)}e^{-2\pi i\omega s}ds. \tag{1.7}$$

The function f can be recovered from its STFT via the inversion formula

$$f(t) = \frac{1}{\|g\|_{L^2}^2} \iint_{\mathbb{R}\times\mathbb{R}} \mathcal{V}_g f(s,\omega)g(t-s)e^{2\pi i\omega t}dtd\omega. \tag{1.8}$$

It is possible to derive the inversion formula (the integral is understood in the mean square sense) from the following formula, which can be seen as an immediate consequence of *Moyal's formula*. In particular, it implies that for a normalized window g

satisfying $\|g\|_2 = 1$ the mapping $f \mapsto \mathcal{V}_g f$ is an isometric embedding from $L^2(\mathbb{R})$ into $L^2(\mathbb{R}^{2d})$

$$\|\mathcal{V}_g f\|_{L^2(\mathbb{R} \times \mathbb{R})} = \|g\|_{L^2(\mathbb{R})} \|f\|_{L^2(\mathbb{R})}. \qquad (1.9)$$

The STFT and the *spectrogram* $|\mathcal{V}_g f(t, \omega)|^2$ have become standard tools in signal analysis. However, the STFT has its disadvantages, such as the limit in its time-frequency resolution capability, which is due to the uncertainty principle. Low frequencies can hardly be depicted with short windows, and short pulses can only poorly be localized in time with long windows; see also Figure 1.4 for an illustration of this fact. These limitations in the resolution were one of the reasons for the invention of wavelet theory. (A recent approach to overcome this drawback is to use multiple analysis windows.)

Another disadvantage for many practical purposes is the high redundancy of the STFT. This fact suggests we ask, if we can reduce this redundancy by sampling $\mathcal{V}_g f(t, \omega)$. The natural discretization for t and ω is $t = na$, $\omega = mb$ with $a, b > 0$ fixed, and n, m in $\mathbb{Z}$, i.e., to sample $\mathcal{V}_g f$ over a time-frequency lattice of the form $a\mathbb{Z} \times b\mathbb{Z}$.

Large values of a, b give a coarse discretization, whereas small values of a, b lead to a densely sampled STFT.

Using the operator notation T_t and M_ω for translation and modulation, respectively,

$$T_t f(x) = f(x - t) \qquad M_\omega f(x) = e^{2\pi i \omega x} f(x), \qquad (1.10)$$

we can express the STFT of f with respect to a given window g as

$$\mathcal{V}_g f(t, \omega) = \int_{\mathbb{R}} f(s) \overline{g(s - t)} e^{-2\pi i \omega s} ds = \langle f, T_t M_\omega g \rangle. \qquad (1.11)$$

Hence, the sampled STFT of a function f can also be interpreted as the set of inner products of f with the members of the family $\{g_{m,n}\} = \{T_{na} M_{mb} g\}$ with discrete labels in the lattice $a\mathbb{Z} \times b\mathbb{Z}$. It is obvious that the members of this family are constructed in the same way as the representation functions $g_{m,n}$ in Gabor's series expansion. Thus, the sampled STFT is also referred to as *Gabor transform*.

Two questions arise immediately with the discretization of the STFT:

- Do the discrete STFT coefficients $\langle f, g_{m,n} \rangle$ completely characterize f (i.e., does $\langle f_1, g_{m,n} \rangle = \langle f_2, g_{m,n} \rangle$ for all m, n imply that $f_1 = f_2$)?

- A stronger formulation is: Can we reconstruct f in a numerically stable way from the $\langle f, g_{m,n} \rangle$?

Recall that in connection with the Gabor expansion of a function we have asked:

- Can any function in $L^2(\mathbb{R})$ be written as a superposition of the elementary building blocks?

- How can we compute the coefficients $c_{m,n}$ of the series expansion $f = \sum c_{m,n} g_{m,n}$?

It turns out that the question of recovering f from the samples (at lattice points) of its STFT with respect to the window g is actually dual to the problem of finding coefficients for the Gabor expansion of f with atom g, using the same lattice to generate the time-frequency shifts of g. Both problems can be successfully and mathematically rigorously handled using the concept of frames and, surprisingly, for both questions the same "dual" Gabor atom has to be used.

1.1.3 Fundamental Properties of Gabor Frames

The theory of frames is due to Duffin and Schaeffer [DS52] and was introduced in the context of nonharmonic Fourier series only six years after Gabor published his paper. Despite this, frame analysis became popular in sampling theory, time-frequency analysis, and wavelet theory much later, ignited by the papers [DGM86] and [Dau90]. Expository treatments of frames can be found in [You80], [Dau92c], and [BW94].

A system $\{g_{m,n}\} = \{T_{na}M_{mb}g\}$ is a *Gabor frame* or *Weyl-Heisenberg frame* for $L^2(\mathbb{R})$, if there are two constants $0 < A \leq B < \infty$ such that for any $f \in L^2(\mathbb{R})$

$$A\|f\|^2 \leq \sum_{m,n\in\mathbb{Z}} |\langle f, g_{m,n}\rangle|^2 \leq B\|f\|^2. \qquad (1.12)$$

For a Gabor frame $\{g_{m,n}\}$ the *analysis mapping* (also called Gabor transform) T_g, given by

$$\mathrm{T}_g : f \mapsto \{\langle f, g_{m,n}\rangle\}_{m,n}, \qquad (1.13)$$

and its adjoint, the *synthesis mapping* (also called Gabor expansion) T_g^*, given by

$$\mathrm{T}_g^* : \{c_{m,n}\} \mapsto \sum_{m,n\in\mathbb{Z}} c_{m,n}\, g_{m,n} \qquad \{c_{m,n}\} \in \ell^2(\mathbb{Z}), \qquad (1.14)$$

are bounded linear operators. The *Gabor frame operator* S_g is defined by

$$S_g f = \mathrm{T}_g^*\mathrm{T}_g f = \sum_{m,n\in\mathbb{Z}} \langle f, g_{m,n}\rangle\, g_{m,n}. \qquad (1.15)$$

We will often drop the subscript and denote the Gabor frame operator simply by S.

According to standard frame theory the family $\{g_{m,n}\}$ constitutes a Gabor frame for $L^2(\mathbb{R})$, if and only if S is a bounded and boundedly invertible operator on $L^2(\mathbb{R})$. In this case any function $f \in L^2(\mathbb{R})$ satisfies $f = S(S^{-1}f) = S^{-1}(Sf)$, or explicitly

$$f = \sum_{m,n} \langle f, g_{m,n}\rangle\, \gamma_{m,n} = \sum_{m,n} \langle f, \gamma_{m,n}\rangle\, g_{m,n} \qquad (1.16)$$

in which $\gamma_{m,n}$ are the elements of the dual frame, given by $\gamma_{m,n} = S^{-1}g_{m,n}$. Equation (1.16) provides a constructive answer to how to recover f from its Gabor transform

$\{\langle f, g_{m,n}\rangle\}_{m,n\in\mathbb{Z}}$ for a given analysis window g and to how to compute suitable coefficients for a series expansion of the form $f = \sum c_{m,n} g_{m,n}$ for a given atom g. It holds for general frames that this method yields to all those coefficients that have minimal "energy" (or ℓ^2-norm), and thus we have enforced uniqueness again in this very natural sense.

This short explanation makes it clear that in order to be able to expand signals f in this way it is crucial to be able to determine the corresponding dual frame $\{S^{-1} g_{m,n}\}_{m,n\in\mathbb{Z}}$.

More results on Gabor frames can be found in [Dau92c, Wal92, FG92b, BW94, Kai95] and in the work of Janssen, and Ron and Shen. Gabor frames for spaces other than L^2 have been studied in [Dau90, BW94, BHW95, FG92a, FG96]. An interesting representation of the Gabor frame operator has been derived by Walnut [Wal92].

A detailed analysis of Gabor frames brings forward some features that are basic for a further understanding of Gabor analysis. Most of these features are not shared by other frames such as wavelet frames.

1.1.4   Commutation Relations of the Gabor Frame Operator

Although it is not difficult to check, the following *commutation relations* are very important for many aspects of Gabor analysis. As mentioned in [Dau90] the Gabor frame operator commutes with translations by a and modulations by b, i.e.,

$$ST_a = T_a S, \quad SM_b = M_b S. \tag{1.17}$$

It follows that S^{-1} also commutes with T_a and M_b, so that

$$\gamma_{m,n} = S^{-1} g_{m,n} = S^{-1} T_{na} M_{mb} g = T_{na} M_{mb} S^{-1} g = T_{na} M_{mb} \gamma. \tag{1.18}$$

Therefore, the elements of the dual Gabor frame $\{\gamma_{m,n}\}$ are generated by a single function γ, analogously to $g_{m,n}$. This observation bears important computational advantages. To compute the dual system $\{\gamma_{m,n}\}$ one computes the (canonically) *dual atom* $\gamma = S^{-1} g$ and derives all other elements $\gamma_{m,n}$ of the dual frame by translations and modulations along the same TF lattice that generates the original Gabor frame.

Because general frames are overcomplete sets, there are many choices for the coefficients $c_{m,n}$, and even different choices of γ are possible. However, in the words of Daubechies, the coefficients determined by the dual frame are the most economical ones, in the sense that they have minimal ℓ^2-norm, and at the same time γ is the L^2-function with minimal norm for which 1.16 holds.

1.1.5   Critical Sampling, Oversampling, and the Balian-Low Theorem

In 1971 it was proved by Peremolov [Per71] and independently by Bargmann et al. [BBGK71] that for Gaussian g the system $\{g_{m,n}\}$ is complete in $L^2(\mathbb{R})$ if and only if $ab \le 1$, i.e., but in this case we can assure that finite linear combinations can be used to approximate any given $f \in L^2(\mathbb{R})$ to any given precision, measured in the L^2-norm. However, this does not imply the possibility of a norm-convergent series expansion, in

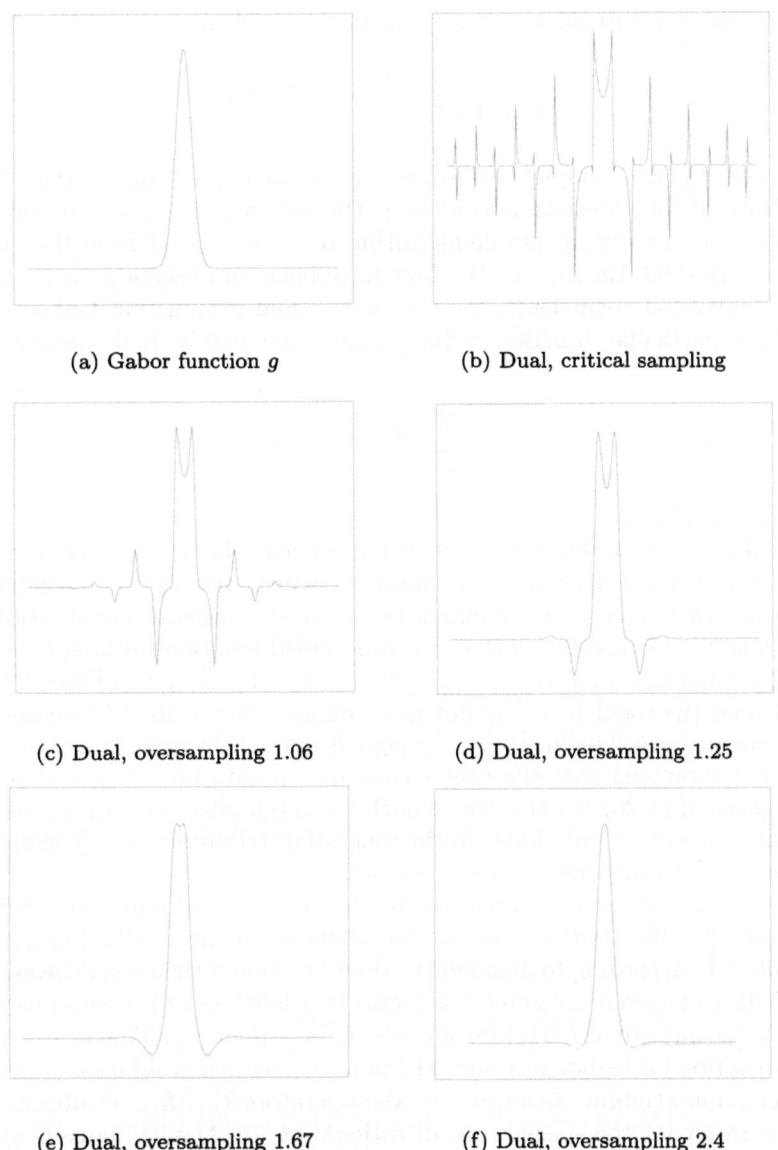

(a) Gabor function g

(b) Dual, critical sampling

(c) Dual, oversampling 1.06

(d) Dual, oversampling 1.25

(e) Dual, oversampling 1.67

(f) Dual, oversampling 2.4

FIGURE 1.5. Dual Gabor functions for different oversampling rates. The dual window approaches Bastiaan's dual function for critical sampling, and it approximates the given Gabor window g with oversampling rate increasing.

which improved approximation can be achieved only by using more terms, but using the "correct" coefficient for a given building block and not choosing a completely new collection of coefficients each time the error has to be reduced. Indeed, in 1975 Bacry, Grossmann, and Zak [BGZ75] showed that if $ab = 1$, then

$$\inf_{f \in L^2(\mathbb{R})} \sum_{m,n} |\langle f, g_{m,n} \rangle|^2 = 0 \qquad (1.19)$$

although the $g_{m,n}$ are complete in $L^2(\mathbb{R})$. Formula (1.19) implies that for Gabor's original choice of the Gaussian and $ab = 1$, the set $\{g_{m,n}\}$ is not a frame for $L^2(\mathbb{R})$. Thus, there is no numerically stable algorithm to reconstruct f from the $\langle f, g_{m,n} \rangle$.

Bastiaans [Bas80b, Bas81] was the first to publish an analytic solution to compute the Gabor expansion coefficients, for $a = b = 1$ and a Gaussian Gabor atom g. He constructed a particular function γ (now called Bastiaan's dual function), claiming that

$$f = \sum_{m,n} \langle f, g_{m,n} \rangle \gamma_{m,n} \qquad (1.20)$$

with $\gamma_{m,n} = T_{na} M_{mb} \gamma$.

Convergence issues of this series expansion, at least for the general case, turn out to be a highly delicate mathematical question, which also indicates that one should not try to use this expansion for numerical purposes, because instabilities are to be expected. Janssen [Jan82] found that γ is a bounded function (although plots give the impression of singularities at the integers) but does not belong to $L^2(\mathbb{R})$. Therefore, as a first difficulty, the coefficients are not well defined (for certain L^2-functions). Even if these coefficients are well defined (e.g., for signals in the Schwartz class of test functions) it cannot be guaranteed that the coefficients are square summable, and consequently the convergence of (1.20) is not clear in such cases (cf. also [DJ93]). Janssen [Jan81] showed that convergence only holds in the sense of distributions (cf. [FZ98] for another detailed analysis of this convergence problem).

Using methods from complex analysis, Lyubarskii [Lyu92] and, independently, Seip and Wallsten [SW92] showed that for the Gaussian g the family $\{g_{m,n}\}$ is a frame whenever $ab < 1$. According to Janssen the dual function γ then is a Schwartz function.

As a corollary of deep results on C^*-algebras by Rieffel [Rie81] it was proved that the set $\{g_{m,n}\}$ is incomplete in $L^2(\mathbb{R})$ for any $g \in L^2(\mathbb{R})$, if $ab > 1$. This fact can be seen as a Nyquist criterion for Gabor systems. The nonconstructive proof uses the properties of the von Neumann algebras, generated by the operators $T_{na} M_{mb}$. Daubechies [Dau90] derived this result for the special case of rational ab. In [Jan94] Janssen showed that the $g_{m,n}$ cannot establish a frame for any $g \in L^2(\mathbb{R})$, if $ab > 1$ without any restriction on ab. One year earlier Landau proved the weaker result that $\{g_{m,n}\}$ cannot be a frame for $L^2(\mathbb{R})$ if $ab > 1$, and both g and $\hat{g}$ satisfy certain decay conditions [Lan93]. His result includes the case of irregular Gabor systems in which the sampling set is not necessarily a lattice.

All these results point to the role of the Nyquist density for sampling and reconstruction of band-limited functions in Shannon's sampling theorem. Hence it is natural to classify Gabor systems according to the corresponding sampling density of the time-frequency lattice:

- *Oversampling* — $ab < 1$: Frames with excellent time-frequency localization properties exist (a particular example are frames with the Gaussian g and appropriate oversampling rate).

- *Critical sampling* — $ab = 1$: Frames and orthonormal bases are possible, but — as we will see — without good time-frequency localization. The time-frequency shift operators, which are used to build the coherent frame, commute with each other (without nontrivial factor) in this case.

- *Undersampling* — $ab > 1$: In this case any Gabor family will be incomplete, in the sense that the closed linear span is a proper subspace of $L^2(\mathbb{R})$. In particular, we cannot have a frame for $L^2(\mathbb{R})$.

Clearly, there are many choices for g, so that $\{g_{m,n}\}$ is a frame or even an orthonormal basis (ONB) for $L^2(\mathbb{R})$. Two well-known examples of functions for which the family $\{T_{na}M_{mb}g\}$ constitutes an ONB are the rectangle function (which is 1 for $0 \le t \le 1$ and 0 otherwise), and the sinc function $g(t) = \sin \pi t/\pi t$, which is obtained by applying the Fourier transform to that box function. However, in the first case $\int \omega^2 |\hat{g}(\omega)|^2 = \infty$, in the second case $\int t^2 |g(t)|^2 = \infty$. Thus, these choices lead to systems with bad localization properties in both time and frequency. Even if we drop the orthogonality requirement, it can be shown that it is impossible to construct Riesz bases for the case $ab = 1$ such that both its elements and the elements of the corresponding biorthogonal family have a good time-frequency localization. One precise statement in this direction is the celebrated Balian-Low theorem [Bal81, Low85], which describes one of the key facts in Gabor analysis and is one of the main reasons Gabor analysis is so different from wavelet theory (in which orthonormal bases with building blocks even with compact support and a given degree of smoothness can be constructed, cf. [DJJ91]).

Balian-Low Theorem: *If the $g_{m,n}$ constitute a Riesz basis for $L^2(\mathbb{R})$, then*

$$\int_{-\infty}^{+\infty} |g(t)|^2 t^2 \cdot \int_{-\infty}^{+\infty} |g(\omega)|^2 \omega^2 = \infty, \tag{1.21}$$

See [BHW98] for an expository treatment of the Balian Low theorem and its consequences.

According to Gabor's heuristics the integer lattice in the time-frequency plane was chosen to make the choice of coefficients "as unique as possible" (unfortunately, we cannot have strict uniqueness because there are bounded sequences that represent the zero function in a nontrivial but only in a distributional sense).

In focusing his attention on the uniqueness problem Gabor apparently overlooked that the use of well-localized building blocks to obtain an expansion $f = \sum_{m,n} c_{m,n} g_{m,n}$ does not imply that the computation of the coefficient $c_{m,n}$ can be carried out by a "local" procedure, using only information localized around (an, bm) in the time-frequency plane. The lack of time-frequency locality of the Gabor coefficients is not only severe in the critical case, but it becomes more serious if we use a sequence of lattices that are close to critical sampling. This becomes clear by observing that the corresponding dual functions lose their time-frequency localization (see also Figure 1.5).

It appears that Gabor families with some (modest) redundancy, which allows a pair of dual Gabor atoms (g, γ), with each function of this dual pair well localized in time and frequency (cf. also Figure 1.5), are more appropriate as a tool in Gabor's original sense. Clearly, under such premises one has to give up the uniqueness of coefficients and even the uniqueness of γ. The choice $\gamma = S^{-1}g$ is in some sense canonical and — as we have seen — appropriate Gabor coefficients can be easily determined as samples of the STFT with window γ.

This observation leads to the question of whether there is a way to obtain an orthonormal basis for $L^2(\mathbb{R})$ with good time-frequency properties based on Gabor's approach.

Wilson observed that for the study of the kinetic operator in quantum mechanics, we do not need basis functions that distinguish between positive and negative frequencies of the same order [Wil87, SRWW87]. Musicians probably would also find it acceptable to make a distinction between sin- and cos-modulated versions of a given envelope (hence also between positive and negative frequencies of the same absolute value), because the human ear does not make any distinction between them (musical notation can also be understood in terms of the "absolute value" of the occurring frequencies).

Thus, we are looking for complete orthonormal systems that are essentially of Weyl-Heisenberg type but use linear combinations of terms $g_{t,s}$ and $g_{t,-s}$. Although such minor modifications are usually considered only as a question of appearance of formulas — if we think of Fourier series expansions in their classical or their modern form (1.1) — it turns out that it makes a substantial difference in the current context. Indeed, a family of orthonormal bases for $L^2(\mathbb{R})$ can be constructed avoiding the Balian-Low phenomenon, the so-called *Wilson bases*. Wilson's suggestion was turned into a construction by Daubechies, Jaffard, and Journé [DJJ91], who gave a recipe how to obtain an orthonormal Wilson basis from a tight Gabor frame for $a = 1/2$ and $b = 1$ (see also [BHW98] and the research articles [Aus94, FGW92, Tac96]). The elements of such a Wilson basis can even be test functions, i.e., functions g with compact support that have continuous derivatives of any order.

The use of redundant frame representations and the fact that by preselecting the TF lattice, means that we may need a comparatively large number of small coefficients to represent a signal that might otherwise have a simple representation by a single term, e.g., some TF translate of the atom g, but with shift-parameters not from the given lattice. This suggests we look for a more flexible way of representing signals, with the aim of minimizing the number of necessary coefficients whenever possible. Theoretically, it is clear that by choosing a very large collection of potential building blocks (a so-called *dictionary*, which may include all TF shifts and dilated versions of a given atom g) we get a better chance to get a "sparse representation" of a given "simple" signal, i.e., one that can be expressed as a finite linear combination of elements from the dictionary. Ideally, only the original building blocks are involved. It is plausible that this aim cannot be achieved by any linear method that maps the signal space to the coefficient space. Indeed, the suitable selection of the required family of atoms from such a huge dictionary has to be controlled by the signal to be represented; hence so-called *adaptive methods* are required, which are controlled in their behavior by signal properties.

The best known algorithm has been introduced by Mallat and Zhang [MZ93] in 1993, the *matching pursuit* for representing highly nonstationary signals. A "greedy" algorithm used building blocks from the dictionary, and the appropriate coefficients are chosen by looking for the strongest correlation between the given signal and all elements of the dictionary. Once a finite sum has been detected it is subtracted from the signal and the remainder is handled in the same way. Despite the popularity of this approach there are a number of theoretical and practical problems with this approach, and new modifications have been suggested in recent literature.

The idea is to expand a given signal into a small number of atoms by selecting atoms from a given *time-frequency dictionary*, which best match the structures included in a signal. The analysis functions of this dictionary are constructed by translations, dilations (like wavelets), and modulations (like Gabor expansions) from a single atom.

Clearly, there is a trade-off between using a huge library of atoms to construct an "optimal" representation of a signal and the computational costs to find the representation functions in this library. Attempts to handle this trade-off comprise multiwavelets and multiwindow Gabor schemes (see [SS94, ZZ97]).

1.1.6 Wexler-Raz Duality Condition

Ignoring mathematical details we say that a system of the form $\gamma_{m,n} = T_{na}M_{mb}\gamma$ is dual to $g_{m,n}$ if every $f \in L^2(\mathbb{R})$ has an L^2-convergent representation of the form

$$f = \sum_{m,n} \langle f, \gamma_{m,n} \rangle \, g_{m,n} \,, \tag{1.22}$$

with a square summable coefficient sequence. Although a frame that is not a Riesz basis (this holds for most Gabor frames) has some built-in redundancy and hence allows many representations of a given signal, it is not obvious that this ambiguity persists if the coefficients have to be of the form $\langle f, \gamma_{m,n} \rangle$ for some $\gamma \in L^2(\mathbb{R})$. If we call any $\gamma \in L^2(\mathbb{R})$ such that (1.22) holds a *dual function* of g with respect to the given time-frequency lattice, it is obvious that the functions $g_{m,n}$ form an affine subspace of $L^2(\mathbb{R})$. In other words, there is a nontrivial linear subspace of $L^2(\mathbb{R})$ such that the difference of any two dual functions (for fixed g and fixed lattice) belongs to that linear space.

The so-called Wexler-Raz theorem (cf. [WR90]) describes this linear space as the orthogonal complement of the family $\{M_{m/a}T_{n/b}g, \ m, n \in \mathbb{Z}\}$. Indeed, Ron and Shen [RS95] were the first to show that this Weyl-Heisenberg family is a Riesz basis if and only if the original family $g_{m,n}$ is a Gabor frame. Moreover, up to normalization, the biorthogonal family to this Riesz basis is again of the same form and is generated by $\tilde{g}$ analogously. Finally, we can show that among all dual functions the *canonical dual* obtained via $\gamma = S^{-1}g$ can be characterized within this affine space by any of the following properties:

1. γ has least energy.

2. It generates the coefficients with minimal ℓ^2-norm for each $f \in L^2(\mathbb{R})$.

3. It is closest to g in L^2-norm.

4. It minimizes the L^2-distance between the normalized versions $g/\|g\|_2$ and $\gamma/\|\gamma\|_2$, i.e., it satisfies the so-called Qian-Chen most orthogonallike condition.

If we want to distinguish it from other duals we denote it by $°\gamma$. The freedom of using alternative dual atoms γ different from $°\gamma$ can be used to optimize different aims. For example, if we want to improve the local concentration experiments, show that this is possible to a limited extent at the cost of loss of frequency concentration.

1.1.7   Gabor Analysis on LCA Groups

Although most of the literature published in the field of Gabor analysis so far (cf. [TA98, FS98b, CHT98, Grö99]) concentrates on Gabor analysis for $L^2(\mathbb{R})$-functions or vectors of finite length (discrete and periodic sequences) and in a few cases on the nonperiodic discrete case or multidimensional settings [Li94, KFPS96, FK97], basically Gabor analysis can be applied to any signal for which an appropriate Fourier transform (in conjunction with a related concept of translation) is available. The general background to such a *conceptual* approach is provided by a mathematical theory, that fundamental results of which were developed around the time of Gabor's paper (i.e., around 1950) and is known by the somewhat unfortunate name of *abstract harmonic analysis*. This section will explain some of the relevant facts and show how the use of "abstract" concepts can help us to better understand the general principles that lead to slightly different (but structurally equal) formulas in different settings. This section is, of course, very close to the book by Ann and Tolimieri [TA98] and the articles [Grö98, FK97] in the Gabor book [FS98b], which are recommended for the reader who is interested in more details on this subject.

Let us first recall that the situation we want to describe is based on an "abstract" approach to the family of Fourier transforms. The ordinary Fourier transform applies to periodic functions in the form of Fourier series, to nonperiodic functions with good decay in the form of an integral transform, or as a generalized Fourier transform defined for (tempered) distributions. Finally, it shows up in the form of a discrete Fourier transform (for short DFT), which applies to complex vectors of length N. As it is easy to combine any two of those Fourier transforms to product domains (e.g., to define the Fourier transform for functions on the d-dimensional Euclidean space $\mathbb{R}^d$, or to pixel images of format $K \times L$) we can say that the most natural setting for Fourier transform theory (resp. harmonic analysis) are functions on so-called *elementary (Abelian) groups* (see [FK97]) that arise as simple products of the cases just mentioned, with a Fourier transform (but also translation) that operates in each coordinate separately. In other words, the group Fourier transform is obtained by iterating the standard Fourier transform to the different coordinates.

As explained in [FK97] we can obtain Gabor expansions not only for functions on $\mathbb{R}^n$ (i.e., of a "continuous" variable), but also for periodic or nonperiodic discrete time series of one or more variables, or, generally speaking, for functions defined on elementary

Abelian groups. However, instead of going by analogy with the most simple case it is the idea of *abstract harmonic analysis* to start from the common general properties of the relevant Fourier transform, in a given context, without taking care of its explicit form. As it turned out, the correct mathematical setting is the theory of *locally compact Abelian groups*, LCA groups; see [Rud62, HR63, Rei68, Kat68, Fol94], basic principles of which are outlined below.

However, right at the beginning we would like to emphasize that it is *not* so much the mathematician's inclination to look for the most general formulation that motivates us to introduce this topic here, but rather the conviction that this unifying language allows us to work at a higher, more *conceptual* level, avoiding a lot of concrete (and in some sense unnecessary) calculations in concrete special cases and getting a better overview of what we have to expect, even as we go to a larger number of variables or to situations in which discrete and continuous variables are mixed. Indeed, the situation may be compared to that of linear spaces, where — at the beginning — we prefer calculations using a particular basis (the particular choice may have an influence on the length of the computation). Later, you may come to the understanding that a more modern and coordinate free way allows for shorter arguments and emphasizes the underlying structure, although it may be more abstract in the sense of ignoring details that are actually unnecessary for the derivation.

In this sense, *abstract harmonic analysis* provides the natural unified framework that allows us to develop key results of Gabor analysis independent of the question, whether variables are "continuous" or "discrete," periodic or nonperiodic, one- or higher-dimensional. Indeed, the basis for this approach is always the interpretation of the class of signals under consideration as functions on some underlying *commutative group* G, with a group law that is usually written additively (hence the neutral element is denoted by 0, and instead of adding the inverse of x to y we write $y - x$). Consequently the concept of translation has an obvious meaning: $T_u(f)$, the translation of a function f by u is the function taking the same values as f, but at positions that are shifted by u compared to the original function. For $G = \mathbb{R}^n$ this unitary, hence isometric or energy-preserving and invertible, transformation is the usual translation.

Thus T_u shifts the graph of f in the direction of u. If f is a bumplike function mostly concentrated near the origin, then $T_u f$ is a function of the same shape concentrated at u. For ordinary vectors of finite length N the natural interpretation is to identify them with functions on the most simple group, i.e., the *cyclic group* of order N. Two (equivalent) concrete models of such a group are the family of remainders $\mathbb{Z}$ mod (N), resp., the group of (complex) unit roots of order N, defined by $\mathbb{Z}_N := \{\exp(-2\pi i k/N), 0 \leq k \leq N-1\}$, forming a group with respect to the multiplication of complex numbers. Therefore, finite sequences of length N have to be identified either with their N-periodic extensions (first model) where translation is the translation of sequences over the integers or translation has to be taken in the cyclic sense (second model), i.e., $T_1([x_0, \cdots, x_{N-1}]) = [x_{N-1}, x_0, x_1, \cdots, x_{N-2}]$. Because the exponential law transforms the law of the first group in a one-to-one way to the addition of exponents $\mod(N)$ the two approaches are obviously equivalent. We think it is easier to understand the correspondence if we label the coordinates of a vector $\mathbf{x}$ of length N as $\mathbf{x} = (x_l)_{l=0}^{N-1}$, which shows that it is naturally identified with a function $k \mapsto x_{k+1}$, for $0 \leq k \leq N-1$.

Clearly, any subgroup of $\mathbb{Z}_N$ is of the form $\mathbb{Z}_M$, with $N = aM$ for some natural number a, which has to be a divisor of N. Of course, a can be understood as a lattice constant describing a (regular) subsampling procedure of $\mathbb{Z}_N$ to $\mathbb{Z}_M$. For digital images of size $K \times L$ the most natural interpretation is to view them as functions on $\mathbb{Z}_K \times \mathbb{Z}_L$, and translation has to be understood in a double cyclic sense: Those parts of an image that move "out of the given frame" to the right or at the top show up again on the left and at the bottom of the image, respectively. Again the alternative is to view images as tiles (of size $K \times L$) that, by double periodic extension cover all of $\mathbb{Z}^2$ and to apply ordinary translation on $\mathbb{Z}^2$.

Although these interpretations may look a bit artificial at the beginning and cause some boundary effect (as is well known from ordinary Fourier analysis) they can be handled relative easily (although one should not neglect them!). However, as a very important payoff we get a full group structure with great practical and theoretical advantages, i.e., for computational aspects (e.g., using FFT) and a unified treatment within harmonic analysis.

Dual Groups and Time-Frequency Planes

Going back to general *Abelian*, i.e., *commutative*, groups (with continuous variables) one has to assume that they are endowed with a suitable topology, turning them into *locally compact Abelian groups* (LCA groups, for short). For the case of $G = \mathbb{R}^n$ this means that for each point $\mathbf{x} \in \mathbb{R}^n$ the closed balls of radius ε are compact but still arbitrary small, in the sense of being suitable to define the concept of convergent sequences in $\mathbb{R}^n$.

Besides the finite-dimensional spaces such as $\mathbb{R}^n$, discrete groups such as $\mathbb{Z}_K \times \mathbb{Z}_L$ or the torus $\mathbb{T} = \{z \in \mathbb{C}, |z| = 1\}$ are important examples. For the torus group multiplication is taken from the complex numbers (note that $z\bar{z} = |z|^2 = 1$ implies $z^{-1} = \bar{z}$ for $z \in \mathbb{T}$). More generally, the so-called *elementary groups* that arise as finite products of these groups have to be mentioned.

An example not falling into this class is any infinite-dimensional vector space, with the standard addition of vectors. It clearly forms an Abelian group, but it will not be possible to provide a topology (compatible with the group structure) that is locally compact.

The local compactness of G implies that there are always "sufficiently many" *characters*, i.e., continuous functions taking complex values of absolute value 1 and satisfying an exponential law of the form

$$\chi(x + y) = \chi(x)\chi(y) \quad \text{for all} \quad x, y \in G.$$

In other words, a function χ is a character on G if it is a group homomorphism from $(G, +)$ to the torus $(\mathbb{T}, \cdot)$. It is easy to verify that these functions, with pointwise multiplication, form a group, the so-called *dual group* $\hat{G}$. Obviously, the constant function $\chi_0(x) = 1$, for all $x \in G$, is the neutral element, satisfying $\chi_0 \cdot \chi = \chi$ for all χ, and $\bar{\chi}$ is the inverse element for a given χ, because $\chi(x)\bar{\chi}(x) = |\chi(x)|^2 = 1 = \chi_0(x)$ in this group. By introducing the topology of uniform convergence over compact sets on $\hat{G}$ (for the general case), $\hat{G}$ is again an LCA group.

Typically, these *characters* $\chi \in \hat{G}$ are — in concrete examples — *pure frequencies* or (complex) *plane waves*. Indeed, for $G = \mathbb{R}^n$ a bounded and continuous function is a character, if and only if it is of the form $\mathbf{x} \mapsto \exp(2\pi i(x_1 y_1 + \cdots + x_n y_n))$ for a uniquely determined vector $\mathbf{y} \in \mathbb{R}^n$. Therefore, it makes sense to identify $\widehat{\mathbb{R}^n}$ with $\mathbb{R}^n$ itself, with the understanding that we take any $\mathbf{y} \in \mathbb{R}^n$, whenever it appears as a "frequency" vector, just as a parameter for the corresponding character $\chi_{\mathbf{y}}$, given by

$$\chi_{\mathbf{y}}(\mathbf{x}) = \exp(2\pi i(x_1 y_1 + \cdots + x_n y_n)) \;\; \forall \mathbf{x} \in \mathbb{R}^n \; . \tag{1.23}$$

Furthermore, it is important to understand that by this identification the abstract group law (multiplication of characters) really corresponds in a one-to-one way to ordinary addition of the parameters (usually named frequencies). Therefore, and to strongly indicate that the dual group is again a commutative group — by the obvious reason that pointwise multiplication does not depend on the order — it is standard to identify the characters defined earlier with their (abstract) labels and to write $\chi_1 + \chi_2$ in order to express the "composition" of the two characters in $\hat{G}$.

This convention is also quite natural for the case of the finite group $\mathbb{Z}_N$, where the characters are simply the mappings of the form $\chi_k : u \mapsto u^k$, for $0 \leq k \leq N - 1$. A simple calculation shows that the obvious identification of χ with its parameter k establishes a natural identification of $\widehat{\mathbb{Z}_N}$ with $\mathbb{Z}_N$ itself. Viewed as vectors of length N these characters are essentially sampled complex exponential functions, or — if one wants to see it that way — just the entries (rows or columns) of the Fourier matrix that describes the (unitary) linear mapping $\mathbf{x} \mapsto \mathrm{FFT}(\mathbf{x})$.

These two most important examples of $\mathbb{Z}_N$ and $\mathbb{R}^n$ should not suggest that the dual group can always be identified with the group itself, as typically a discrete group, like the integers $(\mathbb{Z}, +)$, has a compact dual group, in this case the torus $\mathbb{T}$ via $\chi_z(k) = z^k$, which is different from $\mathbb{Z}$ itself. Conversely, a compact group, such as the torus $\mathbb{T}$, has a discrete dual group, here $\mathbb{Z}$ via $\chi_k(z) = z^k$. However, it is true that $\hat{\hat{G}} = G$ via natural identification.

For the general case, the practical and theoretical importance of these characters is based on the fact that they are exactly the *eigenvectors* for the full family of translation operators and hence also of the family of convolution operators. Because they form something like a (continuous or discrete) basis, the corresponding change of bases, usually denoted as abstract *Fourier transform*, diagonalizes all those convolution operators simultaneously and turns convolution operators into pointwise multiplication. The fact that (again due to the local compactness of G) there are "sufficiently many" characters translates into the (expected) fact that the Fourier transform is a one-to-one mapping (for a large class of functions or distributions), and even a unitary linear mapping between the space $L^2(G)$ of signals of finite energy on G to the corresponding space on $\hat{G}$, i.e., $L^2(\hat{G})$.

Thus, for any such LCA group G the product space $G \times \hat{G}$ takes the role of the (abstract) *time-frequency plane* (TF-plane). There are two interpretations of $G \times \hat{G}$. On the one hand, by viewing at it as a simple product group with addition taking place in each coordinate (like with vectors in $\mathbb{R}^2$) it is another LCA group. On the other hand, we may identify the pairs (x, χ) with frequency shift operators acting on f via multiplication of f by the corresponding character $\chi \in \hat{G}$. By combining these two commutative groups we get a so-called (projective) representation of $G \times \hat{G}$ by "time-frequency" shifts, which we will denote by π. Thus, for $\lambda = (x, \chi)$ the corresponding TF shift $\pi(x, \chi)$ consists of the composition of translation by the element x, followed by multiplication with the character $\chi \in \hat{G}$; i.e., we have

$$[\pi(x, \chi)f](z) = \chi(z)f(z - x). \tag{1.24}$$

Let us assume the following setting. Given an arbitrary nonzero atom $g \in L^2(G)$ (i.e., a signal of finite energy on G) and a fixed TF lattice, and a discrete subgroup Λ in $G \times \hat{G}$ with compact quotient. In this context, **Gabor analysis on G** is concerned with the question

How can we expand general functions $f \in L^2(G)$ (or, more generally, function spaces) in the form of a series

$$f = \sum_{\lambda \in \Lambda} c_\lambda \pi(\lambda)g, \tag{1.25}$$

for suitable ℓ^2-coefficients (c_λ) (resp., with coefficients in an appropriate sequence space indexed by Λ) ?

As we would like to have stability of the expansion we come back to the question of whether $(\pi(\lambda)g)_{\lambda \in \Lambda}$ is a frame for $L^2(G)$. If it is a frame this family is a *Gabor frame* on G generated by the pair (g, Λ).

Of course, besides this basic requirement, some other aspects are important for the usefulness of these representations. For example, such a representation should allow one to "read" the coefficients in the following way. If for some subset of G the function $f \in L^2(G)$ is very smooth this should show up in the Gabor coefficients corresponding to this area in the form of strong decay with respect to the parameter χ. Moreover, storing only a few Gabor coefficients will allow us to have a good approximate representation of the signal in that domain. Such extra requirements (and the so-called *Balian-Low phenomenon*) imply that the otherwise very simple orthonormal bases for $L^2(G)$ that arise from the indicator function of the fundamental domain for some discrete subgroup $H \subseteq G$ (e.g., the box function $\mathbf{1}_{[0,0)}$ for the case $\mathbb{Z} \subseteq \mathbb{R}$) typically are not of much interest in this context. Although they do not form orthonormal bases (unlike wavelet systems), Gabor families with some redundancy are nevertheless of great interest, with blocks $\pi(\lambda)g$ if both g and the Gabor atom $\tilde{g}$ generating the dual Gabor frame are well concentrated in the corresponding TF sense.

As described in [FK97] (for the context of *elementary* LCA groups) the key results of Gabor analysis can be reproduced on the basis of general facts concerning LCA groups. In particular, the so-called *commutation law* for the frame operator, which is now of the form

$$S(f) = S_{\Lambda, g}(f) = \sum_{\lambda \in \Lambda} \langle f, \pi(\lambda) \rangle \pi(\lambda)(g), \tag{1.26}$$

i.e., the fact that S commutes with the family $(\pi(\lambda))_{\lambda \in \Lambda}$, is valid in this more general setting.

It may be seen as the crucial fact behind many properties of Gabor frames, and it is the basis for abstract versions of both Janssen's representation and the Wexler-Raz principle. However, let us mention first that it is responsible for the fact (again in contrast to affine wavelets involving dilations) that S^{-1} commutes with every $\pi(\lambda)$, for $\lambda \in \Lambda$ and therefore the dual frame for a Gabor frame operator is again another Gabor frame, generated by the pair $(\tilde{g}, \Lambda)$, with $\tilde{g} = S^{-1}g$, resp., the solution of the linear equation $S\tilde{g} = g$.

In order to describe the two basic results mentioned earlier we introduce the concept of the *adjoint group* Λ° to a given TF lattice Λ. Λ° is defined as the set (and actually another lattice) of all those TF shifts that commute with all elements of Λ. Not surprisingly, $(\Lambda^\circ)^\circ = \Lambda$. In the current context, which is interesting if Λ is just a nonseparable lattice in $\mathbb{R}^{2d}$ *Janssen's representation* consists of the claim that $S_{g,\Lambda}$ has a series representation (with at least bounded coefficients (c_{λ°), indexed by Λ°), only involving the elements $\pi(\lambda^\circ)$, i.e., of the form $S_{g,\Lambda} = \sum_{\lambda^\circ \in \Lambda^\circ} c_{\lambda^\circ} \pi(\lambda^\circ)$.

On the same basis we derive the most general variant of the so-called Wexler-Raz principle (going back to [WR90] in its original form): A pair of functions from $L^2(G)$, say g and γ, are (weakly) dual to each other if and only if they show a certain form of biorthogonality with respect to Λ°, i.e., if and only if $\langle \pi(\lambda_1^\circ)g, \pi(\lambda_2^\circ)\gamma \rangle = \delta_{\lambda_1^\circ, \lambda_2^\circ}$, for any pair of elements $(\lambda_1^\circ, \lambda_2^\circ)$ in Λ°. Because only for those lattices Λ that show a certain richness (usually described in terms of some *redundancy factor* greater than 1) it is possible that (g, Λ) generates a Gabor frame, the corresponding adjoint lattices Λ° will have some sparsity. It follows that in the typical situations there are many different choices for Λ-dual signals γ for a given atom g (in the case $G = \mathbb{Z}_N$ we simply have an underdetermined inhomogeneous linear equation). More precisely, the collection of so-called *weakly dual Gabor atoms* (see [FZ98]) forms an affine subspace of $L^2(G)$. The usual choice is the so-called *canonical dual window* $\tilde{g} = S_{g,\Lambda}^{-1}(g)$ as suggested by standard frame theory. All the other dual windows differ from this particular choice by an element from the orthogonal complement of the collection $\{\pi(\lambda^\circ)g, \lambda^\circ \in \Lambda^\circ\}$. If a continuous variable occurs we have to take into account that not all of these define dual frames, but if for such a γ the mapping $f \mapsto (\langle f, \pi(\lambda)\gamma \rangle)$ is a bounded linear mapping from $L^2(G)$ to $\ell^2(\Lambda)$ then γ generates a dual frame, in the sense that

$$f = \sum_{\lambda \in \Lambda} \langle f, \pi(\lambda)\gamma \rangle \pi(\lambda)g = \sum_{\lambda \in \Lambda} \langle f, \pi(\lambda)g \rangle \pi(\lambda)\gamma \quad \forall f \in L^2(G), \qquad (1.27)$$

Of course, it is of interest to note that $\tilde{g}$ can be characterized by several different but equivalent properties. Thus, $\tilde{g}$ is the unique Λ-dual signal, which is as close as possible (in the L^2-sense) to g, or, alternatively, to the dual window, which generates those representations among all possible ones, which have minimal ℓ^2-norm, by choosing $c_\lambda = \langle f, \pi(\lambda)\tilde{g} \rangle$, for $\lambda \in \Lambda$, for each signal f.

From a more practical point of view, i.e., with vectors of finite length, this new perspective opens a way to use so-called nonseparable lattices Λ, not just the standard "separable" lattices characterized by a lattice constant a in the time direction and a lattice constant b for the frequency direction (cf. [Li94, FCS95, KFPS96] for early examples in this direction). A typical example of such a nonseparable lattice Λ would be the well-known quincux lattice, which may be seen as a kind of substitute for a hexagonal lattice (which does not exist in the strict sense, in this situation).

Experiments indicate that for a given redundancy factor (e.g., $\mathrm{red}(\Lambda) = 1.5$) those alternative lattices allow for slightly better joint TF concentration of the pair of dual Gabor atoms $(g, \tilde{g})$ than the rectangular lattices. It is natural to associate this phenomenon with the "circular" behavior of typical (Gauss-like) Gabor atoms g in the TF plane and the better properties of the alternative lattices with respect to the sphere packing problem.

1.1.8   Numerical Gabor Analysis

When implementing Gabor analysis methods we can only handle a finite amount of data. Hence, we cannot directly use the infinite-dimensional theory in $L^2(\mathbb{R})$ or $\ell^2(\mathbb{Z})$ but have to set up a finite-dimensional model first.

In [Str98a, Str99] the relation between certain finite-dimensional models used for numerical procedures and infinite-dimensional Gabor theory has been investigated. In $\ell^2(\mathbb{Z})$ the numerical computation of the dual functions

$$\gamma_{m,n}(k) = e^{2\pi imk/M}\gamma(k - na) \tag{1.28}$$

involves the solution of the bi-infinite system of equations

$$Sg = \gamma. \tag{1.29}$$

We certainly cannot solve a system of bi-infinite order, but we can solve it approximately, based on a finite-dimensional model. In [Str98c, Str99] it is shown that the "dual" Gabor functions obtained by solving a finite-dimensional problem converge to the dual Gabor functions of the original infinite-dimensional problem in $\ell^2(\mathbb{Z})$. Probably the most convenient finite-dimensional model that can be used for an approximate computation of the duals is the periodic model.

Hence, we do all our computations in the ring $\mathbb{Z}_N = \mathbb{Z} \bmod N$ (cf. Section 1.1.7). In other words, we consider discrete signals f of length N, extended periodically by $f(k + nN) = f(k)$ for $k = 0, \ldots, N - 1$ and $n \in \mathbb{Z}$. The choice of this model is justified by the theoretical results in [Str98c, Str99].

Our guiding philosophy is to express the underlying structures arising in discrete Gabor expansions in the language of unitary matrix factorization [GvL89, Str98a]. Permutation matrices, Fourier matrices, and Kronecker products constitute the vocabulary of this unifying language. The factorization point of view is notably useful for the design of efficient numerical algorithms.

A few diagonal matrix notations are handy. If $d \in \mathbb{C}^N$, then $D = \mathrm{diag}(d) = \mathrm{diag}(d_0, \ldots, d_{N-1})$ is the $N \times N$ diagonal matrix with entries $d_0, \ldots, d_{N-1}$. If $D_0, \ldots, D_{N-1}$ are $p \times p$ matrices, then $D = \mathrm{diag}(D_0, \ldots, D_{N-1})$ is the block diagonal matrix defined by

$$D = \begin{bmatrix} D_0 & 0 & \cdots & 0 \\ 0 & D_1 & \cdots & 0 \\ \vdots & \vdots & & \vdots \\ 0 & 0 & \cdots & D_{N-1} \end{bmatrix}.$$

A *permutation matrix* is the identity with its columns reordered. If P is a permutation and A is a matrix, then PA is a row-permuted version of A and AP is a column-permuted version of A. Note that $P^* = P^{-1}$. The permutation matrices are thus unitary, forming a subgroup of the unitary group. Among the permutation matrices, the mod p *perfect shuffle permutation* [vL92]

$$P_{p,N} = \left. \begin{matrix} p \text{ rows} \end{matrix} \right\{ \begin{bmatrix} 1 & 0 & \cdots & 0 & 0 & \cdots & 0 \\ & & & & 1 & & \\ & 0 & & & & & \\ & 1 & & & & & \\ \vdots & & & & & & \vdots \\ & & 1 & & & & \\ & & & & & & \\ 0 & & & & & & 1 \end{bmatrix}, $$

$$\underbrace{\qquad\qquad}_{q \text{ columns}}$$

with $N = pq$, shall play a key role in the factorization of the Gabor frame operator. Its transpose $P^*_{p,N}$ is called the mod p *sort permutation* [vL92]. Observe that $P_{p,N} = P^*_{q,N}$. We illustrate the action of $P_{p,N}$ and $P^*_{p,N}$ by means of simple examples with $N = 15 = 3 \cdot 5 \equiv p \cdot q$:

$$P_{3,15}x = [\, x_0\, x_5\, x_{10} \mid x_1\, x_6\, x_{11} \mid x_2\, x_7\, x_{12} \mid x_3\, x_8\, x_{13} \mid x_4\, x_9\, x_{14} \,]^*$$
$$P^*_{3,15}x = [\, x_0\, x_3\, x_6\, x_9\, x_{12} \mid x_1\, x_4\, x_7\, x_{10}\, x_{13} \mid x_2\, x_5\, x_8\, x_{11}\, x_{14} \,]^*.$$

It is not surprising that the *Fourier matrix* is of fundamental importance in the factorization of the Gabor frame operator. The Fourier matrix of order N is the unitary matrix

$$F_N = \sqrt{\frac{1}{N}} \begin{bmatrix} 1 & 1 & 1 & \cdots & 1 \\ 1 & \omega & \omega^2 & \cdots & \omega^{N-1} \\ 1 & \omega^2 & \omega^4 & \cdots & \omega^{2(N-1)} \\ \vdots & \vdots & \vdots & & \vdots \\ 1 & \omega^{N-1} & \omega^{2(N-1)} & \cdots & \omega^{(N-1)(N-1)} \end{bmatrix}$$

with $\omega = e^{-2\pi i/N}$.

If $A \in \mathbb{C}^{p \times q}$ and $B \in \mathbb{C}^{m \times n}$ then the *Kronecker product* $A \otimes B$ is the p-by-q block matrix

$$A \otimes B = \begin{bmatrix} a_{00}B & \cdots & a_{0q-1}B \\ \vdots & & \vdots \\ a_{p-10}B & \cdots & a_{p-1q-1}B \end{bmatrix} \in \mathbb{C}^{pm \times qn}.$$

Note that

$$I \otimes B = \begin{bmatrix} B & 0 & \cdots & 0 \\ 0 & B & \cdots & 0 \\ \vdots & \vdots & & \vdots \\ 0 & 0 & \cdots & B \end{bmatrix}$$

is block diagonal, and I is the identity matrix. If $N = mn$ and $A \in \mathbb{C}^{m \times m}$, then [vL92]

$$P_{m,N}^*(I_n \otimes A) = (A \otimes I_n)P_{m,N}^*. \tag{1.30}$$

If A and B are unitary matrices, then $A \otimes B$ is a unitary matrix, because $(A \otimes B)^* = A^* \otimes B^*$ and $(A \otimes B)^{-1} = A^{-1} \otimes B^{-1}$; see [vL92].

The set of Gabor analysis functions $\{g_{m,n}\}$ is given by

$$g_{m,n}(k) = g(k - na)e^{2\pi imb/N}, \tag{1.31}$$

for $m = 0, \ldots, M-1$, $n = 0, \ldots, K-1$ and $Ka = Mb = N$ with $a, b, K, M \in \mathbb{N}$.

Let G be the $MK \times N$ matrix having $g_{m,n}$ as its $(m+nM)$-th row for $m = 0, \ldots, M-1$, $n = 0, \ldots, K-1$. We write $c_{m,n} = \langle f, g_{m,n} \rangle$ and by slightly abusing our notation we treat the $K \times M$ array c as a column vector of length KM by stacking the columns of c. The Gabor transform of a function f can be written as

$$Gf = c.$$

The case $ab = N$ is usually referred to as critically sampled Gabor transform, whereas the choice $ab < N$ yields an oversampled Gabor transform, the ratio $\frac{N}{ab} = \frac{p}{q}$ is the oversampling rate or redundancy. The case $p = 1$ is referred to as integer oversampling.

Recall that the Gabor frame operator S is defined by

$$Sf = \sum_{m=0}^{M-1} \sum_{n=0}^{N-1} \langle f, g_{m,n} \rangle g_{m,n}.$$

S is a positive definite Hermitian $N \times N$ matrix, which can be expressed by

$$S = G^*G.$$

Due to the commutation relations of Gabor frame operator (cf. Section 1.1.3) it is obvious that these properties translate in the periodic model to the fact that S is block-circulant matrix; see, e.g., [QF95]. More precisely, S can be expressed as

$$S = \begin{bmatrix} A_0 & A_1 & \cdots & A_{K-1} \\ A_{K-1} & A_0 & \cdots & A_{K-2} \\ \vdots & \vdots & & \vdots \\ A_1 & A_2 & \cdots & A_0 \end{bmatrix},$$

the A_k being noncirculant $a \times a$ matrices with $(A_k)_{m,n} = S_{ka+m,ka+n}$ for $k = 0, \ldots, K - 1$ and $m = 0, \ldots, a - 1$, $n = 0, \ldots, a - 1$.

But the Gabor frame operator exhibits even more structural properties. These do not come as a big surprise due to the "symmetry" in the construction of the functions $g_{m,n}$. The following representation of S is a consequence of the *Walnut representation* of S, cf. [HW89].

Lemma 1   *[Str98c] S can be unitarily block-diagonalized via*

$$S = P_{M,N} D_S P_{M,N}^* \tag{1.32}$$

where $D_S = diag(B_0, \ldots, B_{M-1})$ and B_k are $b \times b$ submatrix with entries

$$(B_k)_{mn} = S_{k+mM,k+nM} \tag{1.33}$$

for $m, n = 0, \ldots, b - 1$, $k = 0, \ldots, M - 1$.

A well-known factorization of S can be obtained by combining the sparsity of S as stated in Lemma 1 with the fact that S is of block-circulant type, see [ZZ93, PZZ98]. This factorization of S can be further improved as demonstrated by the following theorem [Str98b].

Theorem 2 (Fundamental Factorization) *Let $\{g_{m,n}\}$ be a Gabor frame for $\mathbb{Z}_N$ with time-frequency shift parameters a, b. Denote $\frac{N}{ab} = \frac{p}{q}$. Then S can be unitarily factorized into the block diagonal matrix*

$$I_p \otimes diag(C_0, \ldots, C_{\frac{N}{pq}-1}),$$

the $q \times q$ submatrices C_j are given by

$$diag(C_{\frac{bk}{q}}, \ldots, C_{\frac{b(k+1)}{q}-1}) = (F_{\frac{b}{q}} \otimes I_q)^* B_k (F_{\frac{b}{q}} \otimes I_q)$$

with B_k as in (1.33).

In other words the Gabor frame operator can be efficiently factorized by properly chosen Fourier transforms and permutations into $N/(pq)$ different submatrices of size $q \times q$; each of these submatrices is repeated p times.

The "classical" result via Zak transform [ZZ93] states that S can be factorized into N/q different matrices of size $q \times q$. Hence, we "gained" a factor p.

In case of integer oversampling (i.e., $p = 1$), Theorem 2 reduces to the well-known diagonalization of the Gabor frame operator by the Zak transform; see for example [AGT91, ZZ93].

Many fast algorithms for computing the dual Gabor function can easily be derived from Theorem 2, because they simply correspond to different factorizations of the frame operator S; see [Str98b] for more details.

Due to the link between Gabor frames and oversampled DFT filter banks (cf. [CV98, BHF98]) the results discussed in this section provide a convenient way for an efficient implementation of oversampled DFT filter bank systems.

1.1.9   Image Representation and Gabor Analysis

Gabor functions are successfully applied to model the response of simple cells in the *visual cortex* [Dau80, Mar80]. A survey on this topic can be found in [NTC96]. In our notation, each pair of adjacent cells in the visual cortex represents the real and imaginary parts of one coefficient $c_{m,n}$ corresponding to $g_{m,n}$. Clearly the Gabor model cannot capture the variety and complexity of the visual system, but it seems to be a key to further understanding biological vision.

Among the people who paved the way for the use of Gabor analysis in pattern recognition and computer vision we certainly have to mention Zeevi, M. Porat, and their coworkers [ZP84, ZP88, PZ89, ZG92] and Daugman [Dau87, Dau88, Dau93]. Motivated by biological findings, Daugman [Dau88] and Zeevi and Porat [PZ88a] propose the use of Gabor functions for image processing applications, such as image analysis and image compression. Ebrahimi, Kunt, and coworkers use Gabor expansions for still image and video compression [EK91]. Many modern transform-based data compression methods try to combine the advantages of Gabor systems with the advantages of wavelets.

1.2   Signal and Image Reconstruction

In the last decade an enormous effort of research in various scientific disciplines has gone into the development of efficient and reliable methods for compression, transmission, analysis, and enhancement of multidimensional signals. Unfortunately, in practice, direct applicability of these methods is often seriously hampered due to following problems:

(i) **Scattered Data Problem:** In many applications, such as exploration geophysics or medical imaging, data of a signal can only be taken at nonuniformly spaced nodes. However, most of the commonly used methods for analysis, compression, or denoising cannot be directly applied to nonuniformly spaced data, but ask for regularly sampled signals. Thus, before further processing can take place, we first have to reconstruct the signal from the given data by computing an approximation on a sufficiently dense regular grid.

(ii) **Missing Data Problem:** A common problem in practice is the loss of data during transmission or recording of signals. The user is then confronted with signals where several data segments are missing or so distorted that they carry no useful information. Because any further processing of those signals, such as feature extraction, segmentation or visualization will be severely affected by these problems, we have to recover the lost information as well as possible. We have to deal with the missing data problem, for example in case of packet loss in coded video bit streams as well as in the restoration of clipped audio signals.

If there is no need to distinguish between these two types of reconstruction problems, we refer to both of them as *nonuniform sampling problem*. In this section we will give an overview on efficient methods for reconstructing signals and images from nonuniform samples. We first give a brief overview of the connection between frames and irregular sampling theory. Then we present efficient numerical algorithms in both one and two dimensions. At the end of this section we demonstrate the performance of the presented methods by applying them to various image reconstruction problems.

1.2.1   Notation

A successful solution of the nonuniform sampling problem requires a priori information about the signal; otherwise the problem is ill-posed. In many cases this a priori knowledge can be derived from physical properties of the underlying process. Such physical properties can often be characterized in terms of the decay of the frequency coefficients of the signal. This model is useful in many applications, for example in speech processing, communication, or geophysics. Other models involve radial basis functions, wavelets, or splines. But in the sequel we will mainly concentrate on reconstruction methods for (essentially) band-limited multidimensional signals.

Before we proceed, we briefly review some basic facts of sampling theory. The space of band-limited signals B_Ω is given by

$$B_\Omega = \left\{ f \in L^2 : \hat{f}(\omega) = 0 \text{ for } |\omega| > \Omega \right\} \tag{1.34}$$

in which $\hat{f}$ is the Fourier transform of f, defined by

$$\hat{f}(\omega) = \int f(t) e^{2\pi i t \omega} \, dt. \tag{1.35}$$

The sinc function defined by

$$\text{sinc}_\Omega(t) = \frac{\sin \Omega t}{\Omega t} \tag{1.36}$$

acts as a *reproducing kernel* on B_Ω, i.e., we have for $f \in B_\Omega$

$$f(t) = \langle f, \text{sinc}_\Omega(\cdot - t) \rangle. \tag{1.37}$$

This property plays an important role in Shannon's sampling theorem [Sha48, Hig96]. Shannon's sampling theorem says that if $f \in B_\Omega$ then for any $\delta \le \frac{\pi}{\omega}$, the signal f can be reconstructed from its regularly spaced samples $\{f(n\delta)\}_{n \in \mathbb{Z}}$ by

$$f(t) = \sum_{n \in \mathbb{Z}} f(n\delta) \frac{\sin \Omega(t - n\delta)}{\Omega(t - n\delta)}. \tag{1.38}$$

It is worthwhile to distinguish between two features provided by Shannon's sampling theorem:

- Shannon's formula gives a unique discrete representation of f in terms of its samples $\{f(n\delta)\} = \{\langle f, \text{sinc}(\cdot - n\delta) \rangle\}$.
- Shannon's theorem also provides an explicit method to reconstruct f from its samples $\{f(n\delta)\}$ by computing the series in (1.38).

If the samples are irregularly spaced, the problem becomes much more challenging. The irregular sampling problem can be stated as follows. Let f be a band-limited signal in B_Ω, and suppose that the values $f(t_n)$ are known at a bi-infinite sampling sequence $\ldots t_{n-1} < t_n < t_{n+1} \ldots$ with $\lim_{n \to \pm\infty}$. Then the question is whether f is uniquely determined by its samples; if yes, how can it be reconstructed?

These questions have inspired many mathematicians, culminating in deep theoretical results due to Duffin, Schaeffer, Beurling, Landau, and others [DS52, Lan67, BM67]. In recent years the attention has focused on practical solutions; see [Mar93, FG93] and the references cited therein. Here the issues are the design of fast and robust algorithms and explicit error estimates.

1.2.2 Signal Reconstruction and Frames

An important role in the investigation of sampling and reconstruction problems from both theoretical and numerical points of view plays the concept of frames [DS52, You80], which has seen a recent resurgence spurred by the papers [DGM86] and [Dau90].

Frames were introduced in Section 1.1.1, defined by (1.6). Figures 1.1 and 1.3 show elementary Gabor functions and how they cover the TF plane, presenting their time-frequency localization. Section 1.1.3 describesd fundamental properties of Gabor frames.

The derivation of conditions under which a system $\{f_k\}_{k \in \mathbb{Z}}$ establishes a frame and estimation of frame bounds play a vital role in harmonic analysis and signal processing [Dau90, Ben92, Chr95, FG93].

From the viewpoint of frame theory the irregular sampling problem can be understood as finding conditions under which the functions $\{\text{sinc}_\Omega(\cdot - t_j)\}_{j \in \mathbb{Z}}$ (or other properly chosen functions) constitute a frame [Fei89, Ben92, Jaf91].

Our numerical methods are based on the following theorem, due to Feichtinger and Gröchenig [FG93].

Theorem 3 *Let $\{x_j\}_{j \in \mathbb{Z}}$ be a sampling set that satisfies*

$$\pi/\Omega > \gamma := \sup_{j \in \mathbb{Z}}(t_{j+1} - x_j). \tag{1.39}$$

Then $\{\sqrt{w_j}\,\text{sinc}_\Omega(\cdot - x_j)\}_{j \in \mathbb{Z}}$ is a frame for B_Ω with frame bounds

$$A = (1 - \frac{\gamma\Omega}{\pi})^2 \ \text{and} \ B = (1 + \frac{\gamma\Omega}{\pi})^2. \tag{1.40}$$

The weights w_j are given by

$$w_j = (t_{j+1} - t_{j-1})/2. \tag{1.41}$$

Let T and T^* denote the analysis and synthesis operators as defined in (1.13) and (1.14) respectively:

$$Tf = \{\langle f, \sqrt{w_j}\text{sinc}_\Omega(\cdot - x_j)\rangle\}_{j \in \mathbb{Z}}, \quad T^*\{c_j\}_{j \in \mathbb{Z}} = \sum_{j \in \mathbb{Z}} \sqrt{w_j}c_j\text{sinc}_\Omega(\cdot - x_j). \tag{1.42}$$

It follows from frame theory that a signal $f \in B_\Omega$ can be recovered from its sampled data $\{x(x_j)\}$ by the following simple iterative procedure, which is also called the *adaptive weights method*:

$$f_n = f_{n-1} + \lambda T^*(T f_{n-1} - \{f(x_j)\}_{j \in \mathbb{Z}}) \tag{1.43}$$

with relaxation parameter $\lambda < \frac{1}{B}$. By exploiting the fact that this frame iteration is identical to *Landweber* or *Richardson iteration* we can conclude that the optimal choice for the relaxation parameter is $\lambda = \frac{2}{A+B}$, see [HY81].

The Richardson iteration is mainly of theoretical interest and should not be used in practice due to its modest rate of convergence. We will discuss faster iterative procedures in the sequel.

1.2.3   Numerical Methods for Signal Reconstruction

In Theorem 3, as in most irregular sampling theorems, we are dealing with an infinite-dimensional problem, by assuming that infinitely many sampling values are given. This is, of course, not the case in practice, where only a finite number of data can be processed. Thus, for the problem to be accessible for numerical solution we first have to create a finite-dimensional model.

There are numerous theorems concerning the reconstruction of a band-limited signal from nonuniform sampling, but most of these theorems do not treat the situation encountered in signal and image processing.

Without loss of generality we can assume that the sampling points are contained in an interval $[0, N]$. Hence let a set of sampling points $\{x_j\}_{j=1}^r$ and sampling values $s_j = f(x_j)$ be given with $f \in \mathbb{B}_M$. Clearly we cannot reconstruct f exactly from a finite set of samples, because $\mathbb{B}_M$ is an infinite-dimensional space, hence our goal is to approximate f as well as possible.

Because no data are provided outside this interval we focus on reconstructing the signal f inside the interval $[0, N]$. Any attempt to design a finite-dimensional model immediately raises the question "what to do at the boundaries" of the interval when we truncate f to the interval $[0, N]$. We extend the truncated signal f periodically across the interval $[0, N]$. As in many other cases, this periodic extension preserves important mathematical properties — such as group structure — which in turn often give rise to efficient numerical algorithms.

Periodic band-limited signals are identical to trigonometric polynomials, thus, we consider the space of trigonometric polynomials of degree at most M defined by

$$P_M = \left\{ p : p(x) = \sum_{k=-M}^{M} c_k e^{2\pi i k x} \right\} \tag{1.44}$$

as a finite-dimensional model for the irregular sampling problem. In [Grö99] it is shown that interpolation and approximation by trigonometric polynomials provide a correct finite-dimensional discretization of the sampling problem for band-limited functions. See [Grö97] for an extension of this result to higher dimensions.

In general the y_j are not the samples of a trigonometric polynomial in P_M, hence we cannot find a $p \in P_M$ such that $s_j = p(x_j)$. We therefore consider the least squares problem

$$\min_{p \in P_M} \sum_{j=1}^{r} |p(x_j) - s_j|^2 w_j. \tag{1.45}$$

Here the $w_j > 0$ are unspecified weights, which can be chosen at one's convenience.

The following theorem, which is due to Gröchenig [Grö93, FGS95] forms the basis for our efficient numerical methods.

Theorem 4 *Given the sampling points $0 \le x_0 < \ldots, x_{N-1} < 1$, samples $\{s_j\}_{j=1}^{N}$, positive weights $\{w_j\}_{j=0}^{N-1}$, and the degree M with $2M + 1 \le N$, the polynomial $\tilde{p} \in P_M$ that solves (1.45) is given by*

$$\tilde{p}(x) = \sum_{m=-M}^{M} a_m e^{2\pi i m x} \in P_M \tag{1.46}$$

in which its coefficients a_m satisfy

$$a = T^{-1} b \ \in \mathbb{C}^{(2M+1)^2}, \tag{1.47}$$

where T is a $(2M + 1) \times (2M + 1)$ Toeplitz matrix with entries

$$T_{lm} = \sum_{j=0}^{N-1} w_j e^{2\pi i (l-m) x_j} \qquad \text{for } |l|, |m| \le M \tag{1.48}$$

and

$$b_m = \sum_{j=0}^{N-1} s_j w_j e^{2\pi i m x_j} \qquad \text{for } |m| \le M. \tag{1.49}$$

If $\{x_j\}_{j=1}^{N}$ is also a stable sampling set with $\max(x_{j+1} - x_j) := \gamma$ and $w_j = (x_{j+1} - x_{j-1})/2$, then the condition number of T is bounded by

$$\kappa(T) \le \left(\frac{1+\gamma}{1-\gamma}\right)^2. \tag{1.50}$$

The main step from a numerical point of view in this theorem is the solution of the linear system $Tb = c$. Because the matrix entries $T_{l,m} = w_j e^{2\pi i (l-m) x_j}$ depend only on the difference $l - m$ it follows that T is a Toeplitz matrix, i.e., the entries of T are constant along its diagonals.

There exist many fast algorithms to solve Toeplitz systems of equations [DH87, AG88]. The most efficient and flexible algorithm for our problem is based on the conjugate gradient method [GvL96, CN96]. By combining the reformulation of the original problem as a *Toeplitz system* with the *adaptive weights method* and the *conjugate gradient acceleration*, we arrive at a fast and efficient reconstruction algorithm [FGS95].

Theorem 5 (and Algorithm) *Let M be the size of the spectrum and let $0 \leq x_1 < \cdots < x_r < 1$ be an arbitrary sequence of sampling points with $r \geq 2M + 1$. Set $x_0 = x_r - 1, x_{r+1} = x_1 + 1$ and $w_j = \frac{1}{2}(x_{j+1} - x_{j-1})$ and compute*

$$\gamma_k = \sum_{j=1}^{r} e^{-2\pi i k x_j} w_j \quad \text{for } k = 0, 1, \ldots, 2M .$$

The associated Toeplitz matrix has $T_{lk} = \gamma_{l-k}$ for $|l|, |k| \leq M$.

To reconstruct a trigonometric polynomial $p \in P_M$ from its samples $p(x_j)$, first compute

$$b_k = \sum_{j=1}^{r} p(x_j) w_j e^{-2\pi i k x_j} \quad \text{for } |k| \leq M ,$$

and set $r_0 = q_0 = b \in \mathbb{C}^{2M+1}$, $a_0 = 0$. Compute iteratively for $n \geq 1$

$$a_n = a_{n-1} + \frac{\langle r_{n-1}, q_{n-1} \rangle}{\langle T q_{n-1}, q_{n-1} \rangle} q_{n-1},$$

$$r_n = r_{n-1} - \frac{\langle r_{n-1}, q_{n-1} \rangle}{\langle T q_{n-1}, q_{n-1} \rangle} T q_{n-1},$$

and

$$q_n = r_n - \frac{\langle r_n, T q_{n-1} \rangle}{\langle T q_{n-1}, q_{n-1} \rangle} q_{n-1} .$$

Then a_n converges in at most $2M + 1$ steps to a vector $\in \mathbb{C}^{2M+1}$, solving $Ta = b$. The reconstruction $p \in P_M$ is then given by $p(x) = \sum_{k=-M}^{M} a_k e^{2\pi i k x}$.

If $\delta < \frac{1}{2M}$ and $p_n(x) = \sum_{k=-M}^{M} a_{n,k} e^{2\pi i k x} \in P_M$ denotes the approximating polynomial after n iterations, then

$$\left(\sum_{j=1}^{r} |p(x_j) - p_n(x_j)|^2 w_j \right)^{1/2} \leq 2(2\delta M)^n \left(\sum_{j=1}^{r} |p(x_j)|^2 w_j \right)^{1/2} . \tag{1.51}$$

Because this algorithm is a combination of the adaptive weights method, the conjugate gradient (CG) algorithm, and the use of Toeplitz matrices, we also refer to it as the **ACT** algorithm.

Computational Complexity: Due to the Toeplitz structure all the information of T is contained in its first row. By using the formulas of Rokhlin and Dutt [DR93, DR95] or Beylkin [Bey95] the entries of T and the right-hand side can be computed in $O(M \log M + r \log(1/\varepsilon))$ operations; ε is the required precision to compute T and b.

The main step in this algorithm is a matrix-vector multiplication in each iteration. Because T is a Toeplitz matrix, this multiplication can be carried out via the FFT in $O(M \log M)$ by embedding T in a circulant matrix [Str86, FGS95]. The rate of convergence of CG is usually much faster than predicted in the theorem, because it essentially depends on the distribution of the singular values of the matrix. If the singular values are clustered, CG will converge quickly if they are not clustered, one can apply one of the many existing Toeplitz preconditioners to achieve clustering (away from zero) of the singular values.

Generalization to Higher Dimensions: An advantage of the proposed approach, besides its numerical efficiency, is the fact that it can be easily extended to multivariate q signal reconstruction. We briefly discuss the two-dimensional case. We define the space of two dimensional trigonometric polynomials P_M^2 by

$$P_M^2 = \left\{ p : p(x,y) = \sum_{j,k=-M}^{M} c_{j,k} e^{2\pi i(jx+ky)} \right\} . \qquad (1.52)$$

To reduce the notational burden, we have assumed in (1.52) that p has equal degree M in each coordinate; the extension to polynomials with a different degree in each coordinate is straightforward.

Let a set of nonuniformly spaced sampling points $\{(x_j, y_j)\}_{j=1}^r$ (we assume without loss of generality that $(x_j, y_j) \in [0,1) \times [0,1))$ and sampling values $s_j = f(x_j, y_j)$ be given. analogous to the one dimensional case, we want to find the trigonometric polynomial of degree M that minimizes the approximation error in a least squares sense.

Similarly to the one dimensional problem we can compute the solution by solving a linear system of equations $Ta = b$, the derivation of the algorithm is essentially the same, for the details the reader may consult [Str97]. We point out that the system matrix T in the two dimensional case is of the form

$$T_{k,l} = \sum_{j=1}^{r} w_j e^{2\pi i(k-l)(x_j+y_j)} , \quad k,l = 0,\ldots 2M . \qquad (1.53)$$

One can easily verify that T is a block Toeplitz matrix with Toeplitz blocks [Str97]. Analogous to the one dimensional case, the multiplication of a block Toeplitz matrix by a vector can be carried out by a two dimensional FFT. Furthermore, the whole information of T is stored in the first and M-th column of T and we can use the formulas in [Bey95] for their fast computation. Only the problem of invertibility of the block Toeplitz matrix is more involved than in one dimensional, see [Str97, Grö97] for more details. We demonstrate the performance of this algorithm and outline some modifications to take advantage of a priori information about specific reconstruction problems.

1.3 Examples and Applications

In order to illustrate the performance of the proposed methods we discuss some image reconstruction problems arising in various scientific disciplines. The method we have presented in the previous section is very flexible, and additional knowledge about a specific reconstruction problem can be easily incorporated. In the sequel we will apply our

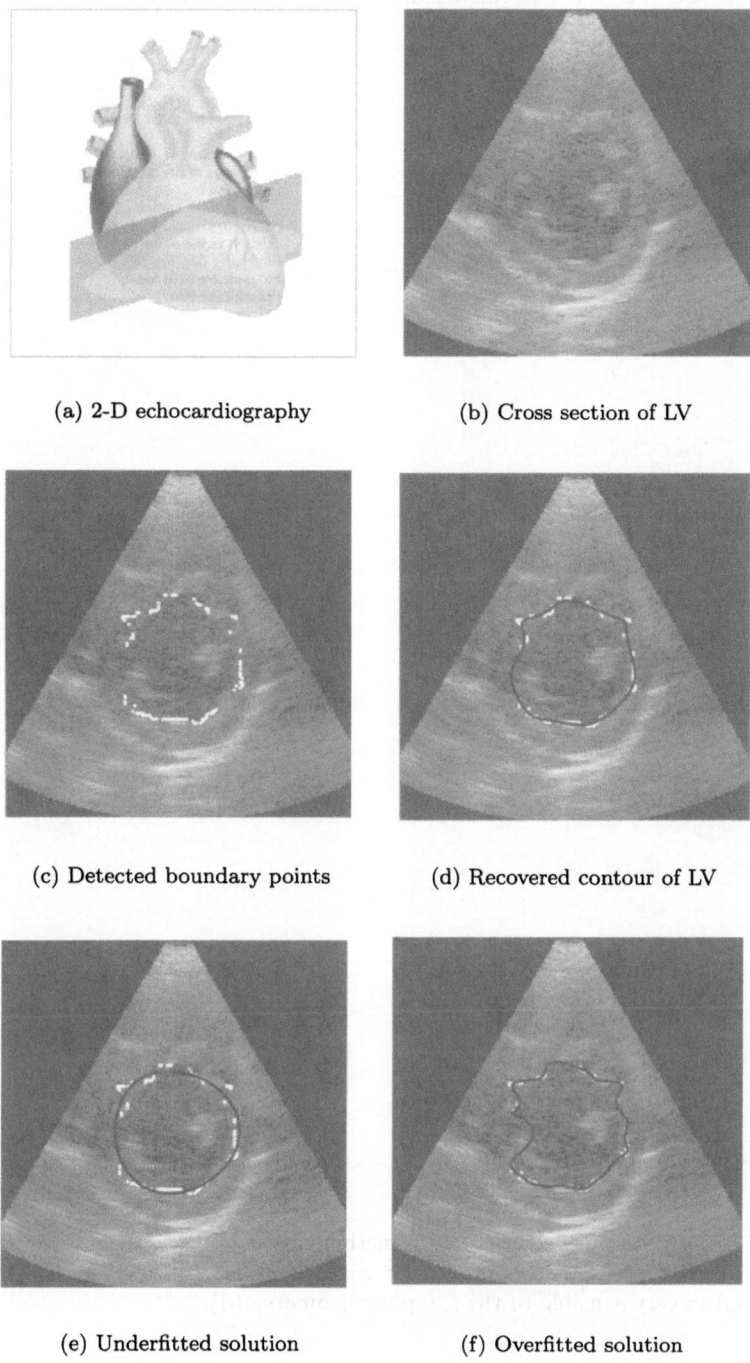

(a) 2-D echocardiography

(b) Cross section of LV

(c) Detected boundary points

(d) Recovered contour of LV

(e) Underfitted solution

(f) Overfitted solution

FIGURE 1.6. The recovery of the boundary of the left ventricle from two dimensional ultrasound images is a basic step in echocardiography to extract relevant parameters of cardiac function.

method to reconstruction problems arising in echocardiography, exploration geophysics, and digital image reconstruction.

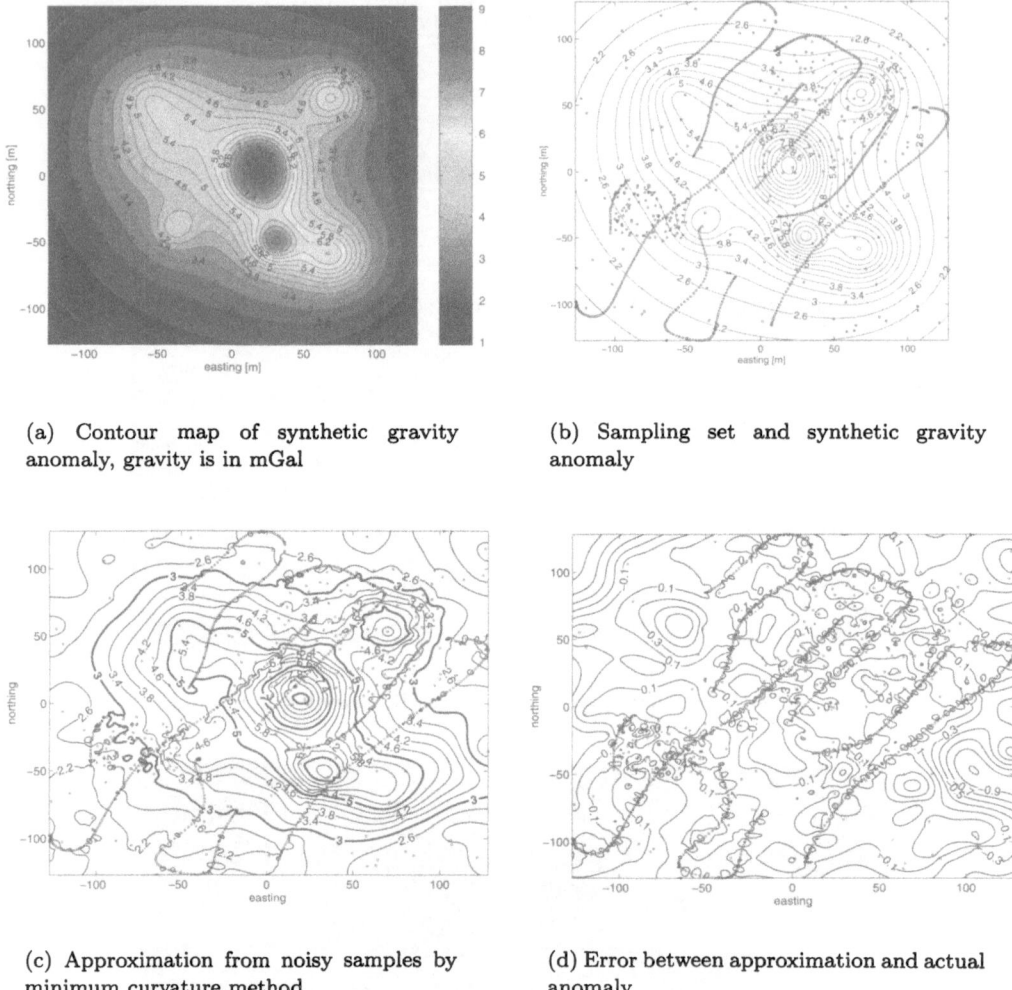

(a) Contour map of synthetic gravity anomaly, gravity is in mGal

(b) Sampling set and synthetic gravity anomaly

(c) Approximation from noisy samples by minimum curvature method

(d) Error between approximation and actual anomaly

FIGURE 1.7. Many existing reconstruction methods used in exploration geophysics produce approximations that are smooth but do not conform to a relevant physical model. These methods are often very sensible to the sampling geometry (d).

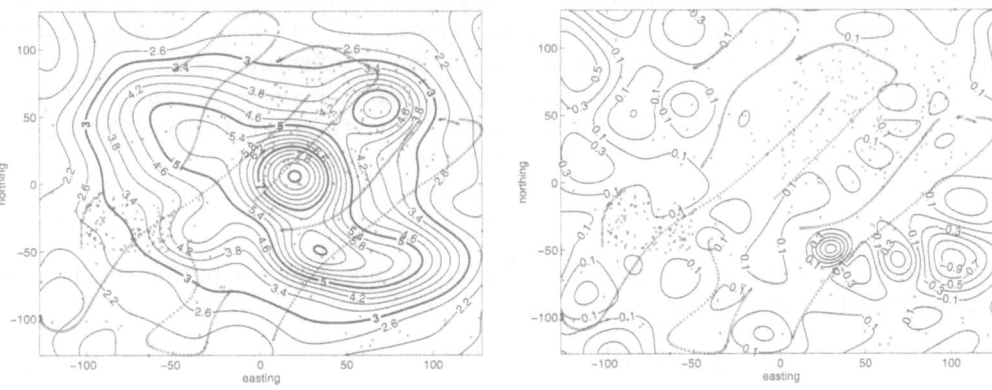

(a) Approximation from noisy samples by the algorithm of Rauth and Strohmer

(b) Error between approximation and actual anomaly

FIGURE 1.8. A priori knowledge about physical properties of potential fields greatly reduced the influence of the sampling geometry, as can be seen by comparing Figures 1.3 (a) and (b) and Figures 1.3 (c) and (d).

1.3.1 Object Boundary Recovery in Echocardiography

Trigonometric polynomials are certainly not suitable to model the shape of arbitrary objects. However, they are often useful in cases in which an underlying (stationary) physical process implies smoothness conditions of the object. Typical examples arise in medical imaging, for example in clinical cardiac studies, in which the evaluation of cardiac function using parameters of left ventricular contractibility is an important constituent of an echocardiographic examination [WGL93]. These parameters are derived using boundary tracing of endocardial borders of the Left Ventricle (LV).

The extraction of the boundary of the LV comprises two steps, once the ultrasound image of a cross section of the LV is given, see Figures 1.6(a)–(d). First an edge detection is applied to the ultrasound image to detect the boundary of the LV; cf. Figure 1.6(c). However, this procedure may be hampered by the presence of interfering biological structures (such as papillar muscles), the unevenness of boundary contrast, and various kinds of noise [SBS+95]. Thus, edge detection often provides only a set of nonuniformly spaced, perturbed boundary points rather than a connected boundary. Therefore a second step is required, to recover the original boundary from the detected edge points, cf. Figure 1.6(d). Because the shape of the left ventricle is definitely smooth, trigonometric polynomials are particularly well suited to model its boundary.

We denote this boundary by f and parameterize it by $f(u) = (x_u, y_u)$; x_u and y_u are the coordinates of f at "time" u in the x- and y-directions, respectively. Obviously, we can interpret f as a one-dimensional continuous, complex, and periodic function; x_u represents the real part and y_u represents the imaginary part of $f(u)$. It follows from the theorem of Weierstrass (and from the theorem of Stone-Weierstrass [Rud76] for higher dimensions) that a continuous periodic function can be approximated uniformly by trigonometric polynomials. If f is smooth, we can fairly assume that trigonometric polynomials of low degree provide an approximation of sufficient precision.

Assume that we know only some arbitrary, perturbed points $s_j = (x_{u_j}, y_{u_j}) = f(u_j) + \delta_j, j = 0, \ldots, N-1$ of f, and we want to recover f from these points. By a slight abuse of notation we interpret s_j as a complex number and write

$$s_j = x_j + iy_j. \tag{1.54}$$

We relate the curve parameter u to the boundary points s_j by computing the distance between two successive points s_{j-1}, s_j via

$$u_0 = 0 \tag{1.55}$$

$$u_j = u_{j-1} + d_j \tag{1.56}$$

$$d_j = \sqrt{(x_j - x_{j-1})^2 + (y_j - y_{j-1})^2} \tag{1.57}$$

for $j = 1, \ldots, N-1$. Via the normalization $t_j = t_j/L$ with $L = u_{N-1} + d_N$ we force all sampling points to be in $[0, 1)$. Other choices for d_j in (1.54) can be found in [Die93] in conjunction with curve approximation using splines. After transforming the detected boundary points as described in (1.54)–(1.57) we can use Algorithm 5 to recover the boundary.

As already mentioned, the detected contour points are distorted by noise. Therefore least squares approximation of the data points is preferred over exact interpolation. This raises the question of choosing the optimal degree of the approximating trigonometric polynomial. In [Str98a, SS98] we have developed a multilevel regularization scheme that iteratively adapts to the optimal polynomial degree.

Figures 1.6(e)–(f) demonstrate the importance of determining a proper degree for the approximating polynomial. The approximation displayed in Figure 1.6(e) has been computed by solving (1.45) with M chosen too small; we have obviously underfitted the data. The overfitted approximation obtained by solving (1.45) using a too large M is shown in Figure 1.6(f). The approximation shown in Figure 1.6(d) has been computed by the algorithm presented in [Str98a]; it provides the optimal balance between fitting the data and smoothness of the solution.

1.3.2 Image Reconstruction in Exploration Geophysics

Exploration geophysics relies on surveys of the Earth's magnetic field for the detection of anomalies that reveal underlying geological features. In geophysical practice it is essentially impossible to gather data in a form that allows direct interpretation. Geoscientists, used to looking at their measurements on maps or profiles and aiming at further processing, therefore need a representation of the originally irregularly spaced (scattered) data points at a regular grid. Gridding is, thus, one of the first and crucial steps in data analysis, and a number of practical constraints such as measurement errors and the huge amount of data make the development of reliable gridding methods difficult.

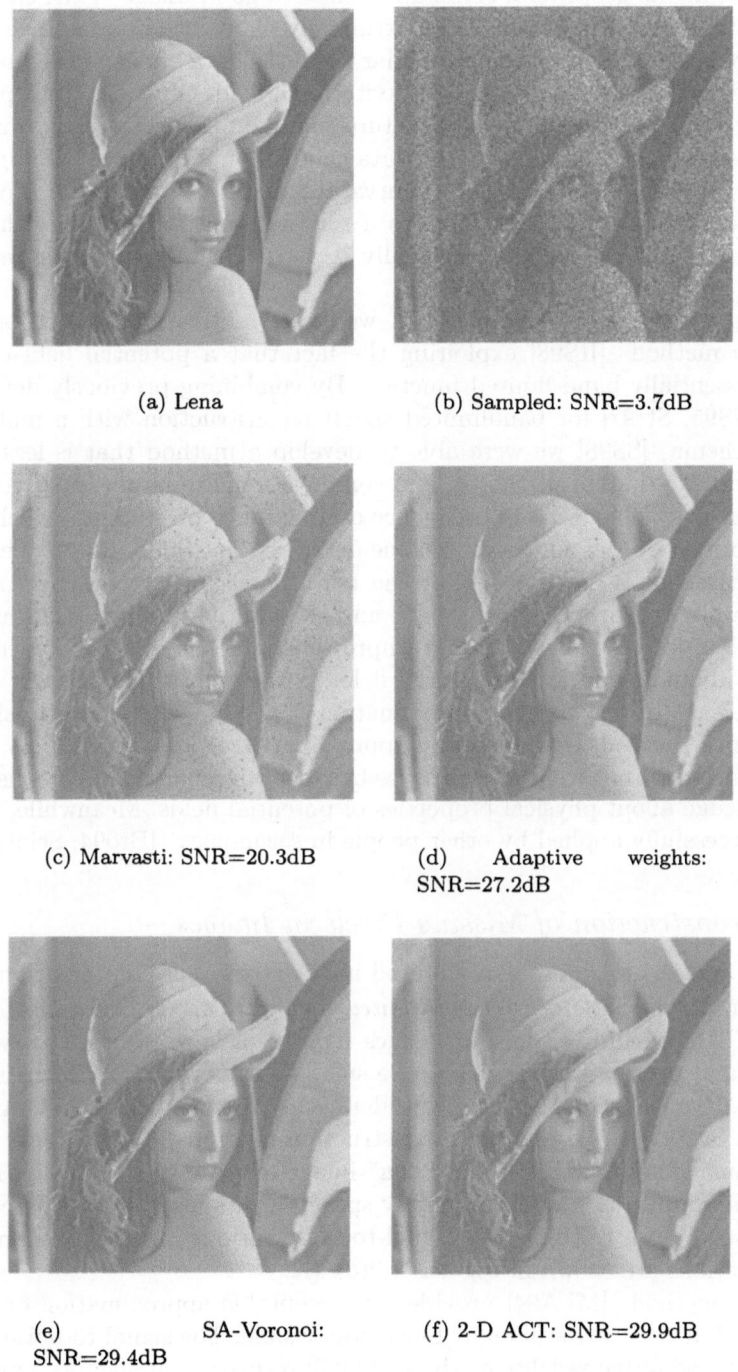

(a) Lena

(b) Sampled: SNR=3.7dB

(c) Marvasti: SNR=20.3dB

(d) Adaptive weights: SNR=27.2dB

(e) SA-Voronoi: SNR=29.4dB

(f) 2-D ACT: SNR=29.9dB

FIGURE 1.9. Nonuniformly sampled Lena and reconstructions.

It is agreed in the geophysics community that "a good image of the earth hides our data acquisition footprint" [Cla98]. Unfortunately many gridding methods proposed in the literature fail in this aspect, in particular when the data are noisy. Figures 1.3(a)–(d) illustrate this problem for a simulated gravitational field. Obviously the approximation obtained by the so-called minimal curvature method [Bri74] is very sensitive to the sampling geometry; it cannot "hide the data acquisition footprints," cf. Figures 1.3(c)–(d). Similar to splines, the minimum curvature method produces an approximation that is smooth but does not conform to a relevant physical model. Other methods, like kriging [Han93], are computationally expensive and require interaction by an experienced operator.

These drawbacks of existing methods were the motivation to develop a new reconstruction method [RS98] exploiting the fact that a potential field can be modeled as an essentially band-limited function. By combining previously developed algorithms [FGS95, Str97] for bandlimited signal reconstruction with a multilevel regularization scheme [SS98] we were able to develop a method that is less sensitive to noise than other gridding methods. The computationally most expensive part of the method is the solution of a nested sequence of Toeplitz-type systems, which can be efficiently performed by the multilevel scheme described in [SS98, RS98]. This multilevel method is based on a combination of the two dimensional reconstruction algorithm described earlier and proposed in [Str97] and the multilevel regularization scheme derived in [SS98]. We achieved further improvement of our method by incorporating information about the decay of potential fields in the algorithm [RS98].

Figures 1.3(a)–(b) display the approximation of the gravitational field shown by the aforementioned method. Obviously the approximation is less distorted by the noise in the data, which does not come as a surprise because our algorithm allows us to exploit a priori knowledge about physical properties of potential fields. Meanwhile, this method has been successfully applied by other people in seismology [Bro94, Sch95b].

1.3.3 Reconstruction of Missing Pixels in Images

In practice, images are rarely band-limited in the strict sense of definition (1.34). But images are often *essentially M-band-limited*, i.e., $\hat{f}(n, m)$ is negligible for $|n| > M$ or $|m| > M$. Representing edges in images requires a large bandwidth, which means that the area of missing samples has to be small to achieve stable reconstruction. The numerical experiments confirm these considerations. We compare the 2-D ACT method, presented in Section 1.2.3, to other reconstruction methods.

Our test image is the well-known "Lena"-image of size 512×512, see Figure 1.9(a). The image is sampled at 150320 randomly spaced locations; about 43 percent of pixels are lost — see Figure 1.9(b) — the signal-to-noise ratio is 3.7dB. The approximations after 10 iterations are shown in Figures 1.9(c)–(f).

Marvasti's method [MLA94] provides an acceptable approximation of most of the lost samples, but there are still many black dots visible. The signal-to-noise ratio (SNR) is 20.3dB. The adaptive weights method [FG93] returns a satisfactory approximation, with SNR = 27.2dB. The ACT method provides a reconstruction with significantly fewer black dots compared to the other reconstructions. In fact there is nearly no visible difference between the approximation provided by our method and the original image, the SNR = 29.9dB. The Voronoi modification of the Sauer-Allebach method [SA87, FS93] provides a reconstruction with comparable quality with SNR = 29.5dB. However, the computational costs for this method are much higher than for the 2-D ACT method [Str97].

It is well known that band-limited functions are not the optimal tool to model arbitrary digital images. Other models, based on wavelets or local trigonometric bases are preferable in many applications. Fast algorithms for the restoration of missing samples using wavelets or brushlets have not yet been developed and are the topic of our future research.

A different approach has been undertaken in [FSS99]. One reason for the success of using Haar wavelets [Mal98] in image analysis is based on the fact that many images can be modeled as piecewise constant functions. This observation suggests using a similar model for reconstructing missing samples in images.

In order to "fill in" gaps in images caused by missing samples, we apply a constant extrapolation of the samples at the boundaries across the gap as follows. To each missing sample we assign the sampling value of its nearest neighbor. In a discrete setting there can be several "nearest" neighbors, in which case we use a weighted combination of these samples. Determination of nearest neighbors can be done by computing the corresponding Voronoi tessellation. Voronoi tessellations are known to be a successful concept in image processing and data interpolation mathematics [FH94, OBS92, AA85]. However, this concept suffers from its computational complexity. In [FS93] we describe an efficient FFT-based algorithm for the approximation of multidimensional Voronoi tessellations which is then used in the image reconstruction algorithm outlined earlier.

In order to preserve edge continuities in the reconstructed images the fast Voronoi reconstruction method can be combined with an adaptive filtering scheme [FSS99]. This algorithm seems to be robust enough to restore large areas of missing samples. A combination of this method with local trigonometric polynomials is currently under investigation.

2

Stochastic Shape Theory

Christian Cenker
Georg Pflug
Manfred Mayer

Stochastic models and statistical procedures are essential for pattern recognition. Linear discriminant analysis, parametric and nonparametric density estimation, maximum-likelihood classification, supervised and nonsupervised learning, neural nets, parametric, nonparametric, and fuzzy clustering, principal component analysis, simulated annealing are only some of the well-known statistical techniques used for pattern recognition. Markov models and other stochastic models are often used to describe statistical characteristics of patterns in the pattern space.

We want to concentrate on modeling and feature extraction using new techniques. We do not model the characteristics of the pattern space but the generation of the patterns, i.e., modeling the pattern generation process via stochastic processes. Furthermore, wavelets and wavelet packets will help us to construct a feature extractor. Applying our models to a sample application we noticed the lack of global non-linear optimization algorithms. Thus, we added a section on optimization, in which we present a modification of a multi-level single-linkage technique that can be used in high-dimensional feature spaces.

2.1 Shape Analysis

A project on offline signature verification shows the need for new approaches. Standard methods do not show the wanted accuracy; nevertheless, they have been implemented at a first stage in order to compare the results. As all signatures of one person are of different but similar shape we look for a description of the similarity and the difference. First, a signature is a special form of curve; we discard all color, thickness and "pressure" information from the scanned signature (cf. [AYF86]), leaving only a thinned *polygonal* shape. We have a connected skeleton of the "contour".

The first problem to solve is the parameterization of the curve, i.e., to get a one-dimensional function that represents the two-dimensional signature, as our constraints are on the one hand to use as little data for storage of the signatures as possible and, on the other hand, to develop fast algorithms. Thus, using only one-dimensional objects (functions) seem to be a feasible solution. We choose a change-in-angle parameterization of the curve, which has the advantages of shift, rotation and scale invariance (cf. [Nie90]). Features are then extracted forming a sampled version of the contour, stored

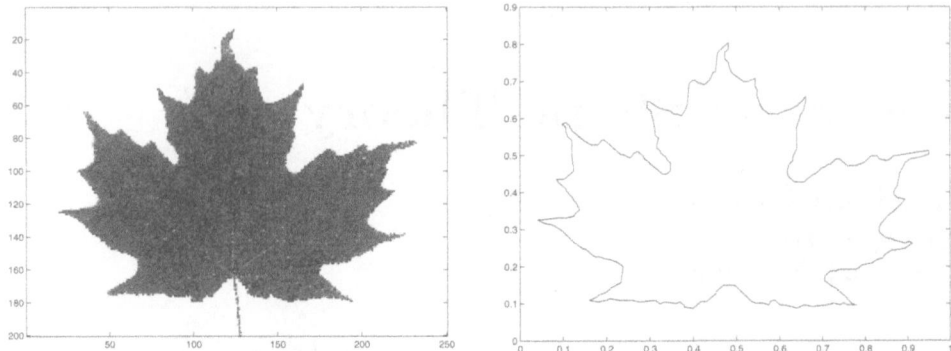

FIGURE 2.1. A maple leaf and its contour.

in a k-dimensional vector, and used for discrimination and classification.

Based on the change-in-angle parameterization we present three different approaches to match the patterns. Starting with the description of classes of signatures and their similarity by stochastic processes, i.e., stochastic deformation processes, describe the generation process of the signatures of an individual (see Section 2.3). Secondly, we want to use new "standard" signal analysis methods to analyze the curve or polygonal shape, i.e., wavelet and frame methods, as they provide fast algorithms that produce patterns that have a nice easy interpretation (see Section 2.5). At last, a straightforward geometrical pattern matching is presented, i.e., calculating the *polygonal distance* between templates when optimally placed on top of each other. This leads to a nonlinear global optimization problem, which we present in Section 2.6. The last approach has been added, as the global optimization techniques are also extensively used with deformable templates, and, at a smaller extent, with wavelet packet feature extraction.

A study of recent and standard literature shows that some work is done on Fourier descriptors of closed curves. Furthermore, biological shapes are dealt with, which are in some way "similar" to our problem, e.g., in the work of Grenander [GK91]. Two parameterizations of closed curves are proposed, a change-in-angle real parameterization and a complex one, using the coordinates as real and imaginary parts (see [Nie90]).

Thus, we look at closed contours first, with the change-in-angle parameterization. This results in periodic functions, and the parameterization is invariant with respect to scale, shifts, and rotations. Thus, a new sample application has to be found that better reflects the idea of closed contours and biologically variable shapes (among "identical" individuals). We will use leaves of broad-leaved trees; to be more exact, to classify leaves by their contour only (see Figure 2.1).

Using these contours of leaves instead of signatures does not change the results concerning stochastic deformations and global optimization, as all algorithms can be applied without change, but, wanting to use wavelet analysis, periodic functions are much easier to handle than nonperiodic functions because we do not have to bother with edge effects, and the results are easier to interpret. The application of the results to signatures will be straightforward, as we may use periodic versions of signatures, i.e,

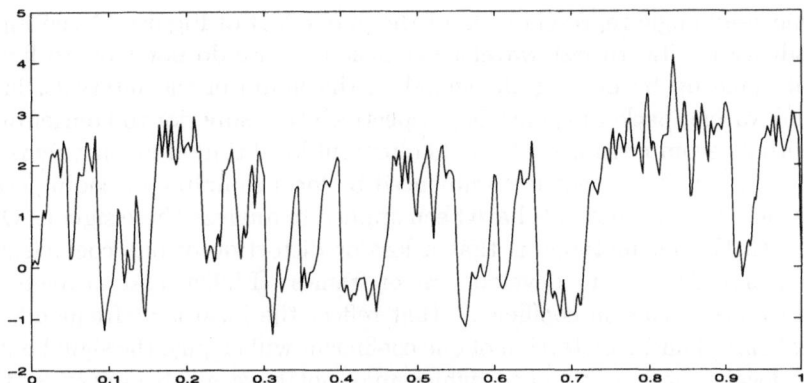

FIGURE 2.2. The change-in-angle parameterization of the maple leaf in Figure 2.1.

the change-in-angle parameterized version of a signature is interpreted as a periodic function starting and ending at zero angle.

2.2   Contour Line Parameterization

Given a closed contour, it is saved as a two-dimensional array of coordinates x and y. This array represents a circular shift-invariant class of contours, i.e., it is independent with respect to the starting point of the digitalization or parameterization, respectively. The contour is then expanded to its *change-in-angle function* by measuring the angle of successive tangents in coordinates (x, y)

$$\gamma(s) = \arctan \frac{x'(a^{-1}(s))}{y'(a^{-1}(s))} - \arctan \frac{x'(a^{-1}(0))}{y'(a^{-1}(0))} - 2\pi s \qquad (2.1)$$

$s \in [0, 1)$ and $a(t)$, $t \in [0, 1)$ being the cumulated arc length

$$a(t) = \frac{\int_0^t \sqrt{x'(u)^2 + y'(u)^2} \, du}{\int_0^1 \sqrt{x'(u)^2 + y'(u)^2} \, du} \; . \qquad (2.2)$$

For a discrete version the integrals have to be replaced by the appropriate sums

$$\begin{aligned} \gamma(a_i) &= \arctan \frac{x_{i+1} - x_i}{y_{i+1} - y_i} - \arctan \frac{x_1 - x_0}{y_1 - y_0} - 2\pi a_i \\ a_i &= \frac{\sum_{j=0}^{i} \sqrt{(x_{j+1} - x_j)^2 + (y_{j+1} - y_j)^2}}{\sum_{j=0}^{n-1} \sqrt{(x_{j+1} - x_j)^2 + (y_{j+1} - y_j)^2}} \end{aligned} \qquad (2.3)$$

in which (x_i, y_i) are the sampled coordinates.

This parameterization results in a circular shift-invariant representation, or, using the periodic continuation, a shift-invariant function with period 1, i.e., on the interval $[0, 1)$

(for the change-in-angle representation of the maple leaf of Figure 2.1 see Figure 2.2). This periodicity is vital to fast wavelet expansions as we do not have to handle edge effects that come up by cutting the signal at the limits of the intervals. Frame and wavelet, and wavelet packet expansions, respectively, are superior to Fourier expansions as the resulting decomposition coefficients represent local time-frequency features of the analyzed function and are thus less influenced by local sampling or coding errors.

For long, only Fourier methods have been applied to analyze these signals. One major drawback with Fourier methods is that a loss or distortion of one coefficient distorts the whole signal. The recent development of frames [FS98a] and wavelets [Mey90] enables us to use expansion coefficients that reflect the local time-frequency behavior of the signal only. Thus, a distortion of one coefficient will change the signal only locally, i.e., only a local feature is changed, which may not have much impact on the whole discrimination and classification process. So far wavelet packet representations are only used to store signals efficiently [Wic91], and there have been attempts to use Gabor frames to analyze textures [PZ88b].

2.3   Deformable Templates

To deal with the deformable templates model we first have to present some minor definitions and the mathematical and statistical framework. We say that a class consists of equivalent shapes or templates, like in nature, where a species may have many different forms.

A two-dimensional shape — a closed contour — is considered to be the equivalence class of closed polygons under rigid motions (rotations and translations). We discuss a model for random shapes, which is used as the basis for probabilistic classifiers. A maximum-likelihood approach is used to deal with the incomplete information given by the knowledge of the equivalence class only.

Notation

A *closed contour* is a simple closed Jordan curve, i.e., a homomorphic image of the interval $[0, 1)$. Let $\mathbf{x} = (x_0, x_1, \dots, x_{n-1})$ be the vector of vertices of a closed polygon in $\mathbb{R}^2$, $x_i = (u_i, v_i)^t$.

The *contour line* of a polygon is the equivalence class of polygons formed by cyclically permuting the indices. This equivalence, however, is not sufficient. We define a *shape* to be the equivalence class of all contours that differ only by rotation or translation.

Let G be the group of *shape-preserving transformations* in $\mathbb{R}^2$, i.e., $G = \{x \mapsto U_\varphi x + d\}$ with U_φ being the rotation matrix of angle φ and $d = (\delta_x, \delta_y)^t$ is a two-dimensional shift vector. G is also called the group of *rigid motions*. Every transformation $g \in G$, or $g_{\varphi, d}$, is a rotation by an angle $\varphi \in [0, 2\pi)$ and a translation by a vector d. These transformations form a group; the inverse of an element g is given by $g_{\varphi, d}^{-1} = g_{-d, U_\varphi^{-1}}$.

A shape-preserving transformation g may not operate only on points but also on polygons, mapping $\mathbf{x} = (x_0, \dots, x_{n-1})$ to $g(\mathbf{x}) = (g(x_0), \dots, g(x_{n-1}))$.

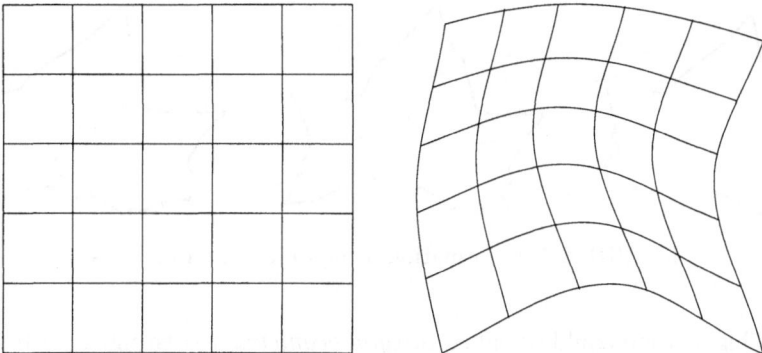

FIGURE 2.3. Stochastic planar deformation process.

The group G is a subgroup of the group of *similarity transformations* $H = \{\mathbf{x} \mapsto \beta \cdot U_\varphi \mathbf{x} + d\}$ that — in addition to G — contains also all scaling transformations with scaling factor β (cf. also [Ken89]).

We call a polygon $\mathbf{x}_1$ *shape equivalent* to another polygon $\mathbf{x}_2$, $\mathbf{x}_1 \sim \mathbf{x}_2$, if there is a transformation $g \in G$ such that $\mathbf{x}_1$ and $g(\mathbf{x}_2)$ are the same contours that differ only by cyclical permutation of the indices. Likewise we define $\mathbf{x}_1$ as *similarity equivalent* to $\mathbf{x}_2$, $\mathbf{x}_1 \approx \mathbf{x}_2$, if there is a transformation $h \in H$ such that $\mathbf{x}_1$ and $g(\mathbf{x}_2)$ are the same contours. The shape equivalence class of a polygon is denoted by $\tilde{\mathbf{x}}$ and the similarity equivalence class by $\tilde{\tilde{\mathbf{x}}}$.

Pattern Classification

When doing pattern classification we are dealing with incomplete information with respect to the pattern. We may not observe $\mathbf{x}$ itself, only $\tilde{\mathbf{x}}$, the equivalence class of $\mathbf{x}$. If the equivalence classes are large this is a considerable reduction of available information.

There are two ways to deal with incomplete information. The first is to calculate the probability density within class i of the equivalence class $\tilde{\mathbf{x}}$ by integration

$$f(\tilde{\mathbf{x}}|i) := \int_{\mathbf{x} \in \tilde{\mathbf{x}}} f(\mathbf{x}|i) \, d\nu(\mathbf{x}). \tag{2.4}$$

The second way is to treat the unknown $g \in G$, which has transformed the unobservable outcome $\mathbf{x}$ to the observation $g(\mathbf{x})$ by a maximum likelihood technique and to set

$$f(\tilde{\mathbf{x}}|i) := \max_{\mathbf{x} \in \tilde{\mathbf{x}}} f(\mathbf{x}|i). \tag{2.5}$$

In both cases we use $f(\tilde{\mathbf{x}}|i)$ instead of $f(\mathbf{x}|i)$. Because the computational effort of Equation (2.4) is beyond every usability, we have decided to use Equation (2.5).

2.3.1 *Stochastic Planar Deformation Processes*

We will use a slightly modified version of the approach of [GK91], which is based on a stochastic model of the random transformation of the plane and leads to shape-invariant

FIGURE 2.4. Deformation using different parameters.

classifiers. This method could be called *integral geometric* to distinguish it from the well-known *differential geometric* analysis of contour lines by polygonal, spline, or Fourier approximation together with descriptors of its local behavior (cf. [BE91, CV90]).

Let $T_\omega(x)$ be a random transformation mapping $x \in \mathbb{R}^2$ to $T_\omega(x) \in \mathbb{R}^2$, ω is the random element. That is, $T_\omega(x)$ is a stochastic vector process on some probability space $(\Omega, \mathcal{A}, P)$ with parameter $x \in \mathbb{R}^2$ and values in $\mathbb{R}^2$. The random image of a (closed) polygon $\mathbf{x} = (x_0, \ldots, x_{n-1})$ under T_ω is the polygon $T_\omega(\mathbf{x}) = (T_\omega(x_0), \ldots, T_\omega(x_{n-1}))$ (see Figures 2.3 and 2.4 for examples).

We develop a stochastic model for the random deformation process $T_\omega(x)$. The explicit notation of the random element ω will be avoided later. Let $V(x) = T(x) - x$, i.e., the elements are shifted to the origin.

The following properties must hold:

1. $E(V(x)) = 0$, i.e., the random deformation is centered at the parameter point (E denotes the expectation).

2. $V(x)$ is invariant with respect to rotations of the image plane.

3. $V(x)$ is invariant with respect to translations of the parameter plane.

4. $V(x)$ is invariant with respect to orthogonal transformations of the parameter plane.

These properties ensure that the random transformation T has the *equivariance property* that $T(g(x))$ has the same distribution as $g(T(x))$, for all $g \in G$ (cf. [Pfl95]).

Thus, $T(g(\mathbf{x}))$ has the same distribution as $g(T(\mathbf{x}))$ for all polygons $\mathbf{x}$ and all shape-invariant transforms $g \in G$. Furthermore, if two polygons $\mathbf{x}_1$ and $\mathbf{x}_2$ are shape equivalent, we may write $T(\tilde{\mathbf{x}})$ as the distribution induced on the shape classes by random deformation of the shape class $\tilde{\mathbf{x}}$.

2.3.2   *Gaussian Isotropic Random Planar Deformations*

Among all stochastic processes $V(z)$ satisfying properties 1 to 4 of above a Gaussian bivariate process with zero mean, independent components, and spherically symmetric covariance structure (isotropic structure) is the simplest. Note that all bivariate Gaussian processes with independent components exhibit property 2 and that a spherically symmetric covariance function implies property 4.

We propose a particular choice of the covariance function for its simple and nice properties:

Let $V(x) = \begin{pmatrix} X(x) \\ Y(x) \end{pmatrix}$, X and Y be two independent univariate Gaussian random processes with parameter $x \in \mathbb{R}^2$, and moments

$$
\begin{array}{rcl}
E(X(x)) = E(Y(x)) & = & 0 \\
\text{Cov}(X(x_1), X(x_2)) & = & \sigma^2 \cdot \exp\left(-\frac{\alpha}{2}\|x_1 - x_2\|^2\right) \\
\text{Cov}(Y(x_1), Y(x_2)) & = & \sigma^2 \cdot \exp\left(-\frac{\alpha}{2}\|x_1 - x_2\|^2\right) \\
\text{Cov}(X(x_1), Y(x_2)) & = & 0.
\end{array}
\tag{2.6}
$$

This process has two real parameters, the variance σ and the parameter $\alpha > 0$ that determines the decrease of the correlation of $X(x_1)$ and $X(x_2)$ as the distance $\|x_1 - x_2\|$ increases. If $\alpha = 0$ then $X(x_1) \equiv X(x_2)$, for all x_1 and x_2, whereas, if $\alpha = \infty$ then all $X(x_i)$ are independent. The same holds for $Y(\cdot)$.

X and Y are two independently identically distributed *stationary processes* (see [Ç75, CL67]) with the spectral density:

$$
(s, t) \mapsto \frac{\sigma^2}{2\pi\alpha} \exp\left(-\frac{\alpha}{2}(s^2 + t^2)\right) \qquad (s, t) \in \mathbb{R}^2.
\tag{2.7}
$$

The process $X(u, v)$ has the Karhunen-Loéve representation (KL)

$$
X(u, v) = \sigma \sum_{k=0}^{\infty} \sum_{l=0}^{\infty} \frac{(\sqrt{\alpha})^{k+l}}{\sqrt{k!\,l!}} u^k v^l \exp\left(-\frac{\alpha}{2}(u^2 + v^2)\right) \cdot \eta_x(k, l),
\tag{2.8}
$$

where $\eta_x(k, l)$ are independent Gaussian $N(0, 1)$ random variables. $Y(u, v)$ has exactly the same representation, but with $\eta_x(k, l)$ replaced by $\eta_y(k, l)$, which are also independent $N(0, 1)$ variables, independent from all η_xs. The KL representation formula (2.8) can be used to calculate the deformation process, replacing the infinite sums by appropriate finite sums.

A comparison with the work of Amit, Grenander, and Piccioni [AGP91] shows that these authors also consider a Gaussian plane process but with the boundaries of the unit square fixed (i.e., the variance at the boundary is 0). Thus, their process is nonstationary and does not exhibit invariance properties 1 to 4.

2.3.3 The Deformable Templates Model

The recognition problem associated with the random deformation model is the following. Assume that $\mathbf{x}^{(1)}, \cdots \mathbf{x}^{(k)}$ are templates representing k classes. We observe polygon $\mathbf{z}$. Under the assumption that $\mathbf{z}$ is in class j it is of the form

$$
\mathbf{z} = U_\varphi(T(\mathbf{x}^{(j)})) + d.
$$

The parameters φ and d are unknown nuisance parameters. The parameters σ and α might be known (if some experience about the deformation process is already gathered)

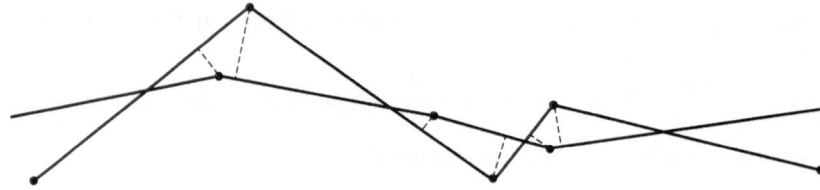

FIGURE 2.5. Calculating the polygonal distance.

or unknown. The estimation of all these parameters is easy, if we know which vertices of the template $\mathbf{x}$ correspond to vertices of the random image $\mathbf{z}$. It is more realistic to assume that this correspondence is unknown and even that the number of vertices of the template and the random image is different (see next section and Figure 2.5).

2.3.4   Maximum Likelihood Classification

In statistical pattern recognition we have to identify a randomly observed object $\mathbf{z} \in \mathcal{Z}$ as a member of one of k given classes. The observation space is some measurable space $(\mathcal{Z}, \mathcal{B}, \nu)$. Usually a Bayesian classifier calculates the posterior probability of each class given the observation and assigns the object to the class that has the highest probability (maximum likelihood). The calculation of this Bayes rule requires the knowledge of

1. $f(\mathbf{z}|i)$, the probability density of the objects within each class i; $i = 1, \ldots k$ with respect to the measure ν and

2. π_i, the prior probability of each class.

The Bayes classifier assigns class i to observation $\mathbf{z}$ if

$$\pi_i \cdot f(\mathbf{z}|i) = \max_{1 \leq j \leq k} \{\pi_j \cdot f(\mathbf{z}|j)\}. \tag{2.9}$$

A widely used technique of pattern recognition extracts an n-dimensional feature vector from the given image and considers this vector as the random object $\mathbf{z}$ in the prior sense.

Polygonal Distance

Let $\mathbf{z}$ and $\mathbf{x}$ be two polygons with possibly different numbers of vertices such that $\mathbf{z} \sim T(\mathbf{x})$. Let $\mathbf{z} = (z_0, \ldots, z_{m-1})$ and $\mathbf{x} = (x_0, \ldots x_{n-1})$. We choose additional points $(\bar{x}_0, \ldots, \bar{x}_{m-1})$ and $(\bar{z}_0, \ldots, \bar{z}_{n-1})$, x_i is the point of the polygon $\mathbf{x}$ closest to z_i, and z_i is the point of $\mathbf{z}$ closest to x_i.

Denote by $\bar{\mathbf{x}}$ and $\bar{\mathbf{z}}$ the polygons resulting from adding new vertices $(\bar{x}_i)$ and $(\bar{z}_i)$ to the old ones, arranged in their natural order. The larger polygons $\bar{\mathbf{x}}$ and $\bar{\mathbf{z}}$ now both have $n + m$ vertices and a natural correspondence. Based on the form of the likelihood function (2.8) we define the distance (see Figure 2.5) as

$$\text{dist}(\mathbf{z}, \mathbf{x}) = (\bar{\mathbf{z}} - \bar{\mathbf{x}}) \Sigma_{\bar{\mathbf{x}}}^{-1}(\alpha)(\bar{\mathbf{z}} - \bar{\mathbf{x}}). \tag{2.10}$$

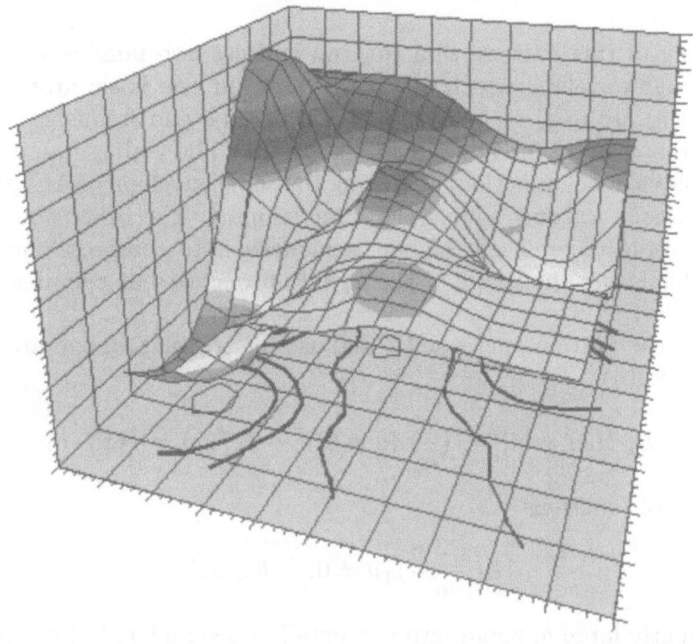

FIGURE 2.6. Objective function of Gaussian deformations.

The maximum likelihood problem (2.5) finds the solution of the optimization problem

$$\text{dist}(g(\mathbf{z}), \mathbf{x}) \to \min \qquad g \in G. \tag{2.11}$$

The density of $\mathbf{z}$ according to the model is

$$f(\mathbf{z}|\mathbf{x}) = (2\pi)^{n/2}\sigma^{-n} \det\left(\Sigma_{\mathbf{x}}^{-1}(\alpha)\right) \exp[-\frac{1}{2\sigma^2}(\mathbf{z} - \mathbf{x})^t\Sigma_{\mathbf{x}}^{-1}(\alpha)(\mathbf{z} - \mathbf{x})]; \tag{2.12}$$

the covariance matrix $\Sigma_{\mathbf{x}}(\alpha)$ is of the form

$$\Sigma_{\mathbf{x}}(\alpha) = \begin{pmatrix} \exp(-\frac{\alpha}{2}\|x_0 - x_0\|^2) & \cdots & \exp(-\frac{\alpha}{2}\|x_0 - x_{n-1}\|^2) \\ \exp(-\frac{\alpha}{2}\|x_1 - x_0\|^2) & \cdots & \exp(-\frac{\alpha}{2}\|x_1 - x_{n-1}\|^2) \\ \vdots & \ddots & \vdots \\ \exp(-\frac{\alpha}{2}\|x_{n-1} - x_0\|^2) & \cdots & \exp(-\frac{\alpha}{2}\|x_{n-1} - x_{n-1}\|^2) \end{pmatrix}$$

Typically, the objective function appearing in Equation (2.11) has several local minima and the optimization must be done very carefully (see Figure 2.6). Thus, we have implemented an adapted stochastic global optimization algorithm (see Section 2.6).

Furthermore, the optimal deformation parameters α and σ and the minimal polygonal distance can be used as additional features for different discrimination algorithms, e.g., classification trees.

2.4   The Wavelet Transform

At the beginning of this part we said that we will use two families of atoms, namely
Gabor frames and wavelets, which are both based on one basic atom. These frames
(see Section 1.1.3) are used to analyze a signal in time and frequency. There are two
approaches to represent different frequencies in time. The Gabor frame approach uses
modulated versions of one function, all having the same envelope (see Figure 1.1), which
are shifted in time, all atoms having the same support. The other possibility, instead
of using modulation, to represent higher frequencies is to compress one signal further
and further. This leaves the shape of the signal untouched but compresses its support
(cf. Figure 2).

Thus, we define a dilation operator D_a and use the translation operator T_b (the same
as in Equation (1.10))

$$D_a f(x) = |a|^{-\frac{1}{2}} f(\frac{x}{a}) \ (a \neq 0) \qquad T_b f(x) = f(x - b) \tag{2.13}$$

to build families of functions

$$\{\psi(\frac{x - b}{a}) \,|\, a \neq 0, \ a, b \in \mathbb{R}\} \tag{2.14}$$

that, for sufficiently large a, zoom into any detail of a signal f, b shifts ψ to any detail
of f.

Similarly to (1.7) and (1.11) we define the *continuous wavelet transform* for an arbitrary $f \in L^2(\mathbb{R})$

$$
\begin{aligned}
\mathcal{W}_\psi f(a, b) &= \frac{1}{\sqrt{C_\psi}} |a|^{-\frac{1}{2}} \int_{\mathbb{R}} f(s) \overline{\psi(\frac{t-b}{a})} ds \\
&= \frac{1}{\sqrt{C_\psi}} \langle f, D_a T_b \psi \rangle \qquad a \neq 0, \ a, b \in \mathbb{R}
\end{aligned}
\tag{2.15}
$$

with the *admissibility condition*

$$C_\psi = \int \frac{|\hat{\psi}(\omega)|^2}{|\omega|} d\omega < \infty, \tag{2.16}$$

which ensures that the continuous wavelet transform

$$\mathcal{W}_\psi : L^2(\mathbb{R}) \to L^2(\mathbb{R}, \frac{da\,db}{a^2}) \tag{2.17}$$

is an isometric transformation onto its image, as

$$
\begin{aligned}
\|\mathcal{W}_\psi f\|^2_{L^2(\mathbb{R}, \frac{da\,db}{a^2})} &= \iint |\widehat{\mathcal{W}_\psi f}(a, \omega)|^2 da\, d\omega \\
&= \frac{1}{C_\psi} \iint |a| |\hat{\psi}(a, \omega)|^2 |\hat{f}(\omega)|^2 \frac{da\, d\omega}{a^2} \\
&= \frac{1}{C_\psi} \iint \frac{|\hat{\psi}(\tau)|^2}{|\tau|} |\hat{f}(\omega)|^2 d\tau\, d\omega \\
&= \frac{1}{C_\psi} \int \frac{|\hat{\psi}(\tau)|^2}{|\tau|} \int |\hat{f}(\omega)|^2 d\omega\, d\tau \\
&= \|f\|^2_{L^2(\mathbb{R})},
\end{aligned}
$$

Thus, the inverse of $\mathcal{W}_\psi$ is its adjoint $\mathcal{W}_\psi^*$, such that $f(x)$ can be reproduced by

$$f(x) = \int_{|a|>0} \int_{\mathbb{R}} \mathcal{W}_\psi f(a,b) \frac{1}{\sqrt{C_\psi}} \psi(\frac{x-b}{a}) \frac{dadb}{a^2}, \qquad (2.18)$$

Remark: The first identity of this type was *Calderon's reproducing formula*, which uses real radial functions $\psi \in L^1(\mathbb{R}^n)$ with zero mean and $\int_0^\infty \frac{|\psi(ax)|^2}{a} da = 1$ and their dilates $\psi_a(x) = a^{-n}\psi(\frac{x}{a})$, $a > 0$, to get (with standard convolution $*$)

$$f = \int \psi_a * \psi_a * f \frac{da}{a} \quad \forall f \in L^2(\mathbb{R}^n) . \qquad (2.19)$$

This identity was 'rediscovered' by A. Grossmann and J. Morlet.

The next section will shed some light on why we had to use a different measure in Equation (2.17) and on the similarity between Gabor and wavelet frames, especially, their roots in group theory.

2.4.1 Atomic Decompositions and Group Theory

As we are interested in analyzing signals by atoms or families of atoms, generated by simple operations from one "mother" atom, we may recall the definitions of the unitary operators of translations T_b, dilations D_a, and modulation (frequency-shift) M_ω (Equations (1.10) and (2.13)). A more elaborate introduction to the group theoretical aspects is presented in [LMR94].

The Affine Linear Group

We will start with the group associated with wavelets, the *affine linear group* G_{al}, which is sometimes also called the $ax + b$ group as its elements are identified with the corresponding affine linear transformations.

Identifying the operators $U_{al}(a,b) = D_a T_b$ with elements $(a,b) \in \mathbb{R} \setminus \{0\} \times \mathbb{R}$ we get a multiplicative group of operators on L^2; the multiplication is the composition of operators

$$U_{al}(a,b) \cdot U_{al}(r,s) \triangleq D_a T_b \circ D_r T_s = D_r T_s D_a T_b = D_{ar} T_{as+b} \triangleq U_{al}(ar, as + b) \quad (2.20)$$

as the *commutation relations*

$$D_a T_b = T_{\frac{b}{a}} D_a \quad \text{and} \quad T_b D_a = D_a T_{ab} \qquad (2.21)$$

hold. In group notation the multiplication law reads

$$(a,b) \circ (r,s) = (ar, as + b) \quad (a,b) \in \mathbb{R} \setminus \{0\} \times \mathbb{R} . \qquad (2.22)$$

The group $G_{al} = (\mathbb{R} \setminus \{0\} \times \mathbb{R}, \circ)$ is called affine linear group.

Remark: Be careful when reading the operational notation. $D_a T_b f(x) = D_a(f(x - b)) = |a|^{-\frac{1}{2}} f(\frac{x-b}{a})$ but $(D_a \circ T_b)f(x) = T_b(D_a f(x)) = T_b(|a|^{-\frac{1}{2}} f(\frac{x}{a})) = |a|^{-\frac{1}{2}} f(\frac{x}{a} - b)$. The same holds for the group notation.

The neutral and inverse elements are

$$U_{al}(1,0) = id \qquad U_{al}(a,b)^{-1} = U_{al}(\frac{1}{a}, -\frac{b}{a}) \; .$$

Thus, we get a unitary irreducible *representation* U_{al} of G_{al} in $L^2(\mathbb{R})$, i.e.,

$$U_{al} : G_{al} \to L^2(\mathbb{R}), \; U_{al}(g_1 \circ g_2) = U_{al}(g_1) \cdot U_{al}(g_2), \; U_{al}(1,0) = id \qquad (2.23)$$

with $g_i \in G_{al}$.

As G_{al} is locally compact there exists an invariant measure. We will show how to derive the left-invariant Haar measure μ_{al}^L as it is responsible for left transforms like the wavelet transform.

We will start with a weighted Lebesgue measure for an $H \subseteq G_{al}$

$$
\begin{aligned}
\mu_{al}^L((r,s) \circ H) &= \int_{(r,s) \circ H} w(a,b) da\, db \\
&= \int_{\tau(H)} w(a,b) da\, db \\
&= \int_H w(r\alpha, r\beta + s) |\det J_\tau(\alpha, \beta)| d\alpha\, d\beta \\
&= \int_H w(r\alpha, r\beta + s) r^2 d\alpha\, d\beta \\
&= \int_H w(\alpha, \beta) d\alpha\, d\beta \\
&= \mu_{al}^L(H)
\end{aligned}
$$

in which we make use of the transformation theorem using the transformation $\tau(\alpha, \beta) = (r,s) \circ (\alpha, \beta) = (r\alpha, r\beta + s)$ with its functional or Jacobi matrix $J_\tau(\alpha, \beta) = \begin{pmatrix} r & 0 \\ 0 & r \end{pmatrix}$.

The weight function $w(\alpha, \beta) = w(r\alpha, r\beta + s) r^2$ solves the preceding relations and thus the left-invariant Haar measure is $d\mu_{al}^L = \frac{da\, db}{a^2}$. There is also a right-invariant Haar measure $d\mu_{al}^R = \frac{da\, db}{|a|}$.

The wavelet transform (2.15) reads in group notation

$$\mathcal{W}_\psi f(a,b) = \frac{1}{\sqrt{C_\psi}} \langle f, U_{al}(a,b)\psi \rangle = \frac{1}{\sqrt{C_\psi}} \langle f, D_a T_b \psi \rangle \qquad a \neq 0, \; a,b \in \mathbb{R} \; . \qquad (2.24)$$

The Weyl-Heisenberg Group

The *Weyl-Heisenberg group* G_{WH} (WH group, for short) is associated with Gabor representations.

G_{WH} has three parameters $(p,q,t) \in \mathbb{R}^2 \times \mathbb{T}$, $\mathbb{T} = \{z \in \mathbb{C}, |z| = |e^{i\xi}| = 1\}$ is the torus, with the group multiplication law

$$(p_1, q_1, t_1) \circ (p_2, q_2, t_2) = (p_1 + p_2, q_1 + q_2, t_1 t_2 e^{i\pi(q_1 p_2 - q_2 p_1)}) \qquad (2.25)$$

with inverse $(p,q,t)^{-1} = (-p, -q, t^{-1})$.

Identifying the operators $U_{WH}(p,q,t) = t e^{-i\pi pq} M_q T_p$ and setting $t = 1$, i.e., redefining $U_{WH}(p,q) = U_{WH}(p,q,1)$, we get the multiplication for Weyl operators

$$U_{WH}(p_1, q_1) \cdot U_{WH}(p_2, q_2) = e^{i\pi(p_1 q_2 - q_1 p_2)} U_{WH}(p_1 + p_2, q_1 + q_2)$$

(see also [Cen89]) we get an irreducible group representation of G_{WH} in L^2.

G_{WH} is also locally compact and a unimodular group; its left- and its right-invariant Haar measures are equal, and in this case equal to the standard Lebesgue measure.

The short-time Fourier transform (cf. Equations (1.11) and (1.25)) essentially reads

$$\mathcal{V}_g f(t, \omega) = \langle f, U_{WH}(t, \omega) g \rangle . \tag{2.26}$$

Group Representations and Orthogonality Relations

First we need an explanation of some technical terms.

U_G is called *representation* of the group G in the Hilbert space $\mathbb{H}_U$ if

$$U_G : G \to \mathbb{H}_U, \ U_G(g_1 \circ g_2) = U_G(g_1) \cdot U_G(g_2), \ U_G(1, 0) = id \tag{2.27}$$

with $g_i \in G$. It is called unitary if the *intertwining operator* that represents U_G is unitary (cf. (2.23)). It is called *continuous* if the intertwining operator is continuous.

Given a continuous unitary group representation U_G of the group G in a Hilbert space $\mathbb{H}_U$ (as earlier) an element $h \in \mathbb{H}_U$ is called *admissible* if

$$\int_G |\langle U_G(g)h, h \rangle|^2 d\mu_G < \infty, \quad g \in G . \tag{2.28}$$

A representation U_G is called *irreducible* if there is no subspace V with $\{0\} \neq V \subsetneq \mathbb{H}_U$, which is invariant under group orbits, i.e., $\{U_G(g)v \mid g \in G, v \in V\} \subseteq V$.

A representation U_G is called *quadratic integrable*, if it is irreducible and there exists at least one admissible element in $\mathbb{H}_U$.

The central theorem is *Moyal's formula*, also called *orthogonality relations*.

Theorem 6 (Orthogonality Relations) *Let U_G be a quadratic integrable representation of the locally compact group G in the Hilbert space $\mathbb{H}_U$. Then there exists a unique self-adjoint operator $\mathcal{A}$ on the set of admissible elements in $\mathbb{H}_U$. Furthermore, the orthogonality relations hold*

$$\int_G \overline{\langle U_G(g)h_1, f_1 \rangle} \langle U_G(g)h_2, f_2 \rangle = \overline{\langle \mathcal{A}h_1, \mathcal{A}h_2 \rangle} \langle f_1, f_2 \rangle \tag{2.29}$$

for any admissible elements $h_1, h_2 \in \mathbb{H}_U$, and all $f_1, f_2 \in \mathbb{H}_U$, $g \in G$.

If G is unimodular, $\mathcal{A}$ is a multiple of the identity id.

As G_{WH} is unimodular we get for admissible h_1 and h_2 and $f_1, f_2 \in L^2$

$$\iint \overline{\langle U_{WH}(p, q)h_1, f_1 \rangle} \langle U_{WH}(p, q)h_2, f, 2 \rangle dp \, dq = \overline{\langle h_1, h_2 \rangle} \langle f_1, f_2 \rangle$$

which can easily be calculated.

In case of the affine linear group G_{al} we have the following for U_{al}

$$\begin{aligned}
\int_{G_{al}} |\langle U_{al}(a, b)h, f \rangle|^2 d\mu_{al}^L &= \int_{\mathbb{R} \setminus \{0\}} \int_{\mathbb{R}} |(D_{-a}\bar{h} * f)(b)|^2 db \frac{da}{a^2} \\
&= \int_{\mathbb{R} \setminus \{0\}} \int_{\mathbb{R}} |\widehat{D_{-a}\bar{h}}(t)|^2 |\hat{f}(t)|^2 dt \frac{da}{a^2} \\
&= \int_{\mathbb{R}} |\hat{f}(t)| \int_{\mathbb{R} \setminus \{0\}} |\hat{\bar{h}}(-at)|^2 \frac{da}{|a|} dt \\
&= \|f\|_{L^2}^2 \int_{\mathbb{R} \setminus \{0\}} |\hat{\bar{h}}(-a)|^2 \frac{da}{|a|}
\end{aligned} \tag{2.30}$$

using that $\frac{da}{|a|}$ is the right- and left-invariant measure of the multiplication group ($\mathbb{R} \setminus \{0\}, \cdot$).

A special case of (2.29) is

$$\int_G |\langle U_G(g)h, h\rangle|^2 d\mu_G = \|\mathcal{A}h\|^2 \|h\|^2,$$

and thus if there is an $h \in L^2(\mathbb{R})$ that is identical zero in a neighborhood of the origin, we have

$$\int_{G_{al}} |\langle U_{al}(a,b)h, h\rangle_{L^2}|^2 d\mu_{al}^L = \|h\|_{L^2}^2 \int_{\mathbb{R}} |\hat{h}(a)|^2 \frac{da}{|a|} \qquad (2.31)$$

which is nothing other than the admissibility condition (2.16) or (2.28).

If $\psi \in L^1$ then $\hat{\psi}$ is continuous by the lemma of Riemann-Lebesgue and thus

$$0 = \hat{\psi}(0) = \int \psi(t) dt,$$

which ensures, together with (2.30), the existence of many admissible functions for the wavelet transform.

Remark: As $\int_{G_{WH}} |\langle U_{WH}(p,q)h, h\rangle|^2 dp\, dq = \|h\|_{L^2}^4$ all functions in L^2 are admissible in case of the Weyl-Heisenberg group G_{WH}, i.e., are window functions for the short-time Fourier transform.

2.4.2 Discrete Wavelets and Multiscale Analysis

The continuous wavelet transform $\mathcal{W}_\psi$ (2.15) is highly redundant. Thus, as in the Gabor or short-time Fourier transform, it makes sense to subsample the transform. As we deal with translations and dilations we cannot use a homogeneous grid as in the Gabor case, but we have to use a grid of the form

$$\{(a_0^m, nb_0 a_0^m) \mid m, n \in \mathbb{Z}\} \subset \mathbb{R} \setminus \{0\} \times \mathbb{R} \qquad (2.32)$$

with $a_0 > 1$, $b_0 > 0$, and $\psi \in L^2$. Thus, we get atoms (wavelets) of the type

$$\psi_{mn}(x) = \psi_{mn}^{(a_0, b_0)}(x) = U_{al}(a_0^m, nb_0 a_0^m)\psi(x) = a_0^{-\frac{m}{2}} \psi(a_0^{-m}x - nb_0), \qquad (2.33)$$

which, for a_0 and b_0 chosen appropriately, form a *wavelet frame* or affine frame with the same definitions as in (1.12), with $g_{m,n}$ replaced by ψ_{mn} (see [Dau92c] for an extensive treatment of wavelet frames and the choice of frame coefficients and constants).

The best choice of a_0 and b_0 so far is $a_0 = 2$ and $b_0 = 1$, which is, for sampled signals f, a shift by 1 in the time domain and a 'doubling' of the sampling frequency by halving the support in the frequency domain with each step. This choice leads to the fast wavelet transform (see also [Chu92c]).

To justify this choice we start with a different idea. If we want to analyze a signal it may be fine to partition it into low- and high-frequency parts

$$f = P^0 f + Q^0 f$$

where P^0 is the ortho-projection onto W_{00} resulting in an approximation of the signal, and Q^0 onto W_{01}, the orthogonal complement of W_{00}, extracting the high frequencies or details

$$f = P^0 f + Q^0 f \qquad \text{and} \qquad W_{-10} = W_{00} \oplus W_{01} \ .$$

Applying this procedure recursively to the approximations of f

$$P^0 f = P^1 f + Q^1 f \qquad \text{and} \qquad P^1 P^0 = P^1, \quad Q^1 Q^0 = Q^1$$

and choosing the projections in a way that the frequency information is split equally between the approximation and the detail of the signals — i.e., resulting in two signals of half the length of the original — we get a multiresolution or multiscale analysis.

A series of closed subspaces $W_{j0} \in L^2(\mathbb{R})$ is called *multiscale analysis* if the following properties hold

1. $\{0\} \subset \cdots \subset W_{2,0} \subset W_{1,0} \subset W_{00} \subset W_{-10} \subset W_{-20} \subset \cdots \subset L^2(\mathbb{R})$

2. $\bigcap_{j \in \mathbb{Z}} W_{j0} = \{0\}$

3. $\overline{\bigcup_{j \in \mathbb{Z}} W_{j0}} = L^2(\mathbb{R})$

4. $f(x) \in W_{j,0} \iff f(2x) \in W_{j+1,0}$ $\hfill (2.34)$

5. $\{\phi_{0,k}(x) = \phi(x - k), \ k \in \mathbb{Z}\}$ is a Riesz basis of W_{00}, for a $\phi \in W_{00}$

   i.e., $W_{00} = \overline{\text{span}\{\phi_{0,k}(x) = \phi(x - k), \ k \in \mathbb{Z}\}}$

   and $0 < A \sum_k c_k^2 \leq \|\sum_k c_k \phi_{0,k}(x)\|_{L^2}^2 \leq B \sum_k c_k^2 < \infty \quad \forall (c_k) \in \ell^2(\mathbb{Z}).$

The function ϕ of a multiscale analysis is called a *scaling function*. Because of property 5, W_{00} is translation invariant, and with property 4 we have

$$f(x) \in W_{j0} \iff f(x - 2^j k) \in W_{j0} \ \forall k \in \mathbb{Z}$$

and, thus, by defining

$$\phi_{jk}(x) = \phi_{jk}^{(2,1)}(x) = 2^{-\frac{j}{2}} \phi(2^{-j} x - k) \qquad (2.35)$$

we get

$$W_{j0} = \overline{\text{span}\{\phi_{jk}(x) \,|\, k \in \mathbb{Z}\}} \ . \qquad (2.36)$$

Defining the orthogonal complements W_{j1} of W_{j0}, with the corresponding ortho-projections

$$W_{j-10} = W_{j0} \oplus W_{j1} \qquad P^{j-1} = P^j + Q^j$$

we get

$$\begin{array}{cc} \bigcap_{j \in \mathbb{Z}} W_{j0} = \{0\} & \overline{\bigcup_{j \in \mathbb{Z}} W_{j0}} = L^2(\mathbb{R}) = \bigoplus_{j \in \mathbb{Z}} W_{j1} \\ W_{j-1,0} = W_{j0} \oplus W_{j1} & W_{00} = W_{J0} \oplus (\bigoplus_{j=1}^{J} W_{j1}) \end{array} \qquad (2.37)$$

and the scaling property inherits to the spaces W_{j1}, i.e.,

$$f(x) \in W_{j1} \iff f(2^j x) \in W_{01}. \tag{2.38}$$

Putting this all together we get a representation of the signal f

$$f = \sum_j Q^j f = \sum_{j>J} Q^j f + \sum_{j \le J} Q^j f = P^J f + \sum_{j=-\infty}^{J} Q^j f, \tag{2.39}$$

i.e., in $W_{J0} \oplus (\bigoplus_{j=-\infty}^{J} W_{j1})$.

So far we only used scaling functions as bases of W_{j0}, but what do the bases of W_{j1} look like? From (2.38) we know that the basis functions of W_{j1} have the same properties as the scaling function ϕ. Thus, we have a look at the so-called *scaling equation*

$$\phi(x) = \sqrt{2} \sum_k h_k \phi(2x - k), \tag{2.40}$$

which holds, as

$$\phi \in W_{00} \subset W_{-10} = \overline{\operatorname{span}\{\sqrt{2}\phi(2x - k), \ k \in \mathbb{Z}\}} \ .$$

Daubechies and others proved that there are not only orthonormal bases, but also orthonormal bases with compact support, i.e., with a finite sequence $(h_k)_{k=0}^{2n-1}$ (see [Chu92c]).

If ϕ_{jk} are an orthonormal basis, then by (2.40)

$$\sum_k h_k h_{k+2l} = \delta_{kl}$$

and by using the Fourier transform we see

$$\hat{\phi}(\omega) = H(\frac{\omega}{2})\hat{\phi}(\frac{\omega}{2})$$

with the high-pass Fourier filter

$$H(\omega) = \frac{1}{\sqrt{2}} \sum_k h_k e^{-2\pi i k \omega} \ . \tag{2.41}$$

We get the corresponding low-pass filter G by

$$G(\omega) = \frac{1}{\sqrt{2}} \sum_k g_k e^{-2\pi i k \omega}, \quad g_k = (-1)^k h_{1-k}, \tag{2.42}$$

resulting in a pair of perfect reconstruction filters

$$HG^* = GH^* \qquad H^*H + G^*G = I, \tag{2.43}$$

so-called *quadratic mirror filters*.

Thus, by defining

$$\phi(x) = \sqrt{2} \sum_{k \in \mathbb{Z}} h_k \phi(2x - k) \qquad \psi(x) = \sqrt{2} \sum_{k \in \mathbb{Z}} g_k \phi(2x - k) \qquad (2.44)$$

we get orthonormal bases (for j fixed)

$$\phi_{j,k}(x) = 2^{-j/2} \phi(2^{-j} x - k) \quad \text{and} \quad \psi_{j,k}(x) = 2^{-j/2} \psi(2^{-j} x - k) \quad j, k \in \mathbb{Z} \qquad (2.45)$$

for

$$W_{j0} = \overline{\operatorname{span}\{\phi_{j,k} | k \in \mathbb{Z}\}} \qquad W_{j1} = \overline{\operatorname{span}\{\psi_{j,k} | k \in \mathbb{Z}\}} . \qquad (2.46)$$

As $\{\psi_{jk}, \ k \in \mathbb{Z}\}$ is an orthonormal basis for W_{j1}, and because of (2.37) $\{\psi_{jk}, \ j, k \in \mathbb{Z}\}$ is an orthonormal basis for L^2, a so-called wavelet basis.

From the definition of the filters H and G and the equations, we see that the high-pass filter H is essentially responsible for the projections Q^j onto W_{j1}, and the low-pass filter G for P^j onto W_{j0}. Furthermore, by (2.44) and the form of the filter coefficients h_k and g_k, we get

$$\int \phi(x) dx = 1 \qquad \text{and} \qquad \int \psi(x) dx = 0 . \qquad (2.47)$$

Remark: There are also wavelets with higher vanishing orders, and thus that are better for approximating smoother functions. The Daubechies wavelets (see Figure 2.7) are compactly supported wavelets with extreme phase and the highest number of vanishing moments for a given support width; the associated scaling filters are so-called minimum-phase filters. The Daubechies wavelet ψ of order n has n vanishing moments, a support width of $2n - 1$, and a filter length of $2n$. Coiflets (see Figure 2.8, by Coifman) are compactly supported wavelets with highest number of vanishing moments for both ϕ and ψ for a given support width. The coiflet of order n has n vanishing moments for both, ϕ and ψ, a support length of $6n - 1$, a filter length of $6n$, and are nearly symmetric (symmetry is impossible because of (2.47)). For examples, definitions, and construction of wavelets see [Chu92c, Mey90].

By reformulating (2.39) we get the *wavelet decomposition* of a signal $f \in L^2$

$$f = \sum_k \langle \phi_{Jk}, f \rangle \phi_{Jk} + \sum_j \sum_k \langle \psi_{jk}, f \rangle \psi_{jk}. \qquad (2.48)$$

We generated a wavelet basis from one *mother wavelet* ψ by choosing a scaling function ϕ, often called *father wavelet*, in a multiscale context, but there are also wavelets without a scaling function, e.g., the Morlet wavelet.

In the following we will only use orthonormal wavelet bases with compact support (see last remark), as they support fast and easy algorithms, the so-called *fast wavelet transform* , implemented in many (mathematical) software packages, i.e., we use finite filter coefficient sequences $(g_k)_{k=0}^{2n-1}$ and $(h_k)_{k=0}^{2n-1}$. Furthermore, $\mathbf{x} = (x_0, \ldots, x_{N-1})$ will be the sampled version of a finite signal f, with $N = 2^m$, which can always be obtained, e.g., by zero or random padding. It will be looked at as a periodic signal in the same sense as in Section 1.1.7. Thus, projection or filter equations

$$(G\mathbf{x})_{k=0}^{2n-1} = \sum_{0 \le k-2l < 2n-1} g_{k-2l}x_l \qquad (H^*\mathbf{x})_{k=0}^{2n-1} = \sum_{0 \le k-2l < 2n-1} h_{k-2l}x_l \qquad (2.49)$$

result in low-pass filtered (approximated) and high-pass filtered (detailed) signals. These signals have to be down-sampled to get the same information content as the original one, which is done by the fast wavelet transform (see [Chu92c, Mey90]).

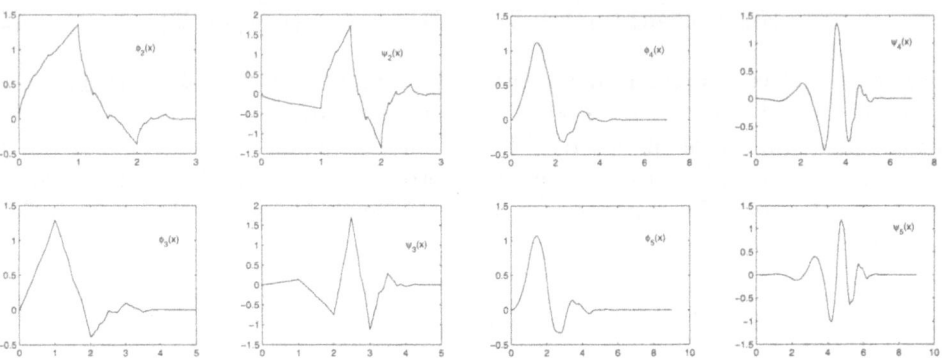

FIGURE 2.7. Daubechies scaling functions ϕ and mother wavelets ψ with vanishing moments of orders 2 to 5 for ψ.

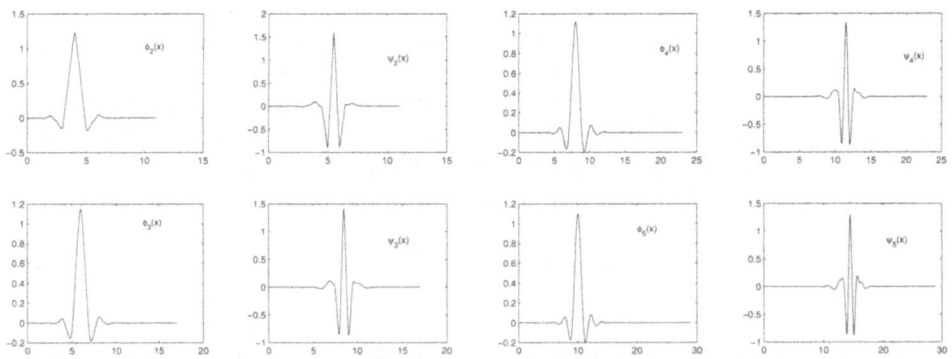

FIGURE 2.8. Coiflets scaling functions ϕ and mother wavelets ψ with vanishing moments of orders 2 to 5 for both, ϕ and ψ.

A discrete signal $\mathbf{x}$ of length N is decomposed by

$$\mathbf{x} = A_J + D_J + D_{J-1} + \cdots + D_1 \quad \in \quad W_{J0} \oplus W_{J,1} \oplus W_{J-1,1} \oplus \cdots \oplus W_{11}$$

or, equivalently, by a wavelet coefficient vector of length N

$$\alpha = (G^J \mathbf{x}, HG^{J-1} \mathbf{x}, HG^{J-2} \mathbf{x}, \dots, HG\mathbf{x}, H\mathbf{x}) \triangleq (A_J, D_J, D_{J-1}, \dots, D_1) . \quad (2.50)$$

Figure 2.9 shows a five-level wavelet decomposition of a synthetic signal (the same as in Figure 1.4) using the Daubechies wavelet of order 8. The signal (level 's') is a 1-second 35 Hz sine wave, sampled at 1 kHz, with a pulse at 0.3 seconds, and chirp, starting at 0 with 25 Hz and ending after 1 second at 140 Hz. The approximating level A_5 shows the sine wave, the pulse appears nicely at the detailed levels D_1 and D_2, whereas the chirp is spread over levels d2 to d5, due to its varying frequency contents (see also the wavelet packet decomposition of the same signal in Figure 2.12).

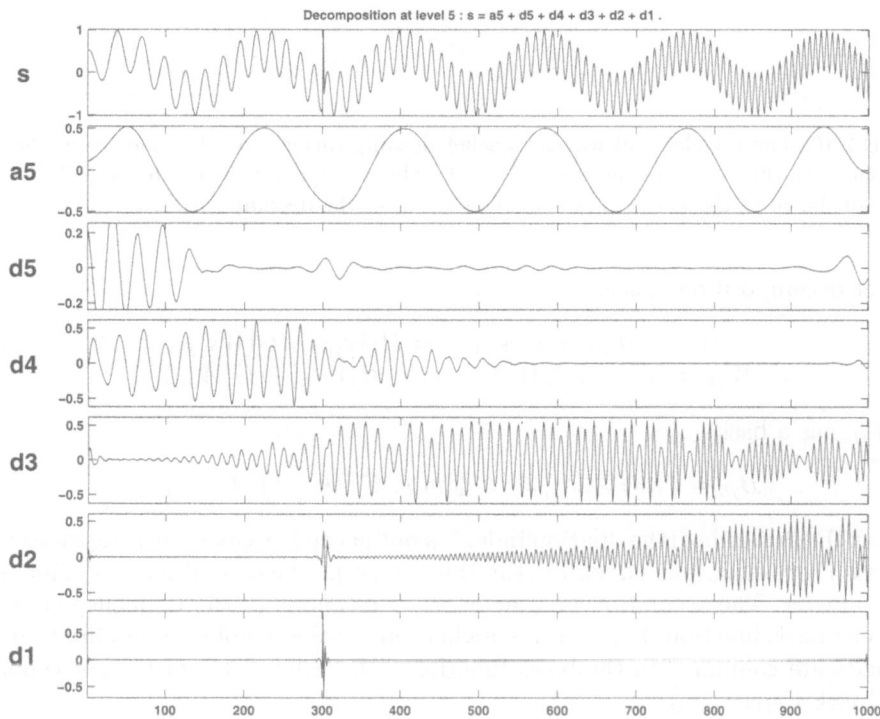

FIGURE 2.9. Daubechies wavelet order 8, five-level decomposition of synthetic signal; see text. Plotted using the `MatLab` wavelet toolbox.

2.4.3 Wavelet Packets

The wavelet packet transform was originally developed to compress images and signals, lossy and nonlossy (see [Top98] and Chapter 3.1).

The wavelet packet transform decomposes not only the approximations A_j (W_{j0}) of the signal at each level, but also all details D_j (W_{j1}). Whereas the wavelet transform only results in a sequence of better and better approximations of the signal representing the smoothness of the input signal, the wavelet packet transform also pays attention to the local high-frequency parts of the image at specific levels (cf. the comparison of the wavelet decomposition tree versus the wavelet packet decomposition tree; Figure 2.10).

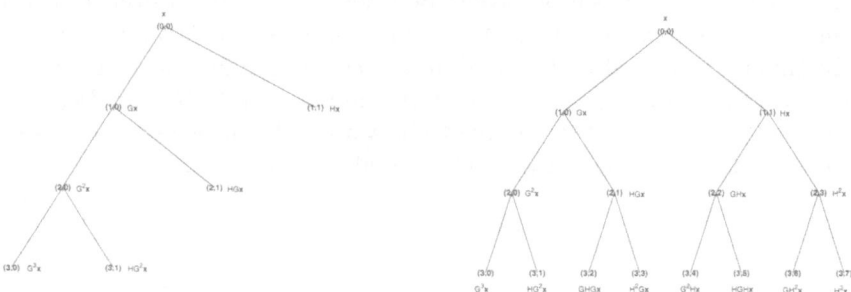

FIGURE 2.10. The wavelet and wavelet packet decomposition tree. The indices of the nodes correspond with the indices of the spaces W_{jk}. Furthermore, a sampled signal $\mathbf{x}$ and its filtered version are shown at the nodes they will show up in in the decomposition.

We get decomposition spaces

$$
\begin{aligned}
W_{j0} &= W_{j+1,0} \oplus W_{j+1,1} = H(W_{j0}) \oplus G(W_{j0}) \\
W_{jk} &= W_{j+1,2k} \oplus W_{j+1,2k+1} = H(W_{jk}) \oplus G(W_{jk}).
\end{aligned}
\tag{2.51}
$$

Each W_{jk} has a basis

$$
B_{jk} = \left\{ \mathbf{w}_{0,\ell,m}(x) \,|\, 2^{-j}k \le m < 2^{-j}(k+1), \ \ell \in \mathbb{Z} \right\}.
\tag{2.52}
$$

Note that the first index (the dilation index) is not needed anymore; it is replaced by the modulation or oscillation index m (the third index). The second index ℓ remains the shift parameter. The oscillation parameter m corresponds to the frequency content of the wavelet basis function. In general, a higher modulation number m implies that more frequencies are contained in the basis functions (cf. Figure 2.11) of the corresponding wavelet packet space W_{jk}.

Comparing wavelet and wavelet packet bases we get

$$
\phi_{jk}(x) = \mathbf{w}_{jk0} \quad \text{and} \quad \psi_{jk}(x) = \mathbf{w}_{jk1};
\tag{2.53}
$$

that is, the wavelet decomposition spaces W_{j0} and W_{j1} have bases

$$
\begin{aligned}
W_{j0} &= \left\{ \mathbf{w}_{0km} \,|\, 0 \le m < 2^{-j}, \ k \in \mathbb{Z} \right\} \\
W_{j1} &= \left\{ \mathbf{w}_{0km} \,|\, 2^{-j} \le m < 2^{-j+1}, \ k \in \mathbb{Z} \right\}
\end{aligned}
\tag{2.54}
$$

whereas the standard wavelet bases are

$$
\begin{aligned}
W_{j0} &= \left\{ \mathbf{w}_{jk0} \,|\, k \in \mathbb{Z} \right\} = \left\{ \phi_{jk} \,|\, k \in \mathbb{Z} \right\} \\
W_{j1} &= \left\{ \mathbf{w}_{jk1} \,|\, k \in \mathbb{Z} \right\} = \left\{ \psi_{jk} \,|\, k \in \mathbb{Z} \right\}.
\end{aligned}
\tag{2.55}
$$

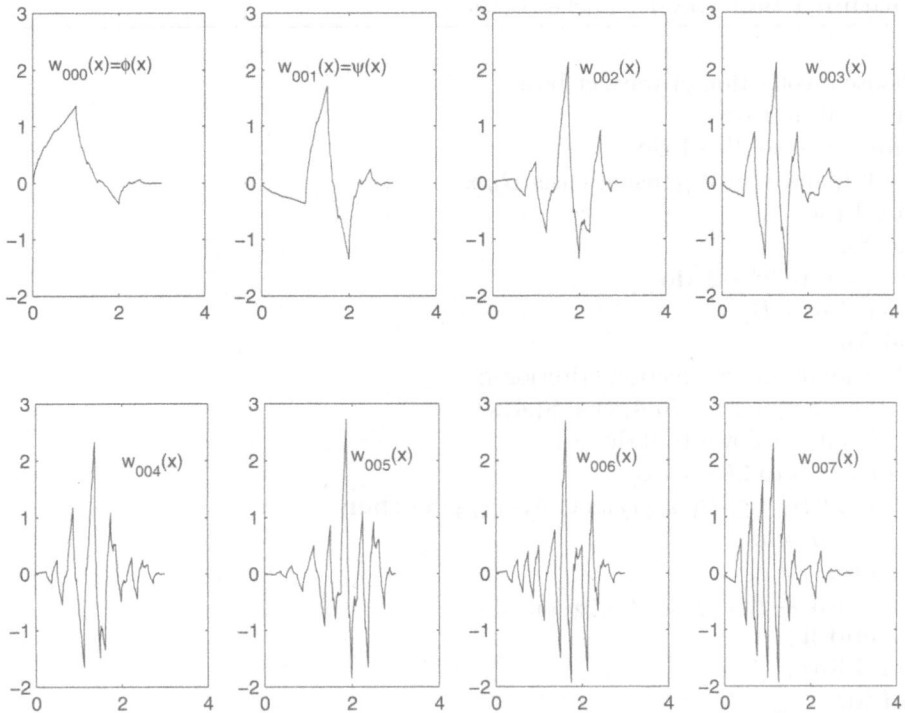

FIGURE 2.11. Wavelet packet basis functions Daubechies order 2, modulations m 0 to 7.

Starting with formula (2.53) we can compute all wavelet packet basis functions of the same kind by

$$\begin{aligned}
\mathbf{w}_{0,0,2m}(x) &= \sum_{k \in \mathbb{Z}} h_k \mathbf{w}_{1km}(x) \\
\mathbf{w}_{0,0,2m+1}(x) &= \sum_{k \in \mathbb{Z}} (-1)^k h_{-k+1} \mathbf{w}_{1km}(x)
\end{aligned} \qquad (2.56)$$

with h_k being the (corresponding) coefficients of the high-pass filter H (cf. formula (2.43)) which corresponds to the wavelet type used.

The (discrete) wavelet packet transform decomposes a discrete signal $\mathbf{x}$ to coefficients

$$\alpha = (G\mathbf{x}, H\mathbf{x}, G^2\mathbf{x}, HG\mathbf{x}, GH\mathbf{x}, H^2\mathbf{x}, \ldots, H^J\mathbf{x})$$

using the same filters as in the wavelet decomposition. This overcomplete representation results in $2^{2^{J-1}}$ possible bases for a reconstruction of $\mathbf{x}$. From these coefficients (bases) the best representation with respect to the selection criterion S is selected by the best basis algorithm (cf. Algorithm 1).

The additive selection criterion S depends on the application. Entropy measures like the nonnormalized Shannon entropy (see Equation (2.57)) are taken for image compression (cf. [Wic93, Top98] and Section 3.1). The compression to information ratio is comparable to fractal image compression algorithms. Furthermore, wavelet compression

---

Algorithm 1 Best Wavelet Packet Basis

Choose a collection of wavelet bases
for $j = 0$ to J **do**
  for $k = 0$ to $2^j - 1$ **do**
    Expand $\mathbf{x}$ in W_{jk} using basis $B_{jk}\mathbf{x}$
  end for
end for
for $k = 0$ to $2^J - 1$ **do**
  Set $A_{Jk} = B_{Jk}$
end for
Select an additive selection criterion S,
i.e., $S(A_i\mathbf{x} \cup A_j\mathbf{x}) = S(A_i\mathbf{x}) + S(A_j\mathbf{x})$
for $j = J - 1$ down to 0 **do**
  for $k = 0$ to $2^j - 1$ **do**
    if $D(B_{jk}) \leq D(A_{j+1,2k}\mathbf{x} \cup A_{j+1,2k+1}\mathbf{x})$ **then**
      $A_{jk} = B_{jk}$
    else
      $A_{jk} = A_{j+1,2k} \oplus A_{j+1,2k+1}$
    end if
  end for
end for
Arrange coefficients with respect to quality of discrimination (PP)
Choose K_0 best components as features (MDL)

---

has won the race for the JPEG2000 image compression standard. For the reconstruction of an image from its wavelet packet decomposition coefficients these coefficients are arranged by their absolute value. For a lossy compression of images only the n absolute largest coefficients are taken, where n depends on the allowed error in the reconstruction (see also Chapter 3 for further details and examples).

Figure 2.12 shows a wavelet packet decomposition of a synthetic signal (the same as in Figure 1.4) using the Daubechies wavelet of order 8 using the best tree algorithm with a Shannon entropy selection criterion for best compression. The signal displayed in the upper right of the figure is a 1-second 35 Hz sine wave, sampled at 1 kHz, with a pulse at 0.3 seconds, and chirp, starting at 0 with 25 Hz and ending after 1 second at 140 Hz. You will first note the white areas (zeros) in the coefficients map on the lower right, which reflects the compression power of the wavelet packet transform. The pulse also shows up in the map in the upper and middle part of the map. The sine wave, reconstructed in the lower left using only coefficients of $W_{4,0}$, is not as well represented as in the wavelet decomposition (Figure 2.9) because the starting frequency of the chirp is almost the same frequency. The coefficients of the sine wave show up in the lowest line of the coefficients map. The coefficients of the chirp are spread over different levels, due to changing frequency content of the chirp.

Thus, the wavelet packet decomposition is optimal for image and signal compression,

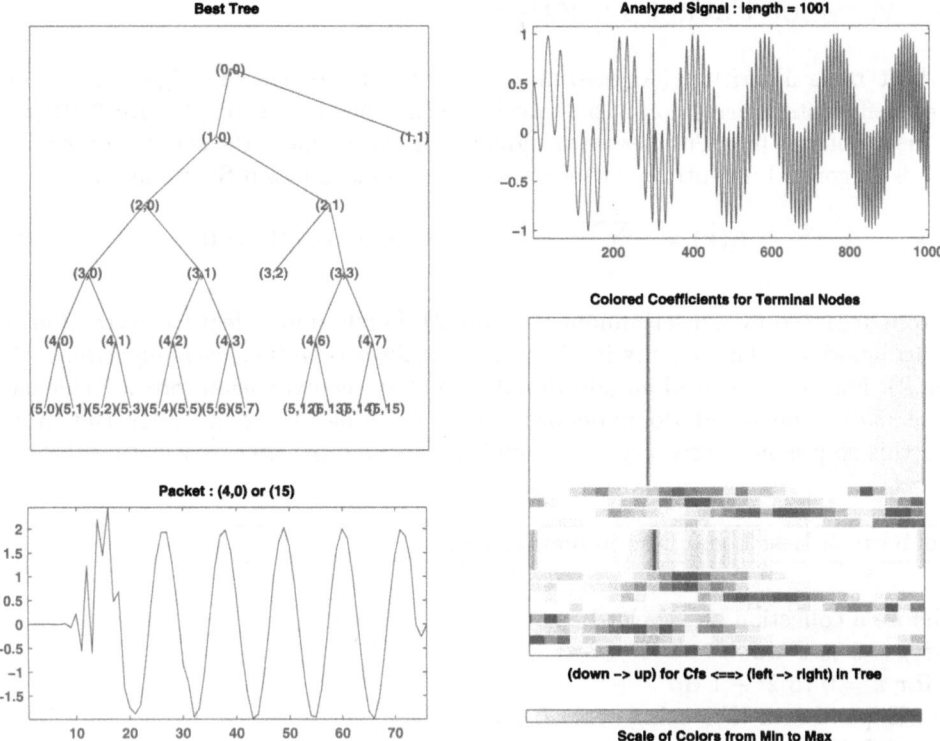

FIGURE 2.12. Daubechies order 8 wavelet packet decomposition of the synthetic signal. The analyzed signal (upper right), the best basis tree (upper left) using the Shannon entropy selection criterion, reconstructed signal using only coefficients of $W_{4,0}$ (lower left), and a map of the absolute values of the wavelet packet decomposition coefficients (lower right).

denoising can easily be done. The next section will present a method for discrimination and feature extraction using the wavelet packet decomposition. Furthermore, one has to admit that the wavelet and wavelet packet transform are not optimal for any task but it serves to solve many different problems, e.g., handling signals of different function spaces or different pattern recognition tasks using the same methods. The solution is then optimal in the wavelet (packet) domain, which is the result has the minimal distance to the mathematical optimal solution, e.g., principal component analysis, or optimal denoising.

The wavelet packet transform and the best basis algorithm can be adapted for pattern recognition tasks (cf. [Sai94]). Depending on different selection criteria, standard pattern recognition methods can be done in the wavelet packet domain. Furthermore, expanding the best basis Algorithm 1 to a best local discrimination basis and feature extraction algorithm local discrimination analysis can be done in the wavelet domain, which results in wavelet descriptors of curves. These are local descriptors, in contrast to Fourier descriptors, which describe the global character of (closed) curves (cf. [Nie90]).

2.5   Wavelet Packet Descriptors

The best basis algorithm (Algorithm 1) can be expanded to an algorithm choosing those coefficients (bases) from the wavelet packet bases tree (cf. Figure 2.10) which best discriminates different classes of signals. For this purpose the selection criterion S, which is in general an entropy criterion like the nonnormalized Shannon entropy

$$E(\mathbf{x}) = -\sum_i x_i^2 \log_2(x_i^2) \qquad \text{with } 0\log(0) = 0 \tag{2.57}$$

has to be replaced by a discriminant measure D. Furthermore, feature extraction steps have to be added. This results in the *best local discrimination basis algorithm* (Algorithm 2). For noise removal an additional step after the expansion into wavelet packet coefficients can be added, doing denoising by wavelet shrinkage [Don92]. But, in most cases, this step is not necessary, as a denoising also happens when selecting the k best features.

Algorithm 2 Best Local Discrimination Basis

Choose a collection of wavelet bases
for $j = 0$ to J **do**
  for $k = 0$ to $2^j - 1$ **do**
    Expand $\mathbf{x}$ in W_{jk} using basis $B_{jk}\mathbf{x}$
  end for
end for
for $k = 0$ to $2^J - 1$ **do**
  Set $A_{Jk} = B_{Jk}$
end for
Select D, an (additive) discrimination criterion
for $j = J - 1$ down to 0 **do**
  for $k = 0$ to $2^j - 1$ **do**
    if $D(B_{jk}) \leq D(A_{j+1,2k}\mathbf{x} \cup A_{j+1,2k+1}\mathbf{x})$ **then**
      $A_{jk} = B_{jk}$
    else
      $A_{jk} = A_{j+1,2k} \oplus A_{j+1,2k+1}$
    end if
  end for
end for
Arrange coefficients with respect to quality of discrimination (PP)
Choose K_0 best components as features (MDL)

The *best local discrimination basis algorithm* (Algorithm 2) is used by a training set of preclassified patterns. These patterns fix the decomposition tree, e.g., Figure 2.10, for the classification of further templates. It has to be mentioned that the decomposition depends on the sampling resolution of the image. Using resolutions that are powers of

2 multiples of one another (e.g., 150 dpi, 300 dpi, 600 dpi) enables one to use the tail of the best basis tree. Furthermore, it is often more applicable to use the *best level tree*, i.e., the level of which the selection or discrimination criterion is best, resulting in both an easier and faster decomposition algorithm and an easier structure of coefficients (features) to be compared.

For the simple case of two classes, two different pattern vectors $\mathbf{x}^{(1)}$ and $\mathbf{x}^{(2)}$ are normalized to length 1, and the Kullback-Leibler distance (relative entropy, cross entropy, or I-divergence)

$$I(\mathbf{x}^{(1)}, \mathbf{x}^{(2)}) = \sum_i \mathbf{x}_i^{(1)} \cdot \log \frac{\mathbf{x}_i^{(1)}}{\mathbf{x}_i^{(2)}} \tag{2.58}$$

may be used as discrimination measure. If one prefers a symmetric measure the J-divergence

$$J(\mathbf{x}^{(1)}, \mathbf{x}^{(2)}) = I(\mathbf{x}^{(1)}, \mathbf{x}^{(2)}) + I(\mathbf{x}^{(2)}, \mathbf{x}^{(1)}) \tag{2.59}$$

may be chosen. These distances are additive and thus are well suited as discrimination criterion D.

Measuring the distance of R classes C_r we sum up combinations of D

$$D(\mathbf{x}^{(1)}, \dots, \mathbf{x}^{(R)}) = \sum_{i=1}^{R-1} \sum_{j=i+1}^{R} D(\mathbf{x}^{(i)}, \mathbf{x}^{(j)}). \tag{2.60}$$

One discrimination criterion used by the best local discrimination basis algorithm (Algorithm 2) can be the energy distribution G of the expansion coefficients given a template $\mathbf{x}_i^{(r)}$ of class C_r

$$G_{jkm}^{(r)} = \sum_i \frac{(\mathbf{w}_{j,k,m}^t \mathbf{x}_i^{(r)})^2}{\sum_i \|\mathbf{x}_i^{(r)}\|^2} \tag{2.61}$$

and the J-divergence may be taken as a discriminant measure. In step 4 the robust version of Fisher's class separability

$$\frac{\sum_r \pi_r |\text{med}(\mathbf{w}_{j,k,m}^t \mathbf{x}_i^{(r)}) - \text{med}_r(\text{med}_i(\mathbf{w}_{j,k,m}^t \mathbf{x}_i^{(r)}))|}{\sum_r \pi_r \text{mad}_i(\mathbf{w}_{j,k,m}^t \mathbf{x}_i^{(r)})} \tag{2.62}$$

($\mathbf{w}_{j,k,m}$ is the basis vectors of basis B_{rs}; cf. formula (2.52)) may serve to calculate the power of the discrimination (cf. [Sai94]).

The advantage of the best local discrimination algorithm is that it is based on a fast and linear decomposition algorithm (the wavelet packet transform) and a binary search tree, the wavelet packet tree, which has to be searched only once due to the additivity of the selection and discrimination criteria. The calculations for the discriminant measures and energy distributions, which are the most time-consuming parts of the algorithm, are *only calculated during the training phase*; the classification and discrimination process

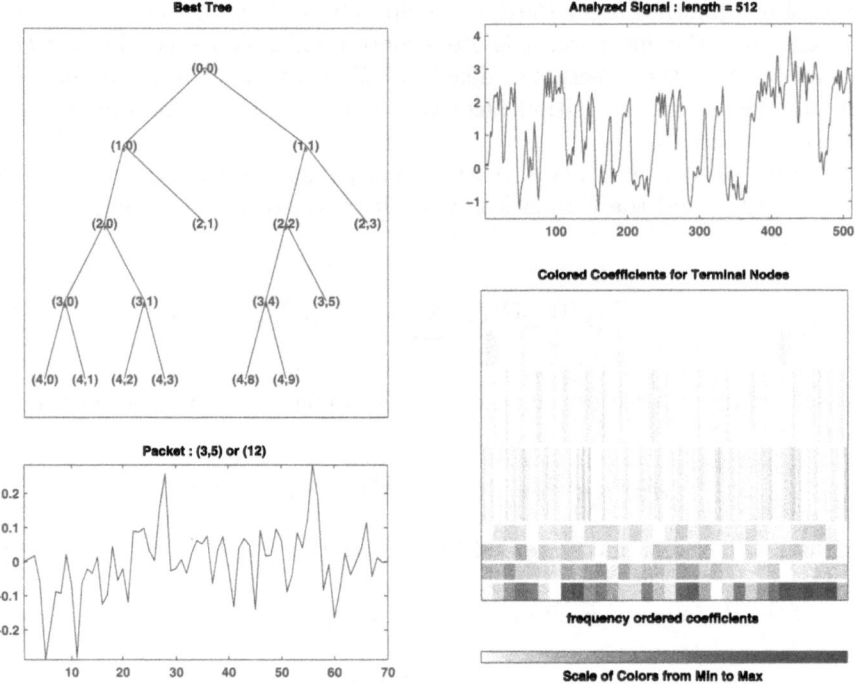

FIGURE 2.13. The wavelet packet best basis decomposition of a change-in-angle parameterized leaf.

uses a simple nearest-neighbor or minimal-distance classifier using only the selected features. During the training process standard techniques and algorithms like the best basis algorithm can be used. For the classification process these algorithms have to be rearranged, and only a small part of the linear basis decomposition has to be used. In the sample application we used, only six bases per class were left; cf. Figure 2.13 (from about 1000 different bases decompositions).

Another typical example, the wavelet packet decomposition of clover with three and four leaves, respectively (see Figure 2.15), even shows easy comparable and interpretable results, as you can see the additional fourth leaf in the coefficients plot.

2.6 Global Nonlinear Optimization

When two templates should be matched by laying one on the top of the other many geometrical parameters have to be optimized. Dealing with the contours of leaves we have parameters like x- and y-shift, rotation angle ρ, and scale parameter s. Assuming the image of the leaf was taken from a three-dimensional scene, viewpoint parameters like elevation h and tilt in two directions (τ_1, τ_2) have to be added, i.e., parameters from a parallel projection. Furthermore, if we add parameters α and σ from the stochastic

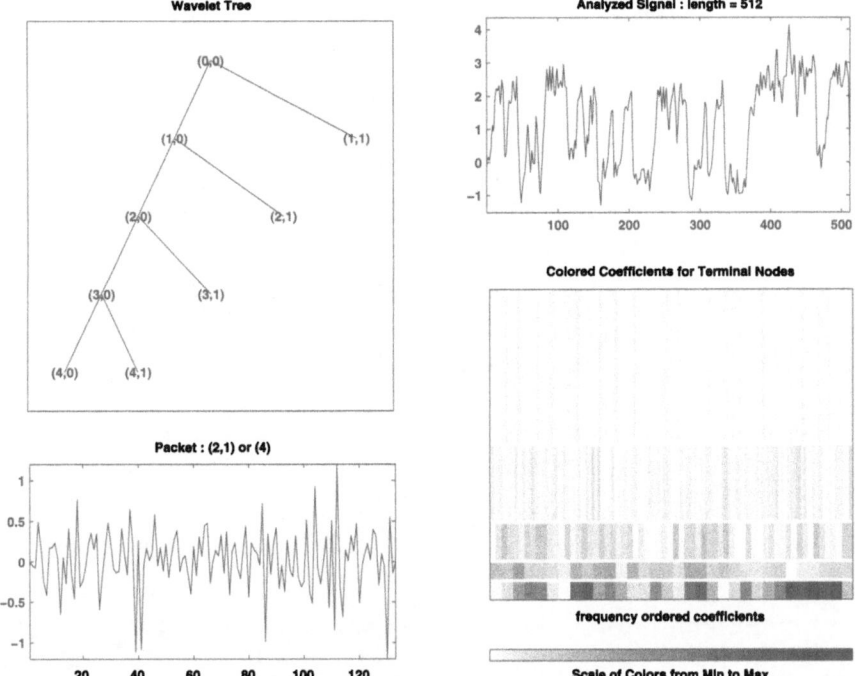

FIGURE 2.14. The wavelet decomposition of a change-in-angle parameterized leaf (same as in Figure 2.13).

deformation process we end with an at least nine-dimensional global optimization problem. All these parameters are variables of the objective function, which in our case is a polygonal distance function; i.e., the polygonal distance between the templates should be minimized (cf. formula (2.10)).

Because the objective function of this optimization problem will have many local minima as the templates themselves have self-similar structures, e.g., a number of similar sub-leaves (see also Figures 2.17 and 2.6).

The aim was to find a fast algorithm that finds the global minimum and does not stop in a local minimum and that has the possibility of decoupling the global and local search routines. The best solution seemed to be a multilevel single-linkage algorithm as in [RKT87a, RKT87b]. Unfortunately, we had to alter the algorithm because in higher dimensions it was very slow and unreliable.

2.6.1   Multilevel Single-Linkage Global Optimization

The multilevel single-linkage (*MLSL*) method of Rinnooy Kan and Timmer [RKT87a, RKT87b], which is a modification of the clustering method of Boender et al. (in [TŽ91]) is a simple method. The global starting algorithm of MLSL is only weakly connected to local optimization procedures (see Algorithm 3). That is, the only information the

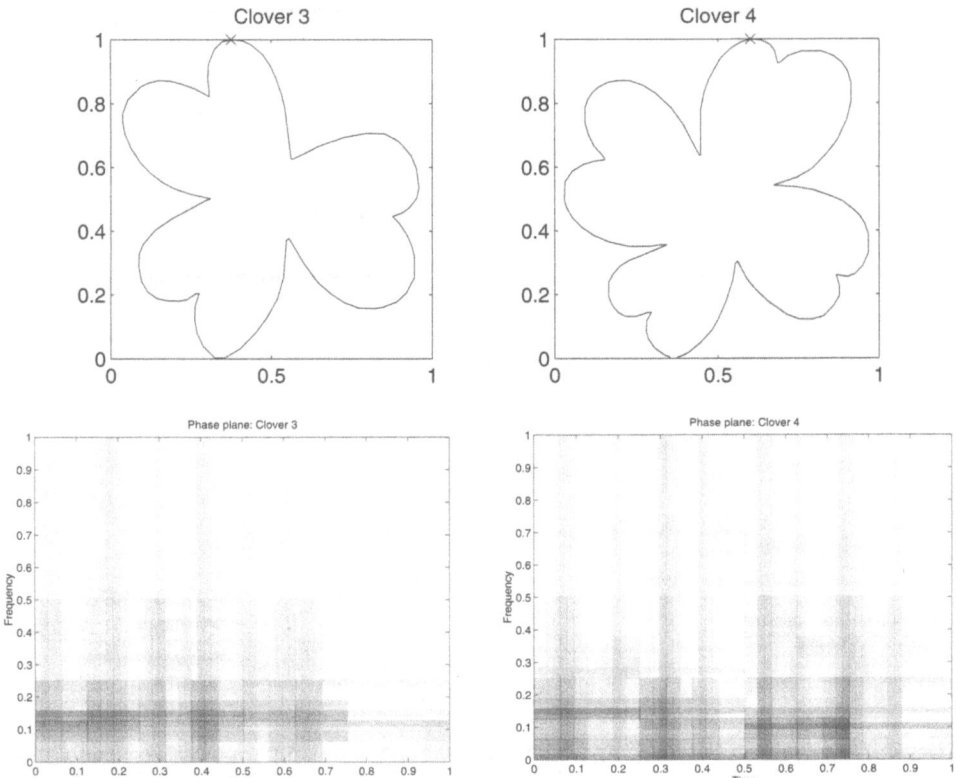

FIGURE 2.15. The wavelet decomposition of two types of clover.

global optimizer passes to the local optimizer is the starting point of the procedure.

In a first step the global clustering algorithm (starting algorithm) tries to identify the regions of attraction of local minima, i.e., regions surrounding local minima so that local optimization procedures started in these regions will converge to the appropriate local minima.

Clusters are usually found by using threshold distances. If a new sample point is within the threshold distance of a cluster, it is assumed that it belongs to the same cluster. Obviously the size of the threshold distance reflects the number of resulting clusters. Thus, if the threshold distance chosen is too small each point will form a cluster of its own, whereas if the threshold distance is too large all points will be included into one single cluster.

In the second step MLSL starts a local optimizer at every sampling point x_i unless there is another sampling point x_j within the threshold distance r_k,

$$r_k = \frac{1}{\sqrt{\pi}} \sqrt[n]{\lambda \, \mu(A) \, \Gamma(1 + \frac{1}{n}) \, \frac{\log k}{k}} \tag{2.63}$$

with a smaller function value. Such an x_i is assumed to belong to the same region of

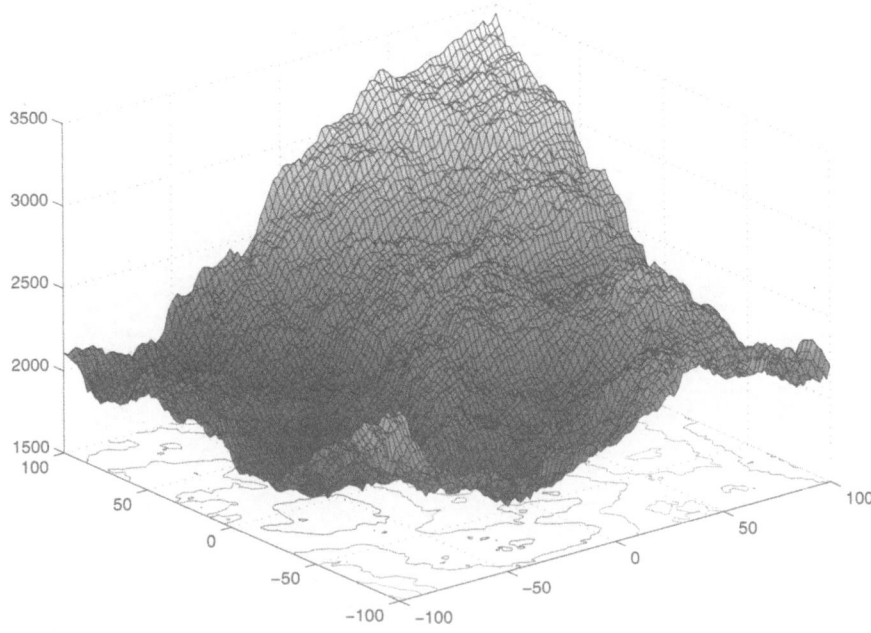

FIGURE 2.16. Projection of x- and y-shift.

attraction as x_j (see Algorithm 3).

If a starting point has been found, a local optimizer is started. The independent structure of our implementation enables us to run many local optimizers in different starting points in parallel. Thus, the algorithm can easily be parallelized.

Almost any known local optimizers may be used. Our implementation of MLSL uses a standardized interface between global and local routines. Unfortunately, many nice optimizers cannot be used, because with our stated problem of contour line matching the objective functions may have steps; thus they are not continuous or differentiable (cf. Figures 2.17, and 2.16).

2.6.2 Implementation

Algorithm 3 schematically describes our implementation of MLSL, which differs slightly from the one found in [TŽ91].

Our implementation of MLSL differs from the original algorithm in the following points:

- New points are sampled in groups of a certain size using the same threshold value for the whole group. This reduces the computational costs.

- Choosing $\gamma = 1$, we decided to abstain from using only the most promising points

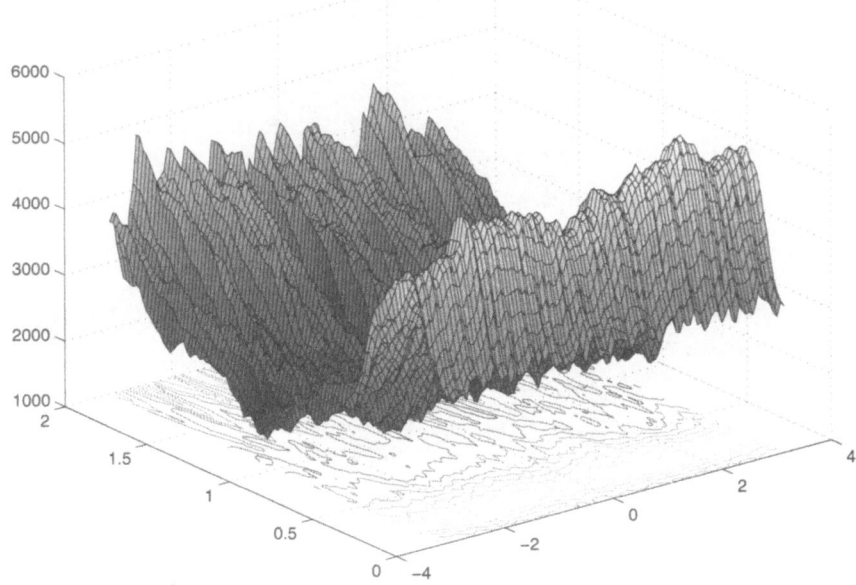

FIGURE 2.17. Projection of rotation and x-shift.

during initialization step (1).

- Because the spiral search algorithm used in the original implementation is becoming more and more inefficient with increasing dimensions, a direct search has been implemented to find the nearest points of the sampling set in the neighborhood of a given point. Thus, the run-time estimations from [RKT87a, RKT87b] are no longer valid.

It can be shown that for $\lambda > 4$ the number of local optimizations started is finite with probability 1, even if the sampling of new points is never stopped. If r_k tends to 0 each local minimum is found within a finite number of iterations with probability 1 (cf. [RKT87a, RKT87b]).

Algorithm 3 MLSL

Choose number of sampling points N

Choose $M_{\max}$, maximal number of expected minima

Choose selection parameter γ

Choose region parameter λ

Initialize set of minima found $X^* = \{\}$

Select N points at random

Choose those $J = \lfloor N/\gamma \rfloor$ points x_i, $i = 1, \dots, J$, with lowest function values

Let $k = \lfloor \gamma N \rfloor$

repeat

   Let $k = k + 1$

   Let $\mu(A)$ be the volume of the 'region of interest'

   Let $r_k = \frac{1}{\sqrt{\pi}} \sqrt[n]{\lambda \, \mu(A) \, \Gamma(1 + \frac{1}{n}) \frac{\log k}{k}}$

   for $i = 1$ to J **do**

      Let StartOpt=true

      Let $j = i + 1$

      while $j \leq J$ **and** StartOpt=true **do**

         if $\|x_j - x_i\| < r_k$ **and** $f(x_j) < f(x_i)$ **then**

            Let StartOpt=false

         end if

      end while

      if StartOpt=true **then**

         Start a local optimizer in x_i that returns, if found, a new minimum NewMinimum

         $X^* = X^* \cup \text{NewMinimum}$

      end if

   end for

until number of minima found is greater than $M_{\max}$, the number of expected minima

---

3

Image Compression and Coding

Josef Scharinger

In recent years the processing of multimedia data has experienced a great deal of interest, which is likely to increase even more in the near future as the Internet continues its growth. Two core technologies for the field are described in this chapter: data compression and data security.

Although in the past most net traffic has been text based, with file sizes measured in hundreds of kilobytes, the use of the HTML protocol to serve multimedia documents has increased file sizes to megabytes. This encroachment of bandwidth results in long delays in accessing documents, limits information availability to fewer users in a given time, and negatively effects net traffic using other protocols such as FTP, mail, or news.

The need to improve effective bandwidth is also motivated by the explosive growth of users and service providers using the Web. In these distributed environments large image files constitute a major bottleneck within systems. Compression is an important component of the solutions available for creating file sizes of manageable and transmittable dimensions and is therefore considered in Section 3.1.

In Section 3.2, on data security, an adequate method for efficient multimedia data encryption is developed. To guarantee security and privacy in speech, image and video transmission, and archival applications, efficient bulk encryption techniques are necessary that are easily implementable in soft- and hardware and are able to cope with the vast amounts of data involved. To this end, the general framework of an iterated product cipher is adopted when developing a novel algorithm for efficient multimedia data encryption applications.

It is worth mentioning that this encryption method based on chaotic mixing might be adjusted to handle requirements in pay-TV applications and fits perfectly as a core component within the general framework of embedding digital watermarks for image copyright protection using chaotic mixing systems.

3.1   Image Compression

Compression algorithms fall into two general classes: lossless and lossy compression. The main shortcoming of lossless compression is that the amount of compression is limited, with typical compression ratios on computer data files being about 2:1. Lossy techniques cause image quality degradation in each compression/decompression step. Careful consideration of the human visual perception ensures that the degradation is often unrecognizable, although this depends on the selected compression ratio. In general, lossy techniques provide far greater compression ratios than lossless techniques. Therefore, only lossy methods are considered in this section dealing with image compression technologies.

3.1.1 Lossy Compression and Machine Vision

Because lossy compression techniques provide far greater compression ratios than lossless, they are usually preferred in image processing applications (except in some areas, e.g., medicine, where legal constraints play an important role). However, as more and more applications of digital image processing have to combine image compression and highly automated image analysis (see, e.g., NASA spacecraft [Whi95], METEOSAT satellite [AG94, AMB95], or FBI fingerprint images [BBH94]), it becomes of critical importance to study the interrelations existing between lossy image compression and subsequent feature extraction.

A study elucidating these interrelations should provide answers to the following questions:

- Which feature extraction algorithm is most stable when preceded by lossy image compression?

- Which lossy compression technique is best in not introducing artifacts later misclassified as features?

- Which lossy compression technique is best in preserving features?

- Which types of features are most difficult to preserve in lossy image compression?

In the sequel we present a systematic comparison of contemporary general-purpose lossy image compression techniques with respect to the most fundamental features, namely, lines and edges detected in images. To this end, the effects of applying the following compression techniques and feature extraction algorithms are qualitatively and quantitatively compared on typical regions of interest:

Compression Methods: vector quantization (VQ), predictive coding (PC), fractal coding (PIFS), cosine transform-based image compression (JPEG), wavelet-based image compression (WAVE).

Edge Detectors: Nevatia and Babu (NB), Burns (BL), Canny (CE), Marr and Hildreth (MH).

Regions of Interest: straight lines (SL), curved lines (CL), parallel lines close to each other (PL), corners and crossings (CC).

Edge Detection

Edges correspond to abrupt changes or discontinuities in certain image properties between neighboring areas. Usually, they are assumed to correspond to discontinuities in the underlying surface or to the maxima and minima of its first (directional) derivative. Therefore, the first part in edge detection is estimating the derivatives. The second is to detect the zeros and extremes of the estimated derivative function. Other issues concern linking edges, forming boundaries, extracting straight lines and so on.

Next, a representative collection of popular edge detection and line extraction algorithms is introduced that will serve as benchmarks for evaluating the lossy image compression methods under consideration.

Nevatia and Babu edge detection (NB)   Edge detection is performed by repeated convolution using a set of six 5×5 kernels proposed by Nevatia and Babu [NB80]. One of the six kernels will cause a maximum response. This value, as well as the current orientation of the mask, is recorded. These two pieces of data, a magnitude and an angle, form a vector. This vector is saved at each pixel and constitutes the basis for the edge selection process.

Burns Line Extraction (BL)   This operator extracts straight lines from regions of similar gradient according to the algorithm proposed by B. Burns [BHR86]. Gradient is measured using a 2×2 mask. Gradient space is arbitrarily divided into a specified number of orientation buckets, and each group of four adjacent pixels falling into the same orientation bucket is labeled a support region. Edge support regions smaller than a given threshold are discarded at this stage. After that, a gradient magnitude weighted least square error plane fit is computed on each support region. Pixels with gradient magnitude below a user-defined threshold are not included in the surface fit. Finally, the points of this surface with intensity equal to the average intensity of the contributing pixels form a straight line.

Canny Edge Detection (CE)   Edge detection is performed using a general technique popularized by Canny [Can86]. First the image is smoothed using discrete Gaussian convolution kernels. Then the gradient is computed using *Sobel* convolution kernels and the gradient magnitude is measured as the square root of the sum of the squares of the two components of the gradient. Pixels that have gradient magnitude greater than neighboring pixels in the direction of the gradient are selected as candidate edges. The final edge selection is made from these candidate edge pixels using thresholding with hysteresis.

Marr and Hildreth Edge Detection (MH)   This operator computes an edge image based on the algorithm proposed by Marr and Hildreth [MH80]. Edge detection is accomplished by finding the zero-crossings of the nondirectional second derivative of the image intensity values. For computing the nondirectional second derivative, the Difference of Gaussians (DOG) method is used.

Lossy image compression methods

Information preserving (lossless) compression is normally able to provide a compression ratio in the range from 2:1 to 10:1. By compromising image quality, lossy image compression is typically capable of reaching substantially higher compression than lossless compression. Next, we provide a sketch of contemporary general-purpose lossy image compression methods, explain their fundamental principles, and give pointers for further reading.

Vector Quantization (VQ)   When applying vector quantization to an image, the image is first broken up into (typically) rectangular pixel blocks. Each of these blocks is a k-dimensional vector. The image is "quantized" by assigning the "closest" vector in a small number of predetermined vectors to each of its blocks. This reduced set of vectors is the *codebook* that is used to encode the image. Instead of the entire block, just the index of the selected codebook vector is stored or transmitted. In other words, vector quantization is the mapping of pixel intensity vectors into binary vectors indexing a limited number of possible reproductions [CORG94, Int95].

For the experiments described in the latter sections, a KBVision implementation [Sch95a] based on software from J. Goldschneider [Gol94] is used.

Predictive Coding (PC)   Binary tree predictive coding uses an image pyramid to represent the data. The design goal of the binary tree predictor is to minimize prediction error variance for estimating every new pixel from four equidistant pixels from earlier levels or bands. Lossy compression is achieved by quantization of prediction errors where each level of the pyramid has its own quantizer.

For the experiments described in the following sections, a KBVision implementation based on software from J.A. Robinson [Rob] is used.

Fractal Image Compression (PIFS)   In simple terms, the aim of fractal compression is to find a small finite set of mathematical equations that describe an image [Bar88, Jac93]. It is based on partitioned iterated function systems (PIFS) and the presence of "affine redundancy" in an image. This is present if a part of the image is similar to another part of the image, providing an arbitrary number of transformations that can be applied to the original part (such as rotations, contractions, skew and moves).

For the experiments described in the following sections a KBVision implementation based on software from Y. Fisher [Fis95] is used.

Cosine Transform Based Image Compression (JPEG)   JPEG (Joint Photographics Experts Group) is a standardized image compression mechanism that has been established by a joint ISO/CCITT committee. It is a transform coding method comprising four steps [Wal91]. First the image is partitioned into blocks of size 8×8 pixels. Then each block is transformed with the discrete cosine transform (DCT) and these frequency coefficients are quantized. Finally, the output is coded with a variable-length lossless encoding method.

For the experiments described in the following sections a KBVision implementation based on software from the Independent JPEG Group (IJG) [Lan95] is used.

Wavelet-Based Image Compression (WAVE)   A wide variety of wavelet-based image compression schemes have been reported in the literature, ranging from simple entropy coding to more complex techniques [VH92] such as vector quantization, adaptive transforms, tree encodings [Sha93], and edge-based coding. According to Jawerth and Sweldens [JS94] all of these schemes can be described in a general framework in which the compressor includes a forward wavelet transform, a quantizer, and a lossless encoder, while the corresponding decompressor is formed by a lossless decoder, a dequantizer, and an inverse wavelet transform.

For the experiments described in the following sections, a KBVision implementation based on software from Said and Pearlman [SP93] (RTS transform, bit-plane ordering, embedded code stream) is used, because it performed best among the three wavelet-based coders considered.

Experimental results

To guarantee a fair comparison between different compression techniques, line and edge detection algorithms, and types of edges, the following experimental setup is chosen:

- equal compression ratio for all compression techniques using the same test image (1:25 compression of *lena*, resolution 512 × 512),

- equal number of edge pixels detected by all line and edge extraction algorithms (20,000 edge pixels),

- equal size for the regions of interest containing the various types of lines and edges (50 × 50 pixels).

In Figures 3.1–3.4, results of image compression and subsequent edge detection on the various regions of interest are arranged as follows (from upper left to lower right): original image, VQ, PC, PIFS, JPEG, and WAVE. The structure of corresponding Tables 3.1–3.4 should be self-explanatory ("less error percentage is better"; AV gives corresponding averages).

Summary

According to the results presented in the preceding section (confirmed and supported by qualitatively similar results obtained from five test images, four regions of interest comprising 50 × 50 pixels, three compression ratios, seven edge detectors and seven compression methods (about 7.35 billion pixels in total!) not detailed in this contribution) satisfactory answers to the questions set forth in the introduction can be found and formulated as follows:

> *Which edge detector is most stable with respect to lossy image compression?* Surprisingly, simple thresholding on gradients computed with rather large masks (NB) does best for all compression techniques considered. If more sophisticated edge detection is needed, CE is highly recommended, while BL and MH must be classified as rather unstable.

> *Which lossy compression technique is best in not later introducing artifacts misclassified as edges?* WAVE performs best for all edge detectors considered. Block-oriented techniques like VQ or JPEG do worst, while PC and PIFS are in between.

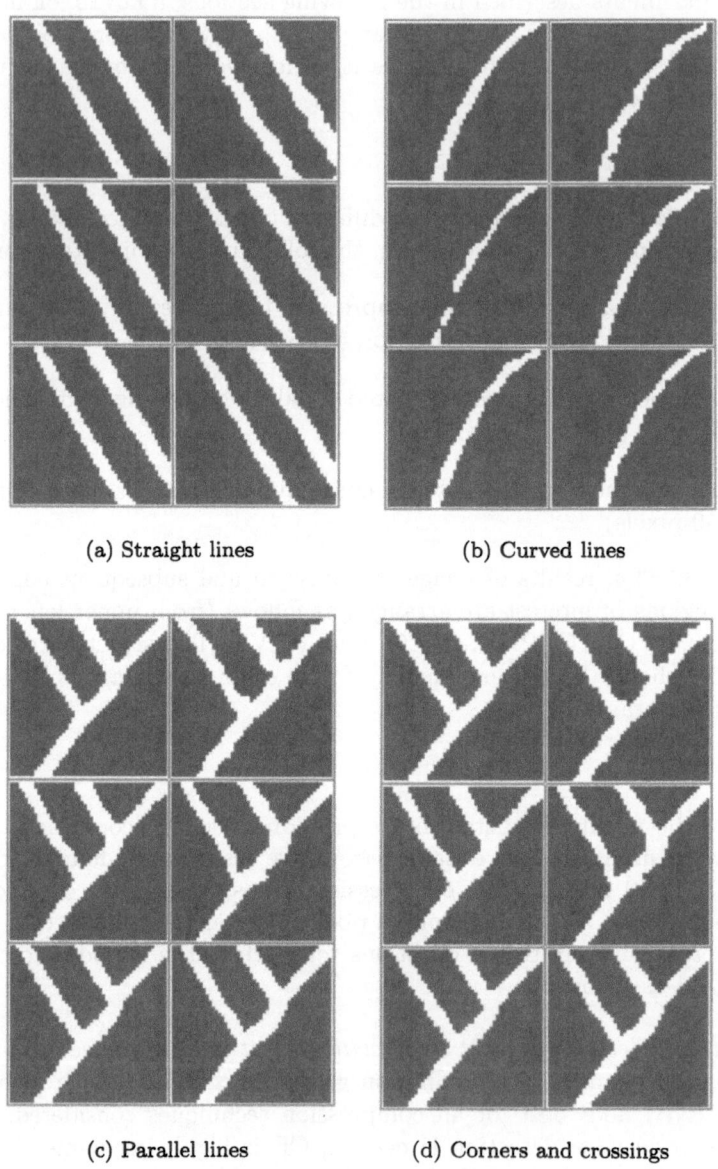

(a) Straight lines   (b) Curved lines

(c) Parallel lines   (d) Corners and crossings

FIGURE 3.1. Impact of image compression and subsequent Nevatia and Babu edge detection.

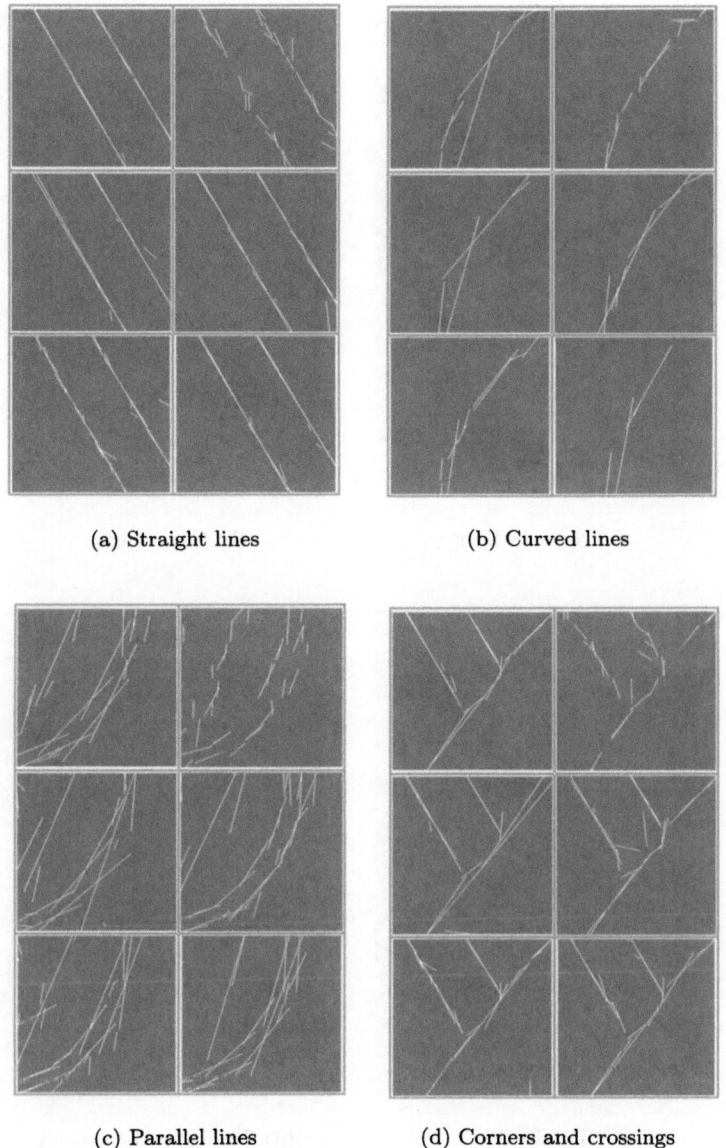

(a) Straight lines

(b) Curved lines

(c) Parallel lines

(d) Corners and crossings

FIGURE 3.2. Impact of image compression and subsequent Burns line extraction.

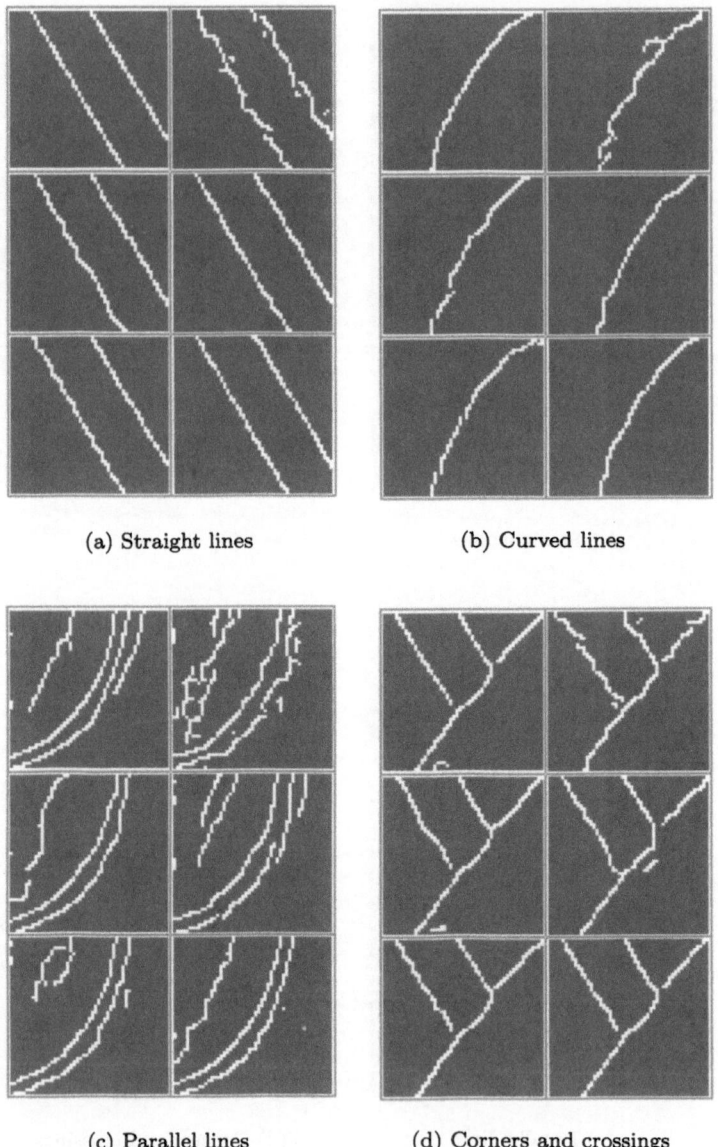

(a) Straight lines   (b) Curved lines

(c) Parallel lines   (d) Corners and crossings

FIGURE 3.3. Impact of image compression and subsequent Canny edge detection.

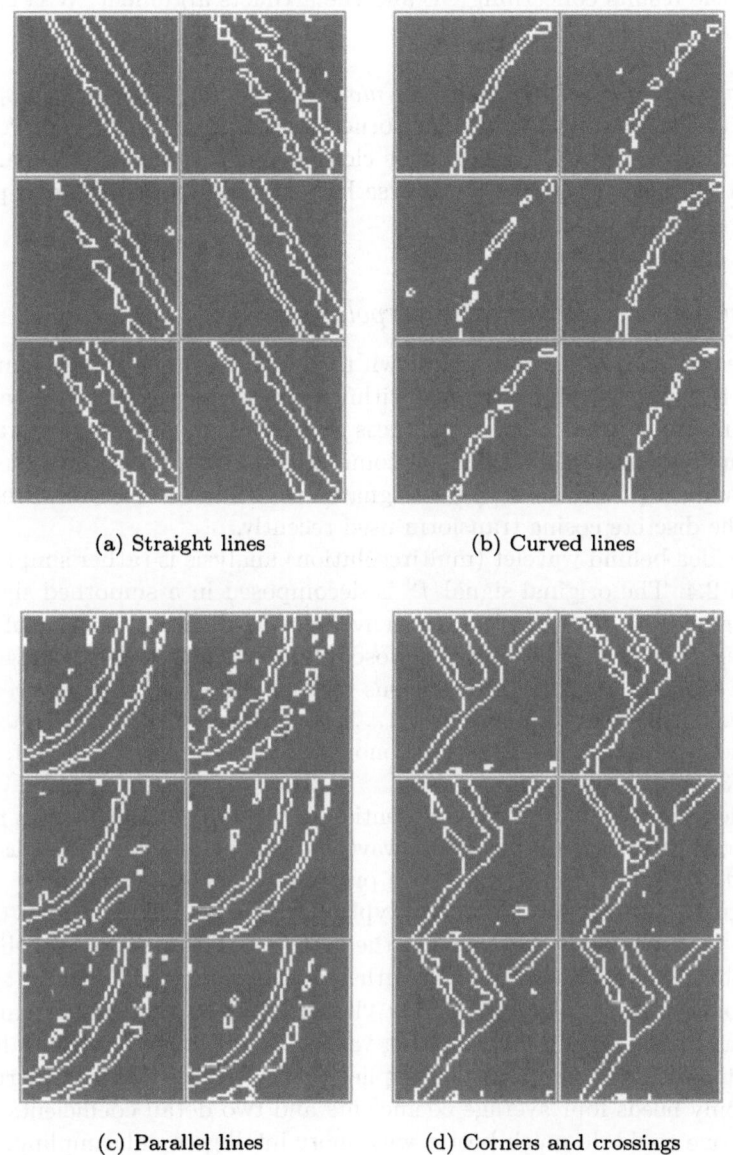

(a) Straight lines

(b) Curved lines

(c) Parallel lines

(d) Corners and crossings

FIGURE 3.4. Impact of image compression and subsequent Marr and Hildreth edge detection.

Which lossy compression technique is best in preserving various kinds of edges? For most edge detectors, the race is tight among PIFS, JPEG, and WAVE with VQ and PC falling off significantly. However, taking into account the results concerning CE and the artifacts argument, WAVE can be rated number one.

Which types of edges and lines are most difficult to preserve in lossy image compression? Straight lines, and corners and crossings are preserved best. Preserving curves and parallel lines close to one another are comparatively hard tasks solved significantly worse by all contemporary general-purpose compression methods.

3.1.2 Multilevel Polynomial Interpolation

In the preceding section it has been shown that wavelet-based image compression systems outperform other compression algorithms not just in terms of their rate/distortion behavior, but also in terms of the robustness when subsequent feature extraction follows the lossy compression step. Therefore, it comes as no surprise that the next generation of the JPEG standard ("JPEG 2000") is designated to include a discrete wavelet transform instead of the discrete cosine transform used recently.

The basic idea behind wavelet (multiresolution) analysis is rather simple [MS94]; see also Section 2.4. The original signal f^0 is decomposed in a smoothed signal f^1 and a difference signal $g^1 = f^0 - f^1$, yielding an average/detail decomposition of the input. In a second step f^1 may be further decomposed in an even smoother average function f^2 and a detail function g^2. After N iterations we thus get a very smooth average function f^N and a sequence of detail functions $g^1, \ldots, g^N$ that allows for excellent (lossy) signal reconstruction from f^N and the most pronounced parts of $g^1, \ldots, g^N$ (cf. also Sections 2.4 and 2.4.3).

Nevertheless, wavelet analysis has potential drawbacks. One of them is related to the fact that for all practical purposes the wavelet transform is computed using a *regular discrete* grid. To see why this might be a problem, consider Figure 3.5.

In this figure the image profile near a typical edge (taken from the hat of the famous *lena* image) is shown in the last pane of the first row. The first pane of the second row gives the subsampling values obtained with the smoothing function of a spline wavelet (stretched by a factor of two for better visibility) while the middle pane shows the profile reconstructed from these sampling values. Important information has been lost, especially at positions 3 and 5, which implies that an acceptable reconstruction of this profile not only needs four average coefficients and two detail coefficients.

However, one could do much better with more intelligent subsampling. By sampling at positions 3 and 5, signal reconstruction (shown in the last pane) can be achieved only using four average coefficients and two sampling positions. Using standard methods [Car88] it is possible to code sampling positions at a rate of about 2 bits per position, while representing a (quantized) detail coefficient usually takes about 1 byte [Sha93]. Therefore, this technique can significantly reduce the need to include detail coefficients in the reconstruction process.

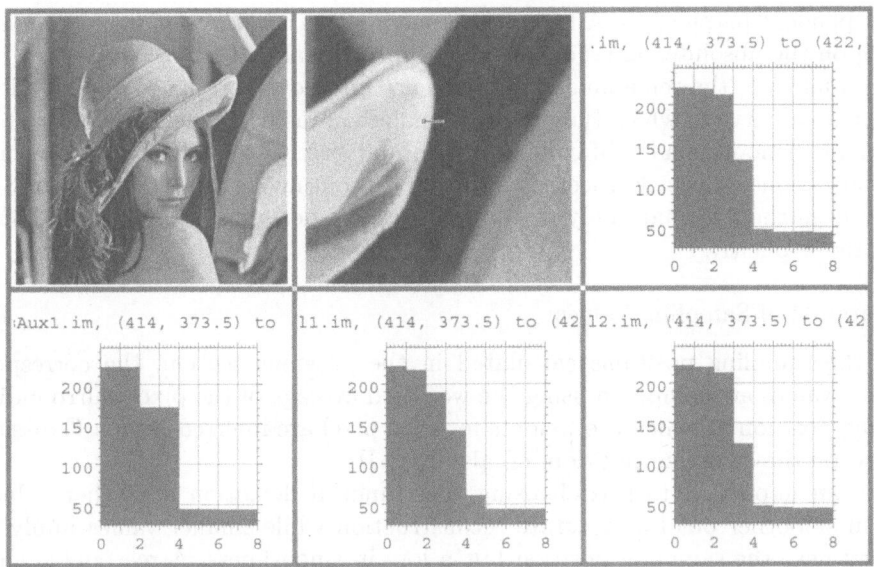

FIGURE 3.5. Problems associated with subsampling and smoothing constrained to a regular grid.

Motivated by this observation the new approach comprises the following steps:

- find appropriate subsampling positions,

- find the corresponding subsampling values (average coefficients), and

- reconstruct the signal from average coefficients and sampling information by polynomial (spline) interpolation. In a well-structured region this should (almost) completely eliminate the need to include additional detail coefficients.

These steps will be executed in an iterative fashion, which means that the subsampled output image of one iteration is, after geometry correction, used as input for the next iteration in order to fully exploit spatial redundancies.

Selection of Sampling Positions

A promising approach is suggested by Figure 3.5. The most suitable sampling position is the point where the profile exhibits the most significant change in direction. Therefore, when subsampling in the x-direction, one has to find points where the *second* directional derivative has a local maximum (minimum) in the x-direction, and when sub-sampling in the y-direction sampling positions are found by maximizing (minimizing) the second directional derivative in the y-direction.

Just selecting local maxima would return too many candidates for sampling positions, because the storage of large bit planes does not come free. Instead, there is a need for a way of selecting the "most significant" positions among all candidate positions whereby the percentage of positions actually selected should be controllable by some compression ratio-dependent parameters. A technique known as *masked thresholding with hysteresis* [Can86] on the absolute values of the second directional derivatives is used.

As a final step, the remaining candidates are filtered according to the length of the local maxima curve to which they belong[1] and are adjusted to yield sampling positions located on a smooth curve. Of course, you do not store these continuous positions, but the binary bitmap of pixels selected. Appropriate continuous sampling positions will be derived from these bitmaps only at compression and decompression time, but they are not stored explicitly.

Computation of Sampling Values

Given the sampling positions calculated in the previous section, the corresponding sampling values are computed using the weighted average of the pixels surrounding the sampling position in which the weights for each pixel are inferred from a Gaussian bell centered on the sampling position; cf. also Part III.

Thus, an important task is choosing the standard deviation σ. Higher values will result in smoother but less accurate reconstruction while smaller values imply higher accuracy near the sampling position but a loss in smoothness. A reasonable choice is based on the requirement that 99 percent of all values lie in the interval $(-0.5, 0.5)$ which is equivalent to demanding that a pixel will be recovered with 99 percent accuracy if the sampling position coincides with the center of that pixel. Using standard statistical arguments this amounts to (approximately) $2.5\sigma = 0.5$ or $\sigma = 0.2$.

Iterative Approach and Geometry Correction

Iterated subsampling of the average component is not that straightforward because irregular subsampling can introduce nasty non-linearities and discontinuities not present at corresponding input locations. These would be difficult to compress in the next levels. Thus, before sub-sampling in the y-direction can be done, a method we call linear geometry correction must be applied.

This is a simple way of projecting irregularly sampled data onto a regular grid. Instead of storing the irregularly spaced sampling values, the linear interpolator sampled on a regular grid is used. This kind of geometry correction is fully invertible and, although quite simple, works remarkably well.

Integrating Wavelet Texture Coding

In structured regions (lines, edges) multilevel polynomial interpolation on an adequately chosen irregular grid can significantly improve coding performance by minimizing the need for storing the detail information resulting from an average/detail decomposition. In highly unstructured regions (noise, texture), however, no adequate subsampling information can be generated and subsampling is done in the middle of each interval, a

---

[1]Using a method developed by Carlsson [Car88] it is possible to code a connected curve comprising n pixels using about $10 + 1.3 * (n - 1)$ bits. This implies that entropy coding at a rate of less than 2 bits per selected pixel should be feasible and that pixels located on long connected curves are to be preferred.

procedure leading to one average and two detail coefficients for each group of two input pixels. Therefore, the *interpolation* approach must be regarded as highly inefficient in textured regions.

In order to overcome this problem, we use wavelet texture coding. Because the proposed image reconstruction process heavily relies on interpolation, only wavelet systems possessing an interpolating scaling function are acceptable. Even under that constraint, excellent solutions can be found based on the Deslauriers-Dubuc [DD89] interpolating scaling functions. Figure 3.6 shows such an interpolating scaling function together with the corresponding wavelet. A valid set of functions biorthogonal to them are displayed in Figure 3.7. Readers interested in the corresponding filter coefficients or interpolating multiresolutions of higher orders are once again referred to the excellent report [Swe94].

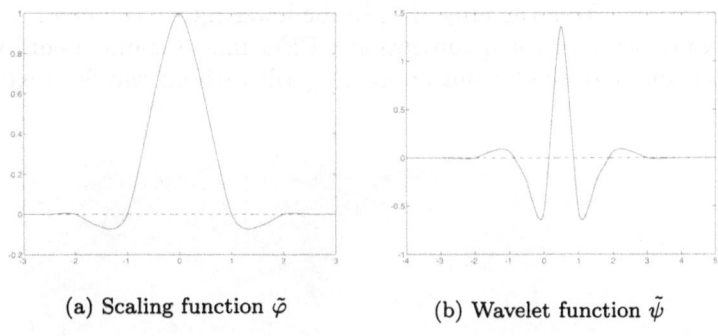

(a) Scaling function $\tilde{\varphi}$ (b) Wavelet function $\tilde{\psi}$

FIGURE 3.6. Deslauriers-Dubuc interpolating scaling function and wavelet of order 4.

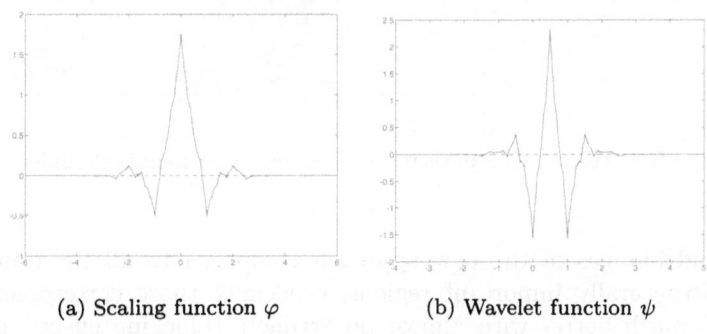

(a) Scaling function φ (b) Wavelet function ψ

FIGURE 3.7. Pair of functions biorthogonal to the Deslauriers-Dubuc system shown in Figure 3.6.

Using the set of finite biorthogonal filters associated with these function, an adequate wavelet-based texture coding system compatible with the approach of image *reconstruction by interpolation* is obtained as follows. Use multilevel polynomial (spline) interpolation for subsampling positions lying on the irregular grid, which can be derived in well-structured regions (lines, edges). In highly unstructured regions (noise, texture), however, no significant subsampling information can be generated. Therefore, subsampling is done in the middle of the interval using the filters pertaining to φ and ψ, while reconstruction is performed by wavelet interpolation using the filters linked to the interpolating scaling function $\tilde{\varphi}$ and the dual wavelet $\tilde{\psi}$.

Summary

To make differences apparent, Figure 3.8 zooms in on Lena's shoulder. In this figure compression results obtained for Lena (512×512, 8 bpp) at a ratio of 20 : 1 are arranged as follows (proceeding from the upper left to the lower right): original Lena image, fractal image compression, vector quantization, JPEG image compression, wavelet-based image compression, and, finally, our approach (still without wavelet texture coding).

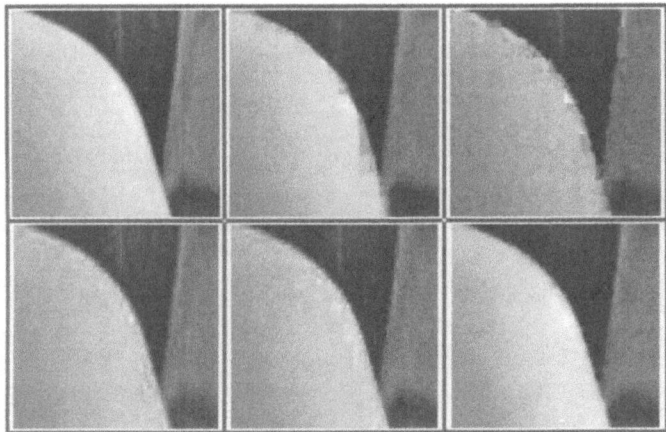

FIGURE 3.8. Comparison by zooming in on Lena's shoulder.

Here, the advantages of the new approach compared to all the other methods is significant: Structurally important regions, especially those corresponding to edges, are recovered much better with almost no artifacts (blocking effects, ringing, Gibbs phenomena) introduced. This is related to the fact that detail information belonging to edges is not added to the signal recovered from the average component afterwards but is directly encoded in the average component and the sampling position information. Therefore, iterative polynomial image interpolation on an irregular grid not constrained to discrete values should definitely improve the performance of wavelet image coders, especially if minimization of degradations of the image contours and unwanted artifacts is a prime interest.

3.1.3   Enhancing the FBI Fingerprint Compression Standard

A contemporary lossy image compression system is usually structured as shown in Figure 3.9. First the image is transformed into a suitable domain (cosine, Gabor, wavelet, etc.) whereby the transformation has to be selected based on criteria like the match to image features, completeness, and computational requirements. Next, the transform coefficients are quantized to certain discrete levels either using scalar quantization or vector quantization, which is the only lossy operation within the whole compression/decompression process. Finally, the quantizer output values are entropy coded usually using Huffman or arithmetic coding. On the other side, the decompression process just inverts these steps in reverse order without introducing any additional loss of information.

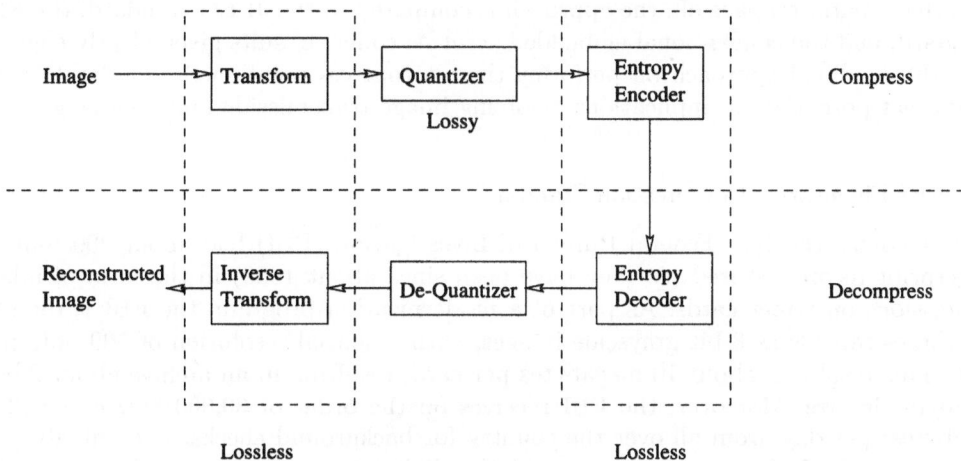

FIGURE 3.9. Image compression system architecture.

Wavelets (see, e.g., [Dau92c, Chu92a, Kai95]) have proven to be excellent bases for transform coding, because they combine adequate time/frequency resolution, efficient implementations, and tolerable artifacts even at highest compression ratios. Additionally, there is a very useful self-similarity of wavelet coefficients in the transform domain that allows for tree-structured entropy coding. Shapiro's [Sha93] famous embedded zerotree coder even goes a step further: It combines quantization and entropy coding, yielding a fully embedded code stream.

The overwhelming success of the embedded zerotree coder has led to the widespread belief that it is no longer necessary to bother with quantization strategies for wavelet-based image coders. It is the intent of this section to give strong evidence that a suitable combination using a dedicated quantization strategy and a *lossless* zerotree coder can outperform other approaches, such as the conventional embedded zerotree coder, a run-length/Huffman coder, or JPEG [Ins91].

To this end, take a closer look at a highly popular example of a wavelet-based image *compression system: the FBI fingerprint compression standard* [oI93, Bri95]. This algorithm uses a very specific wavelet subband decomposition structure and a highly optimized uniform scalar quantization strategy derived as the solution of a nonlinear optimization problem of a high-rate distortion model subject to a linear constraint on the overall bit rate and convex nonnegativity constraints on the individual bit rates used to encode the wavelet subbands, while lossless entropy coding is done using conventional run-length/Huffman coding.

This section demonstrates that the FBI standard can be significantly enhanced if the entropy coder in use is replaced by a lossless zerotree coder. It is essential to notice that this approach differs fundamentally from other applications involving zerotree coders because here zerotree coding is used in a lossless mode just for entropy coding and not for (embedded) quantization, while practically all currently existing zerotree applications do not separate lossy quantization and lossless entropy coding. To emphasize that this separation pays off, the approach is compared to the JPEG standard, the FBI standard, and the conventional embedded zerotree coder. Results given clearly suggest that the modified approach outperforms the alternatives mentioned and should thus offer great potential for applications involving image transmission and archiving.

The FBI Fingerprint Compression Standard

At last count, the U.S. Federal Bureau of Investigation (FBI) had about 200 million fingerprint records, stored (as they have been since about 1900) in the form of inked impressions on paper cards. As part of a modernization program, the FBI is digitizing theses records as 8-bit grayscale images, with a spatial resolution of 500 dots per inch. This results in about 10 megabytes per card, resulting in an archive about 2,000 terabytes in size. Moreover, the FBI receives on the order of 30,000 new cards (300 gigabytes) per day, from all over the country for background checks. Accordingly, the FBI has made data compression part of the digitization process and developed the so-called *wavelet/scalar quantization* (WSQ) standard [Bri95, oI93].

The WSQ algorithm consists of three main steps: a discrete wavelet transform (DWT) decomposition of the source fingerprint image, scalar quantization of the DWT coefficients, and lossless entropy coding of the quantizer indices.

The DWT [SN96, VK95] in the WSQ algorithm is implemented using a two-channel perfect reconstruction linear phase filter bank. Symmetric extension techniques are used to apply the filters near the image boundaries, an approach that allows transforming images with arbitrary dimensions. This two-channel splitting is applied to both the image rows and columns, resulting in a four-channel, two dimensional decomposition. The analysis filter bank is cascaded several times to generate a very specific 64-subband frequency decomposition (see [oI93] for details) that was selected based on fingerprint image power spectral estimation and heuristic evaluations.

The 64 DWT subbands are quantized according to uniform scalar quantization characteristics using a dedicated quantization strategy derived as the solution to a nonlinear optimization problem of a high-rate distortion model subject to a linear constraint on the overall bit rate and convex nonnegativity constraints on the individual bit rates used to encode the wavelet subbands. This bit allocation procedure ensures that the overall quantization distortion is minimized while still maintaining some user-supplied constraint on the overall bit rate and is computed using Lagrange multiplier techniques corrected by an iterative procedure that accounts for discarded subbands [BB94].

As a final step in the compression process, the integer indices output by the quantizer are entropy-encoded by run-length coding of zeros and subsequent Huffman coding. Both the scalar quantizers and Huffman coders are image-specific. The compressed data contains a table of wavelet transform specifications and tables for the scalar quantizers and Huffman coders. The WSQ decoder parses the compressed data and extracts the tables needed in the decoding process. To produce the reconstructed image, the decoded, quantized wavelet coefficients are run through an inverse DWT.

Zerotree Coding

At approximately the same time the WSQ standard was formulated, the embedded zerotree wavelet algorithm (EZW) was published [Sha93]. It is a very simple yet remarkably effective image compression algorithm having the property that the bits in the bit stream are generated in order of importance, yielding a fully embedded code. The embedded code represents a sequence of binary decisions that distinguish an image from the "null" image. Using an embedded coding algorithm, an encoder can terminate the encoding at any point, thereby allowing a target rate or target distortion metric to be met exactly.

The EZW algorithm contains the following features [Sha93]:

- A discrete wavelet transform that provides a compact multiresolution representation of the image to compress.

- Zerotree coding, which provides a compact multiresolution representation of significance maps, that are binary maps indicating the positions of the significant coefficients. Zerotrees allow the successful prediction of insignificant coefficients across scales to be efficiently represented as part of exponentially growing trees.

- Successive approximation that provides a compact multiprecision representation of the significant coefficients and facilitates the embedding algorithm.

- A prioritization protocol by which the ordering of importance is determined, in order, by the precision, magnitude, scale, and spatial location of the wavelet coefficients. Note in particular that larger coefficients are deemed more important than smaller coefficients regardless of their scale.

- Adaptive arithmetic coding, which provides a fast and efficient method for entropy coding strings of symbols and requires no training or prestored tables.

More information and a detailed description of the way the embedded zerotree coder works can be found in [Sha93]. For this purpose it is sufficient to emphasize that Shapiro's coder integrates scalar quantization and lossless entropy coding. Experience has shown that this is a good idea. However, it is not the best thing to do, because the zerotree coder has its strength primarily in entropy coding (and particularly in the efficient way it is able to represent the positions of insignificant coefficients), but it is definitely not an optimum quantizer. To emphasize this fact, take the dedicated quantization strategy incorporated in the FBI fingerprint compression standard and integrate it with a lossless zerotree coder responsible for entropy coding but not for quantization. The results achieved this way significantly outperform the original FBI algorithm as well as the conventional embedded zerotree coder and clearly justify the fundamental message that the role of zerotree coders should be reduced to just doing entropy coding.

Modified Algorithm and Results

This section will give strong evidence that the FBI standard should be redesigned in the sense that the run-length/Huffman entropy coder should be replaced by a lossless zerotree coder. In other words, the dedicated quantization strategy incorporated in the FBI fingerprint compression standard is used and integrated with a lossless zerotree coder just responsible for entropy coding but not for quantization like in Shapiro's EZW approach. Along these lines a modified and enhanced version of the FBI fingerprint compression system has been implemented which is best described by means of Figure 3.10.

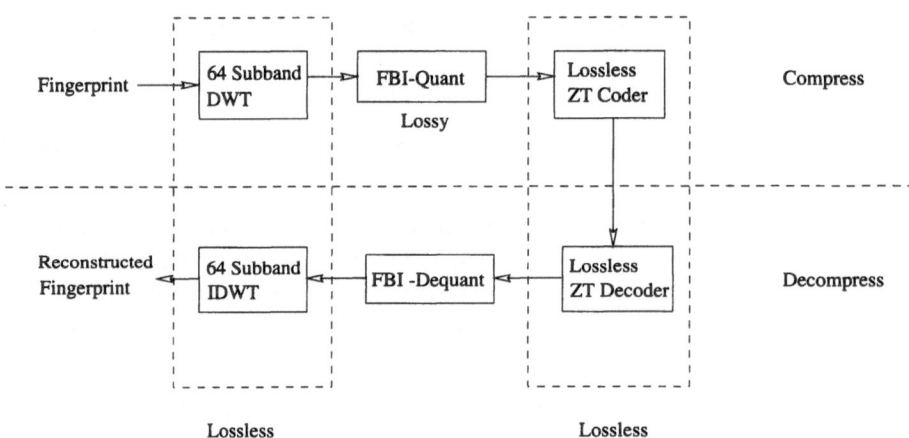

FIGURE 3.10. Structure of our fingerprint compression system.

When compared to the FBI's WSQ standard, the EZW coder, and the JPEG standard, compression results obtained by this modified approach are extremely promising, as shall be shown in the sequel.

Comparison to JPEG   In Figure 3.11 compression results for a 768×768 8-bpp fingerprint image are compared in terms of their appearance. The first row shows the original image, the second row depicts JPEG compression results, and the last row shows compression results with the modified and enhanced algorithm. The first column shows compression results at a compression ratio of 20:1, as does the zoom-in in the second column, while the third and fourth columns display results at a compression ratio of 50:1.

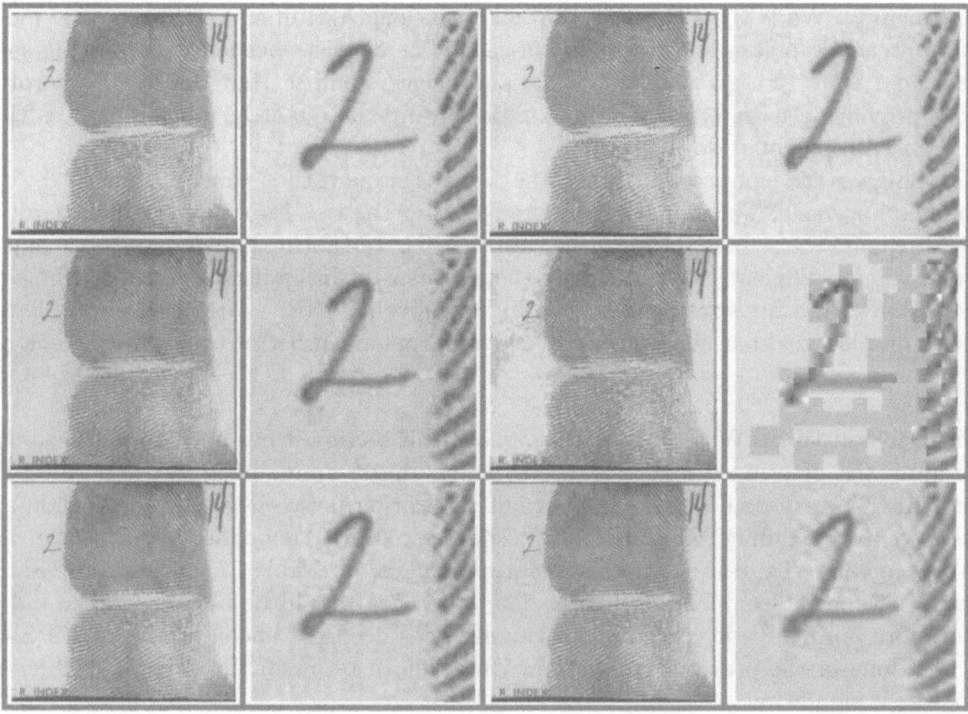

FIGURE 3.11. Fingerprint compression results.

At a compression ratio of 20:1, compression results seem excellent in all cases, but zooming in reveals the superiority of the enhanced FBI coder, which delivers very good results even at high compression rates (50:1), while JPEG falls off significantly. It is important to notice that blocking effects are present in the JPEG compressed image. These blocking effects are a big impediment to automatic fingerprint recognition systems (see [oI84] and the pioneer paper [Fau80]), which have to distinguish principal classes (Arch, Tented Arch, Left Loop, Right Loop, and Whorl) at the first level of fingerprint classification. That is a major reason why the FBI voted in favor of a wavelet-based compression approach.

In Table 3.5, the rate/distortion behavior for the fingerprint shown in Figure 3.11 is analyzed. There it becomes even more obvious that the enhanced version (FBI Enh) significantly outperforms the JPEG standard in terms of the root mean squared error (RMSE; smaller means better) and the peak signal to noise ratio (PSNR; larger means better) distortion measures. Remarkably, the figures for the modified approach at a compression rate of 100:1 are better than the values obtained by JPEG at a ratio of only 50:1, while 100:1 compression is simply not achievable using JPEG.

Comparison to the FBI Standard   The main difference between the modified approach and the FBI standard algorithm lies in the way lossless entropy coding is implemented. While the FBI algorithm uses run-length/Huffman coding, in the modified approach a lossless zerotree coder is used. The file sizes needed for achieving some specified PSNR[2] are given in Table 3.6 and clearly confirm that the lossless zerotree coder provides a more efficient way of representing the quantizer output indices than the FBI entropy coder does.

The higher the compression ratio, the larger the gain that can be achieved by the modified approach. This is related to the fact that the tree-structured lossless zerotree coder exploits the self-similarity present in wavelet transformed images and is thus particularly more efficient in representing the positions of insignificant (zero) coefficients. Inspection of the file sizes needed to achieve a given PSNR, as depicted in Table 3.6, clearly emphasizes that this entropy coder performs much better than the FBI entropy coder.

Comparison to EZW Coder   Throughout this section it has been emphasized that the approach of using a lossless zerotree coder differs fundamentally from the EZW coder in the sense that we take a clear-cut separation between lossy quantization and lossless entropy coding, while the EZW coder integrates embedded quantization and entropy coding. To prove that this separation pays off, Table 3.7 shows comparative results for specific compression ratios. The difference should be obvious and would be even more impressive if you compare the file sizes needed to achieve a certain PSNR, as was done in the previous subsection. But even in terms of the gain in RMSE, the progress is significant.

Summary

The FBI standard could be significantly enhanced if the entropy coder used is replaced by a lossless zerotree coder. In other words, the dedicated quantization strategy incorporated in the FBI fingerprint compression standard is used and integrated with a lossless zerotree coder just responsible for entropy coding but not for quantization like in Shapiro's EZW approach. Along these lines, a modified and enhanced version of the FBI fingerprint compression system has been developed and implemented, which outperforms the alternatives mentioned (JPEG, FBI, EZW) in terms of subjective quality and in rate/distortion behavior.

The research results emphasize that a clear separation between lossy quantization and lossless entropy coding pays off, a bottom line that should definitely be taken into account when designing other compression systems dedicated to a specific class of input images. For general-purpose compression for which no a priori knowledge about the input data is available, the EZW algorithm might remain the method of choice for obtaining high reconstruction fidelity even at highest compression ratios.

---

[2]The PSNRs used in Table 3.6 are chosen due to the fact that the FBI standard encoder achieves compression ratios of 10:1, 20:1, 50:1, and 100:1, respectively, for these PSNR examples.

	% edge pixels not detected						% pixels misclassified as edges					
	VQ	PC	PIFS	JPEG	WAVE	AV	VQ	PC	PIFS	JPEG	WAVE	AV
SL	5	8	7	3	2	5	3	1	1	2	1	2
CL	29	40	11	9	13	20	2	0	1	1	1	1
PL	23	17	13	11	11	15	5	1	4	2	1	3
CC	6	4	8	2	1	4	3	2	1	2	1	2
AV	16	17	10	6	7	11	3	1	2	2	1	2

TABLE 3.1. Impact of Image Compression and Subsequent Nevatia and Babu Edge Detection

	% edge pixels not detected						% pixels misclassified as edges					
	VQ	PC	PIFS	JPEG	WAVE	AV	VQ	PC	PIFS	JPEG	WAVE	AV
SL	29	11	7	25	11	17	4	2	2	2	2	3
CL	79	67	54	58	76	67	3	3	3	3	2	3
PL	64	48	47	51	48	52	6	9	8	10	8	8
CC	48	25	21	28	10	26	3	5	3	3	2	5
AV	55	38	32	41	36	40	4	5	4	5	4	4

TABLE 3.2. Impact of Image Compression and Subsequent Burns Line Extraction

	% edge pixels not detected						% pixels misclassified as edges					
	VQ	PC	PIFS	JPEG	WAVE	AV	VQ	PC	PIFS	JPEG	WAVE	AV
SL	47	24	13	11	11	21	4	2	1	1	1	2
CL	72	46	35	40	27	44	3	1	1	1	1	1
PL	53	48	41	42	36	44	8	4	4	3	3	4
CC	35	22	28	15	13	23	3	2	2	1	1	2
AV	52	35	29	27	22	33	5	2	2	2	2	2

TABLE 3.3. Impact of Image Compression and Subsequent Canny Edge Detection

	% edge pixels not detected						% pixels misclassified as edges					
	VQ	PC	PIFS	JPEG	WAVE	AV	VQ	PC	PIFS	JPEG	WAVE	AV
SL	57	58	40	49	41	49	7	4	4	5	4	5
CL	71	72	46	59	61	62	3	2	2	3	2	2
PL	56	57	46	38	48	49	8	4	6	5	4	5
CC	61	42	51	41	40	47	6	4	5	4	3	4
AV	61	57	46	47	48	52	6	4	4	4	3	4

TABLE 3.4. Impact of Image Compression and Subsequent Marr and Hildreth Edge Detection

Ratio	10:1		20:1		50:1		100:1	
Distortion	RMSE	PSNR	RMSE	PSNR	RMSE	PSNR	RMSE	PSNR
JPEG	5,725	32,976	9,547	28,534	21,496	21,484	n. a.	n. a.
FBI Enh	4,948	34,243	7,739	30,357	12,188	26,413	16,332	23,870
Gain (RMSE)	16%		23%		76%		n. a.	

TABLE 3.5. Rate/Distortion Comparison to the JPEG Standard

PSNR (dB)	33.892	30.057	26.128	23.516
FBI (Byte)	59008	29512	11820	5888
FBI Enh (Byte)	55963	27771	11081	5244
Gain	5%	6%	7%	12%

TABLE 3.6. Comparison to the FBI WSQ Standard

Ratio	10:1		20:1		50:1		100:1	
Distortion	RMSE	PSNR	RMSE	PSNR	RMSE	PSNR	RMSE	PSNR
EZW	5,376	33,522	8,192	29,863	13,343	25,626	17,570	23,236
FBI Enhanced	4,948	34,243	7,739	30,357	12,188	26,413	16,332	23,870
Gain (RMSE)	9%		6%		12%		8%	

TABLE 3.7. Rate/Distortion Comparison to the EZW Coder

3.2   Multimedia Data Encryption

To guarantee security and privacy in speech, image and video transmission, and archival applications, efficient bulk encryption techniques are necessary, which are easily implementable in soft- and hardware and can cope with the vast amounts of data involved. Cryptologic experience has shown that block-oriented symmetric product ciphers constitute an adequate design paradigm for resolving this task. Therefore, because the cryptographic concept is well developed and possible cryptanalytic attacks have been studied in detail, the general framework of an iterated product cipher is adopted to develop a novel method for efficient multimedia data encryption applications.

3.2.1   Symmetric Product Ciphers

The structure of the algorithm is similar to other iterated symmetric product ciphers (DES [Nat77], IDEA [LM90], SKIPJACK (Clipper) [ea93] etc.) that perform a blockwise encryption of the plain-text input to the system by repeated intertwined applications of r rounds of permutations and substitutions, as can be observed in Figure 3.12.

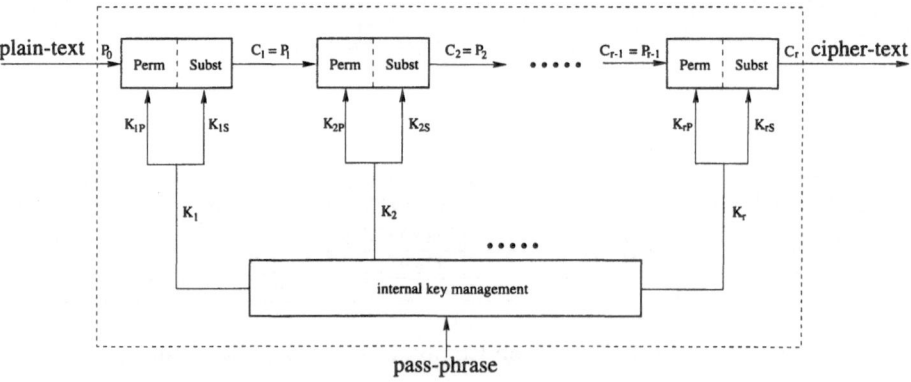

FIGURE 3.12. Structure of an r-round product cipher.

Input to the system is a block of plain-text P_0 and a user-supplied pass-phrase. From this key the internal key management derives the individual keys K_i ($1 \leq i \leq r$) and supplies them to the various encryption rounds. Every round i applies one *permutation* (change the positions of elements within a block) and one *substitution* (change the values of elements within a block) operation to P_{i-1} (keyed by K_{iP} and K_{iS}, respectively) and thus computes the cipher-text block C_i. After executing r rounds, C_r gives the cipher-text output by the r-round product cipher. Although $r = 12$ is recommended more rounds can be used for even greater security or fewer rounds can be thought of for better encryption performance, because the execution of two rounds appears sufficient to ensure that *any* change in input or key modifies *every* output value in a pseudo-random manner.

Important Properties

A single round of an iterated cipher usually involves only simple operations, which would be easy to break by themselves. It is the repeated intertwined application of permutation and substitution steps that accounts for the cryptanalytic strength of the overall system. Provided that certain requirements are met, product ciphers are *computationally secure*, which implies that it is extraordinary unlikely for an intruder to break the system in the near future. Of course, there are many conditions required for a secure cipher, but the following are fundamental and probably most important in applications dealing with multimedia data encryption:

> *Confusion:* Ensures that the (statistical) properties of plain-text blocks are not reflected in the corresponding cipher-text blocks. Instead every cipher-text has to have a pseudo-random appearance to any observer or standard statistical test.

> *Diffusion:*
>
> - In terms of *plain-texts:* Demands that (statistically) similar plain-texts do result in completely different cipher-texts even when encrypted with the same key. In particular this requires that *any* element of the input block influences *every* element of the output block in a complex irregular fashion.
> - In terms of *pass-phrases:* Demands that similar pass-phrases do result in completely different cipher-texts even when used for encrypting the same block of plain-text. This requires that *any* element of the pass-phrase influences *every* element of the output block in a complex irregular fashion. Additionally this property must be valid for the decryption process, because otherwise an intruder might recover parts of the input block from an observed output by a partly correct guess of the pass-phrase used for encryption.

3.2.2 Permutation by Chaotic Kolmogorov Flows

Iterated product ciphers constitute a common basis for almost all contemporary bulk encryption systems (DES, IDEA, and Clipper). However, the security of these systems seems to reside mainly in the substitution parts that depend on the key in a very complex manner. On the other hand, the permutation operations possess *fixed dynamics*, which are usually not influenced by the key. Instead, they just rearrange the elements of the input block in a predefined way specified, once and for all, by the designer of the cipher system.

Obviously, this is a weakness that also counts in the problem that certain iterated ciphers are particularly susceptible to a powerful new attack called differential crypt-analysis [BS91, BS92, LMM91]. A main goal of this section is therefore to improve on this situation and propose a novel approach to how *key-dependent permutations* can be integrated into the general concept of a product cipher.

This will be accomplished by means of so-called *Kolmogorov flows* T_π, a class of extraordinary unstable chaotic systems in which each element of the class is uniquely characterized by the parameter π. Kolmogorov flows can be expected to be particularly useful for scrambling input data blocks because they are the most unstable systems known [Pri80] today!

Continuous Kolmogorov flows

To give a notion why the extraordinary unstable dynamics of a chaotic Kolmogorov flow T_π are so especially suitable for implementing key-dependent permutations in the context of a product cipher, consider the example given in Figure 3.13 in which the parameter is set to $\pi = (0.25, 0.5, 0.25)$.

FIGURE 3.13. The dynamics of the chaotic Kolmogorov flow $T_{(0.25, 0.5, 0.25)}$.

One application of T_π with $\pi = (p_1, p_2, \ldots, p_k)$, $0 < p_i < 1$, and $\sum_{i=1}^{k} p_i = 1$, as shown by passing from pane one to pane two in the first row of Figure 3.13, essentially involves *stretching and folding* the state space of the underlying system (the unit-square $\mathbb{E} := [0, 1) \times [0, 1)$). First, $\mathbb{E}$ is partitioned into vertical strips according to the various p_i in π. Next, every strip of dimension $p_i \times 1$ is dilated by the factor $\frac{1}{p_i}$ to yield a strip of dimension $1 \times p_i$. Finally, theses horizontal strips are stacked on top of each other to end one iteration of T_π.

Formally, the underlying dynamics are defined as follows. Let F_s denote the left border of the vertical strip that contains the point (x, y) that is transformed. Clearly, the following relation holds:

$$F_s = \begin{cases} 0 & \text{for } s = 1 \\ p_1 + \ldots + p_{s-1} & \text{for } s = 2, \ldots, k. \end{cases} \tag{3.1}$$

Then $T_\pi : \mathbb{E} \to \mathbb{E}$ is defined by

$$T_\pi(x, y) = \left(\frac{1}{p_s}(x - F_s), p_s y + F_s \right) \tag{3.2}$$

for $(x, y) \in [F_s, F_s + p_s) \times [0, 1)$.

Iterating T_π generates very complex behavior, as can be seen in Figure 3.13. Actually it is known from the well-developed theory of Kolmogorov flows that there are several important properties that hold for *every* member of that class and provide good reason to use them as confusion/diffusion permutation operators:

Ergodicity: The trajectory connecting the iterates of almost every starting point in $\mathbb{E}$ approaches any other point in $\mathbb{E}$ arbitrarily close [GMC81, AA68]. In cryptographic terms, ergodicity makes it very hard to predict the actual position of a point from its initial position. Even more, after sufficiently many iterations, every position within the whole block is equally likely to be the actual position for almost every starting point (*confusion*).

Mixing Property: Any measurable subset of $\mathbb{E}$ is spread out uniformly across $\mathbb{E}$ [Shi73]. In cryptographic terms this implies that any regular structures contained in an input block will never pass over to the output block. Instead, every input regularity dissipates all over the corresponding output in a pseudo-random manner (*confusion*).

Exponential Divergence: Neighbor points diverge exponentially in the x-direction [Mos73]. This is a characteristic property of chaotic systems where small variations amplify and change the overall systems behavior in a very complex manner. In cryptographic terms, minimum modifications in inputs lead to exponential changes in the corresponding outputs, causing radically different outputs even for highly similar inputs (*diffusion*).

Discrete Kolmogorov Flows

Given a list of positive integers $\delta = (n_1, n_2, \ldots, n_k)$, $0 < n_i < n$, and $\sum_{i=1}^k n_i = n$, the discrete Kolmogorov flow $T_{n,\delta}$ (keyed by δ) for scrambling the data within an $n \times n$ block can be defined under the mild assumption that all $n_i \in \delta$ partition the side length n.

Let the numbers q_s ($s = 1, 2, \ldots, k$) be specified by $q_s = \frac{n}{n_s}$. Due to the constraint that n_s must be an integer divisor of n, all q_s are positive integers and we have the correspondence to the continuous case $q_s \triangleq \frac{1}{p_s}$. Additionally, N_s shall denote the left border of the vertical strip, which contains the point (x, y) that is transformed. Obviously, the following relation holds

$$N_s = \begin{cases} 0 & \text{for } s = 1 \\ n_1 + \ldots + n_{s-1} & \text{for } s = 2, \ldots, k. \end{cases} \tag{3.3}$$

Then, for $(x, y) \in [N_s, N_s + n_s) \times [0, n)$ the definition

$$T_{n,\delta} : [0, n)^2 \to [0, n)^2 T_{n,\delta}(x, y) = \\ (q_s(x - N_s) + (y \mod q_s), (y \div q_s) + N_s) \tag{3.4}$$

constitutes a valid discrete version of continuous Kolmogorov flows, as is easily shown.

The domain and range of the map is changed from the unit square $\mathbb{E}$ to the lattice $[0, n)^2$ in a way that the following asymptotic property holds for $\delta \triangleq n * \pi$, $(x, y) \in [0, n) \times [0, n)$:

$$\lim_{n \to \infty} \|n * T_\pi(\frac{x}{n}, \frac{y}{n}) - T_{n,\delta}(x, y)\| = 0, \tag{3.5}$$

because the measure of the difference (which equals $\frac{1}{n}(y \bmod q_s)$) tends to 0 as $n \to \infty$, as q_s remains constant (on the average) over the scales. In other words, $T_{n,\delta}(x, y)$ differs from $n * T_\pi(\frac{x}{n}, \frac{y}{n})$ only at the least-significant position in the base-q_s representation of x and y, which has measure 0 as the precision of the representation goes to infinity.

For n an integer power of 2 the calculation of $T_{n,\delta}$ can be done by just using addition, subtraction, and bit-shift operations which allow very efficient SW/HW implementations of the permutation. It is worth mentioning that this approach works for arbitrarily sized square blocks and can be extended to handle nonsquare blocks, indicated by results obtained by J. Friedrich [Fri96].

Keys for Selecting Different Permutations

For cryptographic purposes it is vital to know how many possible keys exist for a given encryption system. In the case of permutations by discrete Kolmogorov flows this is reduced to the question, how many different valid parameters δ exist for a given sidelength n. In other words, how many lists of positive integers $\delta = (n_1, n_2, \ldots, n_k)$ $(0 < n_i < n)$ summing up to n can be found under the constraint that every n_i has to be an integer divisor of n?

As presented in detail in [Aig75, Jeg73], a computationally feasible answer to this question can be found using a method based on formal power series expansions leading to a simple recursion formula. If $R = \{r_1, r_2, \ldots, r_m\}$ $(r_1 = 1, r_m < n)$ denotes the set containing all admissible divisors of the sidelength n in ascending order, then c_n, the number of all lists δ constituting a valid key for $T_{n,\delta}$, can be computed using

$$c_n = \begin{cases} 0, & n < r_1 \\ c_{n-r_1} + c_{n-r_2} + \ldots + c_{n-r_m}, & (n \geq r_1) \wedge (n \notin \{r_1, r_2, \ldots, r_m\}) \\ 1 + c_{n-r_1} + c_{n-r_2} + \ldots + c_{n-r_m}, & n \in \{r_1, r_2, \ldots, r_m\}. \end{cases} \tag{3.6}$$

A list of selected results for n an integer power of 2 is given in Table 3.8.

n	#keys	n	#keys	n	#keys
1	0	32	47350055	1024	$\approx 2^{837}$
2	1	64	$\approx 2^{50}$	2048	$\approx 2^{1678}$
4	5	128	$\approx 2^{103}$	4096	$\approx 2^{3325}$
8	55	256	$\approx 2^{209}$	8192	$\approx 2^{6720}$
16	5271	512	$\approx 2^{418}$		

TABLE 3.8. Number of Permissible Keys for Selected Values of n

n	k	# keys	# passed	# failed	% failed
256	2	10000	39677	323	0.8075
256	4	10000	158453	1547	0.966875
256	8	10000	633728	6272	0.98
256	16	10000	2534380	25620	1.00078

TABLE 3.9. χ^2-Testing Checking the Confusion Properties of Permutations Based on Discrete Chaotic Kolmogorov Flows

How do these values compare to the key spaces offered by other systems used today? DES offers 56 bits, SKIPJACK (Clipper) provides 80 bits and IDEA (PES) has 128 bits available. Therefore, as a rough estimate, $n = 64$ ($\rightarrow$ 50 bits) is close to DES and $n = 128$ ($\rightarrow$ 103 bits) is between SKIPJACK and IDEA; $n = 256$ ($\rightarrow$ 209 bits), however, is close to the estimated number of particles in the universe and the exponential growth seen from Table 3.8 ensures that discrete Kolmogorov flows offer key spaces that will *definitely* be sufficient for the foreseeable future.

Confusion and Diffusion

A strong encryption algorithm will behave like a random function of the key and the plain-text so that it is impossible to determine any of the key bits or plain-text bits from the ciphertext bits. To this end, the evaluation team reviewing the security of NSA's SKIPJACK algorithm [ea93] ran two sets of tests aimed at determining whether the algorithm is a good pseudo-random number generator and whether cipher-text bits are not correlated with either key bits or plain-text bits. Here the same setup (chi-square test using a 99 percent confidence level, 10,000 keys) is adopted to check the confusion and diffusion properties of key-dependent permutations based on discrete chaotic Kolmogorov flows.

Given an $n \times n$ input block, the *confusion* property is checked by dividing this block into $k \times k$ subblocks and checking for every individual subblock if the elements within this single sub-block are spread uniformly over all possible sub-blocks (confusion). Table 3.9 summarizes results obtained for $n = 256$ when applying a chi-square test checking the hypothesis that elements are spread according to a uniform distribution after iterating $r = 16$ permutation rounds. Tests are run using a 99 percent confidence level.

Because it is checked for every subblock of the k^2 subblocks, it shows that if the elements within this single subblock are spread uniformly over all possible subblocks, increasing k simultaneously increases the overall number of test cases and the discrimination power of the test. It came out that for the highest value of k exactly 1.00078 percent of the tests failed the 99 percent confidence level chi-square test. This is definitely within a reasonable experimental error of the expected value of 1 percent (actually even closer than the values obtained by the SKIPJACK group) and gives strong statistical evidence that the confusion property is indeed fulfilled by key-dependent permutations based on discrete chaotic Kolmogorov flows.

To check the *diffusion* properties of key-dependent permutations based on discrete chaotic Kolmogorov flows the average diffusion distance was computed for 10,000 pairs of permutation keys (pk_1, pk_2) differing just by a single bit. For every starting point (x, y) within a 256×256 input block the final position after iterating $r = 16$ permutation rounds was calculated under the influence of pk_1 and pk_2 yielding final positions (x_1, y_1) and (x_2, y_2), respectively. Their Euclidean distance obviously is

$$\sqrt{(x_1 - x_2)^2 + (y_1 - y_2)^2}. \tag{3.7}$$

In the optimum case where (x_1, y_1) and (x_2, y_2) are two completely uncorrelated, randomly distributed points within an $n \times n$ block, their average distance is

$$\frac{1}{n^4} \sum_{x_1=0}^{n-1} \sum_{x_2=0}^{n-1} \sum_{y_1=0}^{n-1} \sum_{y_2=0}^{n-1} \sqrt{(x_1 - x_2)^2 + (y_1 - y_2)^2}. \tag{3.8}$$

Evaluating this expression for $n = 256$ yields a theoretically optimum average diffusion distance of 133.479. Extensive simulations (apply 10,000 pairs of permutation keys differing by just a single bit for 16 permutation rounds to every starting point within a 256×256 input block and calculate the average diffusion distance of the respective final positions) amount to an average diffusion distance of 133.457. This is less than 0.02 percent away from the optimum average diffusion distance and gives good evidence to the claim that key-dependent permutations based on discrete chaotic Kolmogorov flows fulfill the diffusion property in the sense that after 16 permutation rounds even the application of keys differing by just a single bit results in completely uncorrelated, randomly distributed final positions (even for the same initial position!).

Summing up, the family of Kolmogorov flows does precisely exhibit the properties required for a good permutation operator within the framework of a product cipher. The existence of valid discrete versions, an impressive number of different possible parameterizations, and highly efficient implementations using only addition, subtraction, and bit-shifts (for n an integer power of 2) give good reason to integrate them in a product cipher for realizing key-dependent (secret) permutations that guarantee adequate confusion and diffusion in a fully systematic and transparent way.

3.2.3 *Substitution by AWC or SWB Generators*

Substitutions replace the elements of an input block primarily based on the element's value. To optimize SW implementations we focus on 32-bit data, but substitutions on other data types can be used with minor modifications.

In a product cipher permutations are complemented by substitution operations. This is essential because no permutation in the world can change important statistical properties (e.g., histogram) of the underlying data. Therefore, besides other tasks, the substitution has to ensure that the output of the overall encryption process is always a block of uniformly distributed pseudo-random data regardless of the distribution of data in the input block.

Popular methods for generating pseudo-random numbers are congruential relations [Knu81], shift registers [Yar88], or lagged-Fibonacci. As emphasized in many papers (e.g., [Ree87]), randomness in cryptography is different from the ordinary standards of randomness in the sense that, for cryptographic purposes, the matter of predictability is most important. This requirement is taken into account by combining substitution based on pseudo-random number generation (PRNG) in an intertwined and iterated manner with permutation operations, as proposed by the general framework of a product cipher.

AWC and SWB Generators

Add-with-carry (AWC) and subtract-with-borrow (SWB) generators [MZ91] are best introduced by revisiting the classical lagged-Fibonacci sequence with lags $r = 2$ and $s = 1$ and the informal description $x_n = x_{n-2} + x_{n-1} \mod b$, but a better formal definition is

$$f(x_1, x_2) = (x_2, x_1 + x_2 \mod b).
\tag{3.9}$$

Including a carry bit c and altering the lags from $r = 2$ and $s = 1$ lead to the general definition of an AWC generator with base b, lags r and s with $r > s$, and a seed vector $x = (x_1, x_2, \ldots, x_r, c)$ generating the sequence x, $f(x)$, $f^2(x)$, $f^3(x)$, $\ldots$ according to the rule

$$f(x_1, \ldots, x_r, c) =$$
$$\begin{cases} (x_2, \ldots, x_r, x_{r+1-s} + x_1 + c, 0) & x_{r+1-s} + x_1 + c < b, \\ (x_2, \ldots, x_r, x_{r+1-s} + x_1 + c - b, 1) & x_{r+1-s} + x_1 + c \geq b. \end{cases}
\tag{3.10}$$

Similarly, the corresponding SWB generator $x_n = x_{n-s} - x_{n-r} - c$ is defined by the iterating function f as

$$f(x_1, \ldots, x_r, c) =$$
$$\begin{cases} (x_2, \ldots, x_r, x_{r+1-s} - x_1 - c, 0) & x_{r+1-s} - x_1 - c \geq 0, \\ (x_2, \ldots, x_r, x_{r+1-s} - x_1 - c + b, 1) & x_{r+1-s} - x_1 - c < 0. \end{cases}
\tag{3.11}$$

Provided that the lags r and s are chosen properly with respect to the base b, AWC and SWB generators are extraordinary efficient and can come up with sequences having outstanding periods at the order of $b^r \pm b^s \pm 1$.

In this section, the choice for implementing a confusion/diffusion substitution operator is based on the SWB generator $x_n = x_{n-24} - x_{n-37} - c \mod 2^{32}$ recommended in Table 2 in [MZ91]. The cipher-text c is computed from the plain-text p according to

$$c[i] = (p[i] + prsp[i] + prsc[i]) \mod 2^{32}
\tag{3.12}$$

and the pseudo-random sequence corresponding to the plain-text is computed as[3]

$$prsp[i] = (p[i-24] - p[i-37] - cp[i]) \mod 2^{32}, \quad (3.13)$$
$$cp[i+1] = I(p[i-24] - p[i-37] - cp[i] < 0), \quad (3.14)$$

and the pseudo-random sequence corresponding to the cipher-text is computed as

$$prsc[i] = (c[i-24] - c[i-37] - cc[i]) \mod 2^{32}, \quad (3.15)$$
$$cc[i+1] = I(c[i-24] - c[i-37] - cc[i] < 0). \quad (3.16)$$

Keys for AWC and SWB Generators

This type of substitution is keyed by the seed vector $x = (x_1, x_2, \ldots, x_r, c)$ instead of the values $c[i]$, $p[i]$ with negative indices needed to compute $prsc[i]$ and $prsp[i]$. For the proposed SWB generator $x_n = x_{n-24} - x_{n-37} - c \mod 2^{32}$ which gives a total of $(2^{32})^{37} * 2 = 2^{1185}$ different keys!

In order to apply the one-dimensional substitution formula to two-dimensional blocks, the rows of the $n \times n$ input block are first concatenated to form an $n^2 \times 1$ array, which is then processed according to the substitution formula given. Furthermore, the direction of substitution is changed in all other rounds, which makes things harder for differential crypt-analysts and increases security against probable-word analysis [Riv87].

Confusion and Diffusion

Provided that the seed vector is not all zero, the SWB in use always produces pseudo-random numbers with the immense period of $\approx 10^{345}$ and passes all the standard tests proposed by Knuth and even more stringent tests included in a test battery called DIEHARD developed by the SCRI [MZ91]. Therefore, the confusion condition obviously holds.

Additionally, contrary to many other generators, AWC and SWB generators possess exponential diffusion. For the sake of simplicity, this shall be explained using the example of the most simple generator, the lagged-Fibonacci sequence with lags 1 and 2 and the informal description $x_n = x_{n-2} + x_{n-1}$.

Suppose that two seed vectors (x_1, x_2) and $(x_1 + d_1, x_2 + d_2)$ differ by $\|d_1\| + \|d_2\|$. Due to the generating relation, these differences amplify exponentially according to the law for the nth Fibonacci number yielding a difference of approximately $\|\frac{\alpha^n}{\sqrt{5}}\|$ after n steps [Wor71]. Thereby, α is the quotient of two successive Fibonacci numbers and, provided that at least d_1 or d_2 is nonzero, it always has a value strictly larger than 1.

Similar arguments can be applied to show that AWC and SWB generators with arbitrary lags have exponential diffusion properties. Differences propagate to higher bit planes and carries occurring at the most significant level are fed back to the least significant level (AWC generators) or propagate to lower bit planes and borrows occurring at the least significant level are fed back to the most significant level (SWB generators),

---

[3] $I(cond)$ gives 1 if the condition $cond$ holds and 0 otherwise.

respectively. In other words, differences in input data are amplified in an exponential manner, which guarantees that the diffusion property holds for the substitution presented.

3.2.4 Security Considerations

In the preceding sections we have clearly indicated how the cipher under consideration achieves both good confusion and good diffusion, the two basic features that contribute to the security of a block cipher. The best measure of security available today for an iterated block cipher is its resistance to attack by differential cryptanalysis [Mas94]. We give two strong arguments why such an attack will not succeed in our case:

- Consider the block size in use. Launching a differential cryptanalytic attack in this case is not computationally feasible. The enormous time and data requirements to mount such an attack put it beyond the reach of any intruder.

- Ciphers having key-dependent (secret) S-boxes are resistant to differential cryptanalysis [Sch93]. The same argument obviously hold true for key-dependent (secret) permutations (P-boxes).

The evidence available today suggests that the cipher proposed is a strong cipher whose strength is well measured by the enormous length of its user-selected key.

3.2.5 Encryption Experiments

Because the permutation and substitution operators in use possess the confusion and diffusion property, it is obvious that the same holds for the overall system. This shall be illustrated by means of some examples interpreting the 256×256 32-bit blocks as 512×512 byte-valued blocks and by graphically representing the values (from $[0..256)$) contained therein as gray levels.

The *first experiment*, which is shown in Figure 3.14, emphasizes the *confusion* property of the cipher under consideration.

In the first row on the left side the famous *lena* image is given, together with its histogram. It is then used as the input image to the cipher. The corresponding output image is shown on the right-hand side of the first row. No similarities can be observed between the input and the output, either in the image domain, or in statistical terms. In the second row on the left side, a completely black (empty) input image is specified. It contains only zeros while values other than 0 do not occur, as is emphasized by the histogram. However, even for this degenerated input image the corresponding cipher image is a uniform distribution of pseudo-random values.

The *second experiment*, which is shown in Figure 3.15, is intended to emphasize the *diffusion* property of the cipher under consideration with respect to small changes in input data.

In the first row on the very left *lena* is given again. Then an image very similar to *lena* is displayed which is in fact equal to *lena* except for *one single pixel* whose value has been increased by one. Of course, these two images have almost equal histograms,

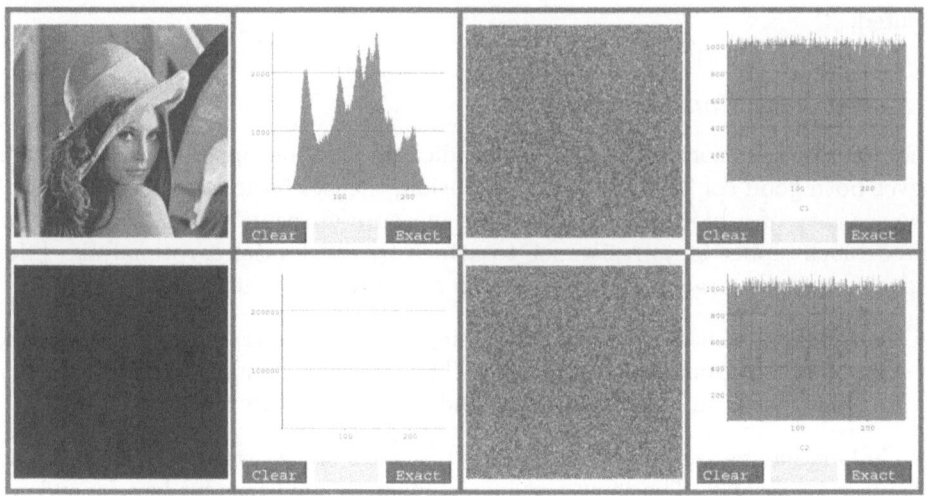

FIGURE 3.14. Experiments validating the confusion property.

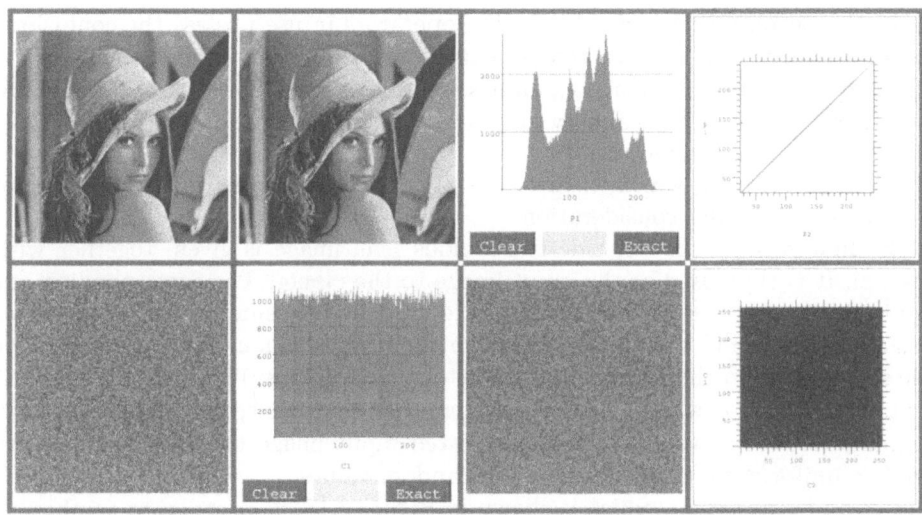

FIGURE 3.15. Experiments validating the diffusion property with respect to small changes in the input data.

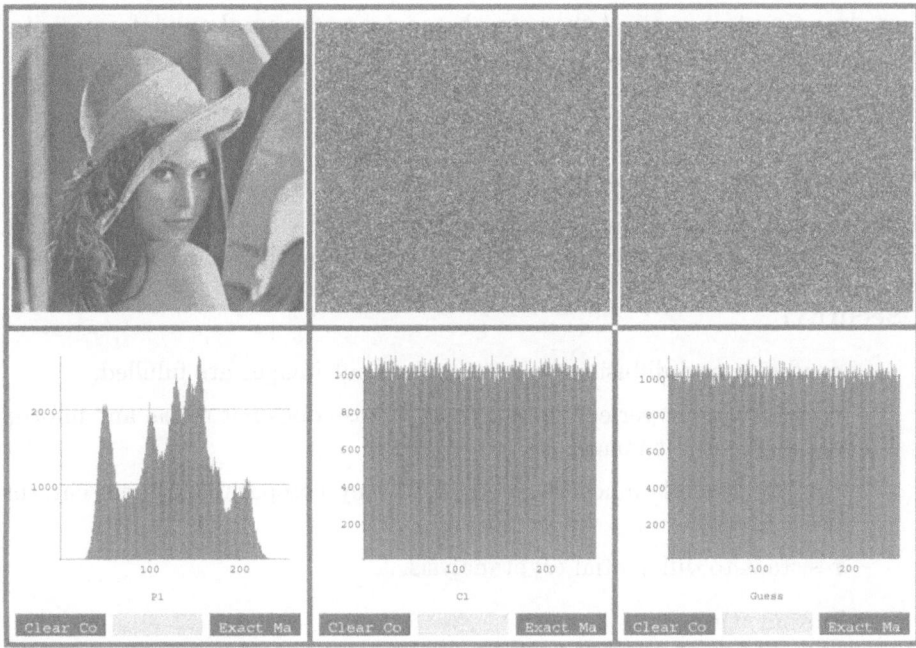

FIGURE 3.16. Attempt to decrypt an image with an almost correct guess of the pass-phrase used for encryption.

so only one is shown. The last pane in the first row shows the correlation of the two input images, which is very strong.

The corresponding output images when encrypting the input images *with the same pass-phrase* are depicted in the second row. On the very left the cipher-text resulting from the encryption of *Lena* is given. Next, we have the histogram of the encryption resulting from modified *Lena*. As expected, they are again pseudo-random uniform distributions. Most important in Figure 3.15 are panes three and four in the lower row. The third pane shows the difference between the ciphers computed when encrypting *lena* and modified *lena* with the same key. Obviously the ciphers show no similarities at all and there is no significant correlation that could be observed from the correlation plot shown in the rightmost pane of the second row.

The *final experiment* given in Figure 3.16 is intended to emphasize the *diffusion* property of the cipher under consideration with respect to small changes in pass-phrases. This is important because otherwise an intruder might reconstruct parts of the input image from the observed output image by a partly correct guess of the pass-phrase used for the encryption operation.

This figure is to be read columnwise. The first column gives the original *lena* image together with the histogram. In the second column the cipher image is depicted if *lena* is encrypted using the pass-phrase *"Max Maier, 0732-2468/9828."* Finally in the third column there is the result when attempting to decrypt with the almost-correct guess *"Max Maier, 0732-2568/9828."* The conclusion to be drawn from this attempt is that even an almost perfect guess of the pass-phrase does not reveal any information about the original image. Instead any attempt to decrypt with a wrong pass-phrase is in fact another encryption operation.

3.2.6 Encryption Summary

Deducing from analytical investigations and supported by experimental validation, the cipher introduced in this section can be characterized by the following properties:

- **Security:**
    - confusion and diffusion properties on input images are fulfilled,
    - even an almost perfect guess of pass-phrase does not reveal any information about the input image,
    - the key space is much larger than for any comparable system currently in use,
    - resistant to differential cryptanalysis.

- **Implementation:**
    - flexibility in implementation and extension; modularity makes it easily adaptable to new needs implied by technological progress or additional cryptanalytical insights,
    - encryption and decryption have the same complexity,
    - only addition, subtraction and bit-shifts involved,
    - efficient HW and SW implementations possible,
    - SW prototype proved to be several times faster than corresponding DES and IDEA implementations.

No cipher can be considered secure unless it has undergone severe scrutiny. However, from the current perspective it does not seem likely that any shortcuts or other weaknesses will be found. Therefore, it can be expected that the system proposed in this section should be of considerable interest in multimedia data encryption applications in which an appropriate combination of efficiency and security plays a major role.

References

[AA68]   V.I. Arnold and A. Avez. *Ergodic Problems of Classical Mechanics*. W.A. Benjamin, New York, 1968.

[AA85]   N. Ahuja, B.J. An, and B. Schachter. Image representation using voronoi tesselation. *Computer Vision, Graphics and Image Processing*, 29(3):286–295, 1985.

[AG88]   G. Ammar and W. Gragg. Superfast solution of real positive definite Toeplitz systems. *SIAM J. Matrix Anal. Appl.*, 9:61–76, 1988.

[AG94]   M. Acheroy and S. Grandjean. Meteosat image compression using the wavelet transform. Technical report, Royal Military Academy, Av. de la Renaissance 30, B–1040 Brussels, Belgium, March 1994.

[AGP91]   Y. Amit, U. Grenander, and M. Piccioni. Structural image restoration through deformable templates. *J. of the Amer. Stat. Ass.*, 86(414):376–387, 1991.

[AGT91]   L. Auslander, I.C. Gertner, and R. Tolimieri. The discrete Zak transform application to time-frequency analysis and synthesis of nonstationary signals. *IEEE Trans. Signal Proc.*, 39:825–835, 1991.

[Aig75]   M. Aigner. *Kombinatorik*. Springer-Verlag, Berlin, Heidelberg, New York, 1975.

[AMB95]   M. Acheroy, J.M. Mangen, and Y. Buhler. Progressive wavelet algorithm versus jpeg for the compression of meteosat data. Technical report, Royal Military Academy, Av. de la Renaissance 30, B–1040 Brussels, Belgium, 1995.

[Amm88]   M. Ammar. Off-line preprocessing and verification of signatures. *Int. J. of Pattern Recognition and Artificial Intelligence*, 2 (4):589–602, 1988.

[Amm89]   M. Ammar. *Feature Extraction and Selection for Simulated Signature Verification*. World Scientific Publ. Co., 1989.

[AO95]   A. Antoniadis and G. Oppenheim, editors. *Wavelets and Statistics*, volume 103 of *Lecture Notes in Statistics*, NY, 1995. Springer-Verlag.

[AR77]   J.B. Allen and L.R. Rabiner. A unified approach to short-time Fourier analysis and synthesis. *Proc. of the IEEE*, 65(11), 1977.

[Aus94]   P. Auscher. Remarks on local Fourier bases. In J.J. Benedetto and M.W. Frazier, editors, *Wavelets: Mathematics and Applications*, 203–218. CRC Press, 1994.

[AYF86]   M. Ammar, Y. Yoshida, and T. Fukumura. A new effective approach for automatic off-line verification of signatures by using pressure features. *Proc. 8th Int. Conf. on Image Analysis and Processing (8ICIAP)*, 566–569, 1986.

[Bal81]   R. Balian. Un principe d'incertitude fort en théorie du signal ou en mécanique quantique. *C. R. Acad. Sci. Paris*, 292:1357–1362, 1981.

[Bar88]   M.F. Barnsley. *Fractals Everywhere*. Academic Press, San Diego, 1988.

[Bas80a]   M.J. Bastiaans. The expansion of an optical signal into a discrete set of Gaussian beams. *Optik*, 57(1):95–102, 1980.

[Bas80b]   M.J. Bastiaans. Gabor's expansion of a signal into Gaussian elementary signals. *Proc. IEEE*, 68:538–539, April 1980.

[Bas81]   M.J. Bastiaans. A sampling theorem for the complex spectrogram and Gabor's expansion of a signal in Gaussian elementary signals. *Opt. Engrg.*, 20(4):594–598, July/Aug 1981.

[BB94]   J.N. Bradley and C.M. Brislawn. The wavelet/scalar quantization compression standard for digital fingerprint images. In *Proc. Int'l. Symp. Circuits Systems*, volume 3, 205–208. IEEE Circuits Systems Soc., June 1994.

[BBGK71]   V. Bargmann, P. Butera, L. Girardello, and J.R. Klauder. On the completeness of the coherent states. *Rep. Math. Phys.*, 2:221–228, 1971.

[BBH94]   J.N. Bradley, C.M. Brislawn, and T. Hopper. The FBI Wavelet/Scalar Quantization Fingerprint Image Compression Standard. Technical report LA-UR-94-1409, Los Alamos National Laboratory, Los Alamos, NM 87545, 1994.

[BE91]   A. Bengtsson and J.-O. Eklundh. Shape representation by multiscale contour approximation. *IEEE Trans. PAMI*, 13 (1):85–93, 1991.

[Ben92]   J. Benedetto. Irregular sampling and frames. In C. K. Chui, editor, *Wavelets: A Tutorial in Theory and Applications*, 445–507. Academic Press, 1992.

[Ben94]   J. Benedetto. Frame decompositions, sampling, and uncertainty principle inequalities. In J. Benedetto and M. Frazier, editors, *Wavelets: Mathematics and Applications*, 247–304. CRC Press, 1994.

[Bey95]   G. Beylkin. On the fast Fourier transform of functions with singularities. *Appl. Comp. Harm. Anal.*, 2(4):363–381, 1995.

[BGZ75]   H. Bacry, A. Grossmann, and J. Zak. Proof of the completeness of lattice states in kq representation. *Phys. Rev. B*, 12(4):1118–1120, 1975.

[BHF98]   H. Bölcskei, F. Hlawatsch, and H.G. Feichtinger. Frame-theoretic analysis and design of oversampled filter banks. *IEEE Trans. Signal Proc.*, 46(12):3256–3268, 1998.

[BHR86]   Burns et al. Extracting straight lines. *IEEE PAMI*, 8(4), July 1986.

[BHW95]   J.J. Benedetto, C. Heil, and D.F. Walnut. Differentiation and the Balian–Low theorem. *J. Fourier Anal. Appl.*, 1(4):344–402, 1995.

[BHW98]   J. Benedetto, C. Heil, and D. Walnut. Gabor systems and the Balian-Low theorem. In H.G. Feichtinger and T. Strohmer, editors, *Gabor Analysis and Algorithms: Theory and Applications*, 85–122. Birkhäuser, Boston, 1998.

[BM67]   A. Beurling and P. Malliavin. On the closure of characters and the zeros of entire functions. *Acta Math.*, 118:79–93, 1967.

[Boo78]   F.L. Bookstein. *The Measurement of Biological Shape and Shape Change*, volume 24 of *Lecture Notes in Biomathematics*. Springer, 1978.

[Bri74]   I.C. Briggs. Machine contouring using minimum curvature. *GEOP*, 39(1):39–48, 1974.

[Bri95]   C.M. Brislawn. Fingerprints go digital. *Notices of the American Mathematical Society*, 42(11):1278–1283, November 1995.

[Bro94]   E.J.F. Broekers. Regridding of irregularly spaced seismic data. Master's thesis, Centre for Technical Sciences, Delft University of Technology, Delft/The Netherlands, 1994.

[BS91]   E. Biham and A. Shamir. Differential cryptanalysis of DES-like cryptosystems. *Journal of Cryptology*, 4(1):3–72, 1991.

[BS92]   E. Biham and A. Shamir. Differential cryptanalysis of the full 16-round DES. In *Lecture Notes in Computer Science No 547: Advances in Cryptology-Crypto'92*, Berlin, Heidelberg, New York, 1992. Springer-Verlag.

[BW94]   J.J. Benedetto and D.F. Walnut. Gabor frames for L^2 and related spaces. In J.J. Benedetto and M.W. Frazier, editors, *Wavelets: Mathematics and Applications*, 97–162. CRC Press, 1994.

[Can86]   J. Canny. A computational approach to edge detection. *IEEE PAMI*, 6(6):679–698, 1986.

[Car88]   S. Carlsson. Sketch based coding of gray level images. *Signal Processing North-Holland*, 15(1):57–83, 1988.

[Ç75]   E. Çinlar. *Introduction to Stochastic Processes*. Prentice Hall Inc., NJ, 1975.

[Cen89]   C. Cenker. *Entwicklung von Distributionen nach kohärenten Funktionensystemen*. Ph.D. thesis, Dept. of Mathematics, Vienna, Austria, April 1989.

[Cen97]   C. Cenker. Wavelet packets and optimization in pattern recognition. In W. Burger and M. Burge, editors, *Pattern Recognition 1997*, Vol. 103 of *Proc. Conf. AAPR*, 49–58. OCG, Vienna, Austria, 1997.

[CGK91]   Y. Chow, U. Grenander, and D. M. Keenan. *Hands: A Pattern Theoretical Study of Biological Shape*, volume 2 of *Research Notes in Neural Computing*. Springer, NY, 1991.

[Chr95]   O. Christensen. A Paley-Wiener theorem for frames. *Proc. Amer. Math. Soc.*, 123:2199–2202, 1995.

[CHT98]   R. Carmona, W.L. Hwang, and B. Torrésani. Practical time-frequency analysis, Gabor and wavelet transforms with an implementation in S, *Wavelet Analysis and Its Applications*. Academic Press, San Diego, 1998.

[Chu92a]   C.K. Chui. *An Introduction to Wavelets*. Academic Press, San Diego, CA, 1992.

[Chu92c]   C.K. Chui, editor. *Wavelets: A Tutorial in Theory and Applications*. Academic Press Inc., Boston, 1992.

[CL67]   H. Cramer and M.R. Leadbetter. *Stationary and Related Stochastic Processes*. J. Wiley and Sons, NY, 1967.

[Cla98]   J. Claerbout. *Geophysical Exploration Mapping*. el. publ., 1998.

[CM97]   C. Cenker and M. Mayer. A MatLab interface for global optimization in pattern recognition. In W. Burger and M. Burge, editors, *Pattern Recognition 1997*, volume 103 of *Proc. Conf. AAPR*, 87–92. OCG, Vienna, Austria, 1997.

[CN96]   R. Chan and M. Ng. Conjugate gradient methods for Toeplitz systems. *SIAM Review*, 38(3):427–482, 1996.

[Coh95]   L. Cohen. *Time–Frequency Analysis*. Prentice Hall, Englewood Cliffs, NJ, 1995.

[CORG94]   P.C. Cosman, K.L. Oehler, E.A. Riskin, and R.M. Gray. Using vector quantization for image processing. Technical report, Univ. of Washington, Dept. of Computer Science and Engineering, Seattle, 1994.

[CR80]   R.R. Coifman and R. Rochberg. Representation theorems for holomorphic and harmonic functions in ℓ^p. *Astérisque*, 77:11–66, 1980.

[CV90]   D. Cyganski and R.F. Važ. Generation of affine invariant local contour feature data. *Pattern Recognition Letters*, 11:479–483, 1990.

[CV98]   Z. Cvetkovic and M. Vetterli. Oversampled filter banks. *IEEE Trans. Signal Proc.*, 46(5):1245–1255, 1998.

[Dau80]   J.G. Daugman. Two-dimensional spectral analysis of cortical receptive field profiles. *Vision Research*, 20:847–856, 1980.

[Dau87]   J.G. Daugman. Image analysis and compact coding by oriented 2-D Gabor primitives. In *SPIE Proc. of Vis. Comm. Image Proc.*, volume 758, 19–30, 1987.

[Dau88]   J.G. Daugman. Complete discrete 2-D Gabor transform by neural networks for image analysis and compression. *IEEE Trans. ASSP*, 36(7):1169–1179, 1988.

[Dau90]   I. Daubechies. The wavelet transform, time-frequency localization and signal analysis. *IEEE Trans. Info. Theory*, 36:961–1005, 1990.

[Dau92c]   I. Daubechies. *Ten Lectures on Wavelets*. Number 61 in CBMS-NSF Series in Applied Mathematics. SIAM, Philadelphia, 1992.

[Dau93]   J.G. Daugman. High confidence visual recognition of persons by a test of statistical independence. *IEEE Trans. Patt. Anal. Mach. Intell.*, 15(11):1148–1161, 1993.

[DD89]   G. Deslauriers and S. Dubuc. Symmetric iterative interpolation processes. *Constr. Approx.*, 5(1):49–68, 1989.

[DGM86]   I. Daubechies, A. Grossmann, and Y. Meyer. Painless nonorthogonal expansions. *J. Math. Phys.*, 27(5):1271–1283, 1986.

[DH87]   F. De Hoog. A new algorithm for solving Toeplitz systems of equations. *Linear Algebra Appl.*, 88/89:349–364, 1987.

[Die93]   P. Dierckx. *Curve and Surface Fitting with Splines*. Monographs on Numerical Analysis. Oxford University Press, 1993.

[DJ93]   I. Daubechies and A.J.E.M. Janssen. Two theorems on lattice expansions. *IEEE Trans. Info. Theory*, 39(1):3–6, 1993.

[DJJ91]   I. Daubechies, S. Jaffard, and J.L. Journé. A simple Wilson orthonormal basis with exponential decay. *SIAM J. Math. Anal.*, 22(2):554–572, 1991.

[Don92]   D.L. Donoho. De-noising by soft-thresholding. Technical report, Dept. of Statistics, Stanford University, 1992.

[DR93]   A. Dutt and V. Rokhlin. Fast Fourier transforms for nonequispaced data. *SIAM J. Sci. Comp.*, 14(6):1368–1394, 1993.

120   References

[DR95]   A. Dutt and V. Rokhlin. Fast Fourier transforms for nonequispaced data II. *Appl. Comp. Harm. Anal.*, 2(1):85–100, 1995.

[DS52]   R. Duffin and A. Schaeffer. A class of nonharmonic Fourier series. *Trans. Amer. Math. Soc.*, 72:341–366, 1952.

[ea93]   E. Brickell et. al. SKIPJACK review interim report: The SKIPJACK algorithm. Posted on sci.crypt; available from NIST, July 1993.

[EK91]   T. Ebrahimi and M. Kunt. Image compression by Gabor expansion. *Opt. Engrg.*, 30(7):873–880, 1991.

[Fau80]   H. Faulds. On the skin-furrows of the hand. *Nature*, 22:605, October 1880.

[FCS95]   H.G. Feichtinger, O. Christensen, and T. Strohmer. A group-theoretical approach to Gabor analysis. *Opt. Engrg.*, 34:1697–1704, 1995.

[Fei89]   H.G. Feichtinger. Coherent frames and irregular sampling. *Proc. Conf. Recent Advances in Fourier Anal. and Its Appl.*, NATO ASI Series C, Vol. 315:427–440, 1989. NATO Conference, Pisa.

[FG89a]   H.G. Feichtinger and K. Gröchenig. Multidimensional irregular sampling of band-limited functions in l^p-spaces. *Conf. Oberwolfach Feb. 1989*, 135–142, 1989. ISNM 90 (1989), Birkhäuser.

[FG89b]   H.G. Feichtinger and K. Gröchenig. Banach spaces related to integrable group representations and their atomic decompositions, II. *Monatsh. Math.*, 108:129–148, 1989.

[FG92a]   H.G. Feichtinger and K. Gröchenig. Non-orthogonal wavelet and Gabor expansions, and group representations. In G. Beylkin, R. Coifman, I. Daubechies, et al., editors, *Wavelets and Their Applications*, 353–376. Jones and Bartlett, 20 Park Plaza, Boston, MA 02116, USA, 1992.

[FG92b]   H.G. Feichtinger and K.H. Gröchenig. Gabor wavelets and the heisenberg group: Gabor expansions and short time Fourier transform from the group theoretical point of view. In C.K. Chui, editor, *Wavelets–A Tutorial in Theory and Applications*, 359–397. Academic Press, 1992.

[FG93]   H.G. Feichtinger and K. Gröchenig. Error analysis in regular and irregular sampling theory. *Applicable Analysis*, 50:167–189, 1993.

[FG96]   H.G. Feichtinger and K. Gröchenig. Gabor frames and time-frequency analysis of distributions. *J. Funct. Anal.*, 146(2):464–495, June 1996.

[FGS95]   H.G. Feichtinger, K. Gröchenig, and T. Strohmer. Efficient numerical methods in non-uniform sampling theory. *Numerische Mathematik*, 69:423–440, 1995.

[FGW92]   H.G. Feichtinger, K. Gröchenig, and D. Walnut. Wilson bases and modulation spaces. *Math. Nachrichten*, 155:7–17, 1992.

[FH94]   T. Foley and H. Hagen. Advances in scattered data interpolation. *Surveys on Mathematics for Industry*, 4(2):71–83, 1994.

[Fis95]   Y. Fisher, editor. *Fractal Image Compression: Theory and Application*. Springer-Verlag, New York, 1995.

[FK97]   H.G. Feichtinger and W. Kozek. Quantization of TF–lattice invariant operators on elementary LCA groups. In H.G. Feichtinger and T. Strohmer, editors, *Gabor Analysis and Algorithms: Theory and Applications*. Birkhäuser, Boston, 1997.

[Fol89]   G.B. Folland. *Harmonic Analysis in Phase Space*. Princeton Univ. Press, Princeton, NJ, 1989.

[Fol94]   G.B. Folland. *A Course in Abstract Harmonic Analysis*. CRC Press, Boca Raton, 1994.

[Fri96]   J. Friedrich. Image encryption based on chaos. Technical report, Center for Intelligent Systems, SUNY Binghamton, NY, 1996.

[FS93]   H.G. Feichtinger and T. Strohmer. Fast iterative reconstruction of band-limited images from irregular sampling values. In D. Chetverikov and W.G. Kropatsch, editors, *Proc. on Computer Analysis of Images and Patterns*, 82–91, Budapest, 1993. Conf. CAIP.

[FS98a]   H.G. Feichtinger and T. Strohmer, editors. Gabor analysis and algorithms: Theory and applications. *Applied and Numerical Harmonic Analysis*. Birkhäuser, Boston, 1998.

[FS98b]   H.G. Feichtinger and T. Strohmer, editors. *Gabor Analysis and Algorithms: Theory and Applications*. Birkhäuser, Boston, 1998.

[FSS99]   H.G. Feichtinger, T. Strohmer, and H. Schwab. Edge-preserving fast Voronoi tesselations for reconstruction of missing data in images, 1999. in preparation.

[Fuk90]   K. Fukunaga. *Introduction to Statistical Pattern Recognition*. Computer Science and Scientific Computing. Academic Press Inc., 1990.

[FZ98]   H.G. Feichtinger and G. Zimmermann. A Banach space of test functions for Gabor analysis. In H.G. Feichtinger and T. Strohmer, editors, *Gabor Analysis and Algorithms: Theory and Applications*, Applied and Numerical Harmonic Analysis, 123–170. Birkhäuser, Boston, 1998.

[Gab46]   D. Gabor. Theory of communication. *J. IEE (London)*, 93(III):429–457, November 1946.

[GK91]   U. Grenander and D.M. Keenan. *HANDS: A Pattern Theoretic Study of Biological Shapes*, volume 2 of *Research Notes in Neural Computing*. Springer, 1991.

[GMC81]   S. Goldstein, B. Misra, and M. Courbage. On intrinsic randomness of dynamical systems. *Journal of Statistical Physics*, 25(1):111–126, 1981.

[GMN97]   J. Goutsias, R. P.S. Mahler, and H.T. Nguyen, editors. *Random Sets: Theory and Applications*, Vol.97 of *The IMA Volumes in Mathematics and Its Applications*. Springer, 1997.

[Gol94]   J. Goldschneider. *Vector Quantization Software Documentation*. Univ. of Washington, Dept. of Computer Science and Engineering, Seattle, USA, 1994.

[GP92]   T. Genossar and M. Porat. Can one evaluate the Gabor expansion using Gabor's iterative algorithm? *IEEE Trans. on Signal Proc.*, 40(8):1852–1861, 1992.

[Gre76]   U. Grenander. *Pattern Synthesis Vol I*. Applied Mathematical Sciences. Springer-Verlag, New York, 1976.

[Gre77]   U. Grenander. *Pattern Analysis Vol. II*. Applied Mathematical Sciences. Springer-Verlag, New York, 1977.

[Grö93]   K. Gröchenig. A discrete theory of irregular sampling. *Lin. Alg. and Appl.*, 193:129–150, 1993.

[Grö97]   K. Gröchenig. Finite and infinite-dimensional models for non-uniform sampling. In *SampTA–Sampling Theory and Applications*, 285–290, Aveiro, Portugal, 1997.

[Grö98]   K. Gröchenig. Aspects of the Gabor analysis on locally compact abelian groups. In H.G. Feichtinger and T. Strohmer, editors, *Gabor Analysis and Algorithms: Theory and Applications*, 211–231. Birkhäuser, Boston, 1998.

[Grö99]   K. Gröchenig. Irregular sampling, Toeplitz matrices, and the approximation of entire functions of exponential type. *Math. Comp.*, 68(226), 749–765, 1999.

[GvL89]   G.H. Golub and C.F. van Loan. *Matrix Computations*. Johns Hopkins, London, Baltimore, 1989.

[GvL96]   G.H. Golub and C.F. van Loan. *Matrix Computations, third edition* Johns Hopkins, London, Baltimore, 1996.

[Han93]   R.O. Hansen. Interpretive gridding by anisotropic kriging. *GEOP*, 58(10):1491–1497, 1993.

[Har28]   R.V.L. Hartley. Transmission of information. *Bell System Tech. J.*, 7(4):535–563, 1928.

[Hig96]   J.R. Higgins. *Sampling Theory in Fourier and Signal Analysis: Foundations.* Oxford University Press, 1996.

[HP95]   R. Horst and P.M. Pardalos. *Handbook of Global Optimization.* Kluwer, 1995.

[HR63]   E. Hewitt and K. Ross. *Abstract Harmonic Analysis, Vols. 1 and 2*, volume 152 of *Grundlehren Math. Wiss.* Springer, Berlin, Heidelberg, New York, 1963.

[HW89]   C. Heil and D. Walnut. Continuous and discrete wavelet transforms. *SIAM Rev.*, 31(4):628–666, 1989.

[HY81]   L.A. Hageman and D.M. Young. *Applied Iterative Methods.* Academic Press, 1981.

[Ins91]   American National Standards Institute. Digital compression and coding of continuous-tone still images, Part 1, Requirements and guidelines, February 1991. ISO Draft 10918-1, (a.k.a. "The JPEG Standard").

[Int95]   PIRA International. Image compression techniques. OII IMSTAND report, Commission of the European Communities, Luxembourg, 1995.

[Jac93]   A.E. Jacquin. Fractal image coding: A review. *Proc. of the IEEE*, 81(10):1451–1465, Oct. 1993.

[Jaf91]   S. Jaffard. A density criterion for frames of complex exponentials. *Mich. Math. J.*, 38:339–348, 1991.

[Jan81]   A.J.E.M. Janssen. Gabor representation of generalized functions. *J. Math. Anal. Appl.*, 83:377–394, 1981.

[Jan82]   A.J.E.M. Janssen. Bargmann transform, Zak transform, and coherent states. *J. Math. Phys.*, 23(5):720–731, May 1982.

[Jan94]   A.J.E.M. Janssen. Signal analytic proof of two basic results on lattice expansions. *Appl. Comp. Harm. Anal.*, 1(4):350–354, 1994.

[Jeg73]   M. Jeger. *Einführung in die Kombinatorik II.* Klett, Stuttgart, 1973.

[JS94]   B. Jawerth and W. Sweldens. An overview of wavelet-based multiresolution analysis. Technical report, Dept. of Math., Univ. of South Carolina, Columbia, 1994.

[Kai95]   G. Kaiser. *A Friendly Guide to Wavelets.* Birkhäuser, Boston, 1995.

[Kat68]   Y. Katznelson. *An Introduction to Harmonic Analysis.* Wiley J., and Sons, New York, 1968.

[KC81]   R.L. Kashyap and R. Chellappa. Stochastic models for closed boundary analysis: Representation and reconstruction. *IEEE Trans. on Inf. Theory*, 27:627–637, 1981.

[Ken89]   D.G. Kendall. A survey of the statistical theory of shape. *Stat. Sci.*, 4(2):87–120, 1989.

[KFPS96] W. Kozek, H.G. Feichtinger, P. Prinz, and T. Strohmer. On multidimensional nonseparable Gabor expansions. In M. Unser, A. Aldroubi, and A.F. Laine, editors, *Proc. SPIE: Wavelet Applications in Signal and Image Processing IV*, 1996.

[KLR95]   J.-P. Kahane and L. Rieusset. *Fourier Seriea and Wavelets*, volume 3 of *Studies in the Development of Modern Mathematics*. Gordon and Breach, Australia, 1995.

[Knu81]   D.E. Knuth. *The Art of Computer Programming*, Vol.2. Addison Wesley, Reading, Mass., 1981.

[KS85]   J.R. Klauder and B.-S. Skagerstam. *Coherent States*. World Scientific, Singapore, 1985.

[KW98]   G.J. Klir and M.J. Wierman. *Uncertainty-Based Information*. Physica-Verlag, Springer, 1998.

[Lan67]   H. Landau. Necessary density conditions for sampling and interpolation of certain entire functions. *Acta Math.*, 117:37–52, 1967.

[Lan93]   H.J. Landau. On the density of phase-space expansions. *IEEE Trans. Info. Theory*, 39:1152–1156, 1993.

[Lan95]   T. Lane. *Using the ICG JPEG Library*. Independent JPEG Group, jpeg-info@uunet.uu.net, 1995.

[Li94]   S. Li. Nonseparable 2D-discrete Gabor expansions for image representation and compression. In *Proc. IEEE ICIP-94*, Austin, 1994.

[LM90]   X. Lai and J. Massey. A proposal for a new block encryption standard. *EUROCRYPT 90*, 389–404, 1990.

[LMM91]   X. Lai, J.L. Massey, and S. Murphy. Markov ciphers and differential cryptanalysis. In *Lecture Notes in Computer Science No 547: Advances in Cryptology-EUROCRYPT'91*, 17–38, Berlin, Heidelberg, New York, 1991. Springer Verlag.

[LMR94]   A.K. Louis, P. Maaß, and A. Rieder. *Wavelets*. Teubner, Stuttgart, 1994.

[Low85]   F. Low. Complete sets of wave packets. In C. DeTar, editor, *A Passion for Physics–Essay in Honor of Geoffrey Chew*, 17–22. World Scientific, Singapore, 1985.

[Lyu92]   Y.I. Lyubarskii. Frames in the Bargmann space of entire functions. *Adv. Soviet Math.*, 429:107–113, 1992.

[Mal98]   S. Mallat. *A Wavelet Tour of Signal Processing*. Academic Press, San Diego, 1998.

[Mar80]   R.J. Marks II. Coherent optical extrapolation of two-dimensional signals: Processor theory. *Appl. Opt.*, 19:1670–1672, 1980.

[Mar93]   R.J. Marks, editor. *Advanced Topics in Shannon Sampling and Interpolation Theory*. Springer Texts in Electrical Engineering. Springer-Verlag, New York, 1993.

[Mas94]   J.L. Massey. SAFER K-64: A byte-oriented block-ciphering algorithm. In R. Anderson, editor, *Fast Software Encryption*, number 809 in Lecture Notes in Computer Sciences, 1–17, New York, 1994. Springer.

[Mey90]   Y. Meyer. *Ondelettes et Opérateurs*. Hermann, Paris, 1990.

[MH80]   D. Marr and E. Hildreth. Theory of edge detection. *Proc. Roy. Soc. of London*, B(207):187–217, 1980.

[MLA94]   F.A. Marvasti, C. Liu, and G. Adams. Analysis and recovery of multi-dimensional signals from irregular samples using nonlinear and iterative techniques. *Signal Proc.*, 36:13–30, 1994.

[Mos73]   J. Moser. *Stable and Random Motions in Dynamical Systems*. Princeton University Press, Princeton, 1973.

[MS94]   P. Maas and H.G. Stark. Wavelets and digital image processing. In *Surveys on Mathematics for Industry*, volume 4, 195–235. Springer-Verlag, 1994.

[MZ91]   G. Marsaglia and A. Zaman. A new class of random number generators. *Ann. of Appl. Prob.*, 1(3):462–480, 1991.

[MZ93]   S. Mallat and Z. Zhang. Matching pursuit with time-frequency dictionaries. *IEEE Trans. Signal Proc.*, 41(12):3397–3415, 1993.

[Nat77]   National Technical Information Service. Data encryption standard. Technical report, National Bureau of Standards, Federal Information Processing Standards Publication, Springfield, VA, 1977. FIPS PUB 46.

[NB80]   R. Nevatia and K.B. Babu. Linear feature extraction and detection. *Comp. Graphics and Image Proc.*, 13:257–269, 1980.

[Nie90]   H. Niemann. *Pattern Analysis and Understanding*. Springer, 1981, 1990.

[NTC96]   R. Navarro, A. Tabernero, and G. Cristobal. Image representation with Gabor wavelets and its applications. In P.W. Hawkes, editor, *Advances in Imaging and Electron Physics*, volume 80, 1–84. Academic Press, Orlando, Florida, 1996.

126   References

[Nyq24]   H. Nyquist. Certain factors affecting telegraph speed. *Bell System Tech. J.*, 3:324–346, 1924.

[OBS92]   A. Okabe, B. Boots, and K. Sugihara. *Spatial Tessellation. Concepts and Applications of Voronoi Diagrams*. John Wiley & Sons, 1992.

[Ogd97]   R.T. Ogden. *Essential Wavelets for Statistical Applications and Data Analysis*. Birkhäuser, Boston, 1997.

[oI84]   Federal Bureau of Investigation. The science of fingerprints, December 1984.

[oI93]   Federal Bureau of Investigation. WSQ gray-scale fingerprint image compression specification, February 1993. IAFIS-IC-0110v2, Drafted by T. Hopper, C. Brislawn, and J. Bradley.

[Per71]   A.M. Perelomov. Remark on the completeness of the coherent state system. *Teoret. Mat. Fiz*, 6(2):213–224, 1971.

[PF77]   E. Persoon and K. S. Fu. Shape discrimination using Fourier descriptors. *IEEE Trans. Sys. Mgmt. Cybern.*, 7:170–179, 1977.

[Pfl89]   G.C. Pflug. Random transformations of the plane and their applications to pattern synthesis and pattern analysis. *Schriftenreihe der OCG, Band 49*, 1989.

[Pfl95]   G. C. Pflug. Random planar shapes and their statistical recognition. *Ann. of Math. and Artificial Intelligence*, 13:267–279, 1995.

[Pri80]   I. Prigogine. *From Being to Becoming*. Freeman and Co., San Francisco, 1980.

[PZ88a]   M. Porat and Y.Y. Zeevi. The generalized Gabor scheme of image representation in biological and machine vision. *IEEE Trans. PAMI*, 10(4):452–468, 1988.

[PZ88b]   M. Porat and Y.Y. Zeevi. The generalized Gabor scheme of image representation in biological and machine vision. *IEEE Pattern Anal. and Machine Intelligence*, 10:452–468, 1988.

[PZ89]   M. Porat and Y.Y. Zeevi. Localized texture processing in vision: Analysis and synthesis in the Gaborian space. *IEEE Trans. on Biomed. Eng.*, BME-36/1:115–129, 1989.

[PZZ98]   M. Porat, M. Zibulski, and Y.Y. Zeevi. Multi-window Gabor schemes in signal and image representations. In H.G. Feichtinger and T. Strohmer, editors, *Gabor Analysis and Algorithms: Theory and Applications*, 381–407. Birkhäuser, Boston, 1998.

[QF95]   S. Qiu and H.G. Feichtinger. Discrete Gabor structure and optimal repre-
            sentation. *IEEE Trans. Signal Proc.*, 43(10):2258–2268, October 1995.

[Ree87]   J. Reeds. "Cracking" a random number generator. In C.A. Deavours,
            D. Kahn, L. Kruh, G. Mellen, and B. Winkel, editors, *CRYPTOLOGY
            Yesterday, Today, and Tomorrow*, 509–515. Artech House, Norwood, MA,
            1987.

[Rei68]   H. Reiter. *Classical Harmonic Analysis and Locally Compact Abelian
            Groups*. Oxford University Press, 1968.

[Rie81]   M.A. Rieffel. Von Neumann algebras associated with pairs of lattices in
            Lie groups. *Math. Ann.*, 257:403–418, 1981.

[Riv87]   R.L. Rivest. Forwards and backwards encryption. In C.A Deavours,
            D. Kahn, L. Kruh, G. Mellen, and B. Winkel, editors, *CRYPTOLOGY
            Yesterday, Today, and Tomorrow*, 433–437. Artech House, 1987.

[RKT87a]   A.H.G. Rinnooy Kan and G.T. Timmer. Stochastical global optimization
            methods Part I: Clustering methods. *J. Math. Prog.*, 39, 1987.

[RKT87b]   A.H.G. Rinnooy Kan and G.T. Timmer. Stochastical global optimization
            methods Part II : Multilevel methods. *J. Math. Prog.*, 39, 1987.

[Rob]   J.A. Robinson. *Binary Tree Predictive Coding, Version 3.* Dept. of
            Systems Design Eng., Univ. of Waterloo, Ontario, Canada. email:
            john@monet.uwaterloo.ca.

[RS95]   A. Ron and Z. Shen. Weyl-Heisenberg frames and Riesz bases in $L_2(R^d)$.
            Technical report 95-03, Univ. of Wisconsin, Madison, 1995.

[RS98]   M. Rauth and T. Strohmer. Smooth approximation of potential fields from
            noisy scattered data. *Geophy.*, 63(1):85–94, 1998.

[Rud62]   W. Rudin. *Fourier Analysis on gGroups*. Interscience Publishers (a divi-
            sion of John Wiley and Sons), New York–London, 1962. Interscience Tracts
            in Pure and Applied Mathematics, No. 12.

[Rud76]   W. Rudin. *Fourier Analysis on Groups*. Wiley Interscience, New York,
            1976.

[SA87]   K.D. Sauer and J.P. Allebach. Iterative reconstruction of band-limited im-
            ages from nonuniformly spaced samples. *IEEE Trans. CAS*, 34(12):1497–
            1506, 1987.

[Sai94]   N. Saito. *Local feature extraction and its applications using a library of
            bases*. Ph.D. thesis, Yale, Faculty of the Graduate School, 1994.

[SBS+95]   M. Süssner, M. Budil, T. Strohmer, M. Greher, G. Porenta, and T. Binder.
            Contour detection using artificial neuronal network presegmention. In
            Proc. Computers in Cardiology, 737–740, Vienna, 1995.

[Sch93]   B. Schneier. *Applied Cryptograpy, Protocols, Algorithms and Source Code in C*. John Wiley and Sons, New York, 1993.

[Sch95a]   J. Scharinger. Implementation of lossy image compression methods in KB-Vision. Technical report, Johannes Kepler Univ., Altenbergerstr. 69, A-4040 Linz, Austria, 1995.

[Sch95b]   J. Schils. Reconstruction of irregularly sampled seismic signals. Master's thesis, Dept. of Mining and Petroleum Eng., Delft Univ. of Technology, Delft/The Netherlands, 1995.

[Sha48]   C. Shannon. A mathematical theory of communication. *Bell System Tech. J.*, 27:379–623, 1948.

[Sha93]   J.M. Shapiro. Embeded image coding using zero-trees of wavelet coefficients. *IEEE Trans. on Signal Proc.*, 41(12):3445–3462, 1993.

[Shi73]   P. Shields. *The Theory of Bernoulli Shifts*. The University of Chicago Press, Chicago, 1973.

[SN96]   G. Strang and T. Nguyen. *Wavelets and Filter Banks*. Wellesley–Cambridge Press, 1996.

[SP93]   A. Said and W A. Pearlman. Reversible image compression via multiresolution representation and predictive coding. In *Proc. SPIE Conf. Visual Communications and Image Processing*, 664–674, Cambridge, MA, Nov. 1993.

[SRWW87]   D.J. Sullivan, J.J. Rehr, J.W. Wilkins, and K.G. Wilson. Phase-space Wannier functions in electronic structure calculations, 1987. preprint.

[SS94]   J. Segmann and W. Schempp. On the extension of the Heisenberg group to incorporate multiscale resolution. In *Proc. Conf. Wavelets and Their Applications*, NATO ASI Ser., Ser. C, 347–361, Il Ciocco, Italy, 1994. Kluwer Academic Publishers.

[SS98]   O. Scherzer and T. Strohmer. A multi-level algorithm for the solution of moment problems. *Num. Funct. Anal. Opt.*, 19(3–4):353–375, 1998.

[Str86]   G. Strang. A proposal for Toeplitz matrix calculations. *Stud. Appl. Math.*, 74:171–176, 1986.

[Str97]   T. Strohmer. Computationally attractive reconstruction of band-limited images from irregular samples. *IEEE Trans. on Image Proc.*, 6(4):540–548, 1997.

[Str98a]   T. Strohmer. A Levinson-Galerkin algorithm for regularized trigonometric approximation. *SIAM J. Sci. Comput.* 22(4), 1160–1183, 2000.

[Str98b]   T. Strohmer. Numerical algorithms for discrete Gabor expansions. In H.G. Feichtinger and T. Strohmer, editors, *Gabor Analysis and Algorithms: Theory and Applications*, 267–294. Birkhäuser, Boston, 1998.

[Str98c]   T. Strohmer. Rates of convergence for the approximation of dual shift-invariant systems in $\ell^2(\mathbb{Z})$. *J. Fourier Anal. Appl.* 5(6), 599–615, 1999.

[Str99]   T. Strohmer. Two or three comments on the solution of Toeplitz systems. manuscript, 2001.

[SW92]   K. Seip and R. Wallsten. Density theorems for sampling and interpolation in the Bargmann-Fock space II. *J. reine angewandte Mathematik*, 429:107–113, 1992.

[Swe94]   W. Sweldens. The lifting scheme: A custom-design construction of biorthogonal wavelets. Technical report, AT&T Bell Laboratories, 600 Mountain Avenue, Murray Hill, NJ 07974, USA, 1994.

[TA98]   R. Tolimieri and M. An. *Time-Frequency Representations*. Applied and Numerical Harmonic Analysis. Birkhäuser Boston Inc., Boston, 1998.

[Tac96]   K. Tachizawa. The pseudodifferential operators and Wilson bases. *Journal de Mathématiques pures et appliquées*, 75:509–529, 1996.

[Top98]   P.N. Topiwala. *Wavelet Image and Video Compression*. Kluwer Academic Pub., 1998.

[TŽ91]   A. Törn and A. Žilinskas. *Global Optimization*. Springer, 1991.

[VH92]   M. Vetteri and C. Herley. Wavelets and filter banks: Theory and design. *IEEE Trans. on Signal Proc.*, 40(9):2207–2232, September 1992.

[Vil48]   J. Ville. Theorie et applications de la notion de signal analytique. *Cables et Transmission*, 2A:61–74, 1948.

[VK95]   M. Vetterli and J. Kovacevic. *Wavelets and Subband Coding*. Prentice Hall, 1995.

[vL92]   C.F. van Loan. *Computational Frameworks for the Fast Fourier Transform*. SIAM, 1992.

[vN55]   J. von Neumann. *Mathematical Foundations of Quantum Mechanics*. Princeton University Press, Princeton, 1932, 1949, 1955.

[Wal91]   G.K. Wallace. The JPEG still picture compression standard. *Comm. of the AMC*, 34(4):30–44, April 1991.

[Wal92]   D. Walnut. Continuity properties of the Gabor frame operator. *J. Math. Anal. Appl.*, 165(1):479–504, 1992.

[WGL93]   D.C. Wilson, E. Geiser, and J. Li. Feature extraction in 2-dimensional short-axis echocardiographic images. *J. Math. Imag. Vision*, 3:285–298, 1993.

[Whi95]   R.L. White. High-performance compression of astronomical images. Technical report, Space Telescope Science Institute, 1995.

[Wic91]   M.V. Wickerhauser. Lectures on wavelet packet algorithms. Unpublished, see wavelet page at http://www.wavelet.org, Nov. 18, 1991.

[Wic93]   Mladen Victor Wickerhauser. Best–adapted wavelet packet bases. In I. Daubechies, editor, *Different Perspectives on Wavelets*, Vol.47, *Proc. of Symp. in Appl. Math.*, 155–171. Amer. Math. Soc., Providence, 1993. From an Amer. Math. Soc. short course, Jan. 11–12, 1993, San Antonio.

[Wig32]   E.P. Wigner. On the quantum correction for thermo–dynamic equilibrium. *Phys. Rev. Lett.*, 40:749–759, 1932.

[Wil87]   K.G. Wilson. Generalized Wannier functions, 1987. preprint.

[Wor71]   N.N. Worobjow. *Die Fibonaccischen Zahlen*. VEB Deutscher Verlag der Wissenschaften, Berlin, 1971.

[WR90]   J. Wexler and S. Raz. Discrete Gabor expansions. *Sig. Proc.*, 21(3):207–221, November 1990.

[Yar88]   V.N. Yarmolik. *Generation and Application of Pseudorandom Sequences*. Wiley, Chichester, 1988.

[You80]   R. Young. *An Introduction to Nonharmonic Fourier Series*. Academic Press, New York, 1980.

[ZG92]   Y.Y. Zeevi and I. Gertner. The finite Zak transform: An efficient tool for image representation and analysis. *J. Visual Comm. and Image Representation*, 3, 1992.

[ZP84]   Y.Y. Zeevi and M. Porat. Combined frequency-position scheme of image representation in vision. *J. Opt. Soc. Am. (A)*, 1:1248, 1984.

[ZP88]   Y.Y. Zeevi and M. Porat. Computer image generation using elementary functions matched to human vision. In R.A. Earnshaw, editor, *Theoretical Foundations of Computer Graphics*, 1197–1241. Springer-Verlag, 1988.

[ZZ93]   M. Zibulski and Y.Y. Zeevi. Oversampling in the Gabor scheme. *IEEE Trans. Signal Proc.*, 41(8):2679–2687, 1993.

[ZZ97]   M. Zibulski and Y.Y. Zeevi. Analysis of multi-window Gabor-type schemes by frame methods. *Appl. Comp. Harm. Anal.*, 4(2):188–221, 1997. Also in: CC Pub. No. 101, Technion–Israel Inst. of Tech., Israel, April 1995.

Part II

Data Handling

Introduction to Part II

In the last few years, due to progress in imaging sensor technology and development of advanced processing methods, the amount of digital image data has greatly increased. The most important applications are industrial inspection and robotics, surveillance, medical imaging, archiving photos or documents, and space-borne earth observation. Handling and exploiting this continually increasing volume of data in an efficient manner are great challenges.

For many applications image analysis is the most critical task and bottleneck in the processing chain. Therefore, even when computing-intensive methods have to be used, the user will still ask for an even faster execution. To satisfy this demand, several strategies may be applied. The most important approaches are hierarchical image analysis, the "active vision" concept, or increasing computing power by parallelization. Each approach has its merits and must be tailored to the specific application and hardware environment. That requires sound experience with all methods and their merits.

In this section, the option of parallelization and the most important related aspects of handling large sets of image data are investigated. As a test bed, this approach has been implemented with various processes applied to an extensive data set of radar remote sensing data. After an in-depth analysis and optimization of the basic code, the algorithms were parallelized by several strategies, according to different scenarios of computing platforms and networking environments available.

Parallelization may be done on dedicated high-performance computers, but also by splitting the given task into independent jobs, which are then executed on different computers. With recent progress in networking technology, the latter aspect is gaining importance. Consequently, this development leads to a flexible architecture, where various computers with specific capabilities and software installed are collaborating. Therefore it is possible to process on demand a huge amount of data, which even may be stored at different locations, according to the actual requirements. Such a scenario is very well suited for maintaining and exploiting large archives of image data.

It also is obvious that cataloging and appropriate retrieval methods are also a very important aspect of data handling. As a typical application, a system for distributed archiving and retrieval of remote sensing data over a high-performance network has been developed. A Java-based graphical interface allows the user to search for image data, according to location and image parameters or any possible combination of descriptors. While this approach is relying on already existing metainformation, there are also many other applications where it is necessary to search for specific properties of image content. Therefore, methods for context-based retrieval from image archives have also been investigated. This more general but more computing-intensive process is browsing a database for pictorial elements. For implementing such a system, image analysis methods have to be performed in the most efficient way.

4

Parallel and Distributed Processing

Alois Goller
Ian Glendinning
Dieter Bachmann
Rainer Kalliany

In order to increase computing times of large image data considerably, algorithms or jobs may be split into packages that may be processed in parallel. For execution, either a machine with inherent parallel architecture or a computer network can be used. The most appropriate solution for a given case will depend on the properties of the algorithm, the hardware available, and the mechanisms of communication between the processors involved. Based on several applications, the relevant key issues have been investigated and will be explained in this chapter.

4.1 Dealing with Large Remote Sensing Image Data Sets

Remote sensing data contain a lot of valuable information on the shape and properties of the surface of the Earth or other planets. Data from radar sensors require elaborate processing before they can be displayed as images–not to mention possible methods of further exploitation. Therefore, these data are an ideal testbed for parallel and distributed processing strategies.

4.1.1 Demands of Earth Observation

Image data from remote sensing spacecraft provide a huge amount of coherent information on our (or other) planet(s) [Kra88]. While meteorological satellites usually capture atmosphere-related parameters at comparatively coarse intervals, the mid- and high-resolution systems of earth observing systems provide resolutions of up to a few meters on the ground.

Among others, important applications of earth observation with medium- and high-resolution imaging sensors are:

- 3D reconstruction of the surface of the Earth;

- generation and updating of topographic maps;

- monitoring of vegetation status;

- surveillance of coastal zones and the oceans;

- documentation of human activities on Earth; and

- detection of natural or manmade hazards.

Further information on earth observation (remote sensing) can be found through links on the CD-ROM.

Remote sensing spacecraft are equipped with either optical sensors, capturing the visible and infrared spectrum, or a synthetic aperture radar (SAR) instrument, recording the backscatter on ground of microwave radiation being emitted by the satellite itself [Kra96]. In any case, the sensor output consists of large matrices of data, where each value corresponds to the amount of radiation backscattered at the corresponding spot on the ground. These grids of physical data are rendered and processed as image data.

Handling of remote sensing images has various aspects, ranging from acquisition, archiving and dissemination (see Chapter 5) to thematic exploitation. In order to obtain the required results, a variety of methods have been and are being developed. Depending on the information actually needed, several image processing and analysis techniques may be applied:

- data compression and decomposition;

- image restoration and radiometric correction;

- image enhancement;

- geometric rectification;

- stereo exploitation;

- image matching;

- multispectral analysis;

- multi-image/multi-sensor fusion;

- feature detection and extraction; and

- many more (sensor-specific) algorithms.

For most tasks, a certain combination and sequence of processing steps is required, often demanding considerable computing resources.

The problem becomes even more evident when the enormous amount of data produced around the clock by each earth observing satellite is considered. For example, the AMI radar sensor on board the European Space Agency's ERS-1/2 satellites produces 8000×560 pixels per second with 32 bits per pixel; a rate of about 18 Mbyte per second [Sch93]. Usually, the satellites can capture data for 20 minutes on each orbit. Applied to ERS-1/2 that results in some 2 Gbyte per orbit or–with about 15 revolutions per day–30 Gbyte in 24 hours. Under these circumstances, only a small fraction of the data obtained are actually processed; the vast majority is just downlinked and archived for possible future exploitation.

Constant automated screening of the images–as soon as they have been captured–may be addressed as the "ultimate goal" of remote sensing. Thus, e.g., environmental changes and possible hazards could be detected at a very early stage. Before the creation of such a surveillance system can be accomplished, not only a lot more knowledge about the various physical phenomena and much improved methods of image analysis are required, but strategies for fast and efficient execution of algorithms are also needed.

Parallelization is a key technique for speeding up the computing process: It may be achieved by either using computers with inherent parallel architectures or by splitting and distributing tasks over a network of distributed computing platforms. In that context, several issues are to be addressed, e.g., the possibility of parallelizing an existing code, and the most appropriate balance between processors computing power and the capability of the connecting network. For each task or algorithm, a different strategy may be required. Therefore, other image processing applications will also benefit from research and development on parallelization of remote sensing procedures.

4.1.2 Processing Radar-Data of the Magellan Venus Probe

For investigating and developing various parallelization strategies, algorithms for processing SAR data from NASA's Magellan spacecraft were analyzed. Magellan mapped planet Venus from 1990 to 1992, acquiring coverage of almost 98% of the surface [LTM92].

The total amount of image data captured was 400 GByte, and it is obvious that full exploitation of all the data will be a very time-consuming effort. The primary goal of processing Magellan data is the generation of a planetary digital elevation model (DEM) and a coherent mosaic of radar images, both at various levels of detail.

For exploitation of the data, NASA provides a collection of sequential algorithms, tailored to the merits of the Magellan system [CM92]. Some key algorithms were analyzed in respect to their ability to be executed on a parallel architecture:

SAR signal processing converts raw Synthetic Aperture Radar (SAR) signal data into images. For the Venus data set a comprehensive software package called the Magellan SAR Processor was developed by NASA [CM91]. To process the data as soon as possible after being downlinked from the probe, this software was run on state-of-the-art hardware at the time of the mission.

However, there is now deeper knowledge of the data set, actual orbits, and other improved supplementary information, and a reprocessing of the original data appears to be desirable. In order to make that operation possible for the whole huge data set within a reasonable amount of time, the software has to be reviewed, optimized, and ported to a contemporary computing environment, preferably a parallel one.

Image matching establishes a regular or irregular grid of corresponding points in two overlapping images. Approaches applied to radar images are mainly based on correlation of pixel arrays. They have to cope with the radiometric differences due to illumination differences; therefore some algorithms use additional information derived from edge filters and local image statistics [GJP+96]. The algorithm we parallelized is called **Xmatch** and was developed by Scott Hensley at JPL [HS94]. The underlying theory is described by Frankot in [Fra90] and [FHS94].

Shape-from-Shading (SfS) is based on the idea that the variation of brightness primary depends on the terrain shape in respect to the direction of illumination by the radar sensor. A DEM becomes locally refined by applying SfS. Various kinds of SfS are described in [HB89]. We parallelized the algorithm developed by John Thomas [TKL91], which is based on work by Frankot and Chellappa [FC89] and performs most calculations in the frequency domain, as outlined in [Gol96].

Visualization and perspective rendering is based on a DEM from stereo and/or SfS (or other sources), and an image mosaic linked to the DEM by terrain correction. By 3D visualization of that data set, any view on the landscape or fly over may be simulated. Because of the large amount of data and frames to be processed, this is a typical parallelization task, being carried out at the very end of the processing chain.

A short video of a virtual flight over a small area on planet Venus can be found on the CD-ROM.

4.2   Parallel Radar Signal Processing

This section deals with strategies and tools that have been used to parallelize the Magellan SAR Processor, the program that implements the digital signal processing operations needed to convert Magellan's raw radar data into an image of the surface of Venus. The program operates on burst data, producing a single-look image framelet per burst and then superimposes the framelets to form a multi-look image data orbit strip.

4.2.1   Parallelization Strategy

The platform for development of a parallel version of the code was the 128-node QSW CS-2 machine at the European Center for Parallel Computing at Vienna (VCPC), and it was decided to perform the parallelization using the message-passing style of programming, using the portable MPI message passing interface [MPI94]. It was quickly realized that the radar bursts represent a natural unit of parallelism in the program, because each one can be processed independently, except for the final stage, called "look buildup", which merges results from overlapping observations in neighboring bursts.

Although the SAR processor is a fairly large program, the bulk of the source code is involved with a preprocessing phase, which takes relatively little time to execute compared to the burst processing for a whole orbit strip. For the sample data set tested on a single CS-2 node at VCPC, the initialization phase takes about 59 seconds, compared to about 2.5 seconds per burst, but there are more than 4000 bursts in the data set, so the burst processing time dominates. Thus, the focus of attention was directed at the main burst processing loop, which is located in the routine that performs the SAR correlator processing, `process_corr`. The main work of the loop is done by calls to the routines shown in Figure 4.1, whose parameters are omitted for brevity.

The final routine `multi_look` is the only one that does not operate independently on each burst, and it is the one that writes the image to disk. The basic strategy is to recode this loop so that each iteration can be executed as a task on a separate processor.

```
call corr_pp       ! Fill processing parameter (pp) common block
call pp_keyvar     ! Copy key pp values to correlator common block
r_nbytes = cread   ! Read raw burst data
call decode_sar    ! Decompress raw intensity values
call range_comp    ! Perform range compression
call corner_turn   ! Perform a non-symmetric matrix transpose
call az_comp       ! Perform the Azimuth compression
call radio_comp    ! Perform the radiometric compensation
call geo_rect      ! Perform a geometric rectification
call multi_look    ! Generate multi-look image
```

FIGURE 4.1. Routines in the main burst processing loop in process_corr

In practice, a pool of "slave" processors, each with code to execute a single burst, would have burst data distributed to them by a "master" process. The resulting image data could be collected by the same master process or by another process, but for simplicity let's assume here that there is a single master controller. In order to be able to recode the loop like this, it is necessary to understand its data dependences. In particular it is necessary to identify:

1. variables that are set before the loop and read inside it, as this implies communication of initial values from the master to worker processes.

2. variables that are set inside the loop and read after it, which implies communication of values from the workers back to the master.

3. I/O, which must be properly sequenced. File handles need special treatment, as you cannot write to a handle opened on another processor.

4. variables whose values are read within the loop, before being updated, as their values depend on an assignment from the previous iteration and imply communication between worker processes. This represents an antidependence from the first statement to the second.

Not only variables that are local to the subroutine containing the loop must be considered, but also any variables in common blocks that are used by either the routine itself, or any other routines that it calls, directly or indirectly.

The source code for the SAR processor consists of approximately 125000 lines of Fortran, divided among approximately 450 subroutines, together with approximately 6500 lines of C, and, although focusing on the main burst processing loop meant that only around 5500 lines (plus included common block declarations) had to be analyzed in depth, this was still a substantial body of code, so manual analysis would have be extremely laborious, and support from parallelization tools was considered essential.

4.2.2   Evaluation of Parallelization Tools

Three tools were evaluated with respect to their suitability for assisting in implementing the parallelization strategy for the Magellan SAR code:

- **FORESYS** (Fortran engineering system), a commercial tool by SIMULOG;

- **IDA** (Inter-procedural Dependency Analyzer), a public-domain tool available from the University of Southampton and VCPC [MR95]; and

- **FORGExplorer**, a commercial tool by Applied Parallel Research.

The most useful feature of FORESYS in the context of this work turned out to be its ability to handle almost all the nonstandard Fortran extensions used in the Magellan SAR processor and to transform the program into equivalent code in standard Fortran 77. Neither IDA nor FORGExplorer accepted these nonstandard extensions, and so it was necessary to use FORESYS to produce a cleanedup version of the code that they could process. However, the program analysis features of IDA and FORGExplorer were found to be more useful than those of FORESYS. Although IDA provided much of the functionality offered by FORGExplorer, FORGExplorer was chosen to perform the code analysis, because its more sophisticated user interface made it much easier to use in practice. It is described in more detail later.

FORGExplorer

FORGExplorer has a Motif GUI and presents a global, interprocedural view of a program. It can perform searches and variable traces, and it features an interactive, interprocedural Distributed Memory Parallelizer (DMP). The features of the tool that were evaluated were code browsing, the DMP option, and the global analysis views.

Code Browsing

Similar facilities to those of FORESYS are provided for code browsing, and they are similarly useful, although there are slightly more options. The Call Subchain display, which represents the call graph as a list of routine names, indented according to their call level, was found to be particularly useful.

Distributed Memory Parallelizer

The idea of an automatic parallelizer was obviously attractive, and so some time was invested in "profiling" the routines that were unknown to the tool, that is, the ones for which it does not have source code, such as the C routines in the Magellan code. The types of their arguments and whether they are read from or written to must be specified. Unfortunately, having profiled the unknown routines, it was discovered that the program was too complex for FORGExplorer to handle, and it looped indefinitely. It may have been possible to get further with the DMP using semiautomatic parallelization options, but it was decided to be less ambitious and to investigate the manual interprocedural analysis features of the basic FORGExplorer tool instead.

Global Analysis Views

Manual analysis of the code using FORGExplorer's global analysis views proved to be a much more fruitful approach than the DMP option, and in particular the variable

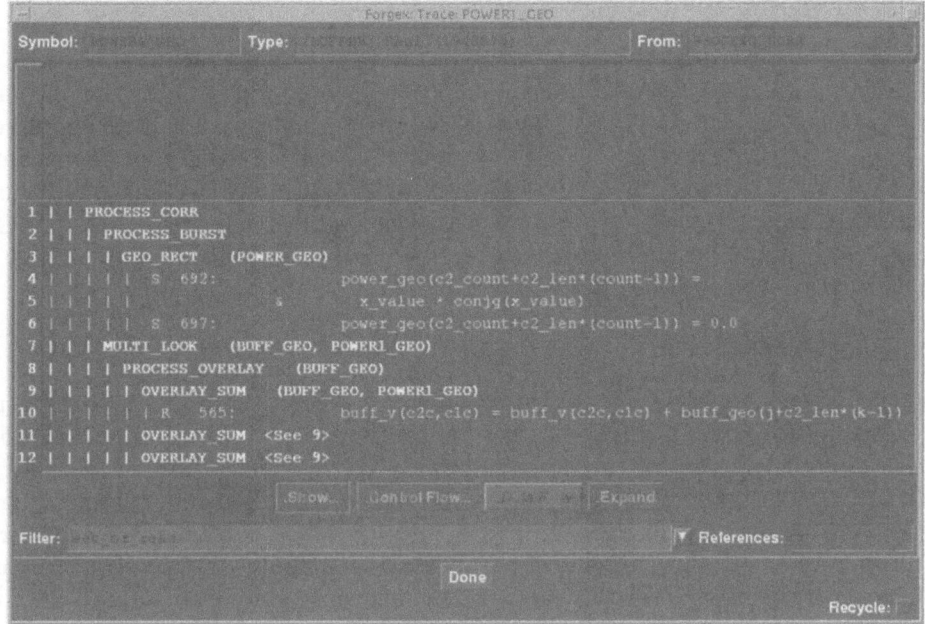

FIGURE 4.2. The FORGExplorer Trace window

tracing and common block usage displays were found to be extremely helpful for identifying dependences. The variable tracing display (Figure 4.2) lists all program lines where a variable is referenced, following the path that items passed through common or subprogram arguments take, and the common block usage display shows a grid of common blocks versus subprograms. At the intersecting cells, usage of the common block by each routine is summarized, according to whether variables are set or read.

4.2.3 Program Analysis and Parallelization

Isolating the Slave Process Code

The first step was to identify which code from the burst loop (Figure 4.1) would be run as a slave process and to localize it in a separate subroutine, giving it a clean interface to the rest of the code, exclusively through common blocks. It was decided to keep the **cread()** statement in the master process, together with the two preceeding routines called, as that represented a particularly clean break in the loop. The remaining routines in the loop were moved into a new subroutine, called **process_burst**. The new routine inherited all the common block and local data declarations from **process_corr**, and all of the local variables were declared to be in a new common block, so that values set in *one routine could be read by the other*.

Using FORGExplorer's "Reference Node"

The next step was to restrict the area of interest to the **process_burst** routine and routines called by it, by setting FORGExplorer's "Reference Node" to it. The "Common Blocks" display shows that the whole program uses 415 routines, 91 of which reference data in common, spread over a total of 61 common blocks. Setting the reference node to **process_burst** reduced the area of interest to 15 routines, referencing 14 common blocks. Potentially that means $15 \times 14 = 210$ common block references, but FORGExplorer showed that in fact there were only 40, and so we succeeded in reducing the size of the problem considerably.

A Simplified Parallelization Strategy

Although the complexity of the program analysis has been much reduced, the dependences within the **multi_look** code were still fairly complex, and in order to obtain an initial parallel version of the code as quickly as possible, it was decided to first construct a simpler parallel version of the code than originally planned, by moving the call to **multi_look()** out of **process_burst** into its calling routine **process_corr**. In this scheme, the maximum amount of parallelization is limited by the sequential code remaining in **multi_look**, but the analysis is significantly simplified, as just eight routines need to be considered in **process_burst**, and there are a total of 14 references to eight common blocks.

Dependence Analysis

The dependences between the master and slave processes were analyzed, so that the communications necessary between them in the parallelized code could be determined. This was done using the common block displays for both **process_burst** and **process _corr**, together with the variable tracing display.

The "Common Blocks" display allows a display of each individual common block to be opened, which shows a table of variables in the common block versus the routines that access them, and for each variable reference it is indicated whether it is read or set. Variables in the common blocks that were referenced within **process_burst** fell into three categories, according to whether they contained variables that were:

1. read but not set within **process_burst**;

2. set within **process_burst** and read afterwards in **process_corr**; or

3. set and then read within **process_burst**, but not used in **process_corr**.

Those in the first category were the easiest to identify, because it was enough that all their references were reads, but for those in the other two categories, it was necessary to check the read and write usage of the individual variables in the common blocks, because different variables set in a common block may or may not be read later. This was done using the variable tracing display, which also revealed accesses to common block variables that were passed to routines as arguments, although the common block was not declared in the routine, in which case the references were not indicated in

	ant_weight	az_comp	cfft	geo_rect	init_fft	process_burst	radio_comp	range_comp
/buffer/						2,3		
/fft_aux/			3		3			
/key_var/	1	1		1		1	1,3	1
/overlay_c12/				2,3				
/pc_loc/						1		
/po_a/				1				
/s_weight/				1				
/test_burst_no/							1	

FIGURE 4.3. Results of dependence analysis–Common blocks vs. routines

the common blocks display. The variable tracing feature was also used to check for antidependences within the burst loop (a variable read followed by a set), but none were found. Figure 4.3 summarizes the results of the dependence analysis, where the numbers in the grid cells correspond to the categories of reading and writing defined earlier.

The communication of variables between master and slave processes can now easily be deduced. Variables in category 1 must be sent to the slave when it starts to execute, those in the category 2 must be sent back to the master when the slave has finished its processing, and those in category 3 require no action.

Parallelization

Although the slave code was isolated from the rest at an early stage in the work, the whole program was kept sequential for as long as possible, so that it could be compiled and tested after each modification, to make sure that it still behaved as before, and so that the global analysis features of FORGExplorer could continue to be used on the whole code. Eventually, having performed the dependence analysis, the code was split into two executables, one for the slave process, containing the code for the **process_burst** routine, and one for the master process containing the rest of the code. Further analysis showed that the large arrays in the common block /BUFFER/ could be split between the master and the slave, which reduced the size of both executables considerably, which is important as they are close to the limit of available memory on the CS-2. Subsequent steps in the parallelization process are the insertion of the MPI communication calls, performance measurement, and final optimization of the code.

4.3 Parallel Radar Image Processing

The previous section explained strategies for parallelization of a given sensor-specific process, generating image data from genuine radar signals. Now we turn to algorithms that are applied to already existing images. Here, appropriate strategies for splitting an image into patches that can be processed independently are a major issue, which is of general importance for digital image processing. Besides, the most efficient strategy for executing such split and merge processes is another key issue.

The parallelization paradigm that was applied is called "Manager/Worker" or "Task-Farm" (e.g., in Fox [FJL+88] or [Edi96]). One process, the manager, loads and stores *all the data and controls the other processors*, the workers. The workers themselves form a pool or "farm," and communication between workers usually is not necessary or allowed.

The execution time for a certain part of the image (patch) may vary, for example, because a match point is found to be insufficiently accurate, and thus additional calculations are necessary to estimate an initial position for the next iteration. Therefore, dynamic load balancing is necessary to obtain good load balancing. However, compared with the benefits, the cost of dynamic data partitioning and redistribution is far too high. Furthermore, the patches are usually the smallest size allowed by the algorithm and cannot be divided any more.

4.3.1 Data Decomposition and Halo Handling

Data decomposition can basically be done in an arbitrary way. However, it is useful to partition regular problems into intervals of similar size. As illustrated in Figure 4.4, one or all dimensions may be partitioned. The shaded area shows the area required by two processors and their surrounding regions (halos). As the halo becomes larger (i.e., wider), it becomes obvious that "squares" reduce the amount of data to be transferred and updated in contrast to "stripes." Especially with matching, the "stripe"- approach would require data to be, collected not only from the neighbors of a certain processor, but from their neighbors neighbors as well.

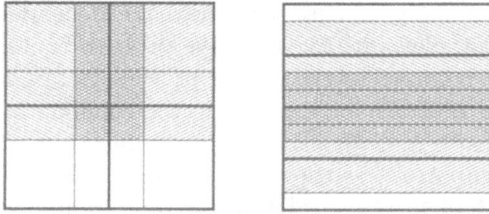

FIGURE 4.4. Impact of halo thickness to data decomposition strategy.

In Figure 4.5 the task farming and decomposition strategy is shown, as implemented in SfS. The manager–sometimes also called the master–reads in the images and performs all necessary work for optimal distribution. After processing by the workers, the manager is responsible for combining the subimages it receives. This is especially difficult in SfS and requires some interpolation and slope alignment computations. As long as the farmer does not get overloaded by either this postprocessing work or the scheduling itself, there is no need to add an extra processor for this job. However, the farmer remains the bottleneck in both, file I/O and communication to the workers. In our experiments, the "task farm" method showed some advantages. The simple communication structure and the well-defined tasks each processor has to perform led to an easy implementation.

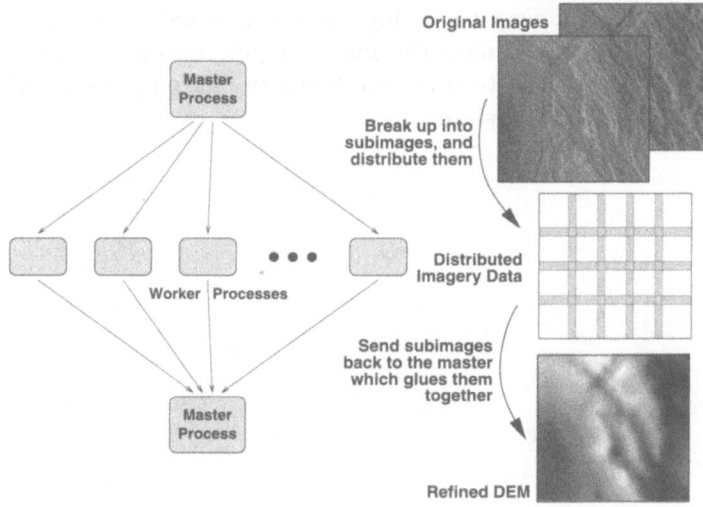

FIGURE 4.5. Data decomposition and distribution.

4.3.2 *Dynamic Load Balancing and Communication Overloading*

If the workers perform tasks unequal in length or if not all workers are equally fast, the tasks cannot be distributed using a static load balancing scheme, which creates a schedule prior to the processing of the subimages. Instead, we used a simple paradigm for dynamic load balancing. The farmer prepares the next outgoing messages while the workers process the data received previously. When a worker sends back its result, this is a request for new work, and the farmer sends the next patch to this worker. At the beginning, or if some workers request new tasks at nearly the same time, they are served in a round-robin fashion. We found task farms well suited to implement dynamic load balancing. An animation illustrating the manager/worker principle in combination with data decomposition can be found on the CD-ROM.

However, this simple way of dynamic load balancing suffers from three problems. First, the tasks are not sorted in order of their expected execution time. Thus, it is possible that the last task submitted is the largest one, leading to the second problem: All workers must wait for completion of each other, and the remaining work cannot be redistributed. These two problems are not really hazardous if there are many more patches than workers in the pool and if the amount of work per task is about the same. While the first restriction can be met only if processing large data sets, the second one is fulfilled implicitly by the SfS algorithm and the distribution policy. Running Xmatch, both restrictions are more difficult to meet. However, we did not put more effort in this direction because the performance results revealed more severe problems with data I/O.

Thirdly, if many workers request tasks concurrently, the farmer is overloaded for a moment. In this case, the workers are served in a round-robin fashion, and some workers are forced to wait until the farmer has time. It is likely that during this time other workers request new tasks, leading to a virtual synchronization of the workers. This problem also occurs at the very beginning. Assuming equally sized tasks, this problem cannot be solved in time, because the manager gets overloaded periodically. These circumstances sometimes lead to dramatic losses in efficiency, especially if processors are interconnected via a bus system.

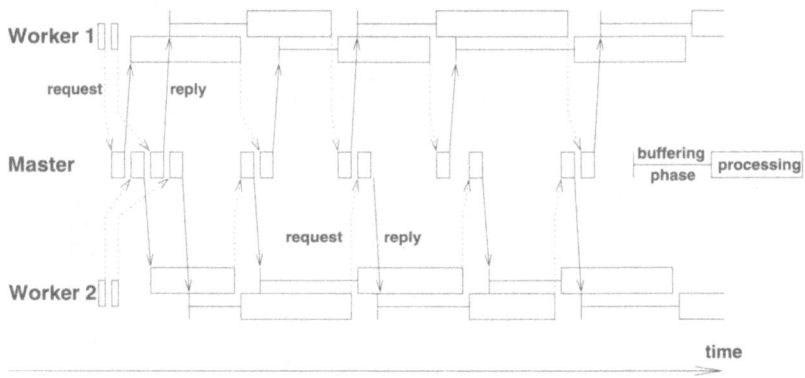

FIGURE 4.6. Double buffering.

To solve this problem, the dynamic load balancing has been extended with a feature called "double buffering" or "buffered task farming" [Edi96]. In Figure 4.6 a farmer is shown with only two workers for simplicity. Initially, every worker requests two pieces of work–one to process immediately and one to process later. This overloads the manager heavily at first, but the workers do not care because they already have tasks to compute. Workers can start their next task immediately after they have finished their former one, and they can request a new task in advance. Provided the master is not overloaded, this method theoretically reduces the idle time of workers to zero. Results show that this is also true in practice, as discussed in Section 4.3.3.

4.3.3 Performance Assessment

Testing two algorithms on several architectures and with different implementations produced a lot of performance figures. Here, we want to emphasize four key elements:

1. CPU use;

2. I/O performance;

3. impact of load balancing; and

4. optimal number of processors.

We found that network bandwidth and latency is of minor interest to our problems. Due to our coarse-grained parallelization approach, this is fairly obvious. The message passing library chosen or other implementation details only affect the time to develop the code and not the performance of the code itself in a measurable manner.

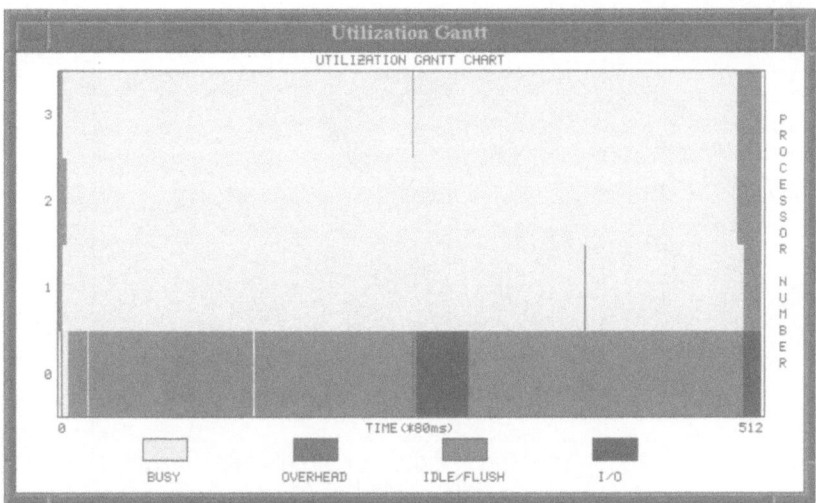

FIGURE 4.7. Gantt chart: CPU Use

Figure 4.7 shows the CPU use during the whole run time of SfS on the Paragon machine. All three workers (numbered 1 to 3) are busy, except at the very beginning and at the end. This points out a good communication policy. We found that double buffering is necessary to obtain such a smooth transition from one task to the next, especially if more than about 16 processors are involved. The rather constant times where only the farmer is working can be seen as the sequential part of the algorithm. Especially on larger data sets, these portions are very small relative to the overall time the workers need for their tasks. Additionally, the farmer (node 0) is idle most of the time. This shows that the farmer can handle many more workers, which consequently guarantees excellent scalability. However, serving three workers already requires the farmer to do extensive data I/O. The black bar in Figure 4.7 denoting this I/O activity is about 10% of the total execution time. Because on the Paragon, I/O and computation can be overlapped, and because reading and writing larger data blocks is faster, we did not experience any I/O bottlenecks even if all processors were used. However, the images were located on a special hard disk which was part of the Paragon machine.

There are two widely used figures to illustrate computers performance: speedup (S) and efficiency (ε), related to each other as $\varepsilon = \frac{S(n)}{n}$. Usually, efficiencies above 50% are considered to represent good performance. In Figure 4.8 the speedup is given for SfS on all architectures. The size of the image is 1000×1000 pixels which results in 121 patches. Sequential execution time is 1421.8s on an SGI Indy, 801.63s on one node of Paragon and 605s on one node of the Meiko CS-2. This image size is common for test images, because it is easy to handle and execution times are rather small; however, real images are $8k \times 7k$ pixels. Load balancing artifacts due to the coarse-grain parallelization–as can be clearly seen with more than 25 processors, especially on Paragon—will therefore not occur in real applications.

The performance of **Xmatch** on the Cray T3D is shown in Figure 4.9. Both speedup and efficiency are given, but neither plot clearly shows the "best" operating point.

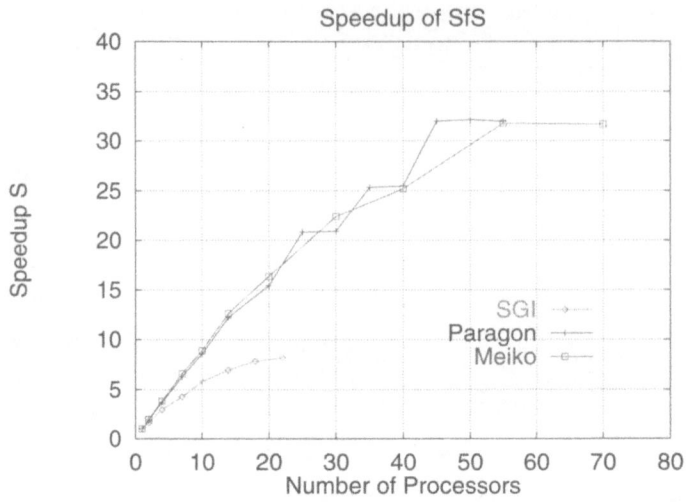

FIGURE 4.8. SfS performance on SGI cluster, Paragon, and Meiko

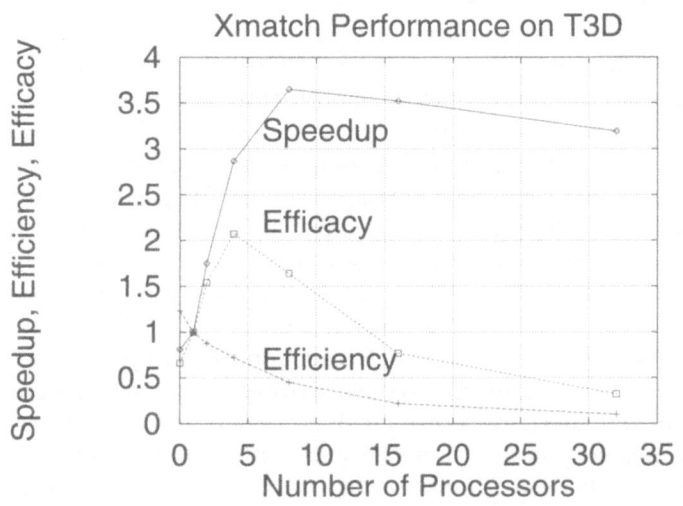

FIGURE 4.9. Xmatch performance: Speedup, efficiency, and efficacy

Taking the maximum, ε would imply not parallelizing at all, and S would allow far too many processors.

Several cost-benefit analyses $\eta = \frac{Benefit\ B}{Cost\ C}$ can be performed to find the best number of processes. A commonly applied technique is to ask for maximum speedup under the constraint of effectiveness, or $B \sim S$ and $C \sim \frac{1}{\varepsilon}$. η then is called efficacy [GST91] and is also plotted in Figure 4.9.

$$\eta = \frac{B}{C} \sim \frac{S}{\frac{1}{\varepsilon}} = S \cdot \varepsilon = \frac{S^2}{n}. \tag{4.1}$$

To get an impression of scalability, we measured execution time, varying the number of processors, and doubling the problem size whenever the number of processors was doubled. Consequently, one processor always performs the same amount of work. Such an analysis bypasses the load balancing problem and inefficiencies caused by the parallelization method and instead shows bottlenecks in the system. This measurement also was performed with Xmatch on the Cray T3D.

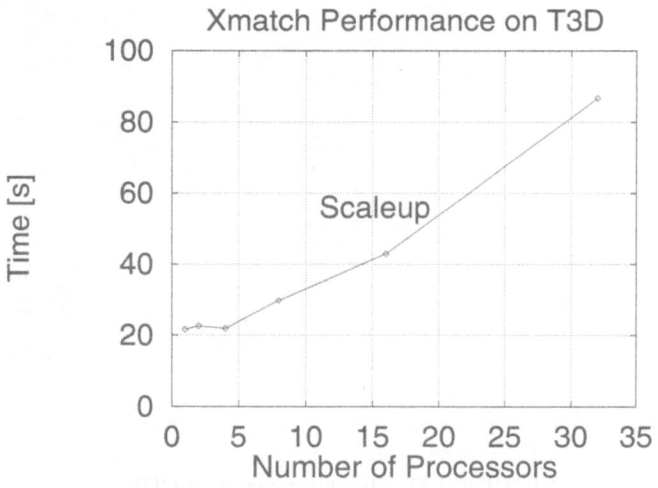

FIGURE 4.10. Xmatch performance: Scaleup

Ideally, the graph is a straight horizontal line. However, in Figure 4.10 this only holds for fewer than four processors, after which execution time scales linearly with the problem size. We found that disk I/O bandwidth was the bottleneck. Note that this observation correlates with the peak of the efficacy η. All files were stored on a single disk, and this disk was connected to the T3D by an ordinary Ethernet 10 Mbit/s line. So far we have not been able put data onto a faster disk. Moreover, even on faster disks the bottleneck would still be disk I/O, but it would become apparent when using a larger number of nodes.

4.4   Distributed Processing

The computation of data products often requires several execution steps. Additionally, the data being handled may be large and therefore both network bandwidth and machine performance influence the overall execution time. Therefore we developed *CDIP* (Concurrent Distributed Image Processing), a system that incorporates high-performance execution hardware, large data storage, and platform-independent clients.

Figure 4.11 illustrates the basic building blocks of CDIP. The three major parts, the front end, the back end, and the broker, with tight connection to the method base are interconnected by an Internet-based network. The central part of CDIP is the broker, which interacts with all other entities and ensures that the network appears transparent to the user. Note that only control connections are shown; data transfer takes place directly between entities.

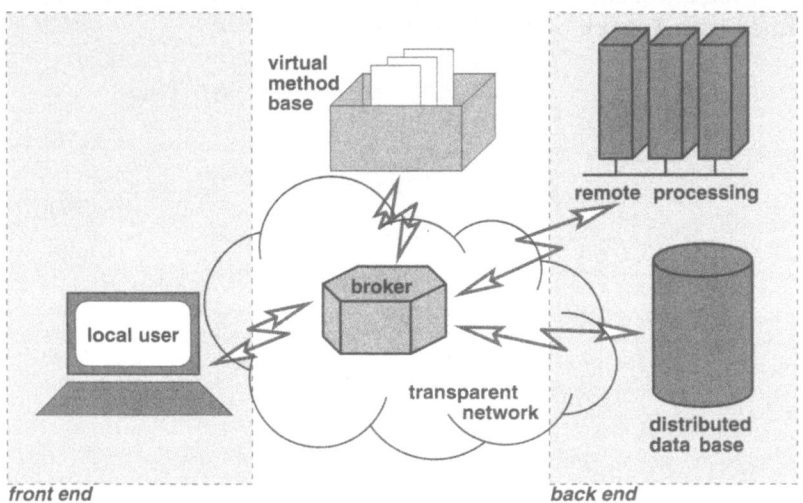

FIGURE 4.11. Overall concept of CDIP.

4.4.1   Front End

The *front end* can be of any kind. It can be a Java applet running within a web browser, a text-oriented command line user interface, or an application programming interface (API) in any language. Our major implementation of the front end is based only on common Internet services such as ftp, email, and http for communication, simple HTML pages for documentation and the help system, and scripts or Java applets for interactive parts. Data is transferred by ftp, either automatically, if a predefined method sequence is chosen, or by filling in an HTML form. Figure 4.12 shows parts of a Java-based graphical user interface (GUI).

4.4.2   Back End

The *back end* may be built of various hardware platforms. It is considered to be a loosely coupled conglomerate of computers of any size and power. The basic idea is to integrate all available computers so that error-prone porting of code is reduced to a

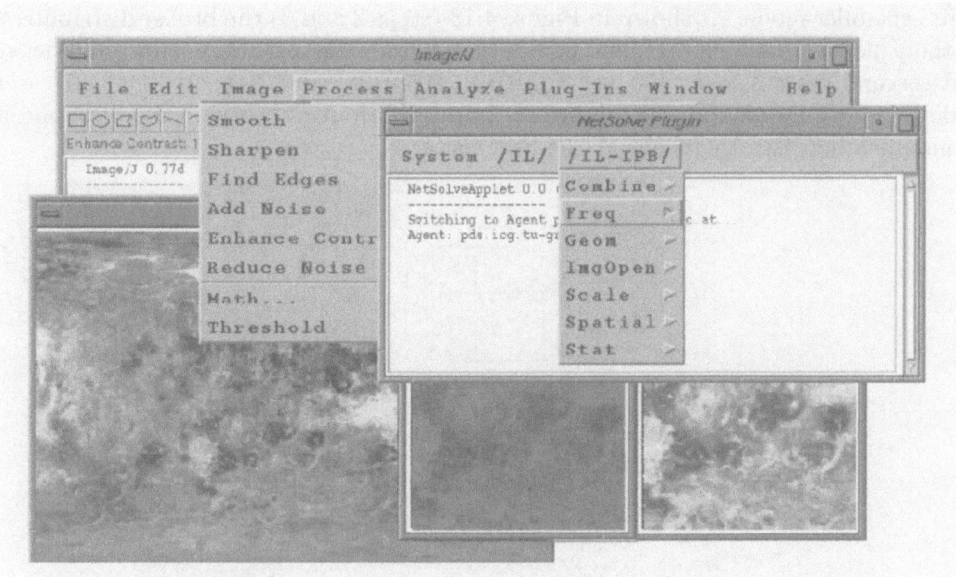

FIGURE 4.12. The Java front end of CDIP.

minimum and fault-tolerance is improved. The back end and its interaction with the broker are discussed more in depth in [NG98a].

Currently, a cluster of workstations, two SGI PowerChallenge shared-memory multiprocessor machines and a Meiko CS2-HA supercomputer are connected. To easily access all these systems, each of them is wrapped into one of the queuing systems DQS [DQS] or Condor [LLM88]; [LBRT97]. Both provide unified access, priority scheduling, and concurrent execution as well as many other features. However, DQS is better suited for high-performance computing as done on supercomputers, and Condor shows its strength on high-throughput computing. Condor also respects on-site interactive users, which makes it very valuable for our cluster of workstations.

4.4.3   Broker

The middle part, the *broker*, is the most critical and intelligent piece. It can range from a simple relational database to a complete decision support system, automatically suggesting the proper sequence of methods for obtaining the desired data product. Whenever a user starts to work with the system and hands in a description of input data and desired output format, the broker–in its agentlike action–collects available algorithms and execution parameters and suggests a few user-specific ways of processing the data. Note that it is not necessary to specify all the details and specific algorithms that are needed to reach the particular goal. We implement this functionality by querying a relational database, holding descriptions of both single methods and sequences of them [Bac98].

Once such a sequence is selected by the user, the broker comes into action again–now in its scheduler mode. As shown in Figure 4.13 (steps 2 and 3) the broker distributes the methods across available back-end computers, minimizing execution time, and network and servers' system load. We use CORBA [COR98] and NetSolve [CD97] as the underlying communications structure for both, distributing work to the back end and communicating with the client at the user's site.

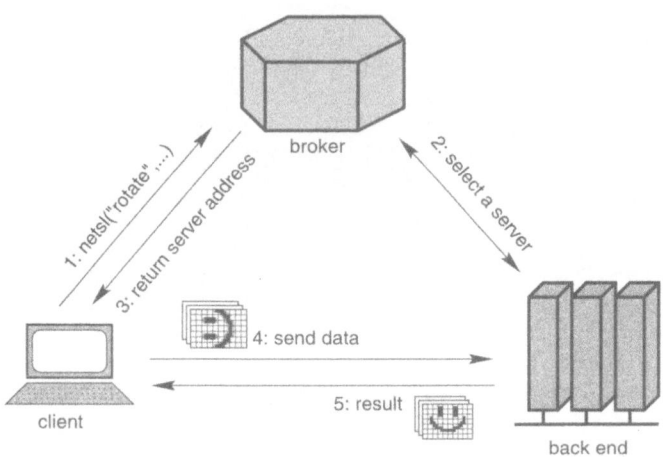

FIGURE 4.13. Example of distributed image processing using a broker: Remote execution of ImageVision via NetSolve.

We implemented two different brokers. They differ in the way they interact with the back end, the interfaces they support, and their own intelligence for scheduling users requests to the proper server. One broker, named DICE [Bac98]–Distributed Image-processing Computing Environment–is implemented on top of CORBA and integrates batchlike methods, currently started via the command line. Because the methods intended for this broker are typically noninteractive and long-lasting, the broker communicates with a queuing system at the backend. The user submits a request and typically does not wait until completion. Instead, a message (email) is sent when the job is finished.

The other broker, DIPS [Obe98]–Distributed Image Processing Shell–extends the functionality of NetSolve [CD97] while still using NetSolve's own agent. It is designed to be highly interactive and connects primarily to remote image processing libraries, for example, to SGI's ImageVision library, which does not run on any other platform. DIPS supports interfaces to C, C++, Matlab, and Java. The most user-centered Java interface was implemented as a plug-in to the Image/J image processing environment, itself exclusively written in Java. Users working with this applet can now transparently use local Image/J methods and functions from ImageVision, which are executed on a remote server. Figure 4.13 illustrates the principle way of working with NetSolve and ImageVision.

4.4.4 Experiences

While CDIP appears similar to the user in all cases, the actual processing depends on the size of the input data set. Raw SAR images are about 10 to 50 Mpixels in size. This amount of data can easily be handled on the CDIP back-end computers and transmitted between them, but so much data is hazardous for a single user's desktop computer and network connection. DICE gracefully handles such situations, keeping as much data as possible at the back end.

Regarding systems issues, CDIP exhibits the following properties:

- **Interoperability** is guaranteed by the Internet Inter-Operability Protocol (IIOP) [COR] which is defined within CORBA.

- **Queuing systems** successfully wrap different hardware platforms and thus provide unified access to a variety of back-end computers through only a few similar interfaces. They also take over basic scheduling tasks, assisting and simplifying the broker.

- Currently, there is no standard for representing method repositories. The interface to the currently implemented **method base** allows any upcoming standard to be easily incorporated.

- The broker only acts as **agent and scheduler** but is not involved in data traffic. Therefore, it primarily acts as a server for meta-information about system parameters. Several brokers can work together, each offering its services to all other brokers.

- Interaction is modular and generic via well-defined **interfaces**. Existing solutions (e.g., distinct parallelizations of SAR algorithms) could easily be integrated and updated, without modifying the structure of CDIP and without necessarily notifying the user.

- As it is based on common and public-domain software, development time was reduced to a minimum, resulting in **fast prototyping**.

Although some test users found it unusual to first specify the task locally and then wait until the remote computers had done their work, this execution model quickly became accepted. Working this way can even help to improve users performance, because jobs are submitted more carefully. DICE proved to work well for dedicated batch jobs and so-called "setup-then-execute" tasks, which are very common when repeatedly processing large similar data sets.

For interactive image processing, DIPS processed requests fast enough that the test-users reported overall good usability. Because images are smaller in this case, it is worth sending them across the network for specialized methods. When selecting method sequences, data traffic is further minimized. DIPS nicely handles very short tasks sending applets to the local machine to compute the images there.

5

Image Data Catalogs

Franz Niederl
Rainer Kalliany
Caterina Saraceno
Walter G. Kropatsch

One of the most significant developments in information technology of the last decade was–and still is–the transition from analog to digital images. On the one hand, any analog image can now be converted into digital form by inexpensive scanning devices, and on the other hand, the number of systems capturing images in digital form is growing considerably: Besides the new digital still and video cameras, in many disciplines (like medicine or material inspection) more and more sensors are generating digital image data. However, remote sensing has been a pioneering area in this development, starting to acquire digital earth observation data 25 years ago with NASA's Landsat satellite program [LMS97].

All those sensors generate a lot of data, which can only be handled because, fortunately, enormous improvements in digital storage capacity have taken place at the same time. Now disk capacities of several gigabytes are available on any desktop and storing even 700 MB of data on a highly portable CD-ROM is no effort at all.

Another innovation of great importance is the Internet. Among many other opportunities, it is a means for fast transfer of large amounts of (image) data to and from almost any computer on the globe.

However, the ability to generate and transmit a lot of image data easily is one issue, but finding the information actually needed is another. While information extraction from an image is an extremely wide field of research and development (which is covered by many other sections in this book), the appropriate organization of catalog and relevant access or query strategies is more specific.

In this chapter, two works on data catalogs are presented. Their contents and approaches address different demands:

- a network-based catalog for browsing a comprehensive distributed archive of remote sensing data and issuing customized requests for data from it; and

- a methodological approach toward automated indexing of and targeted retrieval from a database of portrait images.

In the first case, a huge amount of satellite data has to be administrated in an effective way. An interface is provided, where any remote user may select and order data online. Query criteria are the data's meta-information (e.g., sensor, date, price), location maps, and browse images.

The second task addresses the problem of searching for parameters related to image content, which are not yet defined in an explicit form. Besides solving the given problem of browsing an archive of portraits, such an approach is of fundamental importance and may also be applied to other collections of digital images.

For image data catalogues, all these issues are of great relevance: the structured organization and retrieval, according to existing and standardized parameters, and the approach of searching for certain categories of image content being defined on the fly. Both approaches, explained in the following sections, represent the state of the art in the respective fields.

5.1   Online Access to Remote Sensing Imagery

Online access to remote sensing images is a new service for the operational use of earth observation data sets. Until now many applications that need multitemporal or multisensoral data could hardly be carried out because of lack of information about existing remote sensing images. Other important obstacles are the high costs and the long time between taking an image and the delivery of the desired product. To get quick access to information and the data set we have to pay attention to the following items:

- organization of the data set in a data management system;

- information systems for searching, browsing, and ordering; and

- online product generation and delivery.

5.1.1   Remote Sensing Data Management

Characteristics of Remote Sensing Data

Management of remote sensing data is a special case of the more general problem of managing any visual information. The particular individual characteristics of remote sensing data require special techniques of data storage, query processing, and indexing [Wal96]:

- Image data are the predominant type of information, with single images up to several hundred megabytes in size. Images come in a multitude of formats, each of which has its own characteristics in terms of storage requirements and ease of access to subimages or single spectral bands.

- Metadata contain descriptive information on individual images, like spatial and temporal parameters, radiometric and geometric resolution, sensor characteristics, and data format. Browse products, i.e., thumbnail and quick look images derived from the original data make quick visual interpretation possible. Content information like texture, color, and histogram information is used to describe the image content in a way that allows the use of this information in searches for images by their content (see Section 5.2).

- Sensor-specific procedures play an important role in image processing and image analysis. By integrating this procedural information with the image database, value-added end products can be generated on demand.

The typically very large remote sensing images are managed in an archive, which may be distributed over several places. Because of its size the archive should exist only once, while multiple copies of the catalog may be operated at different locations. The catalog is the metadata database and because of the complexity and diversity of catalog data, it is not possible to manage it without the use of a database system. A detailed description of the procedures is collected in a virtual method base to support online product generation.

Storage Hierarchies

The sheer volume of remote sensing data still provides a challenge for today's system architects. Regardless of increasing disk capacities and decreasing costs of storage media, remote sensing archives are usually too large to be stored entirely on hard disk. Secondary storage devices like magnetic disks are generally used only for mid term storage of data that are likely to be accessed frequently. For long-term archiving of image data, tertiary storage devices like tapes, or CD-ROM are preferred. A variety of storage management methods exist to improve performance and storage use [Jai92]:

- Staging schemes providing automatic transfer of data between different storage media, guided by anticipated user access. An example would be a system that keeps only the latest data on magnetic disk, gradually moving images to tape or CD-ROM as they age.

- Memory caching schemes: Methods such as last recently used (LRU) may not be sufficient and need to be supplemented by strategies taking into account various levels of detail (image pyramids see Section 7.1) or spatial properties of the data. It might be useful to replace images deleted from a disk with a very high compressed (lossy) version of the same image (see Section 3.1). This would allow us to have fast access to browse images for visual inspection of the data before actually retrieving them from the (slow) tertiary storage. The high dimensionality of the data may also require a special caching mechanism that depends not only on syntactical context but also on the semantic context of the application.

- Clustering methods involve placing data that are likely to be accessed together in logically close places in storage. This is even more important for slower storage media like tapes.

To provide automatic access to these archives, robot systems may be used, which can manage different storage media and data formats. This presents a challenge for system integrators, because it requires combining a multitude of hardware and software components, commonly from different vendors, to set up an operational system.

5.1.2 *Image Data Information and Request System*

Information systems that facilitate access to remote sensing data through integration with geographic context information and spatial query processing capabilities are quickly becoming the norm. To provide online access for a world wide user community, many of these systems feature interfaces to the World Wide Web, ranging from simple fill-in forms to clickable multiscale image maps [EL98].

Due to their relatively static nature, traditional HTML-based Web interfaces are rather limited in functionality and suffer from long response times. With the advance of the Java computing platform [J. 96] and the ability to create executable content for the Web, it has become possible to create highly interactive graphical interfaces that provide easy access to remote sensing data catalogs in a platform-independent way.

For the design of an information system for remote sensing image data, the following aspects are considered most important:

- providing easy access to the data set for a wide range of users (professionals and the "casual Web surfer");

- avoiding long response times of conventional Web interfaces; and

- allowing spatial queries to be defined interactively, preferably in a graphical environment.

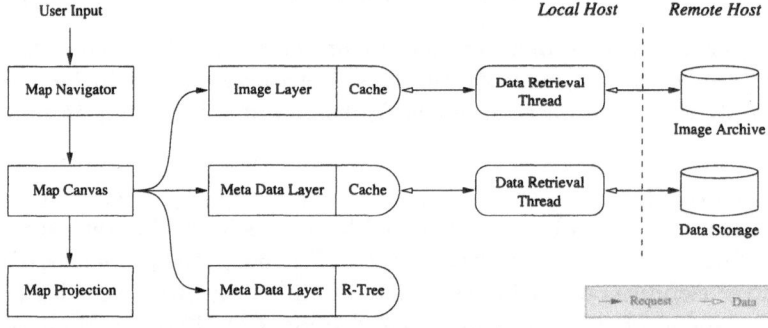

FIGURE 5.1. Framework architecture from [NKWB98].

Access to the image archive is provided through a highly interactive maplike user interface. The framework layered architecture, as depicted in Figure 5.1, makes it easy to selectively display and combine different kinds of data, like image footprints and surface features.

Any combination of several data sources, represented as **map layers**, may be visualized on top of each other. These include an **image layer**, displaying an image map generated from different data sources in the background, and several **metadata layers**, presenting coverage information (image footprints) and geographic context (surface features). Details of the presentation and the current view port of the **map canvas** are controlled by the choice of cartographic projection and navigational user input.

To avoid the performance penalties of traditional HTML-based systems, the framework makes intensive use of Java's multithreading capabilities. Any information that has to be retrieved from the server is loaded asynchronously, using multiple threads of control, and cached using spatial data structures. A specially adopted version of the R-tree [Gut84] is used for this purpose. Where feasible, data are held entirely in an R-tree in the client's main memory to keep access times at a minimum.

There are four basic components from which information systems are usually built. Only components 1 and 4 are necessary to create a fully operational system; parts of components 2 and 3 may be missing.

1. **Query definition and retrieval** of results is the basic function for the generation of queries to the underlying database. In WWW-based systems HTML forms are used for the definition of the query at the user's site and CGI scripts to implement the interface to a relational database.

2. **Map or navigation tool.** Queries for image coverage usually require the definition of a point (POI) or region of interest (ROI). A maplike representation of the area covered by a data set can ease this task considerably. With the possibility of moving around and zooming in and out, regions or points can be defined by point-and-click operations. To visualize the content of a database or the results of a query, one may also overlay the geographical information with outlines and information about any feature with a position or some spatial extent. This can be datalike images, data gaps, topographical features and names, orbit data, and many others.

3. **Preview of data.** To offer the user the possibility of inspecting the data before issuing a request for it, one may have quick looks or reduced versions of images available for downloading. This feature can also save network bandwidth, because it avoids the download of unnecessary data. Also, for copyright reasons, it is often not possible to provide full-resolution images before payment is guaranteed.

4. **Requesting data.** To issue a request, the user must be able to select the desired items from previously retrieved information. While the distribution of data until recently has been done the slow and traditional way of mailing a tape or CD-ROM, online delivery is now becoming feasible.

5.1.3   Online Product Generation and Delivery

Online product generation and delivery are new possibilities to speed up the processing chain between the taking of a scene and the usage of a derived product by the end user.

An important issue is network traffic. By using the Internet for delivering data sets, it is increased, but by introducing high-performance networks like ATM and reducing the data size by sending well-fitted and compressed products, it should not be a big problem in the future. Furthermore the data set can be delivered at any time of the day.

Although security, accounting, billing, and electronic commerce are closely related subjects to this section, we do not cover them here. For a comprehensive discussion of these key points see [NG98b].

Product Generation

Becauseraw data often do not meet user requirements, preprocessing of these data becomes a necessity. This requires either processing all possible data products in advance to provide them for short-term delivery or providing resources for on-demand computation of requested data products. Preprocessing all these data introduces high costs for computation and archiving a static set of standard products. On-demand processing of data products is more flexible and requires less storage space, but makes it difficult to cope with high server loads. A combined approach can be taken to inherit the advantages of preprocessing and on-demand computation, avoiding most of their drawbacks. It allows quick access to raw data and a basic set of pre-processed standard products. Caching is often used to minimize disk usage as well as the required computer power.

We extend the common information system by a broker and a distributed back end. The broker coordinates data retrieval and pre processing performed by the back end. Introducing a database holding the metadata and a virtual method base (a collection of image processing methods), the user can specify exactly which data should be processed in what particular way.

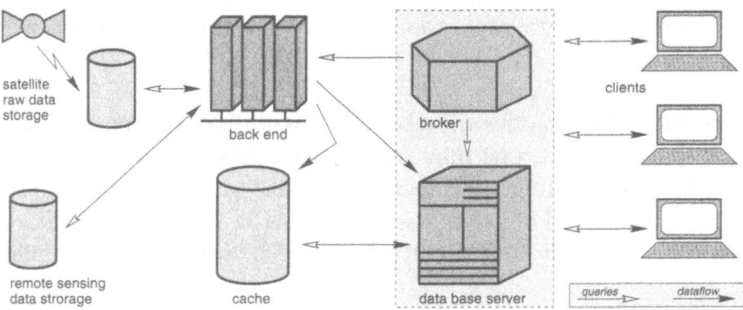

FIGURE 5.2. Combined approach: A broker manages back end servers for on-demand data production and a cache to store often used and intermediate results. From [WNG97].

In many cases, more than one method is needed to produce a tailored product. Many well-known image processing systems like Khoros [Inc98] or KB-Vision [AAI98] provide a tool to set up such a processing chain. Although this directed acyclic graph is quite valuable, this could only be done by a specialist. In contrast to these procedure-based systems we propose a data-driven approach. The key element is a data description platform, where the user can specify the input data and the desired results. According to these specifications, the processing sequence is derived from the virtual method base matching the users constraints. Without the need for in-depth knowledge of the system architecture by the user, a data flow chart will show if and how the required goal can be achieved with the software tools provided (see [NG98b])

The core image processing methods will not be implemented in Java. Some restrictions of Java make it impossible to process large images in an acceptable time. Therefore we decided to use platform-dependent fast image processing software like the Image Vision Library (SGI). We may also use existing noncommercial software and commercial software products, which are well designed and prepared for special tasks. It is obvious that the use of commercial software must be linked with the integration of accounting and billing.

It should also be possible for the user to upload any combination of modules to the computing server he needs for computing his data set. Such alliances of remote servlets, written in pure Java, are hardware independent and managed by the WWW server. To keep the whole system secure, these applications have to run in a secure environment, and their access to the file system has to be restricted.

Delivery Methods

Both online and offline delivery methods are needed. The online method serves for quick access to and availability of the images. Offline methods must be supported for cases of lack of security, bad network connections, and pretty large data sets (> 100 MB). The supported methods are [Nie98]:

- **FTP**, one of the oldest internet services, is a very robust and easy-to-handle method. The ordered data set is automatically transferred to a host specified by the user. The disadvantage is that user name and password can be encoded only with special FTP servers and FTP clients (i.e., [DFD98]).

- For the **WWW** we use a HyperWave server [Gmb98] to provide the images. The product is uploaded to the server with specified access rights so the user can download it via a WWW browser at any time. In this case the user name and password are also transferred as plain text.

- The state-of-the-art media for offline delivery is the **CD-ROM**. This method is used for very large data sets and if the two online methods are not possible for any reason. Delivery time and forwarding expenses are the drawbacks for the user.

The online access and delivery system we developed is demonstrating how WWW-based catalogs of remote sensing data may be organized in a flexible and efficient manner, tailored to system margins and individual user requirements. Links to our systems can be found on the CD-ROM.

5.2   Content-Based Image Database Indexing and Retrieval

Today, computer technology allows for large collections of electronically archived image data. As digital acquisition and storage grow, a number of industrial fields, such as medical imagery, graphic arts, textile and paint, satellite imagery, criminology, and film, *require efficient access to their data*. How can a specific image be efficiently retrieved from a very large database? Examining each single image is certainly not feasible. Traditional database systems store images together with keywords, file identifiers, or textual descriptions to enable their retrieval. However, it is difficult or impossible to fully capture real-world objects by words alone. Furthermore, adding verbal descriptions is time-consuming, error-prone, and not practical or impossible for large-scale image archives. Other approaches must be developed to allow for fast and efficient retrieval of information. Three major needs can be recognized when developing a system for retrieval of information [CJ96]:

- understand the content of the objects within the database;

- extract the information of interest; and

- browse the retrieved information to verify that it matches what is wanted.

If the content of the database objects is extracted, indexes can be created that describe, summarize or represent a subset of database objects with similar content. Such a strategy is called *content-based indexing*. Once indexes are created based on the content of the database objects, a content-based retrieval system can use the indexes to locate the desired information. When dealing with content-based indexing and retrieval, various mechanism for content extraction need to be combined. They must depend on the domain of application and the type of content considered relevant. The retrieval system can then use an interactive query process where the query can be redefined to adapt to the user need [WK98], by enabling content relevance feedback and user-guided navigation within the database.

As a first solution for content-based image database indexing and retrieval, image retrieval by image example has been proposed [ea95, PPS94, SC97], where a query image is given by the user on input. In general, queries based on content similarity to an example object/image in terms of color, texture, shape, etc., is known as Query-by-Example (QBE). When images are entered into the database, each image is segmented manually, semiautomatically, or automatically under human supervision to identify and depict interesting image objects, which are then stored in the database. From there, features of these outlined image objects are extracted and matched with those extracted from the query image.

Recent content-based still image indexing and retrieval systems include IBM's Query-by-Image Content (QBIC) [ea95], MIT's Photobook [PPS94] and WebSEEk from Columbia University [SC97].

QBIC performs a shape-based search using a number of shape features: area, circularity, eccentricity, major axis of inertia, and higher-order algebraic moment invariants. In QBIC, these shape features are combined into a feature vector, and shape similarity is measured by a weighted Euclidean distance metric. These features are sensitive to outliers, and the system is reliable only if the image contains few objects (mainly one object).

WebSEEk integrates texture, color, and shape information for image retrieval using Euclidean distance.

Photobook describes a content-based tool that uses finite element modes to match shapes from a digital database to an example. Later, Sclaroff and Pentland incorporated functions for similarity ranking of objects based on eigenspace decomposition (for more information on eigenspace decomposition, refer to Section 5.2.2). Here, the eigenmodes, computed from a finite element-based correspondence algorithm, are used to describe rigid and nonrigid deformations, so as to align one object with another. The extent of the deformation defines the measure of similarity between two objects. Recently Sclaroff presented a solution that avoids the comparison of query examples with all entries in the database by ordering the shapes of database objects in terms of nonrigid deformations [Scl97].

In the following section the motivations for using eigenspace decomposition to our portrait database are presented, with the main characteristics of the database itself.

5.2.1 The Miniature Portrait Database

The idea is to support art historians or nonexpert users by automatically structuring portrait databases and associating a set with descriptors to the data. This can be used not only to efficiently retrieve a specific portrait, but it can also be used to exploit correlation of specific features among portraits. This will help in defining or exploring similarities in the work of a certain painter or in distinguishing the painting styles of different artists.

Classical face recognition techniques look for facial features that comprise information that is relevant for discrimination of faces and at the same time are robust against different illumination conditions, viewpoint, facial expression, etc. Among the best known approaches for face recognition, big efforts have been devoted to Principal Component Analysis (PCA), considered one of the techniques that provides the best performance [PT91, PMS94]. Instead of explicitly modeling the facial features, they are extracted by PCA from a training set of representative images. In [PT91] the term "Eigenfaces" is used to denote the components of the feature space used for classification.

In the case of portrait miniatures, the artist paints by using his or her own perception of reality, making, therefore, the recognition process even more difficult. Furthermore, in a portrait a face can slightly change due to the style of the painter, whereas eyes remain mostly similar between different portraits of the same person. For this reason and to minimize the variation due to spurious factors such as partial occlusion, different periods, etc., instead of considering whole faces, we are using eigen-eyes. A view-based representation that takes into account different eye poses and pupil positions allows for a more accurate description of our data. The detection of eyes in an image, together with the orientation of each eye, gives immediately the number and location of faces within an image.

These features can then be used to hierarchically organize the database to allow for fast and efficient retrieval, as explained in the following section.

The Hierarchical Database Structure

In order to generate indices that can be used to access an image database, a description of each image is necessary. The key point is to establish a hierarchical data structure

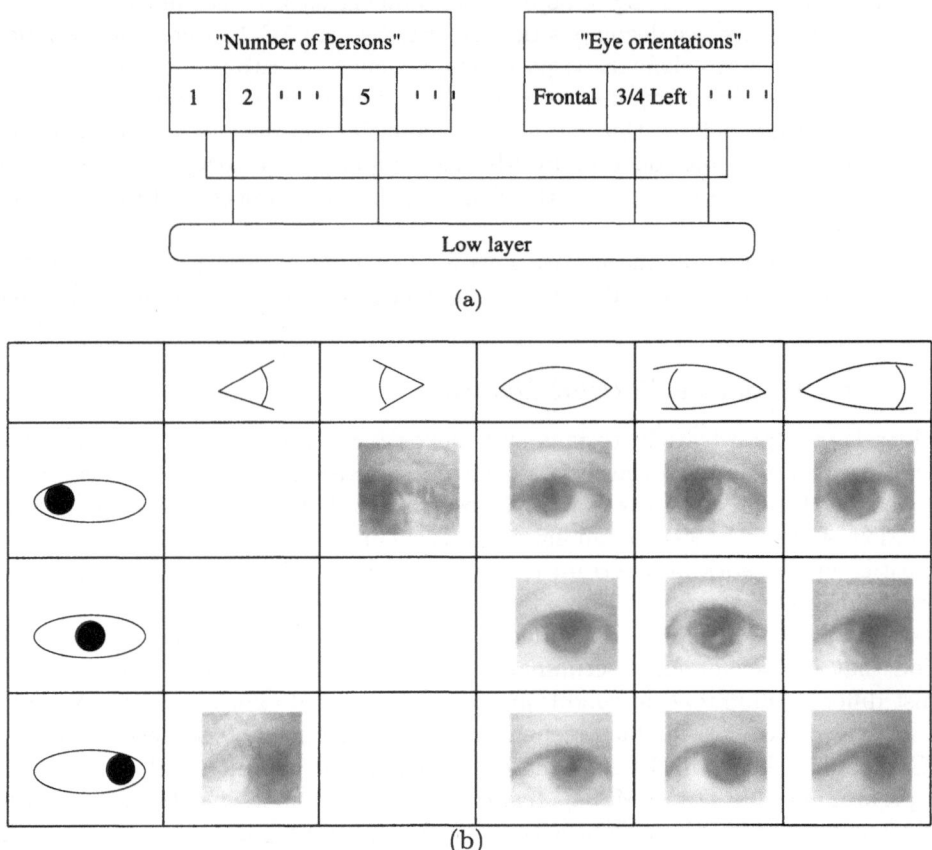

(a)

(b)

FIGURE 5.3. (a) High Layer, (b) low Layer.

(a relational or transition graph) that allows us to handle different levels of abstraction of the visual data. A hierarchical organization of portrait material can, at a low level, characterize the image using low-level features such as color histograms, shape, eigenrepresentation, etc. For each exploited feature, nodes can be created to group images with similar feature values, such as same eye orientation or shape. At a higher level, the images can be characterized based on content-based analysis. Information such as presence of faces, number of faces represented in the image, their location and orientation, etc. can all be stored at this level of abstraction. At this level, nodes are created considering combinations of low- or high-level features. For example, a node can represent a group of images having similar frontal eyes (see Figure 5.3.a).

Then links between nodes can describe the relation between nodes and therefore between features. Additional descriptors may be incorporated to further enable a characterization of the information.

This approach allows us to organize the miniportrait images for subsequent analysis, classification, or indexing task. In the example given in Figure 5.3, the database can

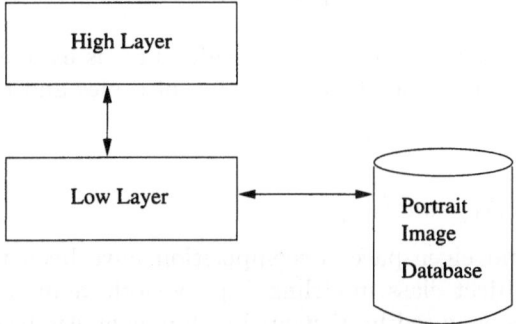

FIGURE 5.4. Connections between layers.

be accessed by requesting the portrait of a specific person. Starting with the retrieved portrait, other portraits having, for example, similar eye orientation can be retrieved.

In the following section, the strategy we have used to structure the database is presented.

The advantage of such a representation is, of course, to have faster access to specific information, allowing for an efficient navigation through the visual data. Operations such as coding or retrieval from specialized queries may all benefit from this type of representation.

Miniature Portrait Database Structure

In order to structure the database, we propose creating two main layers: high and low. In the high layer, nodes are automatically detected using content-based feature analysis, whereas in the low layer, nodes contain low-level features. Possible connections between layers are shown in Figure 5.4.

In the high layer of the hierarchy two types of nodes have been created: nodes that group portraits with the same number of painted faces, and nodes that group portraits with the same eye orientation. Other types of nodes can also be created, if other features are considered. For each of the two classes, a table is created containing a description of the features and nodes representing specific features of that class (as shown in Figure 5.3.(a)).

The table that groups portraits with the same number of faces is identified using eigen-features (see Section 5.2.2). Links connect each node to the corresponding features of the low layer.

Eigenfeatures are also used to group eyes with the same orientation (see Section 5.2.2). Each node of the table "Eye orientation" is connected to low-level feature nodes.

At the low level of the hierarchy, there is a table listing all exploited features. This table can also be used whenever a query on low-level features is proposed to the system. This table contains links to all nodes belonging to this level.

Such a structure can help art historians and nonexpert users exploit similarities *between painters, periods, and painted faces.* For example, the structure can be used to determine painters who prefer to paint frontal eyes or to identify faces with similar eye orientations.

In the following section the role of the eigenfeatures is explained, together with the algorithm that allows for automatically creation of tables and nodes of the two layers of the hierarchy.

5.2.2   The Eigen Approach

Subspace methods and eigenspace decomposition have been used widely for object representation and object class modeling (e.g., generic human face [PT91, MP97]). Essentially a model is acquired by Principal Component Analysis (PCA) [Fuk90] of a set of example images (templates). The PCA allows us to extract the low-dimensional subspaces that capture the main linear correlations among the high-dimensional image data.

In painted portraits, eyes are the most important features for recognizing the depicted person as well as the period and artist of the miniature. In the case of portrait miniatures, after sketching the contour of the face on ivory, in the first step the artist tries to visualize the characteristic personality of the painted person by completely elaborating the eyes.

Eigenspace Decomposition

Given a training set $T_x = \{\mathbf{x}_1, \ldots, \mathbf{x}_M\}$ of N_T image vectors of N^2 dimensionality the eigenvectors $\Phi = \{\mathbf{e}_1, \mathbf{e}_2, \ldots \mathbf{e}_{N_T}\}$ and eigenvalues λ_i of the covariance matrix Σ can be obtained by eigendecomposition (or singular value decomposition). Because usually $N_T << N^2$, Σ is a singular matrix of rank at most $N_T - 1$. The Karhunen-Loeve transform (KLT) $\mathbf{y}$ of a mean normalized image vector $\tilde{\mathbf{x}} = \mathbf{x} - \mu(T_x)$ is defined by

$$\mathbf{y} = \Phi^t \tilde{\mathbf{x}}. \tag{5.1}$$

The original image $\mathbf{x}$ can be obtained using the KL basis Φ by

$$\mathbf{x} = \Phi \mathbf{y} + \mu(T_x) = \sum_{i=1}^{N_T - 1} \mathbf{e}_i y_i + \mu(T_x). \tag{5.2}$$

In PCA the KLT representation $\mathbf{y}$ is truncated approximating $\mathbf{x}$ using only the eigenvectors corresponding to the k highest eigenvalues (the first k eigenvectors):

$$\mathbf{x} = \sum_{i=1}^{k} \mathbf{e}_i y_i + \mu(T_x). \tag{5.3}$$

The KLT is optimal in the sense that the mean square error between the truncated representation and the actual data is minimized. The number of principal components needed to represent $\mathbf{x}$ to a sufficient degree of accuracy depends on the correlation among the images in T_x. We use a fast pattern matching algorithm that uses multiple view-based eigenspaces and Fourier transform [UK97], which allows a fast calculation of the eigenprojections **y** and the normalized correlation

$$C(x_i, x_e) = \frac{x_i x_e}{\|x_i\|} \tag{5.4}$$

between a part of the image x_i and its projection x_e onto the particular eigenspace.

We normalize geometrically by scaling and rotating the images according to two feature points (eye corners). Moreover, data have to be categorized in a way that unimportant factors, which might influence the representation, are eliminated. This can be done using a view-based eigenspace ([PMS94]), where PCA is performed on every subset of images according to certain categories such as left/middle/right pupil and left/right/frontal view. The view-based approach allows a more accurate description of the set of images by multiple independent subspaces.

The images in our database do not have many variations in face orientation. About 90% of them have "three-quarter view," from either the left or right side. A characteristic of these miniatures is that the view of the eyes does not necessarily coincide with the view of the face. As an example, three-quarter faces can also have frontal eyes. This characteristic must be considered whenever an algorithm for face recognition is applied to painted faces.

In our case the eigeneyes are sensitive to different positions of the pupil, different orientations of the eye, and different shading. For this reason, the images have been categorized manually according to these factors, and an eigenspace for each category has been calculated. In particular, we consider three different pupil positions (left, center, and right) and five different eye orientations (left profile, right profile, three-quarter right, three-quarter left, and frontal) for a total amount of eleven different eigenspaces, as shown in Figure 5.3(c). (In the case of profile eyes, only one pupil position is considered.)

In order to index the portrait miniatures according to eye orientation and number of faces per picture, an eigenspace for each of the eleven aforementioned classes must be determined. The eigenspaces will be used to detect the eyes and their orientation, as explained in the following section.

Portrait Miniature Indexing Using Eigeneyes

At this point, all images of the database are analyzed using all eigenspaces. Different resolution and rotation of the testing images are considered by rotating the input image from −30 to 30 degrees in 10-degree steps and scaling with five scaling factors in 10% steps. At each position of the image, the maximum of the normalized correlation between the subimage at this position and its projection on the different eigenspaces is put in a canonical correlation map. Eye locations, poses, rotation angle, and scale can be obtained by thresholding the correlation map.

The images can then be grouped according to eye orientations, i.e., frontal, three-quarter left, three-quarter right, profile left, and profile right. One image will be in more than one group if different eye orientations are detected within the image.

Each group of eyes can be indexed using the eigenvectors. In particular, frontal and three-quarter eyes are represented by the eigenvectors of the three eigenspaces (one for each pupil position), whereas the profile eyes, having only one possible pupil position, are represented by the eigenvectors belonging to one eigenspace. Eigeneyes can also allow us to determine the number of faces within a portrait. The technique to determine the number of faces analyzes the number of detected eyes and their orientations.

One face is detected if one of the following cases occurs:

1. only one eye is detected;

2. two eyes are detected, which can be frontal or three-quarter

In a more general case, N faces are detected if the following case occurs: A are profile eyes and $B \times 2$ are three-quarter and/or frontal eyes, where $A + B = N$ and $A, B \geq 0$. In fact, for profile faces only a profile eye is visible, whereas three-quarter or frontal faces can have either two frontal eyes, or two three-quarter eyes or one frontal eye and one three-quarter eye. In the following section, results of the eye detection and indexing are presented.

5.2.3 Experiments

Five-hundred-eightty-six portrait miniatures have been tested. Most of them have three-quarter faces with frontal eyes. The eye orientations have been classified by art historian experts. Only eighteen miniatures have more than one painted face.

As an example, Figure 5.5 shows a typical input image, the resulting correlation values, the correlation map, and the resulting eye locations.

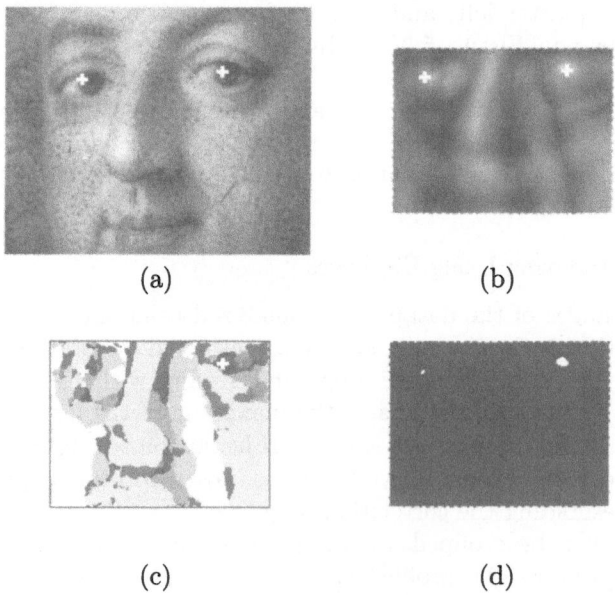

(a)   (b)

(c)   (d)

FIGURE 5.5. (a) Input image, (b) correlation values, (c) indices of eye classes, (d) thresholded correlation values.

TABLE 5.1. Eye Detection Results.

	Number of eyes	Correctly detected	Wrongly detected
Frontal	822	814	42
Three-quarter right	130	94	9
Three-quarter left	166	160	4
Profile right	15	12	0
Profile left	16	14	0

In Table 5.1, the results of detection are presented. Most of the frontal eyes were correctly detected. Only eight of them were detected as three-quarter left or right eyes. Forty-two three-quarter eyes were detected as frontal. Three right-profile eyes were detected as three-quarter right, whereas two left-profile eyes were detected as three-quarter left eyes. However these errors did not have drastic consequences during the indexing procedure. In fact, the number of faces within a portrait does not change if, for example, a three-quarter eye is detected as a frontal eye.

In this section, a hierarchical structure for organizing miniature portrait databases has been presented. Three main layers have been defined. In the high layer, classifications performed by art historian experts are stored. In the middle layer, a content-based analysis of the images is used to index the database. This is performed by using a combination of low-level features (stored in the low layer). Furthermore, an algorithm for indexing art-historical portrait miniatures using Principal Component Analysis (PCA) has been proposed. Eleven different eigenspaces have been created, based on eye orientation and pupil position. These eigenspaces are then used to detect eyes in portrait miniatures. The eigenspaces also allow for determining the orientation of eyes. This information has been used in the middle layer of the hierarchy for automatic content extraction (such as presence and number of faces and their locations).

References

[AAI98]   Amerinex Applied Imaging AAI. The kbvision system. http://www.aai.com/AAI/KBV/KBV.html, 1998.

[Bac98]   D. Bachmann. A distributed image processing back-end. Master's thesis, Computer Graphics and Vision (ICG), Graz University of Technology, Austria, Spring 1998.

[CD97]   H. Casanova and J. Dongarra. Netsolve: A network server for solving computational science problems. *International Journal of Supercomputer Applications and High Performance Computing*, 11(3):212–223, Fall 1997.

[CJ96]   S.K. Chang and E. Jungert. *Symbolic Projection for Image Information Retrieval and Spatial Reasoning*. Academic Press, 1996.

[CM91]   J.C. Curlander and R.N. McDonough. *Synthetic Aperture Radar: Systems and Signal Processing*. Wiley Interscience, 1991.

[CM92]   J.C. Curlander and K.E. Maurice. *Magellan Stereo Toolkit User Manual*. Vexcel Corporation, Boulder, CO, v1.2.6 edition, 1992.

[COR]   Object Management Group (OMG) corba/iiop 2.2 specification. Web page at: `http://www.omg.org/corba/corbiiop.htm`.

[COR98]   Object Management Group (OMG) CORBA 2.0 specifications. Web page at: `http://www.acl.lanl.gov/CORBA/#DOCS`, 1998.

[DFD98]   Differential-filedrive. http://www.filedrive.com/filedrive.html, 1998.

[DQS]   Distributed queuing system. Home page of DQS: `http://www.scri.fsu.edu/~pasko/dqs/dqs.html`.

[ea95]   M. Flickner et al. "Query by image and video content: The QBIC system." *IEEE Comput.*, 28:23–31, 1995.

[Edi96]   Edinburgh Parallel Computing Centre (EPCC), The University of Edinburgh, Scotland. *Course Notes of the Edinburgh Parallel Computing Centre*, 1996.

[EL98]   E. Eliason and S.K. LaVoie. Planetary image atlas. `http://www-pdsimage.jpl.nasa.gov/PDS/public/Atlas` 1998.

[FC89]   R.T. Frankot and R. Chellappa. *A Method for Enforcing Integrability in Shape-from-Shading Algorithms*, 89–122. MIT Press, Cambridge, 1989.

[FHS94]   R.T. Frankot, S. Hensley, and S. Shaffer. Noise resistant estimation techniques for SAR image registration and stereo matching. In *International Geoscience and Remote Sensing Symposium (IGARSS)*, 625–627, Pasadena, CA, 1994. IEEE.

[FJL+88]   G. Fox, M. Johnson, G. Lyzenga, S. Otto, J. Salmon, and D. Walker. *Solving Problems on Concurrent Processors, Vol.1 – General Techniques and Regular Problems*. Prentice-Hall International, London, 1988.

[Fra90]   R.T. Frankot. Registration accuracy for noisy images. In *International Geoscience and Remote Sensing Symposium (IGARSS)*, 1151–53, Maryland, 1990. IEEE.

[Fuk90]   K. Fukunaga. Statistical Pattern Recognition. Computer Science and Scientific Computing. Academic Press, Inc., 2nd edition, 1990.

[GJP+96]   M. Gelautz, G. Jakob, G. Paar, S. Hensley, and F.W. Leberl. Automated matching experiments with different kinds of SAR imagery. In *International Geoscience and Remote Sensing Symposium (IGARSS)*, 31–33, Lincoln, NE, 1996. IEEE.

[Gmb98]   Hyperwave GmbH. Hyperwave information server. http://www.hyperwave.de, 1998.

[Gol96]   A. Goller. Concurrent radar image shape-from-shading on high-performance computers. In *13th International Conference on Pattern Recognition (ICPR)*, volume 4/D, 589–593, Vienna, Austria, August 1996.

[GST91]   D. Goshal, G. Serazzi, and S.K. Tripathi. The processor working set and its use in scheduling multiprocessor systems. *IEEE Transactions on Software Engineering*, 17(5):443–453, May 1991.

[Gut84]   A. Guttman. R-trees: A dynamic index structure for spatial searching. In *Proceedings of ACM SIGMOD Converence on Management of Data*, 47–57. University of California, Berkley, 1984.

[HB89]   B. Horn and M. Brooks, editors. *Shape-from-Shading*. MIT Press, Cambridge, MA, 1989.

[HS94]   S. Hensley and S. Shaffer. Automatic DEM generation using Magellan stereo data. In *International Geoscience and Remote Sensing Symposium (IGARSS)*, 1470–72, Pasadena, CA, 1994. IEEE.

[Inc98]   Khoral Research Inc. Khoros with gui cantata, 1998.

[J. 96]   J. Goslig et al. *Java Programming Language*. SunSoft Press, 1996.

[Jai92]   R. Jain. Workshop report: NFS workshop on visual information management systems. In *Proceedings of the SPIE*, Vol. 1662, 198–218, 1992.

[Kra88]   K. Kraus. *Fernerkundung, Band 1*. Dümmler Verlag, Bonn, 1988.

[Kra96]   H.J. Kramer. *Observation of the Earth and Its Environment. Survey of Missions and Sensors*. Springer-Verlag, 1996.

[LBRT97]   M. Livny, J. Basney, R. Raman, and T. Tannenbaum. Mechanisms for high throughput computing. *Speedup*, 11(1), 1997.

[LLM88]   M. Litzkowand, M. Livny, and M.W. Mutka. Condor–A hunter of idle workstations. In *Eighth International Conference of Distributed Computing Systems*, 104–111, June 1988.

[LMS97]   D. Lauer, S. Morain, and V. Salomonson. The LANDSAT program: Its origin, evolution and impacts. *Photogrammetric Engineering & Remote Sensing*, 63(7):831–838, 1997.

[LTM92]   F.W. Leberl, J.K. Thomas, and K.E. Maurice. Initial results from the Magellan stereo-experiment. *Journal of Geophysical Research*, 97(E8):13675–87, 1992.

[MP97]   B. Moghaddam and A. Pentland. Probabilistic visual learning for object representation. *IEEE Trans. PAMI*, 19(7):696, 1997.

[MPI94]   MPI. Message passing interface forum. MPI: A message-passing interface standard. *International Journal of Supercomputer Applications*, 8(3–4), 1994.

[MR95]   J.H. Merlin and J.S. Reeve. IDA–An aid to the parallelisation of fortran codes. Technical report, Department of Electronics and Computer Science University of Southampton, 1995.

[NG98a]   F. Niederl and A. Goller. Method execution on a distributed image processing back-end. In *sixth Euromicro Workshop on Parallel and Distributed Processing (PDP)*, 243–249, Madrid, Spain, January 1998.

[NG98b]   F. Niederl and A. Goller. Method execution on a distributed image processing back-end. In *Parallel and Distributed Processing, Madrid, Spain*, 1998.

[Nie98]   F. Niederl. Online order and delivery system for remote sensing datasets. In *Proceedings of the Earth Observation & Geo-Spatial Web and Internet Workshop*, Salzburg, Austria, 1998.

[NKWB98]   F. Niederl, T. Kemmer, W. Walcher, and R. Bolter. Diva–Digital interactive venus atlas. In *Proceedings of IGARSS98, IEEE Proceedings 98CH36174*, Seattle, WA, 1998.

[Obe98]   M. Oberhuber. Distributed high-performance image processing on the internet. Master's thesis, Computer Graphics and Vision (ICG), Graz University of Technology, Austria, Summer 1998.

[PMS94]   A. Pentland, B. Moghaddam, and T. Straner. View-based and modular eigenspaces for face recognition. *Proceedings of the Conference on Computer Vision and Pattern Recognition*, 1994.

[PPS94]   A. Pentland, R.W. Picard, and S. Scaroff. Photobook: Tools for content-based manipulation of image databases. *Proc. of Storage and Retrieval for Image and Video Databases II*, SPIE-2185:34–47, 1994.

[PT91]   A. Pentland and M. Turk. Eigenfaces for recognition. *Journal of Cognitive Neuroscience*, 4:71–86, 1991.

[SC97]   J.R. Smith and S.F. Chang. Visually Searching the Web for Content. *IEEE Multimedia*, 4:12–20, 1997.

[Sch93]   G. Schreier. *SAR Geocoding: Data and Systems*. Wichmann Verlag, Karlsruhe, 1993.

[Scl97]   S. Sclaroff. Deformable prototypes for encoding shape categories in image databases. *Pattern Recognition*, 30:627–641, 1997.

[TKL91]   J.K. Thomas, W. Kober, and F.W. Leberl. Multiple image SAR shape-from-shading. *Photogrammetric Engineering and Remote Sensing (PE&RS)*, 57(1):51–59, January 1991.

[UK97]   M. Uenohara and T. Kanade. Use of Fourier and Karhunen-Loeve decomposition for fast pattern matching with a large set of templates. *IEEE Trans. on Pattern Analysis and Machine Intelligence*, 19:891–897, 1997.

[Wal96]   W. Walcher. *Design Aspects of Information Systems for Remote Sensing Image Data*. Ph.D. thesis, Graz University of Technology, 1996.

[WK98]   X. Wan and C.C. Jay Kuo. An interactive approach to image retrieval using multiple seed images. *Proc. of the International Conference on Image Processing*, II, October 1998.

[WNG97]   W. Walcher, F. Niederl, and A. Goller. A WWW-based distributed satellite data processing system. In *Joint Workshop of ISPRS WGI/2 WGII/3*, Boulder, CO, 1997.

Part III

Robust and Adaptive Image Understanding

Introduction to Part III

The human visual system as a functional unit including the eyes, the nervous system, and the corresponding parts of the brain, certainly ranks among the most important means of human information processing. Typical vision tasks that humans perform nearly without any conscious effort are:

- recognition of "interesting" detail in a complex scene (e.g., a good friend on a busy street);

- fast interpretation of local changes and appropriate reaction (e.g., driving a car);

- visual comparison (e.g., identification of a known human face);

- storing and retrieving of pictures (e.g., the local environment where one lives, a mountain scenery).

The efficiency of the biological systems in such areas is beyond the capabilities of today's technical systems even with the fastest available computer systems.

However, there are areas of application where digital image analysis systems produce acceptable results. Systems in these areas solve very specialized tasks, they operate in a very limited environment, and high speed is often not necessary.

The goal of image understanding (IU) is to find semantic interpretations of images, in particular to localize and name objects contained in a scene and to assess their mutual relationships in order to interact with the environment. Image understanding is usually considered at three different levels: (1) Low-level vision deals with the processing of raw image data, e.g., image enhancement; (2) intermediate-level vision derives from the image information related to objects or object parts, typical operations on this level are grouping and segmentation; (3) high-level vision is concerned with scene interpretation, etc. The central problem in IU is to recognize known objects reliably, independent of variations in position, orientation, and size, even when those objects are partially occluded. Although some information is lost by the image formation process, biological vision systems demonstrate that this task can be accomplished reliably and efficiently even under difficult viewing conditions.

In the past 25 years, many specialized techniques have been developed for various aspects of IU without reaching a comparable or even sufficient degree of robustness. We have identified three dominating problem areas that appear to be essential for successful realization of image understanding.

First, there is a clear lack of robust methods for low- and intermediate-level image analysis.*Second*, hierarchies are needed on all levels of the vision process in order to cope with the complexity of images. *Third*, the construction of object models is a too complex task to be done manually and therefore must be supported with suitable tools (*i.e adaptive methods*).

As a solution to these problems we propose a set of methods (tools) that address these problems. One of our goals is to base these methods on sound mathematical theories like graph theory, learning/estimation theory, and robust statistics taking into account the special characteristics of visual images.

The characteristics of the visual images, such as the overwhelming amount of data, high redundancy, and relevant information clustered in space and time, indicate that certain organization and aggregation principles have to be used to reduce the computational complexity of the visual processes and to bridge the gap between the raw data and symbolic descriptions.

A raw digital image consists of a 2D spatial arrangement of pixels, each of which results from measuring the light at a specific location of the image plane. Each pixel results from the projection from the real (3D-) world into the 2D image. Surfaces of 3D-objects reflect the light in a very specific way that somehow "codes" the structure of the object: Reflectivity is a property of material and does not vary much along object surfaces; it changes abruptly between different surfaces or from the object to its background [Mar80].

Computer vision models have in general a parametric and a structural component. While parameters model the quantitative image properties well, the qualitative image and scene properties are better modeled using structural components.

6

Graphs in Image Analysis

Walter G. Kropatsch
Mark Burge
Roland Glantz

6.1   From Pixels to Graphs

We assume a two-dimensional digital image to be a rectangular array of picture elements. These elements are referred to as **pixels**, each of which is associated with a value out of the same finite set. The planar layout of such a two-dimensional digital image suggests the use of **planar graphs** (see Definitions 1 and 2) in order to describe the image. Graphs will be used to represent the topological relations of image parts. See [TS92] for graph theory and [Kro95] for the application of graph theory to images.

Definition 1 (Graph) *A graph $G = (V, E)$ is given by a finite set V of elements called **vertices**, a finite set E of elements called **edges**, and a relation of **incidence**, which associates with each edge e an unordered pair $(v_1, v_2) \in V \times V$. The vertices v_1 and v_2 are called the **end vertices** of e.*

Note that the definition includes graphs with self-loops (i.e., edges with a pair of identical end vertices) and multiple edges (i.e., several edges with the same pair of end vertices).

Definition 2 (Planar Graph, Embedded Graph) *A graph is said to be **planar** if it can be drawn in a plane so that its edges intersect only at its end vertices. A graph already drawn in a surface S is referred to as **embedded in S**.*

Note that in general a graph can be embedded in many ways.

In this chapter we present three ways to map a two-dimensional digital image to a planar graph: While the mapping from images to graphs in the square grid (see Section 6.1.1) is defined for all pixel arrays, the mappings to run graphs and Voronoi graphs (see Sections 6.1.2 and 6.1.3) require binary images. In a binary image the set of pixel values has only two elements.

Mapping an image to a graph, we refer to the **faces** of a graph and the **dual graph**.

Definition 3 (Face, Dual Face Graph) *The planar embedding of a graph divides the plane into regions called **faces**, one of which is infinite. The vertices $\overline{v} \in \overline{V}$ of the*

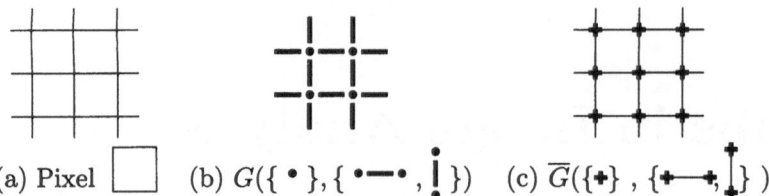

(a) Pixel □   (b) $G(\{\bullet\}, \{\bullet\!-\!\bullet, \vdots\})$ (c) $\overline{G}(\{+\}, \{+\!-\!+, \ddagger\})$

FIGURE 6.1. (a) Pixel grid, (b) neighborhood graph $G(V, E)$, (c) dual face graph $\overline{G}(F, \overline{E})$.

dual face graph *represent the faces, while the edges $\overline{e} \in \overline{E}$ of the dual face graph indicate the neighborhood of pairs of adjacent faces. There is a one-to-one correspondence between the edges of G and the edges of $\overline{G}$.*

6.1.1   Graphs in the Square Grid

In this section we generalize the neighborhood structure of pixel arrays. Figure 6.1 illustrates how a pixel grid can be represented by an image graph $G(V, E)$ and its dual face graph $\overline{G}(F, \overline{E})$. Each vertex in V corresponds to a pixel. Geometrical properties like coordinates or gray values are stored as attributes. Two vertices are joined by an edge, if the corresponding pixels are neighbors.[1] The set F of faces is given by the squares formed by four vertices. Two faces are joined by a dual edge contained in $\overline{E}$ if the corresponding squares are adjacent in G. The vertices of the dual graph $\overline{G}$ are given by the faces of the graph G. There is also a one-to-one relationship between E and $\overline{E}$.

This formalism can be extended to nonregular arrangements of sensors like in most natural vision systems. Thus any tessellation of the image plane is included in this concept (see Section 6.1.3).

6.1.2   Run Graphs

In this section, we present different techniques for representing a pixel array by graphs, where the vertices correspond to vertical or horizontal runs of pixels, rather than individual pixels as in the previous section. These graphs are called **run graphs**. In order to have well-defined runs, we require the image to be binary, i.e., there is an image foreground and an image background. All runs are maximal in the image foreground.

[Bur98] uses run graphs to represent scanned images of documents. The focus is on documents with graphics, where one can see patterns of straight or curved lines. In the following they will be referred to as **line images**. Figure 6.2 depicts two typical line images.

Any particular representation makes certain information explicit at the expense of information that is pushed into the background and may be quite hard to recover [Mar82, p. 21]. Hence, we need to carefully consider the representation of a line image so

---

[1]4-neighbors are used because they make G planar. Pixels $((u_x, u_y), (v_x, v_y))$ are 4-neighbors if $|u_x - v_x| + |u_y - v_y| = 1$.

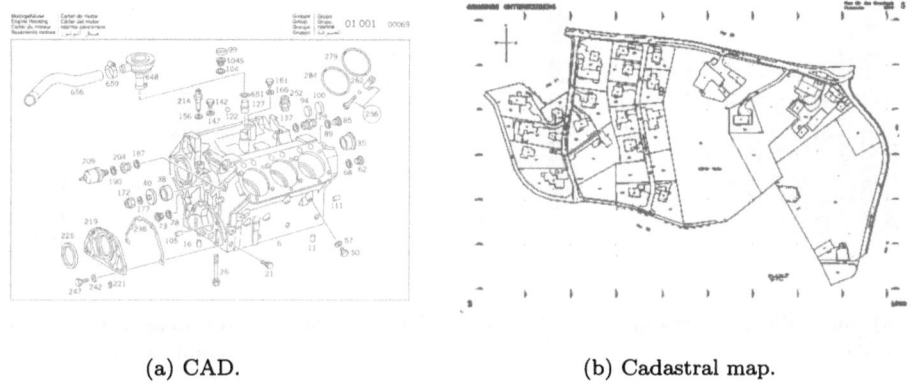

(a) CAD.   (b) Cadastral map.

FIGURE 6.2. Typical line images.

as to maximize the information necessary for document image analysis while minimizing
the cost, in terms of time and space, of acquiring it. There are the following alternatives:
contour, skeleton, and hybrid methods for binary image represention (see [Bur98]).

In a **run-length** or **interval encoding** [AK77] of an image, maximal sequences of
black pixels in a column or row are stored. These $1 \cdot l$ rectangles form an information-
preserving and compressed representation of the image. Both different size rectangles
and maximal squares have been used to extend this representation, the latter being
another representation of the medial axis transform (MAT). The advantages of these
representations are that they are inexpensive to compute, information preserving, and
compressed. Unfortunately it is difficult to extract structural or topological information
from this representation without reencoding it.

A simple reencoding of the run-length representation is the **line adjacency graph**
(LAG) [Pav78], in which vertical columns of pixels are encoded into runs. Each run is
considered a vertex, and adjacent runs are connected by edges. This simple graph reencoding as shown in Figure 6.3(a) does provide access to the local topological structure
of the image, but the shape of an object is only available by examining each of its
vertices. In the LAG every vertical run is a vertex of the graph and graph edges serve
only to connect adjacent runs. [BCB+92] combine vertical runs and construct the
vertical simple graph (VSG) (see Figure 6.3(b). Still, the VSG is built entirely of
vertical runs, and when a line is horizontal it will be encoded inefficiently as a series
of many vertical runs. To remedy this problem graphs built of mixed horizontal and
vertical runs can be constructed [MR93].

The mixed run graph representation (MRG) is built from both vertical runs (e.g., the
VSG and LAG) and horizontal runs. It is a merging of vertical and horizontal simple
graphs, as can be seen in Figure 6.3(c). The definitions for constructing the run graph
are based on the extensions of [MR93] to the formulation by [BCB+92] of the run
graph. First, maximal vertical and horizontal runs are found, then by applying a set
of simple definitions [Bur98] adjacent horizontal runs become an edge and vertical
runs become either a vertex or an edge (Figure 6.4). Vertices are always encoded by

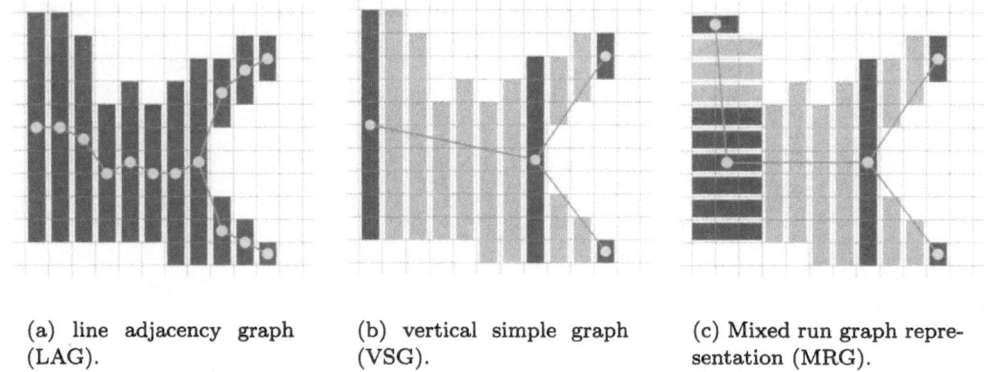

(a) line adjacency graph (LAG).

(b) vertical simple graph (VSG).

(c) Mixed run graph representation (MRG).

FIGURE 6.3. Graph encodings for line images; dark and light runs indicate vertices and edges, respectively.

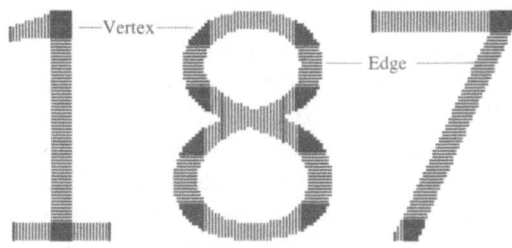

FIGURE 6.4. Line image encoded as a run graph. Dark areas are vertices, and the runs of each edge are shown.

vertical runs, whereas edges are encoded by either horizontal or vertical runs depending on their slope. The run graph can be extended to eliminate some artifact vertices and edges. Often in the run graph, diagonal lines and lines with spurious pixels are divided into a number of small vertex-edge-vertex sequences, some of which can be removed by using simple definitions [Bur98]. *"A good image representation scheme should provide some substantial reduction of storage, while allowing to process the image data directly in the encoded format"* [DZCL96]. It is possible to efficiently compute features (i.e., shape encodings) for recognition, classification, and matching directly from the run graph representation. The run graph is computable directly from the run-length-encoded output of a scanner. Designing algorithms to use the run graph representation results in a saving in both time and space; in fact using these techniques the bitmap representation need never be created. In the following discussions the set of vertices of a run graph is denoted by V, while E denotes the set of edges. Computing features from run graphs, the complexity will be given in terms of:

- n – the larger of the image dimensions,

- $|V|$ – the cardinality of the set of vertices V,

- $|E|$ – the cardinality of the set of edges E,

- c – the number of connected components in the run graph, and

- r – the number of runs in the run graph.

We start with the geometrical features: [DZCL96] give methods for computing the **diameter, convex hull**, and **multiple points** from image elements. The image elements are encoded as vertical simple graphs (VSG) (see Figure 6.3(b)). The authors conclude that the calculation of **local extrema** (i.e., local maximum or minimum) cannot be done using only a vertical simple graph. They can, however, be computed directly from the mixed run graph representation (MRG), where local extrema correspond to extreme point vertices and crossing point vertices. It is possible to use inexpensive approximations of geometric features [Bur98] like the diameter and convex hull for classification of image elements. The convex hull can be approximated from local extrema, which in the run graph are the run vertices. Then any convex hull algorithm (e.g., the algorithm of [ZTA97]) is applicable. The diameter may then be approximated from the convex hull by finding the longest chord between each vertex of the hull.

We proceed with the computation of moment invariants: [Hu62] introduced seven features computable from an object's moments, which are invariant under translation, scaling, and rotation. Normally, computing these features requires examining each pixel in the image, in order to sum its contribution, an $O(n^2)$ operation. An efficient method for binary images makes use of the precomputed information in the run graph. This method, called the (δ) **method**, was introduced by [ZVvK87] for computing moments from binary images using horizontal runs. It can be trivially extended to use horizontal and vertical runs (i.e., using only the starting x and y position and length of each run) to compute moments directly from the run graph in $O(r)$ time.

There is also a link between the run graph representation and the MAT: A simple algorithm exists [Bur98] for computing a discrete version of the MAT efficiently in $O(r)$ time from the run graph representation by taking the middle pixel of each run of each edge, and the centroid of each run graph vertex. This algorithm can also be used to obtain a simple vectorization suitable for display purposes.

We now consider a graph theoretical feature: Finding the connected components (i.e., component labeling) in the iconic image requires $O(n^2)$ time. Starting from the run graph, they can be found in $\Theta(|V| + |E|)$ time[2] using Algorithm 4.

Because the run graph is always a planar graph, the number h of holes in it can be calculated directly from the number c of connected components, as computed in Algorithm 4;

$$h = c + |E| - |V|. \tag{6.1}$$

Locating holes in the image is equivalent to finding cycles in the run graph and can be done in $\Theta(|V| + |E|)$ using depth-first search by labeling **back edges** (i.e., those edges

---

[2]The $O(n)$ notation indicates that the complexity is bounded from above within a constant factor by a function $g(n)$ while the $\Theta(n)$ notation adds the constraint that $g(n)$ is also bounded from within a constant factor from below.

Algorithm 4 Find number c of connected components of the run graph

---

1: $G(V, E)$ is a run graph and $c \leftarrow 0$
2: $V_{\text{visited}} \leftarrow \emptyset$
3: **for all** $v \in V$ **do**
4:     **if** $v \notin V_{\text{visited}}$ **then**
5:         $V_{\text{reached}} \leftarrow$ those vertices reached by Depth First Search from v
6:         $c \leftarrow c + 1$
7:         $V_{\text{visited}} \leftarrow V_{\text{visited}} \cup V_{\text{reached}}$
8:     **end if**
9: **end for**

---

connecting a vertex to an ancestor in the depth-first tree obtained by the depth-first search).

Finally we sketch how to derive further topological information from the run graph. The run graph provides a compact structural representation for line image understanding, but because of its geometric nature it does not explicitly describe the topology of a line image. A new algorithm [BKar] based on dual graph contraction (see Section 6.2.2) transforms the run graph into its minimum line property preserving (MLPP) topological form, which, when implemented in parallel, requires $O(\log(\text{longestcurve}))$ steps. An MLPP graph of a line image complements the structural information in geometric graph representations like the run graph. With such a graph and its dual it is possible to efficiently detect topological features like loops and holes and to make use of relations like containment.

6.1.3   Area Voronoi Diagram

The adjacency relations between regions in an image are typically encoded within a **region adjacency graph** (RAG), where regions of the image are vertices and the edges are connecting adjacent regions. Such a graph encodes the images' topological information, but is of little use in understanding document images as the connections between black image elements are always via a white (i.e., background) region. In general, RAGs are unsuited for images that contain background regions because the relations between image elements are not encoded. In such cases we should replace adjacency with the more appropriate neighboring relation, as in Figure 6.5. The mouth of the screamer in Figure 6.5 consists of two neighboring image elements. This may not be sufficient for understanding, because important global topological relations (i.e., that the smaller part of the mouth is completely contained within the larger) cannot be determined from the graph. Information of this type will be encoded using **arrangements** (see Section 6.2.1).

Voronoi neighborhoods of image elements provide an intuitively appealing definition of proximity. The Voronoi neighborhood of a given image element corresponds to that portion of the Euclidean plane, which is closer to the image element than to any other image element. This simple definition of a neighborhood has been discovered many times and applied to problems in many fields. We list a few examples and refer

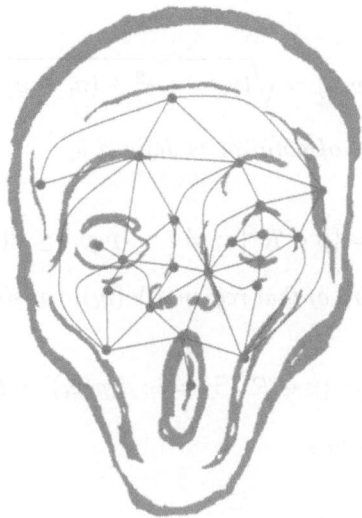

FIGURE 6.5. Graph representing the neighborhood of the black regions in a detail from Edvard Munch's *The Scream*.

the reader to [OBS92] for a comprehensive survey and to [OBS94] for a look at their cross-disciplinary applications.

- In meteorology [Thi11] used an equivalent concept for the spatial interpolation of rainfall estimations.

- In crystallography [Nig27] introduced the equivalent concept of **Wirkungsbereich** (i.e., area of effect) for modeling crystal growth.

- In geology [Sti29] proposed a model of cracking in basalt in which cracks follow the edges of a Voronoi diagram grown from the initial points of hardening.

- In plant ecology [Bro65] defined the area potentially available for a plant's growth with Voronoi diagrams.

- In animal ecology [TH80] modeled the territories of animals with uniform resources and strengths in terms of Voronoi diagrams.

- In computer vision [Ahu82] applied Voronoi diagrams to the analysis of point patterns.

- In astronomy [WI89] model the growth of galaxies using the Voronoi diagram.

The planar ordinary Voronoi diagram is defined for a finite set of $n \geq 2$ distinct planar points $P = \{p_1, p_2, \ldots, p_n\}$. Hence, each image element consists of a single point.

Definition 4 (Voronoi Region, Ordinary Voronoi Diagram) *Using the Euclidean distance*

$$d(p, q) = \sqrt{(p_x - q_x)^2 + (p_y - q_y)^2},\tag{6.2}$$

the Voronoi region, $V(p_i)$, of point p_i is defined by

$$V(p_i) = \{p \in \mathcal{R}^2 | \forall j \neq i : d(p, p_i) \leq d(p, p_j)\},\tag{6.3}$$

which includes the boundary of that region, $\partial V(p_i)$, consisting of the equidistant points

$$\partial V(p_i) = \{p \in \mathcal{R}^2 | \exists j \neq i : d(p, p_i) = d(p, p_j)\}.\tag{6.4}$$

The set of all Voronoi regions

$$\mathcal{V}(P) = \{V(p_1), \dots, V(p_n)\},\tag{6.5}$$

is the ordinary Voronoi diagram of the set of points P.

The vertices of the **Delaunay graph** are the points of P. Two points p_i, p_j create an edge of the Delaunay graph, if and only if $V(p_i)$ and $V(p_j)$ are adjacent in the Voronoi diagram. The Delaunay graph is also referred to as **Delaunay triangulation**, because its faces are triangular (see later).

The **Voronoi graph** is the dual of the Delaunay triangulation (see Definition 3). Its edges represent the line segments of the boundary $\partial V(p_i)$. The vertices of the Voronoi graph are the points, where the line segments meet (see also [PS85]).

In constructing the Voronoi graph, as in Figure 6.6(a), we begin with the simplest case, that of two distinct planar points p_1 and p_2. Equation (6.3) states that the Voronoi region of p_1, $V(p_1)$, consists of all those points that are either closer to p_1 than to p_2 or equidistant from p_1 and p_2. We see in Figure 6.7(a) that all the points that are equidistant from p_1 and p_2 are exactly those that lie on the perpendicular bisector, b_{12} of the segment, $\overline{p_1 p_2}$. Using Equation (6.4) and the definition of a perpendicular bisector, the boundary of p_1's Voronoi region, $\partial V(p_1)$, is exactly b_{12}. All the points on the half-plane containing p_1 and bounded by b_{12} are the points closer to p_1 than p_2, and along with $\partial V(p_1)$ they make up p_1's Voronoi region, $V(p_1)$.

With the addition of a third point, p_3, we construct the triangle $\triangle_{123}$ as in Figure 6.7(b). Again, using the method of perpendicular bisectors on each edge of the triangle (i.e., b_{12} of $\overline{p_1 p_2}$, b_{23} of $\overline{p_2 p_3}$ and b_{31} of $\overline{p_3 p_1}$) we construct the Voronoi graph for $n = 3$.

The dual of the Voronoi graph, the **Delaunay triangulation**, is depicted in Figure 6.6(b). In a Delaunay triangulation, the circumscribed circle of every triangle contains no vertices [PS85]. This is equivalent to the fact that the triangles are as "equilateral" as possible (see [Law77] and [Lee78]), which is a desirable property for models of surfaces (see Chapter 13.5.1). In many cases a set of triangulation edges is pre-specified. Under such constraints the construction of a Delaunay-like triangulation is still feasible.

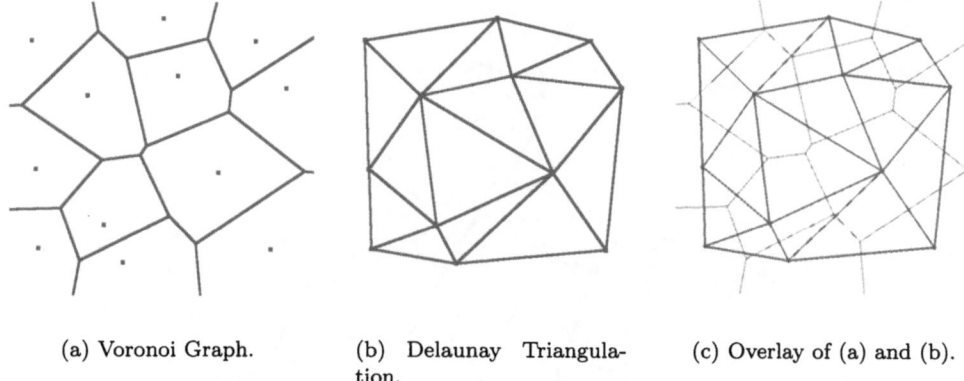

(a) Voronoi Graph.   (b) Delaunay Triangulation.   (c) Overlay of (a) and (b).

FIGURE 6.6. Duality of the Voronoi graph and the Delaunay triangulation.

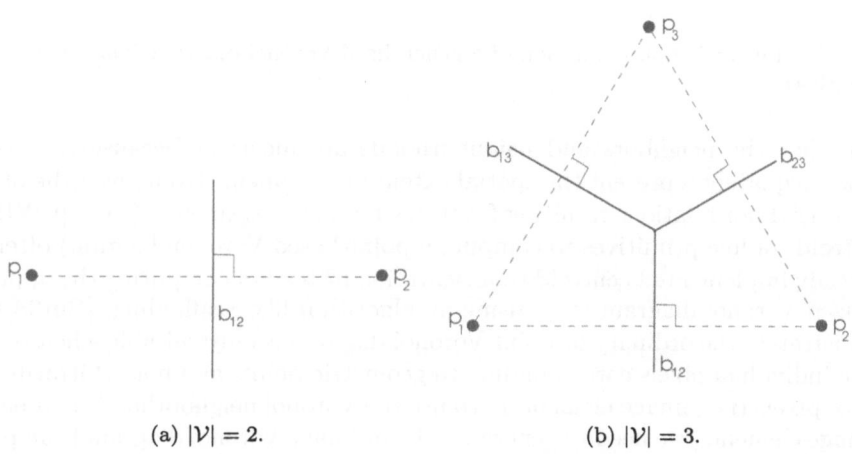

(a) $|\mathcal{V}| = 2$.   (b) $|\mathcal{V}| = 3$.

FIGURE 6.7. The perpendicular bisector method for constructing the Voronoi graph. **(a)** The Voronoi graph of two points p_1 and p_2 is the perpendicular bisector b_{12} of the segment $\overline{p_1 p_2}$. **(b)** The Voronoi graph of three points is formed by the intersection of their perpendicular bisectors. Note that each perpendicular bisector is a ray with a finite endpoint at the intersection point.

The edges are chosen as to make the triangles as "equilateral" as possible. This leads to the constrained Delaunay triangulation used in Chapter 14.2.1 (see also [PS85]).

In the previous section we limited our discussion to the neighborhoods of pointlike image elements. This simplification allowed us to clearly formulate the problem and develop a simple algorithm (i.e., the perpendicular bisection method) for computing the ordinary (i.e., point-based) Voronoi diagram. Unfortunately, for computer vision such simplifications are inappropriate and cause incorrect results. The errors resulting from this simplification can be seen in Figure 6.8, which shows an ordinary Voronoi diagram based on the centroids of line segments. It is immediately apparent in this

FIGURE 6.8. Incorrect approximation of a generalized Voronoi diagram from the centroids of the primitives.

diagram that the neighbors and neighborhoods are incorrect because the **centroid** does not adequately represent the spatial extent of a segment. Even given the obviously incorrect neighbor relations resulting from this method, researchers (e.g., [FWH97] use the centroids of line primitives to compute a point-based Voronoi diagram) often resort to the easily implemented centroid representation instead of computing the appropriate generalized Voronoi diagram (e.g., using an algorithm like Scaffolding [Bur98]).

As illustrated, the ordinary or point Voronoi diagram is only suitable when the primitives are individual pixels corresponding to geometric points and not arbitrarily shaped groups of pixels (i.e., image elements). To use the Voronoi neighborhoods and neighbors with image elements, we need to generalize the ordinary Voronoi diagram from points to arbitrarily shaped image elements. Generalized Voronoi diagrams are defined by generalizing ordinary Voronoi diagrams with respect to the distance measure (e.g., Euclidean or Manhattan), the space (e.g., 2-dimensional or 3-dimensional), or the generators (e.g., point or lines). In the image from Figure 6.8 [FWH97] a generalized Voronoi diagram is approximated from the ordinary Voronoi diagram of the centroid of each primitive. The method is simple to implement and has $O(n \log n)$ time complexity, where n is the number of primitives, but as the centroid is a poor representation of shape for non-round primitives, the resulting generalized Voronoi diagram is incorrect. In computer vision we are primarily concerned with generalizations of the Voronoi diagram in terms of its generators. Efficient implementations for most geometric primitives, though often with simplifying constraints, have been developed:

- **Segments:** [BMS94] give an efficient implementation and [For87b, For97] extends his $O(n \log n)$ plane-sweep algorithm for n possibly intersecting line segments or circles.

- **Circles:** [LD81] introduced an $O(n \log^2 n)$ algorithm for n possibly intersecting circles and [Sha85] a divide-and-conquer algorithm with similar complexity. Ideas for optimizing both algorithms can be found in [DHKP97].

- **Curves:** [Yap87] introduced an $O(n \log n)$ algorithm for n simple non-intersecting curves and [AS95] developed a randomized incremental algorithm with similar complexity.

- **Planar shapes:** [AGSS89] presented a linear-time algorithm for computing the bounded Voronoi diagram (e.g., medial axis) of a convex polygon and [KL96] extended it for simple polygons.

  [SN87] give a detailed exposition of an $O(n \max(\log n, h))$ algorithm, where n is the number of edges on the polygon boundary and h is its number of holes for multiply connected polygons.

  [KMM93] compute in $O(n \log n)$ the Voronoi diagram of n disjoint convex planar shapes using an algorithm based on the $O(n \log n)$ algorithm of [CS88] for n segments in the plane. A divide-and-conquer algorithm with $O(n \log^2 n)$ complexity for the same class of shapes is presented by [LS87].

  [Hel93, Hel94] developed an incremental algorithm for certain classes of planar shapes and both [Cho95] and [MR94] present one for regular polygons.

  [Bur98] developed an $O(n \log n)$ algorithm for arbitrarily planar shapes with holes based on approximating the diagram from the ordinary Delaunay triangulation of the sampled image elements.

For document image analysis [BM95a, BM95b] we use **area Voronoi diagrams** (i.e., generalized Voronoi diagrams using Euclidean distance on a 2-dimensional plane with arbitrarily shaped generators).

Using Equations (6.2) - (6.5) for the ordinary Voronoi diagram as guidelines, we can generalize to the area Voronoi diagram.

Definition 5 (Area Voronoi Region, Area Voronoi Diagram) *The area Voronoi region of an image element i_j is defined by*

$$V_a(i_j) = \{p \in \mathcal{R}^2 | \forall j \neq k : d_a(p, i_j) \leq d_a(p, i_k)\}, \tag{6.6}$$

where the distance between a point p and an image element i_j is given by

$$d_a(p, i_j) = \min_{q \in i_j} d(p, q), \tag{6.7}$$

which is the minimum Euclidean distance (see Equation 6.2) between a point p and any point q within the image element i_j. The area Voronoi region of an image element $V_a(i_j)$ is the point set from which the distance to i_j is less than or equal to the distance to any other image element. Analogous to the ordinary Voronoi diagram, the boundary $\partial V_a(i_j)$ of an area Voronoi region $V_a(i_j)$ is given by

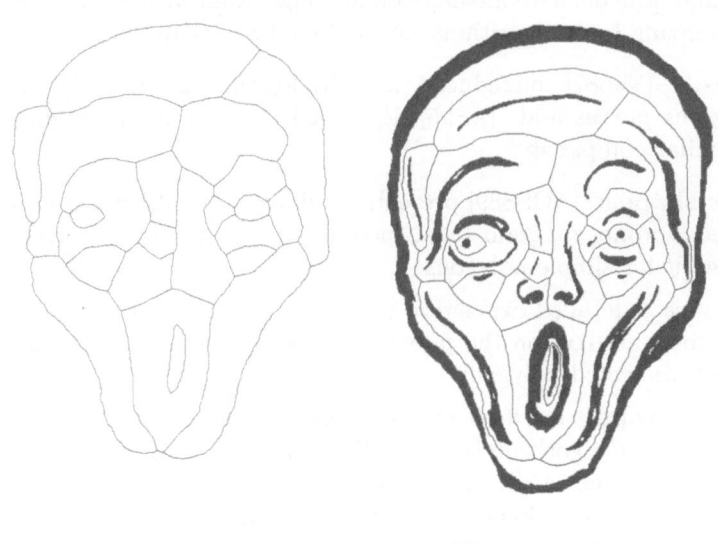

(a) Neighborhoods.   (b) Image overlaid.

FIGURE 6.9. Area Voronoi diagram.

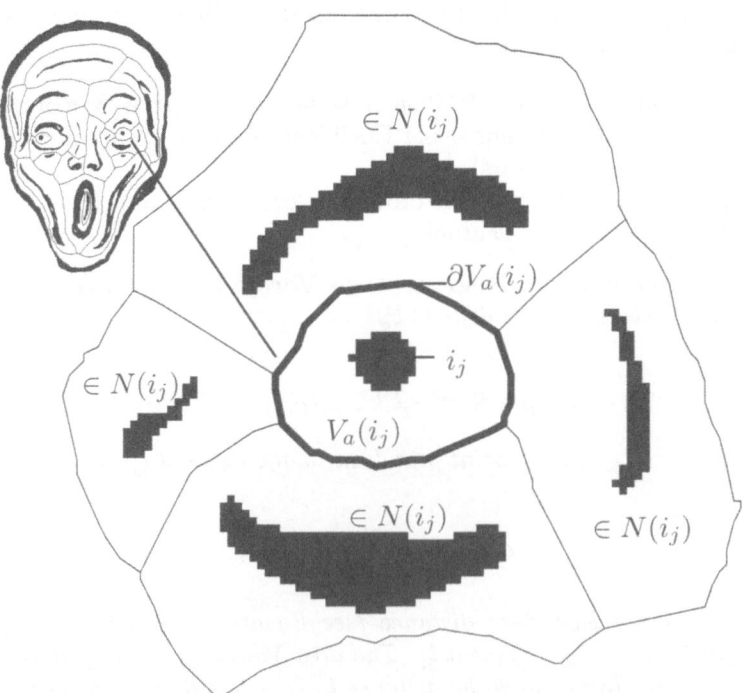

FIGURE 6.10. Area Voronoi diagram with labeled image elements.

$$\partial V_a(i_j) = \{p \in \mathcal{R}^2 | \exists k \neq j : d_a(p, i_j) = d_a(p, i_k)\}. \tag{6.8}$$

The boundary consists of those points that are equally distant from two or more image elements and therefore have no unique nearest image element. In an ordinary Voronoi diagram the boundary shared by two neighboring (i.e., touching) Voronoi regions is always a segment or a line, while in an area Voronoi diagram it is a curve.

The area Voronoi diagram $\mathcal{V}_a$ is the set of all area Voronoi regions (Figures 6.9 and 6.10):

$$\mathcal{V}_a = \{V_a(i_1), \dots, V_a(i_n)\}. \tag{6.9}$$

The **area Delaunay graph** and the **area Voronoi graph** are defined analogously to the Delaunay graph and the Voronoi graph.

6.2 Graph Transformations in Image Analysis

While the previous section was devoted to transformations from images to graphs, we now focus on the generalization of graphs. This generalization serves the purpose of reducing the computational complexity of the visual process and bridging the gap between the image and its symbolic description.

The first section of this chapter addresses the problem of comparing area Voronoi diagrams.

6.2.1 Arrangements of Image Elements

We have seen how area Voronoi diagrams (see Section 6.1.3) can be used to completely describe the spatial arrangement of the elements in an image. In this section we will discuss a simple reencoding of the area Voronoi diagram, which can be used to describe an image in a way that is invariant under translation, rotation, reflection, and scaling.

Definition 6 (Arrangement) *The arrangement of an image element i_j is the list, $A(i_j)$, in a counter clockwise order, of its area Voronoi neighbors, $N(i_j)$ (i.e., those image elements whose Voronoi regions share an edge with its Voronoi region, $V_a(i_j)$).*

We used the Scaffolding algorithm to efficiently calculate arrangements [Bur98] and to describe the spatial relations among large collections [BB96] of arbitrarily shaped image elements, i.e., collections of complex technical diagrams that contain many similar parts for assemblies or multipart symbols (i.e., a spatial arrangement of specific image elements). Searching requires not only an efficient method of computing arrangements, but one for computing the distance between arrangements. [TVJD95] showed how to compute a distance metric between any two arrangements, caused by the embedding *of the same image elements.* The Scaffolding algorithm solves the problem of efficiently

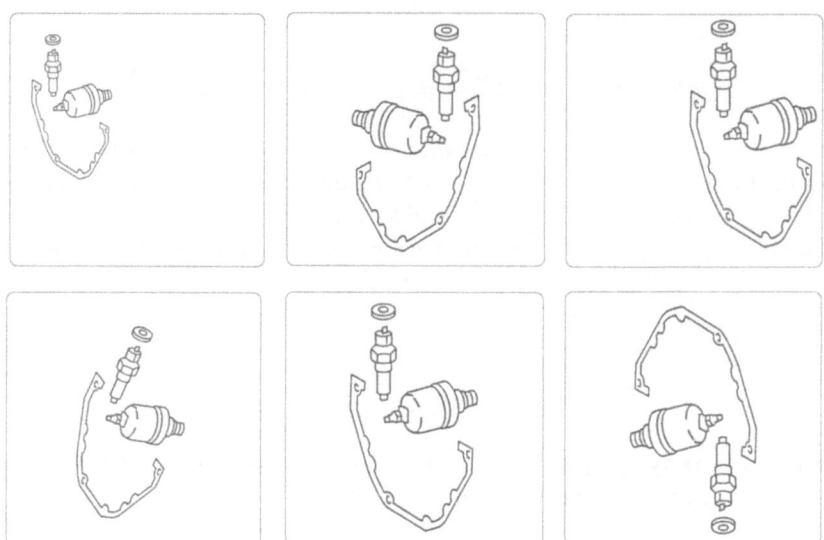

FIGURE 6.11. Arrangement and dispersion measurements. Each figure has the same arrangement but differing dispersion measurements.

computing arrangements, but efficiently computing the distance between two arrangements remains an open problem.

Arrangements describe the location of an image element relative to other image elements, in our case its area Voronoi neighbors, while dispersion measurements consider its location relative to the axis of the plane. Arrangements are invariant under translation, rotation, reflection, and scaling, while dispersion measurements are not (see Figure 6.11 (after [OBS92, p. 408])).

[TVJD95] compare two Voronoi diagrams $\mathcal{V}_x$ and $\mathcal{V}_y$ with the same image elements by converting $\mathcal{V}_x$ into $\mathcal{V}_y$ using the diagonal exchange operator [CH90, For87a] (see Figure 6.12). They proved constructively that there exists a sequence of diagonal exchange operators to convert any Voronoi diagram to any other that has the same number of parts. The diagonal exchange operator may be used to correct changes in the arrangement, which are due to distortions of the image.

The **diagonal exchange operator** (DEO) is a local operation; after application only the relations between four parts are affected while the rest of the diagram remains the same. Another characteristic of the operator is that it is reversible; applying it twice to the same edge results in the original diagram.[3] The minimal number of DEO applications needed to convert an arrangement into another arrangement determines the **distance** of the arrangements. Calculating the distances in less than exponential time remains an open problem.

---

[3]More generally, applying the DEO an even number of times results in no change, and an odd number of times is equivalent to applying it once.

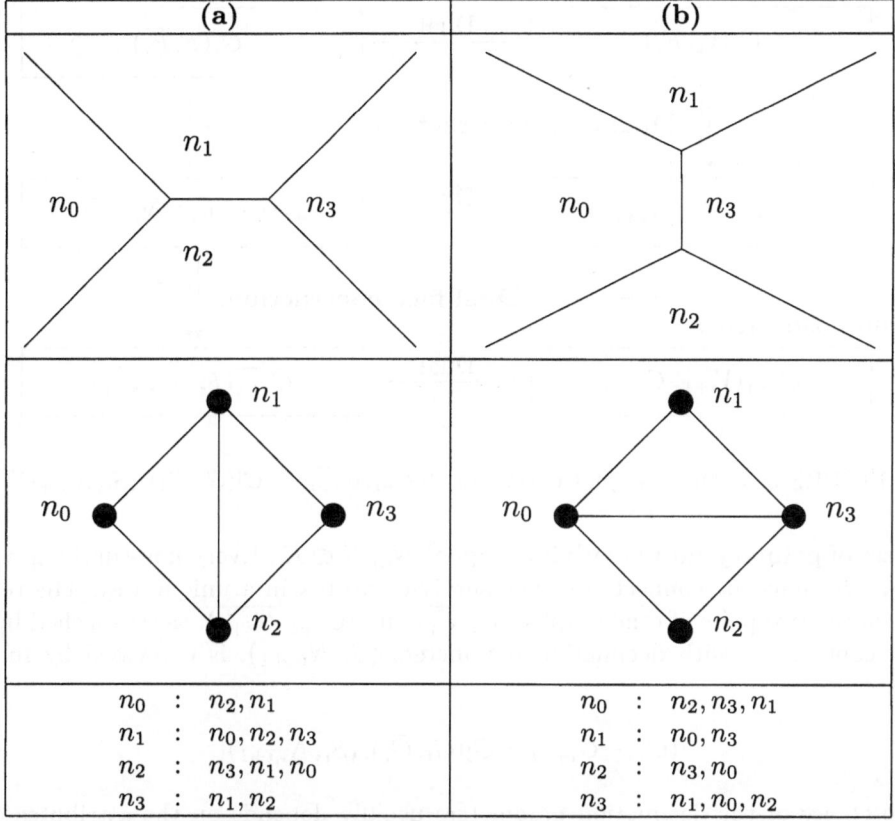

FIGURE 6.12. Diagonal exchange operator: **(a)** The initial configuration of a Voronoi diagram, the corresponding Voronoi graph and the corresponding arrangement. **(b)** Voronoi diagram, Voronoi graph, and arrangement after exchanging diagonal (n_1, n_2) by diagonal (n_0, n_3).

6.2.2   Dual Graph Contraction

In this section, we introduce a transformation for planar graphs (see Definition 2), which reduces the number of vertices and edges while preserving well-defined structural properties. Because the transformation is efficiently computed via contractions of the graph and its dual, it is called **Dual Graph Contraction** [Kro95]. Dual Graph Contraction is used to build the irregular (or graph) pyramids presented in the next chapter. These pyramids are constructed bottom-up, where the graphs are repeatedly contracted level by level. Dual graph contraction proceeds in two basic steps (Figure 6.13): dual edge contraction and dual face contraction. The base of a pyramid consists of a pair of dual graphs $(G_0, \overline{G_0})$ embedded in the plane. Such a pair may be given by an image graph and its dual, a run graph and its dual or the Voronoi graph and the corresponding Delaunay graph. Following **decimation parameters** $(S_i, N_{i,i+1})$ determine the dual edge contraction [Kro95] [Definition 5]: a subset of **surviving vertices** $S_i = V_{i+1} \subset V_i$, and

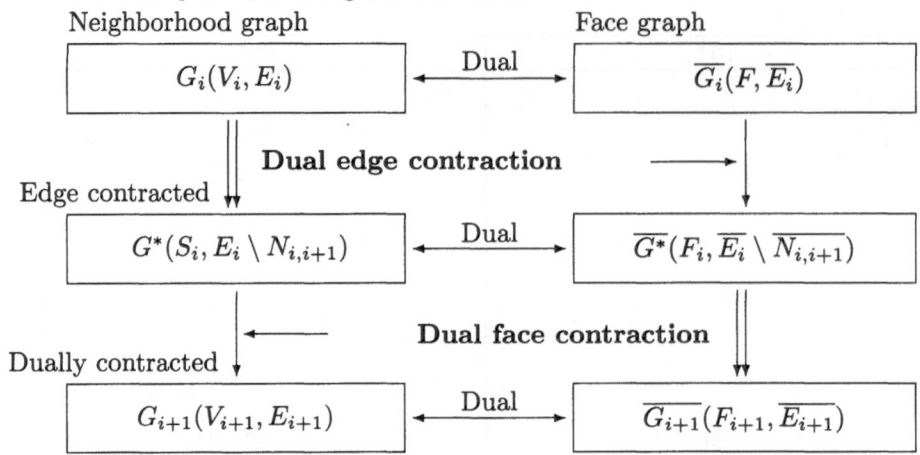

FIGURE 6.13. Dual Graph Contraction: $(G_{i+1}, \overline{G_{i+1}}) = C[(G_i, \overline{G_i}), (S_i, N_{i,i+1})]$.

a subset of **primary non-surviving edges**[4] $N_{i,i+1} \subset E_i$. Every non-surviving vertex, $v \in V_i \setminus S_i$, must be connected to one surviving vertex in a unique way. The relation between the two pairs of dual graphs, $(G_i, \overline{G_i})$ and $(G_{i+1}, \overline{G_{i+1}})$, as established by dual graph contraction with decimation parameters $(S_i, N_{i,i+1})$, is expressed by function $C[.,.]$:

$$(G_{i+1}, \overline{G_{i+1}}) = C[(G_i, \overline{G_i}), (S_i, N_{i,i+1})]. \tag{6.10}$$

The choice of the decimation parameters usually depends on the attributes of the graph and its dual. In case of G being an image graph, these attributes are usually related to the pixel values in the image [GE99].

The contraction of a primary non-surviving edge consists in the identification of its endpoints and the removal of both the contracted edge and its dual edge. Figure 6.14 shows the normal situation (a), the situation where the dual edge contraction creates multiple edges (b), and self-loops (c). Redundancies (lower parts) in cases (b) and (c) are decided through the corresponding dual graphs and may be removed by dual face contractions,[5] where the non-surviving vertices in $\overline{G}$ are identified by their degree being smaller than three. This dual face contraction simplifies most of the multiple edges and self-loops, but not those enclosing any surviving parts of the graph. They are necessary to preserve the correct structure [Kro95]. The example of Figure 6.15 shows two steps of the dual graph contraction. They can be formally written as $(G_1, \overline{G_1}) = C[(G_0, \overline{G_0}), (S_0, N_{0,1})]$, and $(G_2, \overline{G_2}) = C[(G_1, \overline{G_1}), (S_1, N_{1,2})]$. Note that graph G_2 in this example contains both a self-loop and a double edge. In general, the dual face contraction is defined by decimation parameters $(\overline{S_i}, \overline{N_{i,i+1}})$ analogous to the dual edge contraction.

---

[4]Secondary non-surviving edges are removed during dual face contraction.

[5]In figures, $S_i = \{\bullet\}$, $\overline{V_{i+1}} = \{\blacksquare\}$, $V_i \setminus S_i = \{\circ\}$, $\overline{V_i} \setminus \overline{V_{i+1}} = \{\square\}$ and $(\bullet, \circ) \in N_{i,j}$ are indicated by $\longrightarrow$.

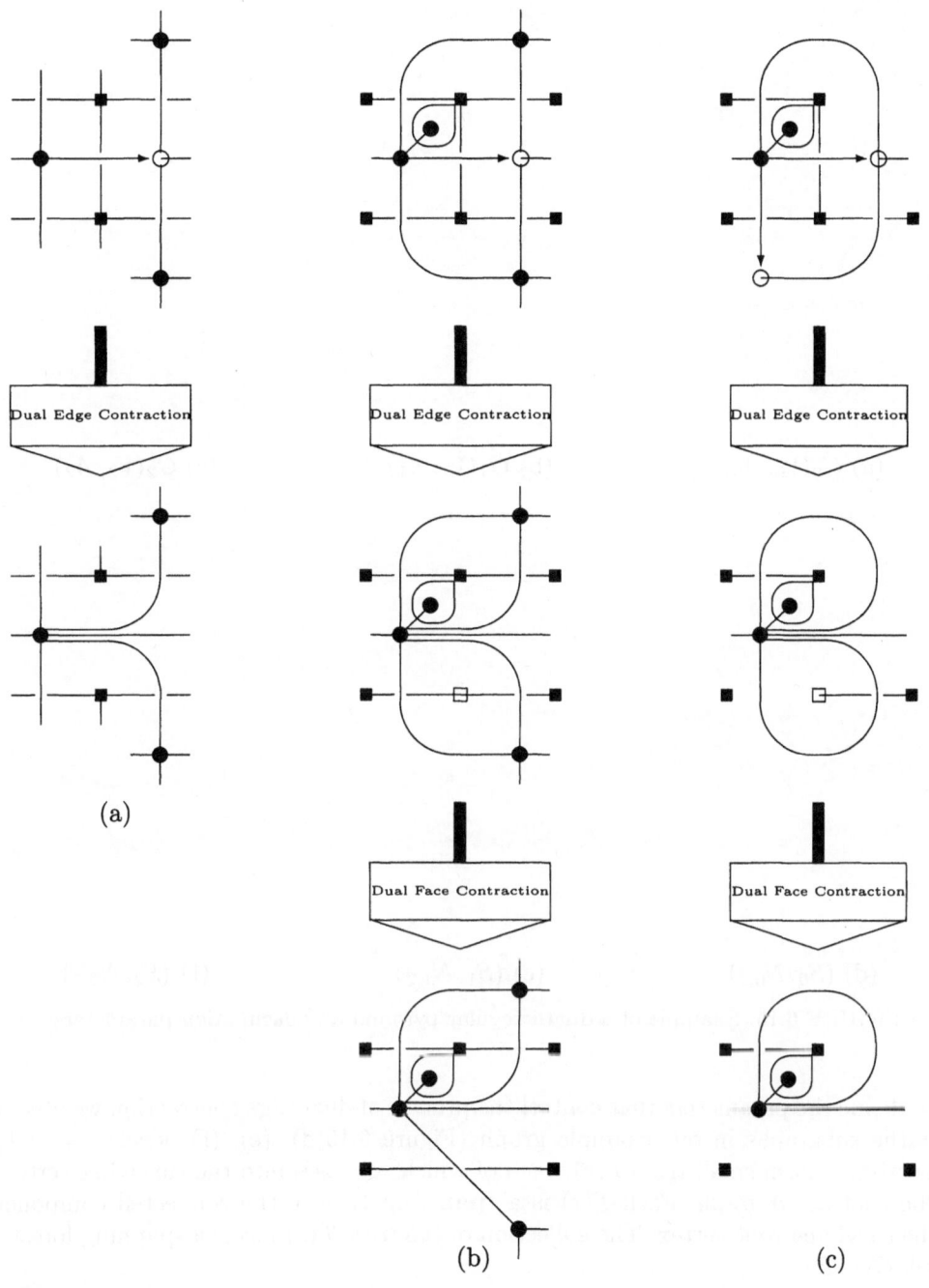

FIGURE 6.14. Three cases of Dual Graph Contraction: (a) normal; (b) multiple edges; (c) self-loops.

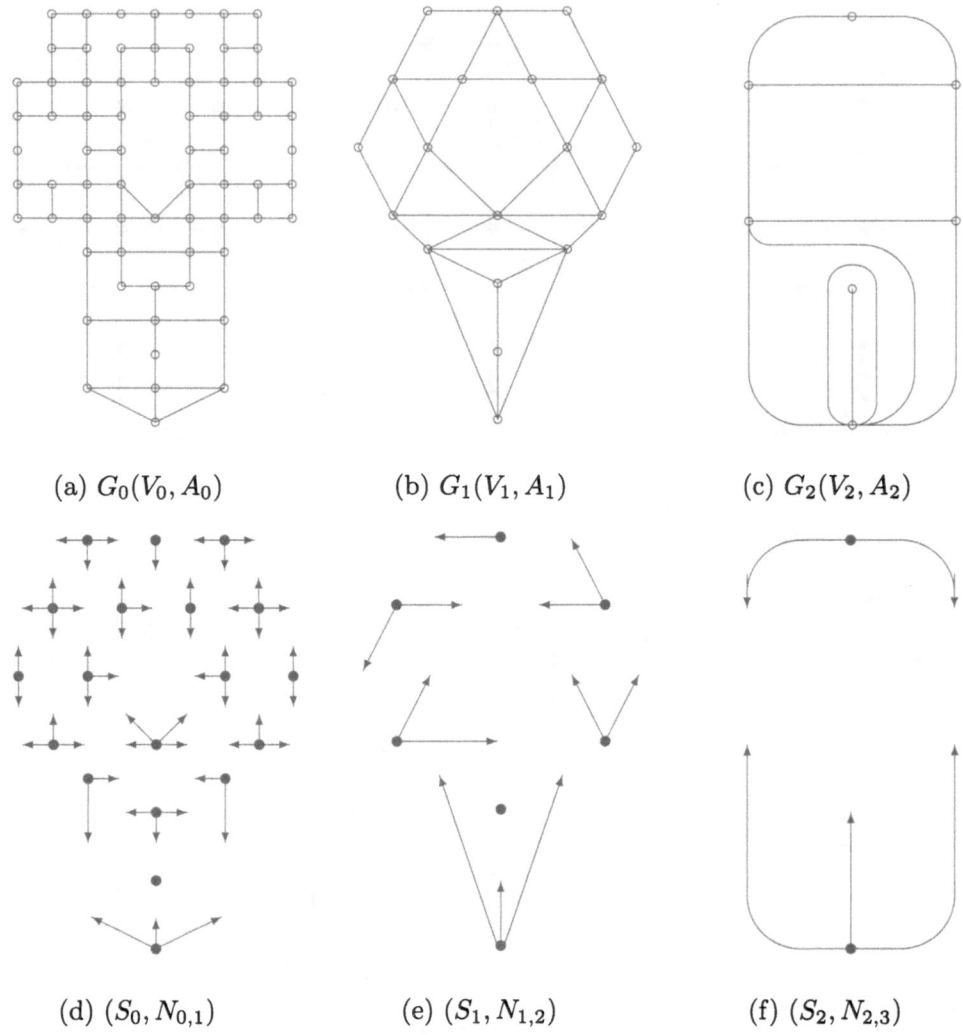

(a) $G_0(V_0, A_0)$ (b) $G_1(V_1, A_1)$ (c) $G_2(V_2, A_2)$

(d) $(S_0, N_{0,1})$ (e) $(S_1, N_{1,2})$ (f) $(S_2, N_{2,3})$

FIGURE 6.15. Example of a dual irregular pyramid and decimation parameters.

To define the parameters that control the process of dual edge contraction we observe that the subgraphs in our example graph (Figure 6.15(d), (e), (f), levels $i = 0, 1, 2$ respectively) form small trees $T(s)$, each of which collapses into the surviving vertex s of the contracted graph. Each $T(s)$ is a **spanning tree** of the connected component of the surviving root vertex. The collection of the trees $T(s)$ forms a spanning forest of graph $G(V, E)$.

Definition 7 (Contraction Kernels) *A decimation of a graph $G(V, E)$ is specified by a selection of* **surviving** *vertices $S \subset V$ and a selection of* **primary non-surviving edges** $N \subset E$ *such that following two conditions are fulfilled:*

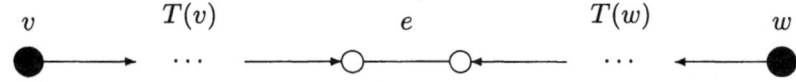

FIGURE 6.16. Decomposition of connecting path $CP(v, w)$.

1. *graph (V, N) is a spanning forest of graph $G(V, E)$; and*

2. *the surviving vertices $S \subset V$ are the roots of the forest (V, N).*

The trees $T(v)$ of the forest (V, N) with root $v \in V$ are called **contraction kernels**.

The connectivity structure of the contracted graph is established by paths connecting two surviving vertices (Figure 6.16):

Definition 8 (Connecting Path) *Let $G(V, E)$ be a graph with decimation parameters (S, N). A path in $G(V, E)$ is called a* **connecting path** *between two surviving vertices $v, w \in S$, denoted $CP(v, w)$, if it consists of three subsets of edges E:*

1. *the first part is a possibly empty branch of the contraction kernel $T(v)$;*

2. *the middle part is an edge $e \in E \setminus N$ that bridges the gap between the two contraction kernels $T(v)$ and $T(w)$. We call e the* **bridge** *of the connecting path $CP(v, w)$; and*

3. *the third part is a possibly empty branch of the contraction kernel $T(w)$.*

Connecting paths $CP_k(v, w)$ in $G_k(V_k, E_k)$ are strongly related to the edges $e_{k+1} = (v, w) \in E_{k+1}$ in the contracted graph $G_{k+1}(V_{k+1}, E_{k+1})$: Two different surviving vertices that are connected by a connecting path in G_k are connected by an edge in E_{k+1}. For every edge $e' = (v, w) \in E_{k+1}$ there exists a connecting path $CP_k(v, w)$ in G_k. Dual edge contraction can be implemented by (1) simply renaming all the non-surviving vertices to their surviving parent vertex, (2) deleting all non-surviving edges N, and (3) their duals $\overline{N}$.

The concept of the contraction kernels and the connecting paths is analogously applied to the dual graph $\overline{G}$. Thus, the implementations of the dual edge contraction and the dual face contraction are the same.

7

Hierarchies

Walter G. Kropatsch
Horst Bischof
Roman Englert

7.1 Regular Image Pyramids

Classical image pyramids were introduced in 1981 and 1982 [BHR81, RK82] as a stack of images of decreasing resolutions. Since then several modifications and additions have been made to the original concept [Kro91] while the main properties are still valid. Image pyramids are efficient data and processing structures for digital image analysis [Ros84, Lev86, Uhr87, Kro91, JR94]. The basic idea is to gradually reduce the spatial resolution of the image and therefore decrease the amount of information. Table 7.1 lists some qualitative consequences of different resolutions.

TABLE 7.1. Image qualities at different resolutions.

	High resolution	Low resolution
Data amount	Huge	Small
Details	Rich and many	Very few
Overview	Bad	Good
Precision	High	Low

An image pyramid combines the advantages of high and low resolution. It is a collection of images of a single scene with exponentially decreasing resolutions [Tan86]. The bottom level of the pyramid is the original image. In the simplest case, each successive level of the pyramid is obtained from the previous level by a filtering operation followed by a sampling operator [HS91]. More general functions can be used to achieve the desired reduction. Therefore, we call them in the following **reduction functions**.

Pyramids have the following merits [BCR90]:

1. reducing the influence of noise by eliminating less important details in lower-resolution versions of the image;

2. making the processing independent of the resolution of the regions of interest in the image;

3. converting global features to local ones;

4. reducing computational cost using the divide-and-conquer principle;

5. finding regions of interest for plan-guided analysis at low cost in low-resolution images, ignoring irrelevant details;

6. visual inspection of large images (see Chapter 15); and

7. increasing speed and reliability of image matching techniques by applying coarse-to-fine strategy (see Chapter 14).

Image pyramids are closely related to the concept of scale space [YP86], in which the scale is introduced as an additional continuous dimension (e.g., as the degree of smoothing). A pyramid is then a logarithmically sampled version of the scale space. Wavelet transformations [Mal89] are closely related to image pyramids, too. For more details on these similarities see [Kro91].

There are three important properties that characterize an image pyramid:

1. structure (see Section 7.1.1),

2. contents of a cell (see Section 7.1.2), and

3. processing performed by the cells (see Section 7.1.3).

In the sequel we demonstrate these concepts on selected examples. We present "fuzzy curve pyramids" (see Section 7.1.4), which are classical in their structure but store fuzzy relations in their cells in order to represent curve information. In the remainder of this chapter graphs take over the role of the regular grid structure of image arrays, particularly pyramids (Section 7.2). The complexity of computing pyramids based on graphs is considered in Section 7.2.1. We demonstrate how a special type of Hopfield neural network (see Section 7.2.2) constructs pyramids on graphs. Then we summarize and illustrate the procedure of dual graph contraction in pyramids by equivalent contraction kernels: The observation that the parameters that control the process form forests is generalized by the concept of contraction kernels. Repeated dual contractions can be replaced by a single dual contraction using equivalent contraction kernels (ECKs, see Section 7.2.3). ECKs enable one to compute any level of an irregular (graph-) pyramid directly from the base. Decimation parameters can be designed now at the base without the need to first generate the lower pyramid levels. Finally, extensions of irregular graph pyramids to three dimensions are sketched (see Section 7.2.4).

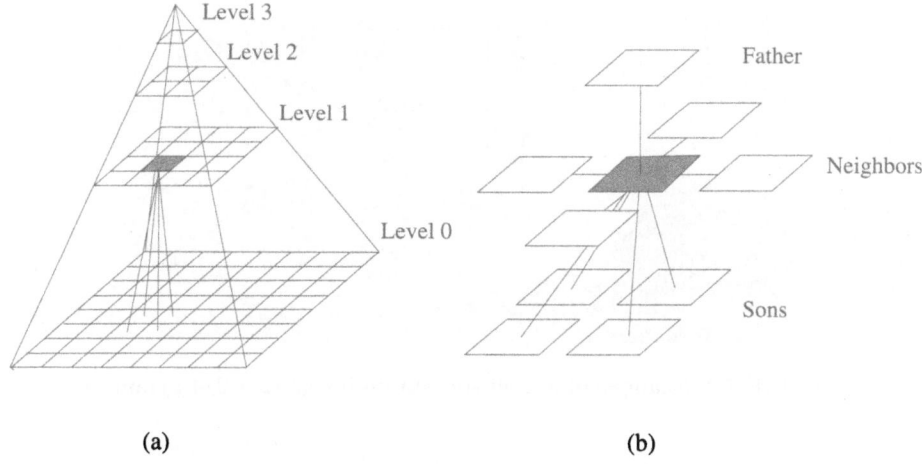

(a)   (b)

FIGURE 7.1. (a) A regular pyramid and (b) a particular cell.

7.1.1 Structure

The structure of a pyramid is determined by the neighborhood relations within the levels of the pyramid and by the "father–son" relations between adjacent levels.

Definition 9 (Cell) *A* **cell** *(if it is not at the base level) has a set of* **children (sons)** *at the level directly below that provides input to the cell. On the same level, each cell has a set of* **neighbors (brothers/sisters)**, *and each cell (if it is not the apex of the pyramid) has a set of* **parents (fathers)** *at the level above.*

Figure 7.1(a) shows a (regular) pyramid and Figure 7.1(b) a particular cell.

Hence, the structure of any pyramid can be described by horizontal and vertical graphs. Each (horizontal) level of a pyramid can be described by a neighborhood graph (see Section 6.1.1).

Definition 10 ((Horizontal) Neighborhood) *The (horizontal) neighborhood of a vertex $p \in V_i$ is defined by*

$$\Gamma(p) = \{p\} \cup \{q \in V_i | (p, q) \in E_i\}. \tag{7.1}$$

The vertical structure (i.e., the connectivity between the levels) can also be described by a (bipartite) graph.

Definition 11 ((Vertical) Neighborhood) *Let $R_i = ((V_i \cup V_{i+1}), L_i)$ and $L_i \subseteq (V_i \times V_{i+1})$. The set of all sons of a cell $q \in V_{i+1}$ is then defined as:*

$$SON(q) = \{p \in V_i | (p, q) \in L_i\}. \tag{7.2}$$

In a similar manner, the set of all fathers of a cell $p \in V_i$ is defined as:

$$FATHER(p) = \{q \in V_{i+1} | (p, q) \in L_i\}. \tag{7.3}$$

Any pyramid (regular or irregular) with n levels can be described by n neighborhood graphs and $n - 1$ vertical graphs. In the following we distinguish between

FIGURE 7.2. Example of a multi-resolution image ($2 \times 2/4$ pyramid).

- regular structures and

- irregular structures (Section 7.2)

depending on whether the structural relations are the same for all pyramid cells (except at the boundary) or whether they may vary from cell to cell.

Regular Pyramids

Two terms describe the structure of a regular pyramid: the **reduction factor** and the **reduction window**. The reduction factor r determines the rate by which the number of cells decreases from level to level. The reduction window (typically a square $n \times n$) associates to a cell in the higher level a set of cells in the level directly below (e.g., the cell's sons). The usual notation for describing the structure of regular pyramids is $n \times n/r$. For example, in the classical $2 \times 2/4$ pyramid, a window of 2×2 forms a new cell of the next lower resolution. Because there is no overlap in this pyramid, as indicated by $2 \times 2/4 = 1$, the number of cells decreases from level to level by a factor of 4. Figure 7.2 shows an example of a regular $2 \times 2/4$ pyramid.

The quadtree [Sam90] is very similar to the $2 \times 2/4$ pyramid. It differs mainly by the fact that a quadtree has no links to neighbors at the same level. Other pyramid structures with overlapping reduction windows (e.g. $4 \times 4/4, 5 \times 5/4, 2 \times 2/2, 3 \times 3/2$) are characterized by $n \times n/r > 1$ and have also been extensively studied (see [Kro91] for an overview). For completeness we mention the case $n \times n/r < 1$, which indicates the existence of cells without any father.

Regular pyramids have one major drawback. Because the structure is the same for any image (i.e., it is independent of the contents of the image), these pyramids cause problems when the image is shifted, rotated, or differently scaled. Bister et al. [BCR90] proved that image segmentation algorithms based on regular pyramids are not shift-invariant. That is, given an image and a slightly shifted image, the resulting segmentations may differ considerably. This result provides the necessary motivation for the study of irregular structures that are allowed to adapt to the contents of the image.

7.1.2 Contents

The content of a pyramid cell is the type of information stored in the cell. Generally speaking, a cell should store information about the region in the image it represents (i.e., its **receptive field**).

Definition 12 (Receptive Field) *Given a sequence of pyramid levels $V_0, \ldots, V_n$, the receptive field RF of a cell $p_i \in V_i$ is defined as those cells in the base level (V_0) that can influence the cell:*

$$RF(p_i) = \{p_0 | p_0 \in V_0, \exists \ edges \ e_1 = (p_0, p_1), e_2 = (p_1, p_2), \ldots,$$
$$e_i = (p_{i-1}, p_i), p_1 \in V_1, \ldots, p_i \in V_i\}. \tag{7.4}$$

In this case, a pyramid cell is considered an observation window through which a subarea of the base level is observed. Kropatsch [Kro91] gave two rules that should be satisfied by the representation in a pyramid cell:

1. The region corresponding to that cell in the image space covers the pictorial entity (e.g., primitive image parts, objects, configuration of objects) completely.

2. No smaller cell (cell at lower level) in the pyramid fulfills property (1).

When these rules are satisfied, each pictorial entity is assigned a unique cell in the pyramid in which it should be represented. The same principles govern the **asynchronous pyramid** [BJ93], where the output is given in the order of the objects identified by rules 1 and 2 in the bottom-up pyramid construction.

In the simplest (and most common) case, a cell stores only one (gray) value. We call such pyramids **gray level pyramids**. In more complicated cases several parameters of general models are stored in a cell [Har84]. But the basic property that numerical values are stored in a cell remains.

Besides numerical values it is possible to store symbolic information in a cell [Kro87a]. A typical example we consider in the next subsection in more detail is the $2 \times 2/2$ curve pyramid [Kro87a]. In this case, we have a finite number of symbols, and a cell contains these symbols or relations among them. We call such a pyramid **symbolic pyramid**.

7.1.3 Processing

The main property of processing in a pyramid is that it occurs only locally, that is, every cell computes from the contents of the sons, the brothers, and/or the parents a new value and transmits it to one or more cells of its pyramidal neighborhood. In the bottom–up construction phase, input comes from the sons, but for some algorithms the flow of information is also in the top–down direction [GJ86].

The type of operations performed by the cells depends, of course, on the type of the cell's contents. Therefore, we distinguish between numerical and symbolic processing.

Numerical Processing

Three types of filters are commonly used as reduction functions in numerical pyramids:

Linear Filters: One way to linearly filter an image is to convolve it with a spatial filter kernel. Most commonly, low-pass filters are used. Because a low-pass filter suppresses high frequencies in an image, the result can be sub-sampled with a larger sampling distance without losing information by sampling. A Gaussian filter kernel has some unique properties [YP86]; it is therefore commonly used in multiresolution representations. Gaussian pyramids are used to generate a Laplacian pyramid by subtracting each Gaussian pyramid level from the next lower level in the sequence. Furthermore, wavelets have been extensively studied [Mal89, PK91]. They combine a low-pass and a high-pass filter in a way that allows the reconstruction of the original resolution from the two filtered and sub-sampled images.

Nonlinear Filters: Among the most commonly used nonlinear filters in image pyramids are the **maximum** and **minimum filters** [BT88]. The purpose and application are similar to linear filters, but nonlinear filters calculate a nonlinear function of the pixel values. Minimum filters, for example, compute the minimum of the values in the receptive field of a cell. This filter has proven to be useful in inspection tasks where a very small and dark spot indicates a surface defect.

Morphological Filters: Haralick, Lin, Lee, and Zhuang [HLLZ87] introduced the concept of a morphological pyramid, which is built by morphological operations [Ser82]. The input image is first morphologically filtered and then sub-sampled to the reduced image size.

Symbolic Processing

If the contents of a cell consist of symbols or relations among these symbols, we must also apply symbolic reduction functions. In the general case, a finite state machine [HU79] may be used to perform symbolic reduction. For special types of symbols and relations, special reduction functions can be used. For example, Kropatsch [Kro87a] introduced curve relations and a reduction algorithm based on the transitive closure of curve relations. We briefly review the basic steps in building this curve pyramid.

2 × 2/2 Curve Pyramid

The basic idea is that linear structures of images are represented by curve relations. A cell of the pyramid is considered an observation window through which the curve is observed. A single curve intersects this window twice. Only the intersection sides (N, E, S, W)[1] are stored in the cell (i.e., a curve relation). We denote a **curve relation** by AB, where $A, B \in \{N, E, S, W, F\}$ (F is the special end code when the curve ends in a cell).

The basic routines of building the next level of the pyramid are (Figures 7.3 and 7.4):

1. split–subdivision of one cell's contents by introducing a diagonal;

---

[1] North, east, south, west.

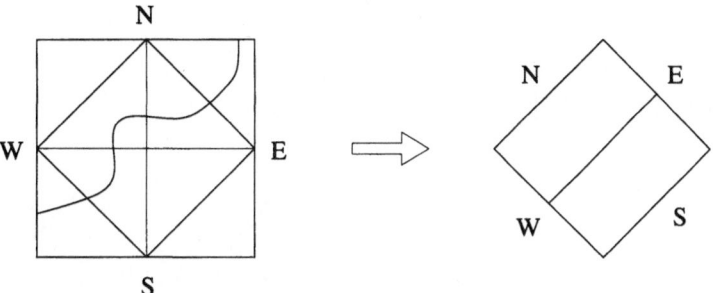

FIGURE 7.3. The reduction step of the $2 \times 2/2$ curve pyramid.

2. transitive closure–the curve relations of the four son cells are merged by computing the transitive closure of all relations (i.e., $AB, BC \Rightarrow AC$); and

3. reduce – the curve relations of the four diagonal elements of the new cell are selected.

Step 1 is based on Jordan's curve theorem because a diagonal is intersected by the curve if and only if it connects opposite sides (with respect to the diagonal).

The $2 \times 2/2$ curve pyramid has several interesting properties. A curve remains connected until it is completely covered by one cell (then it disappears). Very important is the **length reduction property** (i.e., the number of curve code elements decreases after every other reduction step); see [Kro87a]. This important property relates the highest level up to which a curve is still represented to the area traversed by the curve. This implies that short curves will disappear after a few levels, and only long curves will be represented in higher levels of the pyramid (Figure 7.4(d)).

This property has been used for **structural noise filtering** [Kro87b], which first builds the curve pyramid up to a certain level (Figure 7.4(a),(b),(c)) and then deletes all curves that are not represented in the levels below (Figure 7.4(d)).

7.1.4   Fuzzy Curve Pyramid

The (binary) curve pyramid just described has the disadvantage that it can only represent the presence or absence of a curve segment. This binary decision has several demerits:

- We must decide at the base level about the presence or absence of a curve segment. This typically involves the determination of a threshold for an edge detector. This is a problematic step, because either we miss curve segments that cause disconnected curves (and the curve will disappear after a few levels) or we add too many segments, which might connect otherwise disconnected curves.

- Another problem with the binary representation of curves arises when different curves meet in one pyramidal cell. This might cause ambiguities in the representation due to the restricted storage capacity of the pyramidal cells.

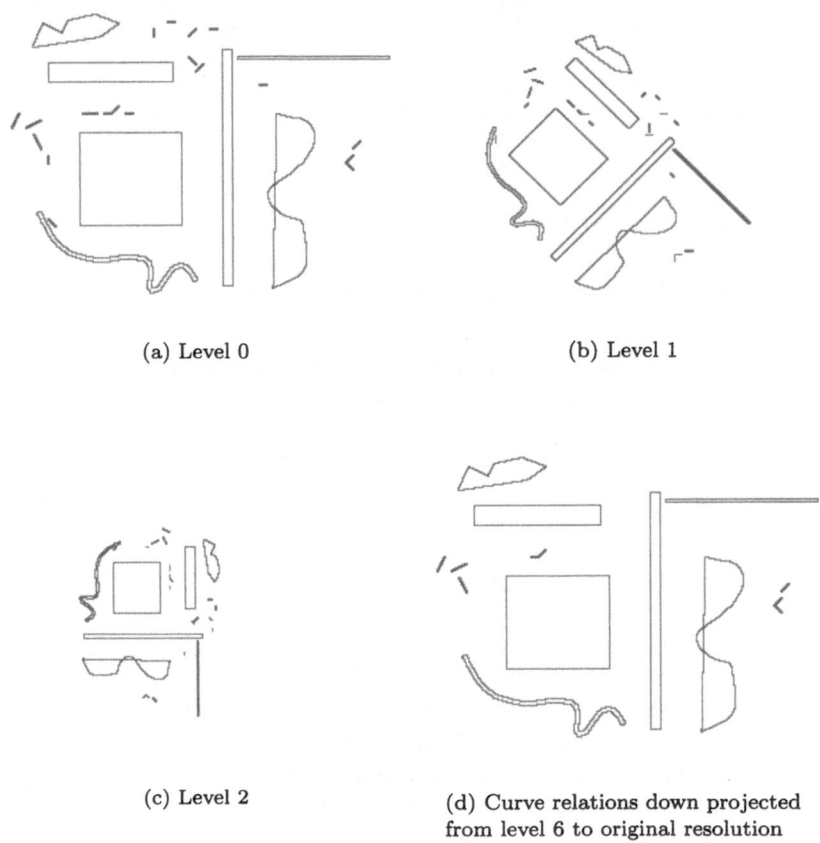

(a) Level 0   (b) Level 1

(c) Level 2   (d) Curve relations down projected
                         from level 6 to original resolution

FIGURE 7.4. Structural noise filtering with the $2 \times 2/2$ binary curve pyramid.

Therefore it would be advantageous to have a nonbinary representation of curves in a pyramid. Because a curve introduces a relation between two sides of a pyramidal cell, a straightforward generalization is to consider fuzzy relations instead of binary ones. The **strength of a curve** is represented by the grade membership of the fuzzy relation.

Definition 13 (Fuzzy Relation) *Let* $X = \{x_1, \ldots, x_k\}$ *be a* $k-$*element fuzzy (or crisp) set. The set* $M \subseteq X \times X \times [0 \ldots 1]$ *is a fuzzy relation. We denote a fuzzy relation between* x_i *and* x_j *with grade membership* $\mu(x_i, x_j)$ *by* $(x_i M x_j, \mu(x_i, x_j))$, *where* $x_i, x_j \in X, 0 \leq \mu(x_i, x_j) \leq 1$.

We say for $\mu(x_i, x_j) = 0$ that there is no relation between x_i and x_j. The relation is symmetric if $\mu(x_i, x_j) = \mu(x_j, x_i) \ \forall x_i, x_j \in X$. In the remainder, relations are assumed to be symmetric.

Let us now describe briefly the individual steps for constructing the $2 \times 2/2$ fuzzy curve pyramid. The steps are generalizations of the binary $2 \times 2/2$ curve pyramid to fuzzy relations. The basic idea is to replace the logical operations (and/or) by min and max operations.

Fuzzy Curve Representation

In [Kro87b] an 8-bit code was suggested to store the curve relations. In order to simplify the discussion we use a simpler code (without end codes); the extension to the equivalent of the 8-bit code is straightforward.

A cell in a pyramid has four sides, labeled N, E, S, W. For each of these sides we use b bits (typically $b = 8$) to store the fuzzy relation. If a curve with strength μ intersects one of these sides we store a value of μ on the corresponding side. Therefore a single curve passing the cell of a pyramid will "activate" two sides of the cell with the same strength. It should be noted that the decisions are only made locally for a particular cell, therefore a neighboring cell may have different strengths. In order to guarantee consistency we require that a curve relation does not end at the side of a cell (e.g., a NS relation in one cell and no relation at the S-neighboring cell). If more than one curve intersects a side of the pyramidal cell we store the maximum of all these curve strengths, indicating the presence of the strongest curve.

Properties of Fuzzy Curve Pyramids

We show several properties of the fuzzy curve pyramid (the proofs can be found in [BK94]).

Property 1 (Length Reduction) *The fuzzy curve pyramid has the length reduction property (i.e., it reduces the number of curve code elements after every reduction step) similar to the $2 \times 2/2$ binary curve pyramid.*

Property 2 (Minimum Strength) *If a single curve intersects the receptive field of a cell at level n, the grade membership of the relation at level n will be the minimum of the grade memberships of the curve segments of the base level.*

For the case when two or more curves pass the receptive field of a cell we can prove a more general property: We define the strength of a curve as the minimum strengths of its segments (see earlier). Then the strength of a fuzzy curve relation AB is the maximum strength of all curves connecting side A with side B. This allows us to formulate the following property.

Property 3 (Maximum Strength) *Let C be a curve in the base of the fuzzy curve pyramid with strength $\mu(C) = \omega_0$. Then this curve will remain connected by the fuzzy reduction process and the strength of all fuzzy curve relations derived from C will be greater than or equal to ω_0, i.e., the strength of the curve is preserved.*

The latter two properties can be combined by the **minmax principle**, which is met by the fuzzy curve pyramid.

Property 4 (Minmax Principle) *The strength of a curve is the minimum of the strength of its segments, and the strength of a side of a cell in the curve pyramid has the maximum strength of all curves intersecting this side.*

7.2 Irregular Graph Pyramids

Irregular pyramids relax the regularity constraint of regular pyramids. These pyramids operate on a general graph structure instead of the regular neighborhood graph as is the case of regular pyramids.

The motivations for the study of such structures are the following:

1. shift variance of regular pyramids as proved in [BCR90] and [BP92];

2. perturbations may destroy the regularity of regular pyramids [MSR88];

3. biological vision systems are not completely regular, e.g., the human retina [Kro92];

4. the high cost of high-resolution CCD sensors (e.g. 2000×2000 pixels) is mainly due to the fact of their low production yield. The sensors could be produced much more cheaply when we allow defective pixels. The resulting sensor geometry would be irregular [Bed92, WOBS93]; and

5. generalization of image processing functions to arbitrary pixel geometries (e.g., log-polar image geometries [RS90, Bed92, HKW$^+$93].

When constructing irregular pyramids we would like to preserve as many properties of regular pyramids as possible. They are due to two processing characteristics:

- all operations are local, and the result does not depend on their order (this allows parallelization); and

- bottom-up construction of the pyramid, with the number of cells decreasing exponentially (contraction property).

In regular pyramids their type (e.g., $n \times n/r$) determines both the geometry and the structure of the reduced levels. Without this regularity we have to define a procedure that derives the structure of the reduced graph G_{i+1} from graph G_i, which is essentially a graph contraction problem. There are two ways to construct irregular pyramids:

1. parallel graph contraction [Ros85] (see also Section 6.2.2); and

2. decimation of the neighborhood graph [Mee89].

Meer [Mee89] introduced an efficient algorithm for building an irregular pyramid by decimation. Because the pyramid is constructed by a random process, it is called a **stochastic pyramid**. Decimation divides the cells in a pyramid level into two categories: Cells that survive form the cells of the next level and cells that do not appear at reduced levels (non-survivors). Meer [Mee89] gave two rules that should be fulfilled by the decimation process.

Definition 14 (Decimation rules)

1. *Two neighbors at the same level cannot both survive, and*

2. *a non-survivor must be a neighbor of a survivor.*

We call a decimation that satisfies these rules a **valid decimation**. In Meer [Mee89] it was shown how a decimation can be computed in parallel by a stochastic algorithm. It is also worth noting that the surviving vertices V_{i+1} of graph G_{i+1} define a maximum independent (vertex) set (MIS) of the graph $G_i = (V_i, E_i)$ if rules 1 and 2 are fulfilled [Chr75].

The algorithm for stochastic decimation proceeds as in Algorithm 5.

Algorithm 5 Stochastic Decimation (in: (V_i, E_i); out: (V_{i+1}, E_{i+1}))

1: Assign uniformly distributed random numbers $\{g(v_i) \in (0, M)\} \subset \mathbb{R}$ to the cells $v_i \in V_i$.

2: Select local maxima of g as surviving cells: $v_i \in V_{i+1}$ if $g(v_i) > g(v_j) \; \forall v_j \in \Gamma(v_i) \setminus \{v_i\}$, where Γ is the horizontal neighborhood.

3: Fill holes, that is, repeat step 2 as long as there are non-surviving cells that have no surviving neighbor:

   (a) set $g(v) := 0 \; \forall v \in V_i : \Gamma(v) \cap V_{i+1} \neq \emptyset$;

   (b) repeat step 2 until $g(v_i) = 0$ for all $v_i \in V_i$.

4: Every non-surviving cell $v_i \in V_i \setminus V_{i+1}$ selects a father $FATHER(v_i) \in V_{i+1} \cap \Gamma(v_i)$. This construction also defines the sons of a surviving node: $SON(v_{i+1}) = \{v_i \in V_i | FATHER(v_i) = v_{i+1}\}$.

5: Construct the neighborhood graph (V_{i+1}, E_{i+1}) of the new level: Two surviving vertices $p_{i+1}, q_{i+1} \in V_{i+1}$ become neighbors at level $i+1$, $(p_{i+1}, q_{i+1}) \in E_{i+1}$ if there exists a vertex $p_i \in SON(p_{i+1})$ that has a neighbor in $SON(q_{i+1})$; that is, $\Gamma(p_i) \cap SON(q_{i+1}) \neq \emptyset$.

6: Set $i := i+1$ and repeat steps 1-6 with new levels until only a single vertex survives, that is, $|V_n| = 1$.

This basic algorithm can be modified to take into account the contents of a cell. The concept of the **adaptive pyramid** [JM92, MB92] selects surviving cells according to the significance of the cell's contents and uses random selection only where the data do not support a decision. This has been used for image segmentation and connected component analysis in logarithmic time complexity [MB92].

Irregular pyramids offer greater flexibility for the price of less efficient access. In [KM92], several properties of irregular pyramids were studied. The main problem of these structures is that the degree of a cell does not remain bounded (for certain configurations, e.g., a tree structure, the degree of a surviving cell increases exponentially).

7.2.1 Computational Complexity

We generalize the computations of a reduction by a transformation $\tau : X \mapsto X'$ that reduces the data size by a factor $\lambda > 1$. It holds

$$|X'| \leq |X|/\lambda, \tag{7.5}$$

while the reduced data set X' preserves some image properties [Kro97d] to compute:

$$\psi(X') = \psi(X). \tag{7.6}$$

Such properties may be the range of gray values, the average gray value, but also the connectivity of regions or their convexity. The application of τ can be repeated on the reduced data set X' until any further reduction would destroy property ψ. Assume that $X^{(n)} = \tau^n(X)$ is the result after n repetitions. From Equation (7.5) it follows that the overall size reduction is bounded by $\lambda^n < \frac{|X|}{|X^{(n)}|}$ and the number n of repetitions:

$$n < \frac{\log|X| - \log|X^{(n)}|}{\log\lambda}. \tag{7.7}$$

Together with constraints (7.5) and (7.6) and the assumption that τ needs only local parallel computations, $\psi(X) = \psi(X^{(n)})$ can be computed in $\mathcal{O}(\log|X|)$ parallel steps [Kro97a].

Classical regular pyramids [JR94] have property (7.5), but in general, counterexamples for property (7.6) can be constructed [BCR90]. It has been demonstrated [KB96] that adaptive pyramids in which the transformation τ depends on the data X overcome the problem. The price to pay is the loss of regularity.

7.2.2   Irregular Pyramids by Hopfield Networks

In the following we will show that we can replace steps 1–3 of the algorithm for stochastic decimation by a modified Hopfield network that works on the neighborhood graph $G = \langle V, A \rangle$.[2] Moreover, we show that the formulation as a Hopfield network is more general than the stochastic decimation, and it naturally includes the concept of the adaptive pyramid.

Let us introduce the notion of a survival state of a cell and an energy function.

Definition 15 (Survival State of a Cell) *The survival state s of a cell $p \in V$ is a function*

$$s : V \mapsto \{0,1\} \text{ with } s(p) = \left\{ \begin{array}{ll} 1, & \textit{if cell } p \textit{ survives,} \\ 0, & \textit{otherwise.} \end{array} \right.$$

Definition 16 (Energy Function)

$$E = -\frac{1}{2} \sum_{\langle i,j \rangle \in A} w_{ij} s(i) s(j) - \sum_{k \in V} I_k s(k),$$

where $w_{ij} \in \mathbb{R}$ is the weight between cell i and j, and I_k is the external input of cell k.

Now we can prove the following theorem, which is a generalization of previous results in [BK93a].

---

[2] We skip the subindices for level i because the algorithm works level by level.

Theorem 7 *The energy function E from Definition 16 obtains a local minimum, E_{min}, with $I_k > 0 \ \forall k \in V, w_{ij} = w_{ji} < 0$ and $I_k < |w_{ij}| \ \forall k \in V, \langle i, j \rangle \in A$ if and only if the assignment of surviving and non–surviving cells, $s(p)$, is a valid decimation (i.e., satisfying rules 1 and 2 of Definition 14) or, equivalently, forms a maximum independent vertex set of G.*

Proof: See [BBB96].

Given the energy function in Definition 16 we can now define a Hopfield network operating on the neighborhood graph that minimizes this energy function and computes valid decimations (according to Definition 14). The update procedure of the cells is as follows:

$$s(p) = \begin{cases} 1, & \text{if } I_p + \sum_{\langle q,p \rangle \in A} w_{qp} s(q) > 0; \\ 0, & \text{otherwise.} \end{cases} \tag{7.8}$$

The initial state of the network can be chosen at random. Theorem 7 states that all the networks that satisfy the conditions on the weights and external input form an equivalence class. That is, as long as the conditions of the theorem are satisfied, the network will end up in the same final state (the initialization and update order must also be identical).

According to the theorem we can produce all possible maximum independent vertex sets of a graph with a Hopfield network. Each produced set depends on the (random) initial state and the (random) order of update of the cells. Because the Hopfield network performs a stochastic gradient descent search on the energy function E, the result is also stochastic. Therefore the resulting pyramid structure will also be stochastic, as in the case of Meer's algorithm. It is not necessary to perform more sophisticated procedures like simulated annealing or mean field theory annealing [GG84] because (at least for regular grids) the global minimum of the energy function is unique (up to symmetries) and corresponds to the maximum number of surviving cells. In this case the pyramid would no longer be stochastic. For example, in the case of a four-connected-pixel grid we would get the $2 \times 2/2$ pyramid, which is regular, and therefore shift-variant.

However, there exist other types of minimization procedures that can be used. For example, a greedy algorithm that calculates for every cell the energy difference gained by changing the state of the cell and then selects the cell with the largest energy difference for update. This algorithm has the disadvantage that it is not local. The other advantage of the formulation as a Hopfield network is that chips for simulating Hopfield networks are available, so it is easy to implement the selection of survivors in hardware.

The essential result is that we can specify an energy function for selecting the survivors. This energy function might be useful for certain proofs about irregular pyramids because it is mathematically easier to handle than the procedure of Meer.

Adaptive Pyramids

We demonstrate how to influence the decimation process by a proper setting of weights of the Hopfield network. If the weights depend on the contents of the image the resulting pyramid structure will be adapted to the image. Therefore it is called an **adaptive pyramid**.

The energy function (Definition 16) has the weights w_{ij} and the external input I_k as parameters that can be changed in order to influence the decimation. The weights w_{ij} between two cells express the constraints on the mutual states of these cells. One should note that as long as $w_{ij} > -I_j$ the behavior of the network is not changed (as can be seen from Theorem 7). The external input I_i can force a single cell to survive or not to survive; e.g., if $I_i > \sum_{j \in \Gamma(i)} |w_{ji}|$ cell i survives, on the other hand if $I_i < 0$ and the weights are negative, then cell i will not survive.

It is interesting to note that the external input I_j can control the number of surviving cells (and therefore the regions found). If I_j is large many cells will survive, if it is small fewer cells will survive, where for positive I_j the limit is a maximum vertex set. We use these observations to build adaptive pyramids [MMR91, JM92]. To determine the connected components of a binary image we set $I_k = 1$ for all $k \in V$, and the weights according to:

$$w_{ij} = \begin{cases} -2, & i \text{ and } j \text{ are neighbors and have the same gray value;} \\ 0, & \text{otherwise,} \end{cases} \qquad (7.9)$$

or expressed differently $w_{ij} = -2(1 - d_{ij})$, where $d_{ij} = |g_i - g_j|$, $g_i \in \{0, 1\}$, are the values of the pixels. In this case the survivors and non-survivors are computed only within a homogeneous region (with identical pixel values). This procedure is equivalent to the algorithm [MMR91], which applied the stochastic decimation only within homogeneous regions.

We generalize this scheme to gray-level images. We set the weights of the corresponding Hopfield network according to the gray value difference of the regions, i.e.,

$$w_{ij} = f(d_{ij}) \text{ and } d_{ij} = |g_i - g_j|. \qquad (7.10)$$

A generalization of function (7.9) is

$$w_{ij} = f(d_{ij}) = \begin{cases} -2, & d_{ij} < \Theta; \\ 0, & \text{otherwise,} \end{cases} \qquad (7.11)$$

which is a threshold function, where Θ is the threshold. In choosing the function f for setting the weights one must be careful that $|w_{ij}|$ is not too small, because for $I_j > \sum_i |w_{ij}|$ the cell will always survive. However, this should happen only in those cases where no similar cell in the neighborhood exists.

With the adaptive pyramid and the setting of weights we are influencing the decimation ratio, i.e., we allow more cells to survive. It is important that we do not alter the property that a non-survivor must be a neighbor of a survivor, because this would make the algorithm nonlocal, which implies that a parallel implementation would be very costly. The modifications we have proposed leave the decimations in homogeneous regions unchanged, but in nonhomogeneous regions more cells are allowed to survive, so that a non-surviving cell has the possibility to select a similar cell as father. This can be proved by the following theorem.

Theorem 8 *Let $I_k > 0$ $\forall k \in V$ and $w_{ij} = w_{ji} < 0$. The following statements are equivalent:*

A: *The assignment of surviving and non–surviving cells, $s(p)$, satisfies Rule 2 of Definition 14; and*

B: *The energy function E from Definition 16 obtains a local minimum E_{min}.*

Proof: See [BBB96].

This theorem is also the basis for the invariance property of adaptive pyramids. Because the survivors depend on the contents of the image, if we shift the image, then the survivors in nonhomogeneous regions will also be shifted, whereas in homogeneous regions it does not matter which cell survives.

The algorithm for the adaptive pyramid controlled by a Hopfield network works as follows (Algorithm 6).

Algorithm 6 Adaptive Hopfield Network

1: Calculate the neighborhood graph of the base level.
2: Initialize the states of the cells at random and compute the weights according to the function f.
3: Update the states of the cells asynchronously according to the update function Equation (7.8) until convergence.
4: Every non-surviving cell ($s(i) = 0$) selects the father with the most similar gray value.
5: Calculate the new neighborhood graph of the next level (according to step 5 of algorithm 5).
6: Repeat steps 2–6 until the graph does not change any more (i.e., all cells are survivors).

We note that the decimation by the Hopfield network naturally includes the concept of the adaptive pyramid with the weights of the neighborhood graph.

Experimental Results

The following results show several experiments obtained with an irregular pyramid controlled by a Hopfield network. Instead of starting from the original image we used in these results the graph of an adaptive Voronoi tessellation as the base level of the pyramid (for more detail see [BBB96]). Figure 7.5 shows the segmentation of Lenna, Figure 7.6 a pyramid constructed by our method, and Figure 7.7 a result obtained with the adaptive pyramid of [MMR91]. Using our technique we need fewer levels in the pyramid, and we end up with a segmentation with fewer regions.

7.2.3 Equivalent Contraction Kernels

How can the Dual Graph Contraction (see Section 6.2.2) be applied to several levels of a pyramid? The combination of two (and more) successive reductions in an equivalent

FIGURE 7.5. Image "Lenna"; final result of the segmentation. Starting with 9033 Voronoi polygons 50 regions remain.

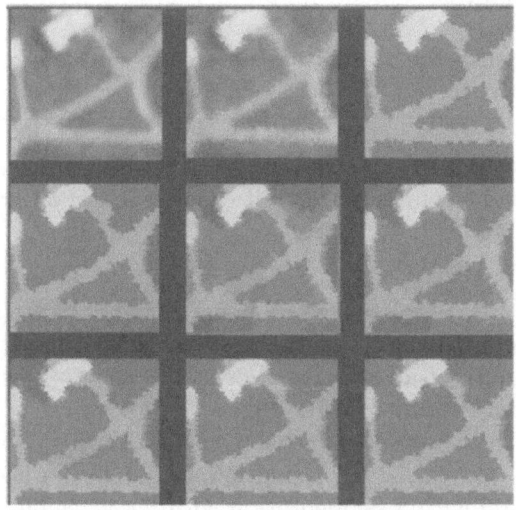

FIGURE 7.6. "Adaptive" segmentation. From left to right and top to bottom: Original image; Voronoi diagram; 1043 polygons; level 8: 12 regions; final result (level 9): 9 regions; level 3: 129 regions; level 4: 123 regions; level 5: 59 regions; level 6: 34 regions; level 7: 19 regions.

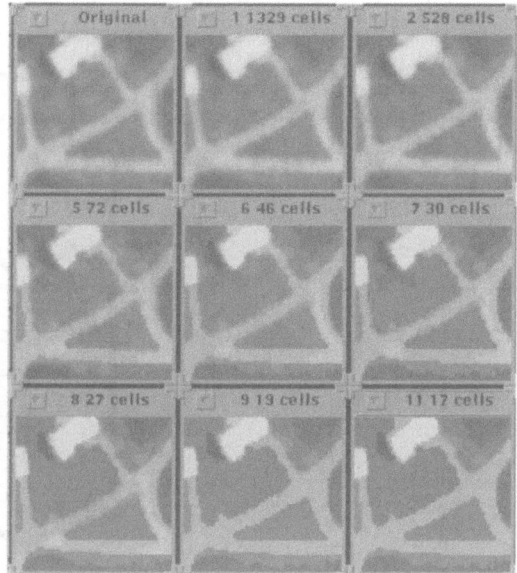

FIGURE 7.7. From left to right and top to bottom: Level 0: original image 4096 pixels; level 1: 1329 regions; level 2: 528 regions; level 5: 72 regions; level 6: 46 regions; level 7: 30 regions; level 8: 19 regions; final result (level 11): 17 regions.

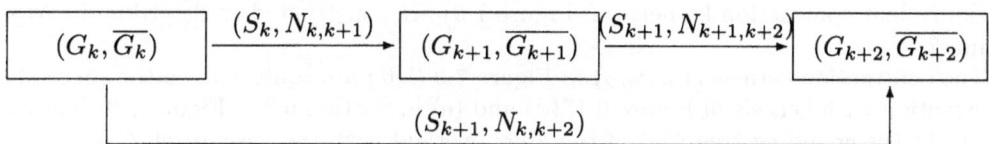

FIGURE 7.8. Equivalent contraction kernel.

weighting function allowed Burt to calculate any level of the pyramid directly from the base [BA83]. Similarly we combine two (and more) dual graph contractions (see Figure 7.8) of graph G_k with decimation parameters $(S_k, N_{k,k+1})$ and $(S_{k+1}, N_{k+1,k+2})$ into one single **equivalent contraction kernel** (ECK) $N_{k,k+2} = N_{k,k+1} \circ N_{k+1,k+2}$ (for simplicity G_i stands for $(G_i, \overline{G_i})$) [Kro97b, Kro97c]:

$$C[C[G_k, (S_k, N_{k,k+1})], (S_{k+1}, N_{k+1,k+2})] = C[G_k, (S_{k+1}, N_{k,k+2})]$$
$$= G_{k+2}. \tag{7.12}$$

The combination of two successive contraction kernels into an ECK is based on a function bridge establishing a 1:1 mapping between connecting path and contraction edge.

Definition 17 (Bridge) *A function* **bridge** : $E_{k+1} \mapsto E_k$ *assigns to each edge* $e_{k+1} = (v_{k+1}, w_{k+1}) \in E_{k+1}$ *one of the bridges* $e_k \in E_k$ *of the connecting paths* $CP(v_{k+1}, w_{k+1})$:

$$bridge(e_{k+1}) := e_k. \tag{7.13}$$

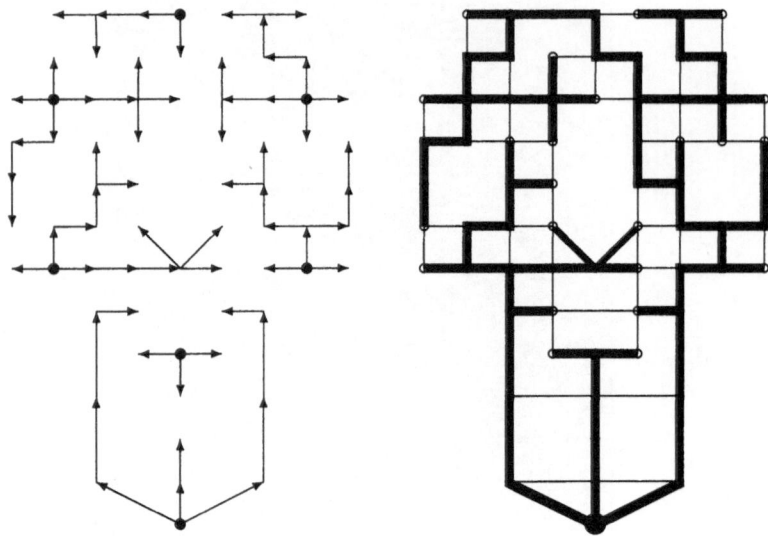

FIGURE 7.9. Example of equivalent contraction kernels: (left) $(S_1, N_{0,2}) = (S_0, N_{0,1}) \circ (S_1, N_{1,2})$ and (right) of the apex: $G_0 \cup N_{0,4}$.

Equivalent contraction kernels (cf. Figure 7.9) are constructed as described in Algorithm 7.

The contraction kernels $(V_2, N_{0,2})$ in Figure 7.9 (left) are equivalent to the successive contraction with kernels of Figure 6.15(d) and (e) in Section 6.2.2. Figure 7.9 shows on the right the spanning tree $N_{0,4}$ of the apex overlaid with the base graph G_0.

7.2.4   Extensions to 3D

The advantages of pyramids should certainly not be restricted to two-dimensional data. The third spatial dimension and the time dimension offer several interesting applications. In these cases the concepts of planarity and duality must be substituted by a higher-dimensional concept that allows decisions whether a cell or a collection of cells is **inside** any other connected agglomeration of cells.

- Four elements can be used to build structures in 3D: **pointels, linels, surfels, and voxels** (cf. e.g. [AAF95]).

  These basic elements describe 0-, 1-, 2-, and 3-dimensional entities in 3D-space. Duality can be established by placing one pointel inside any voxel and by intersecting any surfel by one linel (Figure 7.10).

- **Abstract cellular complexes** of Kovalevsky [Kov93] offer another possibility to reach higher dimensions.

Algorithm 7 Equivalent Contraction Kernels

1: Assume that the dual irregular pyramid $((G_0, \overline{G_0}), (G_1, \overline{G_1}), \ldots, (G_{k+2}, \overline{G_{k+2}}))$ is the result of $k+2$ dual graph contractions. The structure of G_{k+2} is fully determined by the structure of G_{k+1} and the decimation parameters $(S_{k+1}, N_{k+1,k+2})$.

2: Furthermore, the structure of G_{k+1} is determined by G_k and the decimation parameters $(S_k, N_{k,k+1})$. $S_{k+1} = V_{k+2}$ are the vertices surviving from G_k to G_{k+2}. The searched contraction kernels must be formed by edges $N_{k,k+2} \subset E_k$. This is true for $N_{k,k+1}$ but not for $N_{k+1,k+2} \subset E_{k+1}$ if we would simply overlay the two sets of decimation parameters.

3: An edge $e_{k+1} = (v_{k+1}, w_{k+1}) \in N_{k+1,k+2}$ corresponds to a connecting path $CP_k(v_{k+1}, w_{k+1})$ in G_k. By Definition 8 (see Section 6.2.2), $CP_k(v_{k+1}, w_{k+1})$ consists of one branch of $T_k(v_{k+1})$, one branch of $T_k(w_{k+1})$, and one surviving edge $e_k \in E_k$ connecting the two contraction kernels $T_k(v_{k+1})$ and $T_k(w_{k+1})$.

4: Two disjoint tree structures connected by a single edge become a new tree structure. The result of connecting all contraction kernels T_k by bridges fulfills the requirements of a contraction kernel:

$$N_{k,k+2} := N_{k,k+1} \quad \cup \bigcup_{e_{k+1} \in N_{k+1,k+2}} \text{bridge}(e_{k+1}). \qquad (7.14)$$

5: This process can be repeated on the remaining contraction kernels until the base level 0 contracts in one step into the apex $V_n = \{v_n\}$. The edges of the corresponding spanning tree are contained in $N_{0,n}$.

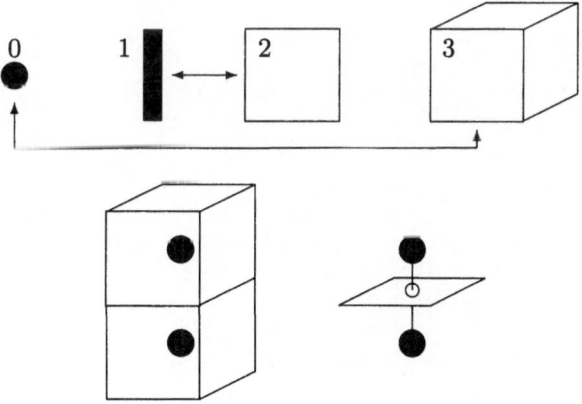

FIGURE 7.10. Duality in 3D: pointels, linels, surfels, and voxels.

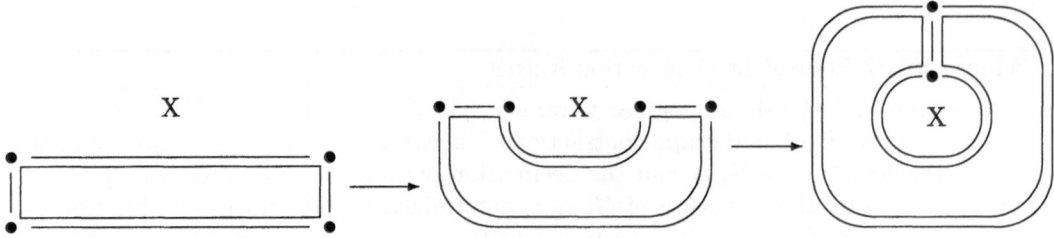

FIGURE 7.11. Bending a cell around a hole region X.

Unfortunately this theory does not yet provide the possibility to represent holes. One idea to integrate holes is to bend a regular cell around the hole region (marked "X" in Figure 7.11).

- The concepts of **star topology** [AAF95] and **boundary graphs** of Ahronovitz [AF94] may be suited to be combined with hierarchical structures. The problem to be solved seems to be the convexity of cells that can be lost during contraction.

Applications of dual contractions within graphs representing three-dimensional objects are described in [EG99, GEK99, GE99] and for pyramids in [PKJ98]. The implementation of the dual graph contraction is depicted in [KBYN98] (cf. also the accompanying CD).

8

Robust Methods

Aleš Leonardis
Horst Bischof

8.1 The Role of Robustness in Computer Vision

The characteristics of the visual signal, such as the overwhelming amount of data, high redundancy, relevant information clustered in space and time, indicate that certain organization and aggregation principles have to be used to reduce the computational complexity of the visual processes and to bridge the gap between the raw data and symbolic descriptions. In computer vision, the data aggregation problem is most commonly approached by fitting models of visual phenomena to image data. Because the image data is inherently unreliable [Sch90], a fitting method should be able to cope with both

- noise that is well-behaved in a distributional sense and

- outliers, which are either large measurement errors or data points belonging to other distributions (models).

It is well known that the least-squares estimator that is based on the assumption of a pure Gaussian noise is very sensitive to outliers in the data set, which may lead to extremely poor results.

In Schunck [Sch90] it is argued that visual perception is fundamentally a problem in discrimination: Data must be combined with similar data and outliers must be rejected. In other words, vision algorithms must be able to combine data while simultaneously discriminating between data that should be kept distinct, such as outliers (errors) and data from other regions. In fact, the data association problem (grouping) makes the task of machine perception fundamentally different from the traditional estimation problems.

The estimators that remain stable in the presence of various types of noise and can tolerate a certain portion of outliers are known under the generic name of *robust estimators* [Hub81, RL87]. These estimators are characterized by the concepts of *efficiency* and *breakdown point*. Efficiency refers to the relative ability of an estimator to yield optimal estimates at the assumed noise distribution. The breakdown point of an estimator is determined by the smallest portion of outliers in the data set at which the estimation procedure can produce an arbitrarily wrong estimate. It is especially the aspect of the breakdown point which is usually emphasized in the design of robust estimators for vision algorithms. This indicates that the use of robust estimators in computer vision is often much more in the function of rejecting outliers than in the function of optimally estimating parameters of the models in the case of non-Gaussian data distributions that may arise from the nature of the physical data.

Some robust local operators [BBW88] can theoretically achieve the maximum breakdown point of 0.5, which means that the estimate remains unchanged if fewer than half of the data are outliers. In practice, the breakdown point may be much lower. Li [Li85], for example, has shown that various classes of robust local operators have breakdown points that are less than $1/(p+1)$, where p is the number of parameters in the regression. Moreover, Kim et al. [KKM+89] have pointed out the infeasibility of using robust local operators in the transition area of two (or more) statistical populations (models). Many of these methods are also sensitive to initial estimates and computationally very expensive. However, their performance can be improved when they are used as building blocks in a more complex method.

Here we present one such method for robust estimation of parametric models. The method can be considered a general framework in which different parameter estimation techniques can be embedded. The method consists of two procedures: model-recovery and model-selection. The first procedure ensures data consistency by iteratively combining data classification and parameter estimation, enabling the rejection of outliers. The overall insensitivity to initial estimates is achieved by systematically recovering a redundant set of parametric models and then passing them to the model-selection procedure, which selects a subset of these models based on their spatial extent, goodness-of-fit, and number of parameters.

8.2   Parametric Models

8.2.1   Robust Estimation Methods

In this section we mention some of the robust estimation methods and point out some of their features. Robust window operators [BBW88, KKM+89, MMRK91, SS92] have been brought into computer vision as an answer to the problems encountered when using standard least-squares methods in windows containing outliers or more than one statistical population. M-estimators, for example, tackle the problems by either rejecting "bad" data points from the calculation of model estimate (*hard redescenders*) or down-weighting their influence on the final result (*soft redescenders* see Section 14.2.2 for a concrete application on feature-based matching). This is achieved by first computing an initial estimate and then refining it by repeated re-weighting of the data points. Several disadvantages can be identified with this approach. Because the information obtained in one window is usually *not* shared among the neighboring windows, the parameter estimation has to start in each window from scratch, i.e., there is no a priori information that data points could, or could not, belong to the model. As the weighting of the data depends on the parameters and vice versa, there is no closed-form solution, and an iterative procedure has to be used for parameter estimation. Another consequence of such a local approach is that the number of outliers that can be tolerated successfully is limited. Also the initial estimates are unreliable because they are based on a small number of data points in a window (if we enlarge the size of the window, we increase the risk of encompassing data that belong to several different models). For certain redescending (non-monotonic) functions there are no guarantees of convergence to a unique solution, which means that the method may not be able to correct the initial errors.

In general, the size of the window plays an important role in the case of robust window operators since it influences the accuracy of the solution and the computational time. Many robust operators are hard to implement and computationally demanding even for neighborhoods of reasonable sizes [MMRK91].

To overcome some of these problems, methods were designed that estimate parameters of the models on domains that are not restricted to prespecified windows [FB81, Bes88, Che89]. While robust window operators have been designed to tolerate a certain portion of outliers, these methods try to prevent the outliers to enter the parameter estimation procedure in the first place. The main idea is that once we have an initial model, we can propagate the information to the neighboring regions. Data points that are found to be consistent with the model are sequentially added, outliers are rejected, and the parameters of the model are re-computed. Depending on the weighting function of the estimator, the new data points that are iteratively added to the model can also be properly weighted [MB93].

The main problem that remains unsolved with these approaches is how to determine an initial set of data points (a seed) that would yield a reliable estimation of initial model parameters. The set of initial data points must be kept small to reduce the probability that the data points would belong to multiple models. As a consequence, the estimation of initial model parameters is unreliable. We can argue that neither extensive preprocessing nor the usage of robust estimators can prevent some of the initial estimates from being incorrect or too crude to be used to guide the data aggregation process.

The other problem is the influence that the developing models have on one another. It has been a common practice to develop models in a sequence and those recovered earlier in the process constrained the ones developed later by restricting their domains only to unclassified data points. Erroneous results are thus propagated through the entire procedure, resulting in an overall faulty output.

In the paradigm, which is described in the next section, we made an attempt to develop a method that can cope with these problems.

8.3   Robust Methods in Vision

8.3.1   Recover-and-Select Paradigm

In this section we present the recover-and-select paradigm. First we describe the *model-recovery* procedure, which includes the strategy for grouping image elements and estimating parameters of the models. We also discuss the selection of the seeds. Then we explain how the models with the best descriptive power are selected by optimizing the quadratic Boolean problem. Finally we describe our approach in combining model-recovery and model-selection in an iterative way, which substantially reduces the computational complexity of the method.

Perhaps closest in spirit to our approach is the work done by Pentland [Pen89], who developed an image segmentation system that first creates a large set of hypotheses about the scene part structure (in terms of binary templates) and then uses a modified Hopfield-Tank network that searches for the subset of those hypotheses that constitute the most likely description of the image.

Model Recovery

We solve the problem of data classification and parameter estimation by an iterative approach, which is conceptually similar to the one described by Besl [Bes88] and Chen [Che89], which simultaneously combines data classification and model fitting. Despite the similarities between our method and, in particular, the one described by Besl [Bes88], our approach differs from the latter in a crucial step, namely, in the selection of initial estimates (seed regions), which then leads to a variety of unique features such as redundancy, parallelism, reduced computational complexity, and provable termination of the algorithm without sacrificing the reliability of the method. Another distinctive feature of our approach is that the individual models are independently recovered, which further increases the robustness. Besides, our method treats the recovered models only as *hypotheses*, which then compete to be selected in the final description.

Seed Selection

As we have discussed, selection of the seeds has a major effect on the success or failure of the overall procedure. Chen [Che89] proposed that a window is moved around in an image searching for an adequate amount of data that is statistically consistent in the sense that the data points belong to the same model. Thus, the requirement of classifying all points from a certain model is relaxed to finding only a small subset. On the other hand, Besl [Bes88] followed the approach of extensive preprocessing to determine the initial estimates. The preprocessing involved computing second-order properties in the local neighborhood of every pixel that is noise sensitive. In the RANSAC paradigm [FB81] the algorithm randomly selects a minimal set of points necessary to fit a model. The resulting model is then tested for validity, which is based on the number of data points in the consensus set of the model.

We argue that despite using elaborate techniques there is no guarantee that every seed will lead to a good result. For example, the seed consistency can sometimes be satisfied on low strength C^0 and C^1 discontinuities. As a remedy we propose an approach that is not sensitive to the selection of inappropriate seeds. The idea is to *independently* build *all possible* models using all statistically consistent seeds, found in a grid of windows overlaid on the image, and then use the recovered models as hypotheses that could compose the final result.

To determine the statistical consistency of a seed, we fit a model[1] to the data points in the seed window. We take the seed as statistically consistent if the goodness-of-fit indicates that there is a high probability that all the data points in the seed window belong to the same model. For each statistically consistent seed we estimate the parameter(s) of the model and proceed with the model-recovery procedure, which simultaneously combines data classification and model fitting.

Data Classification and Model Fitting

The procedure for the recovery of parametric models can be partitioned into three distinct modules. A schematic diagram of the procedure is shown in Figure 8.1.

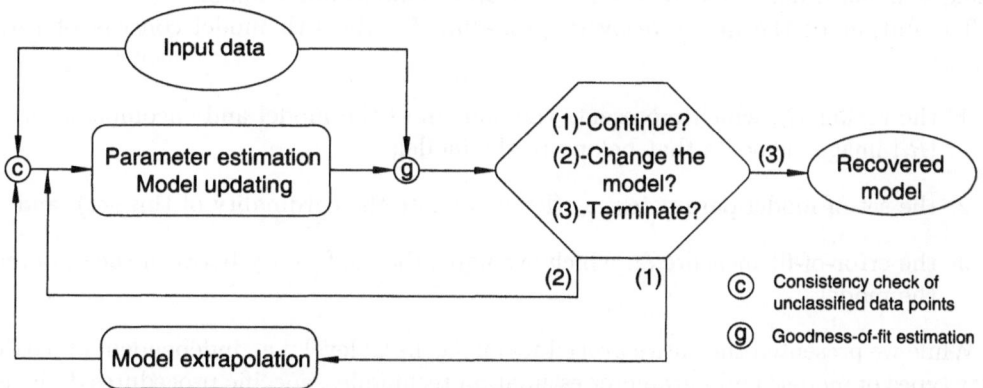

FIGURE 8.1. A schematic diagram outlining the model-recovery procedure.

Data Point Classification

Let us suppose that we have a partially recovered model. An efficient search for more compatible points is performed by extrapolating the current model and testing the new data points for consistency. The consistency check can involve sophisticated methods to establish the compatibility of a data point to the model, or a simple distance measure together with a threshold can be used to classify the data points into inliers and outliers. Additional constraints can be employed, for example, to preserve the topological properties of the models (connectivity). Outliers, which can be classified as either extreme measurement deviations or data points that belong to neighboring models, are rejected. New consistent image elements are temporarily included in the data set and passed to the parameter estimation module.

---

[1]In the case that we have a hierarchy of models of increasing complexity we always start with the hypothesis that the initial data points belong to the simplest model, i.e., the one with the minimum number of parameters. This is due to the limited amount of reliable information that can be gathered in an *initially local* area.

Parameter Estimation

For the given set of data points, the type of parametric model, and the estimation technique we compute the parameters of the model and the goodness-of-fit.

Decision Making

If sufficient similarity is established between the model and the data (goodness-of-fit), we accept the currently estimated parameters, together with the current data set, and proceed with a search for more compatible points. Otherwise a decision is made whether to replace the currently used model with a more complex one (if there is one), calculate a new set of parameters, and re-evaluate the goodness-of-fit, or terminate the procedure. The procedure terminates if the goodness-of-fit does not improve significantly despite using a higher-order model or if no higher-order models are available.

The output of the model-recovery procedure for the i-th model consists of three terms:

1. the region R_i, which represents the domain of the model and encompasses $n_i = |R_i|$ image elements that belong to the model;

2. the set of model parameters $\mathbf{a}_i$ (let N_i denote the cardinality of this set); and

3. the error-of-fit measure ξ_i, which evaluates the conformity between the data and the model.

While we presented the entire procedure on a general level, i.e., independent of particular types of models and parameter estimation techniques, specific procedures designed to operate on individual types of models can differ significantly. Different parameter estimation techniques are due to different dependencies of fitting functions on the set of unknown parameters. For example, a linear or nonlinear parameter estimation procedure can be a direct consequence of the choice in defining the measure of the distance between the model and the data.

Because the model-recovery is performed for all statistically consistent seeds, the complete output of the procedure consists of numerous recovered models, which represent the candidates for the final description of the data.

Model Selection

The redundant set of parametric models obtained by the model-recovery procedure is a direct consequence of the decision that a search for parametric models is systematically initiated everywhere in an image. Several of the models are partially or completely overlapped. The task of obtaining a subset of the recovered models is defined as a selection procedure that considers many competitive solutions and selects those models that produce the simplest global description. The principle of simplicity has a long history in psychology (Gestalt principles), and the formalization of this principle led in information theory to the method of Minimum Description Length (MDL), which has recently found its way to computer science, including computer vision [Lec89, FH89, Pen89]. According to the MDL principle, those models are selected from the set of recovered models that describe the data with the shortest possible encoding. As will be shown in the next subsection, models that provide an efficient encoding should encompass a large number of data points and have a high value of the goodness-of-fit measure. These are exactly the characteristics of the models that contain only the data points belonging to a single statistical population. In contrast, models that incorporated outliers or contain data points that belong to a mixture of data populations either accumulate substantial errors (which prevent them from growing further) or fail to find more compatible points. In any case, these models span a relatively small number of data points and have a poor goodness-of-fit.

In the next two subsections we describe the objective function that encompasses the information about the competing models and the optimization procedure that selects a set of models, respectively.

Objective Function

We want to describe parts of the image, or possibly the whole image, in terms of a selected subset of the set of all recovered models. Let vector $\mathbf{m}^T = [m_1, m_2, \dots, m_M]$ denote a set of models, where m_i is a *presence-variable* having the value 1 for the presence of the model and 0 for its absence in the final description, and M is the number of all models. The length of encoding of an image L_{image} can be given as the sum of two terms

$$L_{\text{image}}(\mathbf{m}) = L_{\text{pointwise}}(\mathbf{m}) + L_{\text{models}}(\mathbf{m}). \tag{8.1}$$

$L_{\text{pointwise}}(\mathbf{m})$ is the length of encoding of individual data points that are not described by any model, and $L_{\text{models}}(\mathbf{m})$ is the length of encoding of data described by the selected models. The idea is to select a subset of models that would yield the shortest length description.

We can translate the equation (8.1) into our particular case using the outcome of the model-recovery procedure

$$L_{\text{image}}(\mathbf{m}) = K_1(n_{\text{all}} - n(\mathbf{m})) + K_2\xi(\mathbf{m}) + K_3 N(\mathbf{m}), \tag{8.2}$$

where n_{all} denotes the number of all data points in the input and $n(\mathbf{m})$ the number of data points that are explained by the selected models. $N(\mathbf{m})$ specifies the number of parameters that are needed to describe the selected models, and $\xi(\mathbf{m})$ gives the deviation between the models and the data that these models describe. K_1, K_2, and K_3 are weights, which can be determined on a purely information-theoretical basis (in terms of bits), or they can be adjusted to express the preference for a particular type of description [Leo93].

So far, the optimization function has been discussed on a general level. More specifically, our objective function, which takes into account the individual models, has the following form:

$$F(\mathbf{m}) = \mathbf{m}^T \mathbf{Q} \mathbf{m} = \mathbf{m}^T \begin{bmatrix} c_{11} & \cdots & c_{1M} \\ \vdots & & \vdots \\ c_{M1} & \cdots & c_{MM} \end{bmatrix} \mathbf{m}. \tag{8.3}$$

The diagonal terms of the matrix $\mathbf{Q}$ express the cost-benefit value for a particular model M_i

$$c_{ii} = \mathrm{K}_1 n_i - \mathrm{K}_2 \xi_i - \mathrm{K}_3 N_i, \tag{8.4}$$

while the off-diagonal terms handle the interaction between the overlapping models

$$c_{ij} = \frac{-\mathrm{K}_1 |R_i \cap R_j| + \mathrm{K}_2 \xi_{i,j}}{2}. \tag{8.5}$$

$|R_i \cap R_j|$ is the number of points that are explained by both models, and $\xi_{i,j}$ is defined as

$$\xi_{i,j} = \max\left(\sum_{R_i \cap R_j} d^2_{M_i}, \sum_{R_i \cap R_j} d^2_{M_j} \right). \tag{8.6}$$

The error terms $d^2_{M_i}$ and $d^2_{M_j}$ are calculated in the region of intersection $R_i \cap R_j$ and correspond to deviations of the data from the i-th and j-th models, respectively.

The objective function takes into account the interaction between different models, which may be completely or partially overlapped. However, like Pentland [Pen89], we consider only the pairwise overlaps in the final solution.

We have formulated the problem in such a way that its solution corresponds to the global extremum of the objective function. Maximization of the objective function $F(\mathbf{m})$ belongs to the class of combinatorial optimization problems (quadratic Boolean problem). Because the number of possible solutions increases exponentially with the size of the problem, it is usually not tractable to explore them exhaustively. It turned out that in our case, for well-behaved inputs (in the sense of being well describable by the chosen set of models), we obtain reasonable solutions by a direct application of the *greedy algorithm*. The algorithm is simple: We start with the state in which no models have been selected. The initial value of $F(\mathbf{m})$ is 0. A successor state is formed by adding a not-yet-selected model to the current description. The selected model is the one that contributes the most to the value of the objective function. The process of adding models to the current description is repeated as long as the value of the objective function can be increased.

Model-Recovery and Model-Selection

After having explained the two major components of our method, namely, the module for model recovery and the module for model selection, we now describe how they can be combined to obtain a fast and efficient overall method. For example, the modules can be applied in succession, as shown in Figure 8.2 (a). All the models are first grown to their full extent and then passed to the selection module. We call this approach *Recover-then-Select*. However, the computational cost of growing all the models completely is prohibitive in most cases. Instead it would be desirable to discard some of the redundant and superfluous models even before they are fully grown. This suggests incorporating the selection procedure into the recovery procedure, as shown in Figure 8.2 (b). We call this approach *Recover-and-Select*. The recovery of currently active models

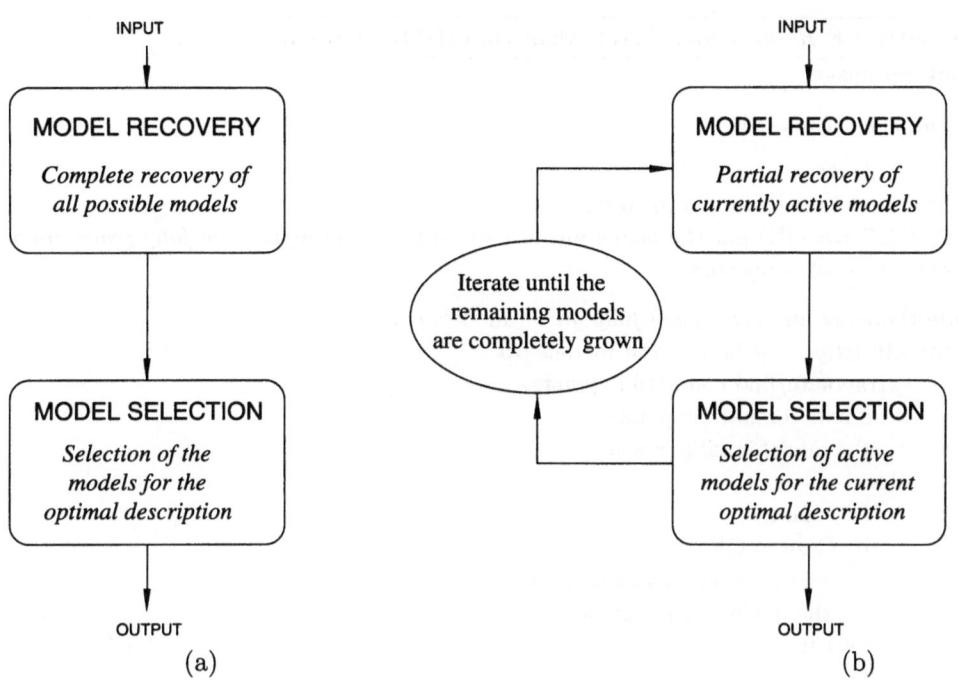

FIGURE 8.2. Model recovery and selection: (a) Recover-then-Select, (b) Recover-and-Select.

is interrupted by the model-selection procedure that selects a set of currently optimal models, which are then passed back to the model-recovery procedure. This process is repeated until the remaining models are completely recovered. The trade-offs involved in the dynamic combination of these two procedures are discussed elsewhere [Leo93]. By properly balancing the trade-offs, a computationally efficient and reliable algorithm is obtained that has the feature of growing mostly well-behaved models (in terms of convergence, error, and number of compatible points) while at the same time lowering the computation time and space complexity of the procedure. The complete algorithm of the method is given in Algorithm 8.

8.3.2 Recover-and-Select applied to

We tested the proposed method on various domains using different parametric models. Here we present some results of recovering variable-order bivariate polynomials and superquadric models in range images and parametric curve models in edge images. Because the main idea of this chapter is to present a general framework for accurate and robust extraction of parametric models of different types and its relation to some other robust estimation methods, here we only briefly mention some of the details pertaining to the particular choice of parametric models and refer the reader to the specific papers (see [LGB95, LSM94, Leo93]).

Algorithm 8 *Recover-and-Select* Algorithm (GOF=Goodness of Fit)

---

input: an image

determine a set of seeds

for all seeds **do**
    fit a model (estimate parameters)
    if (GOF == OK) put the model into the set of currently *active, not fully grown* models
    else the seed is rejected

while there are any *active, not fully grown* models **do**
    for all *active, not fully grown* models **do**
        extrapolate/find compatible points
        if no new compatible points
            the model is *fully grown*
        else
            fit a model
            if (GOF ≠ OK)
                reject the last included points
                the model is *fully grown*
            end if
        end if
    end for

    perform selection among all *active* models for the current optimal description
        (only the selected models remain *active*)

end do

output: description of the image in terms of parametric models

---

Surface Models in Range Images

The Recover-and-Select paradigm has been applied to the problem of estimating variable order bivariate polynomials that are linearly parameterizable in the Euclidean space. We have limited the set of models to planar and second-order surfaces. The surfaces are modeled as functions in the explicit form $z = f(x, y)$. The fitting procedure, which minimizes the sum of squared distances between the data (inliers) and the model in the z-direction, yields a system of linear equations for the unknown parameters of the model. The fitting procedure is computationally efficient because the time complexity for updating the parameters of the model is linearly proportional to the number of data points that are added to the model in each iteration.

The decisions regarding data point classification, model acceptance, and model switching (from planar to curved surfaces) are based on simple well-defined thresholds that are all related to the estimated variance of the well-behaved noise. Several experiments have been carried out to test the noise properties and the stability of the algorithm with respect to perturbations of the thresholds. The interested reader is referred to [LGB95].

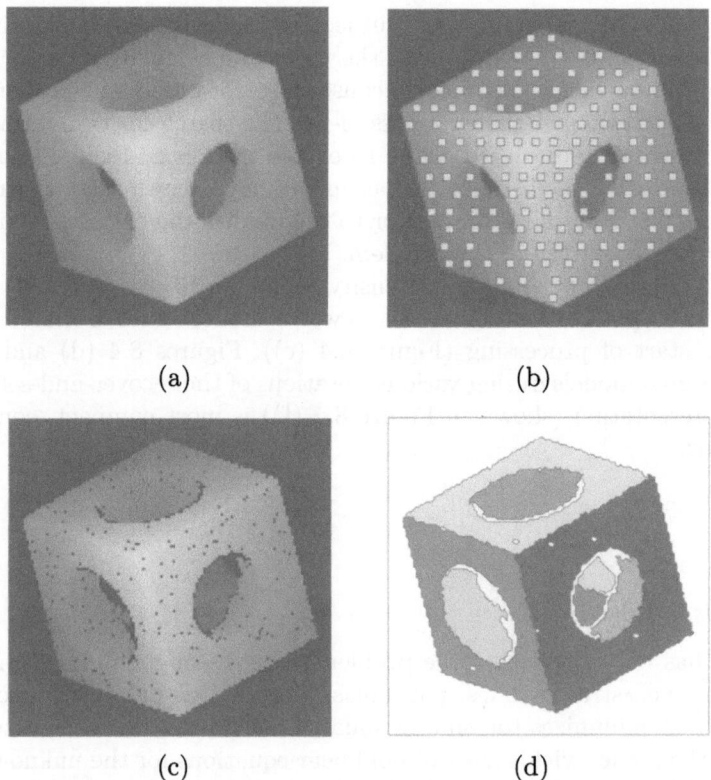

(a)   (b)

(c)   (d)

FIGURE 8.3. (a) Original range image, (b) seed image, (c) reconstructed image, and (d) segmented image.

Figure 8.3 (a) shows a noisy range image of a cube[2] (taken from [Bes88]). The object consists of planar and curved surfaces. 143 models were initiated in the image (the seeds are depicted as white squares in Figure 8.3 (b)). Both planar and curved surfaces are reliably recovered. The data points that were detected as outliers are marked in black (Figure 8.3 (c)). The domains of the individual models are depicted in Figure 8.3 (d).

Superellipsoids in Range Images

We also used the proposed method to *directly* recover superellipsoids, a subset of superquadric models, from unsegmented range images [LSM94]. This approach is in contrast with standard methods that attempt the recovery of volumetric models only after the data has been presegmented using extensive preprocessing. A superellipsoid in general position is defined by an implicit function that involves 11 parameters describing superellipsoid's size, shape, orientation, and position. The parameters of the model are estimated by a nonlinear iterative algorithm [SB90] that minimizes the sum of squares of the algebraic distances between the data points (classified as belonging

---

[2]*The image was provided by Dr. Besl from the University of Michigan.*

to the model) and the superellipsoid, subject to an additional constraint of minimal volume. To decide on the acceptance of the model we calculate an error measure that approximates the Euclidean distance, because the error based on the algebraic distance is inappropriate to evaluate the goodness-of-fit. The search for compatible data points is performed in the neighborhood of the recovered models and is based on the approximation to the Euclidean distance. Experiments have shown that the method is not sensitive to unreliable initial estimates or to the models that get stuck in local minima due to the nonlinear nature of the problem.

Figures 8.4 (a) and (b) show an intensity image and a range image, respectively,[3] of a tube and a cylinder that intersect. Twelve models were initiated on the range image at the start of processing (Figure 8.4 (c)). Figures 8.4 (d) and (e) show the partially recovered models during various iterations of the recover-and-select algorithm. The final representation (shown in Figure 8.4 (f)) is most compact, consisting of two superellipsoids.

Curve Models in Edge Images

The method has been applied to the problem of recovering simple geometric curvilinear structures, i.e., straight lines, parabolas, and ellipses in edge images. The fitting procedure, which minimizes the sum of squared Euclidean distances between the data (inliers) and the model, yields a set of nonlinear equations for the unknown parameters of the model. The main advantage of using the Euclidean distance measure (as opposed to, for example, algebraic distance) is that the recovered models extrapolate accurately in the vicinity of the end points that is necessary for a reliable search for additional consistent data points.

Model acceptance and data point classification are also based on the Euclidean distance measure. Initial models are straight line segments and a more complex curve is used only after the goodness-of-fit indicates the inability of the current model to fit the data. Experiments have shown that the procedure is robust with respect to noise (minor edge elements scattered in images, edge elements caused by multiple responses of the edge detector around certain types of edges, etc.).

Radial Basis Function Networks

The method has been applied to the problem of determining the size of a radial basis function neural network [LB98]. We use axis-aligned Gaussian RBF networks with a single linear output unit.[4] Let us consider an RBF- network as a function approximator:

---

[3]The images were provided by Marjan Trobina from the ETH, Switzerland.

[4]The generalization to other basis functions and multiple output units is straightforward.

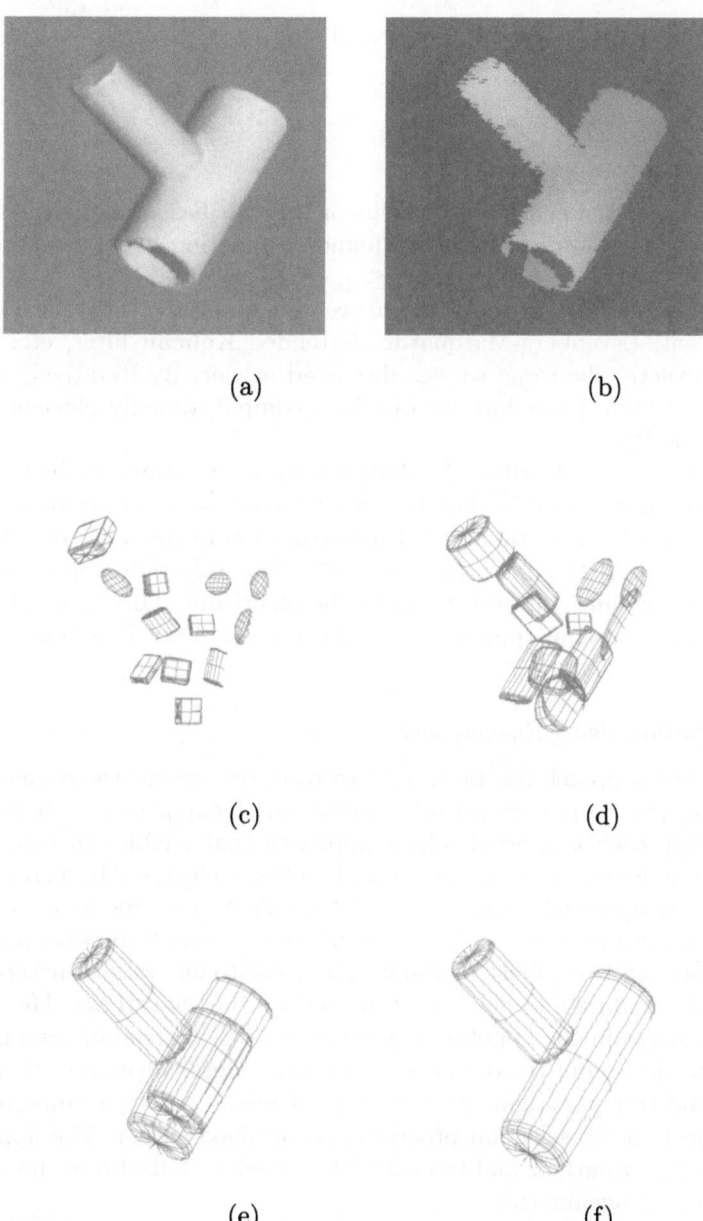

FIGURE 8.4. (a) Intensity image, (b) range image, (c) initial models, (d), (e) selected models after the first and the sixth iteration, respectively, of the recover-and-select algorithm, (f) final result.

$$
\begin{aligned}
y(\mathbf{x}) & = w_0 + \sum_{i=1}^{M} w_i r_i(\mathbf{x}) = w_0 + \sum_{i=1}^{M} w_i e^{-\frac{||\mathbf{x}-\mathbf{c}_i||^2}{s_i^2}} \\
& = w_0 + \sum_{i=1}^{M} w_i e^{-\sum_{j=1}^{d} \frac{(x_j - c_{ji})^2}{s_{ji}^2}} \,,
\end{aligned}
\tag{8.7}
$$

where $\mathbf{c}_i$ and $\mathbf{s}_i$ are the center and widths of the i-th basis function, respectively. We train the network to approximate an unknown function f given a (possibly noisy) training set $TS = \{(\mathbf{x}^{(p)}, f(\mathbf{x}^{(p)})) | 1 \le p \le q, \mathbf{x}^{(p)}, f(\mathbf{x}^{(p)}) \in \mathbb{R}^d\}$.

Instead of the network-growing phase we use a suitable learning algorithm, e.g., gradient descent, Levenberg-Marquardt, Extended Kalman filter, etc. The selection procedure is exactly the same as was discussed earlier. By iteratively combining the training and selection procedure we obtain a computationally efficient algorithm for RBF-network design.

Let us illustrate the algorithm for function approximation; we have used the Hermite polynomial from [Orr95]. The training set consists of 84 samples taken from the function with added noise with a uniform distribution in the range of $[-0.5, +0.5]$. The selection converged at two basis functions after four selection steps. Figure 8.5 shows the intermediate results during the run of the algorithm. This figure shows the training samples, true function, approximated function, and basis functions currently in the network.

Object Recognition Using Eigenimages

A closely related approach has been used to robustly recover the coefficients of eigenimages [LB96] (for more detailed information on eigenimages, see Sections 5.2.2 and 11.3.1). Our approach is a novel robust approach that enables the appearance based matching techniques to successfully cope with outliers, cluttered background, and occlusions. The robust approach exploits several techniques, e.g., robust estimation and the hypothesize-and-test paradigm, which together in a general framework achieve the goal. We have introduced two robust methods. The robust constrained method is computationally less demanding and does not compromise the robustness. The major novelty of our approach lies in the hypothesis generation step. Instead of computing the coefficients by a projection of the data onto the eigenimages, we extract them by a robust hypothesize-and-test paradigm using subsets of image points. Competing hypotheses are then subject to the selection procedure as outlined earlier. The approach enables us not only to reject outliers and to deal with occlusions but also to simultaneously use multiple classes of eigenimages.

The following experiments demonstrate the main features of our method. Figure 8.6 demonstrates that our approach is insensitive to occlusions. One can see that both robust methods outperform the standard method considerably. The visual reconstruction from the robust constrained method is better because we get the exact point on the manifold. Note that the blur visible in the reconstruction is the consequence of taking into account only a limited number of eigenimages.

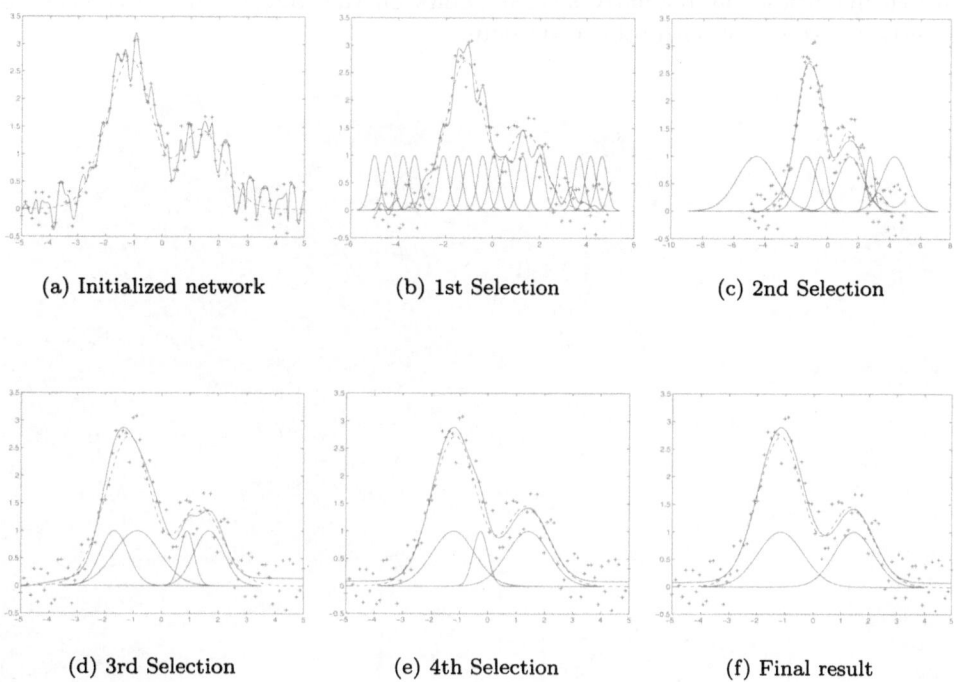

(a) Initialized network   (b) 1st Selection   (c) 2nd Selection

(d) 3rd Selection   (e) 4th Selection   (f) Final result

FIGURE 8.5. Results on Hermite polynomial with superimposed basis functions. "+" denotes training samples, dashed curve denotes original function, and solid curve denotes the approximated function.

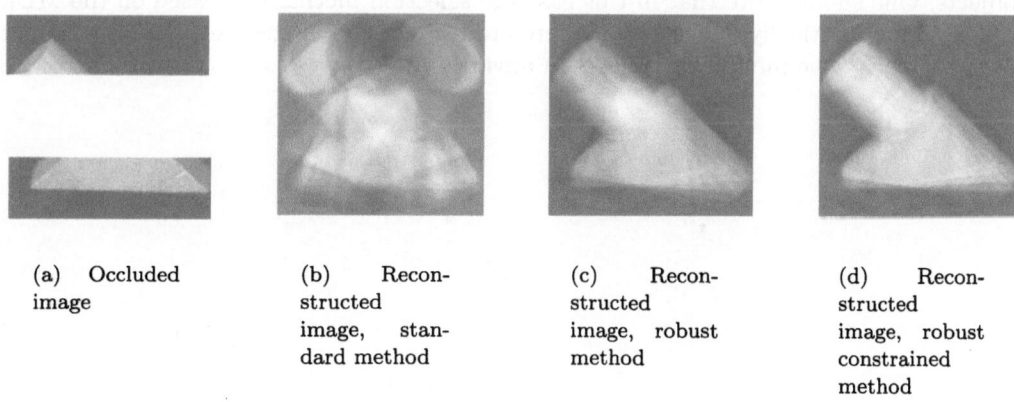

(a) Occluded image

(b) Reconstructed image, standard method

(c) Reconstructed image, robust method

(d) Reconstructed image, robust constrained method

FIGURE 8.6. Demonstration of insensitivity to occlusions using the robust methods for calculating the coefficients a_i.

Figure 8.7 shows several objects on a considerably cluttered background. We initiated multiple hypotheses at regularly spaced points on the image. All objects have been correctly recovered by both robust methods.

FIGURE 8.7. Test objects on cluttered background.

Figure 8.8 demonstrates that our approach can cope with situations when one object occludes another. One can see that both robust methods are able to recover both objects. One should note that in this case the selection mechanism based on the MDL principle automatically delivers that there are two objects in the scene (i.e., we do not need to specify the number of objects in advance).

(a) Two objects occlud-
ing each other

(b) Robust constrained
method, Object 1

(c) Robust constrained
method, Object 2

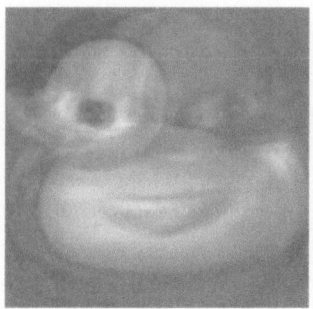

(d) Robust method, Ob-
ject 1

(e) Robust method, Ob-
ject 2

FIGURE 8.8. Two objects occluding each other.

9

Structural Object Recognition

Mark Burge
Wilhelm Burger

Structural object recognition is based on the idea that the appearance of objects can be described by visual primitives (e.g., "features" or "tokens") and the spatial relations between them. In the structural approach, the spatial relations between features are expressed explicitly to improve the specificity of the description. This is why *structural* descriptions are preferred over *evidence-based* descriptions. For the purpose of visual object recognition, we must distinguish between two different forms of structural descriptions:

1. *Object model:* the structure of the *true* object (i.e., in the three-dimensional reality).

2. *Image description:* the structural description of the *appearance* of the object in the image.

9.1   2-D and 3-D Structural Features

Similarly, two different types of image features can be extracted: those that are directly related to the 3-D shape of the part of the object being viewed and those features that result from the 3-D to 2-D down projection. In addition to the problem of detecting both kind of features in intensity images, the latter type can be ambiguous because part of the 3-D shape information is necessarily lost during the projection. The essence of the recognition problem is to relate the structures found in the image with the underlying object models. Other important issues involved in structural recognition are:

- adequacy of the representation for the kind of objects encountered;

- selection and extraction of visual primitives;

- description of the spatial relations between primitives;

- matching image structures to models; and

- inference of structural object descriptions from examples.

9.2   Feature Selection

The selection of suitable shape primitives is of central importance. For efficient recognition, they should be *expressive* in the sense that a combination of only a few of them, or even a single one, can facilitate object identification [Bie87]. On the other hand, the available shape primitives should be *general* enough to model a large range of object categories. They should be detectable from images reliably in a bottom-up fashion and should be *non-incidental*, in the sense that they are unlikely to occur from random configurations in space.

Today, most structural approaches are based on a *single* type of shape primitive, usually straight line segments. Although these features are relatively easy to extract from the image and are well suited for many man-made objects, they are not adequate and reliable for most complex natural scenes. In fact, the poor performance of many image understanding systems in natural environments can be attributed to their reliance on a single feature type.

We call methods using *multiple* feature types for structural object recognition in a cooperative and complimentary fashion the "polymorphic structural approach". The combined use of *multiple* types of structural primitives promises increased recognition performance and reliability and allows covering a broader range of scenes, including complex natural scenes. In this chapter, we want to investigate the full potential of such a "polymorphic" structural approach and develop methods for overcoming the technical difficulties involved.

9.3   Matching Structural Descriptions

When object models are given in the form of structural descriptions, the matching algorithm must solve the following three problems simultaneously:

1. *Selection problem:* determine which image tokens belong to the same object;

2. *identification problem:* determine the identity of the structure (i.e., invoke the correct object model); and

3. *association problem:* assign the correct model component to each image primitive.

Except for trivial configurations, none of these problems can be solved without solving the other two. The selection problem cannot be solved without knowing the identity of the object and collecting those image tokens that are required by the model. Selecting the right model is not possible unless at least some of the image tokens have been assigned to model primitives that, in turn, require solving the identification problem. As a result structural matching is a complex search process within a large space.

Formalized as a graph-theoretic problem, matching structural descriptions is equivalent to finding a *morphism* between the primitives in the image and the model, such that the structure is preserved. This problem is known to be $\mathcal{NP}$-hard [Ull76] (i.e., generally the amount of computation grows exponentially with the number of structural elements).

9.4   Reducing Search Complexity

The search space of the matching process can be reduced in at least three ways:

- *Expressive tokens:* increasing the ability of a token to discriminate between models [Ett88];

- *grouping:* assembling image tokens that are likely to belong to the same object;

- *indexing:* making a good guess for the object's identity; and

- *heuristic constraints:* ruling out unlikely hypotheses at an early stage   [Gri90, Gri91].

In addition, *structural similarity measures* offer a way to match substructures without directly associating their individual elements.

9.5   Grouping and Indexing

When all sensory data under consideration are known to belong to a single known object, the expected amount of search is quadratic in the parameters of the problem and linear in the number of data-model pairings. This assumes that the token selection problem and the indexing problem are correctly solved. Therefore, the pre-selection of scene tokens can effectively reduce the amount of search but, unless pre-selection is perfect (i.e., all selected tokens belong to a single object), the search is still exponential in the worst case. If indexing fails (i.e., the wrong model is used) search is also exponential under otherwise perfect conditions.

Perceptual grouping methods [GB87, Low87, Sau90] are mostly based on:

- single rather than polymorphic primitives; and

- predefined grouping rules rather than rules adapted to the application domain.

Although the resulting simple representations and grouping criteria can be evaluated efficiently and the object descriptions are independent of the problem domain, the traditional grouping approach has several disadvantages:

- Perceptual "saliency" of groupings between different types of primitive features is not used;

- groupings based on a single feature type are inherently brittle; and

- domain-dependent grouping rules are not optimal for unknown and dynamically *changing environments*.

9.5.1 Early Search Termination

Early termination of the search process [Gri91] is based on local unary and binary constraints applied to pairings of scene and model tokens. These constraints are used to rule out interpretations before the full depth of the interpretation tree is reached. In effect, this combines heuristic search with constraint satisfaction or consistent labeling (e.g., constrained tree search). In order to achieve polynomial time recognition algorithms, the ratio of clutter tokens and real object tokens must be kept below a specified bound. This again suggests the use of a pre-selection mechanism for grouping tokens that are likely to belong to a single object.

Using Structural Similarity

Graph morphisms are a very strong notion of *equivalence*. In the strict sense, two graphs are considered equivalent (i.e., isomorphic) when a one-to-one mapping exists between the topology and the attributed labels of the graph. This form of equivalence is not realistic in structural recognition for various reasons. First, it requires a finite set of possible node labels. Node labels, however, represent properties and the spatial relationships of tokens, including distances, angles, etc., from a potentially infinite range of values. Second, to be of practical use, matching must be tolerant against spatial variations to a certain degree. Consequently, instead of searching for structural *equivalence*, the matching process should look for structural *similarity* that can be quantified by a suitable distance measure.

A classic example for such a distance measure is the model proposed by Fischler and Elschlager [FE73], where the spatial relations between tokens are abstracted as elastic springs. The matching distance used is a function of the spring load. This turns the original graph matching problem into an optimization problem, with the goal of finding the "best match" among many possible ones.

Practical graph matching techniques are often characterized by the use of heuristics to avoid exhaustive search. Examples are backtrack search algorithms [BB82], association graph techniques [ABB+75], relaxation labeling [BF84], various hashing schemes [Bre89, LW88, UW97], and genetic algorithms [CWH97]. Considerable work has been done toward structural recognition in industrial environments, particularly under occlusion (i.e., when objects are only partially visible) [AF86, BM87, KJ86].

Other Strategies

Ordering structural tokens can significantly reduce the required search effort when compared to regular combinatorial search. As argued in [SMS87], where tokens are ordered according to their distance from the object's centroid, practical matching algorithms must execute in polynomial and not exponential time. Multi-stage strategies are another alternative to improve matching performance.

The computational advantages of a two-stage matching process are examined in [SR89] in which a subgraph of the model is first selected and then all possible matches with the scene are evaluated. The smaller the chosen subgraph, the fewer matches have to be tried, but the number of acceptable matches, and thus the work necessary at the second level, will be higher. An essential statement is that the threshold for accepting a subgraph match depends on the size of the entire model graph and not on the subgraph only. This guarantees that expanding a rejected subgraph match will never result in an acceptable total match. It is show in [SR89] that the total matching costs are minimal for some fixed subgraph size. However, this is not necessarily the case with geometrically constrained graphs.

9.6   Detection of Polymorphic Features

To successfully use polymorphic features it must be possible to reliably extract them from a broad selection of images under a wide range of conditions. Three classes of primitives: contour-based, region-based, and qualitative 3-D surface primitives have all been successfully applied, and details of their usage can be found in Section 14.2.1.

9.7   Polymorphic Grouping

Grouping is a powerful strategy for combining structural primitives into more expressive aggregates. It can dramatically improve object model indexing and reduce the search complexity. While techniques for grouping primitives of a single type are well developed (e.g., for point sets, straight line segments, and segmented regions), no general methods are available for grouping *different* structural primitives. One of the difficulties involved is that different primitives mostly share only a small set of common properties (e.g., some primitives have an *orientation* property, while others do not). Consequently, a distinct evaluation function is required for each allowed combination of feature types.

However, "polymorphic groupings" offer greater expressiveness than "homomorphic" groupings of the same number of primitives. Thus, to achieve a certain degree of *indexing power*, the number of primitives needed in polymorphic groupings can be kept relatively small. We can therefore be quite selective with respect to the set of permissible feature class combinations, which also reduces the number of distinct evaluation functions. Similarly, the overall complexity of indexing and matching is reduced by using smaller but more expressive assemblies of structural tokens.

It is possible to use *static* grouping rules and grouping evaluation functions specified at the syntactic level for efficient bottom-up detection of salient groupings [DW89, GB87, Sau90]. However, the effectiveness of such general grouping criteria will strongly depend on the relevant objects in the application domain (e.g., searching for parallel lines is effective for certain man-made objects but not in most natural scenes). Thus we want to dynamically adapt the grouping rules to the corresponding application domain, taking into account the objects encountered in this domain, their relative importance *in the given task, and the polymorphic features* used for modeling these objects.

9.8   Indexing and Matching

Indexing and matching are complementary processes in structural recognition and are often incorporated in a hypothesize-and-test strategy:

- *Indexing* is used to narrow down the set of possible object or subpart categories, by evaluating certain properties of a given image feature set. While geometrical invariance is considered important for indexing based on point sets and straight line segments [MZ92], combinations of polymorphic features carry high indexing power. The connection between grouping and indexing is strong, because grouping supplies the token sets for indexing.

- *Matching* is performed by explicitly hypothesizing correspondences between image tokens and object model entries. Indexing can effectively reduce the number of matches to be evaluated. Matching hypotheses requires a *metric* that allows measuring the distance between image features and entries in the model base. In contrast to single feature type approaches, new and specific distance measures must be developed for the polymorphic approach and their combinatorial advantage analyzed and verified under realistic conditions.

9.9   Polymorphic Features

Object models in this approach are viewer-centered descriptions based on the spatial arrangement of structural features. Each object model consists of a set of distinct aspects of the corresponding object. The number of different aspects needed to sufficiently describe an object depends mainly on the object's complexity, viewpoint dependency, and the number of "common views" related to that object. Individual aspects are related to each other by an adjacency relation defined on the "view sphere" such that intermediate aspects can be inferred if necessary. Each aspect is, in general, a multi-scale representation that refers to structural details at a range of different resolutions. In this context, the relationships between polymorphic features at different scale levels present a challenging area of investigation.

To successfully cope with natural objects, the representation must accommodate a certain degree of object variability. The traditional rigid structural descriptions are not adequate for this task. We use structural constraints of varying rigidness for handling object variability:

- *strong:* structural constraints for describing local structural details and

- *weak:* structural constraints for describing larger structural aggregates.

In addition to providing tolerance against object variability, the use of weak structural constraints at the global object level reduces the search complexity during recognition. There is also evidence [Cer86] that similar forms of representations exist in biological vision systems.

9.10   3-D Object Recognition Example

> Then, my dear friend, must not the law-giver also know how to embody in
> the sounds and syllables that name which is fitted by nature for each object?
> Must he not make and give all his names with his eye fixed upon the absolute
> or ideal name, if he is to be an authoritative giver of names? And if different
> law-givers do not embody it in the same syllables, we must not forget this
> ideal name on that account; for different smiths do not embody the form in
> the same iron, though making the same instrument for the same purpose,
> but so long as they reproduce the same ideal, though it be in different iron,
> still the instrument is as it should be, whether it be made here or in foreign
> lands, is it not?—Socrates in Plato's *Cratylus* §389e

As Socrates explained to Hermogenes, we carry a conceptual ideal of many objects in
our thoughts. Indeed the concept of ideals is embedded in our very languages, witness
the almost universal usage of definite and indefinite articles. When we say "a chair",
we envision in a sense the ideal form of a chair. One does not recall an actual chair
but instead a functional description of what a chair does combined with a relational-
structural description of the parts that make up a chair. The IDEAL system [BBM96d,
BB97] attempts to learn from example objects the structural parts and the relations
between them which when recognized in a previously unseen object, enable the system
to probabilistically classify it among its known classes.

Recognizing three-dimensional objects under different viewing and lighting conditions
is arguably the goal of computer vision. The difficulty of the problem depends on both
learning factors such as types of objects, number of classes, and inter- and intra-class
variability, as well as visual problems like the segmentation of multiple object scenes,
the background complexity, and the amount of occlusion. Given the complexity of the
problem many different solutions have been proposed; a comparison of 24 different
approaches is given in [BB97].

We can divide the different recognition approaches for 3-D objects into those using 3-
D models and those based on *appearances* (i.e., on one or more 2-D views of an object).
Our approach is appearance-based and *structural* (i.e., objects are described in terms
of the configurations of their parts [Bie87]). It focuses on learning to recognize single
object scenes of classes (e.g., chair, table, bench), which often exhibit high intra-class
variability.

9.10.1   The IDEAL System

Structural recognition methods are based on both the availability of primitive structural
elements (e.g., blobs, geons, or parametric strokes) and on the assumption that these
elements can be extracted from the image data with sufficient reliability. Regardless of
what the primitives are, the performance of the recognition process depends critically on
how reliably they can be extracted, which is difficult even under ideal viewing conditions
[Bro81]. When images are noisy and cluttered, the extraction of suitable primitives

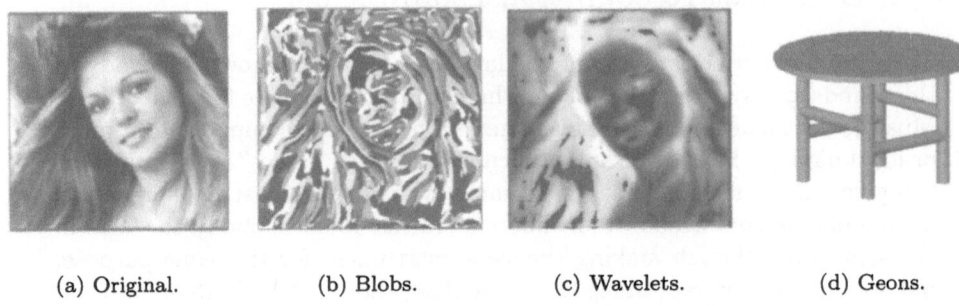

(a) Original.   (b) Blobs.   (c) Wavelets.   (d) Geons.

FIGURE 9.1. Region based initial structural descriptions.

using only local information may not be possible [Low87]. In addition, practically all structural feature extraction schemes work in a rather myopic fashion, trying to assemble larger meaningful structures from scattered pieces using only local evidence and therefore often missing the dominant global structures in the image description (i.e., segmentation).

In practice structural extraction schemes are fragile, and no single method exists that can reliably deliver a good part decomposition, unless the scene domain is very restricted. For these reasons many recognition approaches [BL93] assume a noiseless, pre-segmented image with all parts of the object visible in every view (i.e., no self-occlusion) and models of all objects given a priori. To avoid this reliance on pre-segmented a priori models we combine a powerful initial polymorphic description and machine learning to automatically acquire our models.

9.10.2   Initial Structural Part Decomposition

As we saw earlier in Section 9.2, most structural recognition methods are based on a single type of primitive, commonly straight line segments. Some approaches combine different primitive types of the same *class* of primitives (e.g., a contour class representation might use both straight line segments and circular arcs for primitives). The combination of different primitive classes (e.g., contour and area) is referred to as *polymorphic* [BBM96e].

We attempt to overcome the problem of fragile segmentation in three ways. First, instead of relying on a single type of primitive, we combine three area-based primitives into a single representation and recognition scheme, introducing additional redundancy. Second we do not require structural primitives to be precisely delineated, but only their approximate spatial position and shape properties are needed and parts may be overlapping and ambiguous [BBM96b]. Finally, structural primitives like specific local patterns [LBP95, Bur88] do not need to correspond to "humanly" meaningful parts, it is only necessary that they can be recovered reliably and repeatably from an image. The three area-based features we use (see Figure 9.1)are blobs [Lin93], geons [DPR92b, PBP98], and a class based on Gabor quadrature filters (i.e., wavelets) [BB94].

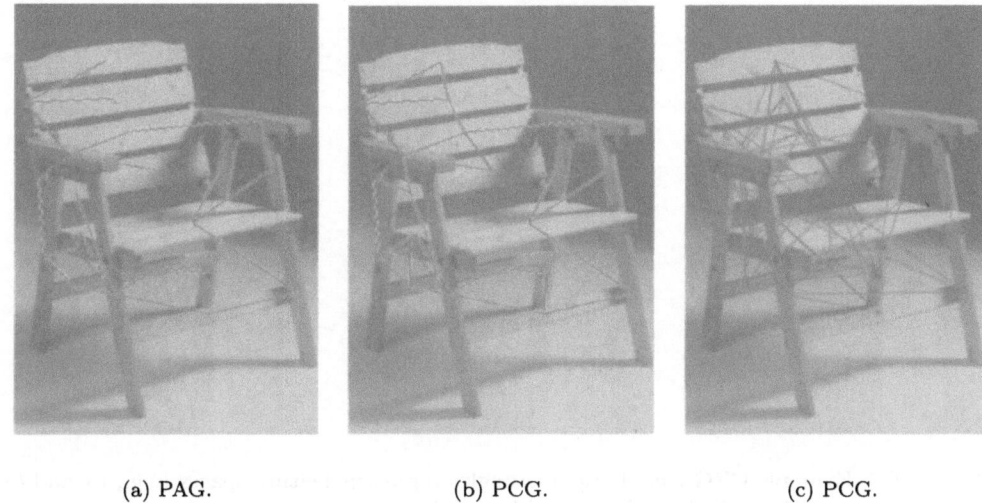

| (a) PAG. | (b) PCG. | (c) PCG. |

FIGURE 9.2. A PAG and two PCGs using different similarity functions.

9.10.3 Part Adjacency and Compatibility Graphs

The problem of label compatibility arises when an object has the same parts and features as a different object. When only unary features are used the problem is more readily apparent, as many objects may have the same parts and unary features (e.g., objects consisting of different arrangements of similar circles and squares). The addition of relations between parts (i.e., binary features) adds structural context. In recognition without labeled parts, one must exhaustively attempt all matchings between unary and binary relations. It is possible to avoid this prohibitively expensive matching problem by encoding the binary relations between the parts during learning in such a way that only *label-compatible* part paths can be generated during both the learning and recognition stages.

Generating only label-compatible part paths can be done by calculating the binary features only between *neighboring* parts of the same object while building the tree [BBM96f]. The tree constructed in this way contains only paths from a part at the root, where all parts are represented in some cluster, through neighboring parts to the final classification leaves. The use of the neighboring relation as a constraint during both the training and recognition stages implicitly solves the label compatibility problem by assuring that any matched sequence must have arisen from a label-compatible sequence. This solution is not sufficient because representative, and therefore important, sequences for recognition occur among *non-neighboring* parts scattered across the image. It is necessary to have a relation that still provides the constraints for solving the label compatibility problem and allows the non-neighboring representative parts to be combined into the same part paths.

The number of paths that can be considered in a view is $\binom{n}{l}$, where n is the number of parts in the view and l is the length of the path. For any given length, l, it is

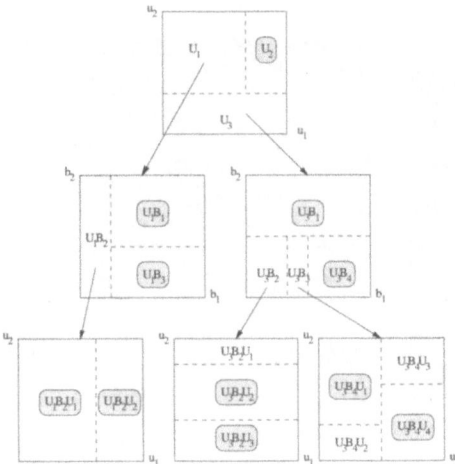

FIGURE 9.3. Example CRG tree. Large rectangles represent feature spaces (e.g., u_1 and b_2), dashed lines determine split boundaries and hatched clusters denote uniqueness.

desirable to choose a subset of all $\binom{n}{l}$ paths, which is minimal but representative of the object. Without a priori knowledge this is not possible, so we must select a function that produces a set with cardinality somewhere between that of the ideal set and $\binom{n}{l}$. Selecting only neighboring parts limits the size of the set but does not achieve the other goal of selecting sufficient representative paths because if the representative parts are separated by more than l neighbors then they will never be included. The problem then is how to select without a priori knowledge a path set of reasonable cardinality that contains representative paths.

A *Part Adjacency Graph* (PAG) $G(V, E)$ contains an edge $e_{i,j}$ between nodes representing the parts p_i and p_j only if the parts are neighbors. Neighborhoods are defined through either physical adjacency or, more generally, spatial proximity (e.g., parts within 10 pixels of each other). Other neighborhood definitions, for example, area Voronoi neighborhoods, are possible but all suffer from the drawback that simply being a neighbor of another part is not necessarily a significant relation for recognition. In a *Part Compatibility Graph* (PCG) $G(V, E)$, a graph edge $e_{i,j}$ denotes a high *similarity measure* between parts p_i and p_j (i.e., the similarity measure replaces the neighboring relation used in the PAG (see Figure 9.2) (see also the Feature Adjacency Graph [FF95]). For details of how to formulate the similarity measure for a given feature set see [BBM96e].

Increasingly, techniques from machine learning are being incorporated into object recognition methods. Using the ability of these techniques to generalize from the training data, previously unseen views can be recognized with increased accuracy. These include methods using the relative frequency of a class in a region as an evidence-based approach [JH88] to generalization while others use neural networks [Ede93], Eigenvalue decompositions [MN95], or decision trees that form the basis for learning in IDEAL.

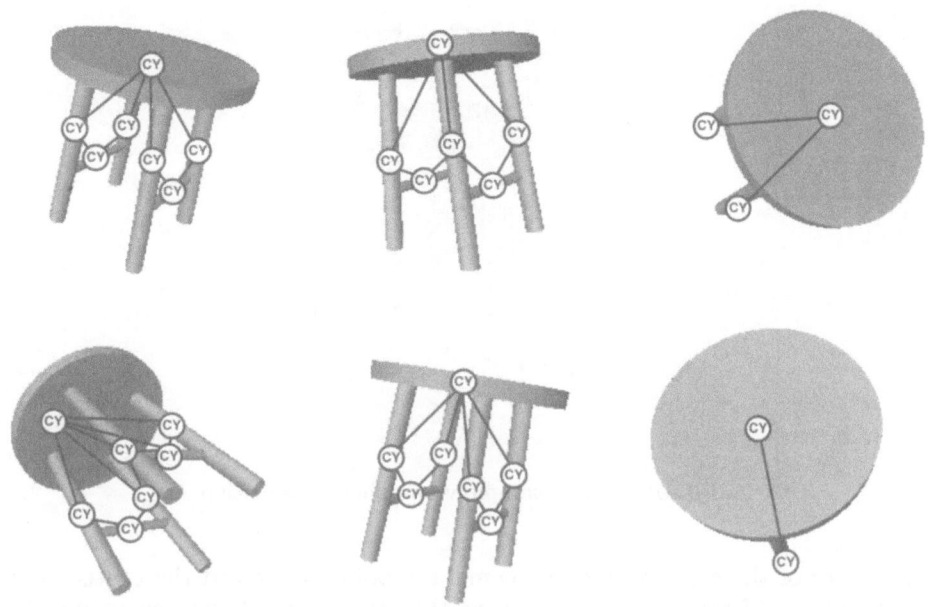

FIGURE 9.4. Examples of initial structural segmentation. The extracted PAG graphs are shown overlaid and nodes are labeled by their geon type (e.g., CY = cylinder).

9.10.4   Automatic Model Acquisition

We use [BC94a] decision-tree based *Conditional Rule Generation* (CRG) for learning and recognition from attributed PAG graphs. In CRG an attributed graph,[1] $G(V, E)$, is constructed from the initial structural segmentation in which each segmented region is a "part" represented by a node in V. These parts are connected by a set of edges E that represent relations between the parts. Each node $v_i \in V$ is attributed by a unary feature vector u_i with a predetermined number of features; each edge $e_{i,j} \in E$ is attributed by a binary feature vector $b_{i,j}$ whose features are computed from the parts p_i and p_j ($i \neq j$). The feature vectors u_i and $b_{i,j}$ form the unary and binary feature spaces U and B, respectively. Figure 9.3 shows an example CRG tree; the root shows the unary feature space U and below it the binary feature spaces UB resulting from the unresolved clusters and the bottom row contains the unary feature spaces UBU computed from the non unique clusters of the UB level.

We adopted a viewer-centered representation for our models where an object is represented by a finite collection of views (see Figure 9.4). The set of views for each model was generated by placing a spherical grid around the object with the origin of the grid and the center of the object coinciding. The center point of each grid facet corresponds

---

[1]With polymorphic features a *Voronoi neighbor graph* (VNG) (see Section 6.1.3) of the primitives is constructed using the Scaffolding algorithm [Bur98] and the Voronoi neighbor relation is used to generate a PAG, it is also possible to use a similarity function [BBM96e] to generate a PCG instead.

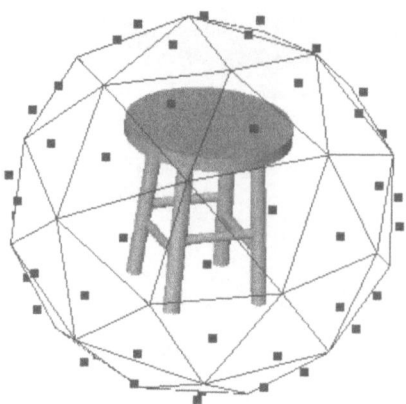

FIGURE 9.5. Example view-sphere tessellation.

to the center of the camera, and the camera is pointing toward the center of the object. The radius of the grid was chosen so that the entire object was visible from all viewpoints on that grid. Figure 9.5 depicts the tessellation of the view-sphere around an example object.

In the *learning* phase the problem is to learn to classify a part p_i into the correct class $C(p_i)$. The training examples are presented separately and sequentially in a supervised fashion. The CRG method works by first classifying all unary features from all parts of all views and all object classes into a unary feature space U. This feature space is then clustered into a number of clusters U_n, some of which may already be unique with respect to class membership (i.e., all parts in a cluster belong to the same class, $\exists_c \forall_{p \in U_n} C(p) = c$, while others will not). Binary features are then calculated between the parts of the non-unique clusters and its neighbors in the graph. The binary feature spaces resulting from the unresolved clusters are again clustered, each forming feature spaces of type $U_n B_m$. For the non-unique clusters the unary feature spaces $U_n B_m U_o$ of the parts of the previous binary relations are determined and clustered. This continues until all clusters are unique or a predetermined maximum depth has been reached.

9.10.5 Object Recognition from Appearances

In *recognition*, the goal is to correctly classify using the CRG tree, the previously unseen objects with possibly occluded and missing parts. First a PAG graph similar to that used in the learning phase is constructed. An evidence accumulation technique is then used where a number (e.g., dependent on the object but typically in the range of 5–10) of small (e.g., typically 3 to 5 nodes in length) paths are extracted starting from each node in the object's graph representation and then matched against the model. Each node (i.e., each part) of the object graph stores the number of times it was assigned to a certain object class.

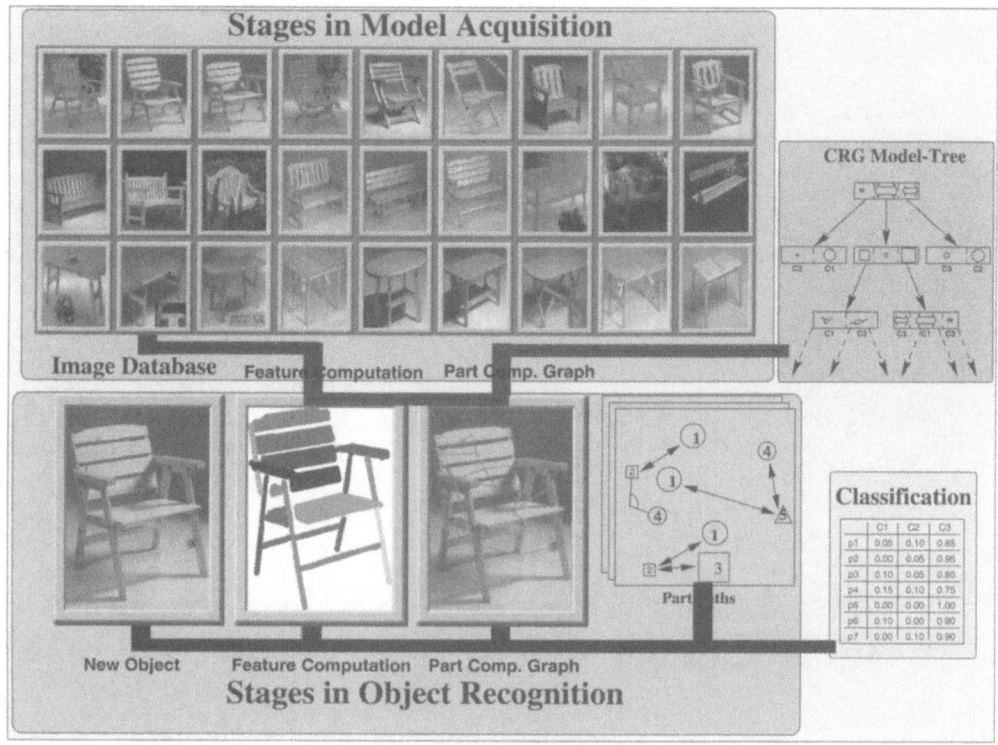

FIGURE 9.6. Flowchart of the learning and recognition process: **Learning path:** Computation of the features from all images in the database; building of a PAG; construction of a classification tree for part paths. **Recognition process:** Presentation of a new image; feature computation; PAG; extraction of part paths; classification of each part path using the classification tree; combining evidence.

9.10.6   Experiments

IDEAL has been tested [BBM96e] on images exhibiting real-world imaging problems such as shadowing and self-occlusion, of generic classes (e.g., chairs, benches, and tables) purposely selected to provide a high degree of structural similarity between classes. The performance with occluded parts is a combination of missing and additional parts, as an occluded part generally causes a missing part and a number of additional parts to occur in the image. If the PCG is used instead of the PAG, the system performs well even when there is a considerable number of missing parts. This is because part paths contained in the PCG extend over larger regions of the object and are therefore more likely to contain non-neighboring significant parts. With both the PCG and the PAG, performance drops when additional parts occurs. A more detailed analysis of these experiments can be found in [BBM96c].

10

Machine Learning

Edward Blurock

An image in its raw form is a set of pixels, i.e., a matrix of numbers. The path toward "recognizing the reality behind these pixels" is a complex interation of algorithms and data structures [PB98, KJ93, CPW93]. One of the tools used to help extract this reality is machine learning [MCM83, Mit97, BC96, Lan96]. Within this process of discovery, one class of techniques relies on the "optimization" or tuning of the algorithms, formulas, and data structures by means of examples, through statistical, pattern recognition, or machine learning analysis techniques [BBM96a].

One of the essential, and highly experimental, problems facing researchers using machine learning is the ability to transform the raw pixel information without loss of essential information needed for learning. Said another way, the abstract relationships hidden within the pixel data need to be transformed to data structures where these relationships are more visible, or more practically, to data structures where they can be manipulated by the analysis techniques to yield the desired concepts to be interpreted by human understanding. As evidenced by the multitude of techniques that have been developed to accomplish the task of "recognition", which algorithms and data structures are necessary is not unique and still involves a great deal of experimentation. It is the task of the researcher to weed through the various of learning algorithms to find a suitable combination that solves the task. An essential prerequisite is to understand the available algorithms and what types of solution they offer.

Due partly to the evolutionary nature of their development, and to the nature of the tasks involved, there are definite relationships between the various machine learning techniques, both structural and operational. In this chapter, first machine learning methods will be defined and contrasted with other analysis techniques. Then they will be categorized in terms of their traditional paradigms. Afterwards, they will be examined in terms of structural and operational points of view. Finally, this latter view will be used as the basis of an object-oriented structuring of the methods that is the basis of the framework being developed. This will be illustrated using the examples of logical structures and clustering.

10.1 What Is Machine Learning?

To give a short answer, *machine learning* represents a class of data analysis methods, i.e., a search for general concepts. From a set of specific examples, a corresponding set of governing principles and generalities are condensed. Their form and how they are *interpreted* depend largely on the methods used.

One common denominator among machine learning methods is that they have something "human" about them (hence the term "learning"). They are more "symbolic" in nature as opposed to numerical or computational (as is statistics). They try to mimic biological, such as neural nets or genetic algorithms, or psychological properties of humans, such as the rule induction methods.

Another common factor is that they are not direct calculational procedures, as with many standard statistical methods, but a "search" through a large complicated space of solutions. This search can take several forms, such as iteration, optimization, or the classic rule-based search of artificial intelligence.

10.1.1   What Do Machine Learning Algorithms Need?

We "learn" by interpreting and generalizing about specific examples we see. Machine learning and data analysis algorithms, in general, are no different. The prerequisite is a set of examples. Associated with each example is a description. The most frequently used description consists of a vector of *attribute-value pairs*. Each element in the vector represents an attribute, i.e., a parameter. The values of these attributes describe the state of the object. The attribute-value pairs are not restricted to simple numbers; they could be discrete characterizations (such as an object identification), entire segments of an image (such as an isolated line), or a graph (such as a run graph or Vornoi description). All learning proceeds from this description.

10.1.2   One Method Solves All? Use of Multistrategy

Image recognition is a complex task that often involves a complex interaction of a series of algorithms for transformations, preprocessing, and analysis. The consequences of this complexity is the necessity of interfacing the input and output data structures to facilitate their use in the next step.

The use of many methods, culminating to a final analysis, is a step toward a general "multistrategy" [MT94] approach. This means that one does not rely on a single analysis technique but recognizes that each analysis method contributes informaton to the problem as a whole, i.e., no information should be thrown away. This approach is especially important for a complex field such as image analysis where a great deal of experimentation is necessary. A consequence of this multistrategic thinking is the emphasis on representation rather than on method. What one is searching for is the optimal representation of the particular recognition task.

A useful result of the multistrategy approach is the developement of methods that combine elements from several machine learning algorithms. A good example is the CRG algorithm, where elements of a generalized decision tree analysis and clustering are combined [BC94b, BBM96a].

10.2   Methods

In this section, machine learning methods are looked at in their "classical" sense, i.e., by the method involved. The philosophy, origin, and purpose of the method is in the foreground. In a certain sense this can be viewed as a historical view of the development of methods:

- **Multivariate statistical**. The statistical methods are the "original" data analysis methods.

- **Distance clustering**. On the basis of a distance function, a set is divided into groups of similar objects. If the groups are successively divided into finer groups, a similarity hierarchy is formed (distance clustering [TG74], CLUSTER/2 [MS83], COBWEB [Fis87, GLF90], self-organizing nets [Koh84, Fri95], vector quantization [BK93b, BLS99], and CRG [BC94b]).

- **Rule induction**. Rule induction methods are based on a logical representation and their philosophies use psychological ideas of learning to form rules to decide concepts (decision trees [Qui86, Qui90a, Qui92, BFS90], version spaces [DM81], AQ [Mic80, MMHL86], FOIL [Qui90b, Qui91], and CN2 [CN89, CN87]

- **Neural networks**. This is an ever-increasing set of methods is based on a "network" of connected nodes in a layered (back-propagation [RM94]) or regular network (self-organizing [Koh84]) arrangement.

- **Genetic**. This class of methods is based on evolutionary optimization. The relationship with machine learning is that a large class of machine learning methods can be formulated in terms of an optimization process [Gol89, Koz92, HHNT89].

- **Probabilistic**. Using Bayesian analysis a network of interdependencies is created between concepts. Each node in the network is a parameter or concept and the directed connections between them denote a dependence of the child node on the parent node [HSC91].

Statistical methods belong to the class of data analysis methods but do not necessarily belong to machine learning. However, many of the operations within machine learning methods stem from statistical and probabilistic analysis. The generalization of concepts from a set of specific examples either directly or indirectly depends on probabilistic principles. An important philosophical difference between machine learning and statistics is that statistics is based on proposing a hypothesis and then testing for its truth given a distribution. Machine learning methods usually assume no distribution, and restrictions on the hypothesis are only indirect given the restrictions of the data structure.

The purpose of clustering is to group together a set of *similar objects* usually through a distance function. Different classes of distance clustering methods are defined by how this distance function is used to form the clusters and whether this is used in an incremental, divisive, or agglomerative way. The definition of similarity is not a flat one-dimensional quantity. There are different grades of similarity. The most accommodating structure for defining levels of similarity is a *tree hierarchy*. This is a tree structure where the top node is all the objects in the original set and as one progresses down the tree, only similar objects stay together.

The *rule induction* methods are based on *logical representations*. The set of parameters are put in *predicate functions,* functions that return a logical value. With the "normal" *two-valued logic,* the logical result is either true or false. These predicate operations are then combined through the operators AND, OR, NOT, etc. to form logical expressions (of *first-order logic*) , such as if-then rules or conjunctions describing a concept.

In machine learning, the result describes under what circumstances, i.e., values of the parameters, a particular condition holds. In clustering, for example, this condition represents a classification specifying when an object belongs to a particular cluster. Associated with each cluster would be different conditions. In learning with a set of known input and output values, as in rule induction, the goal is to find under which conditions a goal parameter is true, the derived formula represents a discriminator specifying what values the describing parameters can take for the goal condition to hold. The goal of rule induction is to form these discriminating formulas as, for example, conjunctions, disjunctions, if-then rules, or decision trees.

The *neural net* algorithms stem from the biological notion of a neuron. In the brain or spinal cord, the neuron receives information from other neurons and decides whether to transmit its information to the next level of neurons. This interconnection of neurons forms a network. In the computer analogy, the neurons are nodes that have connections coming in from one set of nodes and connections going out to another set of nodes. Associated with each connection is a weight as to the effect the connection should have. At the neuron itself, the weights of the incoming nodes are collected and a decision is made whether (or how much) to transmit a signal further. If the neurons are in a layered arrangement (back-propagation), then the net represents a function between vector spaces. If in an ordered network (self-organizing), then the connections reflect similarity.

Genetic algorithms (and *genetic programming*) are two very efficient global optimization methods that play a large role in machine learning because machine learning itself is an optimization process. Evolution, from where the ideas stem, is an optimization process. The goal of the optimization is to find a species that can survive in an environment. The criteria for optimizing is "survival of the fittest". Most learning methods (even for humans) can also viewed as an optimization process. The goal of learning optimization is to find a representation within a learning environment.

10.3   Operational

In the previous section the different paradigms of machine learning (and data analysis in general) were briefly introduced. This section examines the algorithms from an *operational point of view* . This approach not only classifies and puts some order within the multitude of methods, but also clarifies their commonalities and is the first step to a more global definition and generalization of the algorithms.

The examination of the operational structure of the algorithms has two purposes, characterizing and generalizing. Characterizing is achieved when the entire algorithm is examined and classified according to the results it achieves. How it achieves the results is of secondary importance. This characterization of the algorithms determines, for example, which algorithms achieve similar goals and thus can be used interchangeably. Characterizing is one step toward generalizing, where the characteristics between algorithms are examined and commonalities found.

Several classes of operations occur repeatedly within machine learning methods. The classifications listed here are not completely independent. In addition, they are not all used in the same way in terms of characterizing or generalizing an algorithm. The following list should be taken as important operational components and distinctions that occur within and between machine learning methods:

- **Classification algorithms.** The classification process is fundamental to the characterization of an object. The fundamental concept associated with classification is similarity. The result of machine learning is a description of a classification.

- **Discrimination.** Discrimination is determining whether an object, within a measure of certainty, belongs to a "goal" class. It is similar to classification, i.e., the goal is a specific class, but the emphasis is not on classifying an object, but rather on making a decision about an object.

- **Reduction.** An important goal of machine learning is to reduce the original raw information about the system to a smaller manageable form by means of Occam's principle. In addition, through redundancy of information through object and parameter equivalences, the search space can be reduced. A simple form of this is recognizing (and then eliminating) nonsignificant or redundant parameters.

- **Generalization/specialization.** The *most general description* matches all objects and the *most specialized description* matches single (exactly equivalent) objects. Many machine learning algorithms are procedures to specialize the most general description or to generalize the most specific description to describe a class of objects.

- **Heuristic function.** Evaluation functions play a fundamental role in decision making and characterization. The result of a specific algorithm can be highly dependent on the definition of the evaluation function involved. In conjunction with an ordering function they aid in the decision making process (a quality heuristic); with clustering (or characterization) they give a measure of similarity (a distance function); and with result evaluation they give confidence level (a likelihood, accuracy).

- **Optimization and search.** Almost all machine learning methods can be formulated as a search for the "optimum" solution. An optimum solution could be, for example, the best generalization extracted from a set of objects. The optimization methods can be distinguished in terms of "what" is being optimized (search space) and "how" it is optimized (iteration, search, optimization, genetic, etc.).

- **Functional relationship.** After the learning procedure is performed, the result of many methods is simply a function from one domain to another. This is most common in the predictive methods where a function of the input descriptions transformed to the goal descriptions.

- **Logical operations.** The basis of the "rule induction" paradigms is a logical description, a formula of logical operations. The semantic behind the operations depends on the logical paradigm.

- **Incremental/non-incremental algorithm.** In terms of the availability of the data set, there are incremental, where the objects are given to the algorithm one at a time, and non-incremental, where the entire data set must be available at the time of processing.

- **Supervised/unsupervised algorithm.** One of the controlling factors in the learning process is whether outside influences are taken into account. Supervised learning is where the learn optimization is guided through feedback. In practice, this is where the description of the object is used to predict a known goal parameter. Unsupervised learning is where only the description of the object is used to classify and characterize object. It is the nature of the description and the optimization method to "decide" the classification.

10.3.1 Discrimination and Classification

Classification and *discrimination* are fundamental to the characterization and differentiation of objects, respectively. A class represents a set of similar objects to be classified or discriminated. The common properties of a set of specific objects are the defining features of the class. The degree of commonality of the properties between the elements in the class represents the degree of similarity. At the most specific level of classification, the properties are those of the specific objects themselves; two objects belong to the same class only if they are exactly equal (which, in turn, is dependent on the concept of equality). At the most general level of classification is the entire set of objects. How the objects are grouped or classified in the levels between depends on the concept of similarity.

The concept of *discrimination* is similar to classification, but the emphasis is different. Both discrimination and classification deal with differentiating objects between classes. The difference lies in that the purpose of classification is to form a set of classes, and the purpose of discrimination is, given a set of classes and an object, to determine to which class the object belongs. The definition of the classes in discrimination can be defined externally.

10.3.2 Optimization and Search

Optimization and *search* play an important role in machine learning algorithms by finding the best generalized representation of the system. For many rule induction methods, a traditional AI search is made by modifying the current representation at each step according to some (sometimes heuristically based) rules. In optimization, the machine learning method defines a specific "criteria" with which to optimize the representation. The most common optimization used is "iterative", as in neural nets and clustering algorithms, where at each optimization step the current representation is incrementally modified toward the optimum. Often the methods that were originally formulated as a search can be reformulated using basically the same criteria and representations into an optimization. One reason genetic algorithms are often confused as being themselves a machine learning method is that they are a class of very efficient and general global optimization methods.

10.3.3   Functional Relationship

A function takes an input in one domain and transforms it to an output in another domain. The most common use in machine learning is the prediction function with a parameter description of an object as input. The prediction function takes a vector of description parameters and transforms it to a prediction vector of goal parameters. For example, given a numeric vector representation of the object space, the results of regression or neural nets represent a function from n-dimensional input space to m-dimensional result space. The popularity and ease of neural nets can be partially explained by this easy transference of the problem from statistical methods. The decision of whether or not an object belongs to a given class (such as a predicate description or decision tree) is a function from input parameter space to the logical domain.

10.3.4   Logical Operations

A large class of machine learning algorithms create decision making functions. For example, discrimination and classification decide whether a particular object belongs to a particular class. The basis of this decision making process is *first-order logic*. In a parameter description the logical functions are *predicates* in the set of parameters.

Rule induction methods directly manipulate and create logical expressions. For example, from a set of goal and descriptor predicates, the ID3, C4.5, and CART methods form decision trees and the AQ method forms a single logical conjunction. Other methods may create structures whose interpretation can be a predicate. For example, when neural nets are used as a discrimination function, the predicted goal parameter is a logical value.

10.4   Object-Oriented Generalization

An object-oriented structuring of algorithms facilitates their implementation (and extension) by creating a hierarchy of algorithm classes in which the superclasses (classes from which derived classes inherit operators and structures) hold the fundamental operations of similar algorithms [RBP+92, GHJV94]. Differentiation of algorithms occurs through substitution of the necessary algorithms of the superclass (the rest of the superclass remains the same), and adding new structures or operators.

Knowing the operational and structural aspects of an algorithm can aid in the design of the implementation through the recognition of similarity and differences between the algorithms. If a general structure for a class of algorithms already exists, then the experimentation with variances on these algorithms is also facilitated. The strength of the object-oriented philosophy can be used in data structures in two ways:

- **Interchange.** Recognizing similarities within data structures promotes interchange and reuse of the information they contain. Each data structure contains different levels of information. For example, in a cluster tree, at one level, the cluster is a collection of specific objects (common to all clustering methods). In a derived class, additional information such as a description of classification objects could be specified.

- **Algorithm generalization** A generalized algorithm is designed to operate on generalized data objects using only the fundamental properties of the objects. For example, logic-based algorithms would rely on the fundamental logical operations, but would be insensitive to the actual logic, such as crisp or fuzzy logic.

In the design of algorithms, especially in the field of vision, it is not sufficient to rely on one single analysis algorithm. Layers upon layers of sequential, iterative, and optimizing steps are used to reach the goal. This means that the essential information of each step must be transferred to the next. Data and algorithm reuse is implemented in the object-oriented philosophy in two ways:

- **Hierarchical Organization.** Commonalities for a large class of similar algorithms or data structures are put at the top of the hierarchy (superclasses), and as one proceeds downward the algorithms differentiate.

- **Overloading Functions.** Within an algorithm, modular aspects can be defined, which can be exchanged depending on the result desired.

Both are ways to represent the commonalities between algorithms and data.

The use of the object-oriented philosophy in the implementation and organization of the data structures and algorithms will be illustrated in the following sections with logical structures and clustering algorithms, respectively.

10.5   Generalized Logical Structures

The most important data structure in classification (clustering) and decision making (rule induction) is the logical expression. In the original formulations, most analysis techniques are defined in "crisp" terms, usually a binary yes or no; "Yes", this logical statement is true or, "Yes", this object belongs to this cluster. However, experience tells us that one cannot always choose between black and white, there are also gray areas. Fuzzy logic allows this extension [DHR93, KGK94, Zad65].

Most of the rule induction methods use the instances to estimate probabilities within their evaluation functions. The main idea behind the translation of a rule induction method from its classical n-valued formulation to a fuzzy logic formulation is the relaxation and approximation of the probabilistic concepts within an algorithm to a fuzzy logic formulation. The fuzzy logic formulation will continue to hold some "semantic" of the probability concepts, but some of the axioms associated with probability theory will be relaxed.

In the literature fuzzy logic can be described as a "possibility" measure. Furthermore, because a major aspect of machine learning involves the "separation" of objects, the fuzzy concept has a large aspect of "membership" character. The fuzzy function can be thought of as a simplified probabilistic function. The machine learning method is used to provide the first fuzzy guess at a probabilistic description. For example, a Gaussian distribution about a single value would be simplified to a pyramid function. After this first probability based guess, the resulting fuzzy functions could then be optimized by center and width shifts.

The following details how machine learning originally formulated in a crisp logic can be reformulated to a generalized form in an object-oriented approach.

10.5.1 Reformulation

The goal of the generalized approach is to define machine learning methods to allow, for example, the more general logical framework. This is accomplished through the reformulation, i.e., generalization, of the logical operations as they are used in machine learning methods. Within classification, discrimination, and decision making methods there are three important properties that need to be reformulated:

- **Counting and frequencies.** Counting how many objects match a logical description is no longer crisp, in other words, it can be "partially" counted.

- **Partitioning.** Given a classification of several partitions, an object need not belong exclusively to one but may have partial characters of several.

- **Logical operations.** The logical operations have to reflect conjunctions and disjunctions of object distributions.

In the classical formulation, given an object and a partition, the object matches one and only one of the descriptions in question. In a true-false logic, the answer is true for one of the descriptions and false for the others. Given a finite number of objects (which are assumed to be representative of the infinite number of objects), the probability that one of the descriptions is true is found by simply counting the number of objects that match and dividing by the total number of objects.

In the relaxed formulation, given an object and a partition, the object matches all descriptions within the partition, but to varying degrees, with the restriction that the sum of the degrees is one. If the degrees were restricted to only zeros and ones, then the classical formulation would be represented, one for true and zero for false. To calculate the total probability of each description in the partition, in this relaxed formulation, the counting procedure summing is over all of the degrees of the objects in each description. In a crisp logic, this would be summing with ones (true) and zeros (false); otherwise, it would be summing over the "fuzzy" values between zero and one.

An often-used criterion for clustering and decision trees is the minimum length principle, i.e., entropy. The basic term that needs to be calculated is $p_i \ln p_i$, where p is the probability of belonging to partition i. This probability is calculated using the counts of the instances, $\frac{n_i}{n_{tot}}$, where n_i and n_{tot} are the counts within the set of training instances of partition i and all partitions, respectively. The use of this generalized counting to represent probabilities requires that $n_{tot} = \Sigma_i n_i$.

In the classical formulation an object can only be assigned one distinct classification. The conjunction of two classifications reduces down to whether both are true. If the characteristics were of a probabilistic nature, the conjunction of two (evenly distributed) characteristics would be clear:

$$P(A \bigcap B) = P(A) \cdot P(B).$$

Thus, because the characterization of the membership functions of the predicates represents a relaxation of probabilistic concepts, the AND function has the same multiplicative form.

10.5.2   Object-Oriented Implementation

A rule induction algorithm, for example, manipulates logical objects. If the operations on these logical objects are generalized, then the method can be defined independent of the logic used. The data objects, including the logical objects, are represented in a hierarchical fashion to promote interchangeability. The algorithms are formulated in such a way that it is fairly independent of the form of the logical expression and the particular logic used.

A simple example is a nominal attribute representing a set of colors. The superclass is the Logical class. This is the class used in the machine learning methods. Derived from this class is NValuedLogic. An instantiation of this class (as 1.2 is an instantiation of the Real class) is a 3-valued logic, for example, representing the colors red, green, and blue. A specific attribute value (as used within a data set instance) of this type could be, for example, green. The machine learning algorithm would be formulated (compiled) with the Logical class and at run time the Colors class would be used.

Some classes are compound classes consisting of several other classes. The instantiation to a specific attribute type would be the instantiation of the classes making up the compound class. For example, within Figure 10.1 the foundational class NumericPredicate is a predicate function in which a real value is mapped to a logical value. Its main use is to form fuzzy logic predicates. Its definition needs a logic class (Logical) and a numeric function class (FuncRead1D). The logic class specifies the form of the logic that the predicate will return and the numeric function specifies the functional dependence, which, for fuzzy logic, maps the real numbers to a number between zero and one. In the example, the logic class is set to Continuous logic, a fuzzy logic class having a "logic" value from zero to one and the FuncRead1D call is set to PlateauFunction, where eight parameters determine the exact fuzzy relationship. This specifies a new class derived from NumericPredicate. This class could be used to define many fuzzy relationships, each instantiation of which would be a specific set of the eight parameters.

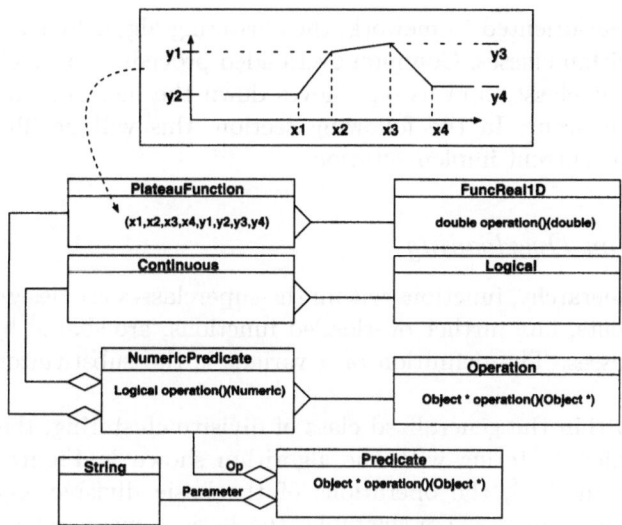

FIGURE 10.1. The interaction and building of a complex data structure from the frame given is shown. The "Predicate" object has two strings for the parameter name (to be found for each example instance) and the logic type of the predicate. The predicate itself is made up of a numeric predicate (a function mapping a number to a logic value). The numeric predicate, in turn, has two slots for the logic type and the numeric function type.

10.6   Generalized Clustering Algorithms

Clustering algorithms, as defined here, create a hierarchy of "clusters", grouping of objects. Each node is a grouping of "similar" objects, and the sons of each node are a further refinement of these similar objects into even more similar objects. There are a wide range of clustering algorithms ranging from k-means, the grouping of vectors into a fixed number of clusters using a Euclidean distance function, to a generalized CRG clustering where a hierarchy of clusters is formed by criteria determined at each level (or node) in the cluster hierarchy.

At one level, the wide variance of clustering methods have characteristics in common. For example, all produce a structure where each node is a grouping of objects. Furthermore, once the clustering hierarchy exists, each has a function that can "classify" a new object, i.e., assign it to a cluster. The two major aspects where the algorithms differentiate are the representations of the descriptions of each cluster and how the clustering hierarchy is created.

Within a similar class of clustering algorithms, certain procedures are common. For example, all divisive clustering methods have the common procedure of splitting the current objects on a node into another set of clusters making up the sons. The similarities are found through the operational examination of the entire set of clustering algorithms. The properties such as whether the method is incremental/non-incremental, divisive or agglomerative, clustering criteria, and object representation are used to group the clustering methods into classes.

Within the object-oriented framework, the clustering algorithms are placed within a hierarchy of algorithm classes. Common overloaded procedures to a class of algorithms are put in the superclasses and as one moves down the hierarchy only the necessary differentiation will occur. In the following section, this will be illustrated with the organization of the current implementation.

10.6.1   Function Overloading

Within the class hierarchy, functions within the superclasses are designed in such a way that the components, i.e., further overloaded functions, are shared by a large portion of the derived classes. The definition of a variant is the substitution of one of these components.

For example, within the generalized class of divisive clustering, the algorithm iteratively optimizes the clustering with the algorithm shown in Figure 10.2. Depending on the clustering method, the operations of the basic divisive algorithm are overloaded in the derived classes. For example, the basic k-means algorithm defines the Initialization routine to choose k seed vectors, the ClusteringInstancesOnNodes would use the distance function to assign the objects to the nodes, AdjustCluster Structure would redefine the node vectors and ContinueClusterIteration checks the change in the node vectors for convergence. In ISODATA and some vector quantization methods, for example, the AdjustClusterStructure operator would eliminate unused nodes in the cluster set. Among other differences, the CRG algorithm would have a more complex ClusteringInstancesOnNodes that would cluster unary and binary features depending on the node level.

Initialization The node is initialized with the appropriate cluster structure.

while(ContinueClusterIteration) The iterative looping continues until convergence is reached based on the current cluster structure. The quality of the structure and the improvement since the last iteration can be used as criteria.

> **ClusteringInstancesOnNodes** Given the current set of instances, current node and the current clustering, the next new clustering structure is created. This routine would be where the distance function could be used to determine the object assignment.

> **ComputeClusterQuality** The quality of the current cluster is evaluated.

> **AdjustClusterStructure** Given the new clustering, the cluster structure is adjusted. As a result, the measure of cluster improvement is calculated (to be used in deciding whether further evaluations are needed).

FIGURE 10.2. The Main Algorithm of Divisive Clustering

Another form of function overloading, which is useful for clustering algorithms, is where the function is not defined in the hierarchy but retrieved externally as an input parameter. The most obvious candidate of this type is the distance function, a mapping from the object and node description to a floating-point number representing the similarity of the object to the node description. In standard distance clustering over real vector spaces, the set of distance functions would calculate the difference between the input vector and the mean vector on the node. Another example in vector quantization where a small representation is searched for is the use of description length (entropy) as the distance function. With data objects beyond vectors, the object could be, for example, graphs, where the definition of the difference between two graphs could be experimented with. This experimentation would occur without distortion to the base clustering algorithm.

Conclusion

A general summary of machine learning has been given from several perspectives. It has been contrasted with other data analysis methods noting that the major differences are that they are based on more humanlike properties and that they are usually a search through the representation space. From a more historical perspective, the major paradigms were outlined, namely, statistical, clustering, rule induction, neural net, genetic, and probabilistic algorithms. A more useful categorization of the methods was given from an operational point of view. This viewpoint was used as a basis to illustrate how they are implemented in an object-oriented framework to expedite the experimentation and developement of the complex algorithms that image analysis requires.

References

[AAF95]   E. Ahronovitz, J.-P. Aubert, and C. Fiorio. The star-topology: A topology for image analysis. In *Cinquième Colloque DGCI*, 107–116. LLAIC1, Université d'Auvergne, ISBN 2-87663-040-0, September 1995.

[ABB⁺75] A.P. Ambler, H.G. Barrow, C.M. Brown, R.M. Burstall, and R.J. Popplestone. A versatile system for computer-controlled assembly. *Artificial Intelligence*, 6:129–156, 1975.

[AF86]   N. Ayache and O.D. Faugeras. HYPER: A new approach for the recognition and positioning of two-dimensional objects. *IEEE Transactions on Pattern Analysis and Machine Intelligence*, PAMI-8(1):44–54, January 1986.

[AF94]   E. Ahronovitz and C. Fiorio. Un système topologique complet pour le traitement d'images. Technical Research Report 94-044, Lab. d'Informatique, de Robotique et de Microélectronique de Montpellier, December 1994.

[AGSS89] A.K. Aggarwal, L.J. Guibas, J. Saxe, and P.W. Shor. A linear-time algorithm for computing the Voronoi diagram of a convex polygon. *Discrete Comput. Geom.*, 4(6):591–604, 1989.

[Ahu82]   N. Ahuja. Dot pattern processing using Voronoi neighborhoods. *IEEE Trans. Pattern Analysis and Machine Intelligence*, 4(3):336–343, 1982.

[AK77]   A.K. Aggarwal and A.V. Kulkarni. A sequential approach to the extraction of shape features. *Comp. Graph. and Image Proc.*, 6(6):538–557, December 1977.

[AS95]   H. Alt and O. Schwarzkopf. The Voronoi diagram of curved objects. In *Proc. 11th Ann. ACM Symp. Comput. Geom.*, 89–97, 1995.

[BA83]   P.J. Burt and E.H. Adelson. The Laplacian pyramid as a compact image code. *IEEE Transactions on Communications*, Vol. COM-31(4):532–540, April 1983.

[BB82]   D.H. Ballard and C.M. Brown. *Computer Vision*. Englewood Cliffs, NJ: Prentice-Hall, 1982.

[BB94]   W. Burger and B. Bhanu. Signal-to-symbol conversion for structural object recognition using hidden Markov models. In *Proc. ARPA Image Understanding Workshop*, 1287–1291, Monterey, CA, November 1994.

[BB96]   M.J. Burge and W. Burger. Qualitative spatial relations using arrange-
           ments for complex images. In *Vision Geometry V*, volume 2826, 152–158,
           Denver, CO, August 4-9 1996. SPIE. mburge@acm.org.

[BB97]   M.J. Burge and W. Burger. Learning visual ideals. In *International Con-
           ference on Image Analysis and Processing*, volume 1310 of *Lecture Notes
           in Computer Science*, 316–323, Florence, Italy, September 1997. Springer-
           Verlag. mburge@acm.org.

[BBB96]   E. Bertin, H. Bischof, and P. Bertolino. Voronoi pyramids controlled by
           hopfield networks. *Computer Vision and Image Understanding*, 63(3):462–
           475, 1996.

[BBM96a]   M. Burge, W. Burge, and W. Mayr. Recognition and learning with poly-
           morphic structural components. *Journal of Computing and Information
           Technology*, 4(1):39–51, 1996.

[BBM96b]   M.J. Burge, W. Burger, and W. Mayr. Generic object recognition us-
           ing weak structural representations. In *3rd Slovenian Speech and Image
           Understanding Workshop*, 167–176, Ljubljana, Slovenia, April 24–26 1996.
           SDRV, Austrian Computer Society. mburge@acm.org.

[BBM96c]   M.J. Burge, W. Burger, and W. Mayr. Learning to recognize generic vi-
           sual categories using a hybrid structural approach. In *Proc. International
           Conf. on Image Processing*, volume 2, 321–324, Lausanne, Switzerland,
           September 16–19 1996. IEEE Press. mburge@acm.org.

[BBM96d]   M.J. Burge, W. Burger, and W. Mayr. Recognition and learning with
           polymorphic structural components. *Journal of Computing and Informa-
           tion Technology*, 4(1):39–51, 1996. mburge@acm.org.

[BBM96e]   M.J. Burge, W. Burger, and W. Mayr. Recognition and learning with poly-
           morphic structural components. In *Proc. International Conf. on Pattern
           Recognition*, volume 1, 19–23, Vienna, Austria, August 25–30 1996. IEEE
           Press. mburge@acm.org.

[BBM96f]   M.J. Burge, W. Burger, and W. Mayr. Where to look next: Using the part
           compatability graph. In *20th Workshop of the Austrian Association for
           Pattern Recognition*, 45–57, Wien, May 1996. ÖAGM, Austrian Computer
           Society. mburge@acm.org.

[BBW88]   P.J. Besl, J.B. Birch, and L.T. Watson. Robust window operators. In
           Proceedings of the 2nd International Conference on Computer Vision, 591–
           600. IEEE, December 1988.

[BC94a]   W.F. Bischof and T. Caelli. Learning structural descriptions of patterns:
           A new technique for conditional clustering and rule generation. *Pattern
           Recognition*, 27:689–697, 1994.

[BC94b]   W.F. Bischof and T. Caelli. Learning structural descriptions of pattern: A new technique for conditional clustering and rule generation. *Pattern Recognition*, 27:689–697, 1994.

[BC96]   G. Briscoe and T. Caelli. *A Compendium of Machine Learning*. Ablex Publishing Corp., Norwood, NJ, 1996.

[BCB+92]   L. Boatto, V. Consorti, M. Del Buono, S. Di Zenzo, V. Eramo, A. Esposito, F. Melcarne, M. Meucci, A. Morelli, M. Mosciatti, S. Scarci, and M. Tucci. An interpretation system for land register maps. *IEEE Computer*, 25(7):25–34, July 1992.

[BCR90]   M. Bister, J. Cornelis, and A. Rosenfeld. A critical view of pyramid segmentation algorithms. *Pattern Recognition Letters*, 11(9):605–617, September 1990.

[Bed92]   B.B. Bederson. *A Miniature Space-Variant Active Vision System: Cortex I*. Ph.D. thesis, New York University, Courant Institute, 1992.

[Bes88]   P.J. Besl. *Surfaces in Range Image Understanding*. Springer-Verlag, 1988.

[BF84]   B. Bhanu and O. Faugeras. Shape matching of two-dimensional objects. *IEEE Trans. Patt. Anal. Mach. Intell.*, PAMI-6(2):137–156, March 1984.

[BFS90]   L. Breiman, J.H. Friedman, R.A. Olshen, and C.J. Stone. *Classification and Regression Trees*. Wadsworthand Brooks, Belmont, CA, 1990.

[BHR81]   P.J. Burt, T.-H. Hong, and A. Rosenfeld. Segmentation and estimation of image region properties through cooperative hierarchical computation. *IEEE Transactions on Systems, Man, and Cybernetics*, Vol. SMC-11(12):802–809, December 1981.

[Bie87]   I. Biederman. Matching image edges to object memory. In *Proceedings of the First International Conference on Computer Vision*, 384–392, London, England, 1987.

[BJ93]   S. Bataouche and J.-M. Jolion. Asynchronous pyramids. In G. Vernazza, A.N. Venetsanopoulos, and C. Braccini, editors, *Int. Conf. Image Processing: Theory and Applications*, 267–270, San Remo, Italy, 1993. Elsevier, Amsterdam.

[BK93a]   H. Bischof and W.G. Kropatsch. Hopfield networks for irregular decimation. In W. Pölzleitner and E. Wenger, editors, *Image Analysis and Synthesis*, volume 68 of *OCG Schriftenreihe*, 317–327. Wien: Oldenbourg-Verlag, 1993.

[BK93b]   J. Buhmann and H. Kühnel. Vector quantizatiion with complexity costs. *IEEE Transactions on Information Theory*, 39:1133–1145, 1993.

[BK94]   H. Bischof and W.G. Kropatsch. Fuzzy curve pyramid. In *Proc of 12th ICPR (Jerusalem)*, volume 1, 505–509. IEEE-Computer Society Press, 1994.

[BKar]   M.J. Burge and W.G. Kropatsch. A minimal line property preserving representation of line images. *Computing*, 62:355–368,1999.

[BL93]   R. Bergevin and M.D. Levine. Generic object recognition: Building and matching coarse descriptions from line drawings. *IEEE Trans. Pattern Analysis and Machine Intelligence*, 1(15):19–36, 1993.

[BLS99]   H. Bischof, A. Leonardis, and A. Selb. MDL principle for robust vector quantization. *Pattern Analysis and Applications*, 2(1):59–72, 1999.

[BM87]   B. Bhanu and J.C. Ming. Recognition of occluded objects: A cluster-structure algorithm. *Pattern Recognition*, 20(2):199–211, 1987.

[BM95a]   M.J. Burge and G. Monagan. Extracting words and multi-part symbols in graphics rich documents. In *International Conference on Image Analysis and Processing*, Lecture Notes in Computer Science, 533–538, San Remo, Italy, September 13–16 1995. IAPR, Springer-Verlag.

[BM95b]   M.J. Burge and G. Monagan. Using the Voronoi tessellation for grouping words and multipart symbols in documents. In *Vision Geometry IV*, volume 2573, 116–123. SPIE, 1995. mburge@acm.org.

[BMS94]   C. Burnikel, K. Mehlhorn, and S. Schirra. How to compute the Voronoi diagram of line segments: Theoretical and experimental results. In *Proc. 2nd Ann. European Symp. Algorithms*, volume 855 of *Lecture Notes Comput. Sci.*, 227–239. Springer-Verlag, 1994.

[BP92]   H. Bischof and A. Pinz. The invariance problem for hierarchical neural networks. In C. Su-Shing, editor, *Neural and Stochastic Methods in Image and Signal Processing*, volume 1766, 118–129. Bellingham, WA: SPIE-The International Society for Optical Engineering, 1992.

[Bre89]   T.M. Breuel. Adaptive model base indexing. In *Proc. Darpa IU Workshop*, Palo Alto, CA, May 1989.

[Bro65]   G.S. Brown. Point density in stems per acre. *New Zealand Forestry Service Research Notes*, 38:1–11, 1965.

[Bro81]   R.A. Brooks. Symbolic reasoning among 3-D models and 2-D images. *Artificial Intelligence*, 17:285–348, 1981.

[BT88]   R.P. Blanford and S.L. Tanimoto. Bright spot detection in pyramids. *Computer Vision, Graphics, and Image Processing*, 43(2):133–149, August 1988.

[Bur88]   P.J. Burt. Smart sensing within a pyramid vision machine. *Proceedings of the IEEE*, 1006–1015, 1988.

[Bur98]   M.J. Burge. *The Representation and Analysis of Document Images*, volume 100 of *Computer Vision and Graphics Dissertations*. Austrian Computer Society, Vienna, 1998. mburge@acm.org.

[Cer86]   J. Cerella. Pigeons and perceptrons. *Pattern Recognition*, 19(6):431–438, 1986.

[CH90]   C. Cherfils and F. Hermeline. Diagonal swap procedures and characterizations of 2D-Delauna and triangulations. *RAIRO-Mathematical Modelling and Numerical Analysis-Modelisation Mathematique Et Analyse Numerique*, 24(5):613–625, 1990.

[Che89]   D.S. Chen. A data-driven intermediate level feature extraction algorithm. *IEEE Transactions on Pattern Analysis and Machine Intelligence*, PAMI-11(7):749–758, July 1989.

[Cho95]   J.J. Chou. Voronoi diagrams for planar shapes. *IEEE Computer Graphics and Applications*, 15(2):52–59, March 1995.

[Chr75]   N. Christofides. *Graph Theory - An Algorithmic Approach*. New York: Academic Press, 1975.

[CN87]   P. Clark and T. Niblett. Induction in noisy domains. In *Progress in Machine Learning*. Sigma Press, 1987.

[CN89]   P. Clark and T. Niblett. The CN2 induction algorithm. *Machine Learning*, 3(4):261–284, 1989.

[CPW93]   C.H. Chen, L.F. Pau, and P.S.P Wang, editors. *Handbook of Pattern Recognition and Computer Vision*. World Scientific, 1993.

[CS88]   K.L. Clarkson and P.W. Shor. Algorithms for diametral pairs and convex hulls that are optimal, randomized, and incremental. In *Proc. 4th Ann. ACM Symp. Comput. Geom.*, 12–17, 1988.

[CWH97]   A.D.J. Cross, R.C. Wilson, and E.R. Hancock. Inexact graph matching using genetic search. *PR*, 30(6):953–970, June 1997.

[DHKP97]   M. Dietzfelbinger, T. Hagerup, J. Katajainen, and M. Penttonen. A reliable randomized algorithm for the closest-pair problem. *J. Algorithms*, 25:19–51, 1997.

[DHR93]   D. Driankov, H. Hellendoorn, and M. Reinfrank. *An Introduction to Fuzzy Control*. Springer-Verlag, 1993.

[DM81]   T. Dietterich and R.S Michalski. Inductive learning of structural descriptions. *Artificial Intelligence*, 16:257–294, 1981.

[DPR92]   S.J. Dickinson, A.P. Pentland, and A. Rosenfeld. From volumes to views: An approach to 3-D object recognition. *Computer Vision, Graphics and Image Processing*, 55(2):130–154, March 1992.

[DW89]   J. Dolan and R. Weiss. Perceptual grouping of curved lines. In *Proceedings of the Image Understanding Workshop*, 1135–1145. DARPA, May 1989.

[DZCL96]   S. Di Zenzo, L. Cinque, and S. Levialdi. Run-based algorithms for binary image-analysis and processing. *IEEE Trans. Pattern Analysis and Machine Intelligence*, 18(1):83–89, January 1996.

[Ede93]   S. Edelman. On learning to recognize 3-D objects from examples. *IEEE Trans. Pattern Analysis and Machine Intelligence*, 15(8):833–837, August 1993.

[EG99]   R. Englert and R. Glantz. Towards the Clustering of Graphs. In *Proc. of the 2nd International Workshop on Graph-Based Representation (IAPR-TC15)*, OCG-Schriftenreihe, Vol. 126, 125–133, 1999.

[Ett88]   G.J. Ettinger. Large hierarchical object recognition using libraries of paramterized model sub-parts. In *Conf. on Computer Vision and Pattern Recognition*, 1988.

[FB81]   M.A. Fischler and R.C. Bolles. Random sample consensus: A paradigm for model fitting with applications to image analysis and automated cartography. *Communications ACM*, 24(6):381–395, June 1981.

[FE73]   M.A. Fischler and R.A. Elschlager. The representation and matching of pictorial structures. *IEEE Transactions on Computers*, 22(1):67–92, 1973.

[FF95]   C. Fuchs and W. Forstner. Polymorphic grouping for image segmentation. In *ICCV95*, 175–182, 1995.

[FH89]   P. Fua and A.J. Hanson. Objective functions for feature discrimination. In *Proceedings of the 11th International Joint Conference on Artificial Intelligence*, 1596–1602, Detroit, MI, August 1989. Morgan Kaufman.

[Fis87]   D. Fisher. Knowledge acquisition via incremental conceptual clustering. *Machine Learning*, 2:139–172, 1987.

[For87a]   S.J. Fortune. A note on Delaunay diagonal flips. Manuscript, AT&T Bell Lab., Murray Hill, NJ, 1987.

[For87b]   S.J. Fortune. A sweepline algorithm for Voronoi diagrams. *Algorithmica*, 2:153–174, 1987.

[For97]   S.J. Fortune. Voronoi diagrams and Delaunay triangulations. In J.E. Goodman and J. O'Rourke, editors, *Handbook of Discrete and Computational Geometry*, chapter 20, 377–388. CRC Press LLC, Boca Raton, FL, 1997.

[Fri95]   B. Fritzke. A growing neural gas network learns topologies. In *Advances in Neural Information Processing Systems*. MIT Press, 1995.

[FWH97]   A.M. Finch, R.C. Wilson, and E.R. Hancock. Matching Delaunay graphs. *Pattern Recognition*, 30(1):123–140, January 1997.

[GB87]   G. Reynolds and J.R. Beveridge. Searching for geometric structure in images of natural scenes. In *Proc. DARPA Image Understanding Workshop*, 257–271, Los Angeles, CA, 1987.

[GE99]   R. Glantz and R. Englert and W.G. Kropatsch. Representation of Image Structure by a Pair of Dual Graphs. In *Proc. of the 2nd International Workshop on Graph-Based Representation (IAPR-TC15)*, OCG-Schriftenreihe, Vol. 126, 155–163, 1999.

[GEK99]   R. Glantz, R. Englert, and W.G. Kropatsch. Contracting distance maps of pores to pore networks. In *Proc. of the 4th Computer Vision Winter Workshop*, 112-121, 1999.

[GG84]   S. Geman and D. Geman. Stochastic relaxation, Gibbs distributions, and the Bayesian restoration of images. *IEEE Transactions on Pattern Analysis and Machine Intelligence*, 6:721–741, 1984.

[GHJV94]   E. Gamma, R. Helm, R. Johnson, and J. Vlissides. *Design Patterns: Elements of Reusable Object Oriented Software*. Addison-Wesley, 1994.

[GJ86]   W.I. Grosky and R. Jain. A pyramid based approach to segmentation applied to region matching. *IEEE Transactions Pattern Analysis and Machine Intelligence*, 8(5):639–650, 1986.

[GLF90]   J.H. Gennari, P. Langley, and D. Fisher. Models of incremental concept formation. In J.G. Carbonell, editor, *Machine Learning: Pardigms and Methods*, 11–61. MIT Press, 1990.

[Gol89]   D.E. Goldberg. *Genetic Algorithms*. Addison-Wesley, 1989.

[Gri90]   W.E.L. Grimson. The combinatorics of object recognition in cluttered environments using constrained search. *Artificial Intelligence*, 44:121–165, 1990.

[Gri91]   W.E.L. Grimson. The combinatorics of heuristic search termination for object recognition in cluttered environments. *IEEE Trans. on Pattern Analysis and Machine Intelligence*, 13(9):920–935, 1991.

[Har84]   R.L. Hartley. *Multi-Scale Models in Image Analysis*. Ph.D. thesis, University of Maryland, College Park, Computer Science Center, 1984.

[Hel93]   M. Held. Incremental generation of Voronoi diagrams of planar shapes. In *Proc. 9th European Workshop Comput. Geom.*, 70–73, 1993.

[Hel94]   M. Held. On computing Voronoi diagrams of convex polyhedra by means of wavefront propagation. In *Proc. 6th Canad. Conf. Comput. Geom.*, 128–133, 1994.

272   References

[HHNT89]   J.H. Holland, K.J. Holyoak, R.E. Nisbett, and P.R. Thagard. *Induction*.
           MIT Press, 1989.

[HKW+93]   G. Hartmann, K.O. Kräuter, H. Wiemers, E. Seidenberg, and S. Drüe.
           Ein distanz- und orientierungsinvariantes lernfähiges Erkennungssystem
           für Roboteranwendungen (A distance– and orientation invariant learn-
           ing and recognition systems for application in robotics). In S.J. Pöppl
           and H. Handels, editors, *Mustererkennung 1993*, 375–382. Berlin: Springer-
           Verlag, 1993.

[HLLZ87]   R.M. Haralick, C. Lin, J.S.J. Lee, and X. Zhuang. Multi-resolution mor-
           phology. In *Proceedings of the First International Conference on Computer
           Vision*, 516–520, London, England, June 1987. IEEE Press.

[HS91]   R.M. Haralick and L.G. Shapiro. Glossary of computer vision terms. *Pat-
           tern Recognition*, 24:69–93, 1991.

[HSC91]   R. Hanson, J. Stutz, and P. Cheeseman. Bayesian classification theory.
           Technical Report FIA-90-12-7-01, NASA Ames Research Center, 1991.

[Hu62]   M.K. Hu. Visual pattern recognition by moment invariants. *IEEE Trans.
           Information Theory*, 8:179–187, 1962.

[HU79]   J.E. Hopcroft and J.D. Ullman. *Introduction to Automata Theory, Lan-
           guages and Computations*. Reading, MA: Addison-Wesley, 1979.

[Hub81]   P.J. Huber. *Robust Statistics*. Wiley, New York, 1981.

[JH88]   A.K. Jain and R. Hoffman. Evidence-based recognition of 3D objects.
           IEEE Trans. Pattern Analysis and Machine Intelligence, 10(6):783–802,
           November 1988.

[JM92]   J.M. Jolion and A. Montanvert. The adaptive pyramid, a framework for
           2D image analysis. *Computer Vision, Graphics, and Image Processing:
           Image Processing*, 55(3):339–348, May 1992.

[JR94]   J.-M. Jolion and A. Rosenfeld. *A Pyramid Framework for Early Vision*.
           Boston: Kluwer, 1994.

[KB96]   W.G. Kropatsch and S. BenYacoub. A revision of pyramid segmenta-
           tion. In W.G. Kropatsch, editor, *13th International Conference on Pattern
           Recognition*, volume II, 477–481. IEEE Comp. Soc., 1996.

[KBYN98]   W.G. Kropatsch, M. Burge, S. Ben Yacoub, and S. Nazha. Dual graph
           contraction with LEDA. *International Journal* COMPUTING-*Archives for
           Informatics and Numerical Computation*, [Suppl.](12):101–110, 1998.

[KGK94]   R. Kruse, J. Gebhardt, and F. Klawonn. *Foundations of Fuzzy Systems*.
           John Wiley and Sons, 1994.

[KJ86]   T.F. Knoll and R.C. Jain. Recognizing partially visible objects using feature indexed hypotheses. *IEEE Journal of Robotics and Automation*, 2(1):3–13, 1986.

[KJ93]   R. Kasturi and R.C. Jain, editors. *Computer Vision: Principles*. IEEE Computer Society Press, 1993.

[KKM⁺89] D.Y. Kim, J.J. Kim, P. Meer, D. Mintz, and A. Rosenfeld. Robust computer vision: A least-median of squares based approach. In *Proceedings of the Image Understanding Workshop*, 1117–1134, Palo Alto, CA, May 1989. DARPA.

[KL96]   R. Klein and A. Lingas. A linear-time randomized algorithm for the bounded Voronoi diagram of a simple polygon. *Internat. J. Comput. Geom. Appl.*, 6:263–278, 1996.

[KM92]   W.G. Kropatsch and A. Montanvert. Irregular pyramids. Technical Report PRIP-TR-5, Technical University Vienna, Department for Pattern Recognition and Image Processing, 1992.

[KMM93]   R. Klein, K. Mehlhorn, and S. Meiser. Randomized incremental construction of abstract Voronoi diagrams. *Comput. Geom. Theory Appl.*, 3(3):157–184, 1993.

[Koh84]   T. Kohonen. *Self-Organization and Associative Memory*. Springer-Verlag, 1984.

[Kov93]   V.A. Kovalevsky. Digital geometry based on the topology of abstract cellular complexes. In J.-M. Chassery, J. Francon, A. Montanvert, and J.-P. Réveillès, editors, *Géometrie Discrète en Imagery, Fondements et Applications*, 259–284, Strasbourg, France, September 1993.

[Koz92]   J.R. Koza. *Genetic Programming*. MIT Press, 1992.

[Kro87a]   W.G. Kropatsch. Curve representations in multiple resolutions. *Pattern Recognition Letters*, 6(3):179–184, August 1987.

[Kro87b]   W.G. Kropatsch. Elimination von "kleinen" Kurvenstücken in der $2 \times 2/2$ Kurvenpyramide (Elimination of "short" curves in the $2 \times 2/2$ curve pyramid). In E. Paulus, editor, *Mustererkennung 1987*, Informatik Fachberichte 149, 156–160. Berlin: Springer-Verlag, 1987.

[Kro91]   W.G. Kropatsch. Image pyramids and curves: An overview. Technical Report PRIP-TR-2, Technical University Vienna, Dept. for Pattern Recognition and Image Processing, March 1991.

[Kro92]   W.G. Kropatsch. Irregular pyramids. In Peter Mandl, editor, *Modelling and New Methods in Image Processing and in Geographical Information Systems*, volume 61 of *OCG-Schriftenreihe*, 39–50. Wien: Oldenbourg-Verlag, 1992.

[Kro95]   W.G. Kropatsch. Building irregular pyramids by dual graph contraction. *IEE-Proc. Vision, Image and Signal Processing*, Vol. 142(6):366–374, December 1995.

[Kro97a]   W. Kropatsch. Property preserving hierarchical graph transformations. In C. Arcelli, L. Cordella, and G. Sanniti di Baja, editors, *Advances in Visual Form Analysis*, 340–349. World Scientific Publishing Company, 1997.

[Kro97b]   W.G. Kropatsch. Equivalent contraction kernels to build dual irregular pyramids. *Advances in Computer Science*:99–107, 1997.

[Kro97c]   W.G. Kropatsch. From equivalent weighting functions to equivalent contraction kernels. In *Czech Pattern Recognition Workshop'97*, 1–13. Czech Pattern Recognition Society, February 1997.

[Kro97d]   W.G. Kropatsch. Property preserving hierarchical graph transformations. In C. Arcelli, L.P. Cordella, and G. Sanniti di Baja, editors, *Advances in Visual Form Analysis*, 340–349. World Scientific Publishing Company, 1997.

[Lan96]   P. Langley. *Elements of Machine Learning*. Morgan Kaufmann Publishers, Inc., 1996.

[Law77]   C.L. Lawson. *Software for C^1 Surface Interpolation*. JPL Publication, 1977.

[LB96]   A. Leonardis and H. Bischof. Robust recovery of eigenimages in the presence of outliers and occlusions. *Journal of Computing and Information Technology*, CIT 4(1):25–36, 1996.

[LB98]   A. Leonardis and H. Bischof. An efficient MDL-based construction of RBF networks. *Neural Networks*, 11(5):963–973, July 1998.

[LBP95]   T. Leung, M. Burl, and P. Perona. Finding faces in cluttered scenes using labelled random graph matching. In *Proc. International Conf. on Computer Vision*, 637–644, 1995.

[LD81]   D.T. Lee and R.L. Drysdale. Generalization of Voronoi diagrams in the plane. *SIAM J. Comput.*, 10:73–87, 1981.

[Lec89]   Y.G. Leclerc. Constructing simple stable descriptions for image partitioning. *International Journal of Computer Vision*, 3:73–102, 1989.

[Lee78]   D.T. Lee. Proximity and reachability in the plane. Technical Report Tech. Rep. No. R-831, Coordinated Sci. Lab., University of Ilinois at Urbana, IL, 1978.

[Leo93]   A. Leonardis. *Image Analysis Using Parametric Models: Model-Recovery and Model-Selection Paradigm.* Ph.D. thesis, University of Ljubljana, Faculty of Electrical Engineering and Computer Science, Ljubljana, Tržaška c. 25, 61001 Ljubljana, Slovenia, May 1993. Also available as Technical Report LRV-93-3, University of Ljubljana, Slovenia.

[Lev86]   S. Levialdi. Programming image processing machines. In S. Levialdi and V. Cantoni, editors, *Pyramidal Systems for Image Processing and Computer Vision*, volume F25 of *NATO ASI Series*, 311–328. Berlin: Springer-Verlag, 1986.

[LGB95]   A. Leonardis, A. Gupta, and R. Bajcsy. Segmentation of range images as the search for geometric parametric models. *International Journal of Computer Vision*, 14:253–277, 1995.

[Li85]   G. Li. Robust regression. In *Exploring Data Tables, Trends and Shapes*, 281–343. John Wiley & Sons, 1985.

[Lin93]   T. Lindeberg. Detecting salient blob-like image structures and their scales with a scale-space primal sketch: A method for focus-of-attention. *International Journal of Computer Vision*, 11(3):283–318, 1993.

[Low87]   D.G. Lowe. The viewpoint consistency constraint. *International Journal of Computer Vision*, 1(1):57–72, 1987.

[LS87]   D. Leven and M. Sharir. Intersection and proximity problems and Voronoi diagrams. In J.T. Schwartz and C.-K. Yap, editors, *Advances in Robotics 1: Algorithmic and Geometric Aspects of Robotics*, 187–228. Lawrence Erlbaum Associates, Hillsdale, NJ, 1987.

[LSM94]   A. Leonardis, F. Solina, and A. Macerl. A direct recovery of superquadric models in range images using recover-and-select paradigm. In J.-O. Eklundh, editor, *Proceedings of the Third European Conference on Computer Vision—ECCV-94*, Stockholm, Sweden, May 1994.

[LW88]   Y. Lamdan and H.J. Wolfson. Geometric hashing: A general and efficient model-based recognition scheme. In *Proc. ICCV-88*, 238–249, Tampa, FL, December 1988.

[Mal89]   S.G. Mallat. A theory for multiresolution signal decomposition: The wavelet representation. *IEEE Transactions on Pattern Analysis and Machine Intelligence*, 11(7):674–693, July 1989.

[Mar80]   D. Marr. Visual information processing: The structure and creation of visual representations. *Philosophical Transactions of the Royal Society London*, Ser. B(290):199–218, 1980.

[Mar82]   D. Marr. *Vision*. Freeman, San Francisco, 1982.

[MB92]   A. Montanvert and P. Bertolino. Irregular pyramids for parallel image segmentation. In H. Bischof and W.G. Kropatsch, editors, *Pattern Recognition 1992*, volume OCG-Schriftenreihe 62, 13–34. Wien: Oldenbourg–Verlag, 1992.

[MB93]   M.J. Mirza and K.L. Boyer. Performance evaluation of a class of M-estimators for surface parameter estimation in noisy range data. *IEEE Transactions on Robotics and Automation*, RA-9(1):75–85, February 1993.

[MCM83]   R.S. Michalski, J.G. Carbonell, and T.M. Mitchell, editors. *Machine Learning: An Artificial Intelligence Approach*. Morgan Kaufmann Publishers, Inc., 1983.

[Mee89]   P. Meer. Stochastic image pyramids. *Computer Vision, Graphics, and Image Processing*, 45(3):269–294, March 1989.

[Mic80]   R.S. Michalski. Pattern recognition as rule-guided inductive inference. *IEEE Transactions on Pattern Analysis and Machine Intelligence*, 2(4):349–361, 1980.

[Mit97]   T.M. Mitchell. *Machine Learning*. WCB/McGraw-Hill, 1997.

[MMHL86]   R.S. Michalski, I. Mozetic, J. Hong, and N. Lavrac. The multi-purpose incremental learning system AQ15 and its testing application to three medical domains. In *Proceedings of the American Association for Artificial Intelligence Conference (AAAI)*, 1041–1045, 1986.

[MMR91]   A.Montanvert, P. Meer, and A. Rosenfeld. Hierarchical image analysis using irregular tesselations. *IEEE-PAMI*, 13(4):307–316, 1991.

[MMRK91]   P. Meer, D. Mintz, A. Rosenfeld, and D.Y. Kim. Robust regression methods for computer vision: A review. *International Journal of Computer Vision*, 6(1):59–70, 1991.

[MN95]   H. Murase and S.K. Nayar. Visual learning and recognition of 3-D objects from appearance. *International Journal of Computer Vision*, 14(1):5–24, January 1995.

[MR93]   G. Monagan and M. Röösli. Appropriate base representation using a run graph. In *Proceedings of the Second International Conf. on Document Analysis and Recognition*, 623–626, Tsukuba, Japan, October 20–22 1993. IAPR, IEEE Computer Society Press.

[MR94]   N. Mayya and V.T. Rajan. Voronoi diagrams of polygons: A framework for shape representation. In *Conf. on Computer Vision and Pattern Recognition*, 638–643, 1994.

[MS83]   R.S. Michalski and R.E. Stepp. *Machine Learning: An Artificial Intelligence Approach*, Chapter 11: Learning from Observation: Conceptual Clustering. Morgan Kaufmann Publ. Inc., 1983.

[MSR88]   P. Meer, C.A. Sher, and A. Rosenfeld. The chain pyramid: Hierarchical contour processing. Technical Report TR-2072, University of Maryland, College Park, Computer Science Center, July 1988.

[MT94]   R. Michalski and G. Tecuci, editors. *Machine Learning: A Multistrategy Approach*. Morgan Kaufmann Publishers, Inc, 1994.

[MZ92]   J.L. Mundy and A. Zisserman. *Geometric Invariance in Computer Vision*. MIT Press, 1992.

[Nig27]   R. Niggli. Die topologische strukturanalsye. *Zeitschrift für Kristallographie*, 65:391–415, 1927.

[OBS92]   A. Okabe, B. Boots, and K. Sugihara. *Spatial Tessellations: Concepts and Applications of Voronoi Diagrams*. John Wiley & Sons, Chichester, UK, 1992.

[OBS94]   A. Okabe, B. Boots, and K. Sugihara. Nearest neighbourhood operations with generalized Voronoi diagrams: A review. *International Journal of Geographical Information Systems*, 8(1):43–71, January 1994.

[Orr95]   M.J. Orr. Regularization in the selection of basis function centers. *Neural Computation*, 7(3):606–623, 1995.

[Pav78]   T. Pavlidis. A minimum storage boundary tracing algorithm and its application to automatic inspection. *IEEE Trans. Systems, Man, and Cybernetics*, 8(1):66–69, January 1978.

[PB98]   J. Peng and B. Bhanu. Closed-loop object recognition using reinforcement learning. *IEEE Transactions on Pattern Analysis and Machine Intelligence*, 20:139–154, 1998.

[PBP98]   M. Prantl, M.J. Burge, and A. Pinz. Recognition of 3-D objects having ambiguous views. In *22th Workshop of the Austrian Association for Pattern Recognition*, 165–174. ÖAGM, Austrian Computer Society, 1998. mburge@acm.org.

[Pen89]   A.P. Pentland. Part segmentation for object recognition. *Neural Computation*, 1:82–91, 1989.

[PK91]   Y.C. Pati and P.S. Krishnaprasad. Discrete affine wavelet transforms. In R.P. Lippmann, J.E. Moody, and D.S. Tourtetzky, editors, *Advances in Neural Information Processing*, volume III, 743–749, 1991.

[PKJ98]   J.-G. Pailloncy, W.G. Kropatsch, and J.-M. Jolion. Object matching on irregular pyramid. In A. Jain, S. Venkatesh, and B. Lovell, editors, *14th International Conference on Pattern Recognition*, volume II, 1721–1723. IEEE Comp. Soc., 1998.

[PS85]   F.P. Preparata and M.I. Shamos. *Computational Geometry*. Springer, New York, 1985.

[Qui86]   J.R. Quinlan. Induction of Decision Trees. *Machine Learning*, 1:81–106, 1986.

[Qui90a]   J.R. Quinlan. Decision trees and decision making. *IEEE Trans. on Systems, Man and Cybernetics*, 20:339–346, 1990.

[Qui90b]   J.R. Quinlan. Learning logical definitions from relations. *Machine Learning*, 5(3):266–293, 1990.

[Qui91]   J.R. Quinlan. Determinate literals in inductive logic programming. In *Proceeding of the Twelfth IJCAI*, 746–750. Morgan Kaufmann, 1991.

[Qui92]   J.R. Quinlan. *C4.5: Programs for Machine Learning*. Morgan Kaufmann, 1992.

[RBP+92]   J. Rumbaugh, M. Blaha, W. Premerlani, F. Eddy, and W. Lorensen. *Object-Oriented Modeling and Design*. Prentice-Hall, 1992.

[RK82]   A. Rosenfeld and A.C. Kak. *Digital Picture Processing*, Vols. 1 and 2. Academic Press, New York, second edition, 1982.

[RL87]   P.J. Rousseeuw and A.M. Leroy. *Robust Regression and Outlier Detection*. Wiley, New York, 1987.

[RM94]   D.E. Rumelhart and J.L. McClelland. The basic ideas in neural nets. *Communications of the ACM*, 37(3):87–92, 1994.

[Ros84]   A. Rosenfeld, editor. *Multiresolution Image Processing and Analysis*. Berlin: Springer-Verlag, 1984.

[Ros85]   A.Rosenfeld. Arc colorings, partial path groups, and parallel graph contractions. Technical Report TR-1524, University of Maryland, Computer Science Center, July 1985.

[RS90]   A. Rojer and E.L. Schwartz. Design of a space variant sensor having a complex log geometry. In *Proceedings of 10th International Conference on Pattern Recognition*, Vol. II, 278–285. Washington: IEEE Computer Society Press, 1990.

[Sam90]   H. Samet. *The Design and Analysis of Spatial Data Structures*. Reading, MA: Addison-Wesley, 1990.

[Sau90]   E. Saund. Symbolic construction of a 2-D scale-space image. *IEEE Trans. Pattern Analysis and Machine Intelligence*, 12(8):355–395, 1990.

[SB90]   F. Solina and R. Bajcsy. Recovery of parametric models from range images: The case for superquadrics with global deformations. *IEEE Transactions on Pattern Analysis and Machine Intelligenc*, 12(2):131–147, 1990.

[Sch90]   B.G. Schunck. Robust computational vision. In *Proceedings of the International Workshop on Robust Computer Vision*, Seattle, WA, October 1990.

[Ser82]   J. Serra. *Image Analysis and Mathematical Morphology*. New York: Academic Press, 1982.

[Sha85]   M. Sharir. Intersection and closest-pair problems for a set of planar discs. *SIAM J. Comput.*, 14:448–468, 1985.

[SMS87]   L.G. Shapiro, R.S. McDonald, and S.R. Sternberg. Ordered structural shape matching with primitive extraction by mathematical morphology. *Pattern Recognition*, 20(1):75–90, 1987.

[SN87]   V. Srinivasan and L.R. Nackman. Voronoi diagram for multiply-connected polygonal domains I: Algorithm. *IBM J. Res. Develop.*, 31:361–372, 1987.

[SR89]   R. Sitaraman and A. Rosenfeld. Probabilistic analysis of two stage matching. *Pattern Recognition*, 22(3):331–343, 1989.

[SS92]   S.S. Sinha and B.G. Schunck. A two-stage algorithm for discontinuity-preserving surface reconstruction. *IEEE Transactions on Pattern Analysis and Machine Intelligence*, PAMI-14(1):36–55, January 1992.

[Sti29]   J. Stiny. *Technische Gesteinkunde für Bauingenieure, Kulturtechniker Land- und Forstwirte, Sowie für Steinbruchtechnicker*. Julius Springer, 1929.

[Tan86]   S.L. Tanimoto. Paradigms for pyramid machine algorithms. In S. Levialdi and V. Cantoni, editors, *Pyramidal Systems for Image Processing and Computer Vision*, Vol. F25 of *NATO ASI Series*, 173–194. Berlin: Springer-Verlag, 1986.

[TG74]   J.T. Tou and R.C. Gonzalez. *Pattern Recognition Principles*. Addison-Wesley, 1974.

[TH80]   M. Tanemura and M. Hasegawa. Geometrical models of territory I. Models for synchronous and asynchronous settlement of territories. *Journal of Theoretical Biology*, 82:477–496, 1980.

[Thi11]   A.H. Thiessen. Precipitation averages for large areas. *Monthly Weather Review*, 39:1082–1084, July 1911.

[TS92]   K. Thulasiraman and M.N.S. Swami. *Computational Geometry*. Wiley, New York, 1992.

[TVJD95]   H. Tagare, F. Vos, C. Jaffe, and J. Duncan. Arrangement: A spatial relation between parts for evaluating similarity of tomographic section. *IEEE Trans. Pattern Analysis and Machine Intelligence*, 9(17):880–893, 1995.

280   References

[Uhr87]   L. Uhr, editor. *Parallel Computer Vision*. Boston: Academic Press, 1987.

[Ull76]   J.R. Ullmann. An algorithm for subgraph isomorphism. *JACM*, 23(1):31–42, January 1976.

[UW97]   M. Umasuthan and A.M. Wallace. Model indexing and object recognition using 3D viewpoint invariance. *PR*, 30(9):1415–1434, September 1997.

[WI89]   R. Van Der Weygaert and V. Icke. Fragmenting the universe II. Voronoi vertices as Abel clusters. *Astronomy and Astrophysics*, 1–9, 1989.

[WOBS93]   R.S. Wallace, P.-W. Ong, B.B. Bederson, and E.L. Schwartz. Space variant image processing. Technical Report 633, New York University, 1993.

[Yap87]   C.K. Yap. An $O(n \log n)$ algorithm for the Voronoi diagram of a set of simple curve segments. *Discrete Comput. Geom.*, 2:365–393, 1987.

[YP86]   A.L. Yuille and T.A. Poggio. Scaling theorems for zero crossings. *IEEE Transactions on Pattern Analysis and Machine Intelligence*, 8(1):15–25, January 1986.

[Zad65]   L.A. Zadeh. Fuzzy sets. *Information and Control*, 8:338–353, 1965.

[ZTA97]   Y. Zimmer, R. Tepper, and S. Akselrod. An improved method to compute the convex-hull of a shape in a binary image. *Pattern Recognition*, 30(3):397–402, March 1997.

[ZVvK87]   M.F. Zakaria, L.J. Vroomen, and P. van Kessel. Fast algorithm for the computation of moment invariants. *Pattern Recognition*, 20(6):639–643, 1987.

Part IV

Information Fusion and Radiometric Models for Image Understanding

Introduction to Part IV

At first glance, the reader might feel that the topics in this part seem unrelated or only very loosely coupled. On the one hand this is true, because Chapter 11 presents rather theoretical work in fundamental areas of Image Understanding (IU), while Chapter 12 deals with more application-driven aspects of IU in remote sensing. However, taking a closer look, there are many interrelations that justify the presentation of these topics in one common part of this book:

- It has been *the* longstanding goal in IU for at least a decade to build generic image understanding systems that are capable of interpreting scenes based on the input of a single 2D image. Remote sensing has been the major application area for these trials (medical IU being the second one).

- More recent developments have led to the idea that on the one hand a more global modeling is required for effective IU. This includes the use of more than one image, leading directly to a bunch of open problems in information fusion covered in Chapter 11, and the accurate understanding and modeling of the radiometric situation when taking an image, which is covered in Chapter 12.

- On the other hand, there is a clear understanding that the complexity of IU applications can be dramatically reduced, if we build more application-specific *purposive* systems or systems that work on a more *qualitative* (vs. metric) basis. This issue is demonstrated for applications in object recognition (Chapter 11) and for specific situations in remote sensing (Chapter 12).

We thus hope that, starting from a general presentation of the theoretical aspects of information fusion in IU, the subsequent two Chapters will provide insight into IU in general, cover in detail the more specific IU problem of object recognition, and finally demonstrate the relevance of the presented techniques in several application areas of remote sensing.

11

Information Fusion in Image Understanding

Jean-Philippe Andreu
Hermann Borotschnig
Harald Ganster
Lucas Paletta
Axel Pinz
Manfred Prantl

It is well known that static, single image analysis constitutes an ill-posed problem. One reason is that the reconstruction of a 3D scene from one 2D image is underdetermined. Interpreting and recovering information from one single image have been the goal of many image understanding systems in the 1980s (e.g., [DCB+89, MH90, Pin89]). While a human has sophisticated image interpretation capabilities–we are in most cases able to correctly infer information about the underlying scene from a photograph–a generic image understanding system is still beyond today's technical capabilities. In the kind of systems mentioned earlier, researchers tried to reach their goals by implementing Artificial Intelligence techniques (expert vision systems, modeling of domain knowledge, modeling of image analysis knowledge, etc.). In 1988–89, a new paradigm of "active perception" or "active vision" [Baj88, AWB87] was introduced and became very popular in the following years, being extended to "active, qualitative, purposive" vision [Alo91]. The main ideas behind these concepts can be subsumed as follows: The ill-posed problem of general vision can become well-defined and easy to solve;

1. if there is an active observer taking more than one image of the scene;

2. if the "reconstructionist" metric approach to vision is relaxed to a qualitative one, where it is sufficient to state, e.g., that object A is closer to the observer than object B;

3. if instead of general vision, a well-defined narrow purpose of the vision system is modeled (leading to a particular solution of a specific application problem); or

4. in the case of any combination of these three items.

The main goal of our work has been the systematic investigation of item 1 from a new perspective: If there is an active vision system taking more than one image of a scene, or even more general, if there are moving observers or objects in the scene and the system is equipped with several sensors, then the essential problem has to be solved of how to *integrate multiple information* from multiple sensors and/or taken at different instances in time. Information to be fused can be imperfect in many ways (wrong, incomplete, vague, ambiguous, contradictory). Mechanisms are required to

- select information from different sources,

- combine information into a new aggregated state,

- spatially and temporally register visual information, and

- integrate information at different levels of abstraction (pixel, feature, symbol level).

While the literature is full of *specific* solutions (e.g., [AS89]) to this general problem of *information fusion in image understanding*, our work is about the first to investigate this problem in a general information theoretic manner and, as a side product, to come up with a new mechanism of control for an image understanding system called *active fusion*. We have worked on metric spatial registration [PPG95], qualitative spatial reasoning [PA98], the evaluation and comparison of several mathematical frameworks for fusion [BPPPnt], and we have applied fusion to medical applications [PBDK98], in remote sensing [PPGB96] and to the task of object recognition [BPB98]. In subsequent sections we briefly present the concept of active fusion and, in more detail, several aspects of active object recognition.

11.1   Active Fusion

Figure 11.1 shows a general schema of processes and representations in image understanding, with a special emphasis (boldface, bold arrows) on the role of fusion within the schema. The process of fusion combines information and *actively selects* the sources to be analyzed and *controls* the processes to be performed on these data; we call it *active fusion*. Fusion can take place at isolated levels (e.g., fuse several input images producing an output image) or integrate information from different representational levels (e.g., generate a thematic map from a map, digital elevation model, and image information). Processing at all levels can be requested and controlled (e.g., selection of input images, choice of classification algorithms, refinement of results in selected areas).

The purpose of the process of active fusion is twofold: generation and control of processing strategies, and selection and combination of information from several representations. The strategy management is required to limit the number of parallel paths, thereby controlling the image understanding system and avoiding well-known problems of computational complexity and combinatorial explosion. For more details of implementations of active fusion based on probability theory, Dempster-Shafer theory of evidence, and fuzzy set theory as well as an application example in remote sensing we refer the reader to [PPGB96].

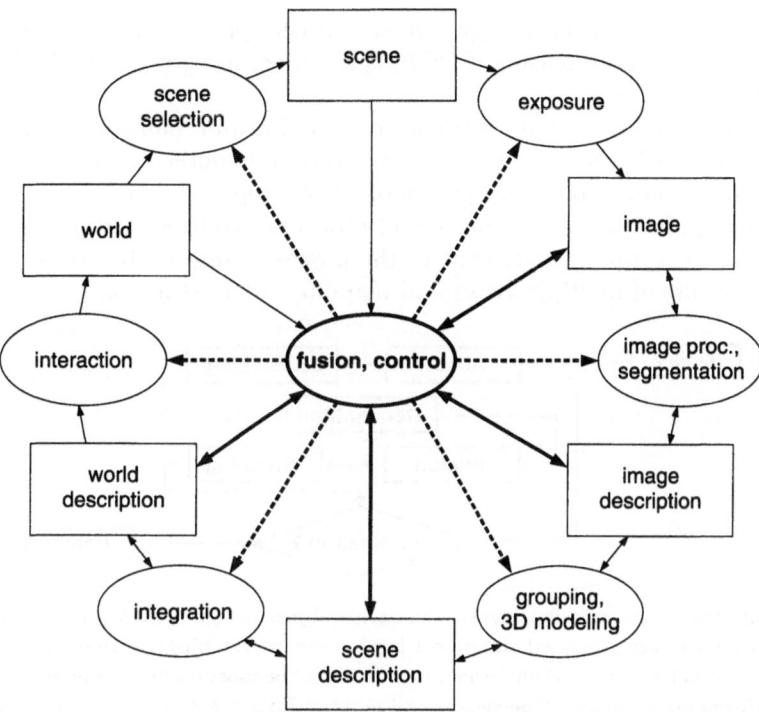

FIGURE 11.1. The concept of *"active fusion"* controlling a general image understanding framework: The active fusion component constitutes a kind of expert system/control mechanism, which has knowledge about data sources, processing requirements, and effective selection and combination of multisource data. The upper half corresponds to the real-world situation, while the lower half reflects its mapping in the computer. Boxes and ellipses denote *levels of representation* and *levels of processing*, respectively. Solid arrows represent the *data flow*, dashed ones the *control flow* in the image understanding system.

11.2   Active Object Recognition

Most computer vision systems found in the literature perform object recognition on the basis of the information gathered from a single image. Typically, a set of features is extracted and matched against object models stored in a database. Much research in computer vision has gone in the direction of finding features that are capable of discriminating objects [Bie87]. However, this approach faces problems once the features available from a single view are simply not sufficient to determine the identity of the observed object. Such a case happens, for example, if there are objects in the database that look very similar from certain views or that share a similar internal representation (*ambiguous objects* or *object data*); this difficulty is compounded when we have large object databases.

A solution to this problem is to use the information contained in multiple sensor observations. *Active recognition* provides the framework for collecting evidence until we obtain a sufficient level of confidence in one object hypothesis. The merits of this framework have already been recognized in various applications, ranging from land-use classification in remote sensing [PPGB96] to object recognition [BPPP98a, PPP98, BPPPnt, PBG$^+$96, GI94].

Active recognition accumulates evidence collected from a multitude of sensor observations. The system has to provide tentative object hypotheses for each single view and combine observations over a sequence of active steps. The fusion of data collected at multiple viewpoints moves the burden of object recognition slightly away from the process used to recognize a single view to the processes responsible for integrating the classification results of multiple views and planning the next action.

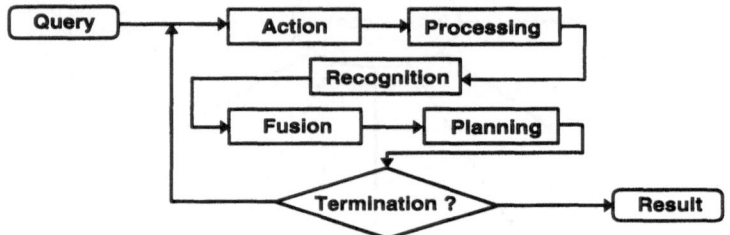

FIGURE 11.2. The major modules involved in active object recognition. A query triggers the first action. The image data are processed and object hypotheses are established. After the newly obtained hypotheses have been fused with results from previous steps the most useful next action is planned and termination criteria are evaluated. The system will perform further active steps until the classification results become sufficiently unambiguous.

In active recognition we have a few major modules whose efficiency is decisive for the overall performance (see also Figure 11.2):

- the object recognition system (classifier) itself;

- the fusion task, combining hypotheses obtained at each active step; and

- the planning and termination procedures.

The work on active recognition was pursued in two different directions inspired by two general object recognition paradigms.

1. **Specific object recognition based on a collection of 2D views.** This work follows the paradigm of appearance-based object recognition. Sections 11.3 and 11.4 present two solutions, namely:

   - *Feature space active recognition*–Objects are represented as a collection of points in a high-dimensional feature space, and view planning tries to minimize the uncertainty contained in the outputs of a classifier. We use a modified version of Murase and Nayar's [MN95] parametric eigenspace as the underlying feature space, and classification uncertainty is measured by Shannon entropy.

   - *Reinforcement learning*–The solution to active recognition using reinforcement learning also uses a feature space representation of the known objects but focuses on the aspect of *learning*. That is, during a training phase the system learns a strategy of how to resolve classification ambiguities by repositioning the camera.

2. **Generic object recognition based on 3D prototype models.** This work follows the paradigm of *generic model based object recognition*. Section 11.5 presents a solution to this difficult problem in the spirit of Biederman's RBC theory [Bie87]. The aim is to establish a generic recognition system that can handle object *classes* rather than specific object *instances* while still using the benefit of an active observer. In order to do so, 3D prototype models are used to infer object identity and estimate its pose. View planning is based on expected part visibility.

11.2.1 Related Research

The general ideas of active vision have already been applied to object recognition by many other researchers.[1] Among them are Hutchinson and Kak [HK92], Callari and Ferrie [CF96], Sipe and Casasent [SC98], Kovačič, Leonardis, and Pernuš [KLP98], and Dickinson et al. [DCTO94]. All of them pursue a similar aim: Given a digital image of an object, the objective of the system is to actively determine the identity of that object and estimate its pose in the scene. The identity or pose of the object may be ambiguous from a given view. The algorithms include mechanisms to detect ambiguities and select viewpoints that resolve these ambiguities.

Hutchinson and Kak describe an active object recognition system based on Dempster-Shafer belief accumulation. The action that minimizes a newly defined measure of ambiguity is performed next. They use various actively controlled sensors such as a range-finder and a CCD camera. The experiments are performed in a blocks-world environment with very simple objects.

Callari and Ferrie base their active object recognition system on model-based shape, pose, and position reconstructions from range data. They estimate Bayesian probabilities for the object hypotheses and choose those steps that minimize the expected ambiguity measured by Shannon entropy.

Sipe and Casasent describe a system that uses an eigenspace representation. They perform probabilistic reasoning for the object hypotheses but do not fuse the pose estimations. In order to derive their active vision scheme they assume the variances of the likelihood distributions to be constant for each object. This is a strong assumption that neglects the variability of the actual data (see Section 11.3.2). For planning they suggest learning for each pair of objects the most discriminating viewpoint.

Kovačič, Leonardis, and Pernuš cluster similar views in feature space. The system calculates the resulting new clusters for each possible action and chooses the action that maximally separates views originally belonging to the same cluster. Doing this off-line for all obtained clusters they compile a complete recognition-pose-identification plan, a tree like structure that encodes the best next view relative to the current one and is traversed during active runs.

---

[1] See for example [TAT95] for a survey of sensor planning in computer vision.

Dickinson et al. present a system that includes active camera viewpoint selection to facilitate object recognition. The control structure of the proposed system offers mechanisms for focusing attention (realized by Bayesian networks) and viewpoint selection (realized by an aspect prediction graph in conjunction with the prediction capabilities of Bayesian networks). The results look promising, although they only presented images where all objects are representable by one single geon (no composite objects).

Previous work has also been reported in planning sensing strategies. Murase and Nayar [MN94] presented an approach for illumination planning in object recognition by searching for regions in eigenspace where object manifolds are best separated. Murase and Nayar limited their approach to an off-line planning phase using no active steps.

11.3   Feature Space Active Recognition

It has been shown that there are no invariant features for 2D projections of a finite, unconstrained set of 3D points ([CJ91, BWR93]). Hence, feature space representations for 3D object recognition usually work in a multiple view context. Objects are represented as a collection of images, and each image in turn is represented as a vector of feature values calculated on it. The resulting set of points in the (usually) high-dimensional vector space then forms the representation for an object as a whole. It is interesting to note that even though the feature space might be very high dimensional (e.g., thousands of dimensions if every image pixel is used as a vector element), the collection of points that represent a specific object forms a manifold representation of much lower dimensionality. Actually, the dimensionality of the manifold is equal to the number of degrees of freedom that were present when the set of images approximating an object (e.g., translations, rotations, illumination changes, scale changes)[2] was recorded. The intrinsically low dimensionality of a feature space representation offers the possibility of using techniques for dimensionality reduction (e.g., principal component analysis) that will result in a more compact representation for the point set forming an object [EI97]. The system presented herein uses the principal component transform [Oja92] to compress the feature space representation for an object.

One problem with multiple view representations is that even with many views a 3D object is only approximated. Each image has to capture the object appearance over a certain range of viewpoint values, where the actual appearance might change. So there is a trade-off between the size of a multiview representation and its accuracy. One way to improve the accuracy is to interpolate between training views to compute additional images [UB91]. Another method is to calculate features on the training images that are *quasi-invariant*, i.e., they remain approximately constant over a certain range of viewpoint values. Our system can be regarded as falling within the first category.

A very attractive feature of multiple view-based object representations is the possibility of acquiring the object models by automatic learning procedures. If a 3D CAD

---

[2]This dimensionality might be further reduced by calculating feature values that are invariant to certain variations (e.g., translation-invariant).

model of the object is available, then this model can be used to construct a multiview (and subsequently a feature space) representation by sampling the view sphere around the object either uniformly or stochastically and to use, for example, techniques from computer graphics to generate the sample images. Alternatively, one can use intensity images obtained from a real object to construct the object model without having to solve the difficult problem of reconstructing the three-dimensional structure. A limitation of this automatic learning procedure lies in the fact that it is exponential in the number of degrees of freedom one would like to model. Usually, rotations in depth are learned explicitly, while, for example, translations or rotations in the image plane, illumination changes or changes in scale are compensated for by preprocessing operations. This makes the number of required training images manageable. We follow the same strategy in our experiments.

We shall now present an active recognition system that uses the parametric eigenspace by Murase and Nayar [MN95] as a specific formulation of the more general notion of a high-dimensional feature space. However, the principal derivations can be applied to other feature spaces without major changes.

11.3.1   Object Recognition in Parametric Eigenspace

The eigenspace approach requires an offline learning phase during which images of all different views of the considered objects are used to construct the eigenspace (see, for example, Figure 11.5). In subsequent recognition runs the test images are projected into the learned eigenspace and assigned the label of the closest model point.

In a preprocessing step it is ensured that the images are the same size and that they are normalized with regard to overall brightness changes due to variations in the ambient illumination or aperture setting of the imaging system. Each normalized image I can be written as a vector $\mathbf{x}(I)$ by reading pixel brightness values in a raster scan manner, i.e., $\mathbf{x} = (x_1, \ldots, x_N)^T$ with N being the number of pixels in an image. $\mathbf{X} := \left(\mathbf{x}_{o_1,\varphi_1}, \mathbf{x}_{o_1,\varphi_2}, \ldots, \mathbf{x}_{o_{n_o},\varphi_{n_\varphi}} \right)$ denotes a set of images with n_o being the number of models (objects) and n_φ being the number of views used for each model.[3] Next, we define the $N \times N$ *covariance matrix* $\mathbf{Q} := \mathbf{X}\mathbf{X}^T$ and determine its eigenvectors $\mathbf{e}_i$ and the corresponding eigenvalues λ_i. See [MN95] for a discussion of various efficient numerical techniques that are useful in the given context. Because $\mathbf{Q}$ is real and symmetric, we may assume that $< \mathbf{e}_i, \mathbf{e}_j > = \delta_{ij}$. We sort the eigenvectors in descending order of eigenvalues. The first k eigenvectors are then used to represent the image set $\mathbf{X}$ to a sufficient[4] degree of accuracy: $\mathbf{x}_{o_i,\varphi_j} \approx \sum_{s=1}^{k} g_s \mathbf{e}_s$, with $g_s = < \mathbf{e}_s, \mathbf{x}_{o_i,\varphi_j} >$. We call the vector $\mathbf{g}_{o_i,\varphi_j} := (g_1, \ldots, g_k)^T$ the projection of $\mathbf{x}_{o_i,\varphi_j}$ into the eigenspace. Under small variations of the parameters φ_j the images $\mathbf{x}_{o_i,\varphi_j}$ of object o_i will usually not be altered drastically. Thus for each object o_i the projections of consecutive images $\mathbf{x}_{o_i,\varphi_j}$ are located on piecewise smooth manifolds in eigenspace parameterized by φ_j.

In order to recover the eigenspace coordinates $\mathbf{g}(I)$ of an image I during the recog-

---

[3]In order to simplify notation we assume $\mathbf{X}$ has zero mean.
[4]*Sufficient in the sense of sufficient for disambiguating various objects.*

nition stage, the corresponding image vector $\mathbf{y}(I)$ is projected into the eigenspace, $\mathbf{g}(I) = (\mathbf{e}_1, \ldots, \mathbf{e}_k)^T \mathbf{y}(I)$. The object o_m with minimum distance d_m between its manifold and $\mathbf{g}(I)$ is assumed to be the object in question: $d_m = \min_{o_i} \min_{\varphi_j} \|\mathbf{g}(I) - \mathbf{g}_{o_i, \varphi_j}\|$. This gives us both an object hypothesis and a pose estimation.

As a way to improve the pose estimation, Murase and Nayar suggested using individual object eigenspaces that are built by taking only images from one specific object for all values of the parameters φ_j. Once the object hypothesis has been obtained using the universal eigenspace the image vector $\mathbf{y}(I)$ is projected into the eigenspace of object o_m and a better estimate of the parameter φ_j is obtained.

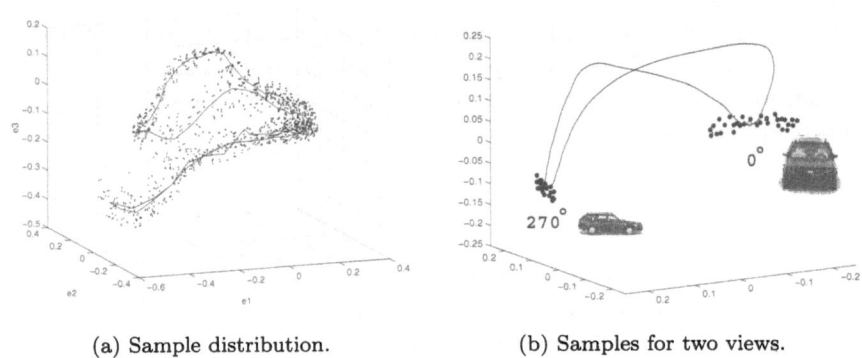

(a) Sample distribution.   (b) Samples for two views.

FIGURE 11.3. (a) Exemplary eigenspace representation of the image set of one object used in the experiments to be described in Section 11.3.7, showing the three most prominent dimensions. (b) illustrates explicitly how different views of an object give rise to likelihood distributions with different standard deviations in eigenspace. The dots indicate the positions of the learned samples for the views 270° and 0° of object o_1.

11.3.2   Probability Distributions in Eigenspace

Before discussing active fusion in the context of eigenspace object recognition we extend Murase and Nayar's concept of manifolds by introducing probability densities in eigenspace (Moghaddam and Pentland [MP97] also used probability densities in eigenspace for the task of face detection and recognition). Let us denote by $p(\mathbf{g}|o_i, \varphi_j)$ the likelihood of ending up at point $\mathbf{g}$ in the eigenspace of all objects projecting an image of object o_i with pose parameters φ_j. The likelihood is estimated from a set of sample images with fixed o_i, φ_j. Figure 11.3(a) depicts the point cloud in eigenspace corresponding to the full set of sample images of a specific object to be used in the experiments. The samples capture the inaccuracies in the parameters φ_j such as location and orientation of the objects; fluctuations in imaging conditions such as moderate light variations; pan, tilt, and zoom errors of the cameras and segmentation errors. With the rule of conditional probabilities we obtain[5]

$$P(o_i, \varphi_j|\mathbf{g}) = \frac{p(\mathbf{g}|o_i, \varphi_j)P(\varphi_j|o_i)P(o_i)}{p(\mathbf{g})}. \tag{11.1}$$

Given the vector $\mathbf{g}$ in eigenspace the conditional probability for seeing object o_i is

$$P(o_i|\mathbf{g}) = \sum_j P(o_i, \varphi_j|\mathbf{g}). \tag{11.2}$$

Murase and Nayar's approach consists in finding an approximate solution for $o_m = arg\max_i P(o_i|\mathbf{g})$ by searching for the minimum distance to the next manifold. We can restate this approach in the framework and thereby make explicit the underlying assumptions. We obtain Murase's and Nayar's algorithm if we

1. Estimate $P(o_i, \varphi_j|\mathbf{g}) = f(\|\mathbf{g}_{o_i,\varphi_j} - \mathbf{g}\|)$ with $f(x) > f(y) \Leftrightarrow x < y$. Thus they assume that the mean of the distribution lies at the captured or interpolated position $\mathbf{g}_{o_i,\varphi_j}$. The distributions have to be radially symmetric and share the same variance for all objects o_i and all poses φ_j. With this estimation the search for minimum distance can be restated as a search for maximum posterior probability:

$$arg\max_{o_i,\varphi_j} P(o_i, \varphi_j|\mathbf{g}) = arg\min_{o_i,\varphi_j} \|\mathbf{g}_{o_i,\varphi_j} - \mathbf{g}\|.$$

2. In the calculation of the object hypothesis the sum in Equation (11.2) is approximated by its largest term:

$$P(o_i|\mathbf{g}) \approx \max_{\varphi_j} P(o_i, \varphi_j|\mathbf{g}) \Rightarrow arg\max_{o_i} P(o_i|\mathbf{g}) = arg\min_{o_i} \min_{\varphi_j} \|\mathbf{g}_{o_i,\varphi_j} - \mathbf{g}\|.$$

The first approximation is error-prone as the variance and shape of the probability distributions in eigenspace usually differ from point to point. This is exemplified in Figure 11.3(b) where the point clouds for the views $\varphi = 270°$ and $\varphi = 0°$ indicate samples of the corresponding probability distributions. The experimentally obtained values for the standard deviations in this example are $\sigma_{270°} = 0.01$ and $\sigma_{0°} = 0.07$, which have to be compared to an average value of 0.04. The second approximation may lead to mistakes if only a few points of the closest manifold lie near $\mathbf{g}$ while many points of the second-closest manifold are located not much further away.

11.3.3   View Classification and Pose Estimation

During active recognition step number n, a camera movement is performed to a new viewing position at which an image I_n is captured. The viewing position ψ_n is known to the system through $\psi_n = \psi_0 + \Delta\psi_1 + \ldots + \Delta\psi_n$ where $\Delta\psi_k$ indicates the movement performed at step k. Processing of the image I_n consists of figure-ground segmentation,

---

[5]We use lowercase p for probability densities and capital P for probabilities.

normalization (in scale and brightness), and projection into the eigenspace, thereby obtaining the vector $\mathbf{g}_n = \mathbf{g}_n(I_n)$. When using other feature spaces we have a similar deterministic transformation from image I_n to feature vector $\mathbf{g}_n$, even though feature extraction may proceed along different lines.

Given input image I_n we expect the object recognition system on the one hand to deliver a classification result for the object hypotheses $P(o_i|I_n)$ while a possibly separate pose estimator should deliver $P(\hat{\varphi}_j|o_i, I_n)$.[6] We obtain through Equation (11.1) the quantity $P(o_i, \hat{\varphi}_j|I_n) := P(o_i, \hat{\varphi}_j|\mathbf{g}_n)$ from the probability distributions in the eigenspace of all objects. From that quantity we can calculate $P(o_i|I_n) := P(o_i|\mathbf{g}_n)$ as indicated by Equation (11.2). The pose estimation for object o_i is then given by

$$P(\hat{\varphi}_j|o_i, I_n) = \frac{P(o_i, \hat{\varphi}_j|I_n)}{P(o_i|I_n)}. \tag{11.3}$$

In order to ensure consistency when fusing pose estimations obtained from different viewing positions, each pose estimation has to be transformed to a fixed set of coordinates. We use the quantity $P(\varphi_j|o_i, I_n, \psi_n)$ to denote the probability of measuring the pose φ_j at the origin of the fixed viewsphere coordinate system after processing image I_n, which is captured at the viewing position ψ_n. In our experiments the system is initially positioned at $\psi_0 = 0°$. Therefore, $P(\varphi_j|o_i, I_n, \psi_n)$ indicates how strongly the system believes that the object o_i was originally placed at pose φ_j in front of the camera. Because the current image I_n has been captured at position ψ_n this probability is related to $P(\hat{\varphi}_j|o_i, I_n)$ through

$$P(o_i, \varphi_j|I_n, \psi_n) := P(o_i, \hat{\varphi}_j + \psi_n|I_n). \tag{11.4}$$

$P(o_i, \varphi_j|I_n, \psi_n)$ will be used for fusion. For ease of notation we shall omit the dependence on ψ_n in the following and write only $P(o_i, \varphi_j|I_n)$.

11.3.4   Information Integration

The currently obtained probabilities $P(o_i|I_n)$ and $P(\varphi_j|o_i, I_n)$ for object hypothesis o_i and pose hypothesis φ_j are used to update the overall probabilities $P(o_i|I_1, .., I_n)$ and $P(\varphi_j|o_i, I_1, .., I_n)$. For the purpose of updating the confidences, we assume the outcome of individual observations to be conditionally independent given o_i and we obtain:

$$P(o_i|I_1, .., I_n) \propto P(o_i|I_1, .., I_{n-1}) P(o_i|I_n) P(o_i)^{-1}, \tag{11.5}$$

$$P(\varphi_j|o_i, I_1, .., I_n) \propto P(\varphi_j|o_i, I_1, .., I_{n-1}) P(\varphi_j|o_i, I_n) P(\varphi_j|o_i)^{-1}, \tag{11.6}$$

$$P(o_i, \varphi_j|I_1, .., I_n) = P(\varphi_j|o_i, I_1, .., I_n) P(o_i|I_1, .., I_n). \tag{11.7}$$

The priors $P(\varphi_j|o_i)$ and $P(o_i)$ enter at each fusion step. In our experiments every object is placed on the turntable with equal probability and $P(o_i)$ is uniform. For the purpose of simplifying the calculations, we also assume $P(\varphi_j|o_i)$ to be uniform even though in general a rigid object has only a certain number of stable initial poses.

---

[6]The reason for the hat on $\hat{\varphi}_j$ will become evident later.

The assumption of conditional independence leads to a very good approximate fusion scheme that works well in most possible cases. Nevertheless, counter-examples exist and lead to experimental consequences. We will discuss such a case in Section 11.3.8.

11.3.5 View Planning

View planning consists in attributing a score $s_n(\Delta\psi)$ to each possible movement $\Delta\psi$ of the camera. The movement obtaining the highest score will be selected next:

$$\Delta\psi_{n+1} := arg \max_{\Delta\psi} s_n(\Delta\psi). \tag{11.8}$$

The score measures the utility of action $\Delta\psi$, taking into account the expected reduction of entropy for the object hypotheses. We denote entropy by

$$H(o_i|\mathbf{g}_1,..,\mathbf{g}_n) := -\sum_{o_i} P(o_i|\mathbf{g}_1,..,\mathbf{g}_n) \log P(o_i|\mathbf{g}_1,..,\mathbf{g}_n), \tag{11.9}$$

where it is understood that $P(o_i|\mathbf{g}_1,..,\mathbf{g}_n) = P(o_i|I_1,..,I_n)$. Other factors may be taken into account such as the cost of performing an action or the increase in accuracy of the pose estimation. For the purpose of demonstrating the principles of active fusion in object recognition, let us restrict attention to the average entropy reduction using

$$s_n(\Delta\psi) := \sum_{o_i,\varphi_j} P(o_i,\varphi_j|I_1,..,I_n)\, \Delta H(\Delta\psi|o_i,\varphi_j,I_1,..,I_n). \tag{11.10}$$

The term ΔH measures the entropy loss to be expected, if o_i,φ_j were the correct object and pose hypotheses and step $\Delta\psi$ is performed. During the calculation of the score $s_n(\Delta\psi)$ this entropy loss is weighted by the probability $P(o_i,\varphi_j|I_1,..,I_n)$ for o_i,φ_j being the correct hypothesis. The expected entropy loss is again an average quantity given by

$$\Delta H(\Delta\psi|o_i,\varphi_j,I_1,..,I_n) :=$$
$$H(o_i|\mathbf{g}_1,..,\mathbf{g}_n) - \int_\Omega p(\mathbf{g}|o_i,\varphi_j+\psi_n+\Delta\psi)H(o_i|\mathbf{g}_1,..,\mathbf{g}_n,\mathbf{g})d\mathbf{g}. \tag{11.11}$$

Here φ_j is the supposedly correct pose measured at the origin of the view-sphere coordinate system and $\psi_n + \Delta\psi$ indicates the possible next viewing position. The integration runs in principle over the whole eigenspace Ω (i.e., over $[-1,1]^k$ because the images are normalized). In practice we average the integrand over samples of the distribution $p(\mathbf{g}|o_i,\varphi_j+\psi_n+\Delta\psi)$. Note that $H(o_i|\mathbf{g}_1,..,\mathbf{g}_n,\mathbf{g})$ on the right-hand side of Equation (11.11) implies a complete tentative fusion step performed with the hypothetically obtained eigenvector $\mathbf{g}$ at position $o_i,\varphi_j+\psi_n+\Delta\psi$.

The score as calculated with Equation (11.10) is multiplied by a mask to avoid capturing views from similar viewpoints over and over again. The mask is zero or low at the recently visited locations and rises to one as the distance from these locations increases. Using such a mask we effectively force the algorithm to choose the action obtaining second-highest score in case the system would decide not to move at all.

The process terminates if the entropy $H(o_i|\mathbf{g}_1,..,\mathbf{g}_n)$ gets lower than a prespecified value or no more reasonable actions can be found (maximum score too low).

11.3.6   The Complexity of the Algorithm

In the following we denote by n_o the number of objects, by n_φ the total number of views used to model an object, and by n_f the number of degrees of freedom of the setup. Because n_φ depends exponentially on the number of degrees of freedom we introduce n_v, the mean number of views per degree of freedom, such that $n_\varphi = n_v^{n_f}$. Finally let us denote by n_a the average number of possible actions. If all movements are allowed we will usually have $n_a = n_\varphi$.

Before starting the discussion of the complexity of the algorithm it is important to realize that many of the intermediate results that are necessary during planning can be computed offline. In Equation (11.11) the quantity $H(o_i|\mathbf{g}_1, .., \mathbf{g}_n, \mathbf{g})$ is evaluated for a set of sample vectors $\mathbf{g} = \hat{\mathbf{g}}_1, .., \hat{\mathbf{g}}_{n_s}$ for each possible manifold parameter $\varphi_j + \psi_n + \Delta\psi$. We denote by n_s the number of samples per viewpoint used for action planning. The corresponding likelihoods $p(\hat{\mathbf{g}}_r|o_i, \varphi_j + \psi_n + \Delta\psi)$ and probabilities $P(o_i|\hat{\mathbf{g}}_r), r = 1..n_s$ are computed offline so that only the fusion step in Equation (11.5) has to be performed online before computing the entropy according to Equation (11.9). Hence the complexity of calculating the score for a particular action $\Delta\psi$ is of order $O(n_o n_\varphi\, n_s\, n_o)$.

On the other hand, the complexity of calculating the score values for all possible actions is only of order

$$O(n_o n_\varphi\, n_s\, n_o + n_o n_\varphi\, n_a) \tag{11.12}$$

if a lookup table is calculated online. The first term $n_o n_\varphi n_s n_o$ expresses the order of complexity of calculating the fused probabilities (and the corresponding average entropies) for all the $n_o n_\varphi n_s$ possible samples that are used as potential feature vectors for view planning (n_s per view with $n_o n_\varphi$ being the total number of views). These average entropies can be stored in a lookup table and accessed during the calculation of the total average entropy reduction. Thus we need only $n_o n_\varphi\, n_a$ additional operations to compute all the scores $s_n(\Delta\psi)$ through Equations (11.10) and (11.11).

We can also take advantage of the fact that only hypotheses with large enough confidences contribute to action planning. This is due to Equation (11.10), where hypotheses with low confidences do not affect the calculation of the score. Hence only the n_l most likely compound hypotheses (o_i, φ_j) may be taken into account. The number n_l is either prespecified or dynamically computed by disregarding hypotheses with confidences below a certain threshold. Usually $n_l << n_o n_\varphi$, for example, $n_l = 10$ (taking $n_l = 2$ imitates the suggestion presented by Sipe and Casasent [SC98]). With this simplification we obtain the following estimate for the order of complexity of the algorithm:

$$O(n_o^2 n_\varphi n_s + n_l n_a) \quad \propto \quad O(n_v^{n_f}(n_o^2 n_s + n_l)). \tag{11.13}$$

This can be lowered again if not all possible actions are taken into account ($n_a < n_\varphi$). The estimates explain why the algorithm can run in realtime for many conceivable situations even though the algorithm scales exponentially with the number of degrees of freedom. In fact, because the contributions of each sample and each action can be computed in parallel a great potential for sophisticated real-time applications exists. In the experiments to be described in Section 11.3.7 a typical view-planning step takes only about one second on a Silicon Graphics Indy workstation even though the code has been optimized toward generality rather than speed and none of the mentioned simplifications has been used.

11.3.7 Experiments

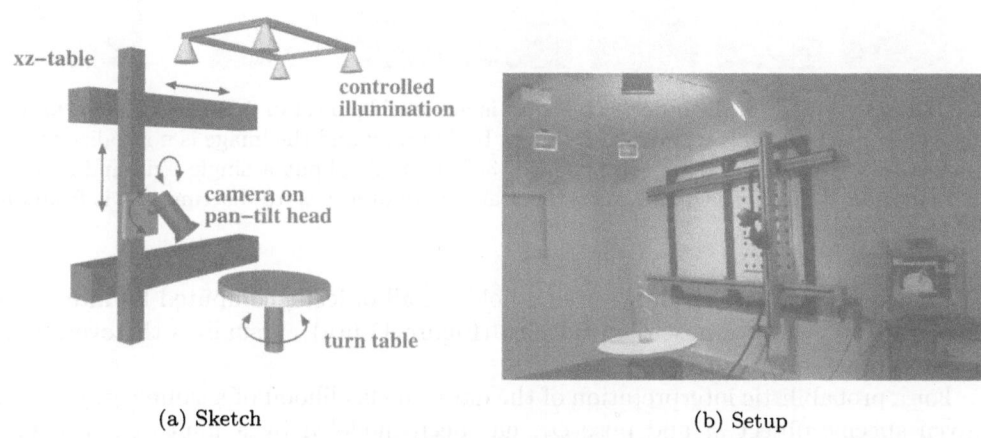

(a) Sketch   (b) Setup

FIGURE 11.4. A sketch (a) plus a picture (b) of the used active vision setup with six degrees of freedom and fiteen different illumination situations. A rectangular frame carrying a movable camera is mounted to one sidewall. A turntable is placed in front of the camera.

An active vision system has been built that allows for a variety of different movements (see Figure 11.4). In the experiments to be described the system changes the vertical position of the camera and the tilt and orientation of the turntable.

Eight Toy Cars:

The proposed recognition system was first tested with eight objects (Figure 11.5) of similar appearance concerning shape, reflectance, and color. For reasons of comparison, two objects o_7 and o_8 are identical and can only be discriminated by a white marker attached to the rear side of object o_8. During the learning phase the items are rotated on a computer-controlled turntable at fixed distance to the camera by 5° intervals. The illumination is kept constant. The object region is automatically segmented from the background using a combined brightness and gradient threshold operator. Pixels classified as background are set to zero gray level. The images are then rescaled to 100×100 pixels and projected to an eigenspace of dimension three. For each view, possible segmentation errors have been simulated by shifting the object region in the normalized image in a randomly selected direction by 3% of the image dimension, as proposed in [MN94].

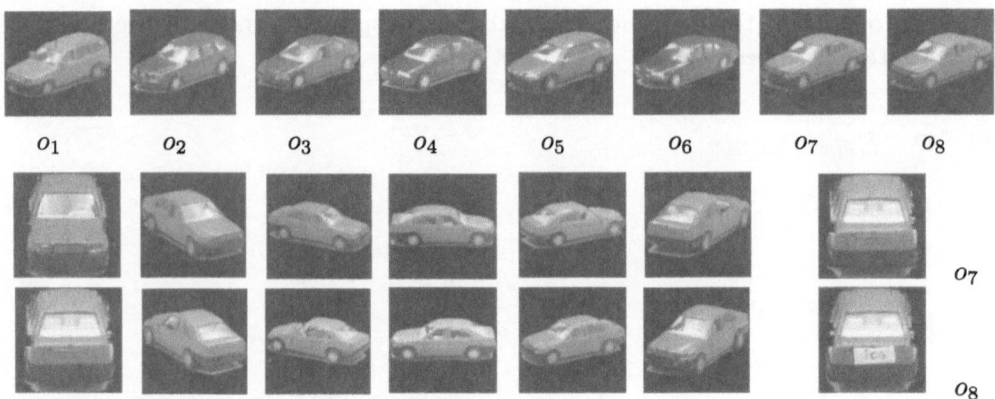

FIGURE 11.5. Each of the objects (*top row*) is modeled by a set of 2-D views (*below*, for object o_1). The object region is segmented from the background and the image is normalized in scale. The pose is shown varied by a rotation of $30°$ intervals about a single axis under constant illumination. A marker is attached to the rear side of object o_8 to discriminate it from object o_7 (*bottom right*).

The significant overlap between manifolds of all objects, computed by interpolation between the means of pose distributions (Figure 11.6(a)), visualizes the overall ambiguity in the representation.

For a probabilistic interpretation of the data, the likelihood of a sample $\mathbf{g}$, $p(\mathbf{g}|o_i, \varphi_j)$, given specific object o_i and pose φ_j, has been modeled by a multivariate Gaussian density $N(\boldsymbol{\mu}_{o_i,\varphi_j}, \boldsymbol{\Sigma}_{o_i,\varphi_j})$, with mean $\boldsymbol{\mu}_{o_i,\varphi_j}$ and covariance $\boldsymbol{\Sigma}_{o_i,\varphi_j}$ being estimated from the data that has been corrupted by segmentation errors. From this estimate both object (Equations (2) and (3)) and pose (Equations (2), (4), and (5)) hypotheses are derived, assuming uniform probability of the priors.

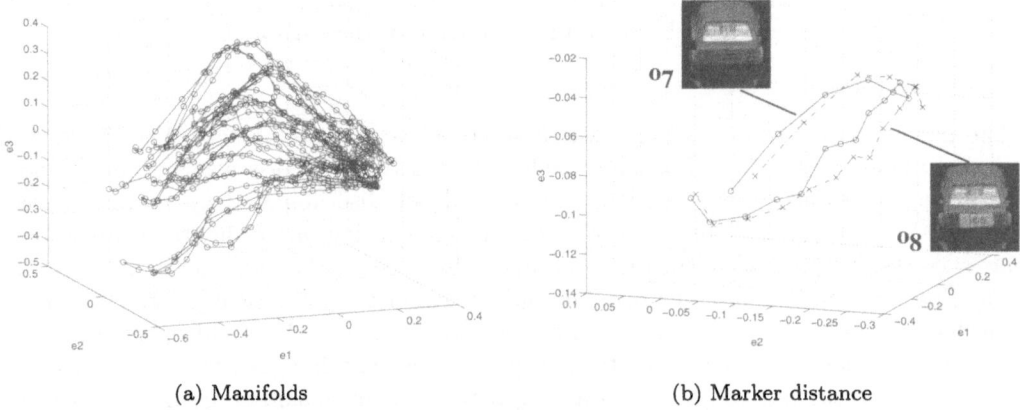

(a) Manifolds   (b) Marker distance

FIGURE 11.6. Manifolds of all eight objects (*a*) and distance between the manifolds of two similar objects introduced by a discriminative marker feature (*b*).

TABLE 11.1. Probabilities for object hypotheses in an exemplary run. See also Figure 11.7(a). P_f are the fused probabilities $P(o_i|\mathbf{g}_1, .., \mathbf{g}_n)$. Object o_7 is the object under investigation.

o_i	$\psi_0 = 0°$		$\psi_1 = 290°$		$\psi_2 = 125°$		$\psi_3 = 170°$	
	$P(o_i|\mathbf{g}_0)$	P_f	$P(o_i|\mathbf{g}_1)$	P_f	$P(o_i|\mathbf{g}_2)$	P_f	$P(o_i|\mathbf{g}_3)$	P_f
1	0.001	0.001	0.000	0.000	0.139	0.000	0.000	0.000
2	0.026	0.026	0.000	0.000	0.000	0.000	0.000	0.000
3	0.314	0.314	0.097	0.203	0.055	0.074	0.091	0.013
4	0.027	0.027	0.096	0.017	0.097	0.011	0.002	0.000
5	0.000	0.000	0.098	0.000	0.335	0.000	0.032	0.000
6	0.307	0.307	0.015	0.031	0.009	0.001	0.224	0.000
7	0.171	0.171	0.354	0.403	0.224	0.597	0.822	0.967
8	0.153	0.153	0.338	0.344	0.139	0.315	0.032	0.019

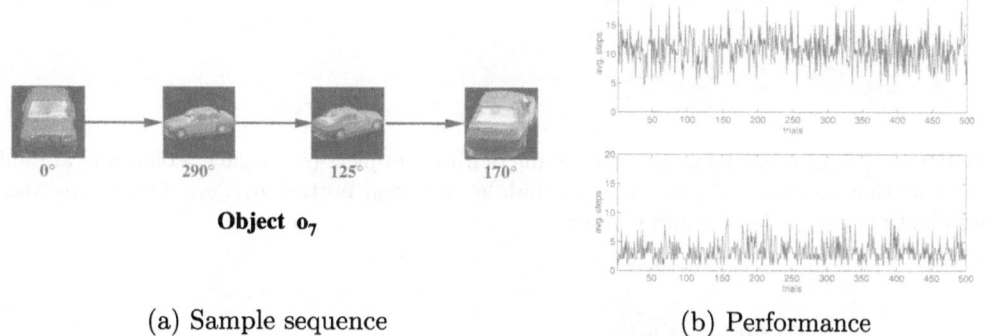

Object o_7

(a) Sample sequence   (b) Performance

FIGURE 11.7. (a) Sample pose sequence actuated by the planning system (see Table 11.1). A comparison of the number of necessary active steps (b) using a random (top) and the presented look-ahead policy ($below$) illustrates the improved performance.

Table 11.1 depicts the probabilities for the object hypotheses in a selected run that finishes after three steps obtaining an entropy of 0.17 (threshold 0.2) and the correct object and pose estimations. Figure 11.7(a) displays the captured images. Object o_7 has been placed on the turntable at pose 0°. Note that the run demonstrates a hard test for the proposed method. The initial conditions have been chosen such that the first image—when projected into the three-dimensional eigenspace—does not deliver the correct hypothesis. Consequently, object recognition relying on a single image would erroneously favor object o_3 at pose $\varphi = 0°$ (pose estimations are not depicted in Table 11.1). Only additional images can clarify the situation. The next action places the system to position 290° and the initial probability for object o_3 is lowered. Objects o_7 and o_8 are now the favored candidates but it still takes one more action to eliminate object o_3 from the list of possible candidates. In the final step the system tries to disambiguate only between objects o_7 and o_8. Thus the object is looked at from the rear where they differ the most.

The results of longer test runs are depicted in Figure 11.7(b) where the number of necessary active steps to reach a certain entropy threshold are depicted for both a random strategy and the presented look-ahead policy. The obtained improvements in performance will also be confirmed in more detail in the following experiment.

Experiments Performed with Fifteen Objects and Two degrees of Freedom

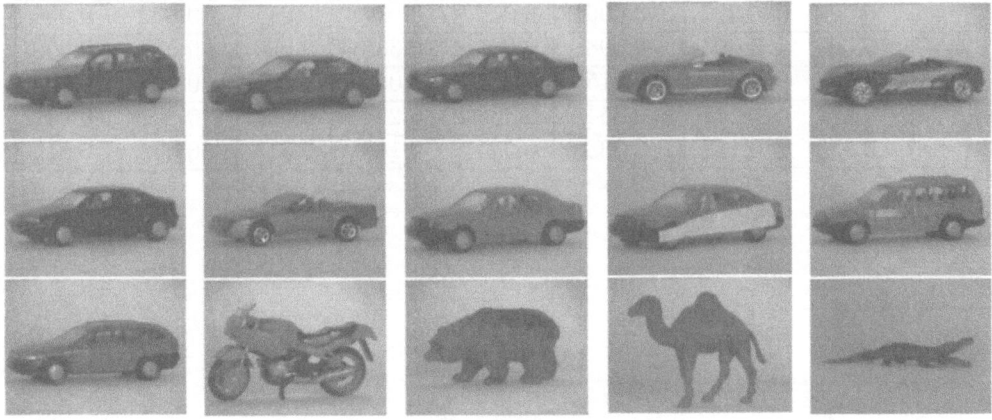

FIGURE 11.8. Extended database consisting of fifteen objects (some cars, a bike, and animals). Top row (left to right): objects $o_1 - o_5$, middle: $o_6 - o_{10}$, bottom $o_{11}..o_{15}$. Objects o_8 and o_9 are identical except for a white marker.

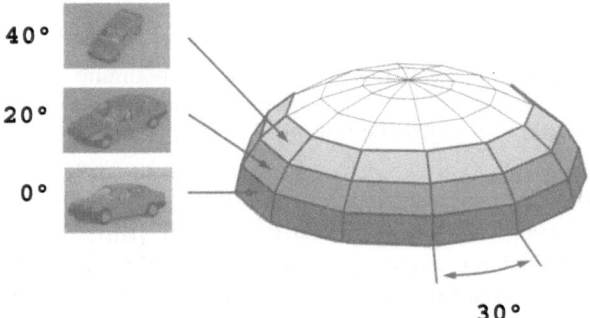

FIGURE 11.9. Top half of the view sphere of two-dimensional rotation about the object (at sphere center). Images are captured at three latitudinal levels ($0°, 20°, 40°$) and at $30°$ longitudinal intervals.

In a second experiment we used fifteen different objects (Figure 11.8) and two degrees of freedom (Figure 11.9) in camera motion. For each of the fifteen objects twelve poses are considered at three different latitudinal positions, amounting to a total of 540 different views. The likelihoods $p(\mathbf{g}|o_i, \varphi_j)$ have been modeled by univariate Gaussian distributions. The mean and variance have been estimated for each view class separately.

Forty additional views of slightly different poses of the objects have been captured for that purpose.

An extensive set of 1440 test runs was performed during which each object was considered for runs with initial poses close to the learned poses ($\pm 5°$). For each initial condition the systems behavior was observed over fifteen steps. The experiment was repeated with eigenspaces of dimensions 3, 5, 7, and 10. Each complete run has been performed twice, once with view planning switched on, and once relying on random motions of the camera. The recognition module has analyzed a total of 21,600 images.

The results of the experiments performed with the whole database of model objects are depicted in Figure 11.10, where recognition rate over the number of active recognition steps is shown for three to ten dimensions of the eigenspace and for planned versus random runs. The following observations can be made:

- A static system that stops after the first observation reaches recognition rates of 30% (3d), 57% (5d), 60% (7d), and 69% (10d). These values have to be compared to 84 % (3d), 96% (5d), 98% (7d), and 99% (10d), which are finally achieved by fusing the results from multiple observations.

- The final recognition level that can be obtained with a three-dimensional eigenspace (84%) lies beyond the recognition rate of a system that relies on a single observation and is using a ten-dimensional eigenspace (69%). Thus multiple observations allow the use of much simpler recognition modules to reach a certain level of performance.

- When comparing the algorithm containing planned actions and the use of a random strategy, attention has to be paid to the increase in recognition rate, especially during the first few observations. The system can come very close to its final recognition rate after $2 - 3$ steps if it plans the next action. In that region the achieved recognition rate lies more than 10% above the level obtained for the random strategy, which usually needs six or more steps to reach its final recognition rate no matter how many dimensions of the eigenspace are used. In Figure 11.10(e) this is reflected in the steep ascent of the surface of recognition rate during planned runs compared to the relatively slow rise in Figure 11.10(f). The beneficial effect of planning can also be inferred from the much faster decrease in average entropy, indicating that the system reaches a higher level of confidence already at earlier stages.

- These results can also be used to compare our approach to a static multi-camera setup. A static system cannot perform the right movement already at the beginning of the recognition sequence but rather has to hope that it will capture the decisive features with at least one of the cameras. We have seen that using a random strategy the system usually needs six or more steps to reach its final recognition level. This fact translates to the assertion that a multicamera system

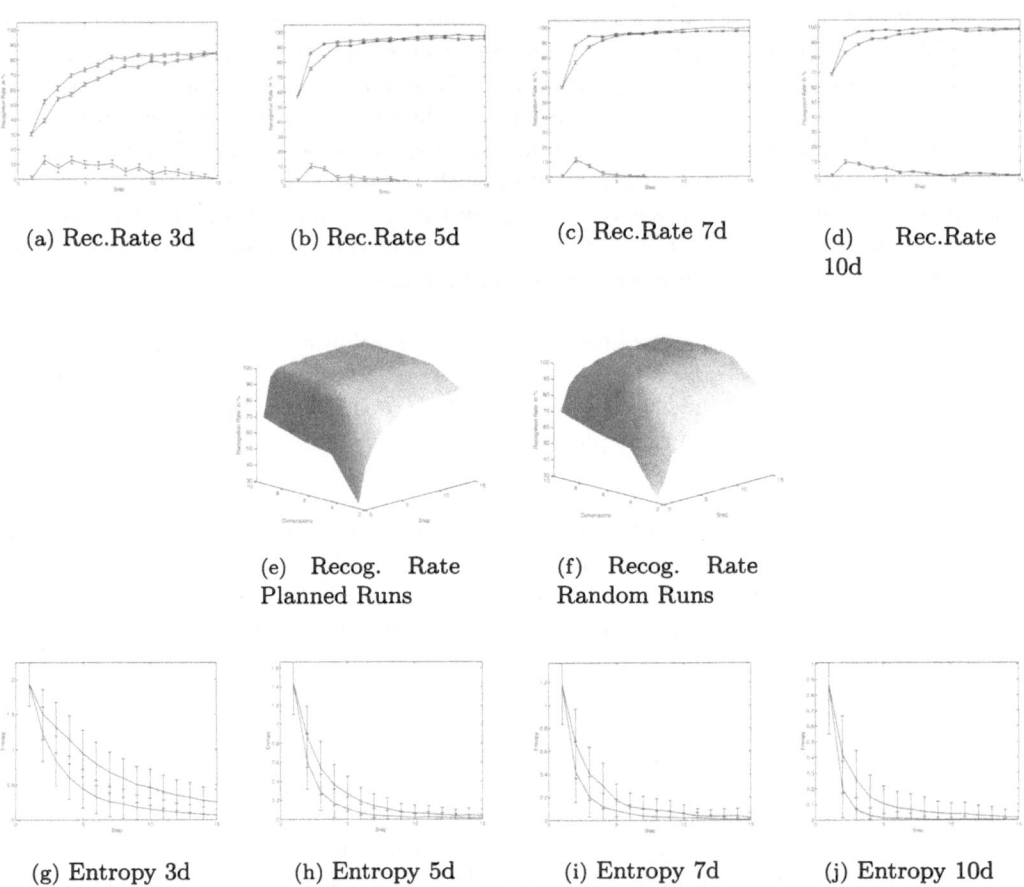

(a) Rec.Rate 3d   (b) Rec.Rate 5d   (c) Rec.Rate 7d   (d)   Rec.Rate 10d

(e) Recog. Rate Planned Runs   (f) Recog. Rate Random Runs

(g) Entropy 3d   (h) Entropy 5d   (i) Entropy 7d   (j) Entropy 10d

FIGURE 11.10. Results obtained with the whole database of toy objects depicted in Figure 11.8. Average recognition rate (top row and middle row) and entropy (bottom row) over number of steps (1–15). Each of the figures (a)–(d) contains three plots: the average recognition rate for runs with action planning switched on (upper plot), for runs relying on a random strategy (middle plot) and the difference of the two recognition rates (lower plot). The number of dimensions of the eigenspace increases from left to right. The two middle row figures (e) and (f) summarize the information in figures (a)–(d) by displaying the average recognition rate (z-axis) over the number of steps (y-axis) and the dimensionality of the eigenspace (x-axis). In the bottom row the average entropy of the probability distribution $P(o_i|I_1,..I_n)$ is depicted for each step n. Each of the figures (g)–(j) shows the entropy for runs with action planning (lower plot) and without action planning (upper plot). Again the number of dimensions of the eigenspace increases from left to right.

with randomly but statically placed cameras will need, on average, six or more cameras to obtain a recognition rate comparable to our active system for the used set of objects.

These observations are even more conclusive when comparing the results obtained with the two Mercedes cars o_8 and o_9. The cars are identical except for the marker on o_9. Even using a seven-dimensional eigenspace the difference in average recognition rate between planned actions and random strategy reaches a maximum beyond 30% at the second step. As the dimensionality of the eigenspace increases to ten the maximum difference is still above 10%.

11.3.8 A Counterexample for Conditional Independence in Equation (11.5)

The case of the Mercedes cars is noteworthy for another reason. We can see from Figure 11.11 that o_9 can be recognized without effort using only a three-dimensional eigenspace. This is in sharp contrast to o_8, which often *cannot* be recognized when using a three-dimensional eigenspace. The situation changes as the dimensionality of the eigenspace increases. The explanation of this effect leads to deeper insight into the fusion process in Equation (11.5).

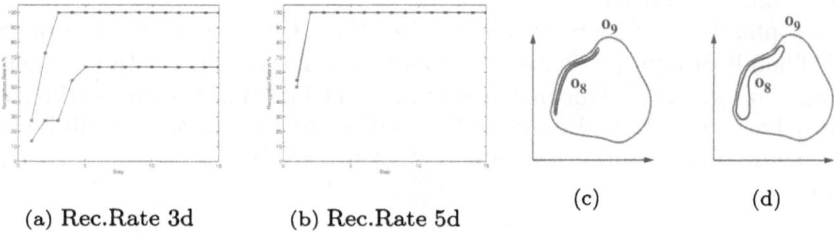

(a) Rec.Rate 3d   (b) Rec.Rate 5d   (c)   (d)

FIGURE 11.11. (a) The average recognition rate achieved for the two Mercedes cars o_8 and o_9 (with marker) in case of a three-dimensional eigenspace. The upper plot corresponds to o_9, the lower plot to o_8. In (b) the eigenspace has five dimensions. (c) and (d) depict manifolds in feature space if all possible observations for object o_8 could stem from object o_9. (c) The case of a practically complete overlap of possible observations for object o_8 with object o_9. Object o_8 has to be symmetric to produce a manifold where each point corresponds to two (or more) views of the object. (d) The case in which o_8 is not fully symmetric, i.e., feature vectors for different views are not equal but only very similar. This can also happen if the chosen feature space is not appropriate for resolving finer details of different views.

This effect occurs because the car without the marker appears to be symmetric under rotations of 180° if one is using only a three-dimensional eigenspace. In other words, there is a significant overlap of $p(\mathbf{g}|o_8,\varphi)$ and $p(\mathbf{g}|o_8,\varphi+180°)$ because the system does not resolve finer details at this level.

If the object database contains two identical objects that appear symmetric under rotation of, e.g., 180° (for example, two blocks) and one of the objects carries a marker on one side, then fusing probabilities according to Equation (11.5) will fail to integrate results correctly when trying to recognize the object without the marker. This can be understood easily if one imagines a static system with an arbitrary number of cameras placed all over the viewsphere observing the object without the marker. Each separate observation will produce equal confidences for both considered objects because each single view may stem from either of the two objects. But the whole set of observations is only possible for the object without the marker because no marker can be found even though images from opposite views have been taken. However, if fusion is based on Equation (11.5), then this fact will not be accounted for. Instead, even after fusing all single results both object hypotheses will achieve equally high probabilities.

The naive Bayesian fusion operator has been applied by different authors working on active recognition tasks [CF96, PPP98, BPPPnt, SC98] because it allows for efficient information integration. We have shown that in some cases the considered fusion scheme will fail to integrate all the encountered hints. The necessary conditions for this to happen may seem to be artificial. All conceivable features for one object must also be possible for another object. But it should not be overlooked that what really counts is *not* the actual visual appearance of the objects but rather the *internal* representation (see also Figs.11.11(c) and (d)). This can also be concluded from the experimental example in which the real car is *not* symmetric under rotations of 180° but its internal representation is symmetric if the eigenspace has only three dimensions. Therefore, the effect disappears if the eigenspace has enough dimensions to capture the data in greater detail (see Figure 11.11(b)).

A more sophisticated fusion scheme requires the estimation or learning of the conditional likelihoods of multiple feature vectors plus corresponding action sequences such as $p(\mathbf{g}_n, \mathbf{g}_{n+1} | o_i, \varphi_j, \Delta\psi_n)$. One may also exploit the fact that the pose estimation for o_9 will usually become more and more uniform while the pose of o_8 can still be estimated precisely (modulo the rotational symmetry). We leave this for future extensions of the algorithm.

11.3.9 Conclusion

We have presented an active object recognition system for single object scenes. Depending on the uncertainty in the current object classification the recognition task acquires new sensor measurements in a planned manner until the confidence in a certain hypothesis obtains a predefined level or another termination criterion is reached. The well-known object recognition approach using eigenspace representations was augmented by probability distributions in order to capture possible variations in the input images due to errors in the preprocessing chain. Furthermore, probabilistic object classifications (instead of hard decisions) can be used as a gauge to perform view planning. View planning is based on the expected reduction in Shannon entropy over object hypotheses given a new viewpoint. The algorithm runs in real time for many conceivable situations. The complexity of the algorithm is polynomial in the number of objects and poses, and it scales exponentially with the number of degrees of freedom of the hardware setup.

The experimental results lead to the following conclusions:

1. The number of dimensions of the feature space can be lowered considerably, if active recognition is guiding the object classification phase. This opens the way to the use of very large object databases. Static methods are more likely to face problems if the dimensionality of the feature space is too low relative to the number of objects represented (due to the overlapping manifolds).

2. Even objects sharing most of their views can be disambiguated by an active movement that places the camera so that the differences between the objects become apparent. Independent of the applied fusion scheme the presented view-planning module successfully identifies those regions in feature space where the manifold representations of competing object hypotheses are best separated.

3. The planning phase is necessary and beneficial as random placement of the camera leads to distinctively worse results.

Future work will focus on the use of different feature spaces, the extension of the fusion scheme, multistep look-ahead planning, and the application of variants of the algorithm to related tasks such as offline camera planning, illumination planning, and robot self-localization.

11.4 Reinforcement Learning for Active Object Recognition

Active object recognition, as introduced in the previous section, involves the observer in a search for discriminative evidence, e.g., by change of its viewpoint. The recognition process, emerging from multiple visual measurements, is here understood as a sequential decision task with the aim of disambiguating initial object hypotheses. Reinforcement learning provides an efficient method to autonomously develop optimal decision strategies in terms of sensorimotor mappings. The benefit in *learning* a strategy, in contrast to explicit reasoning, is to enable the decision maker to extract the probabilistic structure of the control task, i.e., to orient decision making according to control experience, and to weigh this knowledge with a cost measure to focus processing on only the most promising actions. However, this advantage is gained by moving the load of reasoning to an initial training phase, whereas explicit reasoning produces useful results from scratch. Beyond this, reinforcement learning owns the property of integrating concerns about delayed consequences into a current action selection.

We describe an adaptive object recognition system that learns object models from visual appearance and uses a radial basis function (RBF) network for a probabilistic interpretation of the two-dimensional views. The gain of information in fusing successive object evidence provides a utility measure to reinforce actions leading to most discriminative viewpoints. The system is verified in experiments with sixteen objects and two degrees of freedom in sensor motion. Crucial improvements in performance are gained when using the learned in contrast to random camera placements.

Related Work

Active recognition [RAR91, CF96] provides the framework for collecting evidence until

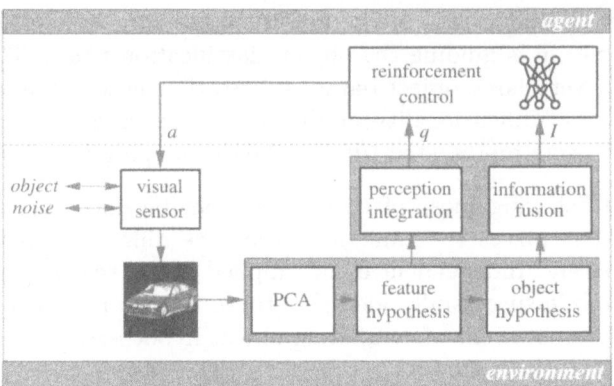

FIGURE 11.12. Closed-loop recognition model: The agent recursively adjusts its discrimination behavior from visual feedback. Actions a and recognition states q are associated with information gains I in the fusion module. This mapping is estimated by a connectionist architecture to recover efficient action selections.

confidence in a particular hypothesis attains sufficient support. The recognition dynamics is actuated, e.g., by controlled camera motion, while other effectors, illumination switches or visual modules might contribute to discrimination as well. Within this context, object recognition can be formulated as an *optimization task* with the objective of finding a sequence of observations to process the most informative features at minimum cost. In purposive and animate vision [Alo90], task-dependent utility measures are considered to evaluate different solution behaviors. Most of the reported applications exhibit exhaustive search over future states or restricted analysis of immediate consequences [Hag90, RB94]. Optimal sequential recognition has been outlined with respect to specific 3-D shape models [CF96] and 2-D objects [BVB$^+$96], whereas evidences from the temporal order of multiple 2-D views has been integrated for classification in [SW92, BG95, Rao97]. A comprehensive analysis on the information content in successive recognition states is given in [SC97].

The contribution of the presented concept is to introduce *reinforcement learning* methods [KM96] for *active* discrimination of arbitrary 3-D objects, with computational costs being orders of magnitude lower than for exhaustive search. This framework complements current methods on active object recognition that use explicit reasoning for viewpoint planning ([PGP96, BPPP98a], Section 11.3.3). The general concept of learning efficient perception-action cycles was introduced by Whitehead and Ballard [WB91]. Draper [Dra97] associated the decision task with the selection of visual modules. Recent research on reinforcement learning in computer vision has focused on classifying single views. Peng and Bhanu [PB98] introduced a closed-loop system that adaptively determines the optimal image segmentation parameters in a recognition task. Bandera et al. [BVB$^+$96] applied learning to optimize saccade sequences in a foveal task. In contrast, the described method provides a working system to select and interpret *multiple views* for 3-D object recognition.

Closed-Loop Recognition Learning

A decision making system, i.e., an *agent* (Figure 11.12), can learn directly from visual interaction with its probabilistic environment. In a sensorimotor feedback loop, the agent develops a sensor planning strategy by reinforcing behavior that will lead to informative viewpoints. Based on a probabilistic interpretation of the visual pattern, each action is evaluated by the degree of disambiguating the current object hypotheses. The proposed recognition system operates *adaptively* and *autonomously*; it automatically acquires the appearance-based object model, develops a mapping from 2-D views to object hypotheses, and learns to selectively fuse the view-based information. The fusion strategy is stored by the parameters of a connectionist architecture, which enables the agent, in contrast to exhaustive planning methods, to *reactively* apply decisions, i.e., in response to perceptive inputs.

11.4.1   Adaptive Generation of Object Hypotheses

Appearance-based models enable objects of arbitrary shape and texture being automatically learned. In contrast, geometric models suffer from matching complexity and fail to work for complex shapes [Ede97]. *Eigenspace representations* (eigenperceptions) result from transformations of intensity images by principal component analysis (PCA) [Oja83, MN95]; they are described in detail in Section 11.3.1. This Section describes how an RBF network [BL88, Low95] is trained to map eigenperceptions to posterior probabilities. The first paragraph investigates eigenspace representations from the point of view of adaptivity and learning. How this feature space is mapped to object hypotheses using an adaptive neural structure is outlined thereafter.

Principal Components Feature Space

On the basis of a process of segmentation and normalization of the image containing the visual information about the object (Section 11.3.1), the question arises how of to build a classifier based on the object appearance, i.e., in terms of the image brightness pattern. Although a number of applications are reported to directly work on the raw pixel input, when trying to construct a classifier they either suffer from high storage requirements or the course of dimensionality [BP97, RBK98].

Feature selection on the basis of a linear transformation has been commonly used by the method of PCA [Fuk90]. This transformation is achieved by finding a rotated coordinate system such that (i) the elements in the new coordinates become uncorrelated and (ii) the variances of the elements in the new vectors own the property of maximum decrease, such that a dimensionality reduction is optimum in the mean-squared error sense. For example, principal components as a basis for neural face recognition is described in [RA97].

The feature space obtained by PCA expansion, called eigenspace, can be iteratively constructed using neural network architectures. Numerous methods have been proposed; the most outstanding are linear PCA networks [San89, Oja92] using unsupervised learning based on Hebbian and orthonormality constraint terms, as well as supervised learning by the backpropagation algorithm, applying multilayer perceptrons in autoassociative mode [BK88, BH89].

These neural network implementations enable us to keep the construction of the object feature space adaptive, in response to a continuous stream of sensor patterns. In combination with the learning structures for probabilistic object classification (Section 11.4.1) and view selection control (Section 11.4.2), the complete recognition system can be designed in terms of a neural network architecture.

Learning Posterior Probabilities

The statistical approach is based on a *closed world assumption* that allows us to assign to each point in eigenspace a probability distribution over all object hypotheses O_k, $k \in \{1, \ldots, \Omega\}$, Ω being the number of objects. A maximum likelihood formulation was outlined by Moghaddam and Pentland [MP97] with respect to distributions in the original sensor space. This paragraph discusses an estimator situating classification directly into the target description space.

As an approximation to the continuous object manifold we sample at discrete positions V_φ in eigenspace (Figures 11.3 and 11.13). For each parameter value φ, the distribution of observations is modeled by a Gaussian function,

$$p(\mathbf{g}_\varphi | V_\varphi) = \frac{1}{(2\pi\sigma_\varphi^2)^{d/2}} \exp\left\{-\frac{\|\mathbf{g}_\varphi - \mu_\varphi\|^2}{2\sigma_\varphi^2}\right\}, \tag{11.14}$$

with mean vector μ_φ and variance σ_φ^2 estimated from the measurements $\mathbf{g}_\varphi$ (Figure 11.13(a)), in eigenspace of dimension d. The local visual error might be alternatively described by elliptical or multimodal Gaussian models, whereas the spherical Gaussian enhances generalization and simplifies matters. A Bayesian estimator of the posterior probabilities is then obtained for any $\mathbf{g}$ by

$$p(O_k | \mathbf{g}) = \frac{p(\mathbf{g}|O_k)p(O_k)}{p(\mathbf{g})} = \frac{\sum_{\varphi=1}^{\Lambda} p(\mathbf{g}|V_\varphi)p(V_\varphi|O_k)p(O_k)}{p(\mathbf{g})}, \tag{11.15}$$

where $p(V_\varphi|O_k)$ and $p(O_k)$ are assumed uniformly distributed and the index φ runs over Λ views V_φ belonging only to object O_k.

The distribution model is refined using a mixture of local estimators, as represented by a radial basis functions (RBF) architecture [Low95] (Figure 11.13(b), see also Section 8.1). Within the context of classification, its network weights $\mathbf{W}$ and the $\Theta = \Omega\Lambda$ basis functions ϕ_j, $j = 1 \ldots \Theta$, are interpreted as quantities of the Bayesian estimator;

$$\phi_j \approx \frac{p(\mathbf{g}|V_j)p(V_j)}{p(\mathbf{g})} = p(V_j|\mathbf{g}), \tag{11.16}$$

$$w_j \approx \frac{p(V_j|O_k)p(O_k)}{p(V_j)} = p(O_k|V_j), \tag{11.17}$$

$$\tilde{p}^k(\mathbf{g}) \equiv \sum_{j=1}^{\Theta} w_{kj}\phi_j, \tag{11.18}$$

$$p(O_k|\mathbf{g}) \approx \hat{p}(O_k|\mathbf{g}) = \frac{\exp \tilde{p}^k(\mathbf{g})}{\sum_j \exp \tilde{p}^j(\mathbf{g})}, \tag{11.19}$$

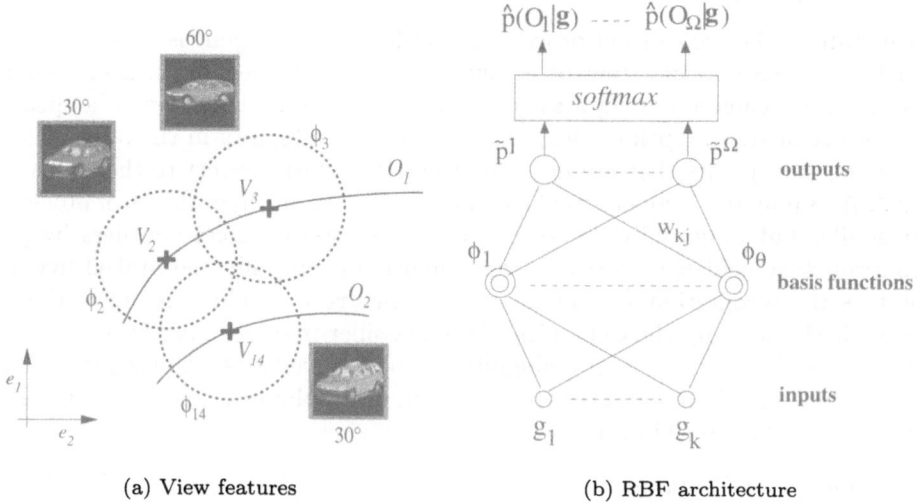

(a) View features   (b) RBF architecture

FIGURE 11.13. (a) Gaussian basis functions ϕ_j model the distribution at each pose, i.e., the view feature V_j. (b) Structural sketch of the RBF mapping from eigenperceptions $\mathbf{g}$ to posterior probabilities $\hat{p}(O_k|\mathbf{g})$.

where the network outputs $\tilde{p}^k$ are normalized by an exponential transformation known as *softmax* to ensure a probabilistic interpretation [Bri90]. Note that the posterior probabilities are estimated over *all* views V_j. The corresponding basis functions ϕ_j operate as local *receptive fields* in eigenspace (Figure 11.13(a)), with their responses being interpreted as characteristic features extracted from the sensor measurements.

During training, the configuration of basis functions is kept constant, whereas the output weights $[\mathbf{W}]_{kj}$ are optimized by gradient descent on the concave error function E

$$E(\mathbf{W}) = -\frac{1}{N} \log P(D|\mathbf{W}) = -\frac{1}{N} \log \prod_{\nu=1}^{N} \hat{p}(O^\nu|\mathbf{g}^\nu), \qquad (11.20)$$

where $P(D|\mathbf{W})$ denotes the likelihood of the training set $D = \{(\mathbf{g}^\nu, O^\nu)|\nu = 1, \ldots, N\}$ and N is the sample size. The RBF mapping (Equation 11.19) outperforms the simple Bayes estimator (Equation 11.15, Section 11.4.3) while its structure provides a basis to minimize complexity with respect to the global error function.

An interesting glance at psychophysical findings about the human visual system indicates that view-invariant representations seem to be driven by view-selective tunings in the visual cortex [BE92]. Pauls et al. [PBL96] conclude from psychophysical and electrophysiological experiments in the inferotemporal cortex (IT) of macaque monkeys that *"learning a novel object from example-views may rely on the formation of new, bell-shaped receptive fields tuned to the trained views"*. In accordance, Poggio and Edelman [PE90] and Logothetis et al. [LVHP94] encode view-invariant recognition by RBF networks, yet in abundance of an explicit probabilistic interpretation.

11.4.2   Learning Recognition Control

In each state of the recognition process, a decision making agent is asked to select an action to drive its classifier toward a reliable decision. For example, a view-planning system provides choices among a set of camera motions that determine a specific sequence of fusion steps. Optimal decisions resolve the ambiguity in the overall classifier by providing viewpoints that are most discriminative with respect to the current state of belief. Accumulated evidence might require us to sort out hypotheses of objects with so far similar but potentially different appearance, or to indicate outliers by providing contradictary evidence. Further, overestimation of initially top-ranked hypotheses might bias the recognition system to support incorrect conclusions. Thus the fusion strategy effects not only the dynamics of the classifier in converging to a reliable decision but also determines whether ambiguity can be resolved at all. Consequently, crucial improvements in performance are reported when using planned, in contrast to random, camera motion (Section 11.4.3).

Optimal Viewpoint Planning

An *optimal* strategy for observer motion results in a sensor trajectory visiting viewpoints that promise a maximum of discrimination from the measurements. The usefulness of actions for view changes is expressed by a user-defined criterion, i.e., the utility function $\mathcal{U}$, that provides evaluative information about actions to the decision maker. It must provide a cost-sensitive measure that might include terms indicating state of ambiguity, reflecting time, and energy expenses of the physical system and including future consequences of a current action.

In each state s_T of the recognition process, the utilities $\mathcal{U}$ of all possible actions a' are compared to select the action of maximum evaluation,

$$a = \arg \max_{a'} \mathcal{E}(\mathcal{U}(s_T, a')), \tag{11.21}$$

$\mathcal{E}(\cdot)$ is the expectation operator. Here we define the utility $\mathcal{U}(s_T, a) = \mathcal{I}(s_T, a)$ as the information gain $\mathcal{I}(s_T, a)$ caused by active step a, using the entropy term

$$\mathcal{I}(s_T, a) = H(\bar{p}_{T-1}) - H(\bar{p}_T), \tag{11.22}$$

where $H(\bar{p}_T)$ represents the entropy in the probability distribution $\bar{p}_T = p(O_k|\mathbf{g}_1, \ldots, \mathbf{g}_T)$, $k \in [1, .., \Omega]$. Explicit evaluation [BPPP98a] of the expected utility needs to quantify the expected information gain by investigating the confidence in every of $\Omega\Lambda$ viewpoints (Section 11.3.5). Each pose-specific investigation requires a provisional fusion evaluation over the entire view-specific receptive field V_φ, computed by means of Σ stored training samples, with respect to Ω object hypotheses. Thus the entire computation results in general in a time complexity of $\mathcal{O}(\Omega^2\Lambda\Sigma)$ (Section 11.3.6).

Active object recognition is now interpreted as a multistep decision task with respect to its discrimination dynamics. The framework of Markov decision processes (MDP [Put94]) provides the mathematical formalism to handle the task of the decision maker. In the context of object recognition, an MDP is defined by a tuple $(\mathcal{S}, \mathcal{A}, \delta, \mathcal{I})$ with state recognition set $\mathcal{S}$, action set $\mathcal{A}$, probabilistic transition function δ, and reward function

$\mathcal{I}$. $\delta : \mathcal{S} \times \mathcal{A} \to \Pi(\mathcal{S})$ describes a probability distribution over subsequent states, given the action $a \in \mathcal{A}$ executed in state $s \in \mathcal{S}$. In each transition, the agent receives reward according to $\mathcal{I} : \mathcal{S} \times \mathcal{A} \to \mathcal{J}$; $\mathcal{I}_t \in \mathcal{J}$, $\mathcal{J}$ is the *reward* space. The agent must act to maximize the utility Q, i.e., the expected discounted reward

$$Q = \mathcal{E}(\sum_{t=0}^{\infty} \gamma^t \mathcal{I}(s_t, a_t)), \tag{11.23}$$

where $\gamma \in [0, 1]$ is a constant controlling contributions of delayed reward. Whereas $\gamma = 0$ is restricted to treating only immediate gain of the current action, increased values of $\gamma > 0$ tend to consider delayed rewards in future states for current decisions. An optimal strategy has to consider not only immediate but also *delayed* consequences of the action in question. Note that an extensive look ahead of the consequences in an entire sequence of length $O(\Lambda!)$ requires $O(\Omega^2 \Lambda! \Lambda \Sigma)$ computations. While explicit reasoning on each planning step investigates responses from tentative fusion steps, an efficient strategy can be *learned* from experience in terms of a sensorimotor mapping.

What we expect from a *learned strategy* is to reduce the complexity of the processing step in making a decision for a useful action. Extensive search over actions has to consider all consequences without any exploitation of experience, for each decision again. In contrast, an adaptive decision maker can adjust a parametric structure, appropriate to the task at hand, that reflects essential statistical dependencies and hence directs the search on the most promising sensor trajectories. An adaptive decision maker thus implicitly aims at constructing a classifier that first categorizes the current recognition state and then restricts reasoning on an appropriate subspace in trajectory space. As a consequence, learning a mapping from recognition states to sensor actions moves the load of reasoning about actions to an initial training phase. The resulting decision function, with the current observation as input, is then evaluated with lower computational costs.

Reinforcement Learning of View Selection Strategies

Reinforcement learning [KM96, SB98] provides the means to construct an optimal action selector from experience while exploring the utility Q by trial and error. In a complex task, extensive search by explicit evaluation of all possible state sequences appears costly, whereas reinforcement learning focuses on visiting those states that have already proved relevance. Furthermore, the use of parametric function approximators to estimate the decision function enables implicit generalization over entire regions in state space. After training, the utilities are stored by use of a parameter set $\mathbf{W}$. Thereafter, viewpoint planning consists in selecting the action a with the largest utility estimate $\hat{Q}$ (Section 11.4.2).

In Q-learning [Wat89, WD92], a derivate of the reinforcement learning philosophy, each state-action pair is associated with the expected utility Q, and the action with the largest Q-value is selected for execution. The estimates $\hat{Q}(\mathbf{s}_t, a_t)$ for the maximum *expected cumulative utility* Q_t received in subsequent steps are recursively updated for residuals of the consistency condition

$$\hat{Q}(\mathbf{s}_t, a_t) \equiv \mathcal{I}(\mathbf{s}_t, a_t) + \gamma \max_a \hat{Q}(\mathbf{s}_{t+1}, a). \tag{11.24}$$

The recognition state s of the active system is represented by a vector $\mathbf{s}_T$ that captures the information from successive observations, by the encountered feature responses. Each measurement in eigenspace generates a vector of confidences in the *feature hypotheses*, $\hat{p}(V_j|\mathbf{g}_t)$, which are integrated over the sequence. Consequently the recognition state is dependent on the vector $\mathbf{f}_T = (f_{T,1}, \ldots, f_{T,\Theta})$, each entry denoting the maximum confidence in a view feature V_j, $j \in \{1, \ldots, \Theta\}$, registered so far, $f_{T,j} = \max_{t \leq T} \hat{p}(V_j|\mathbf{g}_t)$. Because the same set of features can be collected over different state sequences, the effect of perceptual aliasing must be prevented, and thus the recognition state vector $\mathbf{s}_T$ is supplemented by the current eigenperception $\mathbf{g}_T$, giving $\mathbf{s}_T = (\mathbf{f}_T, \mathbf{g}_T)$.

The probabilistic, continuous definition of the recognition state requires the Q-values to be approximated by a universal function approximator Ψ, e.g., by a neural architecture $\hat{Q} = \Psi(\mathbf{s}_t, a_t, \mathbf{W})$. In *residual Q-learning* [Bai95], the free parameters $w = [\mathbf{W}]_i$ of the estimator Ψ are updated by

$$\Delta w = -\alpha \left(\mathcal{I}(\mathbf{s}_t, a_t) + \gamma \max_a \hat{Q}(\mathbf{s}_{t+1}, a) - \hat{Q}(\mathbf{s}_t, a_t) \right) \times$$
$$\left(\phi\gamma \frac{\partial}{\partial w} \max_a \hat{Q}(\mathbf{s}_{t+1}, a) - \frac{\partial}{\partial w}\hat{Q}(\mathbf{s}_t, a_t) \right), \tag{11.25}$$

where α denotes the learning rate. ϕ is the weighting factor between an algorithm performing gradient descent on the mean squared residual of the consistency condition, i.e., the *Bellman residual*, and a direct method similar to temporal difference learning (TD(0) [Bai95, KM96, SB98]). The algorithm guarantees convergence in the limit to the accurate estimates Q [Bai95].

After convergence, the reinforcing controller is assumed to perform a near-optimal strategy with respect to the defined utility measure Q (Equation (11.23)). In response to the current visual observation, the projection to eigenspace $\mathbf{g}_T$ is fused to a new recognition state $\mathbf{s}_T$ and the agent selects the action $a_T \in \mathcal{A}$ with largest $\hat{Q}(\mathbf{s}_T, a)$,

$$a_T = \arg \max_{a'} \hat{Q}(\mathbf{s}_T, a', \mathbf{W}), \tag{11.26}$$

i.e., the action that promises maximum reduction of entropy. The planning step consists of a single feed-forward processing of the neural architecture. The computational cost for a network with Θ hidden and $\Omega\Lambda$ input units then amounts to $\mathcal{O}(\Omega\Lambda\Theta)$. Note that the complexity does not increase for arbitrary look-ahead strategies; instead the load is transferred to an extended training phase.

11.4.3   Experiments

The experiments described here were performed in an active vision setup that enables controlled manipulation by multiple degrees of freedom (Figure 11.4). Using coordinated sensor translation, sensor tilt, and rotation of a turntable, it is possible to investigate observer motion on the view sphere (Figure 11.9).

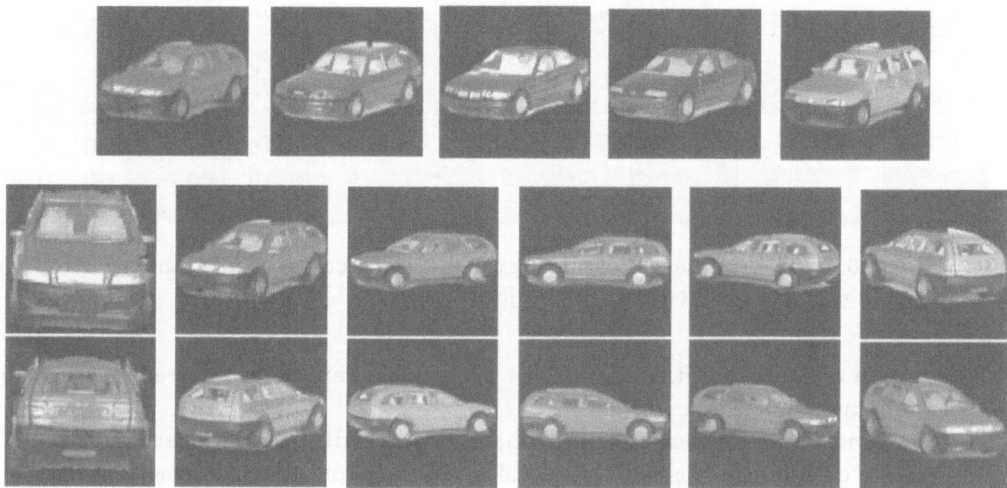

FIGURE 11.14. Illustration of appearance-based object representation with five objects and one degree of freedom. Each object (top row) is modeled by a set of 2-D views (below, for the object top left). This database is a subset of the one depicted in Figure 11.16.

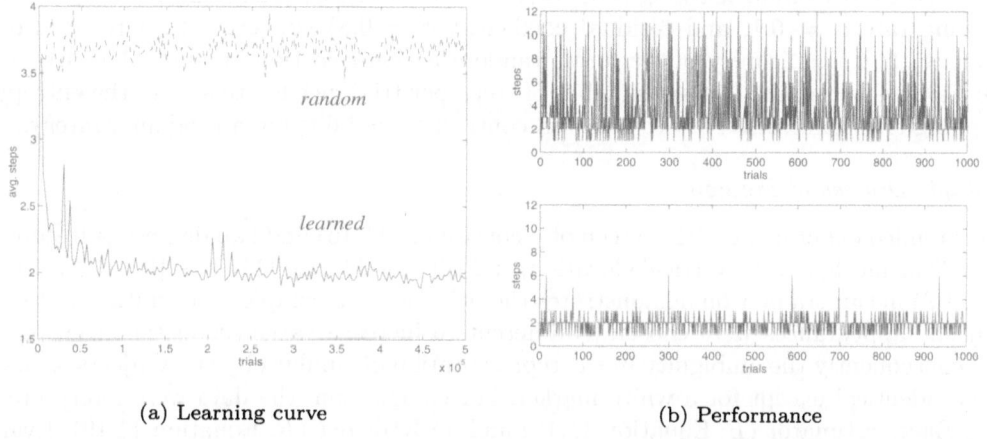

(a) Learning curve   (b) Performance

FIGURE 11.15. Performance of the learned recognition strategy; (a) Stochastic learning curve comparing test results of random (dotted) and learned strategy (line). (b) depicts a comparison of individual trial lengths between a random (top) and a learned (bottom) policy.

Illustrative Environment

In the first experiment, the proposed recognition system was tested with five objects (Figure 11.14), presented on a computer-controlled turntable by 30° intervals, with constant illumination and fixed distance to the camera. The object relevant region was first segmented from the background, rescaled to 100×100 pixels, and projected to an eigenspace of dimension ten. For each view, additional samples were collected, emulating

FIGURE 11.16. Extended database consisting of sixteen objects (cars, bike, animals). Top row (left to right): objects o_1–o_8, bottom row: objects o_9–o_{16}.

segmentation errors by shifting the object region in a randomly selected direction by 3% of the image dimension.

The posterior probabilities are approximated by an RBF network of sixty basis functions, one for each object pose (Section 11.4.1). In the experiments, transitions between states were initiated by table rotations a^k of $k \times 30°$, $k \in \{1, \ldots, 11\}$, to enable direct access to the next promising viewpoint. The Q function for each action a^k was estimated by a multilayer perceptron [RHW86], each network with a hidden layer of five sigmoidal units. For the stopping criterion the threshold on the entropy level in the posterior distribution on object membership was chosen to be 0.5.

The stochastic online learning process (Figure 11.15(a), with discount factor $\gamma = 0.3$, learning rate $\alpha = 0.1$, and residual coefficient $\phi = 0.8$) converges to a recognition strategy that significantly outperforms random action selection (Figure 11.15(b)). In the training phase, the average number of steps per trial, needed to satisfy the entropy stopping criterion, converged to ≈ 1.9 in contrast to ≈ 3.6 using a random strategy.

Multiple Degrees of Freedom

An extended experiment with sixteen objects (Figure 11.16) and two degrees of freedom ($j \times 30°$ azimuth, $k \times 20°$ vertical elevation, and tilt, $j \in \{1, \ldots, 11\}$, $k \in \{0, \ldots, 2\}$, Figure 11.9) in camera motion demonstrates the behavior of a complex recognition system. Objects' appearances were chosen as different to increase variances in the eigenspace and consequently the ambiguity in the representation of similar objects. Objects o_8 and o_9 are identical except for a white marker. For comparison, the data were interpreted by a Bayes estimator (B, Equation 11.15) and an RBF net (R, Equation 11.19). Evaluation of the cross entropy (Equation 11.20, B: 1.12, R: 0.82) proved superior RBF performance. All data were collected from a real scene, with view-specific samples obtained by random deviation in azimuth rotation of $\pm 7°$ amplitude. The fusion strategies were evaluated online in the lab environment.

The described system was tested using an alternative input representation that implicitly records features and actions. The sequence of eigenperceptions $\mathbf{g}_t$ is scanned and compiled into a history vector. The resulting vector $\Gamma = (\mathbf{g}_1, \ldots, \mathbf{g}_T)$ was fed to an RBF network with twelve output nodes representing the utility of azimuth actions and five additional units for relative vertical elevation and tilt actions ($-40°, -20°, 0°, +20°, +40°$). In the experiments, observations in five-dimensional eigenspace are compiled into a sequence of ten vectors, giving an input vector of dimension fifty. The basis layer of

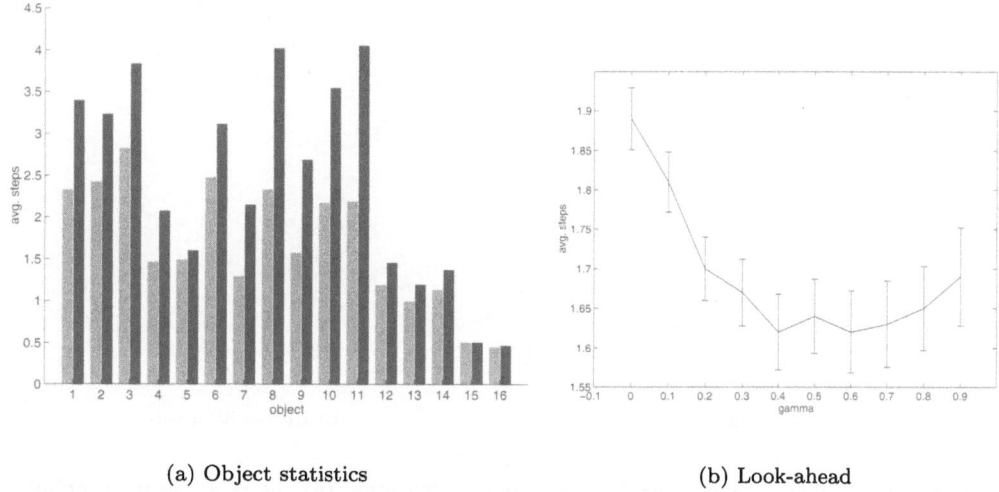

(a) Object statistics   (b) Look-ahead

FIGURE 11.17. Performance statistics: (a) Object-dependent performance (gray and black bars denote learned and random sequence lengths, respectively). (b) Multistep look-ahead policies ($\gamma > 0$) improve on one-step strategies ($\gamma = 0$).

the RBF network consisted of 100 spherical Gaussian basis functions. Using this architecture, the complexity of the network forward pass reduces to $O(\Theta\Phi)$, using Θ basis units and Φ actions ($O(\Theta\Lambda)$ for one degree of freedom). Note that for the described task the complexity of a single action selection, considering no look ahead, decreases from $O(\Omega^2 \Lambda\Sigma) \approx k16^2 \times 10 \times 36 = 92,160$ for explicit view planning to $O(\Theta\Phi) \approx k \cdot 100 \times 17 = 1700$ for the neural network controller, which represents a performance speedup of ≈ 54. The entropy stopping criterion on a single trial was chosen 0.1.

Persistent learning again outperforms random strategies, while performance improvement is merely achieved for ambiguous objects (Figure 11.17(a)). Policies evaluating multistep look-ahead exhibit outperforming strategies concerning payoff collected only at the immediate next step (Figure 11.17(b)). Learned selections needed ≈ 1.62 steps per trial, in contrast to ≈ 2.42 steps for random decisions. The learned strategy not only attains a substantial level of discrimination more rapidly (Figure 11.18(a)), but also associates the true hypotheses to the captured evidences, as recorded by the recognition rate (Figure 11.18(b)). Sample sequences (Figure 11.19) are displayed for comparison between the two action selection policies. We observe that the learned strategy (a) immediately turns its focus to the discriminating marker, whereas the random selection (b) has to integrate multiple ambiguous views until the fusion operator extracts a reliable classification.

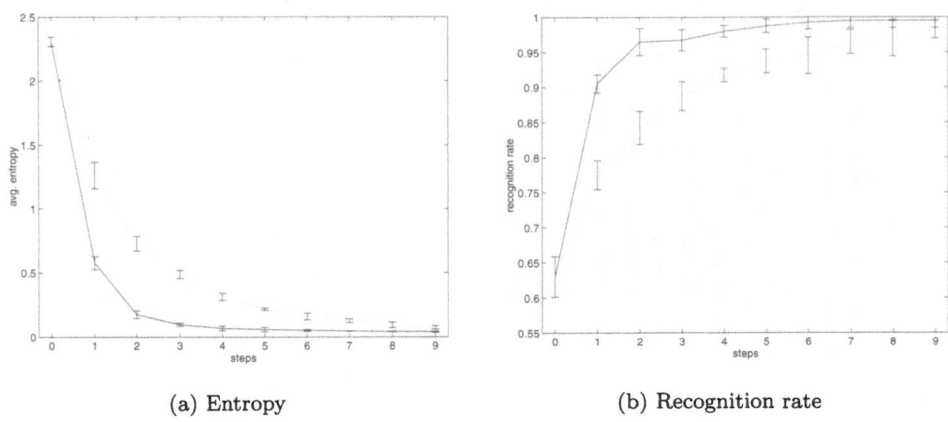

(a) Entropy   (b) Recognition rate

FIGURE 11.18. Convergence rate improvement by learning: (a) the speedup in reaching the entropy goal ($H = 0.1$) by a learned (line) versus a random (dotted) strategy (online evaluation for recognizing object o_{11}); (b) a corresponding acceleration in increasing the recognition rate.

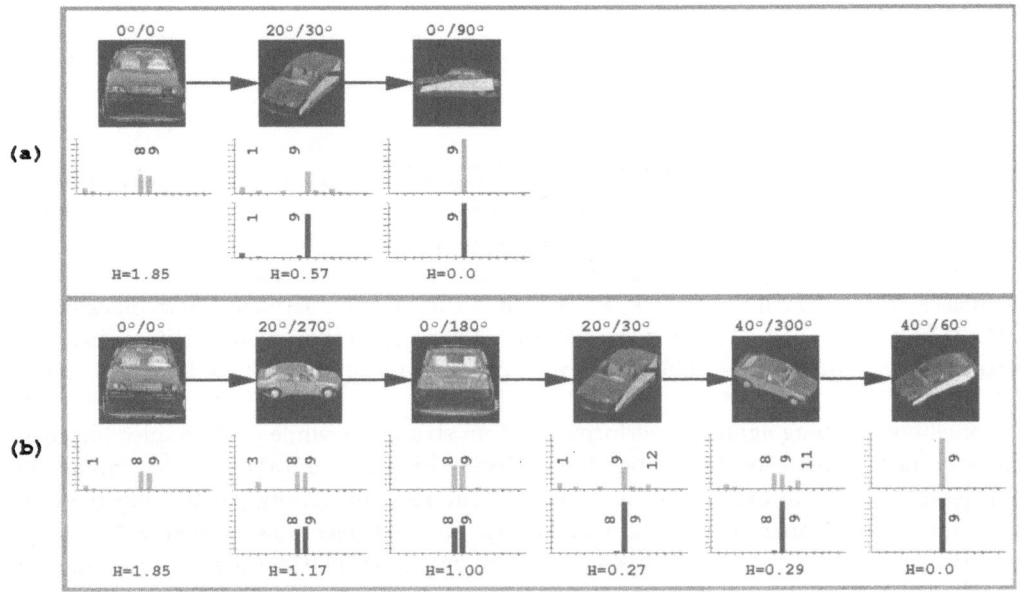

FIGURE 11.19. Sample fusion sequences exhibited on object o_9 (Figure 11.16). The learned (a) and random (b) strategies are compared starting from the same viewpoints. Top to bottom rows: poses (vert. elevation and tilt/azimuth), segmented images, *local* posterior distributions (with marked object hypotheses superimposed), *fused* posterior distributions (Section 11.3.5), entropy values H of fused distributions.

11.4.4 Discussion and Outlook

It has been demonstrated that reinforcement learning provides near-optimal strategies to recognize three-dimensional objects. The appearance-based model is extended by probabilistic decision making that proposes a process to actively increase confidence in the classification, under fusion of the visual evidence. Gaussian modeling of view-specific receptive fields in connection with an RBF optimization framework allows simple and efficient designs of probabilistic inference systems. Eventually, learning viewpoint planning enables us to apply efficient actions in reaction to perceptive inputs. This is a considerable advantage to explicit reasoning methods in case of large data sets. Furthermore, the learning framework proposes autonomous observers that adjust their recognition behavior to varying environmental conditions.

There are many possible applications of this technique. Autonomous robots take advantage from 3-D object recognition to localize their position in the environment, e.g., for navigation purposes. Visual inspection bears the requirement of high confidence in the decision, e.g., in dangerous environments. The representation model permits objects of any appearance, arbitrary shape, and texture, to be included in the database. An important prerequisite is an attention-controlling mechanism to segment relevant information from the background, e.g., using optical flow information in image sequences. Limitations will be due to the complexity of the classifier estimating the posterior distribution and the estimator of action utility. The RBF framework promises relief with currently available methods for global complexity reduction.

Research on learning view selection should develop methods to handle continuous actions, actions toward structures of the interpretation system, and occlusion in a complex scene. The optimization of alternative utility measures, integrating costs on camera motion or processing time, is considered. The described method applies by the same concept to *incremental* sensor motion, i.e., to exploit the information while tracking the object under inspection. This will open a wide area of applications for autonomous systems in uncertain environments.

11.5 Generic Active Object Recognition

This solution to active recognition embodies a dual paradigm approach to generic 3D object recognition from intensity images.

Opposed to recognition by model matching, we want to perform generic object recognition, i.e., recognize objects that belong to the same class i.e., having the same properties (e.g., the objects have the same topological descriptions but differ in their geometry), or are similar to pre-stored models [ZM94].

We use a structural decomposition model where the shape of an object is described in terms of a few generic 3D components joined by spatial relationships. This decomposition is naturally entailed into a graph structure [DPR92b]. Comparison between objects is then resolved mainly by qualitative graph-matching resulting in a correspondence between objects that are identical in their structure but might differ in their *geometry*.

Because part-based descriptions ignore fine (metric or quantitative) distinctions among shapes [Ede97] and, therefore, may not have enough discriminatory power, we introduce a *3D-prototype* that contains all quantitative information needed for the recognition process. The details about the representation of qualitative and quantitative information are given in Section 11.5.1.

11.5.1   Object Models

Basically, objects are represented by a dual model (Figure 11.20) that consists of a qualitative part (graph) and a quantitative part (3D-prototype).

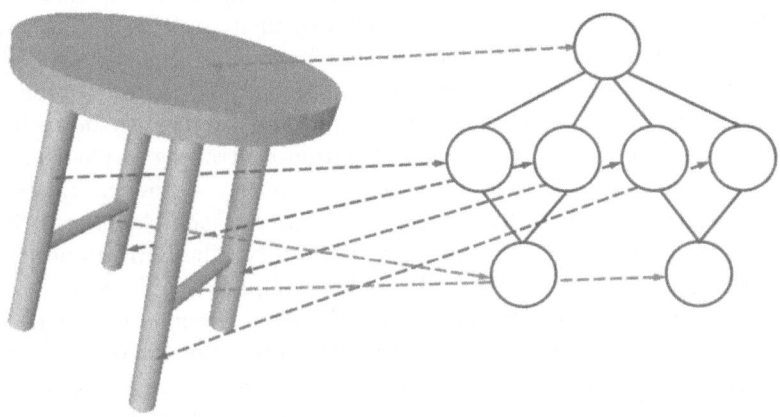

FIGURE 11.20. Dual representation of object models. The direct correspondence between the graph nodes and the primitives of the 3D-prototype is represented with double arcs.

- **Qualitative representation:** The description of the topological information of the objects is achieved by a graph representation. The vertices of the graph represent the volumetric primitives while edges define the connectivity relations between the primitives. In a future stage of system development we plan to add relations for symmetry and parallelism. Furthermore, we intend to extend generic recognition by considering some variations in the primitives, e.g., a vertex in the graph could be either a block or a cylinder.

- **Quantitative representation:**All quantitative information needed for the object recognition process is represented within a 3D-prototype. The 3D-prototype is a CAD model that uses basic elements denoting the volumetric primitives, which have a one-to-one correspondence to the nodes of the qualitative graph. These elements have fixed dimensions in the CAD model, but the dimensions of the primitives in the real object may differ from those in the model. Also the position of the actual primitive attachment in real objects could be different from the position in the CAD model.

The 3D-prototype is used for verifying object hypotheses and in the estimation of viewpoints (Section 11.5.5). In the verification process currently only the topology of the 3D-prototype is investigated (we generate a graph representing an aspect of the 3D-prototype from an estimated viewpoint).

Information that will be retrieved from the CAD model in future stages of system development include

- symmetry relations,

- relative sizes, and

- color and texture information.

11.5.2 Recognition System

The main parts of the generic object recognition system are depicted in Figure 11.21. The three modules shown in the top part are generating object hypotheses and selecting a specific hypothesis to be verified. After selection of a hypothesis a viewpoint reasoning step is performed to derive the actual and the desired next viewpoint as well as the transformation needed to move there in the active step.

The other major part of the recognition system, not depicted in this figure, is the fusion module that integrates the new information.

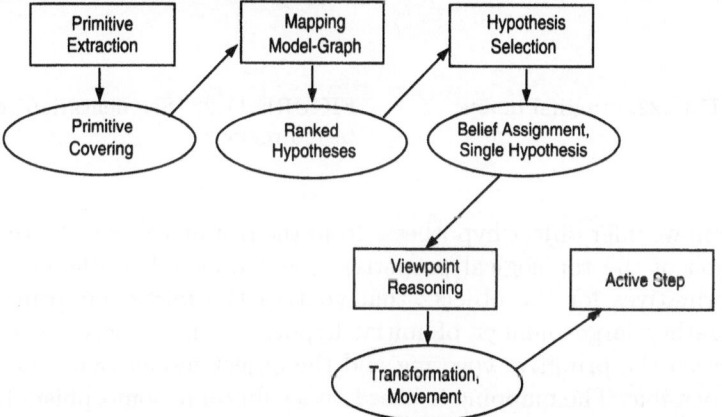

FIGURE 11.21. Generic object recognition system.

11.5.3 Hypothesis Generation

The extraction of primitive elements is an adaptation of the work by Dickinson [DPR92a]. It starts with the extraction of contours from a single 2-D intensity image (Figure 11.22) and classifies them as straight, convex, or concave. These contours are grouped into faces, which are represented by so-called *face-graphs* (Figure 11.24) containing structural properties (parallelism, symmetry, connectivity) in order to describe the nonaccidental properties of the RBC-theory [Bie85]. Grouping of faces results in so-called *aspects* that are used to infer primitive elements. Furthermore, primitives are grouped to give hypothetical interpretations of the scene in terms of graphs, where nodes correspond to primitive elements and arcs contain connectivity information. These interpretations are called *primitive coverings* and are ranked by their assigned score measures. In our example, the best primitive covering (Figure 11.24) does not, due to segmentation problems (cf. Figure 11.23), contain the tabletop and the back leg of the table, which results in a rather low score for the ranking.

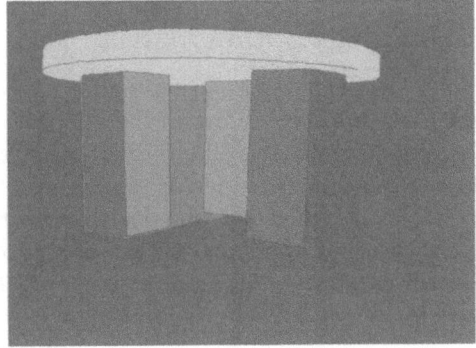

FIGURE 11.22. Original image.   FIGURE 11.23. Segmentation result with detected regions.

In our system we infer object hypotheses from the primitives, which are then verified by investigation of the topological properties. First object hypotheses are generated from single primitives for the objects that contain the particular primitive in their model. This rather large number of initial hypotheses is reduced by establishing a mapping between the primitive covering and the object model that includes as many primitives as possible. The mapping is based on a subgraph isomorphism between a 3D model graph and a 2D primitive covering graph. Due to occlusions, 3D-connections do not appear in the 2D image, therefore, the connectivity relations between the primitives are not investigated in the mapping module.

The result is a list of ranked object hypotheses with a mapping between the object graph (extracted from the image) and the model graph (with direct correspondence to the 3D-prototype). The ranking is established by calculating two values that describe the quality of the match. The first value mq (Equation (11.27)) describes the percentage of recovered primitives of the model. The second measure oq (Equation (11.28))

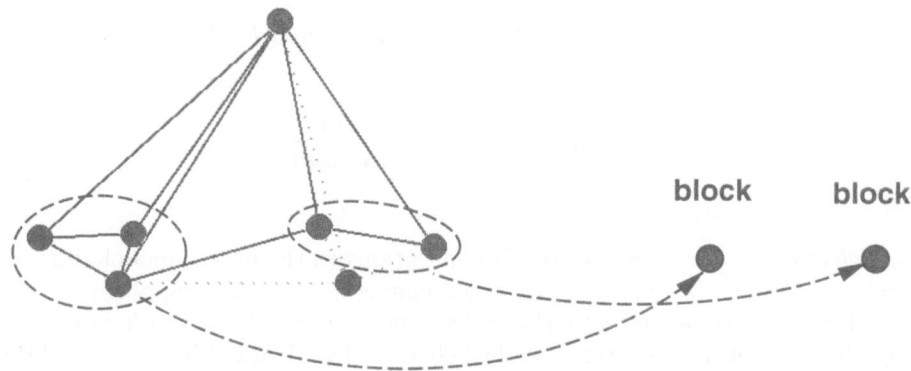

FIGURE 11.24. Face graph on the left. Nodes denote faces, solid arcs represent *adjacency* between faces, and dotted arcs specify *inside* relations. Best primitive covering on the right side. The left block is built by aggregating the three lower-left faces in the face graph; the right block is inferred by the two adjacent faces in the lower-right part of the face graph.

represents the ability of the hypothesis to fit the actual recovered primitives:

$$mq = \frac{modelnum - mapnum}{modelnum}, \tag{11.27}$$

$$oq = \frac{objectnum - hypbel}{objectnum}, \tag{11.28}$$

where

hypbel	...	sum of the score of matched object nodes;
modelnum	...	number of primitives in the object model;
objectnum	...	number of recovered primitive nodes in the hypothesized object; and
mapnum	...	number of matched nodes in the object-model mapping of the hypothesis.

The overall value assigned to the hypothesis is calculated by the following equation

$$r(objhyp) = 1 - a * mq - b * oq, \tag{11.29}$$

where a and b are weighting parameters to give priority to good model estimations or to mappings with a higher number of recovered primitives (in our experiments both parameters are set to one).

As stated earlier the connections are not used in the mapping; however, recovered connections enhance the mapping, and, therefore, they should increase the rank of the object hypothesis. In our system this is achieved by increasing the initial value with a connectivity weight according to the proportion of detected connections given in following formulas:

$$r_c(objhyp) = (1 + confactor) * r(objhyp), \tag{11.30}$$

where

$$confactor = \frac{connum}{modelconnum} \tag{11.31}$$

where

$modelconnum$ ...   number of 3D-connections in the object model and
$connum$ ...   number of verified connections in the mapping.

After building the ranked hypotheses list, the system selects one hypothesis by assessing the list within the transferable belief model (TBM [SK94]). The TBM is a framework to represent the knowledge about the system state within evidence theory. The domain of the model is a finite set of hypotheses called the *frame of discernment* Ω. In our case the frame of discernment is built by all objects in our model database ($\Omega = object \mid object \in modeldatabase$). The knowledge about an actual event is represented by belief assignments. For each hypothesis of the object hypotheses list we calculate a basic belief assignment as follows. Within the TBM a mass of unit one is available for each belief assignment. One part of this mass is given to the single object hypothesis (Equation (11.32)). The rest of the available mass is assigned to the complete frame (Equation (11.33)).

$$\begin{aligned} m(objhyp) &= r_c(objhyp), \tag{11.32}\\ m(\Omega) &= 1 - r_c(objhyp). \tag{11.33} \end{aligned}$$

All these simple belief assignments are then fused by Dempster's rule of combination (Equation (11.35)) which results in a compound belief assignment for the object hypotheses list:

$$\begin{aligned} m^*(A_k) &= (m_1 \oplus m_2)(A_k)\\ &= \frac{1}{1-Conflict} \sum_{A_i \cap A_j = A_k} m_1(A_i)m_2(A_j), \tag{11.34} \end{aligned}$$

$$\tag{11.35}$$

with

$$Conflict = \sum_{A_i \cap A_j = \phi} m_1(A_i)m_2(A_j),$$

where A_i, A_j, and A_k denote sets of object hypotheses.

The final belief assignment for our example shown in Figure 11.22–11.24 is given in Table 11.2. The correct interpretation would be the object named *Table1*, whereas the system is in favor of *Table4*.

The compound belief assignment is transferred into a probability distribution, which is then used to choose the object hypothesis with the highest probability.

TABLE 11.2. Belief assignment after fusing all object hypotheses.

$$\text{bel(Table1)} \quad = \quad 0.2949$$

.
.
.

$$\text{bel(Table4)} \quad = \quad 0.4482$$

.

$$\text{bel(Chair)} \quad = \quad 0.0126$$

.

$$\text{bel}(\Omega) \quad = \quad 0.1382$$

11.5.4   Visibility Space

We want to use spatial relations to qualitatively estimate the current camera position in our active object recognition experiment. Starting from a single intensity image of an object and a corresponding mapping to a 3D CAD prototype, the visibility and the occlusion of parts of the prototype are used to infer possible camera positions on a view sphere (i.e., initial object pose estimation).

Motion planning in robotics, object recognition in computer vision, illumination simulation, or view maintenance in computer graphics are some examples where visibility is a crucial issue. In a review of the field of sensor planning, Tarabanis et al. [TAT95], following the ideas of Maver and Bajcsy [MB93], identified three areas of research in sensor planning: *object feature detection, model-based recognition,* and *scene reconstruction.* The systems in the first area determine the values of the sensor parameters (e.g., position, orientation, optical settings) for which particular features of a known object in a known pose satisfy particular constraints when imaged. The systems in the second area are concerned with the selection of the most useful sensing operations for identifying an object or its pose. The third area is concerned with building a model of a scene incrementally, choosing new sensor configurations on the basis of the information about the world currently available to the system. While our overall approach clearly falls within the second area of this classification we have to notice that estimating the camera position after objects have been hypothesized falls into the first area of this classification. More particularly in computer vision, *aspect graphs* [EBD92] and *characteristic views* [CF82] have been developed to summarize the viewpoints from which an object has the same structure. An *aspect* is defined as a region of space where a set of object features remain simultaneously visible. When moving the sensor or the object, some features may appear or disappear (a situation called *visual event*) and a new *aspect* is generated. The features considered in the literature are mostly contours. Well-known drawbacks of aspect graphs are their inefficient computation ($O(n^6 \log n)$) for a polyhedral object composed of n faces under orthographic projection and $O(n^9 \log n)$ under perspective projection) and their size: $O(n^6)$ and $O(n^9)$, respectively, even though any view within the same aspect can be linearly transformed from its *characteristic view*. Most of the shortcomings of aspect graphs are circumvented by the use of approximate visibility techniques. *Approximate representations* discretize and restrict the domain of sensor configurations as well as the visibility space (possible viewpoints). While scale space could be used to prune the number of aspects retained in an aspect graph [EBD+93], the most widely used approximate visibility technique limits the visibility space to a finite and discrete region of the 3D space surrounding the object being inspected. We also choose such a viewing space because it allows computation of an approximation of the exact aspect graph and a simple intersection of multiple viewing constraints.

We use the surface of a unit viewing sphere, centered around the object (located at the origin of the coordinate system), as a model of the viewpoint space, which we call *view sphere*. This model fits well with orthographic projection while perspective projection would require the knowledge of the viewer-to-object distance. This sphere can be further approximated by a geodesic dome consisting of facets with equal triangular shapes providing a quasiregular tessellation. The viewpoint space is then restricted to the centers of the triangular facets backprojected onto the viewing sphere. Although there are several methods to construct geodesic domes, we simply use a recursive splitting of a triangular facet into four smaller ones, the initial geodesic dome being an icosahedron (20 facets). This enables us to easily adjust the tessellation of our view sphere. Figure 11.25 shows a few examples of geodesic domes having an increasing number of facets.

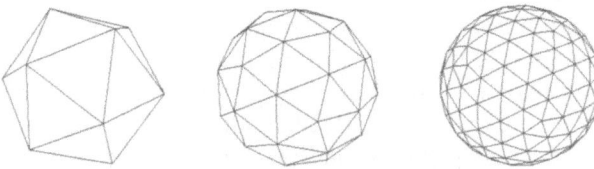

FIGURE 11.25. Examples of geodesic domes at increasing resolution (20, 80, 320 facets).

The visibility of an object (or part of it) is the open set consisting of all viewpoints in free space for which the object is visible. The term *visibility* is inherently vague. We define it here as the set of all viewpoints (consisting of the centers of the facets of a geodesic dome) for which an object is totally or partially visible. *Visibility* can be quantified in either a crisp way or in a fuzzy way. Figure 11.26 shows (transposed to a 2D case) these two possible types of quantification.

Fuzzy logic finds here its natural application in handling *vagueness* (i.e., difficulty in characterizing a particular concept or property with a crisp set): The membership values μ calculated will represent the degree of evidence that an object (or part of it) is visible from a given viewpoint. Considered in the context of the object (Obj) to which it belongs and from a given point of view (Vp_j), the surface area measurement of the part ($Part_i$): $A_{obj}(Obj, Part_i, Vp_j)$ provides a basis for modeling occlusion. Unfortunately, this measure is highly dependent on the shape of the parts and the projection model used. Additional information is needed for normalizing A_{obj}. For example, Figure 11.27 shows the same object part (here a stool leg) from three different viewpoints, where it is obvious that:

$$A_{obj}(Stool, Leg, Vp_a) > A_{obj}(Stool, Leg, Vp_c) > A_{obj}(Stool, Leg, Vp_b).$$

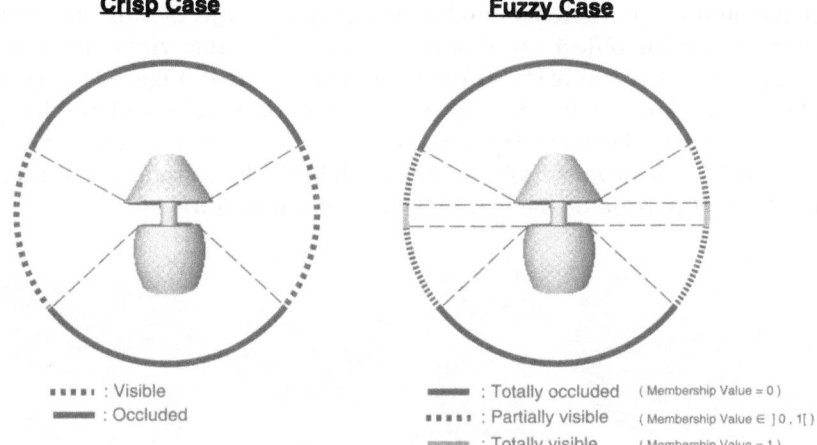

Crisp Case   **Fuzzy Case**

‥‥‥ : Visible
▬▬ : Occluded

▬▬ : Totally occluded   (Membership Value = 0)
‥‥‥ : Partially visible   (Membership Value ∈] 0 , 1[ )
▬▬ : Totally visible   (Membership Value = 1)

FIGURE 11.26. Crisp quantification (left) and fuzzy quantification (right) of *visibility*

Only considering the ordering of $A_{obj}(Obj, Part_i, Vp_j)$ would mislead us to classify the stool leg seen in Figure 11.27(b) as more occluded than in Figure 11.27(c), even though the stool leg in Figure 11.27(b) is clearly not occluded by any other object part.

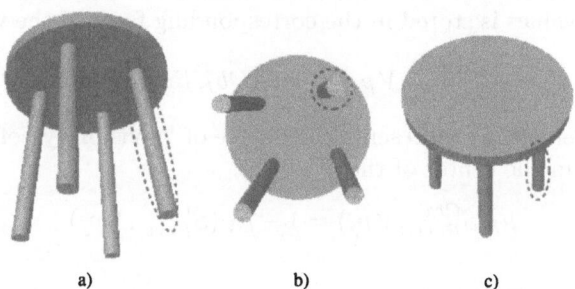

a)   b)   c)

FIGURE 11.27. Visibility of the same stool leg (dotted lines) from different viewpoints.

To avoid this error we introduce a normalizing factor represented by the surface area measurement of the part under inspection in a context where the other parts of the object are hidden: $A_{single}(Obj, Part_i, Vp_j)$. Thus, the normalized value representing visibility from one viewpoint is expressed as:

$$Vis(Obj, Part_i, Vp_j) = A_{obj}(Obj, Part_i, Vp_j)/A_{single}(Obj, Part_i, Vp_j).$$

With the help of this normalizing factor, it can be seen from Figure 11.27 that:

$$Vis(Stool, Leg, Vp_c) < Vis(Stool, Leg, Vp_a) = Vis(Stool, Leg, Vp_b) = 1.$$

Figure 11.28 shows the resulting visibility regions (here displayed on tessellated spheres of 320 facets) of the geometric primitives composing a simple lamp (the darker the facet, the higher the object part visibility) under orthographic projection. In this figure, both the view sphere and the object are represented from the same viewpoint and viewing direction. Figure 11.28(a) shows the visibility of the lampstand, Figure 11.28(b) presents the visibility of the lamp pole, and Figure 11.28(c) the visibility of the lamp shade. Notice that, because of the geometry of the object and the relative size of the different parts, the lampshade is never totally occluded while the lampstand is totally occluded only from a limited portion of the view sphere (polar position).

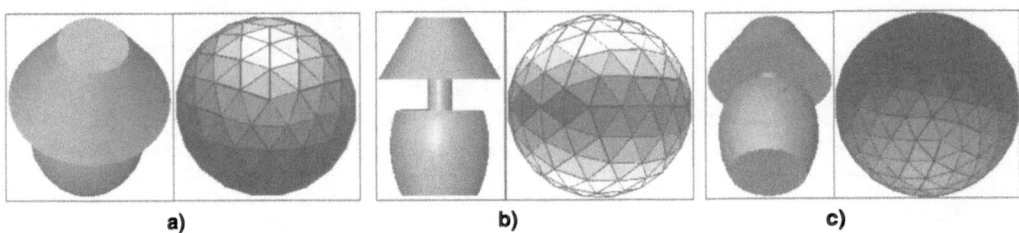

a)   **b)**   **c)**

FIGURE 11.28. Visibility view spheres for the three different parts composing a simple lamp.

We now have visibility of object parts conveyed as fuzzy view spheres interpreting $Vis(Obj, Part_i, Vp_j)$ as a fuzzy membership value μ_V that reflects the degree of visibility of the ith part of the object Obj seen from the center of the jth facet. Each of these membership values is stored in the corresponding facet of the view sphere $S_{Part_i}^{Obj}$:

$$\mu_V(S_{Part_i}^{Obj}, Vp_j) = Vis(Obj, Part_i, Vp_j). \tag{11.36}$$

The fuzzy complement μ_I represents the degree of "invisibility" of the ith part of the object Obj seen from the center of the jth facet:

$$\mu_I(S_{Part_i}^{Obj}, Vp_j) = 1 - \mu_V(S_{Part_i}^{Obj}, Vp_j). \tag{11.37}$$

11.5.5   Viewpoint Estimation

Assuming certain parts are identified in a 2D image of a hypothesized object, an aggregation of the fuzzy view-spheres representing the object parts, visibility can be interpreted as an indication for camera positions.

Basic fuzzy set operators (e.g., complement, intersection, and union) are defined as generalizations of their classical crisp counterparts and must satisfy proper sets of axioms (*commutativity, associativity, monotonicity*) that, however, do not uniquely define them. As a direct consequence, several operators for the same operation are available. This contributes to the richness and flexibility of fuzzy logic, but, on the other hand, the selection of the most suitable operators is often difficult and application-dependent.

We give here three standard and simple intersection operators, but others are available (e.g., Yager class, Dombi class [KF88]):

- Original intersection: $i_1(\mu_A(x), \mu_B(x)) = \mu_{A \cap B}(x) = min(\mu_A(x), \mu_B(x))$,

- Algebraic product: $i_2(\mu_A(x), \mu_B(x)) = \mu_{A \cap B}(x) = \mu_A(x) \cdot \mu_B(x)$,

- Bounded product: $i_3(\mu_A(x), \mu_B(x)) = \mu_{A \cap B}(x) = max(0, \mu_A(x) + \mu_B(x) - 1)$.

Information about single parts can then be aggregated, facet by facet, into a new fuzzy view sphere, specifying for the complete object which parts are visible or invisible and parts for which there is no evidence at all. The aggregation results in:

$$S^{Obj}(R) = \left\{ \cap_i \mu^{Obj}(Part_i, Vp_j), \forall Vp_j \right\} \qquad (11.38)$$

where:

$$\mu^{Obj}(Part_i, Vp_j) = \begin{cases} \mu_V(S_{Part_i}^{Obj}, Vp_j) & \text{if } (Part_i, Visible) \in R \\ \mu_I(S_{Part_i}^{Obj}, Vp_j) & \text{if } (Part_i, Invisible) \in R \\ 1 \text{ (neutral element for } \cap) & \text{if } (Part_i, Irrelevant) \in R \end{cases} \qquad (11.39)$$

with $R(P, ST)$ representing the relation between the two sets:

- $P = \{Part_1, ..., Part_n\}$ set of the parts of the object Obj,

- $ST = \{Visible, Invisible, Irrelevant\}$ set of states for an object part.

Figure 11.29 shows the influence of the three fuzzy intersection operators i_1, i_2, and i_3 described on the resulting aggregation of view spheres. The aggregation is based on the assumption that the tabletop and the first leg are $Visible$ while the other three legs are $Invisible$. Results are displayed on a tessellated sphere of 320 facets, darker gray values reflecting higher membership values. Figure 11.29(a)) shows the aggregation performed using the standard min operator i_1, Figure 11.29(b) using the $algebraic \ product \ i_2$, and Figure 11.29(c) the $bounded \ product \ i_3$.

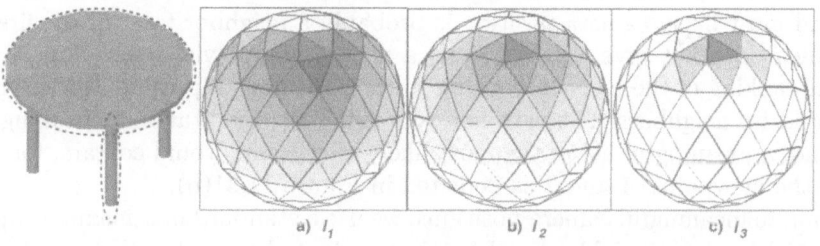

FIGURE 11.29. Influence of fuzzy intersection operators i_1, i_2, i_3.

These three fuzzy intersection operators show increasingly restrictive behavior ($i_1 < i_2 < i_3$): $min(\mu_A(x), \mu_B(x)) < \mu_A(x) \cdot \mu_B(x) < max(0, \mu_A(x) + \mu_B(x) - 1)$.

We give here an example of the influence of the selected configuration ("visual query" in terms of parts $Visible, Invisible$, or $Irrelevant$) on the aggregation result. Figure 11.30 shows the aggregation result (using the $bounded \ product$) for a table lamp (Figure 11.30(a) using two different "visual queries". The first configuration used for calculating the view sphere shown in Figure 11.30(b) was to consider the back of the lamp shade *Visible*, the first articulated pole *Invisible* and the other parts *Irrelevant*. For Figure 11.30(c), the back of the lamp shade was *Visible*, the lamp shade *Invisible* and the other parts were *Irrelevant*. In Figure 11.30(b), the region of the most likely viewpoints is not narrow even though the fuzzy intersection operator used (bounded product) is the most restrictive one. In comparison, Figure 11.30(c) shows a quite compact region, reflecting the more restrictive nature of the query. The accuracy of the resulting visibility regions is thus highly dependent on the "visual query". Stating parts as *Irrelevant* of course brings less discriminating power than considering them *Visible* or *Invisible*.

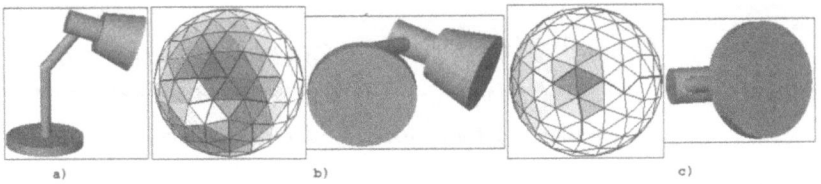

FIGURE 11.30. Aggregation with two different object parts configurations.

We have shown how to aggregate the view spheres of different parts of the same object. This aggregation reflects the visibility constraints of a given objects part configuration. In other words, the resolution of these constraints gives hints to the camera position with regard to a given objects part configuration. Even though the aggregation could result in a very narrow region on the view sphere, the most likely viewpoints do not result in a single facet, making the camera and viewer position estimation difficult.

A first and trivial approach consists in ranking the facets according to their membership value, the most likely camera positions corresponding directly to the center of the sorted facets. This approach is prone to fail due to unfortunate viewpoints. Furthermore, it does not provide a meaningful list of possible camera positions. For example, the second most likely camera position is probably a neighbor facet of the first ranked facet, which does not give, qualitatively, a very different viewpoint. Figure 11.31(a) shows the ranking of the facets according to their membership value. Notice that viewpoint 1 and its neighbors (2–6) are not very different, qualitatively speaking. On the other hand, a meaningful list of the most likely viewpoints would contain, for the same example the viewpoints 1 and 2 as depicted in Figure 11.31(b).

To estimate meaningful camera positions, we use a standard non-maxima suppression algorithm whose local neighborhood has been adapted to match the neighborhood of the view sphere facets.

If several maxima form a connected region on the view sphere we select the most promising one by using a binary distance transform on the region composed of the connected maxima. Among the maxima having the same value, the more distant one from the boundaries of its region is chosen (for results see Figure 11.31(b)). This disfavors unstable regions, i.e., regions associated with configurations seen from a small portion of the viewsphere, which are poor candidates for camera positioning even if they meet the correct configurations. This votes in favor of the region's stability already mentioned

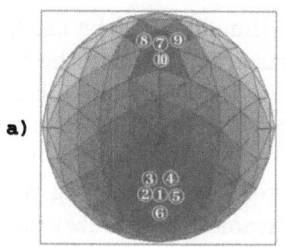 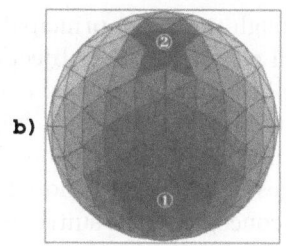

FIGURE 11.31. Camera position estimation methods: (a) simple ranking (b) using non-maxima suppression.

by Trucco et. al. [TDR94].

11.5.6   Viewpoints and Actions

We can infer camera positions but even though viewing directions are now known the rotation angle around the line of sight (between object and viewer coordinate system) remains unknown. Before taking any new action (camera displacement), one should disambiguate the object's pose with respect to the camera's viewing direction (the camera in an orthographic projection is supposed to always point to the object's center). Figure 11.32 depicts the situation where the angular displacements $\Delta\varphi$ and $\Delta\theta$ are planned as next camera action to reach the desired viewpoint. These displacements are a function of the angle Ψ: the rotation angle around the viewing direction (between the camera and the object coordinate systems).

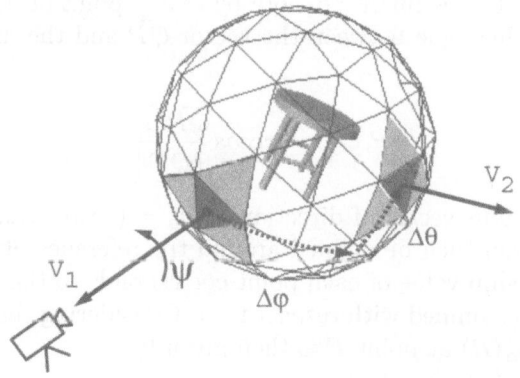

FIGURE 11.32. From the current view V_1, under the knowledge of the camera orientation Ψ, relative angular displacements $(\Delta\varphi, \Delta\theta)$ determine the location of the next viewpoint V_2.

In order to resolve the angle Ψ one might try to use the difference of principal axes between the image under inspection (test image) and the model image seen from the same viewpoint (see Figure 11.33). It is well known that principal axes are undefined for many shapes (such as n-fold rotationally symmetric shapes or mirror-symmetric shapes). Even though universal principal axes [Lin93] could be used, we prefer a more intuitive approach comparing the object's parts embedding in the two images. This is referred to in the literature as *spatial arrangements* [TVJD95]. These spatial relations describe how parts are oriented (e.g., "right to", "above") relative to each other. The similarity (after rotation) of part embeddings can thus be used to infer the orientation between the images. Bloch [Blo97] noted that relative positioning is highly ambiguous; therefore, such a concept is well suited to the framework of fuzzy sets.

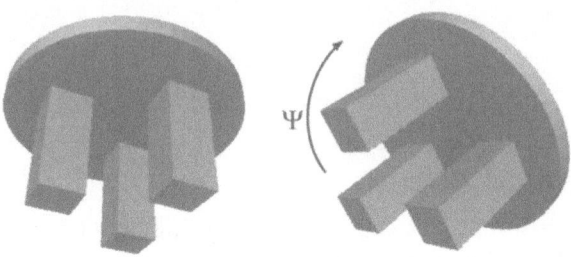

FIGURE 11.33. Model image and test image both seen from the same viewpoint (Ψ: unknown camera orientation).

Following Bloch's approach, we denote by S the Euclidean space where the objects are defined, i.e., 2D discrete space of an image. Let us consider a reference object R and an object A for which the relative position with respect to R along the direction α has to be evaluated. Let us further denote by P any point of S, and by Q any point of R. Let $\beta(P, Q)$ be the angle between the vector $\vec{QP}$ and the direction α, computed in $[0, \pi]$:

$$\beta(P, Q) = arccos\frac{\vec{QP}.\vec{\mu_\alpha}}{\|\vec{QP}\|}, \qquad (11.40)$$

where $\vec{\mu_\alpha}$ denotes the unit vector of direction α: $\vec{\mu_\alpha} = (cos\alpha, sin\alpha)^T$.

A fuzzy landscape can then be defined around the reference object R as a fuzzy set such that the membership value of each point corresponds to the degree of satisfaction of the spatial relation examined with respect to R. Considering the previous definitions, the fuzzy landscape $\mu_\alpha(R)$ at point P is then given by:

$$\mu_\alpha(R, P) = max\left(0, 1 - \frac{2\min_Q \beta(P, Q)}{\pi}\right). \qquad (11.41)$$

Figure 11.34 illustrates the definition of $\mu_\alpha(R)$ for $\alpha = 0$ (i.e., "right-to" relation), where R is a binary hand-sketched region.

As we already mentioned, our objects are represented by a graph structure. We use this graph structure to compute the fuzzy spatial relations between each pair of vertices (i.e., object parts). The orientation space considered is limited to eight directions

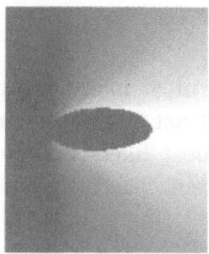

FIGURE 11.34. Fuzzy landscape $\mu_\alpha(R)$ for $\alpha = 0$ (i.e., "right-to" relation). High gray values correspond to high membership values.

(i.e., every 45 degrees) but can be set to a finer or coarser granularity. Figure 11.35 depicts the resulting fuzzy spatial relations computed for a chosen part (highlighted by a dotted line) with an orientation space sampled in eight directions.

FIGURE 11.35. Fuzzy spatial relations between an object part (surrounded by a dotted line) and its neighbors (left: model image, right: test image). The arrows depict the direction of the relation and their length shows the strength of belief that the neighboring object part lays within the considered direction.

Considering this sampled orientation space, one can measure the best similarity measure (correlation) between fuzzy spatial relations stored at the edges of the graph structures extracted from both model and test images. A correlation over the sampled orientation space is performed between each edge of the model graph structure and its corresponding edge from the test graph structure. Because we have fuzzy values (necessity: $N_\alpha^R(A)$, average: $M_\alpha^R(A)$, and possibility: $\Pi_\alpha^R(A)$) for the different orientations, we need a de-fuzzyfication scheme to perform a standard correlation. We simply use:

$$Orientation_\alpha^R(A) = M_\alpha^R(A)(1 - (\Pi_\alpha^R(A) - N_\alpha^R(A))). \tag{11.42}$$

The shift (according to the sampled orientation space chosen) resulting from the best correlation thus approximates the rotation angle difference between the model and the test object.

11.5.7 Motion Planning

In order to verify the derived object hypothesis, a new viewpoint is chosen to get some new data for the fusion step. Two different strategies arise for selecting the new viewing position:

- Like in the estimation of the most likely actual viewpoint, we can use the same visibility sphere to find the least likely viewing position. The image generated from this new position will most likely include object parts not yet seen by the active object recognition system.

- The second strategy would try to verify all parts of the object. It will, therefore, construct a new visibility sphere by generating a new query from the model-object mapping. Now we want to see all the remaining primitives in the model that were not included in the mapping. The most likely viewpoint derived from this query is chosen as the next viewing position.

For the example shown in Figure 11.22–11.24, the resulting belief value for the correct object hypothesis is $bel(Table1) = 0.2949$, but the highest belief value is given to a different object $bel(Table4) = 0.4482$. The reason for this can be seen by investigating the most likely actual viewpoint. In Figure 11.36 the visibility sphere and the model of the best object hypothesis can be seen from the actual viewing direction.

(a) Visibility sphere. Dark facets represent likely viewing positions, the tiny white spots represent the most promising viewing positions with the most likely one in the central facet of the sphere.

(b) Object model from the most likely viewing direction.

FIGURE 11.36. Actual viewing position.

In our example the system selects, by application of the first strategy, a movement to a new viewing position (Figure 11.37), where the tabletop can be seen, and therefore the initial object hypothesis is rejected and the belief for the correct object is increased.

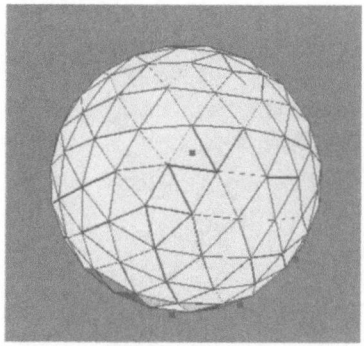

(a) Visibility sphere. White facets represent unlikely viewing positions, dark spots represent the most unlikely ones. The least likely viewing position is in the central facet of the sphere.

(b) Model of the hypothesized object from the least likely viewing direction.

FIGURE 11.37. Next selected viewing position.

11.5.8 Object Hypotheses Fusion

Once the next viewpoint is chosen, the object recognition system will move the camera to this point and gather a new image. This image is then processed by the recognition system, i.e., the image is segmented, face graphs and aspects are extracted, and finally a new primitive covering is built. From this primitive covering, a new list of object hypotheses is derived like in the hypotheses generation Section, which is transferred into a new belief assignment.

The new belief assignment is fused together with the one already derived by applying Dempster's rule of combination (Equation (11.35)). In the case that the initial hypothesis can be verified, the new evidence increases the belief in this hypothesis. The system will further choose new viewpoints and exploit the new information until the belief value for the hypothesis is above a predefined threshold (in our experiments we have chosen a belief value of 85 %) and, therefore, the object is recognized. Otherwise, if the new evidence is contradicting the initial hypothesis it will reduce the belief value for this object hypothesis, and increase a different one. The procedure of selecting new viewpoints and integrating the evidence will again be repeated until the threshold value is exceeded.

Going back to our illustrative example, if we compare the new image (Figure 11.38) taken by the system and the predicted image of the model (Figure 11.37b), we can see that the new information contradicts the initial belief distribution. Due to physical restrictions of the hardware setup, the desired top view of the object was not possible. But the missing tabletop can still be seen clearly now and, therefore, the initially selected hypothesis (*Table4*) will have reduced belief and the correct hypothesis (*Table1*) gains some portion of belief.

FIGURE 11.38. Image of the object from the new viewing position.

11.5.9   Conclusion

In the framework of generic object recognition based on primitive decomposition, a 3D object model consisting of a 3D CAD prototype and a 3D model graph was presented. The 3D CAD prototypes are composed of connected geometric primitives having a high indexing power, while the 3D model graphs represent the spatial relationships between these primitives. While we extract the primitives in a similar way to Dickinson [DPR92a], we differ in the generation of the object hypotheses. In his approach, object hypotheses are inferred by building subgraph isomorphisms, which ignores the fact that 3D connections may disappear in the 2D graphs. We use the recovered connections only to increase the belief in the object hypotheses, not during the establishment of the mapping.

The approach exposed here makes qualitative spatial inference of the camera and viewer position based on the arrangement and occlusion of the parts of the object under inspection. In terms of qualitative spatial reasoning in computer vision, the presented concept of the fuzzy view sphere enables qualitative pose estimation or estimation of the camera position with respect to an object-centered coordinate system. It handles the *vagueness* of the visibility concept in a fuzzy framework and helps after estimating the camera position, in predicting what will be seen after changing the camera viewpoint or, by mean of a history, in incrementally refining the camera position estimation. We thus achieve *active fusion* [PPGB96].

This system is ongoing work and under permanent refinement, therefore, some problems remain to be solved.

Because part-based descriptions are ignoring fine (metric or quantitative) distinctions among shapes, they might not have enough distinguishing power; therefore the basic model (3D CAD prototypes and 3D model graphs) we proposed can be further augmented by including n-ary relations like size, color, and relative size between parts.

As could be seen from the small example the strategy to find new viewing positions is reasonable, because it tries to verify the object by inspection of all parts. Dickinson [DCTO94] in contrast uses a strategy for refining aspects to verify single primitives, which could be used to treat the remaining problems of occlusions and bad or wrong segmentations, which are not resolved in our system directly. At the current stage of system development one hypothesis is selected for the verification process. By considering to investigate the best hypotheses at the same time, it is still an open question to find the strategy for selecting the best viewpoint for multiple hypotheses. In addition, the fusion of the view sphere coming from different viewpoints is under investigation.

12

Image Understanding Methods for Remote Sensing

Joachim Steinwendner
Werner Schneider
Renate Bartl

Remotely sensed images can be interpreted either **visually** by human expert interpreters or **automatically**, by employing digital image processing and pattern recognition methods [KWM99]. The demand for automatic methods mainly stems from two facts:

- A huge number of images continually acquired from Earth observation satellites are waiting for interpretation. At the same time, human interpreters are rare, and their interpretations are costly.

- Humans interpret subjectively. Results obtained by different experts often cannot be compared quantitatively.

Automatic analysis of remotely sensed images is conventionally performed by **pixelwise statistical classification**. These methods are very effective in extracting **multispectral** image information from images of lower and medium spatial resolution such as LANDSAT TM (see Figure 12.1(a)) and outperform the human interpreter in this respect: In multispectral interpretation, the human interpreter relies on color vision. Due to the three-dimensional nature of color space, visual interpretation is restricted to three spectral bands. For example, the spectro-radiometric information content of the four spectral bands of LANDSAT TM shown in Figure 12.2 cannot be fully exploited in visual interpretation.

Pixelwise statistical interpretation, however, completely neglects shape and context aspects of the image information, which are the main clues for a human interpreter. Shape, texture, and context are particularly important in the interpretation of images of high spatial resolution such as IRS-1C (Figure 12.1(b)).

In contrast to pixel-by-pixel techniques, **image understanding (computer vision) methods** try to simulate human visual interpretation. These techniques are based on the conceptual analysis model shown in Figure 12.3.

The model follows the general approach of analytical science and the technology of breaking complex reality down into individual **objects**, identifying these objects, determining their **attributes**, and establishing **relationships** between the objects. Starting from a digital image, "objects" are delimited in the segmentation process. These "image objects" can conceptually be regions, lines, or points. In actuality, the image objects are sets of adjacent pixels having a meaning in the real world depicted.

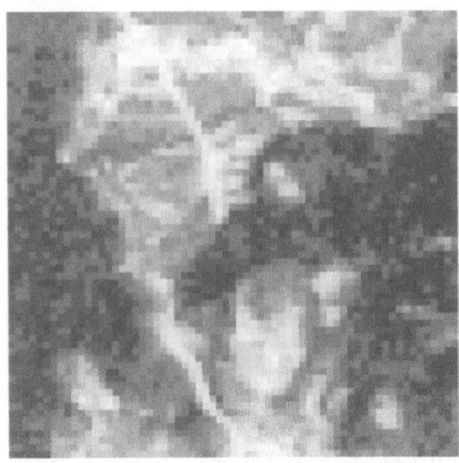

(a) Landsat TM Band 3   (b) IRS-1C Pan

FIGURE 12.1. Satellite images: Differences in geometrical resolution.

The objects of an image are, in a second process, classified, i.e., each object is assigned to a category out of a set of predefined categories. This classification can be seen as a process of **matching** (establishing correspondences) with prototypes stored in a knowledge base and defining the categories.

The process of segmentation may imply a change of representation from the digital image data structure (pixel raster) to a list data structure. Classification (matching) is then performed on the objects represented in the list. The process of converting this list of classified objects (map objects) into a thematic map may again involve a change of representation from the list data structure back to an image data structure. This process of **visualization** is not explicitly shown in Figure 12.3.

The process of classification or matching with prototypes stored in the knowledge base is hindered by the fact that radiometric attributes of the image objects may be image-dependent. The use of a generic knowledge base with image-independent prototypes is therefore made difficult. The solution of this problem is **radiometric calibration** of the images, as discussed in Section 12.1.

Another difficulty occurs in the segmentation process: Depending on the pixel size and the fineness of the spatial land-cover pattern, a considerable fraction of the pixels may be **mixed pixels**, i.e., pixels comprising more than one land-cover type. In the segmentation process, mixed pixels may produce regions without meaning in the real world. To avoid this phenomenon, segmentation based on subpixel analysis (Sections 12.2 and 12.3) may be used.

Section 12.4 illustrates the use of a generic spectral knowledge base for land-cover classification of image objects and addresses the distinction of land cover and land use.

Information derived from remotely sensed images often has to be related to informa-

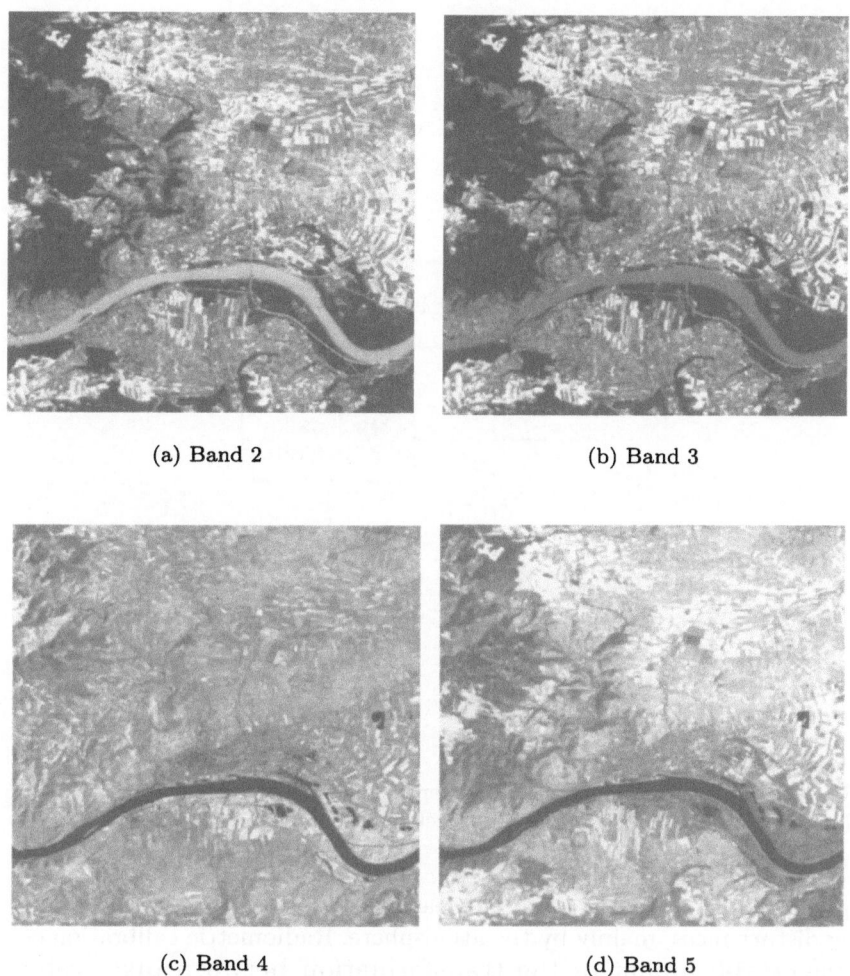

(a) Band 2   (b) Band 3

(c) Band 4   (d) Band 5

FIGURE 12.2. LANDSAT TM image (4 out of 7 bands) of a region near Krems, Austria.

tion from other sources. For example, in the case of land-cover mapping, reference has to be made to the ownership of parcels. The techniques of image information fusion at hand for these purposes are discussed in Section 12.5.

12.1 Radiometric Models

The concept of radiometric calibration is illustrated in Figure 12.4. Every land-cover type is characterized by reflectance values ρ on the terrain. The corresponding pixel

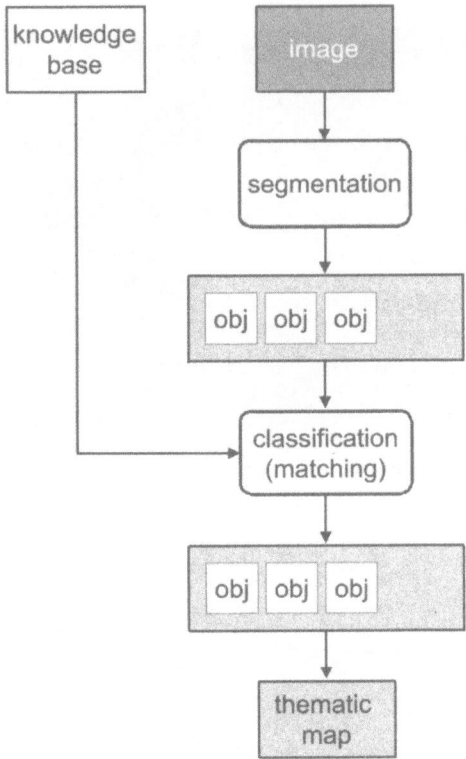

FIGURE 12.3. Conceptual model of computer vision in remote sensing. Classification transforms image objects (im.obj.) into map objects (map obj.).

values p in the image, which should be measures of these terrain reflectances, are influenced by disturbances, mainly by the atmosphere. Radiometric calibration of an image means the **establishment of the transformation between pixel values in the image and reflectance values on the terrain**.

In Figure 12.4, the various paths of radiation in the atmosphere are shown. The radiometric quantities are given for a certain wavelength.

The intensity of the radiation from the sun can be characterized by an irradiance E_S on a plane perpendicular to the incoming radiation at the top of the Earth's atmosphere. This radiation traverses the atmosphere and falls onto the terrain surface. The **specular transmittance** of the atmosphere for this path is τ_{sd} (s for specular, d for downward). The resulting irradiance E_{Gs} of the terrain surface is

$$E_{Gs} = E_S \cdot \tau_{sd} \cdot \cos \vartheta_S, \tag{12.1}$$

where ϑ_S is the zenith angle of the sun. Another portion of the radiation from the sun is being scattered in the atmosphere, i.e., it is deflected from its original direction of propagation, eventually reaching the terrain surface as **diffuse sky radiation**. In anal-

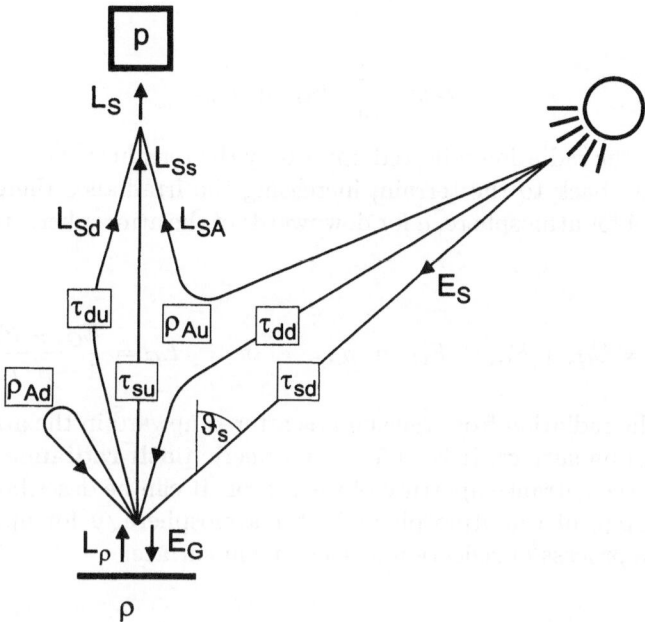

FIGURE 12.4. Influence of the atmosphere on the relationship between terrain reflectance ρ and pixel value p.

ogy to specular transmittance, this scattering process can be described quantitatively by a diffuse transmittance of the atmosphere, τ_{dd}, giving rise to an additional terrain irradiance

$$E_{Gd} = E_S \cdot \tau_{dd} \cdot \cos \vartheta_S. \tag{12.2}$$

A fraction ρ of the radiation falling onto the terrain surface (irradiance E_G) is reflected upward and partly propagates directly to the sensor. The resulting radiance L_{Ss} at the entrance aperture of the sensor is

$$L_{Ss} = \frac{1}{\pi} \cdot E_G \cdot \rho \cdot \tau_{su}. \tag{12.3}$$

The factor $1/\pi$ accounts for the fact that radiance is related to the solid angle (assuming Lambertian reflectance of the terrain surface, see, e.g., [Wol98]). ρ is the reflectance of the surface, and τ_{su} is the **specular transmittance** of the atmosphere for the **upward radiation path**.

Another part of the radiation reflected upward by the terrain surface reaches the sensor not on a direct path, but after being scattered in the atmosphere. Again in analogy to specular transmittance, this scattering process can be described quantitatively by a **diffuse transmittance** of the atmosphere, τ_{du} (d for diffuse, u for upward), giving rise to radiance L_{Sd} at the entrance aperture of the sensor:

$$L_{Sd} = \frac{1}{\pi} \cdot E_G \cdot \rho \cdot \tau_{du}. \tag{12.4}$$

A third part of the radiation reflected upward by the terrain surface is being scattered in the atmosphere back to the terrain, increasing the irradiance there. Introducing a reflectance ρ_{Ad} (A for atmosphere, d for downward) of the atmosphere, the total **terrain irradiance** is

$$E_G = E_{Gs} + E_{Gd} + E_G \cdot \rho \cdot \rho_{Ad} \quad \text{or} \quad E_G = \frac{E_{Gs} + E_{Gd}}{1 - \rho \cdot \rho_{Ad}}. \tag{12.5}$$

A portion of the radiation from the sun is scattered upward in the atmosphere before it reaches the terrain surface. It is called atmospheric **path radiance**. and it causes a radiance L_{SA} at the entrance aperture of the sensor. It can be described quantitatively by a reflectance ρ_{Au} of the atmosphere (A for atmosphere, u for upwards) in direct analogy with the process of reflection at the terrain surface:

$$L_{SA} = \frac{1}{\pi} \cdot E_S \cdot \rho_{Au} \cdot \cos \vartheta_S. \tag{12.6}$$

The total **radiance at the entrance aperture of the sensor** is given by the three terms

$$L_S = L_{Ss} + L_{Sd} + L_{SA}. \tag{12.7}$$

Combining all equations from (12.1) to (12.7) one obtains

$$L_S = \frac{1}{\pi} E_S \cos \vartheta_S \cdot \left(\frac{(\tau_{sd} + \tau_{dd})(\tau_{su} + \tau_{du}) \cdot \rho}{1 - \rho \cdot \rho_{Ad}} + \rho_{Au} \right). \tag{12.8}$$

The resulting pixel value p is linearly related to this radiance L_S by

$$L_S = a_0 + a_1 \cdot p, \tag{12.9}$$

where a_0 and a_1 are the **offset** and **gain** of the sensor, respectively.

Equations (12.8) and (12.9) provide the relationship between pixel value p and reflectance on the ground, ρ:

$$p = p\left(\rho, E_S, \vartheta_S, \tau_{sd}, \tau_{dd}, \tau_{su}, \tau_{du}, \rho_{Au}, \rho_{Ad}, a_0, a_1 \right), \tag{12.10}$$

which is needed for radiometric calibration.

The situation is more complicated in the cases of

(a) Spatially inhomogeneous surfaces: Due to scattering in the atmosphere, radiation from the surroundings of a pixel on the ground will influence the radiance sensed for this pixel (Equation (12.4)). In addition, radiation reflected from the surroundings of a terrain pixel will partly be backscattered by the atmosphere to this terrain pixel (Equation (12.5)). To account for this, ρ in Equations (12.4) and (12.5) has to be substituted by $\bar{\rho}$, which denotes a spatial average of ρ in the surroundings of a pixel. The exact weight function for the averaging depends on atmospheric properties.

(b) Uneven terrain: Equations (12.1) and (12.2) have to be altered to account for the effect of irradiance variations at inclined surfaces. In addition, all atmospheric parameters τ and ρ depend on terrain altitude. A digital elevation model is required to make allowance for this.

(c) Non-Lambertian surfaces: Many natural land-cover types exhibit directional reflectance effects. The main problem is the target-dependence of these effects.

These complications are not further dealt with here. It should only be mentioned that the treatment of spatially inhomogeneous surfaces and uneven terrain is rather straightforward, albeit costly in terms of computing time and input data requirements (digital elevation model). The quantitative treatment of non-Lambertian reflectance on natural surfaces, on the other hand, is a largely unsolved problem.

Equations (12.8) and (12.9) contain a number of parameters whose actual values may come from various sources:

- E_S is known from satellite measurements. (It is not constant, but it shows seasonal variations due to the varying sun-earth distance.)

- ϑ_S can be computed from the exact time of image acquisition.

- τ_{sd}, τ_{dd}, τ_{su}, τ_{du}, ρ_{Au}, and ρ_{Ad} can be modeled quantitatively by computer simulation. Here, the 6S-code (**Second Simulation of the Satellite Signal in the Solar Spectrum**) developed at the Laboratoire d'Optique Atmosphérique of the Université des Sciences et Technologies de Lille [V+97] is used.

- a_0 and a_1 may be considered constant and are provided by the supplier of the satellite images.

The 6S-code allows us to compute the listed atmospheric transmittance and reflectance quantities from other parameters on the gaseous components (e.g., vertical pressure and temperature profiles) and on the aerosol components of the atmosphere (aerosol types, aerosol distribution and aerosol concentration). Typical parameter combinations are compiled in "atmospheric models for gaseous components", M_G (e.g. "midlatitude summer" model), and in "aerosol models", M_A (e.g., "continental" aerosol model). The aerosol concentration, which is highly variable and has a strong impact on radiation processes in the atmosphere, is not included in the aerosol model, but is characterized by an additional parameter, e.g., by the "horizontal visibility" V_h.

To avoid the repeated time-consuming simulation computations of the 6S-code, a polynomial formulation of the dependence of the atmospheric transmittance and reflectance quantities on ϑ_S and V_h has been found for different choices of M_G and M_A by regression from individual data points obtained with the 6S-code:

$$\tau_{sd} = \tau_{sd}(\vartheta_S, M_G, M_A, V_h), \qquad \tau_{dd} = \tau_{dd}(\vartheta_S, M_G, M_A, V_h), \qquad \text{etc.} \qquad (12.11)$$

Inserting Equations (12.11) into (12.10) yields

$$p = p\,(\rho,\, E_S,\, \vartheta_S,\, M_G,\, M_A,\, V_h,\, a_0,\, a_1). \qquad (12.12)$$

Here, the quantities E_S, ϑ_S, a_0, and a_1, which are constant for the image, are known from external sources. M_G, M_A, and V_h are assumed to be constant for the image, but these parameters are unknown.

It is unrealistic to try to obtain these data from field observations and measurements (e.g., with radiosondes) during image acquisition in operational applications. Rather, the aim is to derive this information from the image itself. Such a method of calibration is called **radiometric self-calibration**.

The basic idea of an approach for radiometric self-calibration of remotely sensed images is outlined in Figure 12.5. The relationship between pixel values and terrain reflectance is not formulated for individual pixels, but for image objects. In analogy to Figure 12.3, a distinction is made here between image objects (in the image, with remote-sensing-specific attributes such as pixel values or reflectance values) and map objects (with application-specific attributes such as land-cover). Image objects are obtained by segmentation of an image. Initially, the various attributes of the image objects such as spectral characteristics (mean pixel vector) are image-dependent: The same object may have different attributes on two images (e.g., acquired at different dates). The **image-dependent** attributes are converted to **image-independent** attributes by transformations making use of a **geometric model** and a **radiometric model** of image acquisition (**georeferencing** and **radiometric calibration**). The transition to map objects with application-specific attributes is then accomplished by classification, which is a matching with map object prototypes in a knowledge base.

The main point now is the determination of the parameters of the radiometric model. According to the idea of radiometric self-calibration, this is tried by **simultaneous classification and radiometric model parameter estimation**: Starting from plausible initial values, the radiometric model parameters are varied systematically until a maximum match between image objects and prototype objects in the knowledge base is reached.

It should be pointed out that, in this method of simultaneous calibration and classification, comprehensive use of spectro-radiometric and structural image information can be made for both radiometric calibration and thematic image analysis. For example, shape properties of image objects may influence the radiometric parameters: If an image object, due to its rectangular shape with straight boundaries, is more likely to represent an agricultural field than a forest, this may have some bearing on the radiometric calibration.

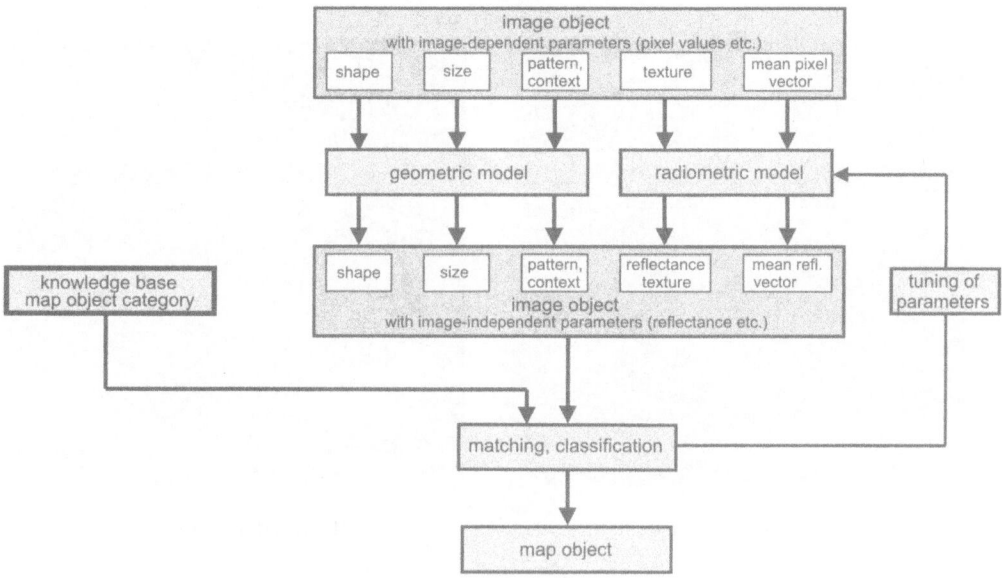

FIGURE 12.5. Simultaneous classification and radiometric calibration.

A simple version of this approach is the "dark-object" method, which tries to estimate V_h from the darkest pixels p_d in every spectral band, while making plausible assumptions on M_G and M_A according to the season of image acquisition and the region depicted. For these darkest pixels, one has, from Equation (12.12):

$$p_d = p\,(0,\, E_S,\, \vartheta_S,\, M_G,\, M_A,\, V_h,\, a_0,\, a_1). \qquad (12.13)$$

From these equations (one for every spectral band), V_h can be determined by least squares estimation. With this value, all pixel values of the image can be converted to terrain reflectance values by using Equation (12.10) or, equivalently, (12.12), i.e., the radiometric calibration can be performed.

Figure 12.6 illustrates the result of radiometric calibration for a part of a Landsat image from the border of Lower Austria and Styria in Austria. In this case, the influence of varying terrain illumination due to uneven terrain has been taken into account. A digital elevation model was used for this purpose. It can be seen that the big differences of the gray values of north-facing and south-facing slopes caused by different sun irradiance in the original image have been largely eliminated in the calibrated image. However, due to the coarse digital elevation model used (250-m raster width), radiometric deviations remain close to topographic discontinuities not resolved by the digital elevation model.

 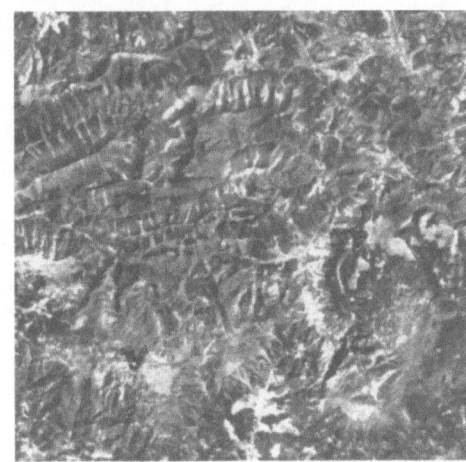

(a) Band 4 original   (b) Band 4 corrected

FIGURE 12.6. Landsat TM image of a region near Mürzzuschlag, Austria, original and radiometrically corrected.

12.2   Subpixel Analysis of Remotely Sensed Images

Conventional image classification techniques assume that all the pixels of an image are pure, i.e., that they represent an area of homogeneous cover of a single land-cover class. This assumption is not justified because there are many situations that lead to pixels having mixed spectral signature ("mixed pixels" or "mixels"), mainly as a consequence of the limited spatial resolution (large pixel size) of the sensor.

To alleviate the mixed pixel problem, two approaches can be taken: **Spectral subpixel analysis** treats every pixel separately, exploiting the spectral pixel pattern. Every pixel vector (whose elements are the pixel values in the different spectral bands) is assumed to be a linear combination of pure "prototype" pixel vectors known in advance. The proportions of the prototype pixels (ground-cover proportions) forming the mixed pixel are estimated. The second method, **spatial subpixel analysis**, will be described in detail here. It exploits the spatial pattern of pixels within a certain neighborhood of a pixel to be analyzed. Geometrically simple real-world situations are assumed, e.g., two homogeneous regions separated by a straight boundary. The real-world scenes are described by a small number of model parameters. Given the pixel distribution within an image window (e.g., a 3×3-cell), spatial subpixel analysis aims at deriving these parameters.

Figure 12.7 illustrates the idea behind spatial subpixel analysis. The aerial photo in the lower left of Figure 12.7 symbolizes the real-world scene from which a model description (two homogeneous regions delimited by a straight boundary) is derived. The parameters of every pixel in the multiband image are estimated from the pixel values of the 3×3 neighborhood. Each pixel value is given by a pixel vector containing the spectral values in the different bands.

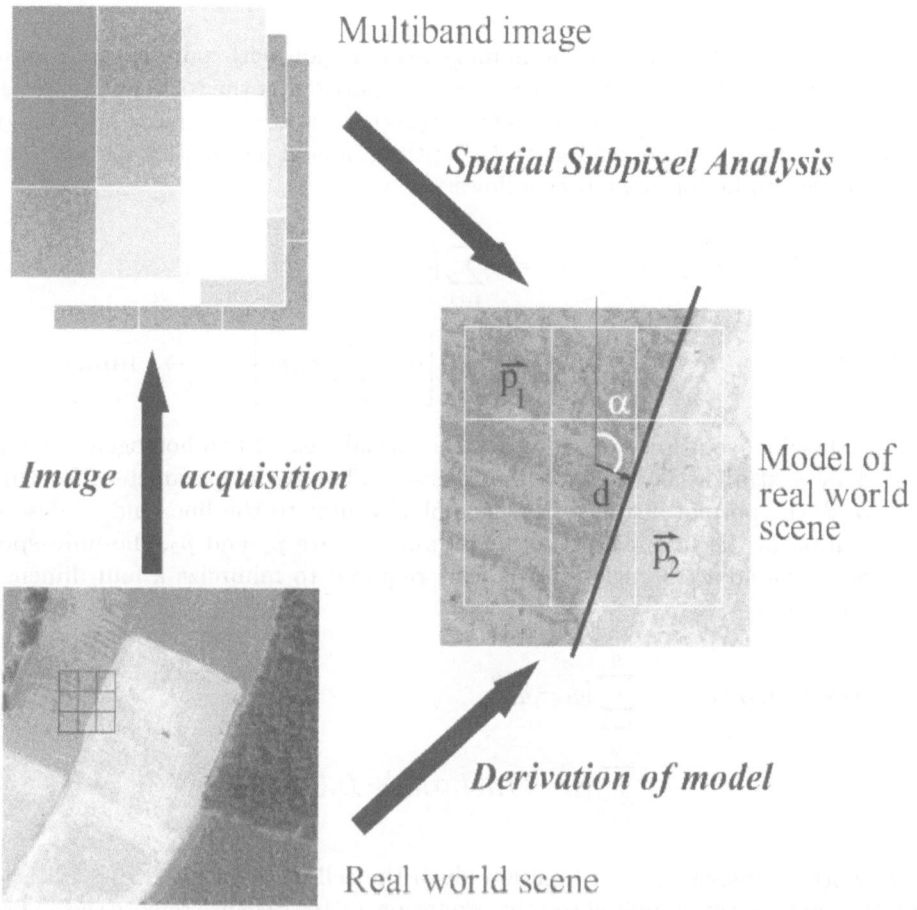

FIGURE 12.7. The relations between real-world scene, its model, and multiband image.

The following discussion is given for one spectral band only. The extension to multiband images is indicated later. In order to estimate the model parameters (spatial: $s_1, s_2, \cdots, s_r$, spectral: $p_1, p_2, \cdots, p_s$) from pixel values $(q_1, q_2, \cdots, q_n)$ in a given image window, a **generalized optimization problem** is formulated. n is the number of pixels in the cell, r is the number of spatial parameters, and s is the number of spectral parameters. In order to find a solution, it is necessary that $r + s < n$. The solution of the optimization problem is the set of estimated parameters giving the minimum error.

It is assumed that each pixel value in the image window is a linear mixture of the pure spectral pixel values $p_1, p_2, \cdots, p_s$. The pixel value q'_i derived according to the model from the estimated parameters is thus given by

$$q'_i = \sum_{k=1}^{s} f_{ki} p_k, \quad i = 1, \cdots, n. \tag{12.14}$$

The scalar f_{ki} gives the area of the homogeneous region with pure spectral value p_k within the pixel with true value q_i, measured as a portion on the total pixel area. Thus, f_{ki} are dependent of the spatial parameters $s_1, \cdots, s_r$ and $\sum_{k=1}^{s} f_{ki} = 1$ for any fixed i. The optimization problem leading to the optimal model parameters within a certain image window can be formulated as follows:

$$
\begin{aligned}
e(s1, \cdots, s_r, p1, \cdots, p_s) &= \sum_{i=1}^{n} [q_i - q'_i]^2 \\
&= \sum_{i=1}^{n} \left[q_i - \sum_{k=1}^{s} f_{ki} p_k \right]^2 \longrightarrow \textbf{min.} \tag{12.15}
\end{aligned}
$$

In the following, solution strategies for the special case of two homogeneous regions delimited by a straight boundary are discussed. The spatial parameters for this example are d, the normal distance from the pixel center to the line, and α, describing the orientation of the line. The spectral parameters are p_1 and p_2, the pure spectral signatures of the adjacent regions. It is thus required to minimize a four-dimensional error function $e(d, \alpha, p_1, p_2)$:

$$
\begin{aligned}
e(d, \alpha, p_1, p_2) &= \sum_{i=1}^{9} [q_i - q'_i]^2 \\
&= \sum_{i=1}^{9} [q_i - (f_{1i}(d, \alpha)p_1 + f_{2i}(d, \alpha)p_2)]^2 \longrightarrow \textbf{min.} \tag{12.16}
\end{aligned}
$$

Figure 12.8(b) displays an error function given the cell of Figure 12.8(a).

Iterative methods are required to solve Equation 12.16. Because remote sensing applications usually deal with large quantities of data, time-efficient strategies are necessary. One possibility of reducing computation time is to begin the optimization process with a **good starting point**. Assuming that long, straight boundaries exist, model parameters to start with may be derived from adjacent pixels where parameters have already been found. If no neighborhood information is available, a fast **neural net method** as described in [SS97, SS98] may also provide a good starting point. Ultimately, either a least-squares method as introduced in [Sch93] or a more time-efficient method involving direct search methods (Fibonacci search) (see [SS98]) is applicable to the solution of the optimization problem. A model is accepted if a minimum error is found that lies below a given threshold.

Object boundaries are hardly detectable in one band but very clearly detectable in others. Figures 12.9(a) and (b) show examples of objects that are distinguishable in only one band. A **multiband approach** helps in this situation: The minimum of

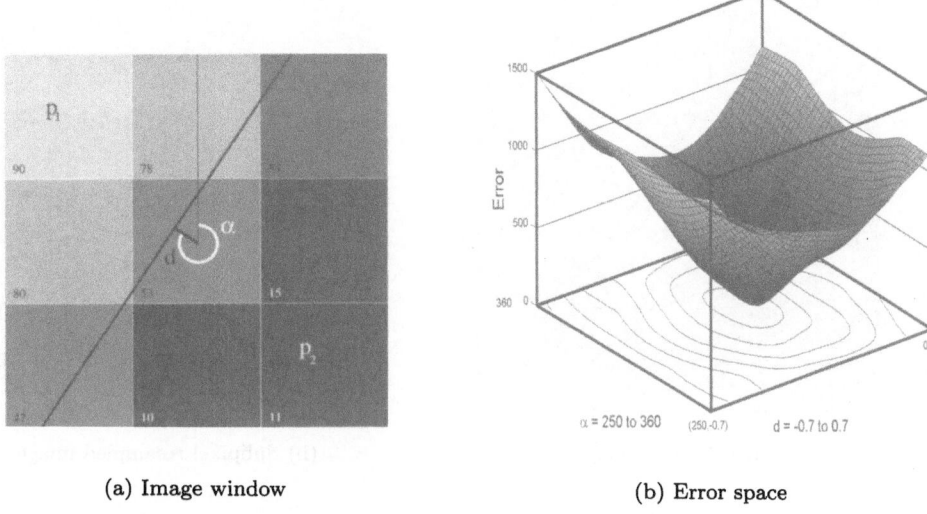

(a) Image window   (b) Error space

FIGURE 12.8. Example of an image window with optimal subpixel line and respective error space.

the error function $e(d, \alpha, p_1, p_2)$ (according to Equation (12.15)) is determined for the image windows of each band separately. The mean values of the spatial parameters are subsequently chosen as final spatial model parameters.

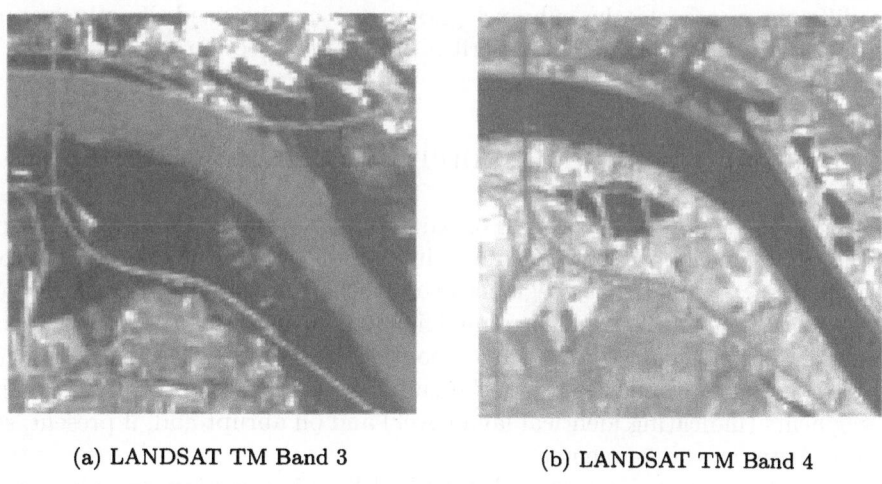

(a) LANDSAT TM Band 3   (b) LANDSAT TM Band 4

FIGURE 12.9. Different discernibility of segments in different bands.

The resultant spatial subpixel information can be used in different ways. The subpixel

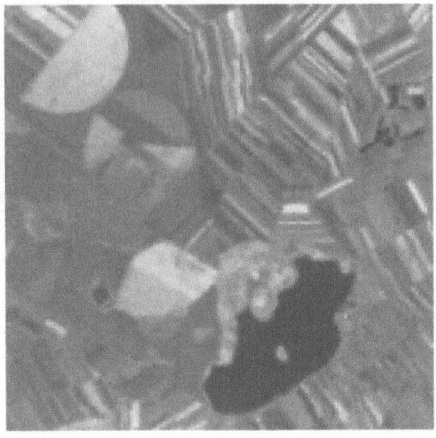

(a) Original image

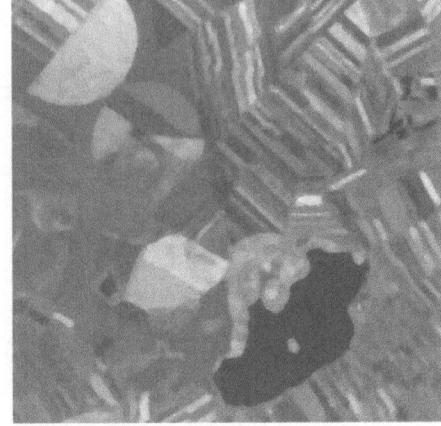

(b) Subpixel resampled image

FIGURE 12.10. Spatial subpixel analysis applied to LANDSAT TM image (only near-infrared band is shown).

parameters can be used to obtain an enhanced image by subpixel resampling. Figure 12.10 depicts an original LANDSAT TM image and the subpixel-resampled image. Each pixel is replaced by a $(k \times k)$ window. The pixels of the window obtain values according to the subpixel parameters. The resultant image is then used as input for further processing, e.g., for segmentation.

In a different approach, the subpixel parameters can be used directly in a special segmentation algorithm, as will be described in the next section.

12.3   Segmentation of Remotely Sensed Images

Segmentation in general is the process of partitioning an image into regions (segments, sets of adjacent pixels) having a meaning in the real world [HS93]. The criteria for selecting pixels to belong to one segment can be spectral or textural similarity, dissimilarity to other segments, geometric simplicity (smoothness) of the boundaries of the segments, or special thematic knowledge about the real-world objects one is interested in. In remote sensing applications, special emphasis is placed on spectral homogeneity of the segments (indicating identical land cover) and on abrupt and, if present, straight boundaries between the segments.

The segmentation process used and described here is a **region growing method**. This process is easily adaptable to multiband images and can be implemented with a variety of homogeneity criteria. Starting from an arbitrary seed pixel, pixels are added, if their spectral differences from the mean of the region existing so far is below a certain threshold. If a region stops growing, a new seed pixel is placed automatically in the

TABLE 12.1. Comparison of spectral parameters of segmented objects.

	Spectral mean values		
	Vector Segmentation	Raster Segmentation	Nominal Value
1	144.8	144.4	145.0
2	126.8	123.4	127.0
3	108.6	104.8	109.0
4	90.6	91.0	91.0
5	53.6	51.5	54.0
6	71.6	69.3	72.0
7	35.7	35.1	36.0

TABLE 12.2. Comparison of spatial parameters of segmented objects for vector and raster segmentation. The nominal values are: area = 115.5, perimeter = 47.

	Vector Segmentation		Raster Segmentation	
	Area	Perimeter	Area	Perimeter
1	114.4	47.1	112.0	46.0
2	113.2	49.2	108.0	54.0
3	111.8	47.4	113.0	60.0
4	112.9	47.6	96.0	44.0
5	113.0	48.0	118.0	56.0
6	112.0	47.4	114.0	62.0
7	111.0	45.7	99.0	60.0

image area not yet assigned to a segment. The main parameters for influencing the mean segment size are the thresholds controlling termination of the growing process. These thresholds specified for the individual spectral bands are adjusted in test runs.

The segmentation generates objects for which shape parameters (e.g., elongation, degree of fill of minimum bounding rectangle, area, perimeter), spectral parameters (mean pixel values), and textural parameters (entropy, energy) can be deduced. These parameters are used for land-cover classification (see Section 12.4), but also for deducing other information, e.g., ecologically relevant attributes of landscape elements represented by the regions.

To achieve segmentation with subpixel accuracy, the region growing algorithm is modified. In addition to the homogeneity criterion, an unconditional stop of the growing process is introduced at pixels for which subpixel parameters have been found in a preceding analysis step. The segment boundaries are then defined in vector form based on the subpixel parameters. The method is termed *vector segmentation* [SSS98].

Apart from alleviating the mixed pixel problem, segments obtained by vector segmentation allow a more reliable determination of shape parameters.

Figure 12.11(a) is a synthetic image displaying a rectangular object and rotated copies with different gray values. This image is segmented by conventional region growing and

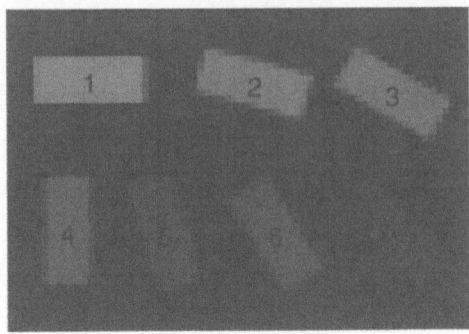

(a) Synthetic image

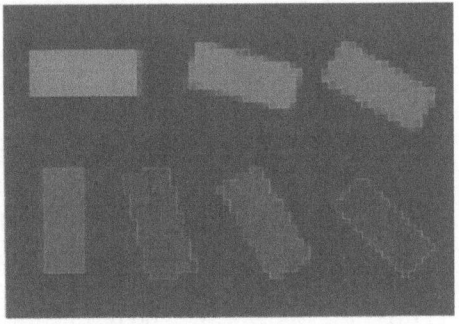

(b) Synthetic image with conventional region growing borders

(c) Synthetic image with vector segmentation borders

FIGURE 12.11. Segmented synthetic image.

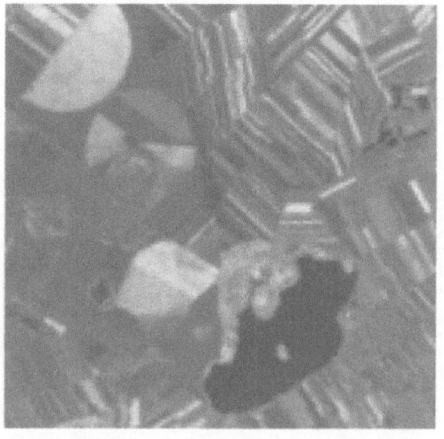 

(a) Original LANDSAT TM (band 4)   (b) LANDSAT TM with vector segmentation

FIGURE 12.12. LANDSAT TM (band 4) and vector segmentation results

by vector segmentation.

Spectral parameters (mean value) and spatial parameters (area and perimeter) of the resultant regions are compared and displayed in Tables 12.1 and 12.2. The parameters of the vector segmentation show a significantly lower deviation from the nominal values compared to the results of the conventional region growing. This example demonstrates the strong distortion of some shape parameters in the case of raster segmentation.

Figure 12.12 shows a LANDSAT TM (band 4) scene with the vector segmentation result superimposed.

12.4   Land-Cover Classification

Land-cover maps and land-use maps are required for many applications such as regional planning, landscape ecology and landscape planning, agricultural management, and forestry.

Land-cover refers to the actual material present on the ground and to the real biophysical conditions of the terrain surface, while land-use includes aspects of the economic and cultural use of the surfaces. For example, a piece of land being composed of land-cover types gravel, concrete, tarmac, vegetated area, and buildings may represent land use type settlement area or industrial area. A clear felling area in a forest may represent land-cover grassland, while its land use is forest. A forest road may be land-cover gravel, while land use is forest, and so on.

Remote sensing can only provide information on land-cover in the first step. Generic knowledge on the spectral characteristics of land-cover types is available for the classi-

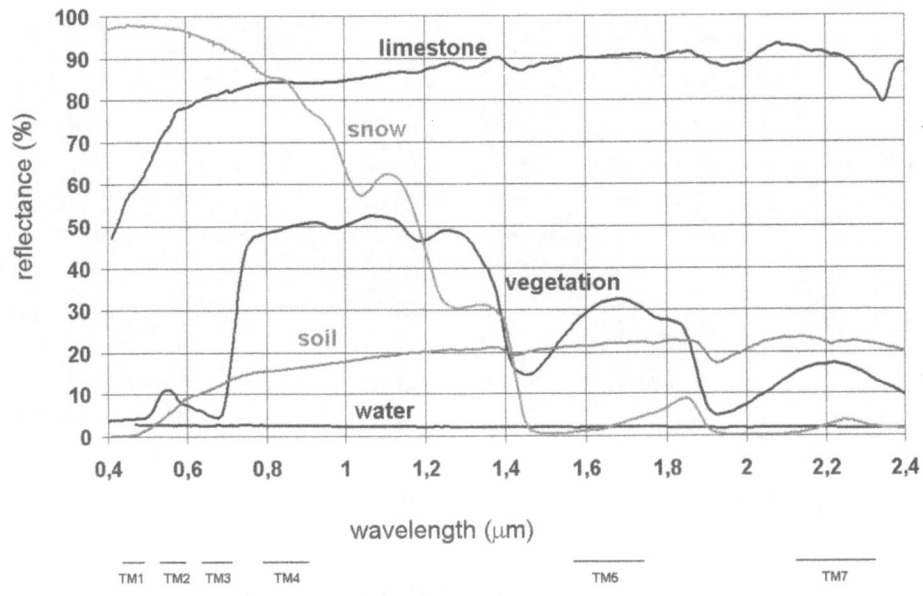

FIGURE 12.13. Spectral reflectance curves of typical land-surface objects.

fication of segments in the radiometrically calibrated image. The coordinate axes represent brightness, wetness, and greenness of the objects on the Earth surface, providing important information about objects. Figure 12.13 shows the spectral reflectance of land-cover categories in the wavelength range from 400 nm to 2400 nm, together with the peak sensitivity of the spectral bands of the satellite sensor LANDSAT TM, TM1, TM2, TM3 (blue, green, red), TM4 (near infrared), TM5, TM7 (midinfrared), TM 6 (thermal infrared).

The following generic rules for classification can immediately be seen from the figure:

- Snow and limestone have a reflectance above 40% in TM3.

- The ratio of reflectances in TM4 and TM3, ρ_4/ρ_3, is positive for limestone and negative for snow.

- Water, soil, and vegetation have reflectance values below 40% in TM3.

- The ratio of reflectances in TM4 and TM3, ρ_4/ρ_3, is negative for water, has small positive values for soil, and is large (above 2.0) for vegetation.

These rules can be formulated in a decision tree classifier (see [SS99]).

In addition to spectro-radiometric knowledge, shape and texture rules can be included in the decision tree (e.g., agricultural parcels are characterized by segments of predominantly rectangular shape with straight boundaries, while grassland exhibits more irregular boundaries).

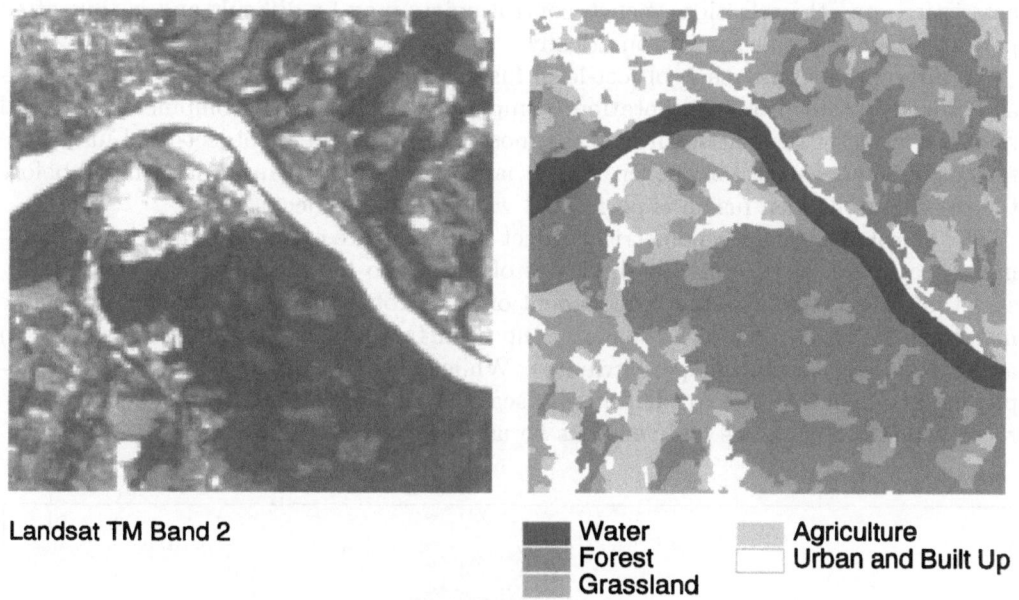

Landsat TM Band 2

- ■ Water
- ■ Forest
- ■ Grassland
- ▨ Agriculture
- ☐ Urban and Built Up

FIGURE 12.14. Classified Landsat TM scene.

An example for land-cover classification based on this method is illustrated in Figure 12.14.

A **land-cover** map can be transformed into a **land-use** map by applying expert knowledge on land use. In many cases, data from additional sources will be necessary for this, e.g., from a digital elevation model, existing maps and GIS data sets (e.g., with administrative boundaries), and the like. This topic is, however, beyond the scope of this book.

12.5   Information Fusion for Remote Sensing

In addition to the application-independent benefits of fusion (as discussed in chapter 11), the combination of data from different acquisition dates and sensors is important in remote sensing, e.g., for

- the interpretation of land-cover types with multiseasonal data showing different states of phenology,

- the detection of land-cover changes during several years, and

- the combination of land-cover data with other data such as cadastral maps.

Traditionally, in a first step, multiple remote sensing data sets are registered using control points. Due to differences in viewing angle, resolution, illumination, sensor characteristics, etc., the selection of such control points may be difficult and is thus often performed manually or semiautomatically.

An alternative approach is object-level fusion [SB97]. Instead of raster images, image objects obtained by segmentation (compare Figure 12.3) are combined. In optical remote sensing of the Earth surface, the most useful objects for object-level fusion are regions of homogeneous land cover. If their land cover already can be determined before the combination, then fusion is performed with the map objects.

The morphological and geometrical object attributes are matched to find corresponding object pairs. Depending on the types of images to be matched, it may be necessary that these attributes are independent of scale, rotation, and translation to enable matching. In figure 12.15, two regions (one from Landsat TM and one from IRS-1C) are shown with certain shape attributes. While pixel-count and perimeter are completely incomparable due to the different scale of the original images, others fulfill the requirement of invariance and can thus be used in matching.

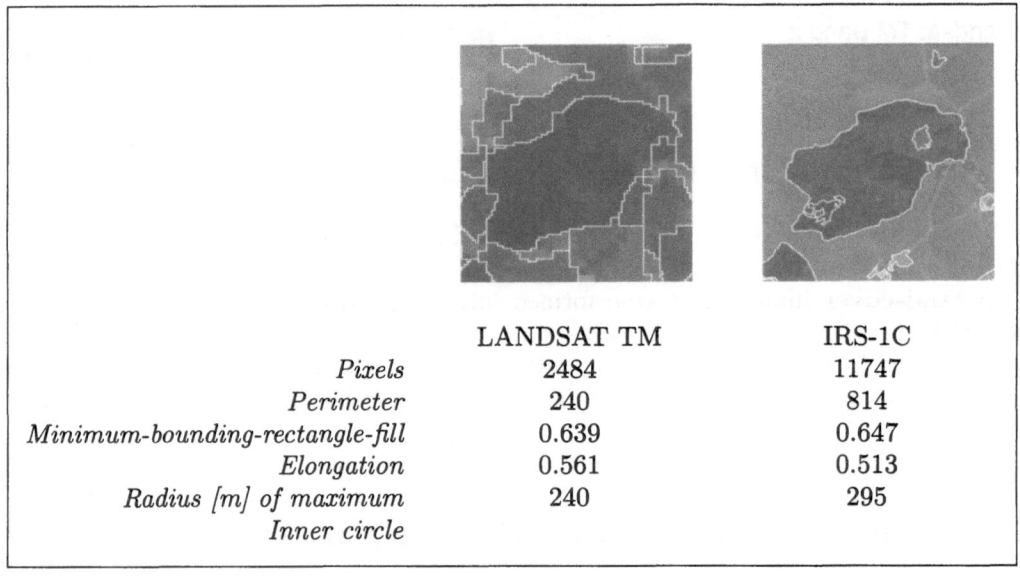

	LANDSAT TM	IRS-1C
Pixels	2484	11747
Perimeter	240	814
Minimum-bounding-rectangle-fill	0.639	0.647
Elongation	0.561	0.513
Radius [m] of maximum Inner circle	240	295

FIGURE 12.15. Regions and their shape attributes.

After matching image objects, the information on correspondences may be used in different ways. One possibility is to derive the geometric transformation parameters between the coordinate systems of the original images. The matched pairs of image objects are thus used as control point pairs. The images may then be registered relative to each other, and subsequent fusion may be performed on a pixel level.

Another approach is to remain on the image object level, e.g., with a list data structure, and to combine attributes of corresponding image objects from different image sources (object-level fusion).

If one data source to be fused is available in vector format, then object-level fusion is most appropriate. An example of interest for agricultural subsidies control is the fusion of satellite image data and a cadastral map [BPCP96]. Agricultural fields with crop-type attributes are identified on the (unregistered) image with an edge detector and a line connecting tool. This information may then be fused with a cadastral map by matching the line segments (see Figure 12.16) and integrating the crop data into the land owner database.

FIGURE 12.16. Matching of line segments from the cadaster (in white) and from the image (in black).

References

[Alo90]   J. Aloimonos. Purposive and qualitative active vision. In *International Conference on Pattern Recognition*, 346–360, 1990.

[Alo91]   J. Aloimonos. Purposive and qualitative active vision. *Artificial Intelligence and Computer Vision*, 455–464, 1991.

[AS89]   J. Aloimonos and D. Shulman. *Integration of Visual Modules: An Extension of the Marr Paradigm*. Academic Press, 1989.

[AWB87]   J. Aloimonos, I. Weiss, and A. Bandyopadhyay. Active vision. In *Proc. 1st ICCV*, 35–54. IEEE Comp. Soc. Press, 1987.

[Bai95]   L. Baird. Residual algorithms: Reinforcement learning with function approximation. In *12th International Conference on Machine Learning*, pages 30–37, 1995.

[Baj88]   R. Bajcsy. Active perception. *Proc. of the IEEE*, 76(8):996–1005, 1988.

[BE92]   H.H. Bülthoff and S. Edelman. Psychophysical support for a 2-D view interpolation theory of object recognition. In *Proc. of the National Academy of Science*, vol. 89, 60–64, 1992.

[BG95]   G. Bradski and S. Grossberg. Fast learning VIEWNET architectures for recognizing three-dimensional objects from multiple two-dimensional views. *Neural Networks*, 8(7/8):1053–1089, 1995.

[BH89]   P. Baldi and K. Hornik. Neural networks and principal components analysis: Learning from examples without local minima. *Neural Networks*, 2:52–58, 1989.

[Bie85]   I. Biederman. Human image understanding: Recent research and a theory. *Computer Vision, Graphics, and Image Processing*, 32:29–37, 1985.

[Bie87]   I. Biederman. Recognition-by-components: A theory of human image understanding. *Psychological Review*, 2(94):115–147, 1987.

[BK88]   H. Bourlard and Y. Kamp. Auto-association by multilayer perceptrons and singular value decomposition. *Biological Cybernetics*, 59:291–294, 1988.

[BL88]   D.S. Broomhead and D. Lowe. Multivariable functional interpolation and adaptive networks. *Complex Systems*, 2:321–355, 1988.

[Blo97]   I. Bloch. Fuzzy relative position between objects in image processing: A morphological approach. Technical report, E.N.S.T (Ecole Nationale Superieure des Telecommunications), 1997.

[BP97]   R. Brunelli and T. Poggio. Template matching: Matched spatial filters and beyond. *Pattern Recognition*, 30(5):751–768, 1997.

[BPB98]   H. Borotschnig, A. Pinz, and I. Bloch. Fuzzy Relaxation Labeling Reconsidered. In *Proc. IEEE World Congress on Computational Intelligence (FUZZ-IEEE section)*, 1417–1423, 1998.

[BPCP96]   R. Bartl, M. Petrou, W.J. Christmas, and P.L. Palmer. On the automatic registration of cadastral maps and Landsat TM images. In J. Desachy, editor, *Proc. Image and Signal Processing for Remote Sensing III, European Symposium on Satellite Remote Sensing*, SPIE 2955, 9–20, 1996.

[BPPP98a]   H. Borotschnig, L. Paletta, M. Prantl, and A. Pinz. Active object recognition in parametric eigenspace. In *Proc. 9th British Machine Vision Conference*, vol. 2, 629–638, 1998.

[BPPPnt]   H. Borotschnig, L. Paletta, M. Prantl, and A. Pinz. A comparison of probabilistic, possibilistic and evidence theoretic fusion schemes for active object recognition. *Computing*, 62:293-319, 1999.

[Bri90]   J.S. Bridle. Probabilistic interpretation of feedforward classification network outputs, with relationships to statistical pattern recognition. In F. Fogelman Soulie and J. Herault, editors, *Neurocomputing: Algorithms, Architectures and Applications*, 227–236. Springer-Verlag, New York, 1990.

[BVB+96]   C. Bandera, F.J. Vico, J.M. Bravo, M.E. Harmon, and L.C. Baird III. Residual Q-learning applied to visual attention. In *13th International Conference on Machine Learning*, 20–27, 1996.

[BWR93]   J.B. Burns, R.S. Weiss, and E.M. Riseman. View variation of point-set and line-segment features. *IEEE Transactions on Pattern Analysis and Machine Intelligence*, 15(1):51–68, 1993.

[CF82]   I. Chakravarty and H. Freeman. Characteristic views as a basis for three-dimensional object recognition. In *SPIE (Robot Vision)*, vol. 336, 37–45, 1982.

[CF96]   F.G. Callari and F.P. Ferrie. Autonomous recognition: Driven by ambiguity. In *Proc. Int. Conf. Computer Vision and Pattern Recognition*, 701–707, 1996.

[CJ91]   D.T. Clemens and D.W. Jacobs. Space and time bounds on model indexing. *IEEE Transactions on Pattern Analysis and Machine Intelligence*, 13(10):1007–1018, 1991.

[DCB+89] B.A. Draper, R.T. Collins, J. Brolio, A.R. Hanson, and E.M. Riseman. The schema system. *Int. J. Computer Vision*, 2(3):209–250, 1989.

[DCTO94] S.J. Dickinson, H.I. Christensen, J. Tsotsos, and G. Olofsson. Active object recognition integrating attention and viewpoint control. In J.-O. Eklundh, editor, *Computer Vision–ECCV'94*, vol. 801 of *Lecture Notes in Computer Science*, 3–14. Springer-Verlag, Berlin, Heidelberg, 1994.

[DPR92a] S.J. Dickinson, A.P. Pentland, and A. Rosenfeld. 3-D shape recovery using distributed aspect matching. *IEEE Transactions on Pattern Analysis and Machine Intelligence*, 14(2):174–198, February 1992.

[DPR92b] S.J. Dickinson, A.P. Pentland, and A. Rosenfeld. From Vvolumes to views: An approach to 3-D object recognition. *Computer Vision, Graphics, and Image Processing*, 55(2):130–154, March 1992.

[Dra97] B.A. Draper. Learning control strategies for object recognition. In K. Ikeuchi and M. Veloso, editors, *Symbolic Visual Learning*, chapter 3, 49–76. Oxford University Press, New York, 1997.

[EBD92] D. Eggert, K. Bowyer, and C. Dyer. Aspect graphs: State-of-the-art and applications in digital photogrammetry. In *Proc. 17th Congress of the Int. Society for Photogrammetry and Remote Sensing*, 1992.

[EBD+93] D. Eggert, K. Bowyer, C. Dyer, H.I. Christensen, and D.B. Goldgof. The scale space aspect graph. *IEEE Transactions on Pattern Analysis and Machine Intelligence*, 15(11):1114–1129, November 1993.

[Ede97] S. Edelman. Computational theories of object recognition. *Trends in Cognitive Science*, 1997.

[EI97] S. Edelman and N. Intrator. Learning as extraction of low-dimensional representations. To appear in D. Medin, R. Goldstone, and P. Schyns, editors. Mechanisms of Perceptual Learning, 1997. Also available at http://eris.wisdom.weizmann.ac.il/~edelman/abstracts.html.

[Fuk90] K. Fukunaga. *Introduction to Statistical Pattern Recognition*. Academic Press, New York, 1990.

[GI94] K.D. Gremban and K. Ikeuchi. Planning multiple observations for object recognition. *Int. J. of Computer Vision*, 12(2/3):137–172, 1994.

[Hag90] G.D. Hager. *Task-Directed Sensor Fusion and Planning*. Kluwer Academic Publishers, 1990.

[HK92] S.A. Hutchinson and A.C. Kak. Multisensor strategies using Dempster-Shafer belief accumulation. In M.A. Abidi and R.C. Gonzalez, editors, *Data Fusion in Robotics and Machine Intelligence*, chapter 4, 165–209. Academic Press, 1992.

[HS93]   R.M. Haralick and L.G. Shapiro. *Computer and Robot Vision II*. Addison-Wesley, 1993.

[KF88]   G.J. Klir and T.A. Folger. *Fuzzy Sets, Uncertainty, and Information*. Prentice Hall, 1988.

[KLP98]   S. Kovačič, A. Leonardis, and F. Pernuš. Planning sequences of views for 3-D object recognition and pose determination. *Pattern Recognition*, 31(10):1407–1417 1998.

[KM96]   L.P. Kaelbling and A.W. Moore. Reinforcement learning: A survey. *Journal of Artificial Intelligence Research*, 4:237–285, 1996.

[KWM99]   I. Kanellopoulos, G.G. Wilkinson, and T. Moons, editors. *Machine Vision and Advanced Image Processing in Remote Sensing*. Springer, 1999.

[Lin93]   J.C. Lin. Universal principal axes: An easy-to-construct tool useful in defining shape orientations for almost every kind of shape. *Pattern Recognition*, 26(4):485–493, 1993.

[Low95]   D. Lowe. Radial basis function networks. In M.A. Arbib, editor, *The Handbook of Brain Theory and Neural Networks*, 779–782. MIT Press, Cambridge, MA, 1995.

[LVHP94]   N.K. Logothetis, T. Vetter, A. Hurlbert, and T. Poggio. View-based models of 3D object recognition and class-specific invariances. Technical Report, AI Memo No.1472, MIT Artifial Intelligence Laboratory, April 1994.

[MB93]   J. Maver and R. Bajcsy. Occlusions as guide for planning the next view. *IEEE Transactions on Pattern Analysis and Machine Intelligence*, 15(5):417–433, May 1993.

[MH90]   T. Matsuyama and V. Shang-Shouq Hwang. *SIGMA: A Knowledge-Based Aerial Image Understanding System*. Advances in Computer Vision and Machine Intelligence. Plenum Press, 1990.

[MN94]   H. Murase and S.K. Nayar. Illumination planning for object recognition. *IEEE Transactions on Pattern Analysis and Machine Intelligence*, 16(12):1219–1227, 1994.

[MN95]   H. Murase and S.K. Nayar. Visual learning and recognition of 3-D objects from appearance. *Int. J. of Computer Vision*, 14(1):5–24, January 1995.

[MP97]   B. Moghaddam and A. Pentland. Probabilistic visual learning for object recognition. *IEEE Transactions on Pattern Analysis and Machine Intelligence*, 19(7):696–710, July 1997.

[Oja83]   E. Oja. *Subspace Methods of Pattern Recognition*. Research Studies Press, Hertfordshire, 1983.

[Oja92]   E. Oja. Principal components, minor components, and linear neural networks. *Neural Networks*, 5:927–935, 1992.

[PA98]   A. Pinz and J.-P. Andreu. Qualitative spatial reasoning to infer the camera position in generic object recognition. In *Proc. ICPR'98*, vol. I, 770–773, 1998.

[PB98]   J. Peng and B. Bhanu. Closed-loop object recognition using reinforcement learning. *IEEE Transactions on Pattern Analysis and Machine Intelligence*, 20(2):139–154, February 1998.

[PBDK98]   A. Pinz, St. Bernögger, P. Datlinger, and A. Kruger. Mapping the human retina. *IEEE Transactions on Medical Imaging*, 17(4):606–619, 1998.

[PBG+96]   M. Prantl, H. Borotschnig, H. Ganster, D. Sinclair, and A. Pinz. Object recognition by active fusion. In *Intelligent Robots and Computer Vision XV: Algorithms, Techniques, Active Vision, and Materials Handling*, vol. 2904, 320–330. SPIE, 1996.

[PBL96]   J. Pauls, E. Bricolo, and N. Logothetis. View invariant representations in monkey temporal cortex: Position, scale, and rotational invariance. In S.K. Nayar and T. Poggio, editors, *Early Visual Learning*, 9–41. Oxford University Press, 1996.

[PE90]   T. Poggio and S. Edelman. A network that learns to recognize three-dimensional objects. *Nature*, 317:314–319, 1990.

[PGP96]   M. Prantl, H. Ganster, and A. Pinz. Active fusion using Bayesian networks applied to multitemporal remote sensing imagery. In *Proc. ICPR'96*, vol. III, 890–894, 1996.

[Pin89]   A. Pinz. Final results of the vision expert system VES: Finding trees in aerial photographs. In A. Pinz, editor, *Wissensbasierte Mustererkennung*, vol. 49 of *OCG-Schriftenreihe*, 90–111. Oldenbourg, 1989.

[PPG95]   A. Pinz, M. Prantl, and H. Ganster. A robust affine matching algorithm using an exponentially decreasing distance function. *Journal of Universal Computer Science*, 1(8), Springer, 1995. Available at http://hyperg.tu-graz.ac.at.

[PPGB96]   A. Pinz, M. Prantl, H. Ganster, and H. Borotschnig. Active fusion–A new method applied to remote sensing image interpretation. *Pattern Recognition Letters*, 17(13):1349–1359, 1996. Special issue on Soft Computing in Remote Sensing Data Analysis.

[PPP98]   L. Paletta, M. Prantl, and A. Pinz. Reinforcement learning for autonomous three-dimensional object recognition. In *Proc. 6th Symposium on Intelligent Robotic Systems*, 63–72. Edinburgh, UK, 1998.

[Put94]   M.L. Puterman. *Markov Decision Processes*. John Wiley and Sons, New York, 1994.

[RA97]   S. Ranganath and K. Arun. Face recognition using transform features and neural networks. *Pattern Recognition*, 30(10):1615–1622, 1997.

[Rao97]   R.P.N. Rao. Dynamic appearance-based recognition. In *Conference on Computer Vision and Pattern Recognition*, 540–546, 1997.

[RAR91]   E. Rivlin, J. Aloimonos, and A. Rosenfeld. Purposive recognition: an active and qualitative approach. In *SPIE 1611 Sensor Fusion IV*, vol. 1611, 225–240, 1991.

[RB94]   R.D. Rimey and C.M. Brown. Control of selective perception using Bayes nets and decision theory. *Int. J. of Computer Vision*, 12:173–207, 1994.

[RBK98]   H.A. Rowley, S. Baluja, and T. Kanade. Neural network-based face detection. *IEEE Transactions on Pattern Analysis and Machine Intelligence*, 20(1):23–38, January 1998.

[RHW86]   D. Rumelhart, G. Hinton, and R. Williams. Learning representations by back-propagating errors. *Nature*, 323:533–536, 9 October 1986.

[San89]   T.D. Sanger. Optimal unsupervised learning in a single-layer linear feedforward neural network. *Neural Networks*, 12:459–473, 1989.

[SB97]   W. Schneider and R. Bartl. Image information fusion in remote sensing: Towards a framework and a consistent terminology. In *Proc. Expert Meeting on Satellite Data Fusion Techniques for Forest and Land Use Assessment*, 16–25. FELIS, Freiburg, Germany, 1997.

[SB98]   R.S. Sutton and A.G. Barto. *Reinforcement Learning*. The MIT Press, Cambridge, Massachusetts, 1998.

[SC97]   B. Schiele and J.L. Crowley. Transinformation of object recognition and its application to viewpoint planning. *Robotics and Autonomous Systems*, 21(1):95–106, 1997.

[SC98]   M.A. Sipe and D. Casasent. Global feature space neural network for active computer vision. *Neural Computation and Applications*, 7(3), 1998.

[Sch93]   W. Schneider. Landuse mapping with subpixel accuracy from Landsat TM image data. In *Remote Sensing and Global Environmental Change, Proc. of the 25th ERIM Symposium*, vol. II, 155–161, 1993.

[SK94]   P. Smets and R. Kennes. The transferable belief model. *Artificial Intelligence*, 66:191–234, 1994.

[SS97]   J. Steinwendner and W. Schneider. A neural net approach to spatial sub-pixel analysis in remote sensing. In W. Burger and M. Burge, editors, *Pattern Recognition 1997, Proc. 21st ÖAGM Workshop, Hallstatt, Austria*, OCG-Schriftenreihe, 265–274, 1997.

[SS98]   J. Steinwendner and W. Schneider. Algorithmic improvements in spatial subpixel analysis of remote sensing images. In Ernst Schuster, editor, *Pattern Recognition and Medical Computer Vision 1998, Proc. of 22nd ÖAGM Workshop, Illmitz, Austria*, OCG-Schriftenreihe, 205–213, 1998.

[SS99]   J. Steinwendner and W. Schneider. Radiometric self-calibration of remote sensing images for generic-knowledge-based image analysis. In M. Vincze, editor, *Robust Vision for Industrial Applications, Proc. of the 23rd ÖAGM Workshop, Steyr, Austria*, OCG-Schriftenreihe, 69–78, 1999.

[SSS98]   J. Steinwendner, W. Schneider, and F. Suppan. Vector segmentation using multiband spatial subpixel analysis for object extraction. *International Archives of Photogrammetry and Remote Sensing*, XXXII(Part 3/1):265–271, 1998.

[SW92]   M. Seibert and A.M. Waxman. Adaptive 3-D object recognition from multiple views. *IEEE Transactions on Pattern Analysis and Machine Intelligence*, 14(2):107–124, 1992.

[TAT95]   K.A. Tarabanis, P.K. Allen, and R.Y. Tsai. A survey of sensor planning in computer vision. *IEEE Transactions on Robotics and Automation*, 11(1):86–104, February 1995.

[TDR94]   E. Trucco, M. Diprima, and V. Roberto. Visibility scripts for active feature-based inspection. *Pattern Recognition Letters*, 15:1151–1164, November 1994.

[TVJD95]   H.D. Tagare, F.M. Vos, C.C. Jaffe, and J.S. Duncan. Arrangement: A spatial relation between parts for evaluating similarity of tomographic section. *IEEE Transactions on Pattern Analysis and Machine Intelligence*, 17(9):880–893, September 1995.

[UB91]   S. Ullman and R. Basri. Recognition by linear combination of models. *IEEE Transactions on Pattern Analysis and Machine Intelligence*, 13(10):992–1006, 1991.

[V+97]   E. Vermote et al. *Second Simulation of the Satellite Signal in the Solar Spectrum (6S)*. Université des Sciences et Technologies de Lille, 1997. Vers. 2.

[Wat89]   C.J.C.H. Watkins. *Learning from Delayed Rewards*. Ph.D. thesis, Cambridge University, 1989.

[WB91]   S.D. Whitehead and D.H. Ballard. Learning to perceive and act by trial and error. *Machine Learning*, 7:45–83, 1991.

[WD92]   C.J.C.H. Watkins and P. Dayan. Q-learning. *Machine Learning*, 8(3):279–292, 1992.

[Wol98]   W.L. Wolfe. *Introduction to Radiometry*, vol. TT29 of *Tutorial Texts in Optical Engineering*. SPIE, 1998.

[ZM94]   M. Zerroug and G. Medioni. The challenge of generic object recognition. In *Object Representation in Computer Vision*, vol. 994 of *Lecture Notes in Computer Science*, 217–232, 1994.

Part V

3D Reconstruction

Introduction to Part V

One central topic of digital image processing is the calculation of three-dimensional (3D) information from two-dimensional (2D) camera data. Depending on the object type, different sensors will be used and the structure of the desired result, i.e., the description method, will differ considerably. Here is an (incomplete) list of applications of 3D reconstruction:

- **Mapping:** The object is the Earth's surface with topographic objects, and the images are taken from aircraft with almost parallel viewing directions (vertical stereo). Depending on the image scale (the ratio of flying height and focal length), one can distinguish "small-scale" aerial images from "large-scale" aerial images. Small-image scales, e.g., 1:30 000, are used for the production of small-scale topographic maps. For these applications, the Earth's surface can be assumed to be smooth, and artificial objects such as buildings are to be plotted in a symbolic form. Large image scales, e.g., 1:4000 are used for the production of precise topographic maps, urban GIS data, or 3D city models. In these applications, man-made objects can be plotted accurately in three dimensions.

- **Architecture:** The object to be reconstructed is a building, especially its façades. The photographs are taken from viewpoints on the Earth's surface ("terrestrial photos"), and the result can be used, e.g.,for reconstruction purposes, damage documentation, or virtual reality models. The representation of this class of objects is task-dependent. However, in general, a 3D representation will be required. Reconstruction has to handle severe problems such as low texture, occlusions, and shadows.

- **Construction:** Deformation analysis is an important topic in construction control. It can be performed by theodolite-mounted CCD cameras. In road/railway construction, mining, and tunnel construction, 3D measurement techniques based on computer vision start to become relevant for planning and quality control.

- **Medicine:** The object is the human body or a part of it, which is photographed from several viewpoints in a close-range setup. Again, true 3D representations are necessary in many cases.

- **Industrial applications:** Three-dimensional reconstruction methods in industrial environments are a quickly growing field. The applications in the following list comprise only a small fraction of the potential set:

  - Quality and/or process control within an industrial production line (e.g., rails, turbine blades, crank shafts, timber manufacturing, car bodies).

– Determination of 3D geometries of metallic objects.

– Target tracking, surveillance, motion detection, and navigation.

All these applications are based on camaras that operate analogous to our human eye, and the system of cameras and software simulate the human biology.

First we consider the human visual mechanism. The inmost membrane of the eye is the retina. When the eye is properly focused, light reflected by objects outside the eyes is imaged on the retina. Over the surface of the retina 110 million to 125 million discrete light receptors (divided in cones and rods) are distributed. The 4 million to 7 million cones are located primarily in the central portion of the retina, called *fovea centralis*, and are highly sensitive to color. We can distinguish three types of pigments that are sensitive for the red, green, and blue parts of the light spectrum. Cone vision is known as the em photopic- or *bright-light vision*. The many rods are not involved in color vision but are sensitive to low levels of illumination. Rod vision is known as the *scotopic-* or *dim-light vision*.

After the perception of light with cones and rods our brain has to interpret the image of our surrounded world. So human visual perception is a complex interaction between the two eyes and different regions of the brain and is composed of three actions:

• perception of shape and color,

• 3D perception, and

• perception of motion.

The perception of color is a sense, not a physical property of objects. It is an effect of electromagnetic waves in our consciousness. Therefore theory of color is an inter-disciplinary field between physics (composition of electromagnetic waves of the light stimulus), physiology, and psychology (response of our visual system to light stimulus). Today two concepts explain the physiology of color vision. These theories and the use of color information for decision making in surface reconstruction are described in Section 17.4.

The 3D perception is the result of the perception of two eyes. Similar to the human visual system, it is possible to generate 3D spatial information from the data of two or more cameras that, from different positions, view the same scene. The exact functionality of this process within the human brain is a yet-unsolved problem. From the mathematical point of view, a camera provides the projection of visual 3D information onto the 2D image space. Attempts to simulate the human biology using two cameras and software have not been very successful. However, for industrial automation tasks and mapping using remote sensing images, specific solutions can be developed that are robust enough for the respective application. Geometrical camera calibration and orientation are essential for each accurate measurement task as it defines the geometrical description of a lens-camera system with respect to the outside world (using "ground truth data" as a basis), which, as a consequence, also allows the fusion between different sensors. Most sensors provide accurate 3D information, but the geometry of the points can be rather complex, depending on the surface viewed (consider a tree, for example). In order to obtain a data description that is usable for further processing, such as making a CAD model of an existing part, consistent modeling or approximation of the surface by primitives becomes necessary.

Therefore, 3D reconstruction can be seen as a process of two stages:

1. Getting individual 3D points (ordered or not, directly from the sensor or as a result of complex image processing) and

2. Deriving a surface model that is usable for the respective measurement task.

The fundamentals of 3D reconstruction from multiple views will be described in Chapter 13. In that Chapter, an overview about sensors that can be used for reconstruction purposes will be given, as well as the fundamental mathematical relationships between 3D object space and 2D image space. In addition, basic principles of object surface modeling will be dealt with. The basic problem that has to be solved in 3D reconstruction is the correspondence problem: In order to reconstruct 3D points, two or more **homologous** (corresponding) points from different images have to be found. An overview of these **matching techniques** can be found in Chapter 14. After that, three sections will deal with specific algorithms and setups for 3D reconstruction from the point of view of three different sciences:

- **Photogrammetry:** High-precision measurement of targeted points and 3D reconstruction from more than two images for photogrammetric purposes are described in Chapter 15. Photogrammetric applications, especially mapping, are often characterized by the enormous amount of image data that has to be handled.

- **Computer vision:** In Chapter 16, algorithms for 3D stereo reconstruction and navigation based on video or CCD cameras will be presented.

- **Engineering geodesy:** In engineering geodesy, video theodolites are applied as sensors to automate 3D reconstruction tasks. Three-dimensional object reconstruction using video theodolites will be dealt with in Chapter 17.

13

Fundamentals

Franz Rottensteiner
Gerhard Paar
Wolfgang Pölzleitner

The large number of 3D reconstruction applications yields an equally large number of approaches to the solution of that problem. These approaches differ in both the instruments and the algorithms used. However, the basic mathematical models are quite similar as they describe the imaging geometry. In this Chapter, these mathematical models and other basic principles will be presented. In Section 13.1, the problems connected with image acquisition are discussed. After that, the basic mathematical model of perspective transformation will be explained in Section 13.2. Section 13.3 gives the basic setup for 3D reconstruction using two images. This concept is generalized to a more complex image setup applying an arbitrary number of photographs in Section 13.4. Finally, Section 13.5 deals with the question of how to represent a more or less complex object on the computer.

13.1 Image Acquisition Aspects

Due to the application-specific requirements regarding speed, accuracy, and object dimensions, different image acquisition methods for 3D reconstruction have to be used. It is the goal of image acquisition to get digital images as depicted in Figure 13.1. A Cartesian coordinate system is attached to these images, which is called **sensor coordinate system**. Its origin is in the center of the left upper pixel, and the axes (r, c) point in the directions of the image rows and columns, respectively. The units of the sensor coordinate system are pixels; thus, the sensor coordinates (r, c) of a point P can be interpreted as its row and column indices, respectively.

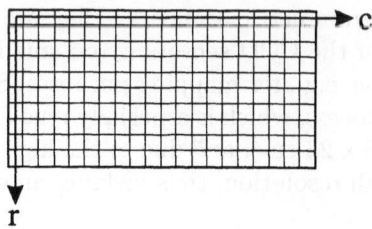

FIGURE 13.1. The sensor coordinate system.

The most commonly used sensors for 3D reconstruction are video cameras, CCD cameras, analog photographic cameras, and remote sensing scanners.

13.1.1   Video Cameras

Video cameras are connected to a PC with a frame grabber that performs conversion of the analog video signal to digital images. The size of these images is typically 768 x 572 pixels, which corresponds to 0.44 MB. These cameras are relatively cheap, and they are well-suited for real-time applications; this is why they are used for industrial and medical purposes. On the other hand, both their sensor size and their resolution are restricted.

13.1.2   Amateur Cameras with CCD Sensors

CCD sensors can be mounted in the image planes of conventional photographic cameras. In addition, such cameras need a device for data storage, e.g. a PCMCIA card. They can then be used just like analog cameras, with the advantage that the images can be checked on a laptop PC immediately after they have been taken, and bad photographs can be replaced by better ones. The sensor size varies considerably between different sensor models: A typical sensor may have about 2000 x 3000 pixels, which corresponds to 6 MB per grayscale image or 18 MB for a true color image. The format of these sensors is about 2.4 x 1.6 cm^2; thus, it is still 33 percent smaller than a common small-format analog photograph. The images in Figure 13.6 were taken using such a sensor. These cameras can be used for architectural applications and basically for everything that can be photographed because their handling is very flexible. However, in order to achieve an economic operating cycle, camera objectives with small focal lengths have to be used that enlarge the aperture angle but bring about geometrical problems due to distortions (Section 13.2).

13.1.3   Analog Metric Cameras

Photographs taken by metric cameras correspond with high accuracy to central perspective images (Section 13.2). These cameras deliver analog images that have to be scanned offline using photogrammetric scanners. They are used for high-precision applications or if the format of the CCD sensors is too small for an economic operating cycle, which is especially true, e.g., for mapping purposes. Scanning offline turns out to be a very time-consuming process, which is especially true for aerial images: The format of aerial images is usually 23 x 23 cm^2, and due to the high demands for accuracy, they have to be scanned with high resolution, thus yielding an enormous amount of data:

- 15 μm: 256 MB per grayscale image (16,000 x 16,000 pixels).

- 30 μm: 64 MB per grayscale image (8000 x 8000 pixels).

The image size for terrestrial metric cameras is typically 12 x 9 cm², which corresponds to 8000 x 6000 pixels or 48 MB per grayscale image at a pixel size of 15 μm.

Some strategies for handling these enormous amounts of data are covered in Chapter 15.

13.1.4 Remote Sensing Scanners

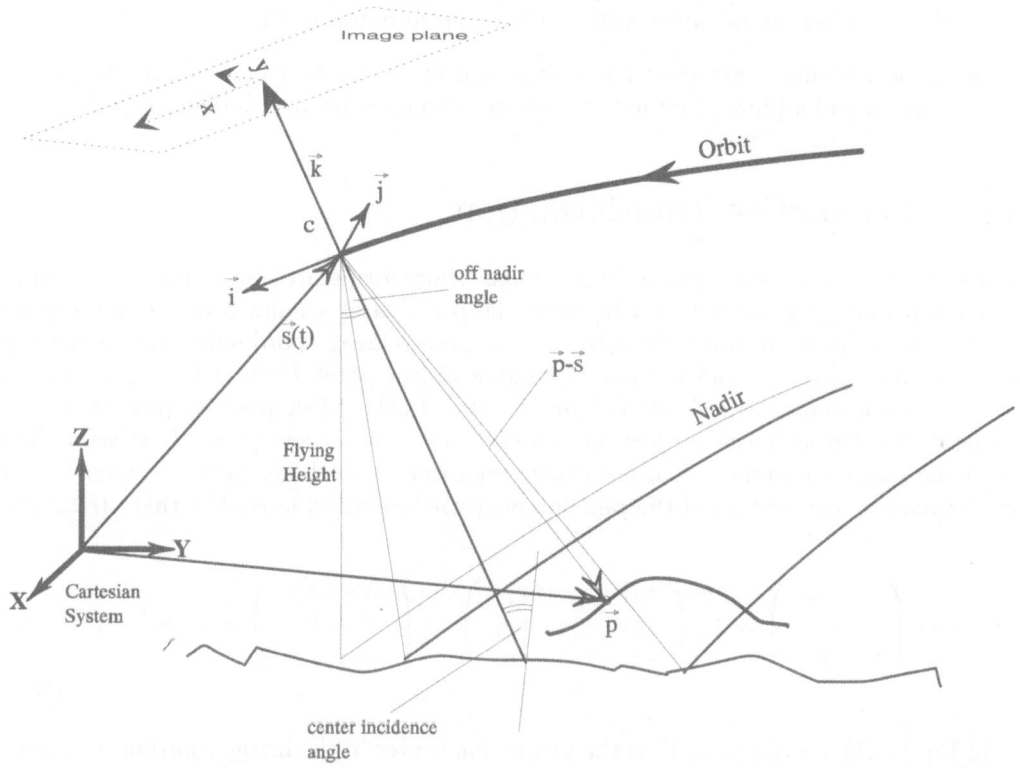

FIGURE 13.2. Image acquisition principle of optical line scanners from satellites or aircraft.

In the case of satellite line scanners [RHR⁺93] (Figure 13.2) a comparable amount of data must be handled. Images consisting of a single line are composed into an "infinite" strip making use of the sensor motion. The platform has its own coordinate system $(\vec{i}, \vec{j}, \vec{k})$, which is dynamically changing with respect to the world coordinate system (X, Y, Z). The sensor is moving in the $\vec{i}$ direction. The transformation between image plane and sensor platform remains fixed. In the standard case, the line scanner is arranged perpendicular to the direction of movement. Each line is oriented individually using the orbit description of the respective satellite. A refinement of these orientations is possible using reference points on the ground. Two line scanners simultaneously looking forward and backward realize a stereo configuration.

Remote sensing images are taken in many different spectral bands of the visible and infrared spectrums with a spatial resolution typically between 5 and 40 m on the ground per pixel. Airborne sensors reach a much higher resolution, but calibration of the data is rather complex due to complicated motion of the sensor.

13.1.5 Other Visual Sensor Systems

- Modern theodolite systems use low-resolution CCD sensors for target localization. These **video theodolites** will be discussed in detail in Chapter 17.

- Optical scanners are used for digitization of analog images, both in the professional area for photogrammetric purposes and for consumer and desktop purposes.

13.2 Perspective Transformation

The photographic imaging process is mathematically formulated by a perspective transformation that gives the relation between the position of a point p in the photograph described by its coordinates $(u, v, 0)$ in a camera-related coordinate system (**image coordinate system**) and the corresponding object point P described by its object or ground coordinates (X, Y, Z) (Figure 13.3). Each object point is projected by a straight line through the projection center C into the image plane I. If we reduce both the image coordinates and the object coordinates to the projection center C, the mathematical formulation of the perspective transformation looks like this [Kra97]:

$$
p - c = \begin{pmatrix} u - u_c \\ v - v_c \\ -f \end{pmatrix} = \lambda \cdot \begin{pmatrix} r_{11} & r_{12} & r_{13} \\ r_{21} & r_{22} & r_{23} \\ r_{31} & r_{32} & r_{33} \end{pmatrix}^T \cdot \begin{pmatrix} X - X_C \\ Y - Y_C \\ Z - Z_C \end{pmatrix} = \lambda \cdot \mathbf{R}^T \cdot (P - C).
$$

$$(13.1)$$

In Eq. (13.1), $c = (u_c, v_c, f)^T$ is the projection center in the image coordinate system, $C = (X_C, Y_C, Z_C)^T$ is the projection center in the object coordinate system, $\mathbf{R}$ is a 3 x 3 orthonormal matrix with three degrees of freedom that describes the rotations between the coordinate systems (u, v, w), and (X, Y, Z); $\mathbf{R}^T$ is the transposed matrix of $\mathbf{R}$. The coefficients r_{ij} of $\mathbf{R}$ can be computed from trigonometric functions of three rotational angles ω, ϕ, and κ [Kra93]:

$$
\mathbf{R} = \begin{pmatrix} \cos\phi\cos\kappa & -\cos\phi\sin\kappa & \sin\phi \\ \cos\omega\sin\kappa + \sin\omega\sin\phi\cos\kappa & \cos\omega\cos\kappa - \sin\omega\sin\phi\sin\kappa & -\sin\omega\cos\phi \\ \sin\omega\sin\kappa - \cos\omega\sin\phi\cos\kappa & \sin\omega\cos\kappa - \cos\omega\sin\phi\sin\kappa & \cos\omega\cos\phi \end{pmatrix}.
$$

$$(13.2)$$

λ is a scaling factor describing the position of P along the projection ray; thus, λ is not constant for all points in the image. This interpretation of λ makes Eq. (13.1) which

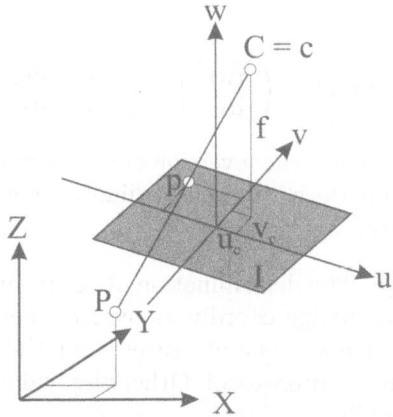

FIGURE 13.3. Perspective Transformation.

formally looks like a spatial similarity transformation, the mathematical formulation of a perspective. If the first two rows of Eq. (13.1) are divided by the third one, λ is eliminated, and we get the common formulation of perspective transformation [Kra93]:

$$
\begin{aligned}
u &= u_c - f \cdot \frac{r_{11} \cdot (X - X_C) + r_{21} \cdot (Y - Y_C) + r_{31} \cdot (Z - Z_C)}{r_{13} \cdot (X - X_C) + r_{23} \cdot (Y - Y_C) + r_{33} \cdot (Z - Z_C)}, \\
v &= v_c - f \cdot \frac{r_{12} \cdot (X - X_C) + r_{22} \cdot (Y - Y_C) + r_{32} \cdot (Z - Z_C)}{r_{13} \cdot (X - X_C) + r_{23} \cdot (Y - Y_C) + r_{33} \cdot (Z - Z_C)}.
\end{aligned}
\tag{13.3}
$$

The mathematical model described by Eq. (13.3) is fulfilled by metric cameras with a variation of a few micrometers. However, if nonmetric cameras are used, there might be considerable deviations from the model, which are called *distortions*. These distortions are larger for small focal lengths; their major component is radial to the image center. The mathematical model can be expanded to hold correctional terms for radial or tangential distortion components, which are usually modeled by polynomial functions of the image coordinates [Kra93, Kra97].

We have not yet considered the relation between the sensor coordinate system (r, c) (Figure 13.1) and the image coordinate system (u, v). For video cameras, cameramounted CCD sensors, and remote sensing images, these coordinate systems can be assumed to be identical, thus $(u, v) = (r, c)$. This is no longer true for photographs from analog metric cameras that were scanned offline. Metric cameras have fiducial marks, i.e., small targets on the camera body that are imaged in the photographs. In this case, the image coordinate system is defined by these fiducial marks; their image coordinates are provided by the camera manufacturer in a **calibration protocol**. The form and the distribution of fiducial marks depend on the camera manufacturer; an example can be seen in Figures 15.1 and 15.3, respectively. If the sensor coordinate system and the image coordinate system are not identical, the relation between them can be described by an affine transformation $\mathbf{T_a}$ [Kra93]:

$$\begin{pmatrix} u \\ v \end{pmatrix} = \mathbf{T_a}(r, c) = \begin{pmatrix} c_{00} \\ c_{01} \end{pmatrix} + \begin{pmatrix} c_{11} & c_{12} \\ c_{21} & c_{22} \end{pmatrix} \cdot \begin{pmatrix} r \\ c \end{pmatrix}. \qquad (13.4)$$

The goal of 3D reconstruction is the inversion of the perspective, i.e., the computation of object coordinates from measured image coordinates. For that purpose, several tasks have to be solved in advance:

- **Camera calibration:** The determination of the position of the projection center $c = (u_c, v_c, f)^T$ in the image coordinate system. For metric cameras, this step is performed by the camera manufacturer, and the calibrated parameters are contained in the calibration protocol. Otherwise, cameras can be calibrated in an offline procedure [Kra93].

- **Inner orientation:** The establishment of the relation between the image coordinate and the sensor coordinate systems. As stated earlier, this is only necessary for scanned analog images. In this case, the sensor coordinates of the fiducial marks have to be measured. As their image coordinates are known, the parameters of the affine transformation (Eq. (13.4)) can be determined. After that step, the position of the projection center relative to the images is given by the camera parameters (u_c, v_c, f) which in this context are often called *parameters of inner orientation*.

- **Outer Orientation:** The determination of the projection center C and the rotations of the image plane relative to the object coordinate system (Figure 13.3). The parameters of outer orientation can be determined from points with known object coordinates (control points). If high precision is required, control points can be targeted. A minimum of three control points are required for the outer orientation of a single image.

Note that camera calibration and outer orientation can be performed in one step (Section 13.4). In this case, at least five control points that must not be coplanar are required [Kra93]. In computer vision, the term **camera calibration** is usually applied to that step.

Another way to describe the perspective transformation is given by the following relation:

$$\begin{pmatrix} U \\ V \\ S \end{pmatrix} = \mathbf{T} \begin{pmatrix} X \\ Y \\ Z \\ 1 \end{pmatrix}. \qquad (13.5)$$

where $\mathbf{T}$ is a 3×4 matrix, namely, the **perspective or calibration matrix** of a camera, $(U, V, S)^T$ the projective coordinates on the image plane, and $P = (X, Y, Z)^T$ the coordinates of the point P in world coordinates [GT90]. In case P does not lie within the focal plane of the camera, the image coordinates (u, v) can be rewritten as

$$\begin{pmatrix} u \\ v \end{pmatrix} = \begin{pmatrix} U/S \\ V/S \end{pmatrix}. \tag{13.6}$$

The 3×4 matrix $\mathbf{T}$ consists of twelve parameters, but these are defined only up to a factor of scale. We need an additional constraint, where the simplest solution is to set t_{34} to 1 (for a discussion of this constraint and the use of other constraints, see [FT86]). We now have eleven unknown parameters. These parameters, the coefficients t_{ij} of $\mathbf{T}$ can be shown to be functions of the parameters from Eq. (13.1) together with two new intrinsic parameters m and d describing a different scaling and a skewness of axes of the image coordinate system. The new mathematical model of the perspective transformation, including additional parameters for describing an affinity of the image coordinate system, looks like this:

$$p - c = \lambda \cdot \begin{pmatrix} 1 & 0 & 0 \\ d & m & 0 \\ 0 & 0 & 1 \end{pmatrix} \cdot \mathbf{R}^T \cdot (P - C). \tag{13.7}$$

A comparison of coefficients yields the relations between the coefficients of the perspective model from Eq. (13.7) and the model from Eq. (13.5). Using $\mathbf{R} = (i, j, k)$ with (i, j, k) being the column vectors of $\mathbf{R}$, $\mathbf{T}$ can be expressed as follows [Kra97]:

$$
\begin{aligned}
(t_{11}, t_{12}, t_{13})^T &= \frac{f \cdot i - u_0 \cdot k}{k^T \cdot C} \\
(t_{21}, t_{22}, t_{23})^T &= \frac{d \cdot f \cdot i + m \cdot j - v_0 \cdot k}{k^T \cdot C} \\
(t_{31}, t_{32}, t_{33})^T &= -\frac{k}{k^T \cdot C} \\
t_{14} &= u_0 - f \cdot \frac{i^T \cdot C}{k^T \cdot C} \\
t_{24} &= v_0 - f \cdot \frac{(d \cdot i + m \cdot j)^T \cdot C}{k^T \cdot C} \\
t_{34} &= 1.
\end{aligned}
\tag{13.8}
$$

Using the mathematical model from Eq. 13.5 has the advantage that no approximations for the parameters t_{ij} are required: If the image coordinates of at least six non-coplanar control points are known, t_{ij} can be computed from linear equations: Each match of an image point p with an associated scene point P gives two linear equations in the eleven unknowns of the matrix T, i.e.,

$$
\begin{aligned}
P^T t_1 + t_{14} - u(P^T t_3 + 1) &= 0 \\
P^T t_2 + t_{24} - v(P^T t_3 + 1) &= 0.
\end{aligned}
\tag{13.9}
$$

where t_{ij} is the (i, j) element of $\mathbf{T}$ and t_i is the vector composed of the first three elements of the row i of $\mathbf{T}$:

$$t_i = (t_{i1}, t_{i2}, t_{i3})^T. \tag{13.10}$$

On the other hand, this model is overparameterized if metric cameras are used, and the orientation procedure will fail if the control points are coplanar or nearly coplanar, which is the case in topographic mapping of flat regions.

However, independent of the formulation of the perspective transformation, it is not sufficient to know the parameters of inner and outer orientation in order to reconstruct a point P: In order to compute its three object coordinates (X, Y, Z) from its image coordinates (u, v), only two Eq. (13.3) are available. The position of P along the imaging ray cannot be determined without additional information. This information can be given by an assumption about the object, e.g., by the assumption that $Z = 0$ for a planar object, or by another ray coming from another image. The 3D reconstruction of points from two or more images will be described in the following sections .

13.3   Stereo Reconstruction

Stereo reconstruction is based on the same principle the human visual system uses for depth recovery. Two cameras viewing the same scene use different perspective transformations. Each scene point is therefore projected on different locations in the two sensors and can be localized using the perspective in Eq. (13.3). The process of searching for corresponding points (projections of the same scene point) in two or more images is called **matching**, which is covered in Chapter 14.

Stereoscopy is a widely used method for surface reconstruction in photogrammetry. Originally, analog cameras were used for image capture, followed by a manual evaluation to get 3D points from stereoscopic images. Growing computational resources enabled the development of systems that strongly support this process, in terms both sensors and of data processing. Stereoscopic machine vision can be split roughly into the following major steps:

1. Image orientation (Section 13.2) to describe the geometry of the sensing devices,

2. stereo matching to get corresponding points in two or more images of the same scene, and

3. 3D reconstruction from the correspondences.

A general stereoscopic system takes at least two different views of the scene to be observed. It can be realized by one moving imaging sensor or by several sensors at different locations.

Figure 13.4 depicts the standard case of two cameras with identical physical properties. The projection center of the left image l is C^l, and the projection center of the

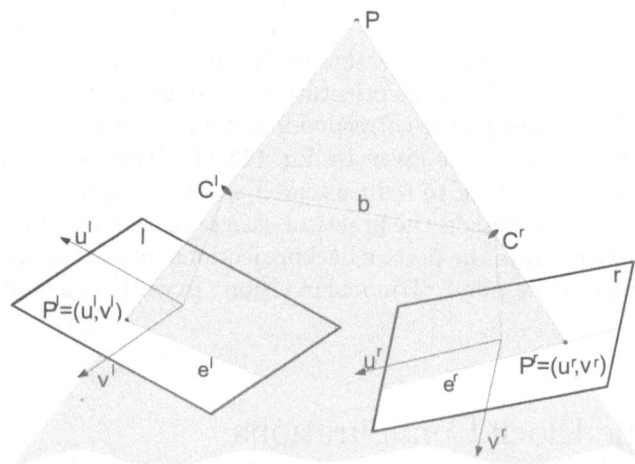

FIGURE 13.4. Geometry of the common two-camera stereo model.

right image r is C^r; the corresponding rotation matrices are $\mathbf{R}^l$ and $\mathbf{R}^r$. The vector $b = C^r - C^l = (b_X, b_Y, b_Z)^T$ is called the **stereoscopic base-line**. If the orientation parameters of both images are known, an object point P can be determined by the intersection of the image rays from two corresponding image points p^l and p^r: each point gives two Eq. (13.3) which can be solved for the unknown object coordinates (X, Y, Z). As there are four equations but only three unknowns, the problem is overdetermined and can be solved by a least squares adjustment. Using the mathematical model given by Eq. 13.5, knowledge of the two calibration matrices $\mathbf{T}^l$ and $\mathbf{T}^r$ (left and right camera) is sufficient to compute the unknown object coordinates from the image points p^l and p^r in quite a similar manner.

An important property of stereo arrangements is **epipolarity** (Figure 13.4): The vectors b, $\overline{C^l P}$ and $\overline{C^r P}$ form a plane called the **epipolar plane**. This plane intersects the image planes in the epipolar lines e^l and e^r. The coplanarity condition can be written as follows [Bra91]:

$$(p^l - c^l)^T \cdot \mathbf{R}^{l^T} \cdot \mathbf{S} \cdot \mathbf{R}^r \cdot (p^r - c^r) = 0 \qquad (13.11)$$

with

$$\mathbf{S} = \begin{pmatrix} 0 & -b_z & b_y \\ b_z & 0 & -b_x \\ -b_y & b_x & 0 \end{pmatrix} \tag{13.12}$$

and c^l and c^r being the projection centers in the image coordinate systems of the left and right images, respectively. If the orientation parameters of both images are known, for a point p^l in the left image, the corresponding point p^r in the right image is situated on the epipolar line e^r, which is given by Eq. (13.11). This is an important property that is used in image matching to reduce search space (Chapter 14).

Using three or more sensors in the practical case reduces errors but increases computational complexity because the point's backprojections into 3D space in general do not intersect in a single scene point. Trinocular vision [Aya91] is a well-known approach in this field.

13.4 Bundle Block Configurations

The stereo configuration described in the previous Section is widely used in 3D reconstruction. Stereo configuration faces problems with occluded object parts and with objects that are too large to be covered by a stereo model. In addition, there is a reliability problem: The depths of points determined from stereo images are not checked by other observations. A more general configuration is **bundle block configuration**. In this case the object is photographed from arbitrary positions so that each part of the object is at least visible in two (better: three) images and the intersection angles at the object points are close to 90° (Figures 13.5 and 13.6).

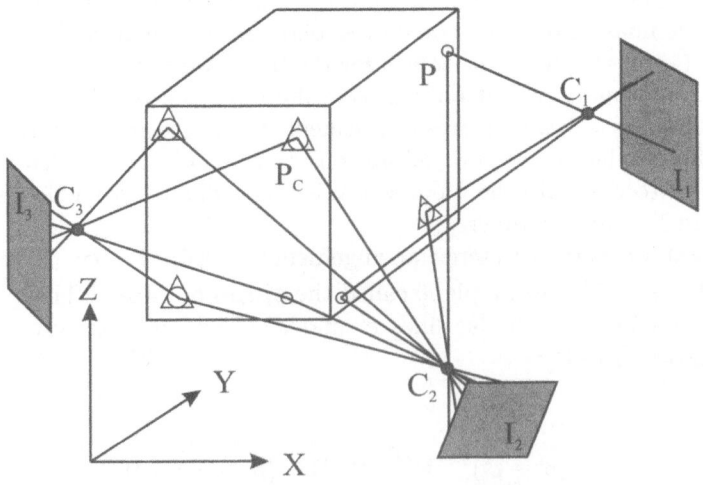

FIGURE 13.5. A bundle block configuration.

In the images, the image coordinates of control points (points with known object coordinates, e.g., P_C) and tie points (points with unknown object coordinates, e.g., P) are measured. ¿From these observations, the orientation parameters of all images I_i and the object coordinates of the tie points P are determined simultaneously by least squares adjustment (**bundle block adjustment**). For each measured image point, two Eq. (13.3) are used in the adjustment, the unknowns being P, C_i, and the three angles determining $\mathbf{R}_i$. As Eq. (13.3) are nonlinear, they have to be linearized using approximate values for the unknowns; adjustment thus has to be performed iteratively. If nonmetric cameras are used, the parameters of inner orientation (u_c, v_c, f) and the additional parameters modeling distortions will be unknown; camera calibration will then be performed "on the job". The concept of bundle block adjustment can be expanded to handle different types of observations such as geodetic observations (angles, distances) or feature observations, e.g., "three points are situated on the same straight line" (**hybrid adjustment**) [Kra93, Kag89].

On the one hand, bundle block adjustment is used for the determination of the orientation parameters of all photographs. On the other hand, bundle block configuration increases both the reliabilty and the accuracy of object reconstruction because an object point P can be determined by intersection from more than two images. For example, if P has been observed in three images, there are six Eq. (13.3) for the determination of its three unknown object coordinates. This local redundancy facilitates the elimination of gross errors in the data.

13.5 From Points and Lines to Surfaces

Automation of surface reconstruction is one of the main current fields of research in 3D reconstruction. Starting from a coarse object model, from the digital images and from the parameters of outer orientation, the surface of the object visible in the images is to be reconstructed. The term *Surface Reconstruction* implies two separate groups of problems that have to be solved:

1. **Matching:** Homologous points or lines have to be found in the images. Feature-based or raster-based matching methods can be applied for that purpose; the result of this step is a list of 3D points or lines. Matching techniques will be discussed in greater detail in Chapter 14.

2. **Modeling:** A point cloud can hardly be considered an appropriate representation of an object surface. Two methods for surface representation are commonly used: 2.5-dimensional digital elevation models (DEM) and 3D triangulations. In any case, the parameters of the surface are to be determined from the matching results. As these results will probably contain gross errors caused by false matches, robust techniques for parameter estimation are required for filtering.

The way to represent object surfaces depends on the task to be solved. In the following Section we will discuss very general object representation techniques that can be used *for the representation of arbitrary surfaces* as they appear in many applications. After

FIGURE 13.6. A photogrammetric block for the generation of a virtual reality model of an architectural object. The original images were taken with a Kodak DCS460. Size of the CCD sensor: 3060 x 2036 pixels; focal length = 15 mm.

that, the representation of man-made objects will be discussed in Section 13.5.2. These representation techniques are less general with respect to their applicability. However, they have their benefits in object reconstruction and visualization.

13.5.1   Representation of Irregular Object Surfaces

Flexibility is a basic requirement for object surface representation methods. Whereas simple geometric entities such as spheres, ellipsoids, or prisms can be represented by a small set of parameters and continuous functions to describe them, this is no longer true for arbitrary surfaces as they appear, for example, in mapping: The terrain cannot be represented in such a way. Descriptions based on discrete points or lines have to be used instead. Representation techniques for arbitrary surfaces can be characterized by several items:

1. **Data structure:** The surface can be described as raster models or by more sophisticated techniques. An important issue is dimensionality, i.e., if a surface model can only handle 2.5-dimensional data or if it is really three-dimensional.

2. **Mathematical model:** The surface has to be modeled between the discrete points of the data. Thus, a functional model for the interpolation of surface points between the discrete data points has to be provided.

3. **Generation:** The surface model has to be generated from a more or less unstructured point cloud. The generation methods can be classified according to whether or not they allow for filtering. Another classification scheme distinguishes local generation techniques and global ones.

Digital Elevation Model (DEM): The DEM is a valuable data source for mapping purposes or can be used as a static database for virtual reality and navigation (tracking and motion detection for robot navigation and surveillance). Figure 13.7 shows the geometry of the selected gridded DEM representation. On the ground plane $Z = z_0$, normal to the Z-axis, a regularly spaced grid is defined by specifying x_0, Dx, dx and y_0, Dy, dy. Here, the first grid point is determined by (x_0, y_0). Dx describes the range, and dx defines the distance between two adjacent grid points in the X-coordinate direction and the direction of grid expansion with respect to (x_0, y_0). By analogy, Dy and dy are defined in the Y-direction. The DEM is stored in a raster image with $C = Dx/dx$ columns and $R = Dy/dy$ rows. The height Z of an arbitrary point P with its planimetric coordinates (X, Y) can be computed from a bilinear interpolation from the corner points of the grid mesh containing (X, Y) [Kra93].

The DEM raster points are interpolated from the arbitrarily distributed object points by least squares interpolation. In order to bridge regions with a low density of points, certain smoothness assumptions have to be made. The least squares interpolation has a filtering effect [Wil83]. For high-quality DEMs, the effect of filtering is, sometimes, too rigid. Considering, for example rough terrain, there are regions with abrupt changes of terrain smoothness. In order to model such terrain edges, a hybrid DEM data structure containing **breaklines** is required: The breaklines are introduced in the generation

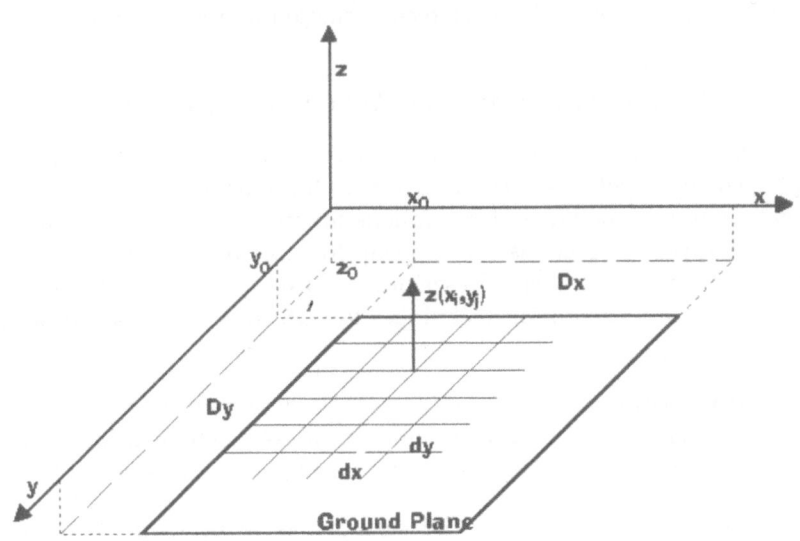

FIGURE 13.7. Geometry of digital elevation models (DEM).

process: Along these lines, no smoothness assumptions are introduced to adjustment. In addition, the breaklines have to be added to the DEM data structure, which will then no longer be a pure raster image [KS86]. Figure 13.8 shows a high-quality DEM from large-scale topographic mapping: The edges of road ditches are introduced as breaklines.

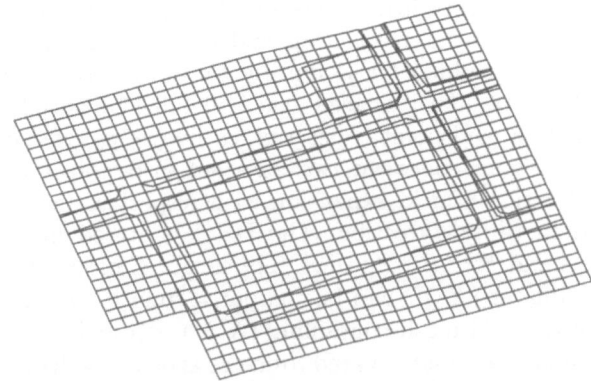

FIGURE 13.8. A high-quality 2.5-dimensional DEM of a topographical surface containing breaklines.

3D Triangulation: It is a drawback of 2.5-dimensional DEMs that vertical and closed surfaces cannot be modeled by them, and the representation depends on the coordinate system. 3D triangulation, which is a generalization of 2D triangulation methods for three dimensions, can be used to overcome these problems. The surface is represented by a set of nodes n and a set of edges e, each connecting two nodes. The 3D coordinates of the measured points are assigned to the nodes, which makes 3D triangulation independent of the selection of a coordinate system. As the "raw" coordinates of the measured points are used, no filtering is performed. The edges of the triangulation determine the neighborhood relations of the measured points. The surface is then approximated by the plane triangles (Figure 13.9).

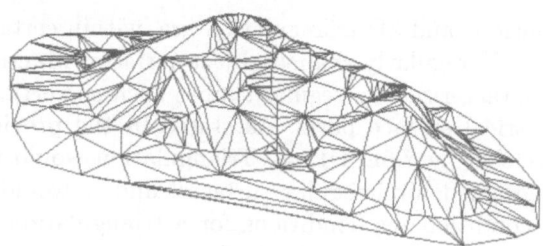

FIGURE 13.9. A perspective view of a 3D triangulation with constraints at the ridge.

In the generation step, the triangulation has to be built incrementally by inserting one point after the other. If a point is inserted, the edges connecting it to its neighbors have to be inserted in such a way that triangles are formed. However, triangulation of a point set is not unique; thus, criteria have to be formulated to achieve an optimal triangulation. The Delaunay criterion, which was described in closer detail in Section 6.1.3, is a well-known optimization criterion in 2D triangulation. The 2D criterion cannot be used here directly because this again would make the results of triangulation dependent on the selection of a coordinate system. One possible approach is to approximate the surface locally by its tangential planes and compute an estimate for the surface normals. For the insertion of a point these surface normals will be used to determine to which triangle the point to be inserted belongs; after that, the point will be connected with all nodes of that triangle. After that, the triangulation has to be modified locally to fulfill the optimization criteria. For that purpose, two criteria can be formulated:

- Maximization of minimum angles of the triangles to gain uniformly shaped triangles. This is the 3D generalization of the Delaunay criterion (cf. Section 6.1.3).

- Maximization of the angle between two neighboring triangle surfaces, i.e., minimization of the angles between the surface normals; this criterion will result in a smooth approximation of the surface.

As with 2.5-dimansional DEMs, breaklines must be considered in order to obtain a high-quality representation of the surface. At breaklines, there is a discontinuity of the first derivatives, thus, for points at a breakline, there exist two surface normals; the smoothness criterion described earlier is not to be used. In addition, we want the breaklines to appear as edges in the triangulation. This is done by making them constraints in the triangulation: Two nodes connected by a breakline in object space have to be connected by an edge in the triangulation even if the shape of the triangles will then no longer be optimal in the sense of the first criterion.

For very complex surfaces such as urban areas, this algorithm might fail. In that case another algorithm has to be used, or constraints to model the surface have to be introduced [HHK96].

13.5.2 Representation of Man-Made Objects

DEMs with 2.5 dimensions and 3D triangulation are, within certain limits, well-suited for the representation of irregularly shaped object surfaces. Man-made objects such as buildings are often characterized by regular shapes such as vertical or parallel planes, rectangles, or symmetrical surface parts. As stated in the previous Section, vertical planes cannot be modeled by 2.5D DEMs. Triangulation would overcome that problem; however, it is designed for irregular surfaces, and it would be very difficult to formulate regularity conditions as conditions for a triangulation to be fulfilled as we did with breaklines. In addition, semantic attributes are often connected to man-made objects. Thus, for the representation of man-made objects, different techniques from those described in Section 13.5.1 are often used. Figure 13.10 shows four possibilities for the representation of buildings characterized by increasing complexity [Bru98]:

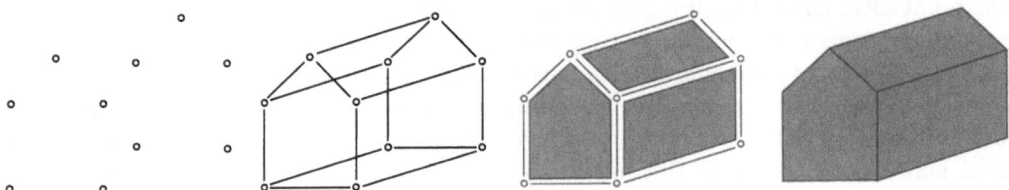

FIGURE 13.10. Object representation methods (*left to right*): Point cloud, wireframe model, boundary representation, solid model.

1. **Point cloud:** This certainly is not a sufficient way of representing objects, which was the first statement of this Section already.

2. **Wireframe model:** Wireframe models are widely used in CAD applications. The object is represented by the corner points and the edges connecting them. There is no information about surfaces. However, surface information is a desirable feature, especially for visualization tasks.

3. **Boundary representation:** In addition to points and edges, surfaces are used to model the object. Boundary representations are well suited for modeling 3D objects.

4. **Solid models:** Objects can be modeled as the combination of simple primitives represented by solid models. Constructive solid geometry provides the techniques necessary for formulation of such models.

Boundary Representations: Boundary representations offer a very flexible tool for modeling man-made objects. They consist of surfaces, edges, points, and the topological relations of these features. The surfaces, edges, and points are the (labeled) nodes of a graph, and the direct neighborhood relations are described by the edges of the graph (Figure 13.11):

- edges have two neighboring surfaces that intersect at the edge;

- surfaces thus have a set of neighboring edges by which they are bordered;

- edges have two neighboring points; and

- points have a set of neighboring edges that intersect at them.

Indirect neighborhood relations can be derived from the direct ones: Two edges are indirect neighbors if they share a common point neighbor, two surfaces are indirect neighbors if they share a common edge neighbor, and a point is an indirect neighbor of a surface if one of its edge neighbors is a neighbor of that surface. Thus, all topological relations can be determined from the graph. The object coordinates (X, Y, Z) of the points are attributes of the point nodes, and the geometrical parameters of the surfaces are attributes of the surface nodes. The surfaces need not necessarily be planar; thus, curved objects can be modeled as boundary representations, too.

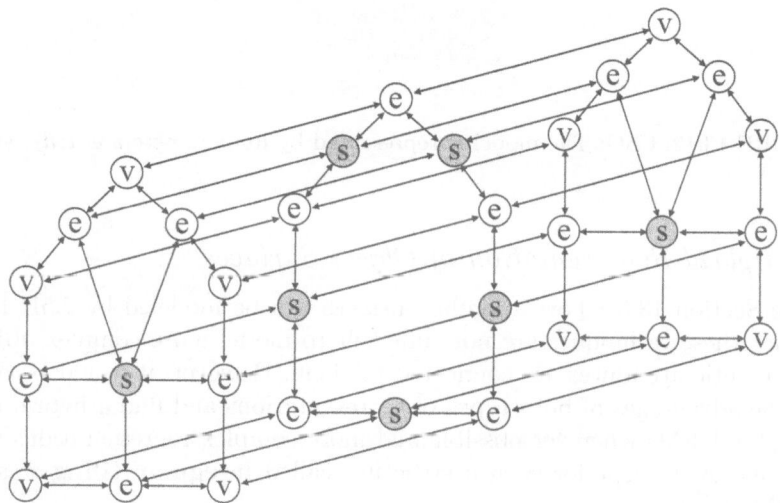

FIGURE 13.11. Boundary representation: A graph with nodes of type s (surfaces), e (edges) and v (points) and their topological relations.

It is the main drawback of boundary representations that similarities cannot be modeled easily; they would have to be added to the geometrical descriptions of a model [Vel98].

Constructive Solid Geometry (CSG): It is the concept of CSG to provide solid 3D primitives that describe a set of parameters reflecting the object dimensions (Figure 13.12). The CSG primitives are simple objects such as cubes, boxes, tetrahedrons, or quadratic pyramids, and more complex objects are composed of a set of primitives by logical operations: union, intersection, and difference [Mül98]. A minimum set of parameters can be chosen for the description of each primitive, and symmetries are thus modeled implicitly, which makes CSG a suitable technique for modeling man-made objects. For certain applications, a boundary representation is to be derived from a CSG model. The appropriate surface parameters and point coordinates can be derived from functions of the CSG parameters; this functional model is also a part of the CSG description. CSG is a very powerful concept to be used e.g., for object modeling in automation procedures for building extraction and for 3D city models, especially for objects that are relatively simple and show symmetries. However, CSG is not as flexible as boundary representations: The applicability of CSG depends on the primitive set that can be used [Mül98, Vel98]. If an inappropriate set of primitives is chosen, object modeling using these primitives will become difficult.

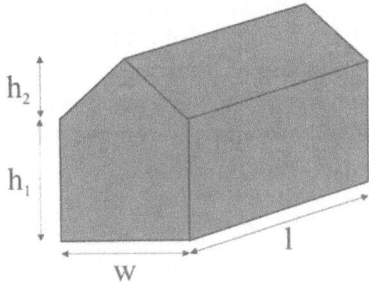

FIGURE 13.12. CSG: The model is represented by its parameters w, l, h_1, and h_2.

13.5.3 Hybrid Representation of Object Surfaces

We saw in Section 13.5.1 how irregular surfaces can be modeled by 2.5D DEMs, and we saw that these techniques are not sufficient to model more complex objects, especially if semantic attributes are connected to them. However, it would be desirable to combine the advantages of both types of representations and find a hybrid data structure using 2.5 DEMs wherever possible and more complex representations where they are necessary. A concept for such a structure called **irregular tiling** was presented by [MWW96].

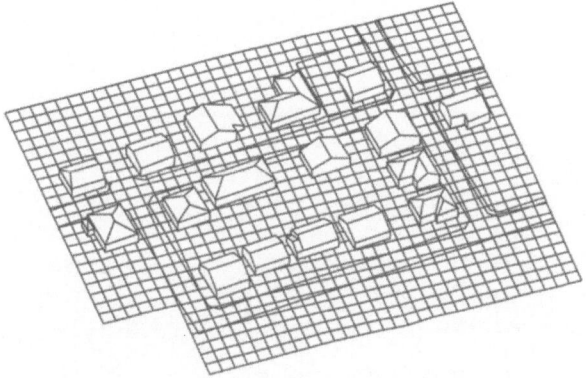

FIGURE 13.13. A hybrid representation: Boundary representation for houses and a high-quality DEM for the terrain.

14

Image Matching Strategies

Gerhard Paar
Franz Rottensteiner
Wolfgang Pölzleitner

One of the central tasks in photogrammetry and computer vision concerned with both the location of objects and the reconstruction of object surfaces with digital images is to solve the **correspondence problem**, i.e., the establishment of a relation either between two or more images or between one or more images and an object to be reconstructed or located.

In case of stereo reconstruction that means finding pixel coordinates in one image that can be located in the other stereo partner describing the same world location. The coordinate shift of two **corresponding (homologous) points** $P^l = (u^l, v^l)$ and $P^r = (u^r, v^r)$ is designated by a **disparity vector** $\vec{d}$,

$$P^r = P^l + \vec{d}^{lr}, \tag{14.1}$$

at which the exponents l and r, respectively, denote the left and right image coordinate space. Usually, for searching correspondences, the left image is selected as reference and the right one as search image.

To solve the local correspondence problem, a large variety of core methods for matching have been published for many applications. Probably the bestknown approach uses local correlation coefficients to describe local similarities [BNL90]. To overcome the numerical complexity for a single match, some of the older implementations used first-order statistics such as Laplacians of Gaussians on selected points [Gri85]. The idea to use local features evolved to a large variety of different local attributes like edges [II86], corners [WAH92] and local phase [Jen91]. Syntactic methods like labeling [MN95] or contour detection [HA89] still decrease the numerical effort but introduce combinatoric complexity. Most of the newer approaches rely on hybrid algorithms or active vision [AA93]. Almost all known matching approaches use multiresolution techniques to decrease search space and preserve robustness.

Depending on the geometric models used for the mapping functions (Figure 14.1, taken from [LF98]), two cases can be distinguished:

1. **Object Space Matching:** In this case, the object O is reconstructed directly by inverting the perspective transformations T_{O1} and T_{O2}. An explicit model for O has to be available, and the problem is solved by establishing correspondences between image features and features of the object model. Object space matching techniques have the advantage that they are closer to physical reality so that they may be capable of handling occlusions if sophisticated object models are used.

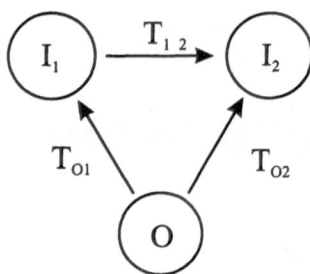

FIGURE 14.1. Matching versus object reconstruction.

On the other hand, the number of parameters to be estimated in the inversion process can be very high in some cases [LF98].

2. **Image Matching:** Image matching techniques directly relate the images I_1 and I_2 by a mapping function T_{12}. In this case, the object model is implicitly contained in the formulation of T_{12}, which will be very complex in general but can be locally approximated by an affine transformation if the object surface can be assumed to be smooth, thus yielding a reduction of computational complexity compared to object space matching. However, in the presence of occlusions the smoothness assumption will be hurt, and image matching algorithms will have to face problems [LF98, Gül94].

This section will concentrate on describing strategies for image matching. Image matching algorithms can be characterized by the **image model** they use [Gül94]:

- **Raster-Based Matching:** These algorithms use a raster representation of the image, i.e., they try to find a mapping function between image patches by directly comparing the gray levels or functions of the gray levels. They offer the highest potential for accuracy, but they are very sensitive to occlusions [Ack84, LF98, Gül94]. Raster-based matching techniques will be presented in Section 14.1.

- **Feature-Based Matching:** In this case, a symbolic description of the images is derived in a first step by extracting salient features from the images using some feature extraction operator, e.g., the Förstner operator [FG87]. After that, corresponding features from different images have to be found under certain assumptions regarding the local geometry of the object to be described and the mapping geometry. These algorithms are more flexible with respect to surface discontinuities and requirements for approximate values than raster-based techniques [Krz95, Gül94]. Feature-based matching will be discussed in closer detail in Section 14.2.

- **Relational Matching:** Relational or structural matching techniques rely on the similarity of topological relations of features that are stored in feature adjacency graphs rather than on the similarity of gray levels or of point distributions. This is motivated by the fact that topology is an image property that is invariant under perspective transformation. Matching of relational descriptions or relational matching is thus a very powerful concept that might work in rather general cases. However, its computational complexity is very high because it leads to rather complex search trees [Vos95]. Structural matching techniques and their application in object recognition were described in detail in Chapter 9.

One of the main reasons to enhance the idea of using local features for matching instead of area-based correlation or syntactic methods was the high density of matching points required for 3D surface reconstruction that would have exceeded the available computational resources for these approaches. Therefore a new matching method, coming from space research [Paa95], relies on a combination of local features to describe the surrounding of each pixel. The so-called **hierarchical feature vector matching (HFVM)** (Sections 14.3.1 and 14.3.4) turned out to be robust and accurate enough to be a valid tool in a stereo vision-based 3D reconstruction processing chain.

14.1   Raster-Based Matching Techniques

Raster-based matching techniques use the gray levels themselves or functions of the gray levels as the description of the images. It is the goal to estimate the parameters of the transformation T_{12} between two images (Figure 14.1). One of the images is chosen to be the reference image (the **template**), its gray levels will be denoted by g_R; the other image will be called search image and its gray levels denoted by g_S. T_{12} can be a dense parallax field. In this case, the whole images will be used as reference and *search images*, respectively. However, raster-based matching can also be applied to small image patches only. In this case, the reference image is either a synthetical one derived from a given target description or a small image patch in a region surrounding a feature previously extracted by a feature extraction algorithm or provided by a human operator. The search image is then an image patch limited by approximations.

14.1.1   Cross Correlation

Cross correlation is an algorithm for the location of corresponding image patches based on the similarity of gray levels. A reference point is given in the reference image, and its coordinates are searched for in the search image. That is why, the reference image is moved in the search image, and the position of maximum similarity of gray levels is searched for. For that purpose, at each position of the reference image in the search image, a similarity value, e.g., the cross-correlation coefficient $k_{R,S}$ of the gray levels is calculated [Rot93]:

$$k_{R,S}(\Delta r, \Delta c) = \frac{\sum_{r_R, c_R} [g_R(r_R, c_R) - \bar{g}_R] \cdot [g_S(r_R + \Delta r, c_R + \Delta c) - \bar{g}_S]}{\sqrt{\sum_{r_R, c_R} [g_T(r_R, c_R) - \bar{g}_R]^2 \cdot \sum_{r_R, c_R} [g_S(r_R + \Delta r, c_R + \Delta c) - \bar{g}_S]^2}}. \quad (14.2)$$

In Eq. (14.2), $\bar{g}_R$ and $\bar{g}_S$ denote the arithmetic mean gray level in the reference image and the part of the search image covered by the reference image, respectively. All sums are to be taken over all pixels of the reference image. In order to speed up computation, Eq. (14.2) can be rewritten as follows using the shorthand $g_R = g_R(r_R, c_R)$, $g_S = g_S(r_R + \Delta r, c_R + \Delta c)$, and $k_{R,S} = k_{R,S}(\Delta r, \Delta c)$:

$$k_{R,S} = \frac{\sum g_R \cdot g_S - \sum g_R \cdot \sum g_S}{\sqrt{[\sum g_R^2 - (\sum g_R)^2] \cdot [\sum g_S^2 - (\sum g_S)^2]}}. \tag{14.3}$$

In Eq. (14.3), the expressions $\sum g_R$ and $[\sum g_R^2 - (\sum g_R)^2]$ are constant, and most terms of $\sum g_S^2$ and $\sum g_S$ remain so, too. Thus, as the reference image moves over the search image, only the sum of g_S and g_S^2, respectively, of one row or column has to be added and another one removed. Only $\sum g_R \cdot g_S$ has to be fully recomputed for every new position of the reference image. The position of the point corresponding to the reference point is given by the position of the maximum of the similarity measure; the result is only accepted if a certain threshold is met by the similarity measure. In case the cross-correlation coefficient is used, the threshold can be chosen rather easily (e.g., 0.7) because that coefficient is bounded by -1 and 1. Thus the position of that point can be determined with a resolution of one pixel. ¿From Eq. (14.2) it can further be seen that T_{12} in this case just comprises two shifts:

$$T_{12} : \begin{pmatrix} r_S \\ c_S \end{pmatrix} = \begin{pmatrix} r_R \\ c_R \end{pmatrix} + \begin{pmatrix} \Delta r_{max} \\ \Delta c_{max} \end{pmatrix}. \tag{14.4}$$

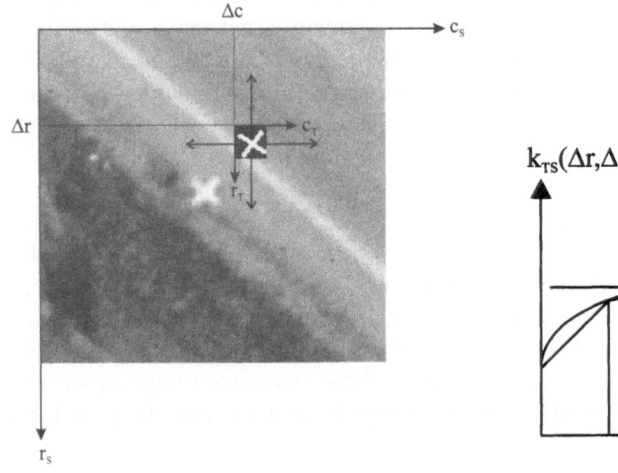

FIGURE 14.2. Cross correlation.

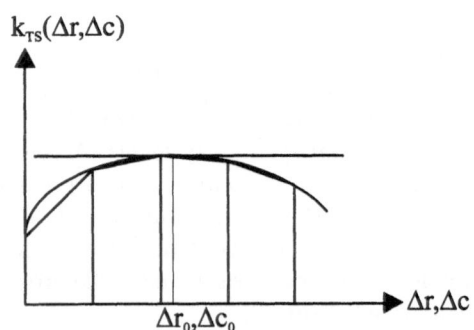

FIGURE 14.3. Subpixel estimation.

Subpixel estimation can be performed by approximation of the correlation coefficients $k_{R,S}$ by a second-order polynomial function:

$$k_{R,S} = a_0 + a_1 \cdot r + a_2 \cdot c + a_3 \cdot r \cdot c + a_4 \cdot r^2 + a_5 \cdot c^2. \tag{14.5}$$

The coefficients a_i in Eq. (14.5) can be determined from the correlation coefficients in a small, e.g., 3 x 3 pixel^2 window by least squares adjustment. The subpixel shift vector $(\Delta r_{max}, \Delta c_{max})^T$ can then be computed as the position of the maximum of the polynomial function from its differentials:

$$\left(\begin{array}{c} \frac{\partial k_{R,S}}{\partial r} \\ \frac{\partial k_{R,S}}{\partial c} \end{array} \right) = \left(\begin{array}{c} a_1 \\ a_2 \end{array} \right) + \left(\begin{array}{cc} 2 \cdot a_4 & a_3 \\ a_3 & 2 \cdot a_5 \end{array} \right) \cdot \left(\begin{array}{c} r_{max} \\ c_{max} \end{array} \right) = \left(\begin{array}{c} 0 \\ 0 \end{array} \right). \qquad (14.6)$$

The accuracy of subpixel estimation was empirically determined to be about ± 0.2 to ± 0.3 pixel for targeted points.

Cross correlation is tolerant with respect to the quality of the approximations; problems may arise with repeating patterns because in this case there will be different positions with high similarity. The algorithm will also fail if the images are not similar, which will happen in several cases [Rot93]:

- The approximations are too bad. New approximations have to be provided by a human operator in order to overcome that problem. In some cases measurement can also be aborted. The important thing is that failure is detected at all.

- T_{12} from Eq. (14.4) cannot be used because the image is rotated or scaled. If the rotation is unknown, the search can be repeated with successively rotated reference images until the correct position has been found. In the second case, better approximations for the scale are required.

- The image patch is too big. In this case, the search has to be repeated with a smaller patch size.

- There are occlusions. This is one of the greatest problems with raster-based matching techniques and can hardly be handled by them; in applications where occlusions are to be expected it is better to use feature-based matching techniques.

14.1.2   Least Squares Matching

Least squares matching (LSM) is the most accurate image matching technique [Ack84, Pri95]. Just as in cross correlation, it is based on the similarity of gray levels. However, T_{12} is more complex in this case. Assuming the image patch in question is small and the object surface is smooth, T_{12} can be modeled as an affine transformation $\mathbf{T_a}$ from Eq. (13.4):

$$T_{12}(r_R, c_R) = \left(\begin{array}{c} r_S \\ c_S \end{array} \right) = \mathbf{T_a}(r_R, c_R). \qquad (14.7)$$

If the parameters c_{ij} of T_{12} were known exactly and there were no radiometric errors, the gray levels of the search image and the reference image transformed by T_{12} according to Eq. (14.7) are assumed to be identical up to randomly distributed noise n [Ack84]:

$$g_R(r_R, c_R) + n = g_S(r_S, c_S) = g_S[T_{12}(r_R, c_R)]. \tag{14.8}$$

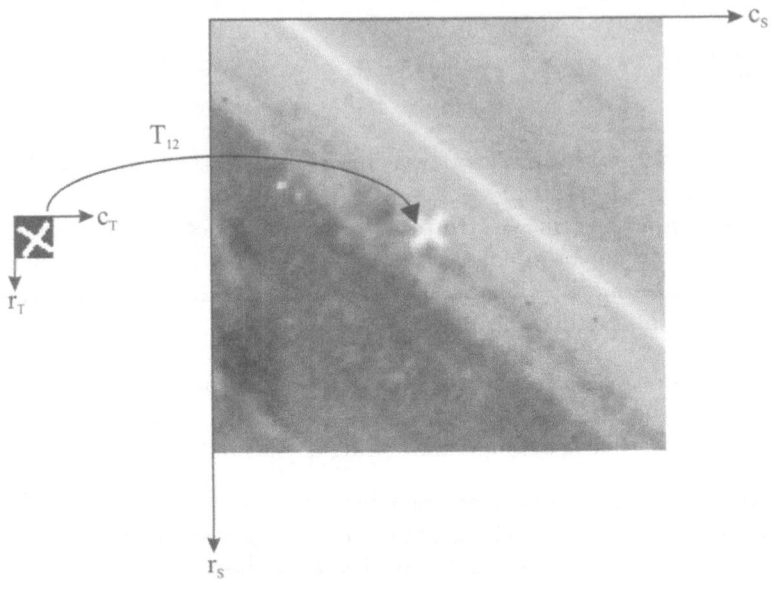

FIGURE 14.4. Least squares matching.

The reference image is transformed to the search image using approximate values c_{ij}^0 for the parameters of T_{12}. Due to radiometric errors and the fact that the parameters of T_{12} are not known exactly, there will be gray level differences between the two images. It is the basic idea of LSM to estimate the parameters of T_{12} from these observed gray level differences by a least squares adjustment. Equation (14.8) is linearized using the approximate values c_{ij}^0 and setting $c_{ij} = c_{ij}^0 + \delta c_{ij}$. Approximating the first derivatives of the gray levels of the search image $\partial g_S / \partial r$ and $\partial g_S / \partial c$ by the differences of gray levels of the reference image $\Delta g_{R_r}, \Delta g_{R_c}$ gives the observation equations, which can be established for each pixel [Pri95]:

$$n = \sum_{i,j} (\Delta g_{R_r} \cdot \frac{\partial r_S}{\partial c_{ij}} + \Delta g_{R_c} \cdot \frac{\partial c_S}{\partial c_{ij}}) \cdot \delta c_{ij} - \{g_R(r_R, c_R) - g_S[T_{12}^0(r_R, c_R)]\}. \tag{14.9}$$

Least squares adjustment using the observation in Eq. (14.9) delivers the unknown corrections δc_{ij} for the transformation parameters. Due to the nonlinearity of Eq. (14.8), least squares has to be iterated using the corrected transformation parameters of the previous adjustment as approximations for the successive one. Iteration implies the calculation of $g_S[T_{12}^0(r_R, c_R)]$ by resampling. The mathematical model can be expanded to other transformations T_{12} and to handle radiometric parameters. However, radiometric parameters might prevent iteration from convergence. Thus, it is better to apply radiometric corrections before stepping into the LSM algorithm [Pri95]. Due to the great number of observations (one observation per pixel of the reference image), LSM is the most accurate image matching technique. The transformation parameters can be estimated with an accuracy of up to ± 0.1 pixel [Ack84]. However, it is very sensitive with respect to the quality of the approximations. They have to be known with an accuracy of a few pixels. For that reason, LSM is often used to improve accuracy as a final step following another matching step, e.g., cross correlation, for establishing the approximations T_{12}^0. Just as in cross correlation, LSM will fail if the two image patches are not similar; it is especially confronted with problems if there are occlusions due to surface discontinuities. Additional care has to be taken on the determinability of the parameters c_{ij}. Analyzing Eq. (14.9) it can be seen that pixels in homogeneous regions with Δg_{R_r} and Δg_{R_c} close to zero do not deliver any information for the determination of the parameters. Some parameters cannot be determined if there are certain dependencies between the gray level differences, e.g., for a circular target, the rotations cannot be determined.

LSM can be expanded to more than two images. In case N images are used, $\frac{N \cdot (N-1)}{2}$ transformations T_{ij} with $1 \leq i < j$ can be established because the gray levels of each image pair can be compared. However, these transformations are not independent. Again, one image, e.g., I_1, is chosen to be the reference image. Now all transformations T_{ij} with $1 < i < j$ can be expressed as $T_{ij} = T_{1j}(T_{1i}^{-1})$, which leads to more complex normal equation systems. In addition, geometrical constraints can be included in the mathematical model [Bal91, Tsi92].

14.2 Feature-Based Matching Techniques

Feature-based matching techniques do not use the gray levels themselves as the description of the images but rather an abstract image representation derived from a feature extraction algorithm. The form of the description and the type of features used for matching (points, lines, homologous patches) depend on the task to be solved. In any case, the correspondence problem between features from different images has to be solved. Again, the parameters of the transformation T_{12} between two images (Figure 14.1) are to be estimated in order to solve this problem. In Section 14.2.1 a framework for the extraction of points and lines from digital images will be presented. Section 14.2.2 shows how abstract descriptions from different images can be matched.

14.2.1 Feature Extraction

Many techniques for feature extraction have been proposed in the literature. These techniques differ by the type of primitives to be extracted, e.g., points, lines, homogeneous regions, or wavelet coefficients, and they also apply different image models, e.g., analysis of first or second derivatives. Following is an (incomplete) list of different feature extraction schemes:

1. **Contour-Based Primitives:**

- straight line segments [BWR89, BHR86];

- parameterized curve segments [FH88, Leo93];

- corners [BR92, CVK91, GD91, MN90]; and

- multiscale curve descriptions [LE92, Sau90].

2. **Region-Based Primitives:**

- classical region segmentations [KR84];

- local homogeneous blobs [Bur88, Heu92, LE92, RS88]; and

- oriented wavelet patterns [BGER92, Mal89].

3. Qualitative 3-D surface primitives using invariance characteristics derived from differential geometry, based on the promising results from [Sar92, Sar93].

A framework for simultaneous extraction of point and line features is polymorphic feature extraction based on the Förstner operator [FG87, Fuc95]. The framework is based on analysis of the gray level gradients $\nabla g(r, c)$:

$$\nabla g(r, c) = \left[\begin{array}{c} \Delta g_r(r, c) \\ \Delta g_c(r, c) \end{array} \right] = \frac{1}{2} \cdot \left[\begin{array}{c} g(r+1, c) - g(r-1, c) \\ g(r, c+1) - g(r, c-1) \end{array} \right]. \qquad (14.10)$$

¿From the gray level gradients ∇g of a small window, e.g., 5 x 5 pixels^2, a measure W for texture strength can be calculated as the average squared norm of ∇g [Fuc95]:

$$W = L \star ||\nabla g||^2 = L \star (\Delta g_r^2 + \Delta g_c^2), \qquad (14.11)$$

with L being a linear low pass filter, e.g., a 5 x 5 Gaussian filter. W will be high in windows containing great gray level differences. An additional measure Q for isotropy of texture can be computed from the gray level gradients ∇g. Q can be derived from the equations for LSM (Section 14.1.2). If the affine transformation T_{12} in Eq. (14.7) is replaced by a simple shift by setting $c_{11} = c_{22} = 1$ and $c_{12} = c_{21} = 0$, the normal equation matrix N derived from the observation Eq. (14.9) looks as follows if the observations are weighted by L:

$$N = \left(\begin{array}{cc} L \star \Delta g_r^2 & L \star \Delta g_r \cdot \Delta g_c \\ L \star \Delta g_r \cdot \Delta g_c & L \star \Delta g_c^2 \end{array} \right). \qquad (14.12)$$

Note that the normal equations can be derived from the gray levels of one image only. The standard deviations of the resulting shifts can be estimated a priori from the inverse $\Sigma = N^{-1}$ of N. In addition, the error ellipse can be analyzed a priori. Its axes are proportional to the square roots of the eigenvalues λ_1 and λ_2 of Σ. Thus, the ratio $\frac{\lambda_1}{\lambda_2}$ gives a measure for the isotropy of texture. In [För91], the following measure for Q is proposed:

$$Q = 1 - \left(\frac{\lambda_1 - \lambda_2}{\lambda_1 + \lambda_2}\right)^2 = \frac{4 \cdot \det(N)}{trace^2(N)}, \tag{14.13}$$

where Q from Eq. (14.13) is bounded by 0 and 1; it equals 0 if all the gradients in the small image patch are parallel, and it is 1 if the gradient directions are equally distributed. Figure 14.6 shows the W and Q images derived from the image in Figure 14.5 with L being a 5 x 5 Gaussian filter.

FIGURE 14.5. Original image.

FIGURE 14.6. Left: W image. Right: Q image. White: $Q = 0$; black: $Q = 1$, or Q is undetermined.

By applying thresholds W_{min} and Q_{min} to W and Q, each pixel can be classified as belonging to a homogeneous region, a point region, or a region containing a line:

1. $W < W_{min}$: the pixel is inside a homogeneous region;

2. $(W \geq W_{min}) \wedge (Q < Q_{min})$: the pixel is inside an edge region;

3. $(W \geq W_{min}) \wedge (Q \geq Q_{min})$: the pixel is inside a point region.

FIGURE 14.7. Left: Classified image: point regions (black), line regions (light gray), homogeneous regions (dark gray). Right: Extracted points and lines superimposed to the original image.

As the classification result is especially sensitive to the selection of the threshold W_{min} for texture strength, this threshold is selected in dependence on the image contents, e.g., $W_{min} = j \cdot median(W)$ [För91], with j being a constant for a certain class of images. The selection of Q_{min} is less critical because Q is bound by 0 and 1. Thus, Q_{min} can be chosen to be, e.g., 0.7. The results of classification have to be thinned out. Points are found at the positions of relative maxima of texture strength W in the point regions. Line pixels are relative maxima of texture strength in the direction of the gradient of the gray levels. Neighboring line pixels have to be connected to line pixel streaks by an edge-following algorithm [Ker95, KDFR95]. Finally, these streaks are to be thinned out and approximated by polygons. For both line pixels and points, their coordinates are estimated with subpixel accuracy [För91, Fuc95].

Evidently, by just describing the image by an unstructured cluster of such features, a considerable amount of information would be thrown away. Having in mind nonstereo configurations and surface discontinuities, structural matching considering similarity of topology for generation of correspondence hypotheses might be a convenient approach. That is why it is a good idea to also extract the topological relations between the features to create a feature adjacency graph (FAG) [Fuc95]. The basis is a 2D Delaunay triangulation of the extracted points and the line vertices. To the Delaunay triangulation the lines are added as constraints, i.e., the vertices of the polygons have to be connected by edges (labeled as line edges) in the graph in the way described in Section 6.1.3. Obviously, the new graph describes the original image better than the Delaunay graph [HHK96, MR97].

As experience shows, errors due to noise are contained in the extracted features. In the future, topological relations will be used to perform consistency tests in order to eliminate these errors.

14.2.2 Matching Homologous Image Features

As already stated, it is the goal of feature-based matching to establish correspondences of features from different images rather than to establish correspondences between pixels. Thus, the raster images are replaced by a symbolic description of the images,

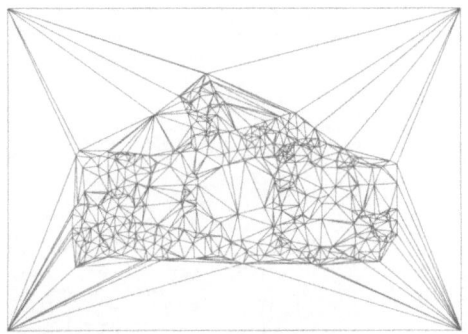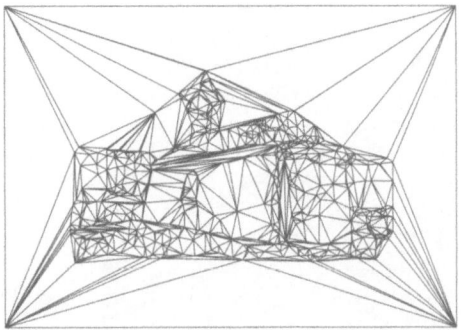

FIGURE 14.8. Left: Delaunay triangulation of the extracted points and line vertices. Right: Constrained triangulation: Line vertices are connected by edges.

which can be more or less complex depending on the difficulties of the task to be solved, as was described in Section 14.2. Having detected features in two or more images, correspondences between homologous features from different images have to be found. Again, a model for the transformation T_{12} is required. Under the assumptions made in Section 14.1.2, the affine transformation (Eq. (14.7)) can be used again. However, the image patches used for feature-based matching are usually larger (e.g., 200 x 200 pixels^2) than those used for raster-based techniques; on the other hand, the result is not a single point or a raster of displacement vectors but a set of homologous points or lines from which a set of 3-D points or lines in object space can be computed. These 3D features can be used to derive a description of the object surface. A useful approach for establishing correspondences is given by the hypothesis generation and verification paradigm, which splits the task into two subtasks [Krz95, TPO$^+$96, LF98]:

1. the generation of correspondence hypotheses–find initial matches between features from different images.

2. the evaluation of hypotheses–eliminate *false* under the assumption of a transformation T_{12} (which implicitly contains a model of the object surface). Only hypotheses consistent with T_{12} will be accepted.

In the following sections we will assume that the problem of finding homologous image patches has already been solved. As the size of the object usually exceeds the patch size for matching, the object is split into object patches, which one after the other provide homologous regions of interest in the images.

Generation of Hypotheses: If no other information were available, each feature from image I_1 could correspond to each of the features from the other image I_2. This would obviously lead to too great a number of possible matches; methods for the restriction of the number of possible matches have to be searched for. First of all, the number of possible matches can be considerably reduced by geometric constraints, both of them corresponding to knowledge about T_{12}:

- **Epipolar Constraints:** A feature in I_2 homologous to a certain feature in image I_1 has to be situated along the epipolar line (Section 13.3). Thus if the orientation

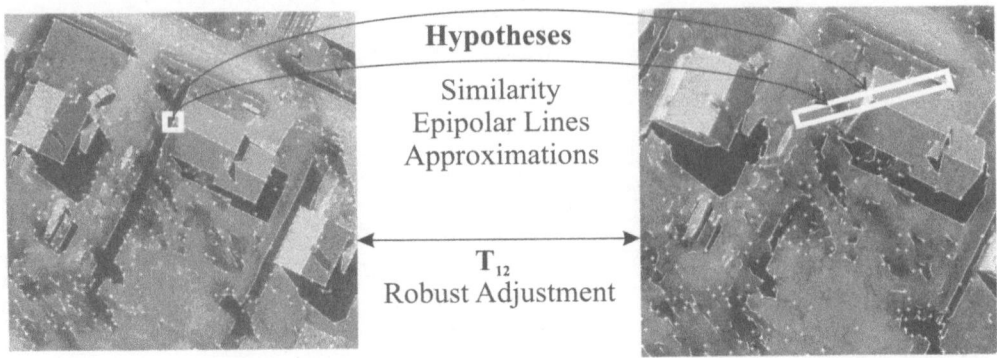

FIGURE 14.9. The principle of feature-based matching.

parameters of the images were known exactly, only points along the epipolar line would be possible candidates. If the orientations are only known approximately, the search space is still restricted to a band centered at the epipolar line; its width depends on the quality of the approximations.

- **Approximations for the Object:** They reduce search space along the epipolar lines. These approximations can either be specified by the user, e.g., in the form of limits for the object's distance from the images, or they can be derived automatically from hierarchical procedures (Section 15.3.1).

In this way, the search space for one feature is reduced to a more or less small rectangular area (Figure 14.9). The remaining possible hypotheses have to be assigned weights based on a measure of similarity S of the corresponding images. Depending on the contents of the symbolic image information and on the feature type, there are several possibilities for assigning weights:

- **Similarity of Gray Levels:** The cross-correlation coefficient of the gray levels from small image patches can be used as a similarity measure for point features from different images, e.g., [Tsi92].

- **Similarity of Neighborhood:** A similarity measure can also be derived from the topological relations.

- **Similarity of Lines:** Lines can be parameterized by their length l, and a measure for similarity can be derived from a comparison of the curvatures $\Psi_1(l), \Psi_2(l)$ [LST91].

In any case, the number of hypotheses can further be reduced by excluding hypotheses that fail to meet a certain threshold for their similarity measure. As a result, we get a set of weighted correspondence hypotheses that, however, is not consistent because it might contain multiple matches and because it still contains false matches.

Evaluation of Hypotheses: As stated earlier, those correspondence hypotheses contradicting to our model of the image transformation T_{12} have to be eliminated.

We will show this, assuming that we want to search homologous points. In this case, the parameters of T_{12} can be estimated by least squares adjustment. Each correspondence hypothesis gives two observation equations based on the mathematical model in Eq. (14.7). The coordinates of the feature from image I_2 are the observations (u, v), and the parameters of T_{12} are the unknowns to be determined in the adjustment. The weight p_i of the observation pair from point i is chosen to be proportional to the similarity measure S_i, thus $p_i = c \cdot S_i$. The more similar two features from different images are, the greater is their influence on the determination of the parameters of T_{12}. However, least squares adjustment is not robust with respect to gross errors in the data, thus it offers no possibility for eliminating false matches. Robust estimation techniques are required for that purpose. A more general overview on robust estimation techniques was given in Section 8.1; in this section we will restrict ourselves to maximum likelihood (ML)-type robust estimators ("soft redescenders" in the context of Section 8.1), which are often used for matching purposes because the number of parameters to be estimated is not restricted by them [För98].

Robust Estimation: It is the idea of ML-type robust estimation techniques to minimize a function of the residuals d other than the weighted sum of squares. This is equivalent to assuming a probability distribution different to the normal distribution. However, the routines for least squares adjustment can be used for that purpose because the goal of minimizing different functions can also be achieved by making the weights functions of the residuals in least squares adjustment. As stated earlier, the initial weights p_{u_i} and p_{v_i} for the two observations (u, v) of correspondence hypothesis i was given by $p_{u_i} = p_{v_i} = c \cdot S_i$, and a least squares adjustment was carried out using these weights. After adjustment, the residuals d_j with $j \in \{u_i, v_i\}$ can be computed. They are normalized by their initial weights; thus the normalized residuals r_j are calculated from Eq. (14.14):

$$r_j = s_0^2 \cdot \frac{d_j}{\sqrt{p_j}}. \tag{14.14}$$

In Eq. (14.14), s_0 denotes the a posteriori rms. error of unit weight. If we want to apply robust estimation, adjustment will be iteratively applied with the weights $p_{j,n+1}$ in iteration $n+1$ being modulated by weight functions $w(r_{j,n})$ of iteration n according to:

$$p_{j,n+1} = w(r_{j,n}) \cdot p_j. \tag{14.15}$$

The weight functions w should fulfill several requirements [För98]:

- An observation with $r_{j,n} = 0$ should receive its initial weight, thus $w(0) = 1$;

- w should be monotonously decreasing;

- The influence of gross errors on the results of adjustment should be reduced, thus $\lim_{r_{j,n} \to \infty} w(r_{j,n}) = 0$; and

- In order to completely eliminate observations marked as gross errors, w should be cut off at a certain threshold t: $w(r_{j,n}) = 0$ for $r_{j,n} > t$.

A weight function fulfilling these criteria is [Kra97]:

$$w(r_{j,n}) = \frac{1}{[1 + (\frac{r_{j,n}}{h})^4]^2}. \tag{14.16}$$

Parameter h is the size of a normalized residual causing weight modulation to give an observation half its original influence. If redundancy is great enough, blunders, i.e., observations not fitting our mathematical model, will successively lose influence by receiving a lower weight. However, an observation with a low influence according to Eq. (14.16) can be rehabilitated in the next iteration step if another, this time the true blunder, has in the meantime been eliminated. Convergence speed depends on h; h can be selected a bit smaller than the greatest residual. In addition, $w(r_{j,n}) = 0$ for $r_{j,n} < h$. Adjustment is repeated with h being reduced at each step until h reaches a given threshold. In order to make robust adjustment work, a high redundancy is required and the number of outliers should not exceed 30 percent.

After iteration is finished, there may still be multiple false correspondences in the data. Robust estimation should not be used rigorously in the preceding context if the mathematical model, e.g., an affine transformation T_{12}, is not very exact. However, this shows one of the strengths of feature-based matching compared to raster-based techniques: It works even if the mathematical model is not rigorously fulfilled. Thus, feature-based matching is, to a certain extent, less sensitive to occlusions than raster-based matching. Multiple matches are resolved by accepting the match with the best fit, i.e., the one receiving the smallest residuals. False matches will be propagated to object space, and again robust techniques have to be applied in object space to eliminate false 3D features [Gül94].

14.3   Hierarchical Feature Vector Matching (HFVM)

14.3.1   Feature Vector Matching (FVM)

Many published matching techniques deal with just one, or at most two, different properties of an image. These include grey levels, edges, corners, and other local primitives. A natural extension of this property-based matching philosophy is a combination of many of these features that would lead to a significant improvement of the stereo matching step, especially in terms of robustness. Such a method combines the advantages of several image features, whereas the particular disadvantages are compensated by the large variety of features. This new stereo matching approach is based on the idea of creating a **feature vector for each pixel** and comparing these features in the images to be registered.

In the following context a *feature* is a value that numerically describes the neighborhood of a pixel location. Most of the features used here are described as *convolutions* or can be approximated by means of convolutions [PP91]. Calculating a certain feature for all pixels of an image results in a so-called *feature image*. In the following a method is presented that matches pixels by comparing a number of features.

Suppose there are m features. All features of one location are collected in the *feature vector $\vec{f}$* for this pixel. From the contents of the feature images this vector can be derived for each pixel of the stereo image pair. Finding a match is performed by comparing a feature vector of the reference image, the *reference vector*, to all feature vectors of the search area that is a part of the search image. The reference image and the search image are named r and s, respectively, and the "images" consisting of the corresponding feature vectors $\vec{r}$ and $\vec{s}$, respectively. Then, for a point p, $\vec{r}(p)$ is the feature vector of p in the reference image and $\vec{s}(p)$ is the feature vector of p in the search image. The lth component of a vector $\vec{f}$ is denoted by $\vec{f}_l$. Table 14.1 lists a set of features currently in practical use. In order to compare a reference vector to a search vector, the *feature*

TABLE 14.1. FVM feature set (example); n_i are normalization factors, w_i are weights.

f_i	Property	Kernel	n_i	w_i
f_0	Horizontal high pass	2 1 0 -1 -2	4	2
f_1	Vertical high pass	$(2 \quad 1 \quad 0 \quad -1 \quad -2)^T$	4	2
f_2	Horizontal band pass	1 0 -1 0 1 0 -1	2	3
f_3	Vertical band pass	$(1 \quad 0 \quad -1 \quad 0 \quad 1 \quad 0 \quad -1)^T$	2	3
f_4	Horizontal band pass	2 1 0 -1 -2 -1 0 1 2 1 0 -1 -2	8	3
f_5	Vertical band pass	$(2\,1\,0\,-1\,-2\,-1\,0\,1\,2\,1\,0\,-1\,-2)^T$	8	3
f_6	Local variance [Han89]			10
f_7	Gaussian	0 1 2 1 0 1 3 5 3 1 2 5 8 5 2 1 3 5 3 1 0 1 2 1 0	56	4

distance between the two vectors is computed. The feature distance is defined such that each component of the vectors is weighted. If the weight of feature l is denoted as w_l, then the feature distance between the vectors $\vec{f}$ and $\vec{g}$ is defined as the Euclidian distance:

$$|\vec{f} - \vec{g}| = \sqrt{\frac{\sum_{l=1}^{m}((\vec{f}_l - \vec{g}_l) \cdot w_l)^2}{\sum_{l=1}^{m} w_l^2}}. \tag{14.17}$$

It could be shown that the absolute difference can be used instead of Euclidian distance without loss of accuracy. Computing, for a point p, the distance between $\vec{r}(p)$ and *each* vector in the search image is generally too expensive. In practice, a search can be restricted to a certain *search space* σ_p. This search space is defined by the search area, i.e., the center $(i,j)_p$ (which is assumed to be given) and the extensions δ_h and δ_v (which are the same for all points):

$$\sigma_p = \{\ \vec{s}(q)\ |\ q \in [i - \delta_h, i + \delta_h] \times [j - \delta_v, j + \delta_v]\ \}. \tag{14.18}$$

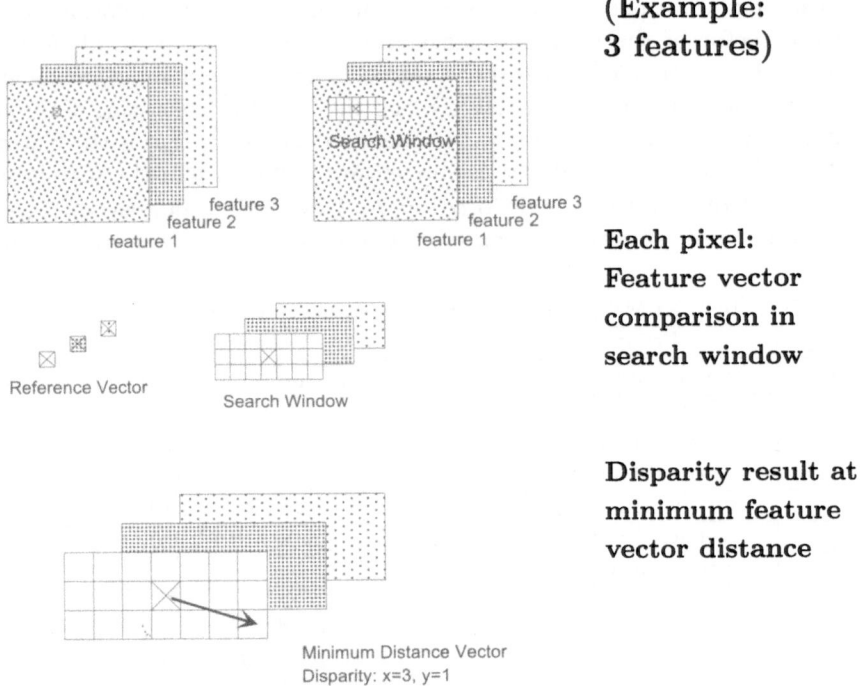

FIGURE 14.10. Feature vector matching principle.

For a point p, the best correspondence is found at position q in the search space, where the distance between the reference vector and the search vector is minimal, i.e.,

$$|\vec{r}(p) - \vec{s}(q)| = \min_{\vec{f} \in \sigma_p} |\vec{r}(p) - \vec{f}|. \tag{14.19}$$

The principle of feature vector matching is depicted in Figure 14.10. The algorithm is split into the following parts:

1. Create feature images for both the reference and the search image.
2. Compare each reference vector to all search vectors of the search space. Best correspondence is found where the feature distance is minimal. The difference in x- and y-coordinates is stored as a disparity vector. If the minimum feature distance exceeds a given threshold, the correspondence is invalid and the reference pixel is not matchable. As a result, the disparity for the reference pixel remains undefined.
3. Remove errors and interpolate undefined disparities.

14.3.2 Subpixel Matching

Within the search space σ_p of each reference pixel p (Eq. (14.18)) the feature vector distances $|\vec{r}(p)-\vec{s}(q)|$ (Eq. (14.19), $q \in \sigma_p$) describe a small image. Around the minimum location q_{min}, the neighboring feature vector distances are used for a linear interpolation in each direction (row and column).

It turns out that the distribution of subpixel disparities between -0.5 and 0.5 is not equal. Therefore a lookup table is defined that maps subpixel values in the interval $(-0.5, 0.5)$ onto itself to get an equal distribution. This can be done by one learning step, i.e., applying FVM on some typically textured images and analyzing the histogram of the subpixel values.

14.3.3 Consistency Check

To measure the consistency of the disparities, matching from right to left is also performed. This is called *backmatching*. On each point l of the left image, the left disparity map is applied. The result is r. Next, the right disparity map is applied on r resulting in l'. The match is invalid when the distance between l and l' exceeds one pixel.

14.3.4 Hierarchical Feature Vector Matching

In order to evaluate the center of the search area for each point and to improve robustness and efficiency of the matching algorithm, *pyramids* of the input images are generated (see also Part III in this book). Level 0 of the pyramid is the original image. To create the next level, the average grey level of four pixels in a square is computed and stored as one pixel in a new image. Matching starts at the top level of the pyramid with large search areas for each pixel. The resulting disparity map is smoothed and undefined disparities are interpolated before it is used as input initial disparity map (defining the centers of the search areas) for matching the next lower level of the pyramid. Incorporating pyramids, backmatching, and filter algorithms leads to *hierarchical feature vector matching* [PP92b]. The major steps are as follows (Figure 14.11):

1. Build the pyramid.
2. Compute the feature images for each pyramid level.
3. Match the top level of the pyramid.
4. Filter the resulting disparity map.
5. Check matching consistency by backmatching.
6. Interpolate the undefined disparities.
7. Use the resulting disparity map as the initial disparity map to match the next lower pyramid level.

Steps 4 through 7 are repeated until a disparity map at level 0 is computed.

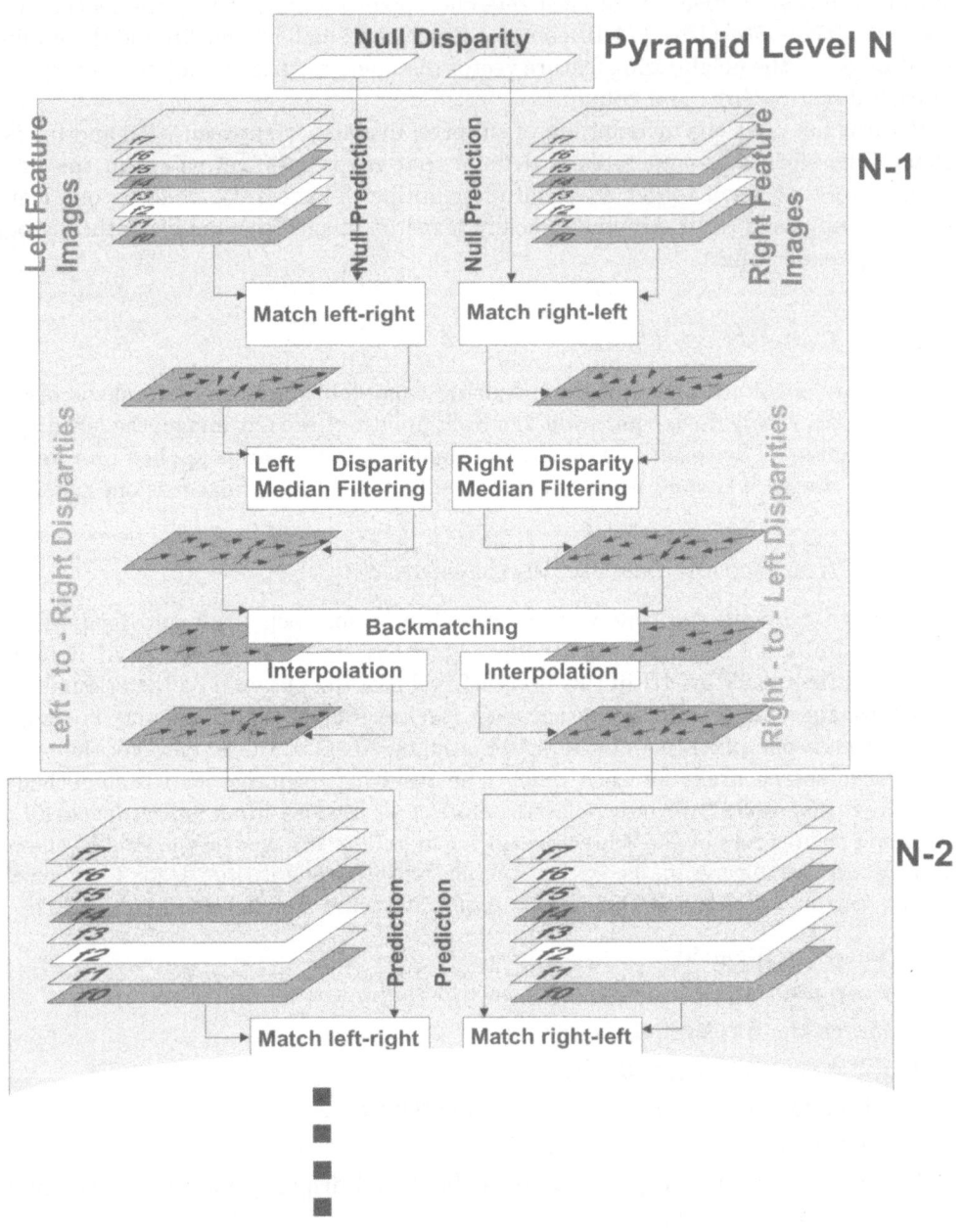

FIGURE 14.11. Hierarchical feature vector matching from pyramid level N to $N-1$.

15

Precise Photogrammetric Measurement: Location of Targets and Reconstruction of Object Surfaces

Franz Rottensteiner

Digital photogrammetry is photogrammetry with digital images in contrast to analog photogrammetry, where the analog photographs are used for measurement. There are several advantages connected with using digital images:

- Digital soft copy workstations running on standard computers can be used for working with digital images rather than expensive plotting devices requiring special hardware.

- Data transfer is simpler with regard to plotting results because they can be post-processed on the same computer.

- Digital image processing techniques can be used for image enhancement.

- Digital image processing techniques render possible the automation of photogrammetric measurement tasks.

However, there are problems connected with image acquisition. For many applications the format of CCD sensors, which are commercially available, is too small or the sensors are too expensive.

The enormous amounts of data involved in digital photogrammetry require specific strategies to be applied for image processing techniques because the image cannot necessarily be kept in computer RAM. In addition, visualization of great images cannot be done straightforwardly for the same reason. This is why Gaussian image pyramids (section 7.1) are used. Figure 15.1 shows a visualization of a digital image: In an overview window, a coarse level of the Gaussian pyramid is displayed. This overview window is used for navigation: With a mouse click, the zoom window can be placed and a small section of the pyramid level with the finest resolution is displayed.

In order to achieve precision comparable to those achieved in analog photogrammetry, point location has to be done with an accuracy better than one pixel ("subpixel accuracy"). Subpixel accuracy can be achieved because of the information contained in "mixed pixels": Their gray level is a mixture of the gray levels of the neighboring homogeneous regions. In addition, algorithms aimed at achieving subpixel accuracy for a certain task can be designed to use a greater number of pixels and thus redundant

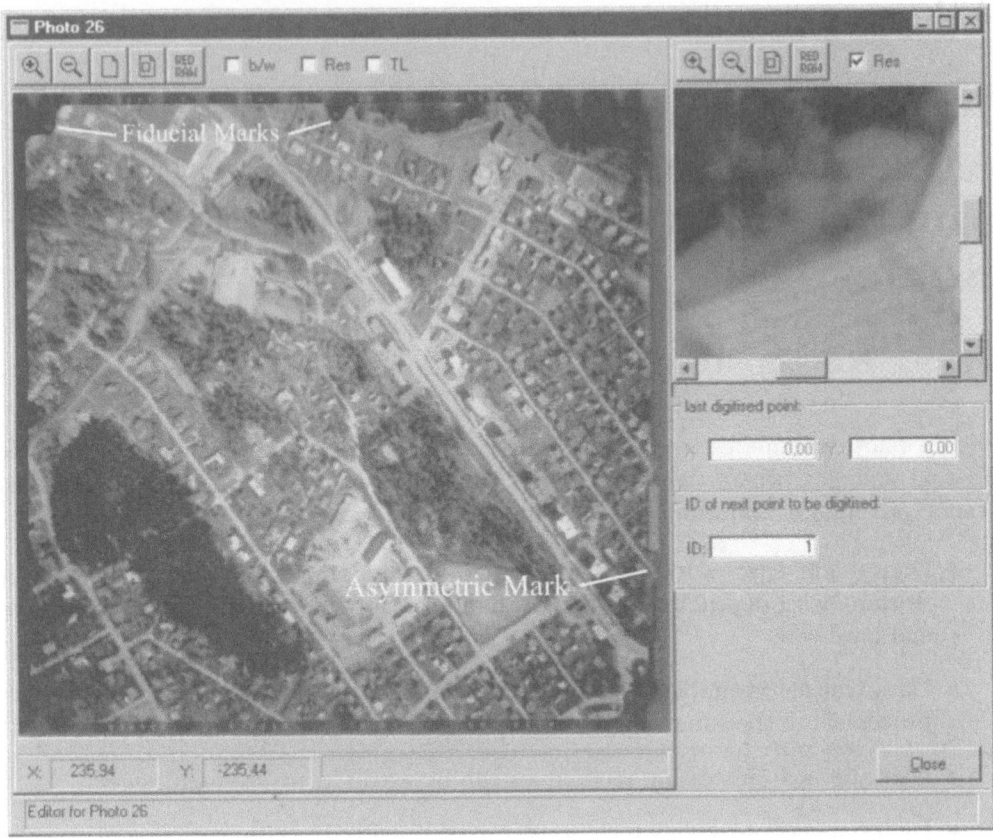

FIGURE 15.1. Large-scale aerial image: Image scale = 1:4000, original pixel size = 15 μm. In the right upper window, a zoom window shows a small part of the image at full resolution. Two fiducial marks are indicated; the others are on the corresponding places on the other image borders and in the other corners.

information. Figure 15.2 gives an idea that there is a higher potential for accuracy available in the images than the image resolution.

The following section gives an overview of automation in inner and outer orientation. In subsequent sections, two groups of tasks will be discussed in greater detail: The localization of targets as used in inner orientation and for the detection of targeted object points will be discussed in Section 15.2, and in Section 15.3, a general framework for object reconstruction will be presented together with its application to DEM generation for topographic mapping. Finally, no other application of that general framework, namely, semiautomatic building extraction, is dealt with in Section 15.4 due to its great importance in data acquisition for GIS.

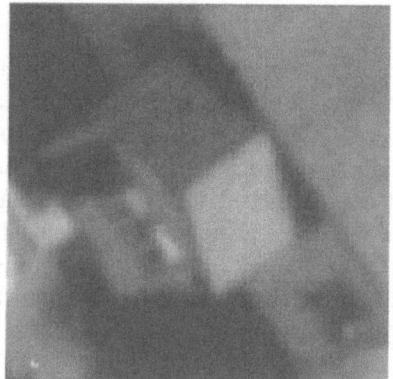 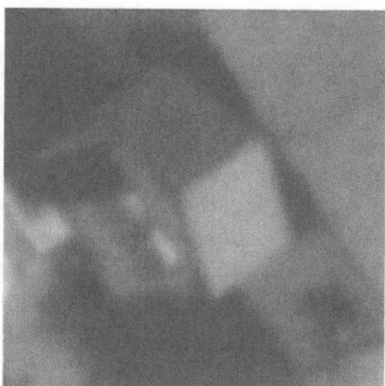

FIGURE 15.2. A small section of an aerial image scanned at 15 μm and enlarged in a zooming viewer. *Left*: Nearest neighborhood resampling; *right*: Bilinear resampling. The right image looks significantly smoother which shows that subpixel information is contained in the image.

15.1   Automation in Photogrammetric Plotting

The goal of current research in the field of vision-based 3D reconstruction is the automation of both orientation and object reconstruction tasks by applying digital image processing or, to be more precise, image matching techniques (Chapter 14). Two strategies can be applied for that purpose, depending on the complexity of the task to be solved and the semantics involved:

- **Data-driven or bottom-up strategies:** These algorithms start with low-level feature extraction from all images and then typically search for homologous features from different images. There is no semantic meaning assigned to the features: Data-driven processes do not care which features are found as long as they come from identical object features. Knowledge about the object depicted in the images is used for matching; however, it is not very detailed and is often given implicitly in the algorithm, e.g., by the assumption that the object surface is flat. Typical examples for this strategy are surface matching for the generation of DEMs in topographic mapping [Gül94, Krz95] and automatic measurement of tie points for image orientation [TPO+96].

- **Model-driven or top-down strategies:** Features are extracted from the images, but in this case, an explicit object model is provided in a knowledge base, and the model is to be adjusted to the data, i.e., model features have to be matched with image features. Typical examples for this strategy are automatic inner orientation [SP96], automation of measurement of targeted control points [RP96] or untargeted control points [Sch92], and building reconstruction from aerial images [GMLR98, Rot98].

Data-driven and model-driven strategies can be combined. For example, an algorithm could start with feature-based matching aimed at 3D lines and then match the 3D lines with an object model from a task-specific knowledge base.

15.1.1 Automation of Inner Orientation

The term *automation of inner orientation* is a synonym for the automation of fiducial mark measurement. Fiducial marks are available on metric cameras only (Section 13.2). Metric cameras are usually analog cameras because no CCD chips of appropriate size are currently available. Automation of inner orientation is a typical model-driven process. On the one hand, a camera model is required that contains the positions of the fiducial marks and the borders of the camera body, and on the other hand, models of the fiducial marks are required. The positions of the fiducial marks are usually symmetric with respect to the axes of the image coordinate system. Automatic inner orientation basically consists of three stages [SP96, Rot93]:

1. **Coarse location of the fiducial marks:** Image pyramids (Section 7.1) can be used for that purpose. If only one photograph per image data file is permitted, the search can start at standard positions (e.g., the corners) [SP96]. Another possibility is the detection of the camera borders by Hough transformation [Rot93].

2. **Fine location of the fiducial marks:** At this stage, any target location algorithm can be applied (Section 15.2).

3. **Determination of the camera pose:** An analog photograph can be put into a scanner in eight different ways (four different rotation states, geometrically positive or negative). A nonsymmetric feature on the camera body has to be located for that purpose. This could be one of the auxiliary features visible at the image borders; modern metric cameras have an asymmetric mark on the camera body (Figure 15.1). From the results of the previous step, eight sets of transformation parameters can be derived, each giving an approximate position for the asymmetric feature. This feature is searched for in all those areas; the area with the best fit corresponds to the correct set of transformation parameters [SP96].

Note that steps 1 and 3 would be unnecessary with digital metric cameras (if such cameras were available). Whether fiducial marks are required for digital metric cameras depends on the construction principle. If the CCD chip were mounted in a stable connection to the camera body, no fiducials would be necessary.

15.1.2 Automation of Outer Orientation

The automation of outer orientation comprises two steps that have to be treated in different ways [Hei97]:

1. **Automatic measurement of tie points:** Being a typical data-driven process, this task is solved by multiimage feature-based matching techniques (Section 14.2): There is no emphasis on which features are detected as long as the same features are found in different images. Current procedures work well in near-normal case configurations as they appear in aerotriangulation (orientation of aerial images) [TPO+96]; in other situations, e.g., in the configuration from Figure 13.6, they might fail. Automatic measurement of tie points is basically a

task similar to the generation of DEMs (Section 15.3), the difference being the fact that only coarse approximations for the orientation parameters are available. Automatic measurement of tie points is often referred to as *automatic relative orientation* [Hei97].

2. **Automatic measurement of control points:** This is a model-driven process. Automatic measurement of targeted control points will be explained in Section 15.2. Automatic measurement of nontargeted control points is very difficult because the structures of the models involved are different, depending on the object used as a control point. Most algorithms aim at using one specific class of objects. [Sch92] gives an example for the automation of control point measurement using a countrywide control point database containing wire-frame models of houses that are matched to imaged data. Another example is given in [DR96], where the control points are manhole covers. In this case, the model of the control points is given implicitly as a radiometric model that is the basis for a search for candidates in the images. The candidates are matched to a GIS database containing all manhole covers of the given area. Automatic measurement of control points has been solved for certain classes of objects but not yet in as general a manner as the measurement of tie points [Hei97].

15.2   Location of Targets

In close-range applications, points on the object surface are sometimes targeted if no or hardly any contrast is available and high precision is required. If the object is small enough and it is a bright color, the targets can also be projected. Figure 15.3 shows two examples for targeted object points in the center and on the right-hand side.

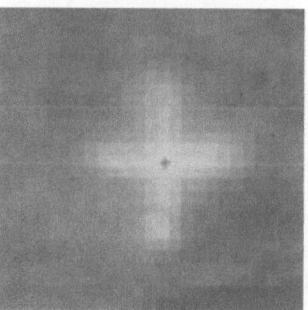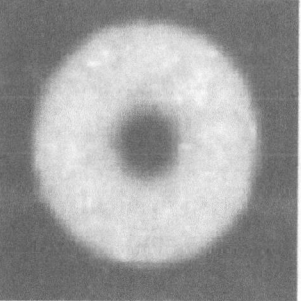

FIGURE 15.3. Targets in photogrammetry. *Left:* A fiducial mark at 15 μm pixel size. *Center:* A targeted control point in an aerial image: Image scale = 1:4000, pixel size = 15 μm, target size = 60 cm. *Right:* Circular symmetrical target used in a close-range application; diameter of the central circle = 2.5 mm.

In the sense discussed in Section 15.1, target location is a model-driven task. Thus, *the shape of the signal in object space must be given*. In addition, approximate values for the position of the targets in image space are given to reduce search space and to avoid false matches. The algorithms that can be used for target location can be classified according to the way of modeling the targets:

- **The target model is given implicitly:** In this case, a special algorithm is designed for a special target shape. These algorithms are very fast and efficient; however, they lack flexibility because for obvious reasons they fail if the target is shaped differently from the given form. An example for this class of algorithms is given in Section 15.2.1.

- **The target model is given explicitly:** In this case, a uniform description method is provided. With the help of this description method, arbitrarily shaped targets can be modeled; the algorithms used for target locations have to be designed to handle the uniform description method rather than a specific target shape. This subject will be discussed in greater detail in Section 15.2.2.

In the course of photogrammetric plotting, automation of target localization occurs at three stages:

1. Location of fiducial marks for inner orientation;

2. Location of targeted control or tie points for outer orientation; and

3. Location of targeted object points for high precision surface reconstruction, e.g., for deformation analysis.

In analog photogrammetry, targets can be located in the images with an accuracy of $\pm$ 4 μm. In digital photogrammetry, analog images are usually scanned at 30 μm or 15 μm, the pixel size of the CCD chips described in the introductory text to this chapter is about 11 μm. This means that if we do not want to lose accuracy in switching to digital techniques, subpixel accuracy is required in any case.

15.2.1   Location of Circular Symmetric Targets by Intersection of Gradient Vectors

This is a very simple algorithm that works with circular or nearly circular targets only. In addition to circular shape, the algorithm requires the absence of greater disturbances (e.g., occlusions, parts of other objects) in the image and approximate values in the sense that a window has to be known that contains one and only one target.

The algorithm starts with the determination of the gray level gradient vector $\nabla g_{r,c}$ in each pixel (r, c) from Eq. (14.10). $\nabla g_{r,c}$ is considered to be the direction of a straight line $l_{r,c}$ through pixel (r, c). As the gray level gradient points to the direction of the greatest change of the gray levels, it is orthogonal to a gray level edge; this only holds for pixels where such an edge exists (Figure 15.4). In other pixels in homogeneous areas, it is only influenced by noise, thus its direction is arbitrary. The distance d of the center $p = (r_p, c_p)^T$ of the circle can be computed from the Hesse form of the straight line equation. If p is on $l_{r,c}$, d has to be 0:

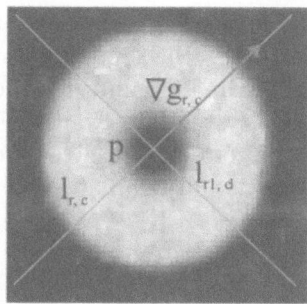

FIGURE 15.4. Location of circular symmetric targets by intersection of gradients.

$$d = 0 = \frac{\Delta g_c \cdot r_p - \Delta g_r \cdot c_p - (\Delta g_c \cdot r - \Delta g_r \cdot c)}{\sqrt{\Delta g_r^2 + \Delta g_c^2}}.$$ (15.1)

Equation (15.1) can be interpreted as an observation equation: The distance of the center p of the circle from the line $l_{r,c}$ through pixel (r, c) is observed to be 0. The coordinates (r_p, c_p) of p can be determined by intersection of all straight lines $l_{r,c}$ by a least squares adjustment. For each pixel in the given image window, one equation can be added to the adjustment system. If the observations are weighted by the norm of the gradient vectors $P_{r,c} = \sqrt{\Delta g_r^2 + \Delta g_c^2}$, the influence of noise is reduced as only pixels at significant gray level edges will influence the adjustment. Under these assumptions, the normal equations for the determination of (r_p, c_p) look as follows [FG87]:

$$\begin{pmatrix} \sum \Delta g_r^2 & -\sum \Delta g_r \Delta g_c \\ -\sum \Delta g_r \Delta g_c & \sum \Delta g_c^2 \end{pmatrix} \cdot \begin{pmatrix} r_p \\ c_p \end{pmatrix} = \begin{pmatrix} \sum r \Delta g_c^2 - \sum c \Delta g_r \Delta g_c \\ \sum c \Delta g_r^2 - \sum r \Delta g_r \Delta g_c \end{pmatrix}.$$ (15.2)

If the requirements of the algorithm are fulfilled, it can give results with an accuracy of ± 0.1 pixel. If the requirements are not fulfilled, the results can be completely wrong. In order to make the algorithm more robust, robust estimation techniques as described in Section 15.3.3 can be used: Those observations that deviate from the circular model can be eliminated by successively modulating their weights.

This model is mainly used in close-range applications, e.g., for camera calibration in a laboratory or in industrial surveying tasks. In both cases, circular retroreflective targets can be used. An example dealing with deformation analysis of wooden doors will be given in Section 15.2.4.

15.2.2 Location of Arbitrarily Shaped Targets

In this case, the target model is given explicitly by a vector description, e.g., a CAD model. This model can consist of simple geometric primitives such as circles, circle arcs, circular rings, and closed polygons, which are to be filled with a given gray level. A raster image can be derived from the vector description, taking into consideration the pixel size. This is sufficient for fiducial marks because their rotation with respect to the pixel coordinate system is known; targeted object points first have to be transformed from object to image space using approximate values for the outer orientation parameters and can be sampled in the sensor system afterwards (Figure 15.5). As an alternative, raster images representing the targets can be given from the beginning in a certain resolution; from these images, the actual templates can be calculated by resampling.

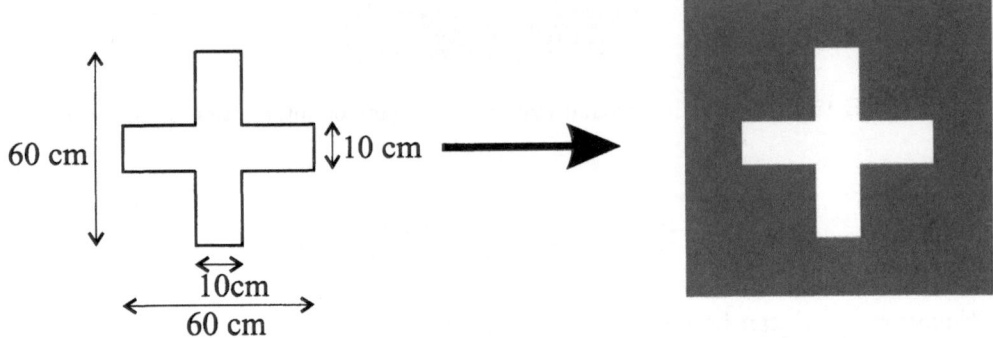

FIGURE 15.5. Vector-raster conversion for target models.

In addition to the raster image representing the target, approximate values for the location of the targets are required in order to speed up computation and avoid false matches. The approximate positions can be found in two ways:

1. If relatively good approximations for the parameters of outer orientation and the target position in object space are known, they can be found by transformation using the perspective Eq. (13.3).

2. Coarse interactive location by a human operator if this is not the case.

The raster image is used as a template for a raster-based image matching algorithm, e.g., cross correlation (Section 14.1.1) or least squares matching (Section 14.1.2) or both: As LSM requires relatively good approximate values, cross correlation can be used for a first location, and the results can be improved by LSM [Rot93].

With respect to targeted object points, another problem has to be solved: If they are not circular, their rotation in object space has to be determined, too. The raster-based matching algorithms will not work if the rotation is not at least approximately known. This problem can be tackled by repeating cross correlation in the first images with different rotation states of the template that are created from the original one by a rotation and bilinear resampling (Figure 15.6).

The matching algorithms can be sped up significantly if image pyramids (Section 7.1) can be used: In this case, a coarse-to-fine strategy can be applied. However, image pyramids can only be used if the targets are great enough that they are still visible in the higher pyramid levels. For fiducial marks, this is usually the case. Targeted object points are very often too small. In Section 15.2.3, an example for a project where cross-shaped targets were to be located in high-resolution digital images will be given.

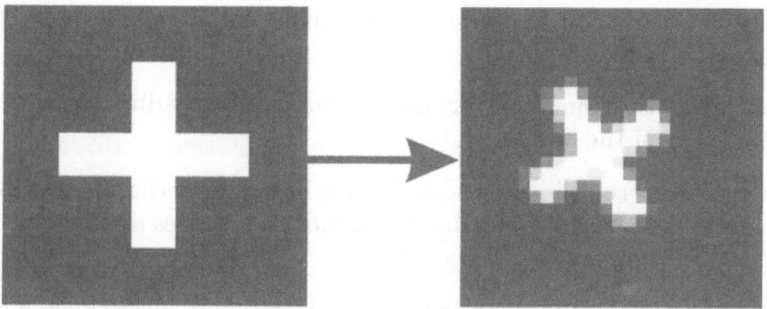

FIGURE 15.6. Rotation of the template from Figure 15.5 by 30°.

15.2.3   The OEEPE Test on Digital Aerial Triangulation

A test on digital aerial triangulation was initiated by the European Organization for Experimental Photogrammetric Studies (OEEPE) in 1995. The OEEPE provided a test block covering the small town of Forssa in southern Finland. The block consisted of 28 aerial images at an image scale of 1:4000, which were scanned at two resolutions (15 μm and 30 μm); Figure 15.1 shows one of the images. About 100 targeted points (crosses about 60 cm wide; Figure 15.7) were visible in up to six images each, and these targets were located by cross correlation and LSM. A few of the targets were used as control points in bundle block adjustment; the others were simply tie points. However, their ground coordinates were known from geodetic measurements, so that they could be used as check points for the determination of empirical accuracy values [Pri95, RP96, JS96].

FIGURE 15.7. *Left*: One of the targets at 15 μm. *Right*: The same target at 30 μm.

Table 15.1 sums up the empirical accuracy measures for the check points. The values are rms errors of the differences between the geodetically derived coordinates of the check points and the matching results. About 80 coordinates were compared; differences greater than three times their rms errors were excluded from computation. The rms errors of the object coordinates were computed from the rms errors of the coordinate differences under the assumption that both techniques are equally accurate. From Table 15.1, several conclusions can be drawn [RP96]:

1. *The empirical accuracy improves* with resolution; however, the improvement is

not linear. This is due to the increasing influence of noise with decreasing pixel sizes.

2. Although robust estimation was used in bundle block adjustment, there are still (few) outliers in the data.

3. With respect to the 15 μm images, LSM is both more accurate and more reliable than cross correlation. This is due to the fact that it does not only consider shifts, but also scale and rotation parameters.

4. With respect to the 30 μm images, cross correlation is surprisingly more accurate and reliable than LSM. This is caused by the fact that the signals are already quite blurred in the 30 μm images (Figure 15.7 shows actually a good example), and the rotations and scales for LSM can no longer be determined well.

TABLE 15.1. CC = Cross correlation. Res. = Resolution. $m_{\Delta x}$, $m_{\Delta y}$, $m_{\Delta z}$ = rms errors of the differences between geodetically derived coordinates and matching results. m_x, m_y, m_z = rms errors of the object coordinates derived from the matching results. Out.: number of eliminated coordinates.

Alg.	Res. [μm]	$m_{\Delta x}$ [mm]	m_x [mm]	Out.	$m_{\Delta y}$ [mm]	m_y [mm]	Out.	$m_{\Delta z}$ [mm]	m_z [mm]	Out.
CC	30	23	16	1	30	21	1	35	25	2
LSM	30	36	25	2	36	25	2	48	34	3
CC	15	27	19	3	24	17	5	37	26	1
LSM	15	23	16	1	24	17	1	37	26	1

15.2.4 Deformation Analysis of Wooden Doors

In a joint research project carried out at the Institute of Photogrammetry and Remote Sensing with the Austrian Timber Research Institute, procedures for automatic derivation of surface models were tested. The goal of the project was to derive exact models of the surfaces of wooden doors for an exact deformation analysis for quality control. The accuracy to be achieved should fulfill the criteria of the accuracy required by European norm EN 79: an accuracy of $\pm$ 0.5 mm for this kind of quality control measurement. The Timber Research Institute aims at an even better accuracy of $\pm$ 0.2 mm. In order to achieve this accuracy, a metric camera had to be used. As the wooden doors are often dark and hardly structured, small retroreflective targets had to be fixed on them manually in a 10 x 10 cm^2 raster. One door dummy was photographed twice: first in its initial position and then in a deformed one. At each epoch, five images had to be taken, some of them are quite convergent (Figure 15.9). Figure 15.8 shows one of the frontal images.

The diameter of the retroreflective targets was about 2.5 mm (the inner circle in the right part of Figure 15.3). They were measured in the images by intersection of gradients, which worked well in the frontal images but less well in the convergent ones:

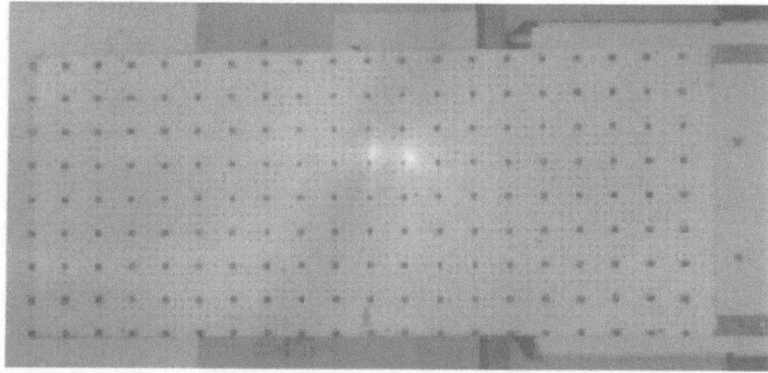

FIGURE 15.8. One of the images taken from the door.

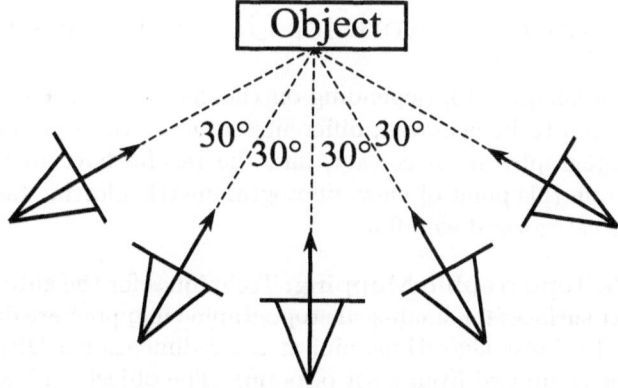

FIGURE 15.9. Image configuration.

In the convergent images, the circular targets appear as ellipses, which do not fit well to the circular model. Measurement was carried out in two steps. In the first step, only four points per image were measured interactively by the human operator. The images were oriented using these observations. In a second step, the target points could be projected into the images, and starting at these approximate positions, they could be located automatically.

Using the 3D coordinates of the target points, 2.5-dimensional DEMs (Section 13.5.1) could be calculated for both epochs. These elevation models had to be transformed to an identical coordinate system in order to be compared. Four points in the door corners were used for transformation. After that the differential model could be calculated (Figure 15.10; the absolute size of the deformation was about 3.5 mm). The preliminary results achieved by this method are quite promising. The rms error of the calculated height differences was estimated to be ± 0.15 mm.

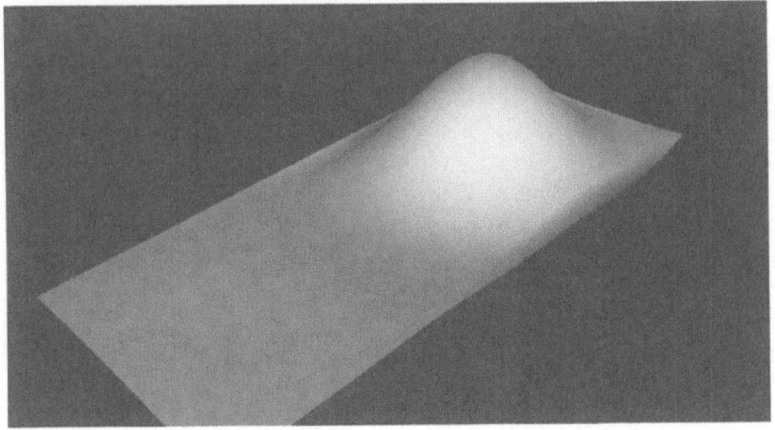

FIGURE 15.10. A shaded view of the differential model.

15.3   A General Framework for Object Reconstruction

As we have seen in Chapter 13, depending on the class of object to be reconstructed and the level of detail to be achieved, different sensors have to be used, different configurations of photographs are necessary, and the results have to be represented in different ways. ¿From this point of view, photogrammetric plotting tasks that are to be automated can be categorized as follows:

- **Small-Scale Topographic Mapping:** Techniques for the automatic reconstruction of object surfaces for small-scale topographic mapping are described in Chapters 14 and 16. Most algorithms aim at a 2.5-dimensional DEM (Section 13.5), which can be computed from a set of points. The object surface can be assumed to be smooth, and the image configuration is usually close to the stereo case with two images covering each surface patch (Figure 15.11). The images are analogous aerial images that have to be scanned offline.

 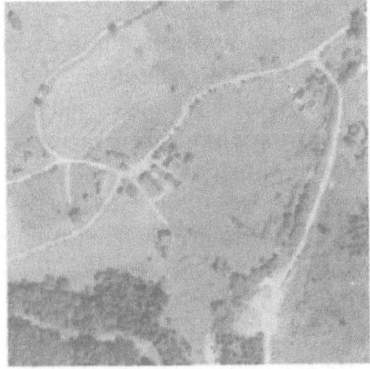

FIGURE 15.11. Two homologous image patches used for small-scale topographic mapping.

- **Large-Scale Topographic Mapping:** A 2.5-dimensional DEM will no longer be sufficient to describe the Earth's surface, especially if we think of built-up areas. 3D modeling techniques useful for man-made objects were described in Section 13.5. If topographic objects such as houses are to be reconstructed, a point cloud will no longer be sufficient to derive an object description; this task requires surfaces and lines as well as topological information. As is obvious from the image patches in Figure 15.12, the object surface can no longer be assumed to be smooth so that we have to deal with occlusions and surface discontinuities. This is why two images might no longer be sufficient for the automation of this task. Again, the images are scanned analogous aerial images.

FIGURE 15.12. Two homologous image patches from a large-scale photo flight.

- **Close-Range and Industrial Applications:** Depending on the actual object class, close-range and industrial applications have to face different problems. Flat building facades can more or less be treated similar to the way described for small-scale topographic mapping; in other applications, surface discontinuities and occlusions must be handled. Especially in architectural and industrial applications, nonstereo (bundle) configurations are typically used to increase accuracy and reliability (Section 13.4). Some classes of objects might be better described by points and others by lines (e.g., Figure 15.13). In most cases, 3D representations will be required.

In this section, we first want to describe a general framework for object reconstruction that relies on robust hybrid photogrammetric adjustment and consistent 3D modeling. After that, an example will be given showing the application of that framework to DEM generation for topographic mapping. Another example for the application of the framework is given in Section 15.4.

15.3.1 Hierarchical Object Reconstruction

Considering the great variety of objects that can be reconstructed by photogrammetric techniques, it appears to be impossible to find one algorithm capable of handling all possible cases. However, it does make sense to investigate common strategies for object

FIGURE 15.13. Three images for the reconstruction of a car's door.

reconstruction and common structures for object modeling, in order to create a framework for object surface reconstruction into which specific algorithms can be inserted easily rather than try to find one single algorithm capable of handling all possible cases. Such a framework is to be based on the following considerations [Rot96, Rot98]:

- **Hierarchical Object Reconstruction:** In order to make the algorithms work with quite coarse approximations, a hierarchical coarse-to-fine strategy using image pyramids (Section 7.1) has to be applied.

- **MultiImage Solution:** Two images might be sufficient for topographic applications, but in case of more complex tasks, occlusions will enforce the usage of more, e.g., four, images.

- **Feature-Based Matching:** As stated in Section 14.2, feature-based matching is more flexible with respect to occlusion and surface discontinuities than raster-based matching.

- **Consistent Object Modeling:** A consistent way of object modeling in the reconstruction process provides a powerful tool for treating different applications in a similar way in a framework based on the hypotheses generation or verification paradigm.

- **3D Representation of Results:** The problem of object representation was discussed in Section 13.5. As long as the hybrid approach combining 2.5-dimensional raster techniques and 3D techniques is not available, 3D triangulation is a good compromise capable of modeling most objects.

A coarse approximation for the object is assumed to be given, which can either be provided by the human operator in a semiautomatic system or from project parameters such as flying height in topographic mapping. Object reconstruction is then first applied to the upper level $i = N$ of the image pyramids with approximate values derived from

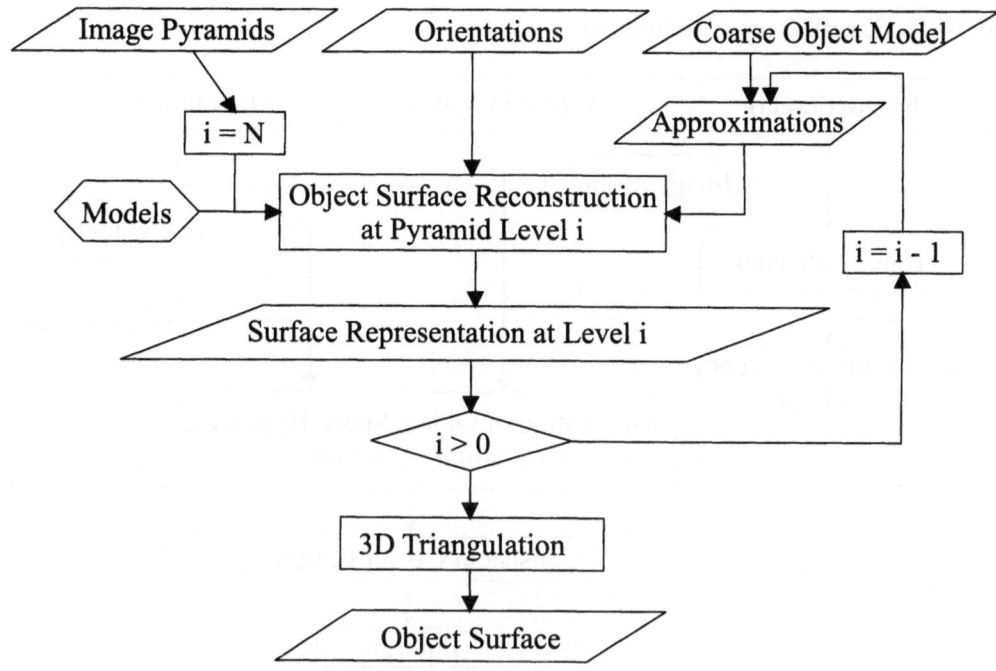

FIGURE 15.14. A flowchart of hierarchical object reconstruction.

the coarse object model. The resulting representation of the object surface is now used as an approximation for a reduction of search space at the next lower pyramid level, and so on. The process is terminated as soon as the lowest level of the image pyramids (i.e., the level with the highest spatial resolution; $i = 0$) has been reached (see the flowchart in Figure 15.14); this hierarchical concept is common to all applications, which is not the case for the reconstruction step itself.

Object Reconstruction at a Given Pyramid Level: Feature-based matching techniques are applied for object reconstruction at pyramid level i (Figure 15.15). Thus, the first step required at each level is the extraction of salient features (points and/or lines) together with their topological relations, which is a process controlled by a model of what we expect to find in the images. The result of feature extraction applied to an image is a feature adjacency graph (FAG) by which the image is described on a symbolic level (see Section 14.2.1 for more details on feature extraction).

Having detected features in two or more images, the correspondence problem has to be solved. Contrary to Section 14.2.2, where the relation between two images was given by a functional model T_{12} for a transformation between two images, a more general approach will seek correspondences in object space, as was indicated in the introductory section of Section 14, because these methods are more flexible with regard to handling occlusions and surface discontinuities. Instead of the functional model T_{12}, a task-dependent local model of the object surface is provided, and false correspondences are detected from bad fits to that model in object space. Thus, despite these differences, the *same principle of hypotheses generation and verification* as described in Section 14.2.2

can be used, with some modifications:

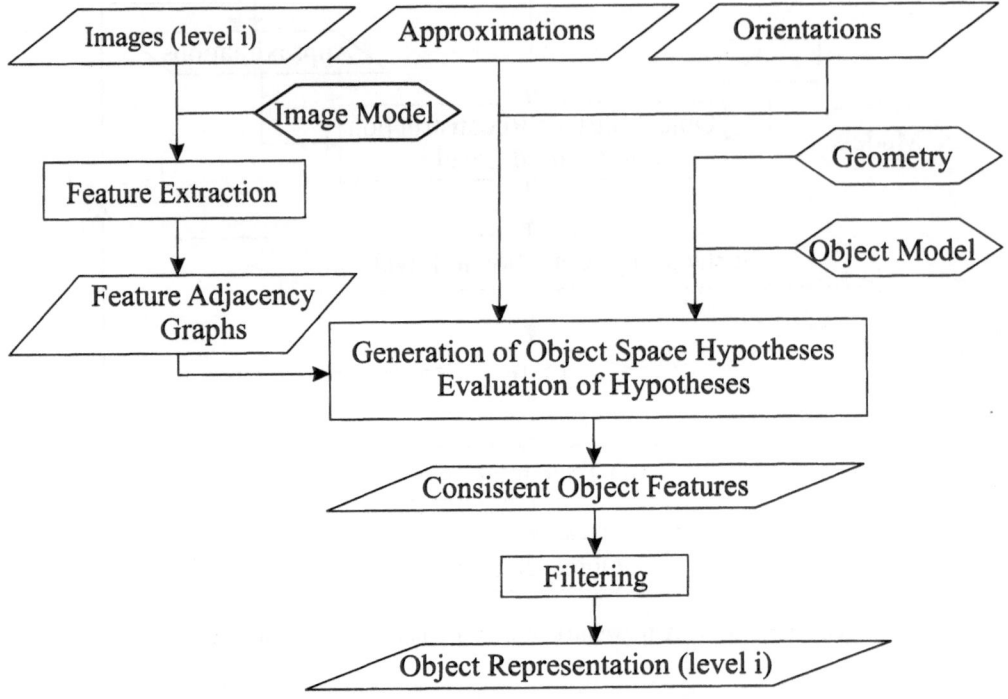

FIGURE 15.15. A flowchart of object reconstruction at pyramid level i.

1. The generation of correspondence hypotheses makes use of approximate values and the orientation parameters assuming a model of imaging geometry in order to reduce search space (Section 14.2.2). Depending on the object class, different algorithms can be used for that step. A correspondence hypothesis can be (Figure 15.16):

   (a) a correspondence between two points or lines from different images, such a correspondence is propagated to object space and can be assigned to a feature of the local surface model.

   (b) a correspondence between a point or line and a point or line of the local surface model.

2. The evaluation of these hypotheses is performed under the assumption of the (predefined) local surface model in object space: Only hypotheses consistent with the model will be accepted. Using a uniform mathematical formulation of these local surface models makes this step independent of the object class.

The selection of an appropriate local surface model mainly depends on the class of object to be reconstructed. For each object class, a knowledge base of possible models

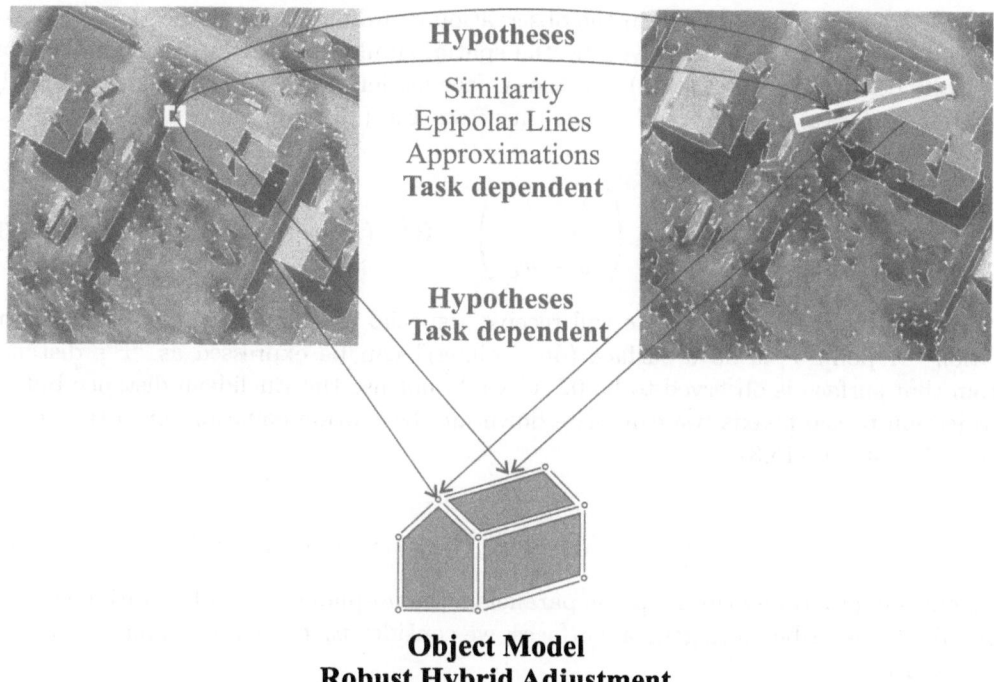

Hypotheses

Similarity
Epipolar Lines
Approximations
Task dependent

Hypotheses
Task dependent

Object Model
Robust Hybrid Adjustment

FIGURE 15.16. Generation and evaluation of correspondence hypotheses.

is prepared; the decision about which of the models is to be used has to be taken by user interaction. In some applications, model selection can be automated. The way the object models are represented in the reconstruction process differs from the way we represent the final output: 3D triangulation is a very flexible technique to represent object surfaces, but for object reconstruction it brings about overparameterization as even planar surfaces are split into several triangles; thus, triangulation is not "rigid" enough for hypothesis evaluation. **Boundary representation** (cf. Section 13.5.2) can be used instead because practically all objects can be described by a set of surfaces and their topological relations. In Section 15.3.2, the mathematical formulation of the local surface models will be described. Hypothesis evaluation by robust hybrid adjustment using the mathematical model of that section will be explained in more detail in Section 15.3.3 [Rot98].

15.3.2 Mathematical Formulation of the Object Models

Boundary representations are graphs as depicted in Figure 13.11. As stated in Section 15.3.1, the local surface models have to be used in a robust hybrid adjustment. This means that the mathematical model for "fictitious observations" (observations made without a measuring device) is to be formulated from which observation equations for a least squares adjustment can be derived. The surface models are formulated in a local 3-D Cartesian **observation coordinate system** (u, v, w) (Section 13.2), and the transformation, between the observation coordinate system and the object co-ordinate system (X, Y, Z) is given by the spatial similarity transformation which can formally be written as Eq. (13.1). For the surface models, the reference point is formally written as $c = (u_c, v_c, w_c)^T$ and $\lambda = 1$, thus from Eq. (13.1) we get:

$$p - c = \begin{pmatrix} u - u_c \\ v - v_c \\ w - w_c \end{pmatrix} = \mathbf{R}^T \cdot (P - C). \tag{15.3}$$

The internal reference point c will receive a special interpretation later. The observation "A point P is on a surface (on a plane)" can be expressed as "P's distance from that surface is observed to be 0." If we do not use the Euclidean distance but its projection to the w-axis, we can write down an observation equation for w taking the third line of Eq. (15.3):

$$w = 0 = w_c + r_{13} \cdot (X - X_C) + r_{23} \cdot (Y - Y_C) + r_{33} \cdot (Z - Z_C). \tag{15.4}$$

Equation (15.4) describes a plane parallel to the uv-plane in the observation system. In order to describe more general surfaces, we consider w_c to be a polynomial function in u and v:

$$w_c = \sum_{i,j=0}^{n,n} c_{i,j} \cdot u^i \cdot v^j \tag{15.5}$$

with u, v from Eq. (15.3), n being the maximum degree of the polynomial and assuming $u_c = v_c = 0$. Similar considerations can be made for u and v. In addition, the mathematical model has to be expanded to handle symmetries; the observation coordinate system can be mirrored by one of its principal planes. Thus, the observation that a point P is on a surface can be formulated in one of the following ways:

$$
\begin{aligned}
u &= 0 = s_u \cdot u_R + \sum_{j,k=0}^{n,n} a_{j,k} \cdot (s_v \cdot v_R)^j \cdot (s_w \cdot w_R)^k; \\
v &= 0 = s_v \cdot v_R + \sum_{i,j=0}^{n,n} b_{i,k} \cdot (s_u \cdot u_R)^i \cdot (s_w \cdot w_R)^k; \\
w &= 0 = s_w \cdot w_R + \sum_{i,j=0}^{n,n} c_{i,j} \cdot (s_u \cdot u_R)^i \cdot (s_v \cdot v_R)^j.
\end{aligned}
$$

$$\tag{15.6}$$

Equation (15.6) is yielded by replacing w_c Eq. (15.4) by the sum in Equation 15.5, u_c and v_c by analogous equations, and by using the short-hand $p_R = (u_R, v_R, w_R)^T = \mathbf{R}^T \cdot (P - C)$ for the right-hand side in Eq. (15.3). The polynomial coefficients $a_{j,k}, b_{i,k}$ and $c_{i,j}$ describe the surface in the observation coordinate system [Kra97]. The parameters

(s_u, s_v, s_w) can take two values: $s_q \in \{-1, 1\}$ for $q \in \{u, v, w\}$. By assigning identical parameters but different values of s_q to different surfaces, symmetries with respect to the coordinate planes of the observation coordinate system can be modeled. It is one of the benefits of this way of mathematical formulation that geometrical constraints between surfaces can be modeled with it: For example, by assigning identical coefficients and identical but unknown rotations r_{ij} to a set of surfaces, parallelism can be enforced, and rectangularity of two planes can be obtained by formulating them as being the $uv-$ and vw-planes of the same coordinate system, respectively.

Three-dimensional polynomial curves can be formulated as the intersection of two surfaces by using a set of two of the Eq. (15.6), and a 3D point is determined by the intersection of three surfaces, i.e., by all three Eq. (15.6).

Using these techniques of formulation, **task-dependent knowledge bases** can be built. The knowledge base contains a set of predefined object models (**primitives**) that make sense in the context of the task to be solved; in Sections 15.3.4 and 15.4, examples for such knowledge bases will be given. Each primitive, i.e., each object model in the knowledge base, is a graph as described in Figure 13.11. The following information has to be provided to build that graph:

1. a set of surfaces s. For each surface, a subset of the coefficients $a_{j,k}, b_{i,k}, c_{i,j}$ defining the mathematical formulation of the surface or a reference to a symmetrical surface and the symmetry have to be provided;

2. a set of corner points v; and

3. a set of edges e. For each edge, its starting and endpoints and the surface neighbors have to be defined.

In object reconstruction, an appropriate surface primitive is selected, and points or lines are assigned to points, edges, or surfaces of the primitive in the hypothesis generation step. Hypothesis verification by robust hybrid adjustment is described in the following section.

15.3.3 Robust Hybrid Adjustment

By **hybrid adjustment** we mean a simultaneous least squares adjustment of different types of observations. In the context of object reconstruction as described here, for each correspondence hypothesis, two types of observations are basically used:

1. **Image coordinates:** For each image point and for each vertex of an image line that is one of the partners of a correspondence hypothesis, two Eq. (13.3) are inserted in the adjustment. As the orientation parameters are assumed to be known, only the coordinates of the object point $P = (X, Y, Z)^T$ are unknown.

2. **Surface observations:** For a point on a surface, one, and for each vertex of a line attached to an edge, two Eq. (15.6) are inserted in the normal equation system. In these observation equations a subset of all possible parameters $(P, C, \mathbf{R}, a_{j,k}, b_{i,k}, c_{i,j})$ is unknown.

The observations are weighted by $p_i = \frac{c^2}{m_i^2}$, m_i, and c being the a priori rms errors of the observation (an image coordinate or a point's distance from a surface or curve) and of the weight unit (an observation with weight 1), respectively. By selecting an appropriate rms error for the surface observations, the "rigidity" of the object models can be tuned. Starting from coarse approximate values, all unknown parameters are determined by iterative simultaneous adjustment of all observations. If only planar surfaces are used, adjustment will converge within a few iterations.

There are dependencies between the coordinates of C and the constant coefficients and between the rotations $\mathbf{R}$ and the linear coefficients; the way these dependencies are treated is task-dependent. With respect to edges, care has to be taken on the determinability of the coefficients of the intersecting surfaces. For example, thinking of a straight line being the intersection of two planes, the tilts of the planes orthogonal to the line have to be either determined by other observations or be declared constant. It is worth mentioning that no homologous points are required to determine a curve in object space: A point being observed in one image and on one curve gives four equations, three of which are required to determine its object coordinates. The fourth equation will give support for the curve parameters; thus the curve will be determined by intersection of two or more bundles of rays.

As soon as convergence has been achieved, robust estimation by modulating weights by the weight function in Eq. (14.16) described in Section 14.2.2 is used to eliminate the outliers. The arguments $r_{j,n}$ of the weight function $w(r_{j,n})$ in Eq. (14.16), i.e., the normalized residuals, are in this case given by $r_{j,n} = \frac{d_{j,n}}{m_j}$. As described in Section 14.2.2, it is the goal of robust adjustment to eliminate false matches; the observation equations corresponding to false matches, i.e., hypotheses contradicting the surface model, are successively eliminated from adjustment. The results of hybrid robust adjustment is an estimation for the surface parameters, the object coordinates, and (if desired and possible) of C and $\mathbf{R}$. In addition, blunders are marked in the data. In order to make robust adjustment work, a high redundancy is required, and the number of outliers should not exceed 30 percent.

The hybrid photogrammetric adjustment system ORIENT [Kag89], which was developed at the Institute of Photogrammetry and Remote Sensing at Vienna University of Technology in the mid-1970s, is used for the implementation of the object reconstruction framework described in this section. ORIENT offers the possibility of simultaneous hybrid least squares adjustment of different types of observations, including image coordinates, control points, model coordinates, and surface observations. The great number of observation types it can handle and its possibilities for blunder detection are the most important reasons for ORIENT's flexibility, which makes its application in object reconstruction possible [Rot98].

15.3.4   DEM Generation for Topographic Mapping

A digital elevation model for small-scale topographic mapping can be derived from a point cluster in object space. In the framework described in the previous sections, the whole area of interest is divided into surface patches that are treated individually.

Within a patch, the object surface can be approximated by one or more almost horizontal planes, depending on whether we want to model smooth terrain, a ridge edge, or a step edge. Which model is eventually used is decided by user interaction, depending on the kind of terrain available in the area of interest.

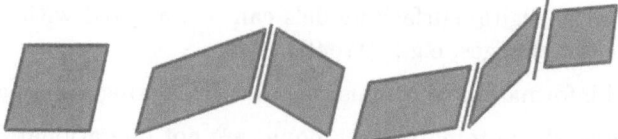

FIGURE 15.17. Surface models for DEM generation: A flat surface (*left*), a ridge (*center*), and a step edge (*right*).

Points are extracted from the digital images, and each point of the first image is compared with each point of the other image situated on or close to the epipolar line. Given the approximations from the previous pyramid level, the search space (i.e., regions where we compare points) is reduced along the epipolar line, so that a point corresponding to a feature from the first image has to be within a flat rectangle parallel to the epipolar line; all points within that rectangle are possible candidates. Similarity of gray levels is used to assign weights to the correspondence hypotheses and to exclude hypotheses failing to meet a certain similarity threshold. Having done that, each correspondence hypothesis gives a 3D point P, which is assigned to one of the planes comprising the local object model. Thus, each hypothesis gives five observations:

- four image coordinates (two per image), and

- one surface observation.

Each hypotheses adds three new unknowns to the adjustment, the point's object coordinates, and there are three additional unknowns per object plane to be determined. Thus, the system is highly redundant, an important prerequisite for robust estimation.

15.4   Semiautomatic Building Extraction

The great demand for 3D city models, 3D GIS, and virtual reality models collides with the enormous costs of data acquisition. Thus, automation of extraction of buildings from large-scale aerial images is a very desirable and challenging yet equally difficult task because of the great number of possible building forms, even in a rather homogeneous cultural region such as central Europe. In principle, automatic building extraction consists of two steps [Bru98]:

1. **Building detection** gives an answer to the question "Where is a building?"; thus it comprises methods to detect regions of interest for subsequent building *reconstruction*. Automation of building detection is not yet operational due to

the great complexity of the task. The application of different data sources seems to be most promising:

(a) digital images: Grouping of extracted image features to find rectangular structures or color-based segmentation methods, e.g., [BM97].

(b) high-quality digital surface models can be analyzed with respect to sudden local height changes, e.g., [Wei97].

(c) 2D GIS information can be used to locate existing buildings, e.g. [HBA97].

(d) As long as the automated techniques are not operational, interactive determination of the regions of interest will be inevitable. In this section, we will only describe interactive methods for building detection.

2. **Building reconstruction** gives an answer to the question "What does the building look like?", it is the determination of the geometrical parameters of a building located in a given region of interest. The fact that there is a building in the region of interest is assumed to be answered by a previous detection step. In order to automate building reconstruction, the computer has to learn what a building is. Thus, a knowledge base containing one or more models of what a building is has to be made available. This knowledge base can be provided explicitly by giving a set of building primitives, or it can be provided implicitly by declaring rules for feature grouping. Two strategies are followed in current research involving different degrees of automation:

- fully automatic building reconstruction; and
- semi-automatic building reconstruction.

Fully automatic building reconstruction: In fully automatic building reconstruction, data-driven and model-driven techniques have to be combined. In a first step, feature aggregates have to be found by a grouping process. This step is driven by implicit assumptions on which structures are typical for all buildings, e.g., characteristic patterns of intersecting edges. In a second step, the feature aggregates have to be combined using information from a knowledge base. The knowledge base gives the possible combination of aggregates that make sense with respect to the task. In [FKL97], the feature aggregates are 3D corners with neighboring edges combined by applying a knowledge base containing typical building forms. [HBW+96] aggregate the bounding edges of homogeneous image patches and derive 3D planar surface blobs that are combined by a consistency check considering the neighborhood relations of adjoining blobs.

Semiautomatic building reconstruction: Due to the complexity of the task, fully automatic building reconstruction is not yet operational. That is why semiautomatic systems are currently being developed [Mül98, Vel98, Rot98] to offer a compromise between the great demand for automation in data extraction and the fact that the problem has not yet been completely solved. Semiautomatic systems provide a knowledge base of building primitives typical for a certain cultural region, and they offer tools for the automation of precise determination of the building parameters as well as for efficient interactive adaptions. The workflow for the reconstruction of a certain building looks as follows [Mül98]:

1. interactive selection of an appropriate building primitive from the knowledge base by the human operator;

2. interactive determination of approximations for the building parameters;

3. automatic fine measurement and adjustment of the building parameters to the image data; and

4. visual inspection of the matching results and interactive editing in case the automation tools failed to achieve correct results.

In this section, the realization of semiautomatic building extraction within the framework given in Section 15.3 is described.

15.4.1 Building Models

In Section 15.3.2 the mathematical model for describing surface primitives was described. If we analyze the task of building extraction in the context of surface reconstruction as discussed in Section 15.3.1, there are three possibilities for providing local object surface models [Bru98] in a knowledge base:

- Parameterized models: Basic primitives such as hip roof buildings or saddleback roofs (Figure 15.18). The topology of these primitives is provided by the knowledge base; only the geometrical parameters have to be adjusted.

- Prismatic model: This type of model provides a construction rule rather than a fixed topology; a prismatic building is characterized by two horizontal planes (roof and bottom) and a set of n vertical planes (walls).

- Combinations of simple primitives in order to model more complex buildings. This means that "gluing tools" are required.

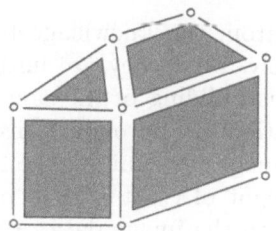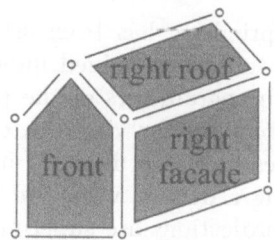

FIGURE 15.18. Surface models for building reconstruction: A hip-roof building (*left*) and a saddleback roof building (*right*).

Both parameterized models and the prismatic model can be expressed in the same way in the framework of Section 15.3.2, the difference being only the initialization phase. Taking the saddleback roof as an example, the following formulation would be adequate:

- The reference point C must be in the center of the floor. Its object coordinates determine the position of the house in object space.

- The coordinate system is parallel to the building facades; thus only one rotation κ around the Z-axis is required to determine the orientation of the building in object space.

- The model consists of seven surfaces:

    1. floor (not visible): $w_c = 0$.
    2. front facade: $v_c = a_{000}$.
    3. back facade: identical parameters as front facade, mirrored by the uw-plane.
    4. right facade: $u_c = b_{000}$.
    5. left facade: identical parameters as right facade, mirrored by the vw-plane.
    6. right roof plane : $w_c = c_{000} + c_{100} \cdot x_T$.
    7. left roof plane: identical parameters as right roof plane, mirrored by the vw-plane.

Although the building primitive is formulated as a boundary representation, it is determined (apart from its position and orientation in the object coordinate system) only by a small set of parameters that can be easily interpreted: the building length $l = 2 \cdot |a_{000}|$, the building width $w = 2 \cdot |b_{000}|$, the gutter height $h = |c_{000}|$, and for the obliquity angle δ of the roof we get $tan(\delta) = |c_{100}|$. Using the formulation method described in Section 15.3.2, the boundary representations behave in a way similar to CSG models, and the overparameterization usually connected with boundary representations is avoided.

15.4.2   Interactive Determination of Approximations

As soon as the primitive has been selected from the knowledge base, the building parameters have to be determined interactively. First they are initialized by default values, e.g., by the parameters of the previous building of the same type. Typically, two images will be open for visual determination of approximations. As soon as one point on the eaves has been digitized in an image, the building can be positioned in object space using a default value for the height of C; it is then projected into the images and the projections are superimposed to the image data. As soon as the first point has been measured in the second image, the object coordinates are computed and the shifts can be initialized (Figure 15.19, upper row). If a second point of the eaves is measured in one of the images, the rotations and the building length can be

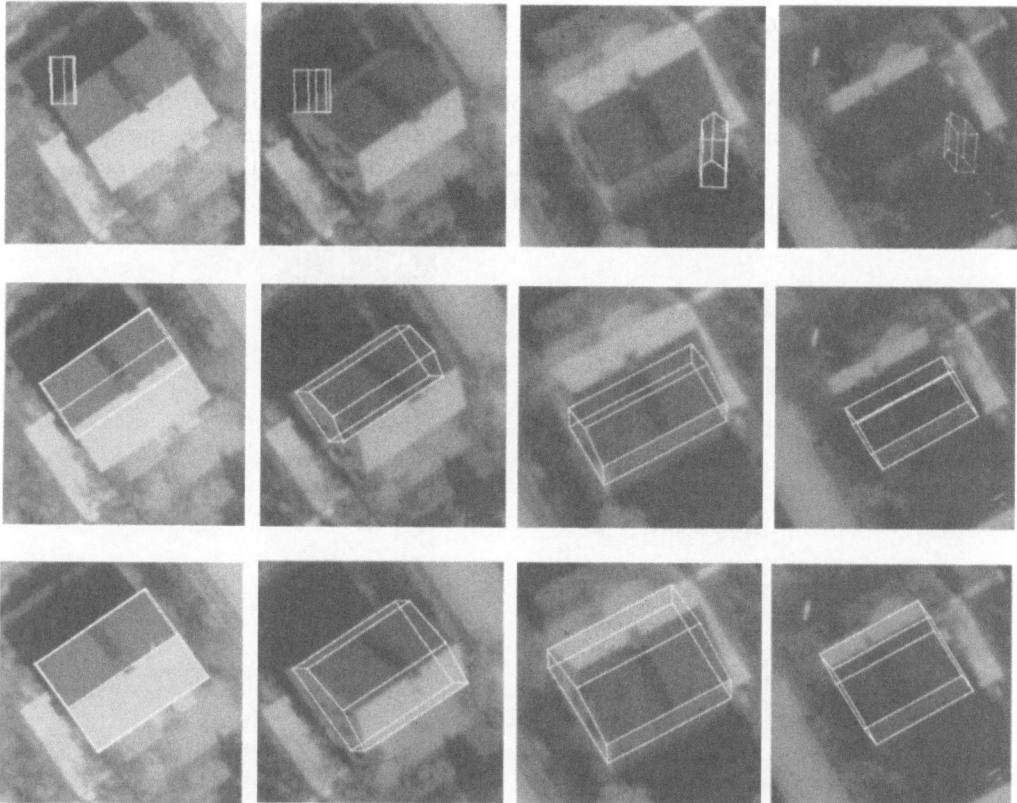

FIGURE 15.19. Semiautomatic building extraction: *Upper row*: One point has been measured in the left two images. *Second row*: A second point has been measured in the left image. *Third row*: A third point has been measured in the left image. The house primitive is backprojected to all images in which the house is visible.

determined (Figure 15.19, second row); a third point finally gives the building width, and the model is approximately positioned in object space (Figure 15.19, last row).

Of course, the rest of the parameters are still initialized by defaults. The procedure described earlier relies on the eaves being horizontal, a condition that is not necessarily fulfilled for all buildings. A more general and very elegant approach which sets up rules for directly modifying the building parameters in dependency of changes of the image coordinates of the corner points is described in [Mül98]. Another possibility is given by introducing observations for the building parameters and performing robust hybrid adjustment after each mouse click; by robust estimation the observations for building parameters that have been determined by image rays can be eliminated so that the model fits optimally to the interactively determined corner coordinates.

15.4.3 Automatic Fine Reconstruction

As soon as it is requested by the human operator, fine adjustment of the building parameters is to be performed in the sense of the framework described in Section 15.3.1. The surface model and the approximations are provided by interactive measurement. First, the building model is projected into all images to determine the regions of interest. In these regions of interest, features are extracted (Figure 15.20).

FIGURE 15.20. Semiautomatic building extraction: Features extracted in the region of interest.

In a subsequent step the features have to be matched to the corners and edges of the building models: Hypothesis generation comprises both the assignment of extracted image lines to building edges and extracted image points to corner points of the model. Thus, we get four observations for each image line vertex assigned to an object line:

- two image coordinates; and
- two surface observations.

For each image point assigned to a building corner, we get five observations:

- two image coordinates; and

- three surface observations.

Each hypothesis (each line vertex and each corner point) adds three unknowns to the adjustment, the point's object coordinates, and there are three additional unknowns per object plane to be determined. Note that we do not need homologous points for determination of lines! As each line vertex adds four observations and three unknowns to the adjustment, it increases redundancy by one. The line parameters are actually determined by intersection of two or more bundles of rays. Again, adjustment is highly redundant; in order to speed up computation, a preliminary elimination of the unknown object point coordinates is desirable. Even if the automatic determination of the building parameters fails, the workflow of building extraction is sped up significantly by providing a knowledge base of building primitives because symmetries are used in interactive positioning and the topology of the building is also given by the primitives.

15.5   State of Work

In the previous sections, strategies for the automation of photogrammetric measuring tasks were discussed and examples given. The degree of automation that could be achieved depended on the complexity of the task to be solved: In some cases, especially in extracting buildings from digital images, human interaction remained an important part of the system, even though the amount of work to be done by the human operator could be considerably reduced. A part of the work described in the previous sections has already been finished; other parts are currently in the implementation phase. The latter holds true for surface reconstruction: The components of the framework described in Section 15.3 have been implemented in the course of the Austrian Research Program on Digital Image Processing in C++ and in object-oriented design. Current work does not only comprise the specialization for DEM generation but also semiautomatic building extraction. A prototype of the knowledge base for building extraction has been made available; the matching algorithm described in Section 15.4 is about to be implemented.

In order to increase the degree of automation that can be achieved in photogrammetric plotting in the future, several strategies can be followed:

- **Modeling:** In order to automate 3D reconstruction tasks, knowledge about the objects to be reconstructed has to be converted into a form that can be understood by computers.

- **Multiimage solutions:** In photogrammetry, stereo configurations are still commonly used, and many algorithms for surface reconstruction rely on that. By increasing the number of images, automation of more complex tasks might become easier.

- **Multisensor solutions:** Sensors other than photographic cameras can provide valuable information, which can be applied for the automation of 3D reconstruction. This especially holds true for laser scanners.

16

3D Navigation and Reconstruction

Gerhard Paar
Wolfgang Pölzleitner

16.1 High Accurate Stereo Reconstruction of Naturally Textured Surfaces for Navigation and 3D-Modeling

16.1.1 Reconstruction of Arbitrary Shapes Using the Locus Method

Stereoscopy is one of the widely used techniques for passive three-dimensional (3D) measurements. With known sensor geometry, the projection of one scene point into different locations within the stereo images is used to reconstruct the scene surface (see Section 13.3). In addition to correspondence analysis, which concerns the matching of points in two perspective views of a scene so that the matched points are projections of the same scene point (Section 14), the surface reconstruction process is one of the essential tasks in stereo image processing.

Many publications address the topic of *registration* or *alignment* between 3D point clouds and given surface models (see [SS89] for a survey). The application in the case described in this section is different because the geometrical properties of the measured data and the reference are exactly known from sensor calibration. This makes it a *3D inspection* task.

Traditional recovery of scene topography for stereo vision using *spatial forward intersection* [BK78] is not satisfying for many applications. When corresponding image points are directly projected into Cartesian object space using triangulation, the resulting elevation description is sparse and nonuniform with all the problems attached thereto.

The *stereo locus reconstruction method* is based on an approach by Kweon and Kanade [KK92] for multiple range finder data. The fundamental concept of working in image space rather than object space is extended to the stereo disparity mapping case. Having dense disparities (i.e. on each pixel of the input images), the locus method can be applied in a straightforward and efficient way to gain a robust 3D reconstruction of the observed surface.

Usually point clouds are the result of a spatial forward intersection step and need to be projected on the given surface patches. Some operational systems need manual assistance [UP95b, Len96] for tasks that is not acceptable for fast and cheap industrial inspection. It is one of the advantages of the locus method that the problems induced by *triangulation, spatial forward intersection,* and *interpolation* do not affect the measurement. Ambiguities, occlusions, and especially uncertainties caused by calibration and matching errors can be detected, which is an essential property of industrial measurement systems.

In the following we assume that the orientation of the stereo camera system is exactly known with respect to the surface model. This is the case in any standard medium-range stereophotogrammetric system [BUv96].

The surfaces to be inspected are a combination of discrete primitives (patches) that can be described analytically in 3D space. Planes, spheres, superquadrics, or cylindric shapes are well-known examples. In addition, the position and orientation of each patch are known exactly. The basic aim of the inspection process is to measure the deviation of the measured surface to the model. One of the simplest scenarios for such a task is the generation of a digital elevation model (DEM: Section 13.5.1) from remotely sensed stereo images. Here the locus method already proved to be a valid tool [BP93]. However, the general problem is sparsely represented in literature. We claim that the simplicity of DEM reconstruction is the reason why operational solutions in the field of stereo reconstruction exist mainly in the remote sensing domain.

A result of HFVM (Section 14.3) is a set of disparity images with the same geometry as the input images. Each pixel defines a parallax between corresponding points on the left and right images of the stereo pair. They can be considered the basic database for the locus reconstruction.

The idea of incorporating the known image orientation into the matching process [Gru95] could be applied to improve the matching robustness. Because the locus consistency provides a very similar measure of matching correctness, this has not yet been done for the current HFVM implementation. Furthermore it would significantly reduce the matching speed.

The fundamental concept of the *locus reconstruction approach* is to work in image space rather than object space. It requires knowledge of correspondence between the left and right image spaces. For this reason it is well suited to exploit dense and uniform disparity maps computed with HFVM.

The elevation at an *arbitrary* reference position is found by intersecting a hypothetical line at this location with the object's surface (Figure 16.1). The line is projected into the stereo images (*left* and *right locus*). The image information at the locus location characterizes a profile curve on the object's surface. The corresponding location in the other image is found by mapping the locus using the given disparities. The elevation is determined by the most consistent intersection between the locus and the profile curve projection, taking into account the well-known height of the curves [BP93]. The stereo locus reconstruction algorithm operates as follows:

1. Define a discrete grid on the reference model shape. For every point do steps 2–(6:

2. Construct a hypothetical vertical straight line to the reference surface.

3. Determine the maximal possible deviation from the reference shape on this point to restrict the search space.

4. Determine the stereo images whose field of view includes the search line.

5. Project this line section into both stereo images (*left* and *right locus*).

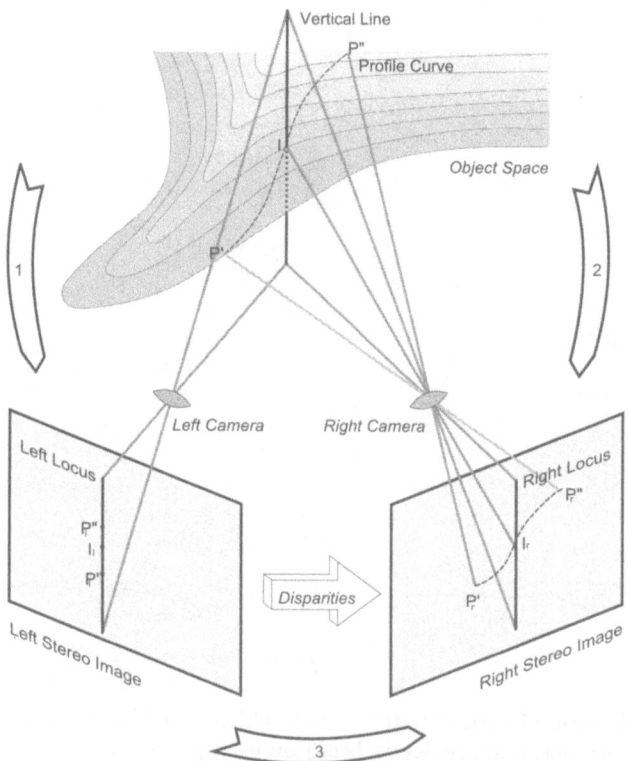

FIGURE 16.1. Stereo locus reconstruction: Project straight line at desired grid location into left (1) and right stereo image space (2). Map left locus into right image using disparities (3). Intersect left locus projection and right locus to yield surface point.

6. Look at the disparity of each image pixel that covers the left locus. If it points at a right image pixel covering the right locus, this is a candidate for describing the "elevation" (surface normal distance) at this location. Consistency checks for both the disparity and the given elevation at the respective locus location lead to the best fit elevation. Several simple constraints can be applied to decide whether or not a valid candidate exists.

Using simple neighborhood relationships and the pyramid structure to gradually refine the reference surface resolution permits a drastic reduction of the search space for consistent elevations. The adaptation to the multiresolution HFVM disparity map structure makes it possible to provide a rough elevation description for a general view.

A consistency check allows us to evaluate the quality and accuracy of both the elevation and the disparity map and calibration. The locus approach shows less sensitivity to noise in the disparities than the spatial forward intersection method.

The result is an elevation map projected on the reference surface. The byproduct is an ortho image, the gray level projection of the images acquired on the reference surface.

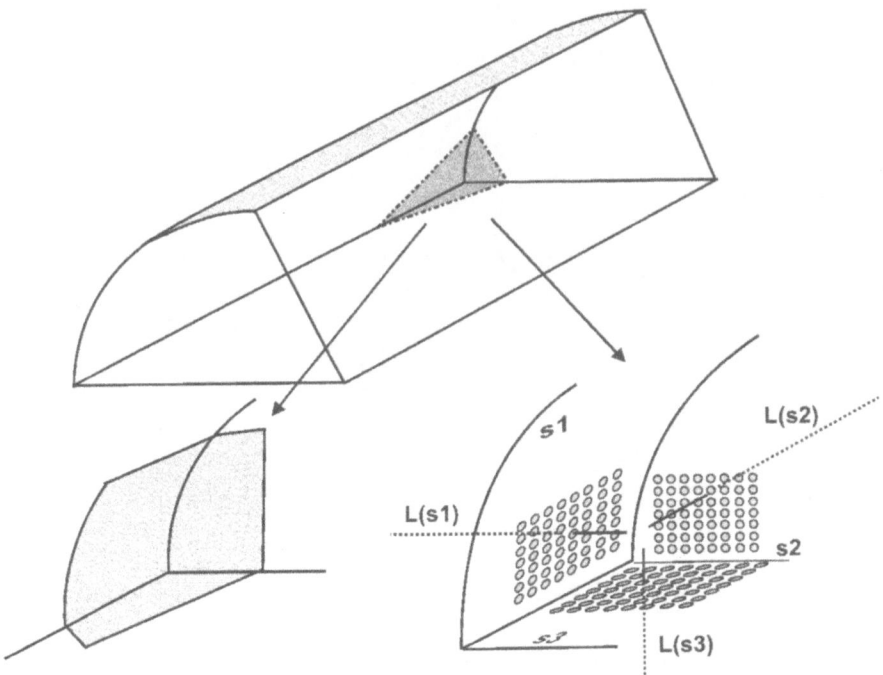

FIGURE 16.2. Combination of surface patches. *Left:* Camera field of view; *right:* example for a regular grid on the patches, and one locus $L(s_n)$ on each patch s_n.

For many measuring applications, it is important to easily project the measured surface to any analytically describable shape. The locus reconstruction method can handle arbitrary global shapes: In object space, straight lines perpendicular to a reference surface are defined. By preference for a dense reconstruction, they are arranged in a regular grid thereon. Generally, the interesting locations can be selected without restriction on a reference surface in object space (Figure 16.2). This allows us to individually inspect specific regions with different reference resolutions but the same height resolution. Another task is to use stereo image sequences acquired from different locations and viewing angles to view the same target. The locus reconstruction approach can handle and merge a set of stereo images in a direct and efficient way. Without any further processing, it combines the results of many stereo configurations that can cover arbitrarily distributed parts of the surfaces. A *disparity data base* and a *surface data base* can be taken into consideration within a single processing step (Figure 16.3).

The advantage is that the reconstruction starts to inspect the target locations in object space but evaluation is done in image space. For that purpose it is possible to predict whether the search location is relevant for a specific stereo geometry.

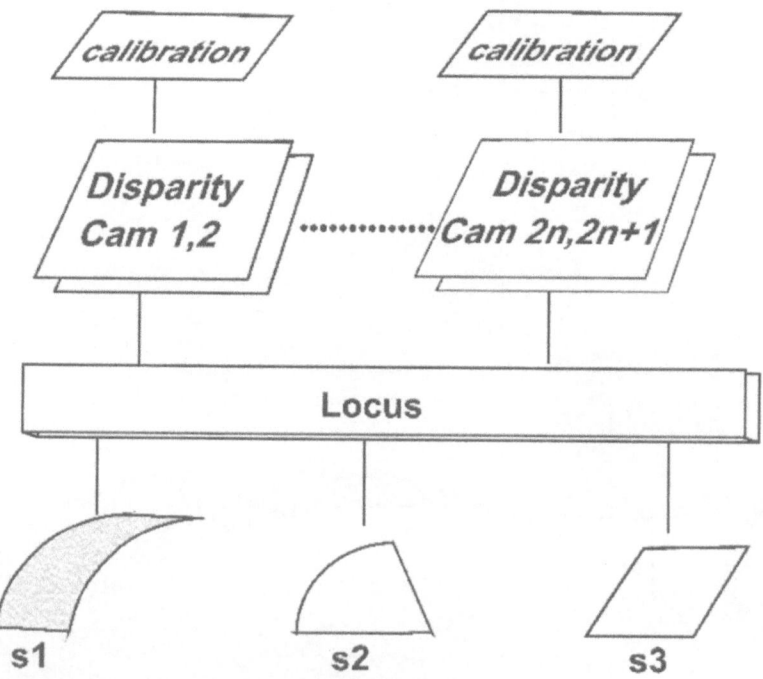

FIGURE 16.3. 3D inspection database: Each set of disparities and camera calibration represents a stereo camera setup. The locus method combines all setups into one process and calculates for each given surface patch s_n the deviations.

16.1.2   Using the locus Method for Cavity Inspection

The process of cavity construction needs thorough correctness checking of the current cavity shape. Figure 16.4 shows such a geometric scenario. Three stereo setups are used to monitor different parts of the surface. Stereo images of a plane P and two views c_1 and c_2 of a cylinder surface C are acquired. HFVM is performed on the three image pairs. Disparity images and locus reconstruction results are depicted in Figure 16.5 for the plane P and in Figure 16.6 for the cylinder surface C.

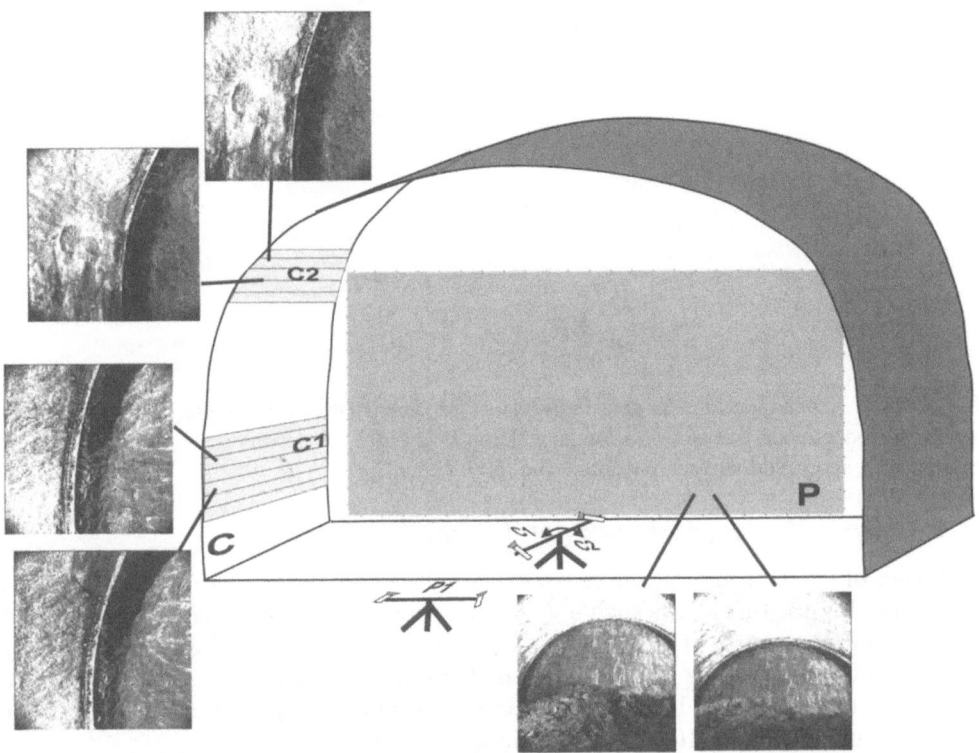

FIGURE 16.4. Cavity inspection scenario: One stereoscopic view p_1 of plane P and two views c_1 and c_2 of a cylinder surface C. Image size is 1000×1000 pixels.

FIGURE 16.5. *Left*: Row disparity image for plane P; *right*: locus reconstruction results (*top*: ortho image, *bottom*: isolines of surface structure with 40 mm depth spacing). Scene size is about 10×5 m.

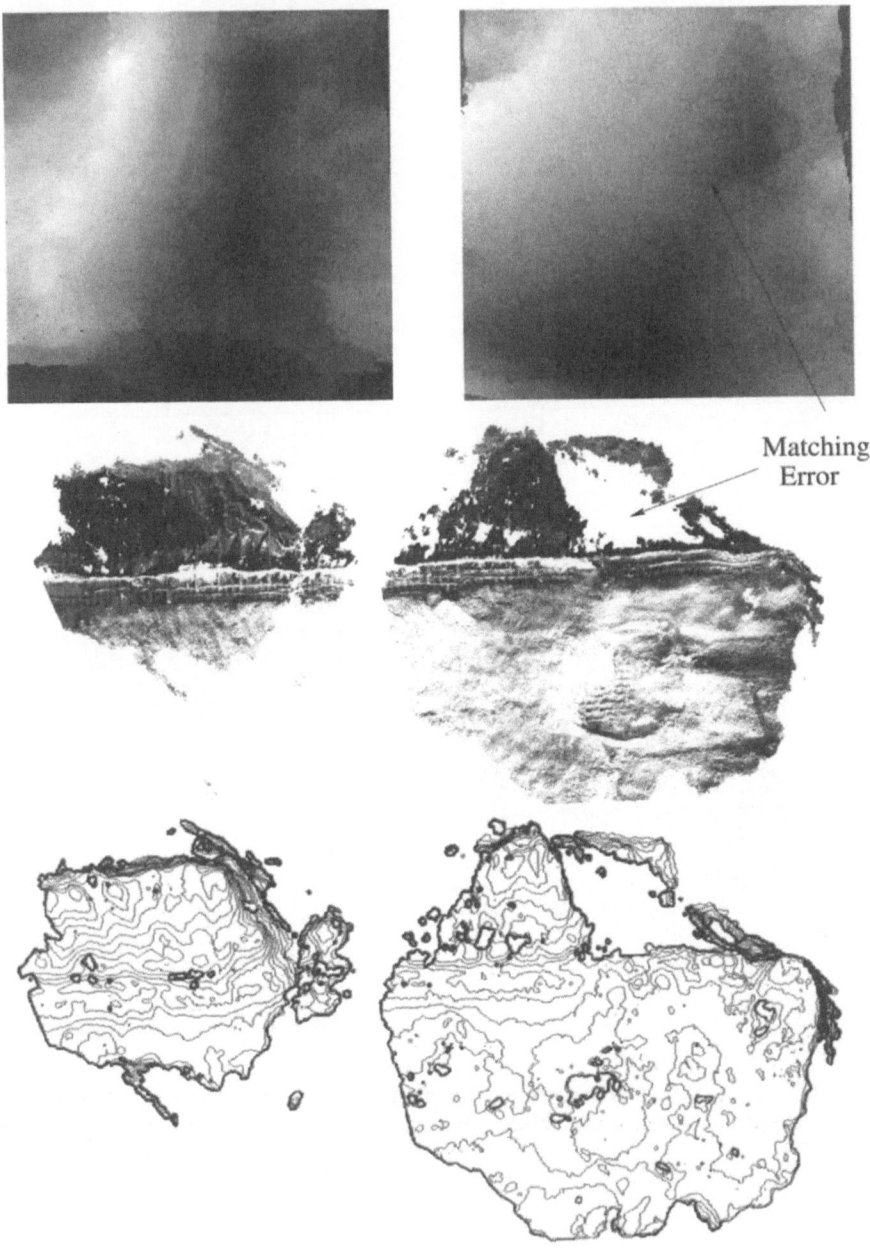

FIGURE 16.6. Row disparity images (*top*) and locus reconstruction results for cylinder C (*center*: ortho image, *bottom*: isolines of surface structure with 40 mm depth spacing). The results of views c_1 and c_2 have been merged. A large area of erroneous matching was detected in the c_2 reconstruction. Scene size is about 8×4 m.

16.1.3   Stereo Reconstruction Using Remote Sensing Images

Operational solutions in the field of stereo reconstruction exist mainly in the remote sensing domain. Most of the commercially available remote sensing data processing and GIS packages provide subtools that support DEM generation from satellite and aerial stereo imagery. One of the most widely used data set is generated by the Landsat [U.S84] or SPOT [spo88] satellites. In Figure 16.7 an example for a stereo pair from a mountainous region in Austria is displayed. The stereo reconstruction results of two different stereo matching methods are depicted in Figure 16.8. An evaluation of the errors introduced by the matching process is given in Tables 16.1 and 16.2. The results indicate that feature-based techniques in this field are superior to standard correlation techniques (see Chapter 14).

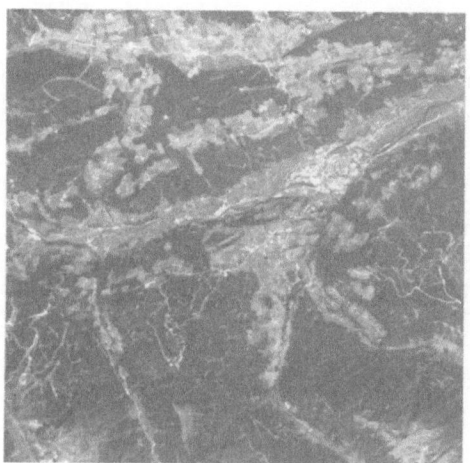

FIGURE 16.7. 1024 × 1024 pixel stereo partners, part of SPOT *TADAT* test site. The two subareas mentioned in Table 16.1 are marked in the right image with subarea RAMSAU being inside the upper rectangle.

The example in Figure 16.8 was generated using a system by an Austrian distributor [RHR+93]. As one representative in the GIS domain, the OrthoMax system should be mentioned [Vis96], which also provides automatic DEM generation from two images from the same sensor. Several other products have entered the market during the last ten years, most of them for the DEM generation from SPOT stereo pairs [GR93]: see [TVD94, BT91] for comparison. The reconstruction accuracy lies in the range of pixel resolution, i.e, in case of the SPOT panchromatic sensor (10 m/pixel) a height error of 10 m can be expected.

A list of all available systems for remote sensing applications would go far beyond the scope of this book. However, it must be stated that an overall solution has not been

TABLE 16.1. 1024×1024 pixels part of SPOT *TADAT* test site: Comparison between errors (m) of reconstruction using three different HFVM pyramid levels and traditional cross-correlation approach for disparity generation. Reference is a DEM manually generated from topographic 1:25.000 maps.

	HFVM L. 0	HFVM L. 1	HFVM L. 2	Correlation
Nb. of points matched	1000000	227300	59200	2200
Nb. of points used	26490	25258	14800	1197
Proc. time (disparities)	32 min	8 min	2 min	13 min
Image resolution (m)	10	20	40	10
Standard Deviation error (m)	**15.5**	**19.2**	**29.2**	**21.1**
Mean error	1.78	0.9	2.1	1.7
Max error	151	178	199	110
Min error	−129	−104	−159	−202

TABLE 16.2. Comparison between errors (m) of reconstruction using HFVM (Section 14.3) and cross correlation (Section 14.1.1) for disparity generation on subareas SCHLADMING (urban area) and RAMSAU (field and forest area).

	SCHLADMING		RAMSAU	
	HFVM L. 0	Correlation	HFVM L. 0	Correlation
Standard Deviation error (m)	**12.3**	**16.8**	**10.6**	**16.5**
Mean error	2.09	1.77	4.76	4.23
Max error	77	80	50	70
Min error	−52	−87	−51	−87

published yet and the necessary amount of interaction and manual corrections are, for good reason, not mentioned in the advertisements for the respective systems.

Reference DEM

 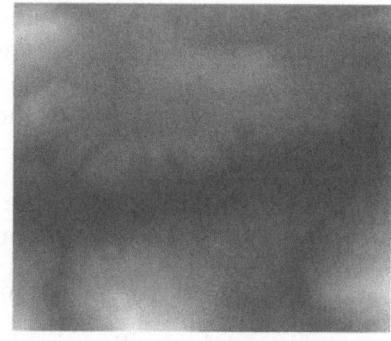

DEM from HFVM level 0 disparities

 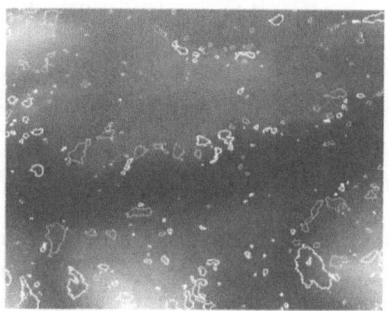

DEM from correlation disparities

 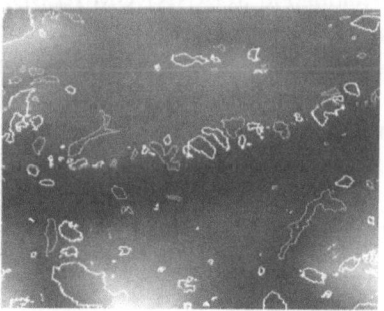

FIGURE 16.8. *Left:* Contour plots (δz=40 m) of TADAT test area DEMs; *right:* heights coded as grey levels overlaid with regions of height error > 30 m. Thin lines represent negative error regions; thick lines represent positive error regions.

16.1.4   Stereo Reconstruction for Space Research

Unmanned space research requires the highest amount of autonomy for all data processing tasks. Therefore, so far, stereoscopy has only been used with other methodism in this domain. Nevertheless, a set of prototypes has been developed in Europe, the US and Japan to demonstrate the feasibility of autonomous navigation systems and robotic applications:

- Medium-sized rovers are able to reconstruct the environment using onboard stereo cameras and processing resources [HZF93].

- Comet exploration models foresee stereo mapping from near orbits [de 90].

- A testbed for landing simulation of unmanned spacecraft was developed. Automatic surface stereo mapping from orbit is followed by closed loop vision-based navigation [Paa95, PP92a].

- A stereo vision testbed for robotic operations [SIR94] shows real-time capabilities in tracking artificial 3D objects.

- The advantages of trinocular stereoscopy were shown on a robotic vehicle called *Dante* for reconstruction of its environment [Ros93].

16.1.5   Operational Industrial Stereo Vision Systems

Most advancements in steoroscopic measurements for industry were gained in the field of industrial quality control, mainly in the automotive and aircraft industries. High-precision photogrammetric methods use a new generation of high-resolution digital cameras as well as digital theodolites in integrated systems [BD93, Hoe93]. The field of application is mainly offline: the texture observed is covered with reference points for single high accuracy measurements (1/200.000 of object dimensions).

One example of the new generation of stereoscopic surface reconstruction systems was developed at JOANNEUM RESEARCH in Graz, Austria [PPB95]. It is capable of fully automatic reconstruction of rocklike surfaces with included error detection. Results of several reconstructions are merged and projected on selected analytically described surfaces as raster data (DEM and gray levels, namely, *ortho images*). Figure 16.9 shows an example of input images and disparities as a result of HFVM (Section 14.3). A reconstruction result is shown in Figure 16.10. The prototype system is able to generate a 10×10 m grid of 10 mm density with a height accuracy of 10 mm in half an hour on standard PC hardware.

FIGURE 16.9. Image examples: Left and right stereo partner and row disparity image (disparities coded as gray levels) of a concrete surface.

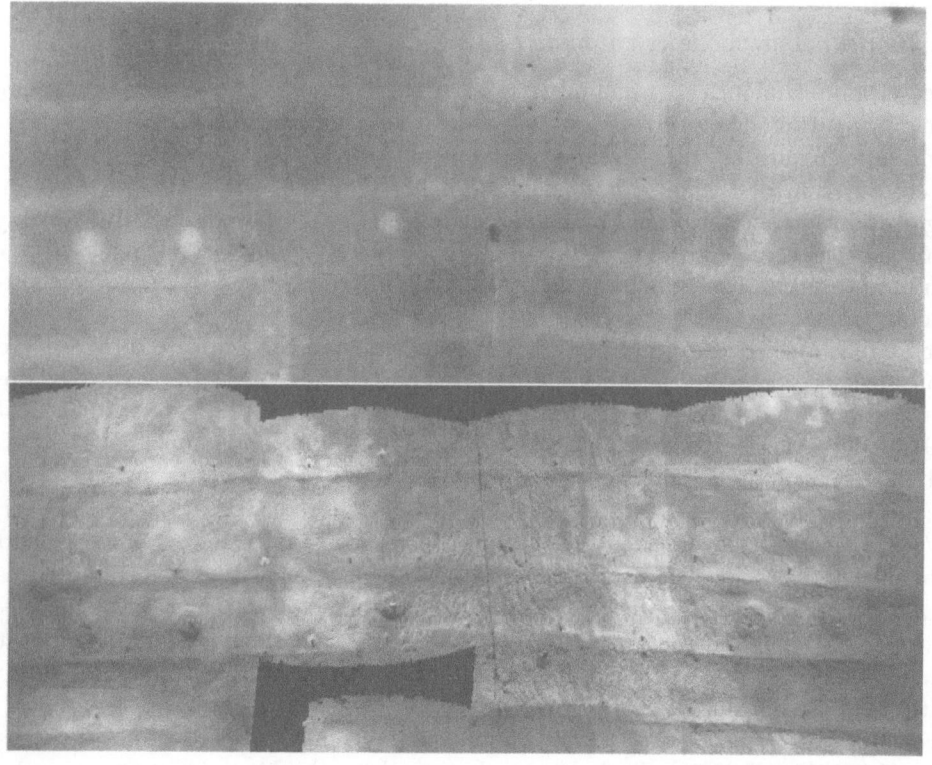

FIGURE 16.10. Result of merging four stereo reconstructions: Ortho image and raster DEM (gray level coded) projected on a cylindric surface.

16.2   A Framework for Vision-Based Navigation

A vision-based navigation system is a basic tool to provide autonomous operations of unmanned vehicles. For offroad navigation that means that the vehicle equipped with a stereo vision system and perhaps a laser ranging device shall be able to maintain a high level of autonomy under various illumination conditions and with little a priori information about the underlying scene. The task becomes particularly important for unmanned planetary exploration with the help of autonomous rovers.

Major advances in autonomous navigation based on computer vision techniques have opened the possibility of using autonomous rovers to explore the planets. The implementation of the recent technological achievements to planetary rovers was outlined in the previously withdrawn LEDA moon exploration project [Eur95]. Three roving control modes should be supported by the vision-based navigation (VBN) system according to LEDA mission objectives:

1. teleoperating mode of ground-based piloting;
2. medium autonomy mode or autonomous piloting and ground-based navigation; and
3. full autonomy mode or autonomous navigation.

Stereo vision techniques offer a number of advantages in solving the task of autonomous vehicle navigation. They rely on low-cost video technology, which uses little power; the sensor is mechanically reliable and emits no signature (unlike laser rangefinding).

A stereo system also allows more flexibility. Most of the work during stereo range image production is performed by software that can easily be adapted to a variety of situations. The same applies to the path planning software block: The logic of the path planning procedure can easily be changed depending on a goal to be approached on a planetary surface.

There have been several attempts by different teams in the world to integrate stereo vision into the rover navigation system. The construction of the first wheeled rover, named Robby, that successfully used stereo was completed in December 1989 at JPL [LB91]. Another early stereo vehicle was developed by Nissan and named PVS [OOK89]. With faster computers and advanced algorithms new perspectives in stereo vision have been opened. Robust stereo systems have been realized on the robotic truck NAVLAB [Tho90] developed by Carnegie Mellon University. More time-demanding trinocular stereo vision has been employed on the eight-legged walker Dante [Ros93] also developed at Carnegie Mellon. The idea to use three stereo cameras was justified in the work by Dhond and Aggarwal [DA91], who found that the increase in computation due to a third camera was only 25 percent while the decrease in false matches was greater than 50 percent.

French teams have been working on autonomous navigation systems for several years [PHF+93, PLSN93]. Their approach proved for the Marsokhod rover combined the chain of sequential operations such as stereo reconstruction, obstacle location, and path planning. Nevertheless both Dante and the French system imposed a parallel geometry condition by the stereo reconstruction algorithms used. This condition weakens the whole system, because parallel stereo geometry is practically difficult to arrange and maintain. Even small distortions in epipolar stereo image geometry cause immediate impact on the reliability of stereo matching. Therefore, an additional rectification procedure must be employed before [BHP⁺92].

In the following we present a concept for the fully autonomous mode of the rover equipped by an active/passive imagery sensors setup. Our approach combines both stereo and mono vision techniques. The 3D stereo reconstruction algorithm is based on almost arbitrary stereo geometry, which makes it stable against accidental distortions on the vision system arrangement. Tracking techniques are employed during the path execution step to control the vehicle locomotion along the local path. It can be stated that optimized versions of the algorithms involved in a closed-loop processing chain are suitable for onboard implementation. The reliability of the proposed algorithmic solution is demonstrated during simulation sessions with the help of an accurate robot and a lunar terrain mockup.

16.2.1 Vision Sensor Systems

Experiences of several teams working on autonomous navigation have proved that parallel geometry of stereo cameras is difficult to arrange and maintain. A special platform has been designed to adjust and maintain parallel geometry for three stereo cameras on Dante, the autonomous vehicle for Antarctic applications [Ros93]. In case of the Russian Marsokhod rover [Kol94] both stereo cameras were fixed on top of a special device performing accurate three-angle rotation.

Evidently, the parallel stereo geometry can be easily distorted by vibrations during motion or day/night temperature variations. Therefore a 3D stereo reconstruction approach based on almost arbitrary stereo geometry looks more preferable and reliable. Consequently, the necessary calibration procedure for the stereo system comprises three steps:

1. Inner orientation (Section 13.2). It is performed on the ground during system compilation and is considered unchanged (or recalculated depending on the known temperature conditions) during vehicle operation.

2. Initial calibration of camera positions and orientations with respect to the vehicle frame. One important parameter is the distance between the stereo cameras, which can be considered unchanged. This sensor description is performed during system integration and can be used for 3D reconstruction of the environment and as prediction during navigation. However, a very accurate relative orientation between the cameras can be accomplished using results from stereo matching [UP95a].

3. Online extrinsic (camera position and orientation) calibration. These parameters must be updated with respect to a given coordinate system while the vehicle is moving. Auxiliary sensors can help to avoid drifts and provide predictions for attitude parameters.

Auxiliary sensors (measurement units) are integrated in the vehicle navigation system to provide additional independent information regarding vehicle position and orientation. These are:

- magnetometer to know the general orientation of the vehicle and make it follow in the desired direction.

- wheel odometers and accelerometers as additional control units. The vehicle operations are stopped immediately if the data obtained from the sensors are above predefined safe thresholds.

- star tracker for independent self-localization of the vehicle on a planetary surface other than Earth.

- gyroscope/inclinometer, the only source of rotation data, used for both ortho DEM generation based on stereo matching and the image sequence tracking procedure. The tracking itself does not presume any relative rotation between subsequent image frames. In case relative rotation between two frames cannot be omitted, one can use sensor rotation data to derotate corresponding image frames.

- laser range-finding (ladar). This optional sensor can be effectively used for quick monitoring and obstacle detection near the vehicle.

16.2.2   Closed-Loop Solution for Autonomous Navigation

The vehicle vision-based navigation (VBN) system must operate under a set of specific conditions and requirements that are present on a planetary surface where immediate human intervention is in fact impossible. These are:

1. automatic initial calibration of the vision sensors;

2. absence of accurate reference points or landmarks for precise self-calibration;

3. low angle illumination conditions;

4. low angle viewing conditions; and

5. no a priori information about the underlying terrain.

On the other hand there are two conditions that simplify the operation of the vehicle VBN system:

1. low speed of the vehicle operations. The vehicle can move in a stop or thinking mode, thus performing time-consuming stereo reconstruction while it is stopped.

2. static environmental conditions. The vehicle's VBN system operates in a still scene if no moving objects within its field of view are expected.

To accomplish a fully autonomous vehicle navigation mode we suggest using a combination of stereo and mono vision techniques. Time-consuming stereo matching processing is employed during the stop thinking vehicle mode to calculate a DEM, to classify the underlying scene, and to generate a safe local path. A less time-consuming tracking procedure is employed during the path execution mode to control the vehicle displacements along the path. Summarizing, we propose the following approach to accomplish the vehicle's autonomous mode:

1. **Initialization phase.** This step is performed only once to initialize the operational units of the vehicle. These are: initial calibration of the imagery sensors (laser, stereo cameras) and measuring units (wheel odometer, accelerometer, inclinometer sensors, gyroscope, star tracker) and self-localization of the vehicle position with respect either to a given global map of the surface or another vehicle.

2. **Operational phase.** This step consists of the following operations implemented in the cycle:

   Stop thinking mode: 1. stereo image acquisition;

   2. DEM reconstruction;

   3. risk map generation;

   4. local path generation;

   Path execution mode: 5. consecutive image acquisition;

   6. landmark tracking; and

   7. update vehicle position (calibration update).

16.2.3 Risk Map Generation

A risk map is generated on the basis of a DEM, which has been generated using the HFVM (Section 14.3) and locus (Section 16.1.1) algorithms. The DEMs and ortho images are reconstructed in a world coordinate system considered fixed at the motion initialization point of the vehicle. Therefore elevation models from different vehicle positions can be merged to get a full 3D description of the surrounding vehicle path. Figure 16.16 shows an example of a merging result of nine subsequent stereo reconstructions.

The basic idea for generating a trajectory risk map is to select steep slopes and elevated areas from the DEM and to mark them as hazardous and unsuitable for the vehicle motion by comparing to some predefined safe threshold. The algorithm evaluates the minimal and maximal heights on the DEM in a local window and then calculates the local inclination. It takes $O(N)$ calculations per pixel in the optimized version of the algorithm (where N is the local window size).

16.2.4 Local Path Planning

A path based on a Voronoy diagram [BL91] is an equal distance from obstacles but is computationally expensive. Our idea is to consider the points of the risk map located outside hazardous areas as the nodes of a directed graph [Kol95]. The path is generated from a predefined start point and should reach a specified target point on the local map in such a way to minimize the length of a subgraph (Dijkstra algorithm [Dij59], Figure 16.11).

The start point of the path, e.g., the current position of the vehicle, is considered the graph origin. The length of the graph edges are positive values (weights) defined as the height difference between the subsequent vertices. As usual, the length of a particular path that joins any two given vertices of the graph is defined as the sum of the edge weights composing the path. Because the real local path must follow continuously

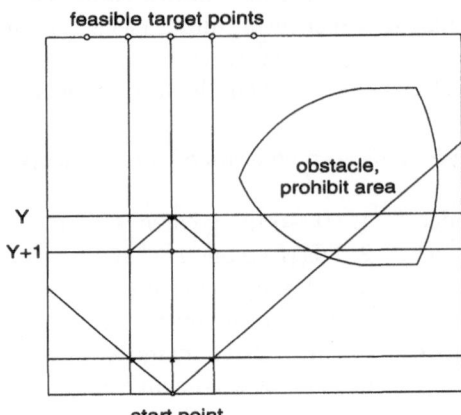

FIGURE 16.11. Path planning task: Directed graph on the image field. Each node in the image row Y can be connected only with the three nodes from the previous row Y+1.

through the image field, the graph edges must be connected in a directed way: Each node on the graph can be connected only with the three nodes from the previous image row. Under this restriction, the number of operations for searching the shortest path from the start point to the possible destination points is equal to $O(N)$, where N is the image size.

16.2.5   Path Execution and Navigation on the DEM

The accuracy of **initial localization** for the vehicle in a given world coordinate system depends on the accuracy of the available auxiliary sensor systems or a global map. After vehicle deployment, a local map with respect to the vehicle (its position will specify the beginning of the local coordinate system) can be used on board for further vehicle operations. The vehicle position and orientation shall be constantly controlled on board in the local coordinate system. That can be done with the help of the vision system, as described herein.

A **landmark tracking** algorithm [PSP95] is used to follow on the tracks of homolog points (interest points) in two subsequent images. Corresponding displacements between the Interest Points are then used as a database for the calibration update. To extract the interest points from the original image a derivative of the Moravec operator [Mor77] is used. Using auxiliary sensors (Section 16.2.1) it is only possible to make coarse predictions of the motion between two consecutive images (frames) taken while the vehicle is moving. Therefore, we propose using a hierarchical approach to identify corresponding interest points on subsequent frames. As a first iteration, the disparities of all points on the image are calculated in coarse resolution. In the following, this information is used to calculate the disparities only for the interest points in high resolution using feature vector matching. Figure 16.12 depicts this process: In a search window

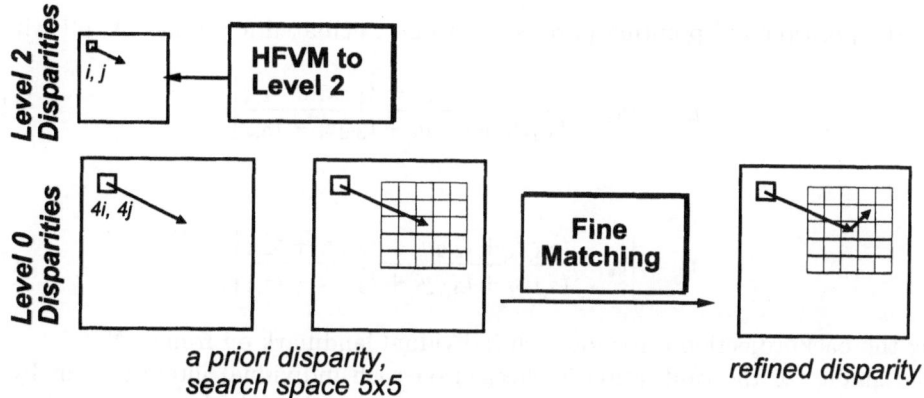

FIGURE 16.12. Coarse-to-fine tracking using HFVM results from higher pyramid levels.

around the coarse location of the point the best match of the old feature vector within the new image is searched for in the highest resolution. Because of the coarse tracking step, the search window needs only to be approximately 8×8 pixels, which implicates relatively low computational effort.

The essence of the **calibration update** method (i.e., identifying an instant camera position and pointing parameters along the vehicle path) is the following. Let us consider two consecutive images (frames N and $N + 1$) taken from the vehicle during motion. The 3D coordinates of the interest points on frame N are calculated from the DEM and the calibration matrix of frame N. Having 3D coordinates of interest points acquired from Frame $N(x_i, y_i, z_i)$ and their 2D coordinates (u_i, v_i) on frame $N + 1$ (from landmark tracking between frame N and Frame $N + 1$), a calibration can be performed to obtain position and pointing parameters of frame $N + 1$. The calibration method keeps the intrinsic camera parameters fixed and gains only an update for extrinsic camera parameters.

Assume the lens distortion has already been corrected to gain perfect perspective geometry. Having a_u, a_v–the focal length divided by pixel sizes in column and row directions–and u_0, and v_0–the coordinates of the principal point–as intrinsic parameters (assuming an orthogonal pixel coordinate system), we use the perspective projection matrix for the pinhole camera model [PU93]:

$$T := \begin{pmatrix} a_u r_{11} + u_0 r_{31} & a_u r_{12} + u_0 r_{32} & a_u r_{13} + u_0 r_{33} & a_u t_1 + u_0 t_3 \\ a_v r_{21} + v_0 r_{31} & a_v r_{22} + v_0 r_{32} & a_v r_{23} + v_0 r_{33} & a_v t_2 + v_0 t_3 \\ r_{31} & r_{32} & r_{33} & t_3 \end{pmatrix}, \quad (16.1)$$

where (t_1, t_2, t_3) is the translation vector (camera position) and $\mathbf{R} = (r_{ij})$ is the rotation matrix from Eq. (13.2) with the three pointing angles ω, ϕ, and κ. The minimization of

$$\sum_i (\mu_i + \nu_i) \quad (16.2)$$

gains the position and pointing parameters to be calculated for frame $N + 1$ with

$$\mu_i = \left| u_i - \frac{t_{1,1}x_i + t_{1,2}y_i + t_{1,3}z_i + t_{1,4}}{t_{3,1}x_i + t_{3,2}y_i + t_{3,3}z_i + t_{3,4}} \right| \qquad (16.3)$$

and

$$\nu_i = \left| v_i - \frac{t_{2,1}x_i + t_{2,2}y_i + t_{2,3}z_i + t_{2,4}}{t_{3,1}x_i + t_{3,2}y_i + t_{3,3}z_i + t_{3,4}} \right| \qquad (16.4)$$

being the backprojection error for each individual landmark on frame $N + 1$.

The quality of the calibration is checked on each individual interest point by projecting its 3D coordinates back into the image using the calculated calibration. The deviation of the corresponding 2D coordinates to the original image coordinates of the respective interest point is again calculated using Eq. (16.3) and (16.4) and is a measure of consistency. The calibration is iterated with the most inconsistent interest points removed, until this error gets below a certain threshold for all interest points.

Reflex obstacle detection is done in the following way: Any unexpected obstacle whose size is above a given threshold as well as unknown areas (shadowing, specular reflection) have to be detected during the vehicle motion at a minimum distance equal to two times the stopping distance of the vehicle. The fact that a bright stripe from the laser is easily recognized on the image field can be used to detect obstacles in the vicinity of the vehicle. A well-known approach is to analyze the shape of the laser stripe on the images taken during the motion. High curvy portions of the trace can be detected as parts of hazardous areas on the underlying scene.

A passive method for quick obstacle detection using images is described in [PSPS93]. The approach is based on a shadow and bright area detection mechanism that estimates the location and size of possible hazards with respect to the viewed image. It uses low-level image processing in connection with a highly dedicated syntactic object detection process that is robust against noise and adaptive in terms of various possible surface properties.

16.2.6 *Prototype Software for Closed-Loop Vehicle Navigation*

The vehicle's on-board software should be designed as a combination of separate algorithmic solutions (software blocks) that minimize intermediate data exchange. It is especially important to separate those software blocks that will need data from the vehicle sensors as input. All necessary processing shall be sorted into on-board and remote parts after on-board computational resources are clarified. The software blocks that need data from the vehicle sensors as input are preferable to be put on board. The computational complexity of the algorithms to be developed is a good starting point in a trade-off regarding necessary on-board computational power.

The current software organization is depicted in the left side of Figure 16.13. Table 16.3 gives raw estimates for the computational performance of the currently used modules on standard hardware.

Process	Parameters	CPU time (sec)
Stereo matching HFVM	Image size 570 × 520, every pixel	40
DEM/ortho image locus reconstruction	600 × 300 pixels	20
Risk map generation		1
Path planning	1 path	1
Tracking	200 landmarks	5
Calibration	10 iterations	5

TABLE 16.3. Processing time for the simulation software modules (Pentium 166 MHz, Windows NT).

16.2.7 Simulation Results

This section describes data and processing results collected during the sessions simulating vehicle operations on the moon surface. The hardware used for simulation (CamRobII, Figure 16.13) includes an accurate robot holding two cameras that can be moved with seven degrees of freedom within a 2 m x 1 m x 1.5 m wide volume. The motion is performed by seven step engines. CamRobII is controlled by software running on a SPARC workstation. A software interface enables an operator to move the camera on an interactive-command basis to capture images and store video data with the camera position and orientation data. In addition, CamRobII can be accessed via a programmable interface. A model of the lunar terrain was placed in a 1.6 m x 2 m bed mockup. The whole setup is designed to simulate a scale factor of 1:10 to reality.

For the vehicle motion simulation session both cameras were placed in the lowest position and directed forward and slightly downward. The positions of the cameras are detected with respect to the world coordinate system. The correspondence between CamRobII and world coordinate systems is given by a transformation matrix. Initial coordinates for the very first position of the left stereo camera and the stereo basis for the stereo pairs in the sequence are taken as known. The relative orientation of the stereo configuration based on stereo correspondences was performed using a fixed baseline between the cameras to obtain a certain scale factor. The following sequence of operations has been performed with the help of the system described earlier:

1. stereo sequence image acquisition;

2. stereo matching and DEM generation;

3. risk map generation and local path planning; and

4. landmark tracking and calibration update.

A long **sequence of stereo images** (40 pairs) was taken. The left image frames with odd image indices are taken by the left camera whereas even frames are regarded to the right camera (Figure 16.14). Both stereo cameras are set close to the mockup surface and directed slightly downward (15–20 degrees) to obtain a convergent low viewing angle perspective stereo pair of the mockup terrain. After the first pair is acquired both cameras are moved one step forward (15–20 mm) to catch the next stereo pair

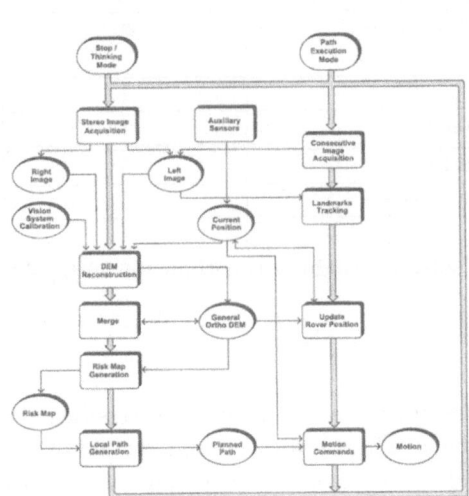

FIGURE 16.13. *Left:* Software components currently used for simulations; *right:* CamRobII camera motion device with a mockup simulating the lunar surface.

and so on. The whole camera path is straight for the case presented in the illustrations.

A general **elevation model** of the mockup terrain (ortho DEM) is generated on the basis of each fifth stereo pair (called *basic stereo pairs*) from the sequence. Intermediate left image frames (e.g., taken by the left camera) between the subsequent basic stereo pairs are used for the tracking and calibration update for the left camera. The frequency of the basic stereo pairs is defined by the necessary overlap between the reconstructed ortho DEMs to keep 3D coordinates known on the underlying surface (about 70 percent). The ortho DEMs calculated from the subsequent basic stereo pairs are merged to generate the entire ortho DEM for the underlying terrain. The stereo pairs are matched automatically (Figure 16.15); the locus method is applied for the 3D reconstruction. DEM resolution in x and y is selected 1 mm.

The left side of Figure 16.16 depicts the merging result of the nine ortho images calculated from the nine subsequent basic stereo pairs. Occluded and undefined areas are marked as white.

Path planning was done independently from the tracking simulation to demonstrate the robustness of the proposed approach for the moonlike terrain. A local path has been generated on the basis of the once reconstructed DEM. The generated local path is shown in the right side of Figure 16.16. Hazardous areas unsuitable for the vehicle motion are marked on the DEM as black. The start and destination points for the vehicle path are specified by an operator. A safe path is generated automatically within safe areas on the basis of the DEM slopes.

The goal of the landmarks (interest points) **tracking** is to calculate actual displace-

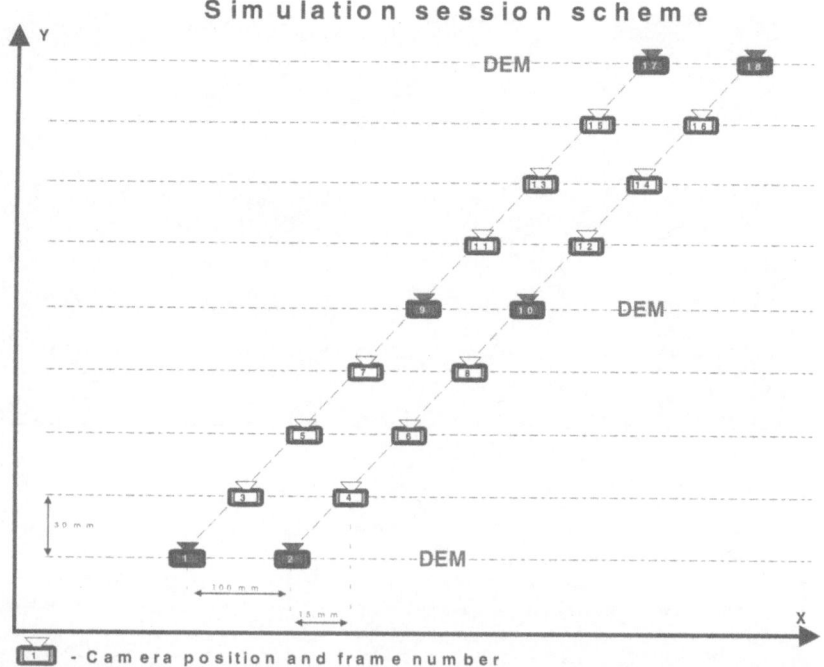

FIGURE 16.14. Every fifth stereo pair is used for the reconstruction of a new DEM.

ments between the CamRobII positions (calibration update) on the basis of tracking information for each subsequent image frame. The calibration update results have been compared with the actual CamRobII coordinates. The image sequence used for the tracking and calibration update is composed with the ten basic stereo pairs (20 frames) and four intermediate left image frames between each of them (40 frames). A relative calibration procedure based on stereo matching [UP95a] is used to calculate the coordinates of the right camera for each basic stereo pair. This simulates the process of self-calibration for the case of slight mechanic changes of the stereo system.

A calibration update procedure [PSP95] based on the interest points (landmarks) tracking is used to maintain the coordinates of the four intermediate frames known. Each forth intermediate frame comprises the left image for the next basic stereo pair, starting the next calibration loop.

The actual CamRobII trajectory used for the stereo sequence acquisition is a straight line. An offset between subsequent odd and even frames is 15 mm in the X direction and 30 mm in Y direction (Figure 16.14). The stereo basis (SB) for the basic stereo pairs is equal to 97 mm. An example of the tracking paths between corresponding interest points in four subsequent frames is shown on Figure 16.17. The major parameters during interest points tracking are the number of landmarks and their backprojection error as a measure of the calibration consistency. The most inconsistent interest points are rejected and not used for calibration. Experiments showed that the optimum number of landmarks necessary for the reliable calibration is about 200 points; however, a smaller

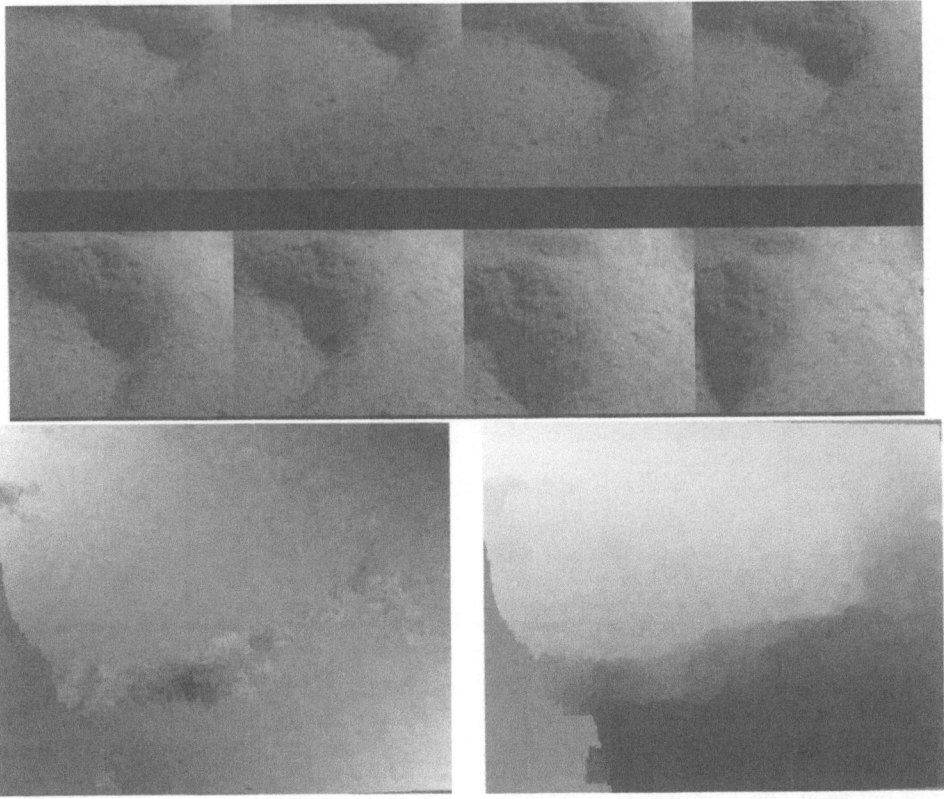

FIGURE 16.15. Four subsequent stereo pairs (*top*) and HFVM matching result of first stereo pair. *Left*: Row disparities; *right:* column disparities, gray level coded. Occluded areas around the image center rows caused matching errors.

set of landmarks (<200) still leads to robust tracking.

Figure 16.18 displays the trajectory calculated on the basis of tracking and calibration update for the cameras. The position offsets are presented in the right side of Figure 16.18. They show that the discrepancy between CamRobII coordinates and tracking positions have not considerably accumulated along the path. The fact that Y offset values are always above 30 mm is explained by the uncertainty in the scale factor chosen with the estimated stereo baseline.

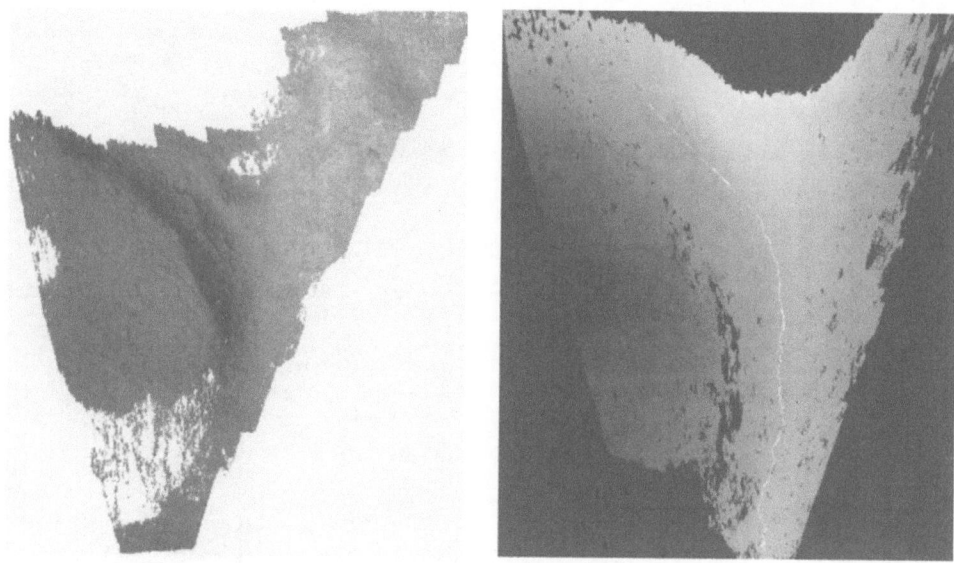

FIGURE 16.16. *Left:* Ortho image merged from nine stereo configurations; *right:* local path put on the DEM. Elevations are gray coded, bright areas are high. Unknown and hazardous areas are marked black.

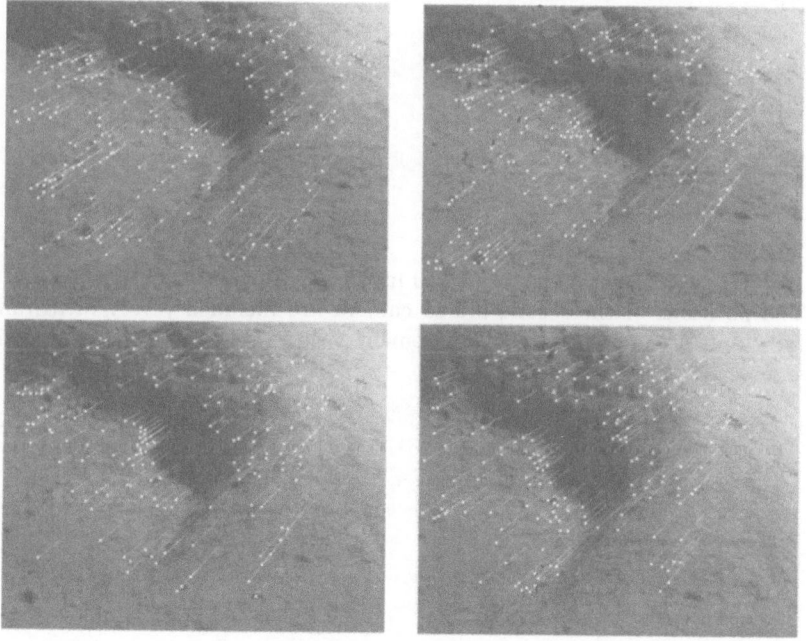

FIGURE 16.17. Four consecutive image frames and landmark tracking paths.

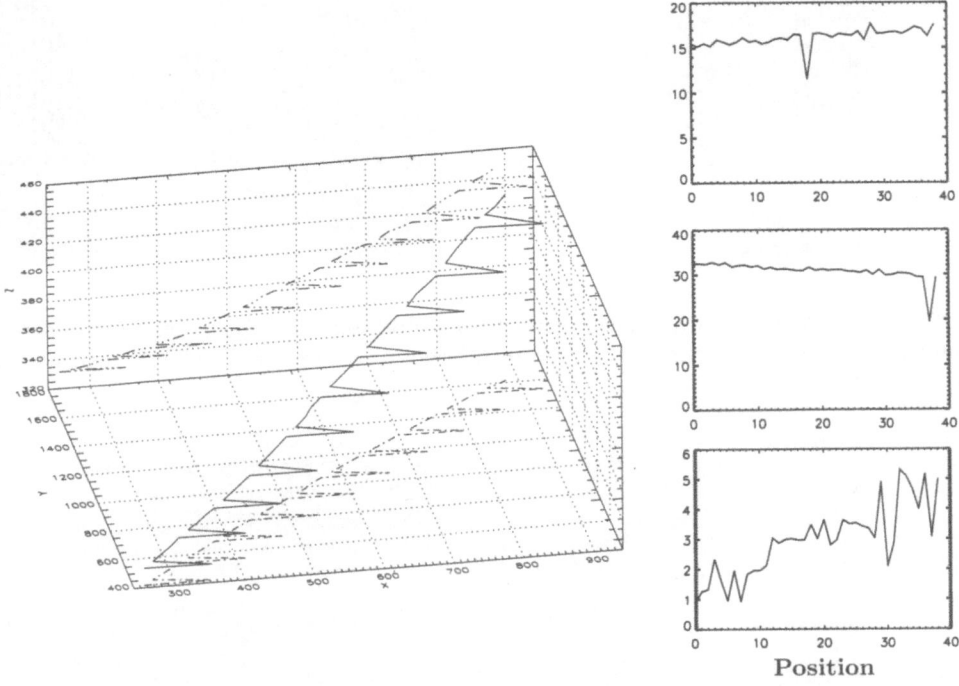

FIGURE 16.18. *Left:* Camera trajectory (~40 frames) as calculated on the basis of landmark tracking. The positions of the second stereo camera are included (every fifth frame). *right, from top:* x, y and z components of displacement vectors between successive positions. All values in mm.

3D Object Sensing Using Rotating CCD Cameras

Heribert Kahmen
Anton Niessner
Andrea de Seixas

Scientists, managers and planners in the industry and governmental offices increasingly need 3D representations of objects in the built environment. The demand for 3D data and real imagery of the environment is ever increasing.

Typical application areas are:

- quality control for production lines;

- facility management;

- construction management;

- 3D geographical information systems (GIS);

- hazardous site survey;

- accident site survey;

- general site survey;

- building interior survey; and

- archaeological site survey.

Theodolite- and image-based measurement systems using videometric methods can help to fulfill these demands.

17.1 Concept of Image-Based Theodolite Measurement Systems

A theodolite measurement system makes use of the intersections provided by a series of pointings to the same points (targets) by several theodolites to determine coordinates of the points measured (Figure 17.1). For the computation of the point coordinates, we *use the angle readings on the scale circles* of the theodolites pointing to the target.

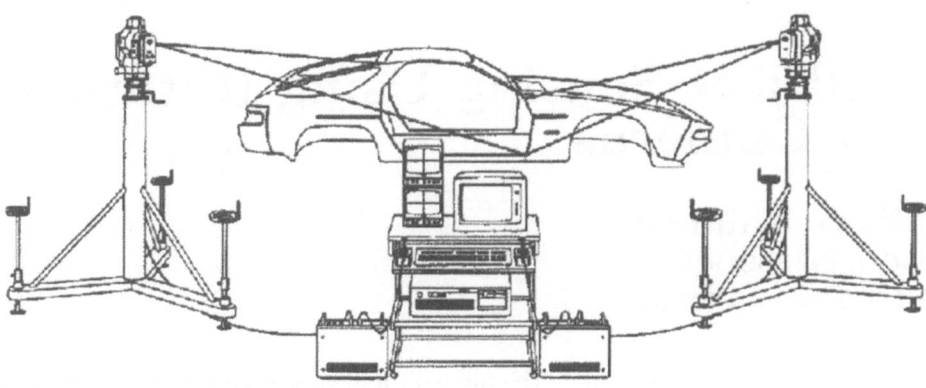

FIGURE 17.1. Theodolite measurement system consisting of two theodolites.

The coordinates of the measured points and the instrument stations are determined by a three-dimensional network adjustment. The system is oriented in a given coordinate system by reference to control points that form part of that system. In addition, these control points provide the scale of the system.

The measurement system is a combination of different components:

- theodolites used as sensors;

- computer system;

- software; and

- accessories.

The sensors used to capture data are computer controlled video theodolites. A video theodolite has a CCD camera in its optical path (Figure 17.2). The horizontal and vertical axes carrying the telescope and the CCD camera, are driven by motors. The motors are controlled by a computer.

The images of the telescope's visual field are projected onto the camera's CCD chip. They consist of the target object and a frame in the focus plain of the telescope replacing the standard telescope reticule. The CCD camera is capable of capturing mosaic panoramic images through camera rotation. With appropriate calibration these images are accurately georeferenced and oriented as the horizontal and vertical angles of rotation are continuously measured by electronic angle measuring systems and fed into the computer. The oriented images can then be used directly for direction measurements with no need for object control points or photogrammetric orientation processes. The image resolution can be chosen by selecting different camera lenses and should be limited only by the angular precision of the total station. In practice, the camera system should have a two-camera lens systems. A wide angle system should provide overview images to support the organization of the measurements and a narrow angle system

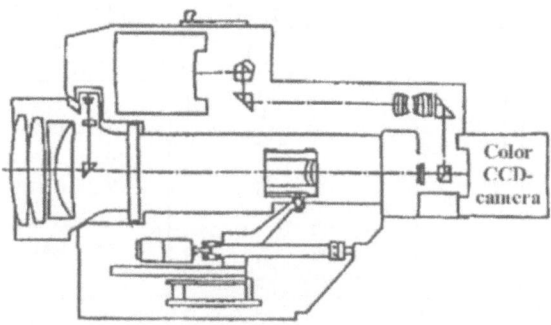

FIGURE 17.2. Optical path of a video theodolite.

that provides images for the measurements. The focal length of the narrow angle lens system should be chosen so that the image pixel angle is compatible with the angular precision of the theodolite.

In addition to the motor drives for both theodolite axes, the focusing drive is also motorized. The search for an optimal autofocus distance is controlled by an autofocus function.

17.2   The Videometric Imaging System

17.2.1   The Purpose of the Videometric Imaging System

A videometric imaging system consists of a light source, image sensor, components for image acquisition and image processing, a computer for system control, and some output devices. The electrooptical sensor converts an optical image into a video signal. Especially if high resolution is required, a CCD camera should be used as the image sensor. An example of an electrooptical setup, based on a CCD camera, is shown in Figure 17.3.

In videometric imaging systems sensing and computer technologies are merged. The sensor acquires electromagnetic energy from a scene and converts it into an alternate form (voltage), that the computer can use. The computer then extracts information from the data, compares the information with the previously developed standards, and outputs the result, usually in the form of a response.

Videometry may be defined as follows: the use of devices for optical sensing to automatically receive and interpret an image of a real scene, to obtain geometrical information, and to control direction information, the particular location, or orientation of a part in an assembly, the simple presence or absence of an object, or part of an assembly.

Based on videometry, theodolite measurement systems can be developed, which can perform their measurements with and without targeting. The basic idea behind the second method is to use the texture on the surface of the objects to define targets (natural targets). If both methods are available, the theodolite measurement systems are much more flexible. This will be described in the following.

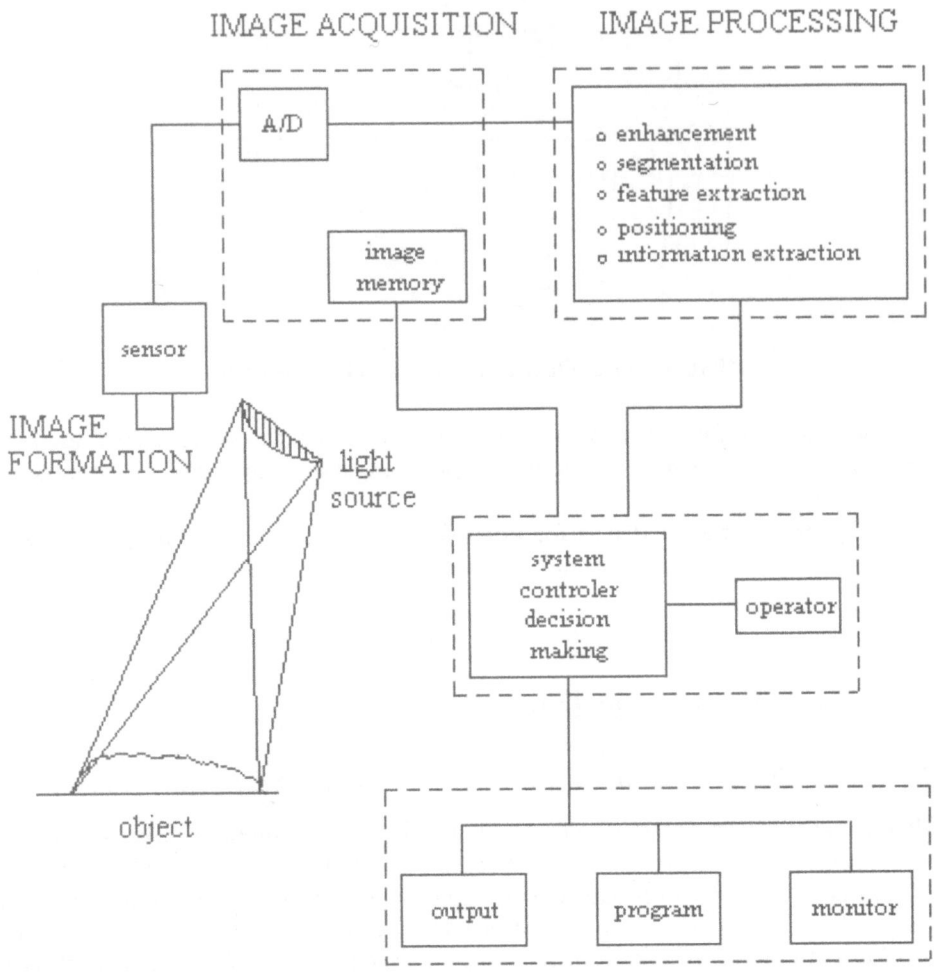

FIGURE 17.3. A simplified concept of a videometric imaging system.

In combination with theodolites, CCD matrix sensors can be used to produce automatic coordinate determination systems, based on the reduction of direct angular readings to x-, y- and z- coordinates. If a CCD camera is integrated into the telescope of the theodolite, automatic direction measurements can be performed with the system depicted in Figure 17.4. A special frame in the focus image of the theodolite's telescope is used there as an "interface" to combine the theodolite system with a camera system. With the frame, the orientation and translation parameters are determined, describing the relationship between the sensor and the telescope coordinate system. As these parameters are determined frequently, the system can be considered free of temperature-influenced drift. The first such system was developed by Leica in Heerbrugg.

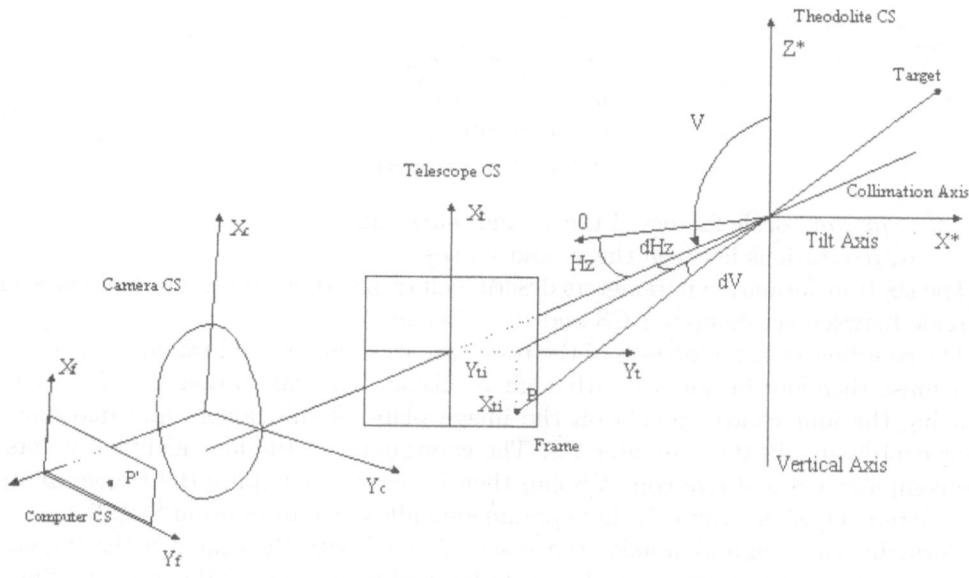

FIGURE 17.4. CCD camera combined with the telescope of a theodolite.

A suitable definition of the telescope coordinate system (CS) is given, if it is located in the focus plane of the objective system and perpendicularly intersected by the collimation axis.

The direction measurement process then consists of the following steps:

1. The coordinates of the geometrical center of the target are determined by image processing procedures in the computer CS.

2. The coordinates of the computer CS have to be transformed into the telescope CS.

3. If the collimation axis is not aligned with the center of the target, the target coordinates in the telescope CS are used to correct the direction readings of the theodolite.

The three steps comprise the inner orientation (intrinsic parameter) whereby Step 2 can be considered an affine transformation:

$$\begin{bmatrix} x_{ti} \\ y_{ti} \end{bmatrix} = \begin{bmatrix} c_{01} \\ c_{02} \end{bmatrix} + \begin{bmatrix} c_{11} & c_{12} \\ c_{21} & c_{22} \end{bmatrix} \bullet \begin{bmatrix} x_{ri} \\ y_{ri} \end{bmatrix}. \tag{17.1}$$

with x_{ri}, y_{ri}–coordinates of the computer CS;
x_{ti}, y_{ti}–coordinates of the telescope CS;
c_{01}, c_{02}–translation parameters;
c_{11}, c_{22}–rotation parameters; and

$$m_x = \sqrt{c_{11}^2 + c_{12}^2},$$
$$m_y = \sqrt{c_{21}^2 + c_{22}^2},$$
$$\alpha = \arctan(c_{12}/c_{11}), \tag{17.2}$$
$$\beta = \arctan(c_{21}/c_{22}),$$

m_x, m_y–scale factors of the x- and y-axes and
α, β–rotations between the x- and y-axes.

The six transformation parameters describe all translations, rotations, and variations in scale between the computer CS and the telescope CS.

The coordinates of the corners of the frame are used for the calibration of the camera and must therefore be known with high precision. The calibration is performed by imaging the four control points on the image plane of the camera and determining their coordinates in the computer CS. The coordinates of the four identical points in the computer CS and telescope CS can then be used to compute the transformation parameters. Once determined, these parameters allow one to perform Step 2.

Normally, the collimation axis need not be aligned with the center of the target. In that case, the coordinates (x_{ti}, y_{ti}) have to be used to correct the direction readings of the theodolite (Figure 17.4). If the theodolite has a panfocal telescope, the corrections are given by:

$$\begin{bmatrix} \tan dH_z \\ \tan dV \end{bmatrix} = (C_1 D^2 + C_2 D + C_3)^{-1} \begin{bmatrix} x_{ti} \\ y_{ti} \end{bmatrix}, \tag{17.3}$$

where C_1, C_2, C_3 are the parameters obtained from the calibration of the telescope and D is the path length the focus lens was moved away from an intial point.

Starting at an initial point, the focus lens can be moved by a DC motor (see Figure 17.2). The desired path length that the focus has to be moved can be determined with an autofocus function.

Finally, the corrected angles are used to compute the object coordinates of the target. The measurement process is automated by incorporating motors to drive the horizontal and vertical axes of the theodolites and to focus the telescope.

With the measurement process described earlier only a small part of the information produced by the camera for the detection of the targets is used. Therefore a new type of measurement system was under investigation, which enables not only fast and accurate pointing of targets but also allows object reconstruction without targeting by using nearly all the information the images contain. Without targeting pointing shall be possible on two ways: either interactively performed by an operator or automatically, controlled by a computer. In the following, both methods will be described.

17.2.2   An Interactive Measurement System–A First Step

The key element of the first system is vision software that supports the operator to find "natural targets" (extracted features) on the object [Roi96]. The diagram of the videometric system is shown in Figure 17.5. The main steps are image formation, image

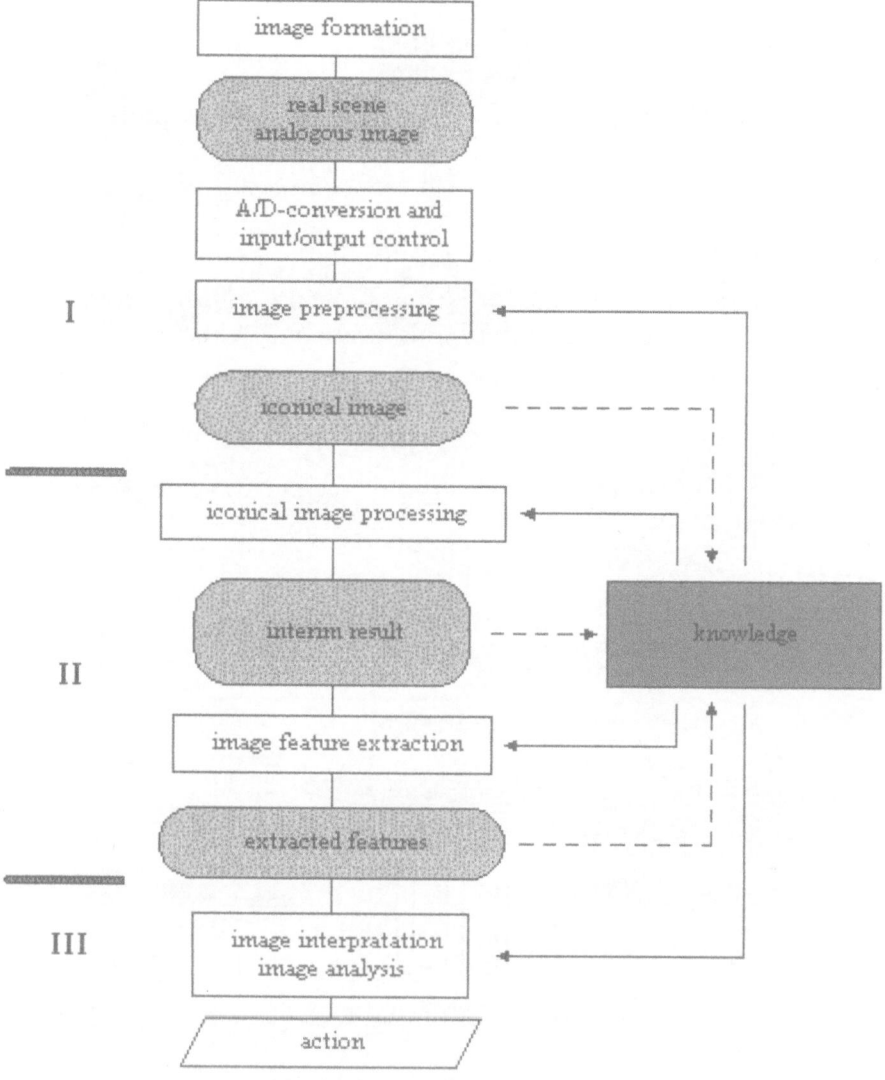

FIGURE 17.5. Diagram of videometric system of the theodolites.

preprocessing, iconical image processing, image feature extraction, image interpretation, and image analysis.

Image formation involves the light source and the object reflecting the light. The optical image is transformed into a two-dimensional function of the object and stored as a matrix of gray values. The hardware contains amplifiers, A/D converters, frame grabbers, and other devices. The preprocessing software enables improvement of the radiometric quality of the images and enhancement. Enhancement includes improvement of the geometric quality of the image and data reduction by applying digital filters to

FIGURE 17.6. (a) Facade original; (b) after applying histogram equalization and Sobel-operator; (c) after applying thresholding.

support the feature extraction and positioning phase. Iconical image processing is used to create new images, finally resulting in sets, containing the desired information. Image feature extraction (segmentation) comprises searching the objects of interest from the rest of the scene with the aim of partitioning the image into various clusters. Thresholding is a special method in region segmentation assigning "white" to each pixel in the image with gray scale above a particular value. All pixels below this become "black" (Figure 17.6).

Finally the operator has to extract feature information from the enhanced and seg-

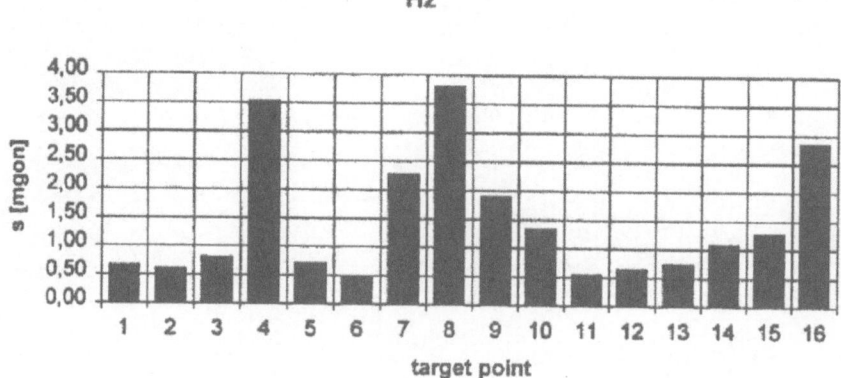

FIGURE 17.7. Standard deviation of the horizontal direction.

mented images and analyze whether they can be used as targets.

There is no standard telescope reticule in the telescope's visual field; it is replaced by a reference frame. Therefore, for interactive pointing a recticule (identical to the coordinate axes of the telescope coordinate system) has to be added to the optical system by special image processing software. This recticule then can be used for the alignment of artificial and natural targets on the object.

To test the measurement system, a facade was monitored. Instead of targeting, the videometric system described in Figure 17.5 was used. Sixteen selected edges were monitored (Figure 17.6(a)). To enhance the edges a Sobel operator was used with histogram equalization and thresholding (Figure 17.6(b) and (c)). Figure 17.7 depicts the standard deviations of the horizontal directions we got after we monitored the detected edges. The facade was monitored with two video theodolites. The distance between the object and the theodolites was about 33 m; that leads to an accuracy of the determined edges of ±2 mm (1 σ). The accuracy was only limited by the roughness of the surface. In addition, the observations were performed with only the standard theodolite without using image processing. Then the standard deviations increased to about ±5 mm (1 σ). Other projects showed that the videometric system can also sucessfully be used for extremely accurate measurement and shape fit of small industrial objects (Figure 17.8). Accuracies of about 0.1 mm (1 σ) are possible [KR95, Roi96]. The results encouraged us to start with the development of an automatic system.

17.2.3 An Automatic System–A Second Step

The most effective way to develop an automatic system is to use the theodolites in a master and slave mode. Then one theodolite (master) scans the object while the second theodolite (slave) tracks it by automatically searching for homologous regions.

Two different scanning procedures were developed:

- The first method is based on the subposition that there are patterns on the surface

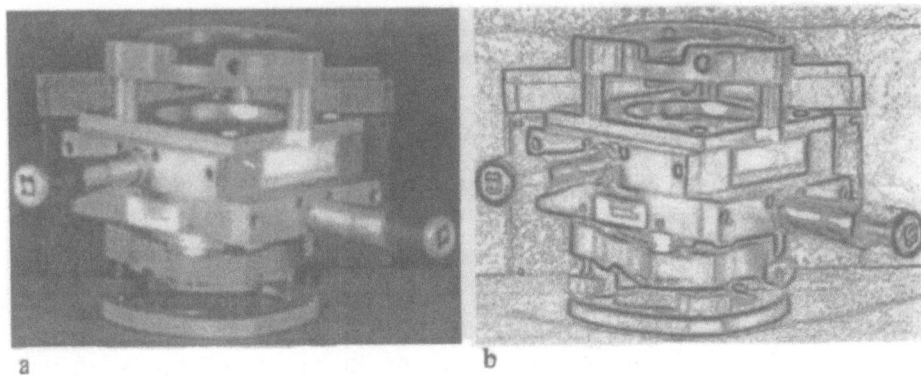

FIGURE 17.8. (*a*) Tripod original; (*b*) after applying image processing.

of the object to be scanned or that the object is composed of different structural parts so that corners, intersections of lines, or other wellmarked points can be detected.

- The second method can be applied without any of these subpositions.

The first scanning method works with an interest operator, the second with different grid-line methods.

A Scanning Method Based on an Interest Operator: The procedure is described in Figure 17.9 [Mis97].

Scanning of the object is started with the master theodolite; scanning means that points of interest have to be detected, which finally can describe the 3D surface of the object. This can be performed with interest operators. We decided to take the Förstner operator. With the Förstner operator a wide field of different points can be located with subpixel accuracy:

- points on lines or edges;

- centers of symmetrical figures;

- intersections of lines; and

- edges.

The speed, accuracy, and reliability of the Förstner operator depend on the quality of the images, the number of pixels to be processed, and limiting parameters chosen by the user. In our systems it is possible to use the operator for the total image or a predestined region of interest.

For all points identified with the Förstner operator on the surface of the object, image coordinates are stored in a list. In addition, they can be marked on the screen to help the operator decide if they should be used for object reconstruction.

While the master theodolite is scanning the object, the slave has to track it in order to find homologous regions and, finally, the homologous points. For the tracking procedure the collimation axis of the master theodolite is used (Figure 17.10).

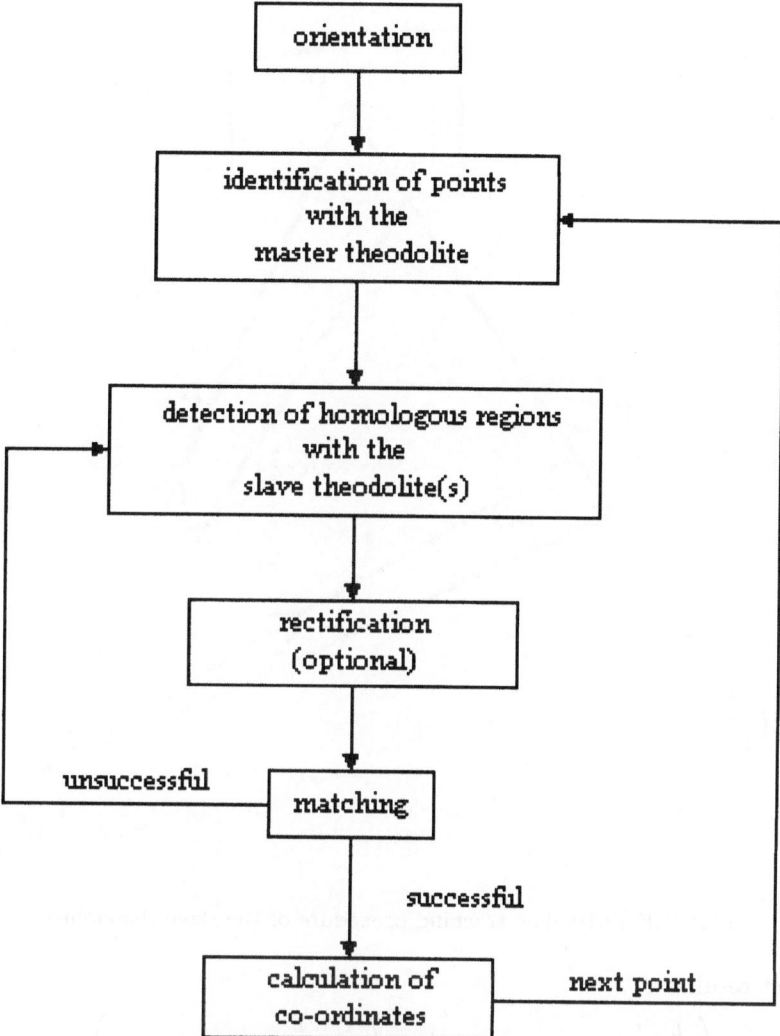

FIGURE 17.9. Diagram of the automatic measurement system.

This method is very time-consuming if there are no approximate coordinates of those points P_i of interest available that the master theodolite had identified. These approximate values can be calculated with the approximate distance $\overline{T_I P_i}$ we get from the autofocus function of the master.

A new autofocus function was developed [MW95, Mis96]. The main idea behind the mathematical model is the fact that a sharply defined image is only formed at the focal plane of the telescope. In view of digital image processing this means the sum of the absolute values of all gray value gradients becomes maximum in the focal plane. First experiments showed, for practical use, the following approximation model, which leads

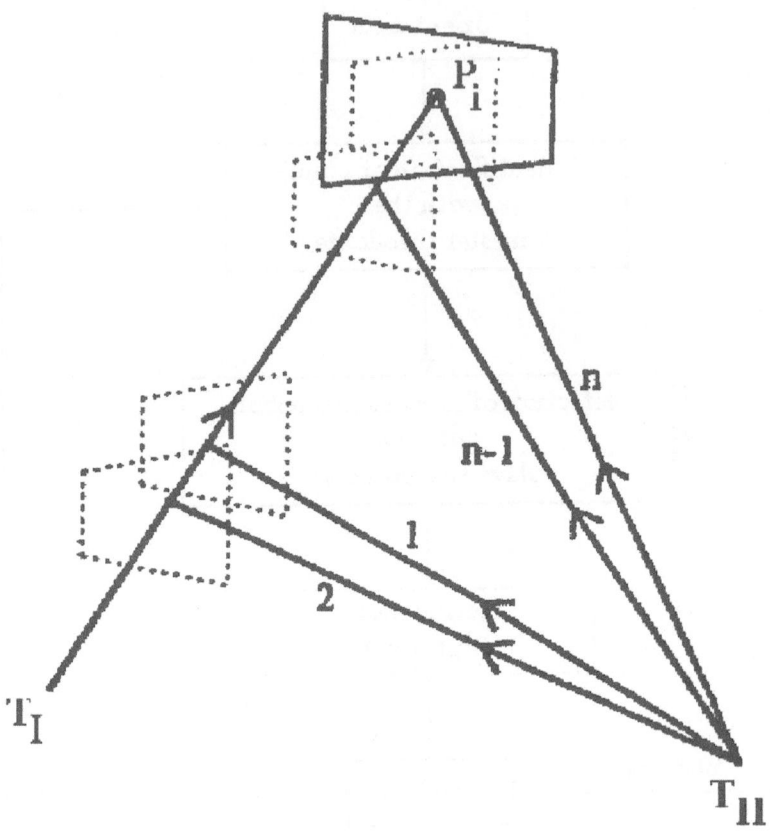

FIGURE 17.10. The tracking procedure of the slave theodolite.

to sufficient results:

$$\Phi_I(F_{opt}) = \left(\sum_{i=1}^{L} \sum_{j=2}^{C} (g_{i,j} - g_{i,j-1})^2 \right) + \left(\sum_{j=1}^{C} \sum_{i=2}^{L} (g_{i,j} - g_{i-1,j})^2 \right) = \max. \quad (17.4)$$

In Eq.(17.4) gray value gradients are only computed for lines and columns to get a better effectiveness of the algorithm. This can be done without loss of accuracy. A further simplification and less time-consuming solution is possible by not using every column and line but only every $a - th$ line and $b - th$ column:

$$\Phi_{II}(F_{opt}) = \left(\sum_{i=1}^{L/a} \sum_{j=2}^{C/b} (g_{a*i,b*j} - g_{a*i,b*(j-1)})^2 \right)$$
$$+ \left(\sum_{j=1}^{C/a} \sum_{i=2}^{L/b} (g_{b*i,a*j} - g_{b*(i-1),a*j})^2 \right) = \max. \quad (17.5)$$

If focusing has been performed accurately, we get not only a sharply defined image but also an image with the smallest dimensions. An object imaged with minimum dimensions shows minimum properties of gray value variations. This is taken into consideration by normalizing function Φ_{II} by dividing it through the number of the registered gray value variations:

$$\Phi_{III}(F_{opt}) = \frac{\Phi_{II}(F_{opt})}{N_\Delta}; \tag{17.6}$$

with N_Δ = number of the $\Delta g \neq 0$.

Besides influences of refraction can disturb the autofocus procedure. This can be avoided if only gray value differences below a certain threshold s are used for the computations. Then, finally, the autofocus function is given by

$$\Phi(F) = \frac{M}{N}; \tag{17.7}$$

with $M = \sum\limits_{i=1}^{L/a} \sum\limits_{j=2}^{C/b} \left\{ \begin{array}{l} t_1^2 \text{ for } t_1 \geq s \\ 0 \text{ otherwise} \end{array} \right\} + \sum\limits_{j=1}^{C/a} \sum\limits_{i=2}^{L/b} \left\{ \begin{array}{l} t_2^2 \text{ for } t_2 \geq s \\ 0 \text{ otherwise} \end{array} \right\},$

$N = \sum\limits_{i=1}^{L/a} \sum\limits_{j=2}^{C/b} \left\{ \begin{array}{l} 1 \text{ for } t_1 \geq s \\ 0 \text{ otherwise} \end{array} \right\} + \sum\limits_{j=1}^{C/a} \sum\limits_{i=2}^{L/b} \left\{ \begin{array}{l} 1 \text{ for } t_2 \geq s \\ 0 \text{ otherwise} \end{array} \right\},$

$t_1 = \left| g_{a*i,b*j} - g_{a*i,b*(j-1)} \right| \qquad t_2 = \left| g_{b*i,a*j} - g_{b*(i-1),a*j} \right|.$

For the slave theodolite a very fast tracking algorithm has been developed by making use of the epipolar line geometry (see Chapter 13). An epipolar line is given by the intersection of two plains. Here one plain is defined by the points T_I, T_{II}, and P_i and the second plain is given by the CCD array of the slave. T_I and T_{II} are the intersection points of the principal axes of the theodolites. Figure 17.11 shows how the intersections of the epipolar line and the frame of the CCD array can be used to control the slave theodolites. After the coordinates of the intersection points are determined with respect to the theodolite, coordinate system correction angles can be calculated by which the collimation axis of the slave can be moved along the epipolar line.

This tracking procedure starts at one intersection point and stops at the other. If the searching procedure was without success the axes of the theodolite have to be moved for some steps and further epipolar lines have to be determined in the neighborhood of the first one.

Simultaneous with the tracking procedure, a search algorithm is used to detect homologous regions and points with respect to the master theodolite by a matching procedure. In our case least squares matching (see section 14.1.2) was used.

With the image coordinates determined with the camera of the master and slave, horizontal and vertical angles of the theodolite measurement system are calculated (see Section 17.2.1), which can then be used to compute the object coordinates by spatial intersection or three-dimensional network adjustment.

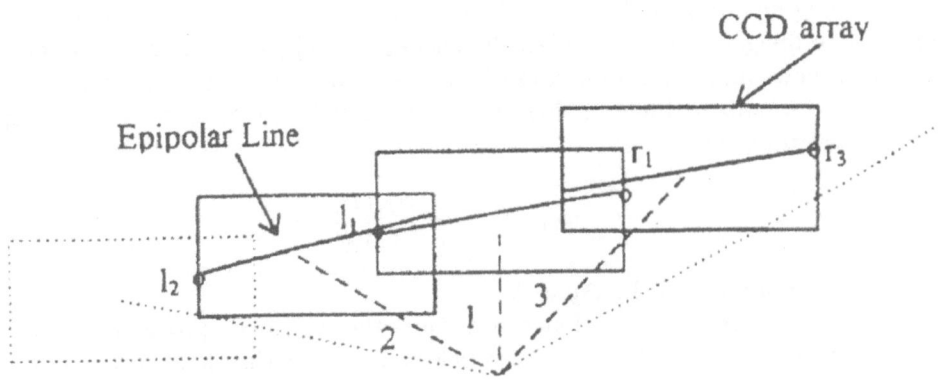

FIGURE 17.11. The tracking procedure by using the epipolar line.

A Scanning Method Based on Different Grid-Line Methods. For this method, the measurement system has to be modified in such a way that regularly arranged virtual grid lines of the 3D object coordinate system can be created. The grid lines can be chosen a priori and shall intersect the surface of the object to be reconstructed. Figure 17.12 depicts, with a very simple example, how regularly arranged grid lines of a Cartesian coordinate system intersect an object, which has the form of a cuboid.

We get grid lines parallel to the y-axis, if the x- and z-coordinates are kept constant, grid-lines parallel to the x-axis, if the y- and z-coordinates are kept constant; and grid lines parallel to the z-axis, if the y- and x-coordinates are kept constant. The intersection points can then be used for 3D object reconstruction. The density of the points of interest depends on the density of the grid lines and should be chosen such that 3D reconstruction of the object is possible without loss of accuracy.

The modified measurement system consists of a laser theodolite (master) and a video theodolite (slave). The laser theodolite is coupled to a laser generator of a visible laser beam that projects target points on the object. To ensure maximum contrast between the target and the surface of the object during measurement, the intensity of the laser should automatically be adjusted.

The video theodolite is automatically pointed at the same time as the pointer theodolite. As soon as the target point appears in the visual field, the video theodolite identifies it and determines its position on the CCD array. Computation of the point of intersection P_i of the two space directions that represent the two lines of sight produces the effective point coordinates.

Figure 17.13 shows the surface of an object and point P_i, where the laser hits the surface. While scanning the object, the laser target point has to be moved until it is identical with points P_s, where the grid line intersects the surface.

Different iterative methods were developed to get the intersection points by scanning [Sei99]. All methods are in common with that the shortest distance

$$d = \sqrt{(\Delta x_{is})^2 + (\Delta z_{is})^2} \qquad (17.8)$$

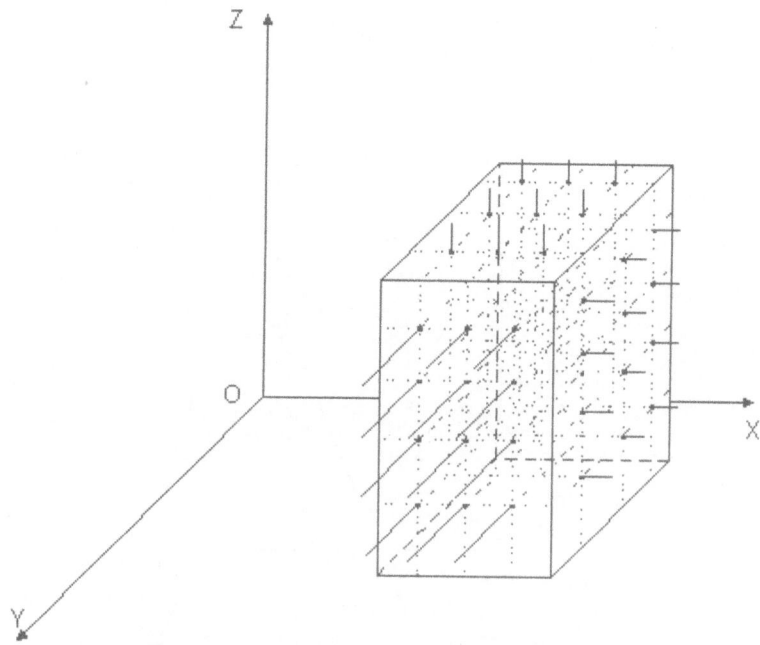

FIGURE 17.12. Lines intersect the surface of an object.

between the laser beam, and the grid line y_k has to be minimized. The coordinate differences are defined as

$$\Delta x_{is} = x_i - x_s = \rho \cos H_z \sin V - x_k \,;$$
$$\Delta z_{is} = z_i - z_s = \rho \cos V - z_k \,. \tag{17.9}$$

H_z (horizontal angle) and V (vertical angle) are measured with the laser theodolite. ρ is the distance between the position P_{Th} of the laser theodolite and P_i. As the coordinates of P_{Th} and P_i are known from the intersection procedure, ρ is well known. Consequently d can be written

$$d = f(H_z, V) \,. \tag{17.10}$$

Here only the gradient method shall be mentioned. If $P_i(x_i, y_i, z_i)$ is a point in the neighborhood of the searched minimum, then the new point $P_s(x_s, y_s, z_s)$ is searched in the direction of the gradient of $f(H_z, V)$ by:

$$\begin{bmatrix} H_{z_{k+1}} \\ V_{k+1} \end{bmatrix} = \begin{bmatrix} H_{z_k} \\ V_k \end{bmatrix} + h_k \frac{g_k}{|g_k|} = \begin{bmatrix} H_{z_k} \\ V_k \end{bmatrix} + h_k u_k \tag{17.11}$$

with $g_k = \mathrm{grad} f(H_z, V) \,.$

The minimization procedure comprises seven steps:

I. computation of point P_i by spatial intersection;

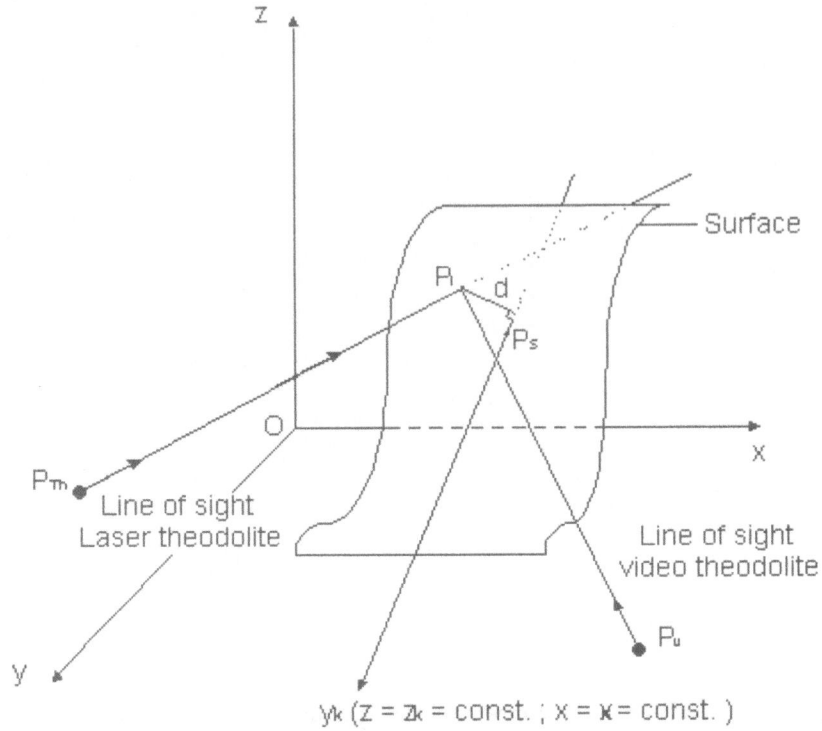

FIGURE 17.13. Principle of the measurements with laser and video theodolite.

2. evaluation of the gradient $\mathrm{grad} f(H_z, V) = g_k$ at point P_i;

3. computation of the search direction $u_k = -g_k/|g_k|$;

4. performance of a linear search in the search direction by choosing h_k;

5. generatation of a new point $x_{k+1} = x_k + h_k u_k$;

6. the process must then be repeated iteratively by setting $k = k+1$ and going back to Step 2; and

7. the iterative process is stopped if step $h_k u_k$, taken at iteration k, is less than the positioning error caused by resolution of the angle measurement systems of theodolites.

If the object to be monitored is rotationally symmetrical or a sphere it can be advantageous to use a cylindrical or spherical object coordinate system for 3D object reconstruction. In that case the grid lines have to be adapted to these coordinate systems. Sometimes it can be useful to combine different coordinate system. Then complex surfaces, like that shown in Figure 17.14, can be covered with regularly arranged measurement points.

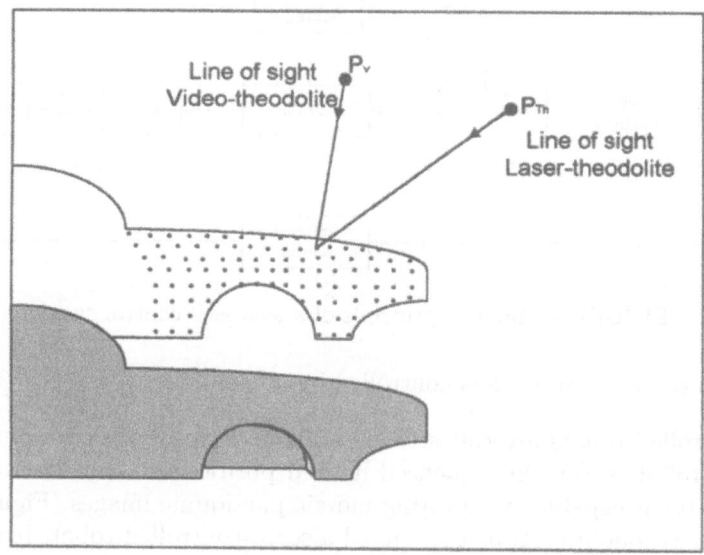

FIGURE 17.14. An application of scanning complex surfaces with the grid-line method.

17.3   Conversion of the Measurement System into a Robot System

In order to increase productivity, reduce product and personal costs, and improve product quality and reliability in many branches of the industry, new highly automated measurement systems for 3D object recognition had to be integrated into the production processes. Because during measurement tasks a lot of repetitive work often has to be done, it seemed necessary to study the impact robot techniques could have on measurement systems. Although everyone uses the word *robot* it has been difficult to find a usable, generally agreed-upon definition of a *measurement robot*.

With the help of the definition of the industrial robot we can define:

A *measurement* robot is a programmable feedback controlled multifunctional device with several axes designed to both move and orientate measurement devices to perform specific measurement tasks along variable programmed paths [Kah97].

Move and *orientate* means the measurement devices have to be rotated around the axes or moved along axes to be, e.g., prepared for automatic target finding. *Measurement devices* are, e.g., electronic sensors for angular, range, or range rate measurements. *Measurements tasks* are tasks applying triangulation, trilateration, or interferometric techniques.

The theodolites of the measurement system, described in Section 17.2, can work like servo-controlled robots, if

- their axes are driven by servo motors,

- automatic target finding is performed by electronic sensors, and

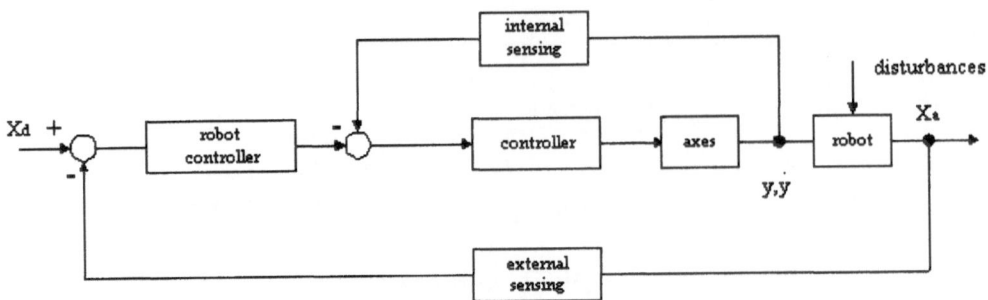

FIGURE 17.15. The principle of a feedback control system.

- the measurement process is controlled by a computer.

Servo-controlled robots are run in a closed loop. A feedback control system is used to drive the robot to certain sequenced desired positions so that the camera fixed at the manipulator is capable of capturing mosaic panoramic images (Figure 17.15).

The master theodolite can be considered a servo-controlled robot. It is programmed by storing a series of positions along a path so that the search for points of interest is possible. The positions can be gained in a teaching mode in two ways:

- by taking the information from a theoretical 3D model of the path or

- by walking the robot through the operational mode and storing a series of coordinates along the path.

Conversion of the measurement system into a robot system shall here only be described for the scanning method, based on an interest operator. One closed loop is used to scan the object by internal sensing in such a way that it is covered with overlapping mosaic images (Figure 17.16).

After the position of a mosaic image has been founded, an on line search for all points of interest is started within this image with a second closed loop. This searching procedure is based on an interest operator.

The slave theodolite is also moved simultaneously with the master. It gets the approximate coordinates of the point of interest from the master. Based on this information the slave can be moved to an approximate position with the first closed loop. Then a search for homologous points of interest can be started with the second closed loop using the epipolar line geometry, a matching procedure, and the interest operator.

17.4   Decision Making

The measurement system shall apply further decision making for 3D surface reconstruction and exchanging or varying programs to be executed. Decision making is based on how close the representation from the present object being examined compares to the original or standard representation. To keep the system in action a "goodness of fit"

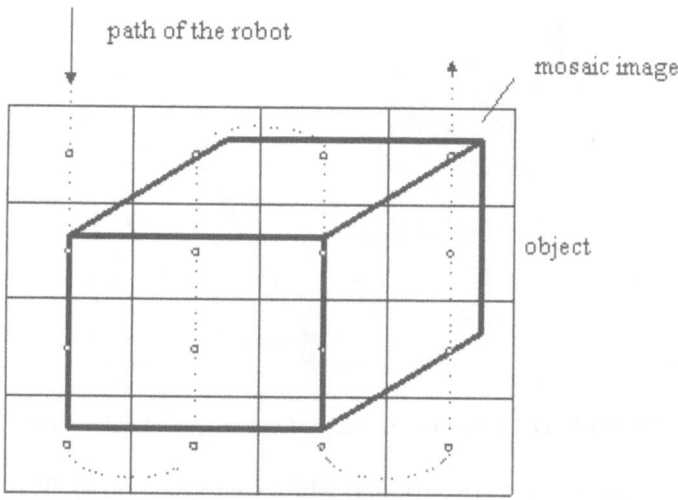

FIGURE 17.16. Scan of object with overlapping images.

has to be defined based on certain tolerance criteria. The goodness-of-fit criteria can be defined with different criteria.

In the case of semantic analysis vision methods emulate how humans would characterize the image and make decisions. For human vision, perception of color is of great importance. How this can be used for decisions is described in the following.

Two concepts of physiology of color vision have been developed since the beginning of the nineteenth century:

- three-component theory of T. Young and H. Helmholtz; and

- opponent theory of E. Hering.

The three-component theory drafted by Thomas Young and Herman Helmholtz explains color vision by three basic colors (red, green, and blue). The opponent theory of Ewald Hering sets the hypothesis that three contrary processes determine vision of color (bright-dark, red-green, and blue-yellow). Red-green and blue-yellow constitute pairs of colors and the colors of a pair cannot be a part of an intermediate color. Both concepts explain different aspects of human color vision and have come in competition. Today we know that both theories are correct in principle but they describe different levels in the process of visual perception. The three-component theory describes processes on the level of light receptors, and the opponent theory comprises further steps of our human visual perception system.

Analogous to the eye, the CCD camera produces a three-component signal with a red, green, and blue part of the light spectrum. Every color is a combination of these components, and that is well represented by the color cube (see Figure 17.17). The three base vectors point to the pure basic colors red, green, and blue. The origin of the axes means black. The other corners of the cube mean the mixed colors yellow (red-green),

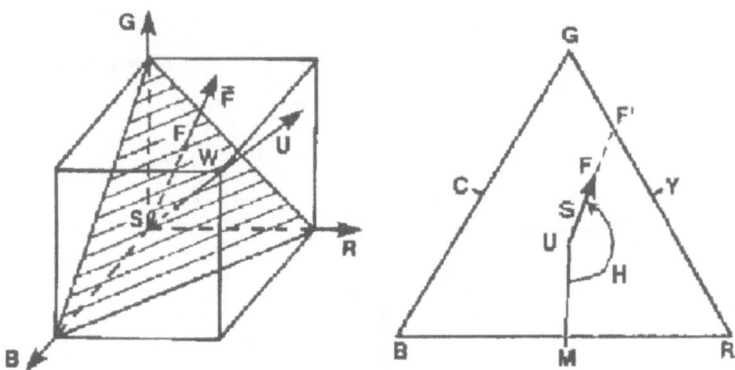

FIGURE 17.17. Representation of colors in the color cube.

cyan (green-blue), magenta (blue-red), and white (red-green-blue). The gray values are situated on the diagonals between the point of black and the point of white.

A cut through the cube furnishes the color triangle named by James Clerk Maxwell with the corners red, green, and blue. The center of this triangle is uncolored. All colors in this triangle have the same value of intensity I (Figure 17.18), which is defined by

$$I = \frac{R+G+B}{3} \qquad \begin{array}{l} R = \text{red } [0,255], \\ G = \text{green } [0,255], \\ B = \text{blue } [0,255]. \end{array} \qquad (17.12)$$

The consideration of this triangle offers the possibility of defining two other quantities:

- the saturation S as the weighted distance from the center to the boundary line of the triangle, which is calculated by

$$S = \left(1 - 3 \cdot \frac{min\{R,G,B\}}{R+G+B}\right) \cdot 255, \qquad (17.13)$$

describes the "strength" of color (Figure 17.19); and

- the hue H as the angle between an arbitrary zero line and the line between the center and color point describes the "kind" of color (Figure 17.20).

At the zero line the hue value H leaps from 255 to 0, so neighboring colors have large different values. In practice it is necessary to choose an unimportant color region for the position of the zero line. If this line is used between the center and magenta, the transformation equations are written as:

$$H = \tfrac{2\pi}{3} + \arctan \tfrac{\sqrt{3}(G-R)}{(G-B)(R-B)} \qquad \text{for } R > B \text{ and } G \geq B$$

or

$$H = \tfrac{4\pi}{3} + \arctan \tfrac{\sqrt{3}(B-G)}{(B-R)(G-R)} \qquad \text{for } G > R \qquad (17.14)$$

or

$$H = \arctan \tfrac{\sqrt{3}(R-B)}{(R-G)(B-G)}.$$

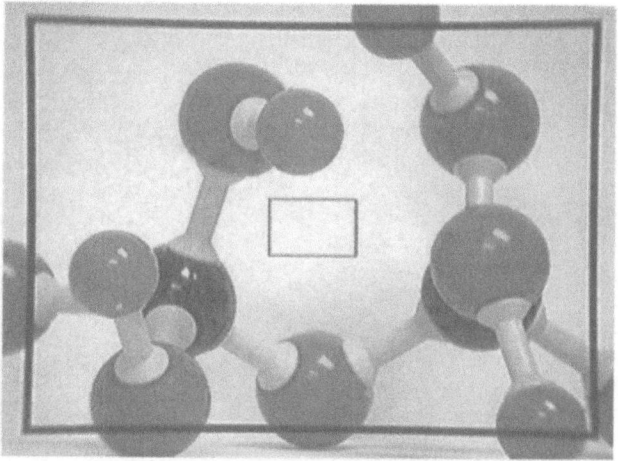

FIGURE 17.18. Intensity I of a scene.

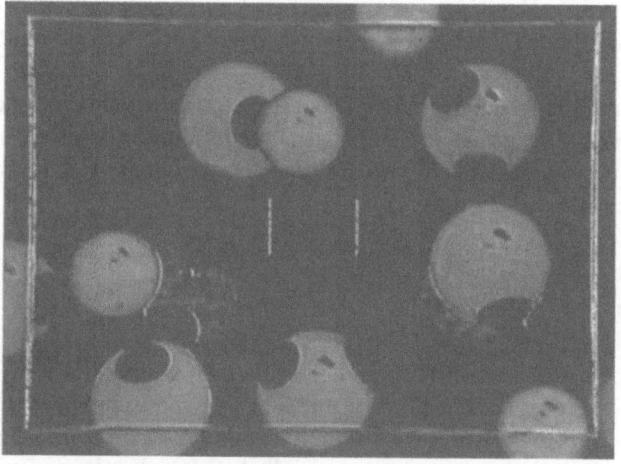

FIGURE 17.19. Saturation S of a scene.

The transformation of the CCD image from RGB to ISH is the basis of color-based digital image processing because a direct extraction of the kind of color is possible. An important pillar of color-based feature extraction is the segmentation of an image according to colors. The search for significant objects and interesting features or parts of these objects is simplified by the use of color information.

The comparison of the three figures (Figure 17.18, Figure 17.19, and Figure 17.20) shows that the balls are only distinguished by hue H, because this quantity furnishes the "kind" of color. The information of intensity I and saturation S restricts the candidates for interesting regions. For details of the process of segmentation look at the CD-ROM.

Semantic analysis also applies methods to make decisions based on pieces of an object. With this analysis, e.g., the object can be represented as a graph of primitive patterns

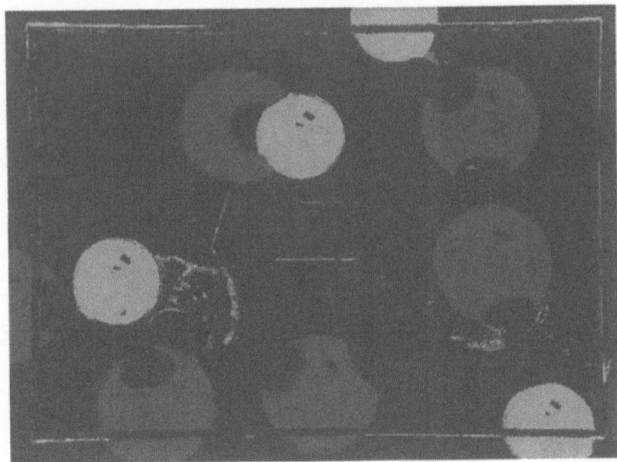

FIGURE 17.20. Hue H of a scene.

and their relationships. Decision making is then based on local feature analysis using a collection of features (e.g., curves, angles, and lines) with spatial relationships between various combinations.

On the other hand, the object can be represented by an ensemble of simple geometrical forms (e.g., spheres, cubes, cones). Decision making in that case is based on local form analysis using a collection of the simple forms with spatial relationships between various combinations.

17.5   Outlook

Surveying objects with a complex surface will only be possible if all the knowledge is available, and the operator normally adds to the measuring system. Then decision making of the measurement system will be possible, based on semantic analysis. Further investigations of a knowledge-based system will therefore be the main goal in the future. Complex surfaces, as shown in Figure 17.1 or 17.6 and, e.g., frameworks, as depicted in Figure 17.21 can then be reconstructed.

FIGURE 17.21. Automatic deformation monitoring of frameworks as an example of a main goal for future research.

References

[AA93] N. Ahuja and A.L. Abbott Active stereo: Integrating disparity, vergence, focus, aperture, and calibration for surface estimation. *IEEE Trans. Patt. Anal. Mach. Intell.*, 15(10):1007–1029, October 1993.

[Ack84] F. Ackermann. High precision digital image correlation. In *Proc. 39th Photogrammetric Week*, Vol. 9 of *Schriftenreihe der Universität Stuttgart*, Stuttgart, 1984.

[Aya91] N. Ayache *Artificial Vision for Mobile Robots*. MIT Press, 1991.

[Bal91] E. Baltsavias. *Multiphoto Geometrically Constrained Matching*. Ph.D. thesis, Institute of Geodesy and Photogrammetry, ETH Zürich, 1991. Mitteilungen Nr. 49.

[BD93] J. Brown, and J. Dold. V-STARS–A system for digital industrial photogrammetry. In A. Gruen, and H. Kahmen, editors, *Optical 3-D Measurement Techniques II*, 12–21, Zürich, Switzerland, October 4–7, 1993. ISPRS, Wichmann.

[BGER92] A.C. Bovik, N. Gopal, T. Emmoth, and A. Restrepo. Localized measurement of emergent image frequencies by Gabor wavelets. *IEEE Trans. Information Theory*, 38(2):691–712, 1992.

[BHP+92] L. Boissier, B. Horz, C. Proy, O. Faugeras, and P. Fua. Autonomous planetary rover: On-board perception system concept and stereo vision by correlation. In *Proc. IEEE International Conference on Robotics and Automation*, 1992.

[BHR86] J.B. Burns, A.R. Hanson, and E.M. Riseman. Extracting straight lines. *IEEE Trans. Pattern Analysis and Machine Intelligence*, 8(4):425–455, 1986.

[BK78] H.P. Bopp, and H. Krauss. An orientation and calibration method for non-topographic applications. *Photogrammetric Engineering & Remote Sensing*, 44(9):1191–1196, September 1978.

[BL91] J. Barraquand, and J.C. Latombe. Robot motion planning: A distributed representation approach. *IJRC*, 10, December 1991.

[BM97] E. Baltsavias and S. Mason. Automated shack reconstruction using integration of cues in object space. In *Proc. ISPRS Commission III/IV Workshop*, Vol. XXXII-3-4W2 of *International Archives of Photogrammetry and Remote Sensing*, 96–105, Stuttgart, 1997.

[BNL90] G. Brookshire, M. Nadler, and C. Lee. Automated stereophotogrammetry. *Computer Vision, Graphics, and Image Processing*, 52:276–296, 1990.

[BP93]   A. Bauer, and G. Paar. Stereo reconstruction from dense disparity maps using the locus method. In A. Gruen, and H. Kahmen, editors, *Proc. 2nd Conference on Optical 3-D Measurement Techniques*, 460–466, Zürich, Switzerland, October 4–7 1993. ETH Zürich, Wichmann Verlag.

[BR92]   S. Baugher and A. Rosenfeld. Corner detection and localization in pyramid. In *Proc. Computer Vision and Image Processing*, 103–121, 1992.

[Bra91] G. Brandstätter. Notitzen zur voraussetzungslosen gegenseitigen Orientierung von Meßbildern. *Österreichische Zeitschrift für Vermessungswesen und Photogrammetrie*, 79/4:273–280, 1991.

[Bru98] A. Brunn. Techniques for automatic building extraction. In *Third Course in Digital Photogrammetry* [Ins98].

[BT91]   D.C. Brockelbank, and A.B. Tam. Stereo elevation determination techniques for SPOT imagery. *Photogrammetric Engineering & Remote Sensing*, 57(8):1065–1073, August 1991.

[Bur88] P.J. Burt. Smart sensing within a pyramid vision machine. *Proc. of the IEEE*, 1006–1015, 1988.

[BUv96] H.A. Beyer, V. Uffenkamp, and G. van der Vlugt. Quality control in industry with digital photogrammetry. In *Proc. 2nd Workshop on 3-D Image Processing*, Stuttgart, January 25–26 1996. ABW.

[BWR89] M. Boldt, R. Weiss, and E. Riseman. Token-based extraction of straight lines. *IEEE Trans. Systems, Man, and Cybernetics*, 19:1581–1595, 1989.

[CVK91] J. Cooper, S. Venkatesh, and L. Kitchen. Early jump-out corner detectors. In *Conf. on Computer Vision and Pattern Recognition*, 688–689, 1991.

[DA91]   U.R. Dhond, and J.K. Aggarwal. A cost benefit analysis of a third camera for stereo correspondence. *International Journal of Computer Vision*, 6(1):39–58, 1991.

[de 90] J. de Lafontaine. Autonomuous spacecraft navigation and control for comet observation and landing. In *Astrodynamics Conference*, Portland, OR, 1990. European Space Agency.

[Dij59] E.W. Dijkstra. A note on two problems in connection with graphs. *Numerical Mathematics*, 1(5):269–271, October 1959.

[DR96]   C. Drewniok and K. Rohr. Automatic exterior orientation of aerial images in urban environments. In *Proc. of the XVIII. ISPRS Congress* [ISP96], 146–152.

[Eur95] European Space Agency. LEDA assessment report: LEDA-RP-95-02. Technical report, European Space Research and Technology Centre, Noordwijk, The
Netherlands, June 1995.

[FG87] W. Förstner and E. Gülch. A fast operator for detection and precise location
of distinct points, corners and centres of circular features. In *ISPRS Inter-
commission Workshop*, 281–305, Interlaken, 1987.

[FH88] P. Fua and A.J. Hanson. Extracting generic shapes using model-driven optimization. In *Proc. DARPA Image Understanding Workshop*, 994–1001, 1988.

[FKL97] A. Fischer, T. Kolbe, and F. Lang. Integration of 2D and 3D reasoning for
building reconstruction using a generic hierarchical model. In W. Förstner, editor, *Proc. Workshop on Semantic Modeling for the Acquisition of Topographic
Information from Images and Maps (SMATI'97) at Bonn*. Birkhäuser Verlag,
Basel, 1997.

[För91] W. Förstner. *Statistische Verfahren für die automatische Bildanalyse und
ihre Bewertung bei der Objekterkennung und -Vermessung*, volume C-370.
Deutsche Geodätische Kommission, München, 1991.

[För98] W. Förstner. Robust estimation procedures in computer vision. In *Third
Course in Digital Photogrammetry* [Ins98].

[FT86] O.D. Faugeras and G. Toscani. The calibration problem for stereo. In *Proc.
CVPR'86*, 15–20, Miami Beach, Florida, 1986. IEEE.

[Fuc95] C. Fuchs. Feature extraction. In *Second Course in Digital Photogrammetry*
[Ins95].

[GD91] G. Giraudon and R. Deriche. On corner and vertex detection. In *Conf. on
Computer Vision and Pattern Recognition*, 650–655, 1991.

[GMLR98] E. Gülch, H. Müller, T. Läbe, and L. Ragia. On the performance of semiautomatic building extraction. In *Proc. ISPRS Commission III Symposium*
[ISP98], 331–338.

[GR93] L. Gabet, and L. Renouard. 3-D high resolution elevation model for exploring
planetary bodies. In *Proc. Workshop on Computer Vision for Space Applications*, 140 146, Antibes, France, September 22–24, 1993. European Space
Agency.

[Gri85] W.E.L. Grimson. Computional experiments with a feature-based stereo algorithm. *IEEE Trans. Patt. Anal. Mach. Intell.*, 7(1):17–34, January 1985.

[Gru95] A. Gruen. High accuracy object reconstruction with least squares matching.
In R.-J. Ahlers, editor, *Bildverarbeitung 95: Forschen, Entwickeln, Anwenden*,
277–296, Esslingen, Nov. 29–Dec. 1, 1995. Technische Akademie Esslingen.

492   References

[GT90] W.I. Grosky, and L.A. Tamburino. A unified approach to the linear camera calibration problem. *IEEE Trans. Patt. Anal. Mach. Intell.*, 12(7):663–671, July 1990.

[Gül94] E. Gülch. *Erzeugung digitaler Geländemodelle durch automatische Bildzuordnung*. Ph.D. thesis, Institute of Photogrammetry, University of Stuttgart, 1994. Deutsche Geodätische Kommission Vol. 418.

[HA89] W. Hoff, and N. Ahuja. Surfaces from stereo: Integrating feature matching, disparity estimation, and contour detection. *IEEE Trans. Patt. Anal. Mach. Intell.*, 11(2):121–136, February 1989.

[Han89] M.J. Hannah. A system for digital stereo image matching. *Photogrammetric Engineering & Remote Sensing*, 55(12):1765–1770, December 1989.

[HBA97] N. Haala, C. Brenner, and K.-H. Anders. Generation of 3D city models from digital surface models and 2D GIS. In *Proc. ISPRS Commission III/IV Workshop*, vol. XXXII-3-4W2 of *International Archives of Photogrammetry and Remote Sensing*, 68–75, Stuttgart, 1997.

[HBW+96] O. Henricsson, F. Bignone, W. Willuhn, F. Ade, O. Kübler, E. Baltsavias, S. Mason, and A. Grün. Project AMOBE: Strategies, current status and future work. In *Proc. of the XVIII. ISPRS Congress* [ISP96], 321–330.

[Hei97] C. Heipke. Automation of interior, relative, and absolute orientation. *ISPRS Journal of Photogrammetry and Remote Sensing*, 52(1):1–20, 1997.

[Heu92] M. Heumel. Ein nicht-linearer Operator zur Detektion fleckförmiger Strukturen in Bildern. Master's thesis, Johannes Kepler University, Linz, Austria, 1992.

[HHK96] A. Halmer, D. Heitzinger, and H. Kager. 3D-surface modelling with basic topologic elements. In *Proc. XVIII. ISPRS Congress* [ISP96], 407–412.

[Hoe93] R. Hoelting. Leica ECDS3, a solution for extended measuring tasks in aircraft manufactoring. In A. Gruen, and H. Kahmen, editors, *Optical 3-D Measurement Techniques II*, 22–28, Zürich, Switzerland, October 4-7 1993. ISPRS, Wichmann.

[HZF93] B. Hotz, Z. Zhang, and P. Fua. Incremental construction of local DEM for an autonomous planetary rover. In *Proc. Workshop on Computer Vision for Space Applications*, 33–43, Antibes, France, September 22-24 1993. European Space Agency.

[II86]   M. Ito and A. Ishii. Three-view stereo analysis. *IEEE Trans. Patt. Anal. Mach. Intell.*, 8(4):524–532, July 1986.

[Ins95] Institute for Photogrammetry at Bonn University and Landesvermessungsamt Nordrhein-Westfalen. *Second Course in Digital Photogrammetry*, Bonn, Germany, 1995.

[Ins98] Institute for Photogrammetry at Bonn University and Landesvermessungsamt Nordrhein-Westfalen. *Third Course in Digital Photogrammetry*, Bonn, Germany, 1998.

[ISP96] *Proc. XVIII. ISPRS Congress*, International Archives of Photogrammetry and Remote Sensing, Vienna, 1996.

[ISP98] *Proc. ISPRS Commission III Symposium*, vol. XXXII-3/1 of *International Archives of Photogrammetry and Remote Sensing*, Columbus, OH, 1998.

[Jen91] M.R.M. Jenkin. Techniques for disparity measurement. *Computer Vision, Graphics, and Image Processing*, 53(1):14–30, January 1991.

[JS96] J. Jaakola and T. Sarjakoski. *Experimental Test on Digital Aerial Triangulation*, vol. 31 of *Official Publication of the OEEPE*. Finnish Geodetic Institute, Helsinki, Finland, 1996.

[Kag89] H. Kager. ORIENT: A universal photogrammetric adjustment system. In A. Grün, and H. Kahmen, editors. *Optical 3-D Measurement*, 447–455, Karlsruhe, Germany, 1989. Herbert Wichmann Verlag.

[Kah97] H. Kahmen. *Vermessungskunde*. De Gruyter Lehrbuch, Berlin, 19th edition, 1997.

[KDFR95] M. Kerschner, L. Dorffner, G. Forkert, and F. Rottensteiner. Using freeformed spatial curves for object reconstruction from digital images. In F. Solina and W. Kropatsch, editors. *Visual Modules, Proc. 19th OeAGM and 1st SDRV Workshop*, vol. 81 of *Schriftenreihe der OCG*, 150–159. R. Oldenbourg Verlag Wien–München, 1995.

[Ker95] M. Kerschner. Kantenextraktion aus digitalen Bildern und Verfolgung glatter Linien. Diploma Thesis, Institute of Photogrammetry and Remote Sensing, Vienna University of Technology, 1995.

[KK92] I.S. Kweon, and T. Kanade. High-resolution terrain map from multiple sensor data. *IEEE Trans. Patt. Anal. Mach. Intell.*, 14(2):278–292, February 1992.

[Kol94] M. Kolesnik et al. Possibilities of stereo vision for solving scientific and technological tasks. In *Proc. 2nd International Symposium on Missions, Technologies and Design of Planetary Rovers*, Moscow, St. Petersburg, May 15–21, 1994. CNES, RSA.

[Kol95] M. Kolesnik. Vision and navigation of marsokhod rover. In *Proc. ACCV'95*, III-772–III-777, Dec. 5–8, 1995.

[KR84] L. Kitchen and A. Rosenfeld. Scene analysis using region-based constraint filtering. *Pattern Recognition*, 17(2):189–203, 1984.

494   References

[KR95]   H. Kahmen and M. Roic. A new generation of measurement robots for object reconstruction without targeting. In A. Grün and H. Kahmen, editors, *Optical 3-D Measurement III*, 251–262, Karlsruhe, Germany, 1995. Herbert Wichmann Verlag.

[Kra93] K. Kraus. *Photogrammetry Volume 1. Fundamentals and Standard Processes.* Dümmler Verlag, Bonn, Germany, 4th edition, 1993. With contributions by P. Waldhäusl.

[Kra97] K. Kraus. *Photogrammetry Volume 2. Advanced Methods and Applications.* Dümmler Verlag, Bonn, Germany, 4th edition, 1997. With contributions by J. Jansa and H. Kager.

[Krz95] P. Krzystek. Generation of digital elevation models. In *Second Course in Digital Photogrammetry* [Ins95].

[KS86]   A. Köstli and M. Sigle. Die SCOP Datenstruktur zur Verschneidung und Korrektur von Geländemodellen. In *Proc. ISPRS Commission III Symposium*, vol. XXVI-3 of *International Archives of Photogrammetry and Remote Sensing*, Rovaniemi, 1986.

[LB91]   D. Lavery, and R.J. Bedard. 1991 NASA planetary rover program. In *Proc. 42nd Congress of the IAF*, Montreal, October 5–11, 1991. IAF.

[LE92]   T. Lindeberg and J.O. Eklundh. Scale-space primal sketch: Construction and experiments. *Image and Vision Computing*, 10:3–18, 1992.

[Len96] W. Lenz. Mit PhotoModeler vom Foto zum 3D-Modell. In *Proc. 2nd Workshop on 3-D Image Processing*, Stuttgart, January 25–26, 1996. ABW.

[Leo93] A. Leonardis. *Image Analysis Using Parametric Models.* Ph.D. thesis, Faculty of Electrical Engineering and Computer Science, Univ. of Ljublijana, Slovenija, 1993.

[LF98]   F. Lang and W. Förstner. Matching techniques. In *Third Course in Digital Photogrammetry* [Ins98].

[LST91] J.-C. Li, T. Schenk, and C. Toth. Towards an autonomous system for orienting digital stereopairs. *Photogrammetric Engineering and Remote Sensing*, 57(8):1057–1064, August 1991.

[Mal89] S.G. Mallat. A theory for multiresolution signal decomposition: The wavelet representation. *IEEE Trans. Pattern Analysis and Machine Intelligence*, 11:674–693, 1989.

[Mis96] A. Mischke. Distanzmessung mittels Autofokusfunktion einer CCD–Kamera. *AVN*, 1:31–39, 1996.

[Mis97]   A. Mischke. *Entwicklung eines Videotheodolit-Meßsystems zur automatischen Richtungsmessung von nicht signalsisierten Objektpunkten.* Ph.D. thesis, Department of Engineering Surveying, Vienna University of Technology, 1997.

[MN90]   R. Mehotra and S. Nichani.   Corner detection.   *Pattern Recognition,* 23(11):1223–1233, 1990.

[MN95]   G. Medioni, and R. Nevatia. Matching images using linear features. *IEEE Trans. Patt. Anal. Mach. Intell.,* 6(6):675–685, November 1995.

[Mor77]   H.P. Moravec. Towards automatic visual obstacle avoidance. In *Proc. 5th International Conference on Artificial Intelligence MIT,* Cambridge, MA, 1977.

[MR97]   A. Mischke and F. Rottensteiner. Feature extraction in an on-line engineering surveying system. In W. Burger and M. Burge, editors. *Pattern Recognition 1997, Proc. 21th OeAGM Workshop,* vol. 103 of *Schriftenreihe der OCG,* 143–149. R. Oldenbourg Verlag Wien–München, 1997.

[Mül98]   H. Müller. Experiences with semiautomatic building extraction. In *Third Course in Digital Photogrammetry* [Ins98].

[MW95]   A. Mischke and A. Wieser. Automatic target-area-collimation with videotheodolites. In A. Grün and H. Kahmen, editors. *Optical 3-D Measurement III,* 263–271, Karlsruhe, Germany, 1995. Herbert Wichmann Verlag.

[MWW96] L. Molnar, J. Wintner, and B. Wöhrer. DTM System SCOP in a new technological generation. In *Proc. XVIII. ISPRS Congress* [ISP96], 569–574.

[OOK89]   T. Ozaki, M. Ohzora, and K. Kurahashi. An image processing system for autonomous vehicle. In *SPIE Vol. 1195 Mobile Robots IV.* SPIE, 1989.

[Paa95]   G. Paar (ed.). Planetary body high resolution 3D modeling. Final Report of ESTEC Contract 9195/90/NL/SF, Joanneum Research, CAE, Matra Marconi Space, Noordwijk, November 1995.

[PHF+93] C. Proy, B. Hotz, O. Faugeras, P. Garnesson, and M. Berthod. Onboard vision system for a mobile planetary exploration robot. In *Proc. Workshop on Computer Vision for Space Applications,* 2–8, Antibes, France, September 22–24, 1993. European Space Agency.

[PLSN93] C. Proy, M. Lamboley, I. Sitenko, and T.N. Nguen. Improving autonomy of Marsokhod 96. In *Proc. 44th Congress of the IAF,* Graz, Austria, October 16–22, 1993. IAF-93-U.6.584.

[PP91]   G. Paar and W. Pölzleitner. Stereovision and 3D terrain modeling for planetary exploration. In *Proc. 1st ESA Workshop on Comp. Vision and Image Processing for Spaceborne Applications,* Noordwijk, The Netherlands, June 1991. European Space Research and Technology Centre.

[PP92a] G. Paar and W. Pölzleitner. Descent and landing phase: Vision based spacecraft motion estimation and elevation modeling. In *Proc. Int.Symp. on Missions, Technologies and Design of Planetary Mobile Vehicles*, Toulouse, September 28–30, 1992.

[PP92b] G. Paar and W. Pölzleitner. Robust disparity estimation in terrain modeling for spacecraft navigation. In *Proc. 11th ICPR*. International Association for Pattern Recognition, 1992.

[PPB95] G. Paar, W. Pölzleitner, and A. Bauer. A system for on-line 3D measurement of rough natural surfaces. In *Proc. Photonics East*, Philadelphia, October 22–26, 1995. SPIE The International Society for Optical Engineering.

[Pri95] R. Prinz. Aerotriangulation mit digitalen Bildern. Diploma Thesis, Institute of Photogrammetry and Remote Sensing, Vienna University of Technology, 1995.

[PSP95] G. Paar, O. Sidla, and W. Pölzleitner. Natural feature tracking for autonomous navigation. In *Proc. 28th International Dedicated Conference on Robotics, Motion and Machine Vision*, Stuttgart, Germany, October 1995. ISATA.

[PSPS93] G. Paar, G. Schwingshakl, W. Pölzleitner, and O. Sidla. Automatic landing site selection by computer vision. In *Proc. 43rd Congress of the IAF*, Graz, Austria, October 16–22, 1993. International Astronautical Federation. IAF-93-U.6.582.

[PU93] W. Pölzleitner and M. Ulm. Robust dynamic 3D motion estimation using landmarks. In *Optical Tools for Manufacturing and Advanced Automation, Videometrics II*, 1993.

[RHR+93] H. Raggam, W. Hummelbrunner, E. Riegler, A. Almer, and D. Strobl. *RSG–Remote Sensing Software Package Graz*. JOANNEUM RESEARCH, Graz, Austria, release 2.4 edition, January 1993.

[Roi96] M. Roic. *Erfassung von nicht signalisierten 3D-Strukturen mit Videotheodoliten*, volume 43 of *Geowissenschaftliche Mitteilungen der Studienrichtung Vermessungswesen*. Department of Engineering Surveying, Vienna University of Technology, 1996. Ph.D. Thesis.

[Ros93] B. Ross. A practical stereo vision system. In IEEE Computer Society, editor, *1993 IEEE Computer Society Conference on Computer Vision and Pattern Recognition*, 148–153, New York, June 15–18, 1993. IEEE Computer Society Press.

[Rot93] F. Rottensteiner. Area-based matching of fiducial marks in scanned images. In W. Pölzleitner and E. Wenger, editors, *Image Analysis and Synthesis, Proc. of the 17th OeAGM Workshop*, vol. 68 of *Schriftenreihe der OCG*, 163–172. R. Oldenbourg Verlag Wien–München, 1993.

[Rot96]   F. Rottensteiner. Three dimensional object reconstruction by object space matching. In *Proc. XVIII. ISPRS Congress* [ISP96], 692–696.

[Rot98]   F. Rottensteiner. Object reconstruction in a bundle block environment. In *Proc. ISPRS Commission III Symposium* [ISP98], 177–183.

[RP96]   F. Rottensteiner and R. Prinz. Aerotriangulation mit digitalen Bildern: Der Testblock FORSSA der OEEPE. *Österreichische Zeitung für Vermessung und Geoinformation*, 2/96:189–195, 1996.

[RS88]   A. Rosenfeld and A.C. Sher. Detection and delineation of compact objects using intensity pyramids. *Pattern Recognition*, 21(2):147–151, 1988.

[Sar92]   R. Sara. The surface structure of 3-D curved objects. In H. Bischof and W. Kropatsch, editors, *Proc. 16th OAGM Workshop*, 129–138, Vienna, May 1992. R. Oldenbourg.

[Sar93]   R. Sara. The impact of smooth surface perception capability to the structure of a vision system. *Cybernetics and Systems*, 1993. (to appear).

[Sau90]   E. Saund. Symbolic construction of a 2-D scale-space image. *IEEE Trans. Pattern Analysis and Machine Intelligence*, 12(8):355–395, 1990.

[Sch92]   W. Schickler. Feature matching for outer orientation of single images using 3-D wireframe controlpoints. *International Archives of Photogrammetry and Remote Sensing*, XXIX-B3:591–598, 1992.

[Sei99]   A. Seixas. *3D Object Reconstruction with Different Grid-line Methods*. Ph.D. thesis, Department of Engineering Surveying, Vienna University of Technology, 1999. in preparation.

[SIR94]   SAGEM, INRIA, and RIT. Stereovision, final report. ESA Contract Report 8019/88/NL/PP, Document AS94-039, European Space Research and Technology Centre, Noordwijk, The Netherlands, May 1994.

[SP96]   W. Schickler and Z. Poth. The automatic interior orientation and its daily use. In *Proc. XVIII. ISPRS Congress* [ISP96], 746–751.

[spo88]   SPOT 1 image utilization assessment results. Technical report, Centre National D'etudes Spatiales, France, 1988.

[SS89]   W. Strasser and H.P. Seidel. *Theory and Practice of Geometric Modeling*. Springer, Berlin, Heidelberg, 1989.

[Tho90]   C.E. Thorpe (ed.). *Vision and Autonomous Navigation. The Carnegie Mellon NAVLAB*. Kluwer Academic Publishers, 1990.

[TPO+96] L. Tang, Z. Poth, T. Ohlhof, C. Heipke, and J. Batscheider. Automatic relative orientation–Realization and operational tests. In *Proc. XVIII. ISPRS Congress* [ISP96], 843–848.

[Tsi92]   V. Tsingas. *Automatisierung der Punktübertragung in der Aerotriangulation durch mehrfache digitale Bildzuordnung*. Ph.D. thesis, Institute of Photogrammetry, University of Stuttgart, 1992. Deutsche Geodätische Kommission Vol. 392.

[TVD94]   J.C. Trinder, A. Vuillemin, and B.E. Donnelly. A study of procedures and tests on DEM software for spot images. In *Proc. ISPRS Commission IV Symp.*, Georgia, May 1994. ISPRS.

[UP95a]   M. Ulm and G. Paar. Relative camera calibration from stereo disparities. In *Proc. 3rd Conference on Optical 3-D Measurement Techniques*, Vienna, Austria, October 2–4, 1995. ISPRS.

[UP95b]   P. Uray and A. Pinz. Semiautomatic triangulation of irregular 3D point data. In F. Solina, editor, *Proc. International Workshop on Visual Modules*, 197–204, Maribor, Slovenia, May 11–13, 1995. Oesterreichische Arbeitsgemeinschaft fuer Mustererkennung, Oesterreichische Computer Gesellschaft.

[U.S84]   U.S. Geological Survey, Alexandria. *Landsat 4 Data Users Handbook*, 1984. 233 pages.

[Vel98]   H. Veldhuis. Performance analysis of two fitting algorithms for the measurement of parametrised objects. In *Proc. ISPRS Commission III Symposium* [ISP98], 400–408.

[Vis96]   VisionInternational, ERDAS Inc, Earth City, MO; Atlanta, GA. *IMAGINE OrthoMAX*, 1996. Version 8.2.

[Vos95]   G. Vosselman. Applications of tree search methods in digital photogrammetry. *ISPRS Journal of Photogrammetry and Remote Sensing*, 50(4):29–37, 1995.

[WAH92]   J. Weng, N. Ahuja, and T.S. Huang: Matching two perspective views. *IEEE Trans. Patt. Anal. Mach. Intell.*, 14(8):806–825, August 1992.

[Wei97]   U. Weidner. *Gebäudeerfassung aus digitalen Oberflächenmodellen*. Ph.D. thesis, Institute of Photogrammetry, University of Bonn, 1997. Deutsche Geodätische Kommission Vol. 474.

[Wil83]   E. Wild. *Die Prädiktion mit Gewichtsfunktionen und deren Anwendung zur Beschreibung von Geländeflächen*. Ph.D. thesis, Institute of Photogrammetry, University of Stuttgart, 1983. Deutsche Geodätische Kommission Vol. 217.

Index